South Africa's Alternative Press

This book examines South Africa's alternative press, which has played a crucial but largely undocumented role in the making of modern South Africa. Mirroring political realities that differed substantially from those projected by the established, white-owned commercial presses, the alternative press had its origins in African mission journals from the 1860s and 1870s. By the 1880s, an independent African protest emerged. South Africa's Coloured and Indian communities were represented by their own protest publications from the early 1900s, while South Africa's expanding black urban working-class population communicated their concerns through various socialist publications in the first decades of the twentieth century. Only in the 1950s did a nonracial resistance press emerge. Representing South Africa's marginalized communities to themselves and to the outside world for more than a century, these newspapers, newsletters, journals, and magazines constitute a unique political, social, and literary archive – the oldest, most extensive and varied collection of indigenous publications this kind in sub-Saharan Africa.

"This study is a major contribution to scholarship. I greatly appreciate the extensive primary research and analysis that has gone into the collections.... The articles significantly add to our knowledge of African political movements and will serve as an important complement to the basic texts of South African studies."

– Robert Edgar, *Howard University*

CAMBRIDGE STUDIES IN THE HISTORY OF MASS COMMUNICATIONS

Cambridge Studies in the History of Mass Communications includes books that examine the communications processes and communications systems within social, cultural and political contexts. Inclusive of empirical, effects-based research, works in this series proceed from the basis that the histories of various media are an important means to understanding their role and function in society. The history of a medium – its pattern of introduction, diffusion, acceptance and effects – varies in each society, interacting with, and, in turn, shaping its culture. Moreover, each society reacts differently to the introduction of a medium, and regulatory policies are shaped by both political and cultural forces. The detailed study of various communications forms and their complex message systems is now understood to be the key to unraveling the evolution of modern society and its culture.

Other books in the series:

Hollywood's Overseas Campaign: The North Atlantic Movie Trade, 1920–1950, by Ian Jarvie

Ronald Reagan in Hollywood: Movies and Politics, by Stephen Vaughn

Hollywood Censored: The Catholic Legion of Decency and the Hays Code, by Gregory Black

South Africa's Alternative Press

Voices of Protest and Resistance, 1880s–1960s

Edited by

Les Switzer

University of Houston

CAMBRIDGE UNIVERSITY PRESS

In memory of my mother, Aileen

PUBLISHED BY THE PRESS SYNDICATE OF THE UNIVERSITY OF CAMBRIDGE
The Pitt Building, Trumpington Street, Cambridge CB2 1RP, United Kingdom

CAMBRIDGE UNIVERSITY PRESS
The Edinburgh Building, Cambridge CB2 2RU, United Kingdom
40 West 20th Street, New York, NY 10011–4211, USA
10 Stamford Road, Oakleigh, Melbourne 3166, Australia

First published 1997

Printed in the United States of America

Typeset in Sabon

Library of Congress Cataloging-in-Publication Data
South Africa's alternative press: voices of protest and resistance, 1880s–1960s
/ edited by Les Switzer.
p. cm. – (Cambridge studies in the history of mass
communications)
Includes index
ISBN 0–521–55351–2
1. Underground press – South Africa – History. 2. Journalism –
Political aspects – South Africa. I. Switzer, Les. II. Series.
PN5477.U53S68 1996
070.5′0968 – dc20 95–44814
CIP

*A catalog record for this book is available from
the British Library.*

ISBN 0 521 55351 2 hardback

Contents

Map and Photographs

Photographs

Figures and Tables

Figures

Tables

Notes on Contributors

Mohamed Adhikari is a lecturer in the Department of History at the University of Cape Town (South Africa). He is the author of *Let Us Live for Our Children: The Teachers' League of South Africa, 1913–1940* (1993).

R. Neville Choonoo received his Ph.D. in English from Columbia University in New York. A South African citizen, he has taught in the Department of English at the University of Durban-Westville (South Africa) and is currently an associate professor in the Department of English and Black-Hispanic Studies at the State University of New York at Oneonta.

R. Hunt Davis, Jr., is professor of History and African Studies and interim director of International Studies and Programs at the University of Florida, where he served previously as director of the Center for African Studies. Davis is also the former editor of the *African Studies Review* (1980–1988). His numerous publications include "John L. Dube: a South African Exponent of Booker T. Washington," *Journal of African Studies* (1975), and *Mandela, Tambo, and the African National Congress* (1991), coedited with Sheridan Johns.

Elizabeth Ceiriog Jones is a Ph.D. candidate in the London School of Economics. A Canadian citizen and a journalist by profession, she has worked as a reporter for the London bureau of *Newsweek* magazine, and as a reporter for the Canadian Broadcasting Corporation and the British Broadcasting Corporation. Jones is currently a freelance radio and television reporter working primarily in East and Central Africa.

Uma Shashikant Mesthrie lectured in the Department of History at the University of Durban-Westville (South Africa) and was a Research Fellow in the Department of Sociology at the University of Cape Town (South Africa) before moving to the University of the Western Cape (South Africa), where she is currently a lecturer in the Department of History. She is coauthor (with Vertree Canby Malherbe) of *Not Slave Not Free: Indentured Labour* (1992).

Donald Pinnock has worked as a print and broadcast journalist in England, Rhodesia (now Zimbabwe) and South Africa. He was director of the Media

Research and Training Unit and a senior lecturer in the Department of Journalism and Media Studies at Rhodes University (South Africa) before moving to the University of Cape Town (South Africa), where he is a senior lecturer and researcher in the Institute of Criminology. His numerous publications include *Private Labour Recruiting in South Africa* (1981), *The Brotherhoods: Street Gangs and State Control in Cape Town* (1984), and *They Fought for Freedom: Ruth First* (1995).

Les Switzer has worked as a journalist in South Africa and the United States, and taught at California State University at Los Angeles, Rhodes University and the University of the Western Cape (South Africa). He is currently professor and head of the Journalism program in the School of Communication, adjunct professor in the Department of History, and co-director of the Center for Critical Cultural Studies at the University of Houston. His numerous publications include *The Black Press in South Africa and Lesotho: A Descriptive Bibliographic Guide, 1836–1976* (1979), coauthored with Donna Switzer; *Media and Dependency in South Africa* (1985); and *Power and Resistance in an African Society: The Ciskei Xhosa and the Making of South Africa* (1993).

Ime Ukpanah, a Nigerian-American citizen, recently completed an interdisciplinary Ph.D. in the Department of History at the University of Houston. He has taught in the African American Studies program and the Department of History at the University of Houston and in the Department of History at Texas Southern University in Houston.

Preface

This book is the first major study of the most significant collection of alternative political publications in sub-Saharan Africa. I also believe it is one of the first attempts in communication research to offer a set of procedures for employing both non-quantitative and quantitative methods in analyzing texts produced by marginalized communities over time. These texts sustained a critique of South Africa's white-dominated social order for more than a century, but they retained distinct linguistic, ethnic, social, cultural and even geographical identities. In a sense, the texts function as a mediated history of South Africa by its subaltern communities, and can be compared with similar mediated histories of the United States and other culturally diverse societies by their subaltern communities.

This book is the product of several ventures in scholarly research on the South African press. It is in part the long-anticipated followup to a book I co-authored, *The Black Press in South Africa and Lesotho, 1836–1976*, published in 1979, that first described the hundreds of African, Coloured and Indian publications associated with more than 150 years of the black press in South Africa. It is also in part the product of a conference on the resistance press held at the University of the Western Cape in 1991, "A Century of the Resistance Press in South Africa," where early drafts of many chapters published in this volume were first presented. The conference was organized by André Odendaal, director of the Mayibuye Centre at UWC–South Africa's central archive for the anti-apartheid movement. André and I were coconvenors of this conference, and I am grateful to him for his steadfast support during the years it took to complete the project.

Finally, this book is the product of a diverse group of contributors of different national, ethnic and cultural backgrounds. I owe a special debt of gratitude to each of these contributors–to Mohamed Adhikari, Neville Choonoo, Hunt Davis, Elizabeth Jones, Uma Mesthrie, Don Pinnock and Ime Ukpanah–who did their best to respond to every editorial query.

The University of Houston provided a grant to cover the costs of preparing the index. UH's African American Studies Program provided a grant to cover the costs of the map and some of the photographs, and a number of individuals at the university were most helpful in preparing the manuscript for publication. My thanks to Martha Steele, Keiko Horton and the staff in University Access Services, who obtained essential primary and secondary sources for me in an efficient and timely manner, to Bill Ashley and his colleagues Joel Howell and Tommy Leo in University Media services, who prepared the map, the final draft of the figures and some of the photographs for publication. I'm also grateful to colleagues in the School of Communication: Mike Ryan helped me refine the language used in describing the figures, tables and appendix; William Linsley provided me with a computer-generated draft of the figures; and Barry Brown and Jennifer van Akin assisted me administratively in getting various drafts of the manuscript packaged and sent to the publisher.

My thanks also to Gordon Metz and especially Graham Goddard at the Mayibuye Centre for their help in obtaining so many photographs reproduced in this book, to Naomi Shapiro Barnett for the photograph of herself, to the late Bernice Wardell-Ngubane and Margaret Marshall for the photograph of Jordan Ngubane, to Roni Snitcher of the South African Library, and especially to Uma Mesthrie and Mohamed Adhikari for their help in locating a number of photographs in various archival collections.

In addition, Mohamed, Uma, Bob Edgar, Tom Karis, Dorothy Woodson, Peter Limb, James Campbell, Ron Gwamanda, Catherine Nawa-Gwamanda and Moore Crossey and his colleagues at Yale University Library assisted me in following up numerous factual details. James Zug allowed me access to his unpublished manuscript on the *Guardian*, and Colin Bundy did the same with two unpublished essays on Govan Mbeki that he produced for seminars at Yale's Southern Africa Research Program in 1992. I also wish to thank Christie Lerch, who was meticulous in copyediting the manuscript, Cynthia Green, who helped with the proofreading, and Elisabeth Hughes, who prepared the index.

John McNamara, my friend and coworker at the Center for Critical Cultural Studies, scrutinized the Introduction, pinpointed missing sources and raised several editorial questions that needed to be resolved. A special word of gratitude goes to Bob Edgar and Bill Hachten, who read the entire manuscript and made a number of important suggestions that were incorporated into the final draft. My colleagues Ken Short and Garth Jowett, coeditors of Cambridge University Press's Mass Communication Series, were steadfast in their support of the project, and Ken shepherded the manuscript to publication.

As always, my wife Hazel allowed me to ignore numerous household obligations to work on the book. She helped with the proofreading and provided essential moral support when I most needed it.

Les Switzer
University of Houston
May 1995

Acknowledgments

The editor would like to thank the following individuals and institutions for permission to reproduce the photographs:

Photographs 1, 4, 18, 21, 22, 24, 25, 26, 27, 29, 30, 31, 32, 33, 34, 37, 38, 39, 40, 41, 42 and 43 were obtained from the Mayibuye Centre for History and Culture in South Africa (University of the Western Cape). Photographs 2, 3, 5, 14, 15, 16, 17, 19, 20, 35 and 36 were obtained from the South African Library (Cape Town). Photographs 6, 7, 8, 9, 10, 11, 12 and 13 were obtained from the University of Durban-Westville Documentation Centre (Durban). Photograph 28 was obtained from Naomi Shapiro Barnett's personal collection and Photograph 23 from the late Bernice Wardell-Ngubane's personal collection.

Introduction

South Africa's Alternative Press in Perspective

Les Switzer

South Africa's alternative press has played a largely unrecognized role in the making of modern South Africa. Nevertheless, these newspapers, newsletters, journals and magazines have sought to interpret South Africa's subordinated black (meaning African, Coloured and Asian) communities both to themselves and to the outside world since the beginning of the new era in the 1860s.[1]

Publications intended for Africans were actually produced from the beginning of the European mission enterprise in the early nineteenth century. They were controlled by the missionaries but written and later edited largely by African converts. Publications independent of European mission control were produced by the African Christian community from the 1880s and 1890s. Publications representing other population groups–the Asian (mainly Indian) and Coloured communities–were produced from the early 1900s. They were targeted for separate African, Coloured and Indian audiences, but collectively they comprised South Africa's pioneer black protest press. Circulation rates remained low–apparently below 5,000 before the 1930s (except for the *Workers' Herald*, a trade union monthly), and below 30,000 before the 1980s (except for the *Guardian*, a socialist weekly)–although carry-on readerships (literates reading to nonliterates or passing publications on to other literates) were much in excess of these figures.[2]

African protest journals dominated the alternative press until the 1930s, but control over the means of publication remained limited. African journalists were deprived of opportunities to accumulate capital legally, and they had little access to printing equipment, paper, buildings, skilled tradesmen and distribution networks. The purchasing power of African readers remained low, and there were very few black entrepreneurs who had surplus capital to use to advertise in these publications. They were also denied access to conventional political and public affairs news, both before and after the creation of the Union of South Africa in 1910, including news generated by white political parties, by city councils, provincial legislatures and the national parliament, and by government departments and the prime minister's office. The dominant economic and social institutions of white South Africa were off limits to scrutiny by African journalists, and they were harassed even in their coverage of African community news.

African protest journals remained fragile as periodicals and provincial in audience, if not outlook, but during the first half of the twentieth century the potential pool of readers gradually increased. According to census figures, the literacy rates among Africans rose slowly from an estimated 6.8 percent of the adult population in 1911 to 9.7 percent in 1921, and it was estimated unofficially at 12.4 percent in 1931.[3] Very few independent African political publications, however, survived the decade of the 1930s. In a climate of economic depression and political repression–highlighted by the loss of the African franchise in the Cape and renewed efforts by the state to institutionalize segregation and retribalize the whole of the African population–there was much less tolerance for an African protest press.

As the urban African population grew and the literacy rate gradually rose, white entrepreneurs began buying up independent African newspapers and establishing other publications aimed at African readers. The traditional African protest press, starved of capital and unable to compete against white-owned African commercial newspapers like *Bantu World* and its imitators, in effect collapsed. The number of African newspapers registered with the government had reached a high of 19 in 1930, but there were only 7 by 1954–all owned and controlled solely by whites.[4] Outside of *Inkundla ya Bantu* and a few African township newsletters with limited circulations, no independent African political journals were left by the 1940s.

The vacuum created by the demise of the independent African protest press was largely filled by a number of socialist journals. The flagship newspaper of the Communist Party of South Africa (CPSA) in the 1940s–Johannesburg's *Inkululeko*–attracted a multiracial readership that extended far beyond the CPSA's minuscule membership. The *Guardian*, another socialist weekly independent of the party, was the most popular alternative publication between the 1940s and early 1960s, when the apartheid govemment, in attempting to silence all public criticism of its policies, finally forced the last of these protest-cum-resistance journals to cease publication.

The alternative press throughout its history mediated social realities that differed substantially from the social realities mediated by the white-owned and controlled commercial press, which will celebrate its two-hundredth anniversary in the year 2000. The established white press has been owned and controlled by whites, aimed at or intended for whites, concerned almost exclusively with the political, economic and social life of the white population, and consumed mainly by whites for most of this two-hundred-year history.[5]

Mainstream white publications in South Africa sought on the whole to imitate their counterparts in the Western metropoles in constructing middle-class versions of modernity for their readers. Although English-language newspapers did represent themselves as an "opposition" press during the apartheid era, the targets of dissent were carefully selected and comprised an insignificant proportion of the news.[6] African journalists were given permanent employment in a few of these newspapers only from the 1960s and 1970s, and they worked almost exclusively on subordinate, segregated and decidedly paternalistic inserts or supplements targeted for black audiences. African journalists, moreover, had no control over and virtually no access to other media of mass communication before the 1960s.[7]

Anti-apartheid critics of the English-language commercial press have claimed that these "opposition" newspapers (1) focused on "safe" anti-apartheid news stories and on personalities and events rather than issues, ignoring the conditions and contexts in which these stories took place; (2) practiced widespread self-censorship as part of their response to the government's attempt to censor and control communication media; (3) did nothing to deracialize and democratize their own institutions, inside and outside the newsroom; (4) omitted, trivialized or downplayed news that might threaten the economic and political interests of those corporate groups who owned or otherwise controlled these publications; and (5) played the role of a community press that served the cultural interests of their largely white, English-speaking readership in much the same way as the white Afrikaans press, which was perceived to be the mouthpiece of the Afrikaner community and the National Party. Even during the apartheid era, few if any mainstream newspapers consistently attacked the government's policies and activities before the 1980s.[8]

South Africa's alternative press, then, constitutes a unique political, social and literary archive–the oldest, most extensive and varied collection of indigenous serial publications of this kind in sub-Saharan Africa. There have been four phases in the history of the alternative press:

1. The African mission press (1830s–1880s), which represented the pioneer missionary societies and their converts living and working primarily in mission station and outstation communities. The earliest African protest literature can be traced to a few mission journals in the last three decades or so of this era.

2. The independent protest press (1880s–1930s), which represented primarily the black petty bourgeoisie. African nationalist newspapers were the dominant organs of news and opinion. The origins of an indigenous black literary tradition in English, Afrikaans and various ethnic African languages can also be traced to this period. It would take many forms, including personality profiles and essays devoted to African language, literature and history, humor and advice columns, poetry, short stories, plays, sermons, and even the words to hymns and other musical compositions.

3. The early resistance press (1930s–1960s), which gradually embraced a popular, nonracial, nonsectarian and more militant alliance of left-wing working- and middle-class interests. At the same time, traditional protest publications were bought out, closed down or depoliticized and merged with a new captive black commercial press controlled by white entrepreneurs.

4. The later resistance press (1970s–1980s), which represented primarily the Black Consciousness movement and its press (1970s) and the so-called progressive community press (1980s). Resistance media changed dramatically in form and content during these decades. They embraced (1) various commercial publications still aimed at segregated black and/or white audiences; (2) progressive academic journals and student publications from historically "white" universities, adult literacy texts, published oral narratives, personal memoirs and popular histories; and (3) a variety of literary, musical and performance texts generated mainly in segregated African townships, informal settlements and historically "black" or "homeland" university settings that were now fully engaged in the struggle for South Africa.[9]

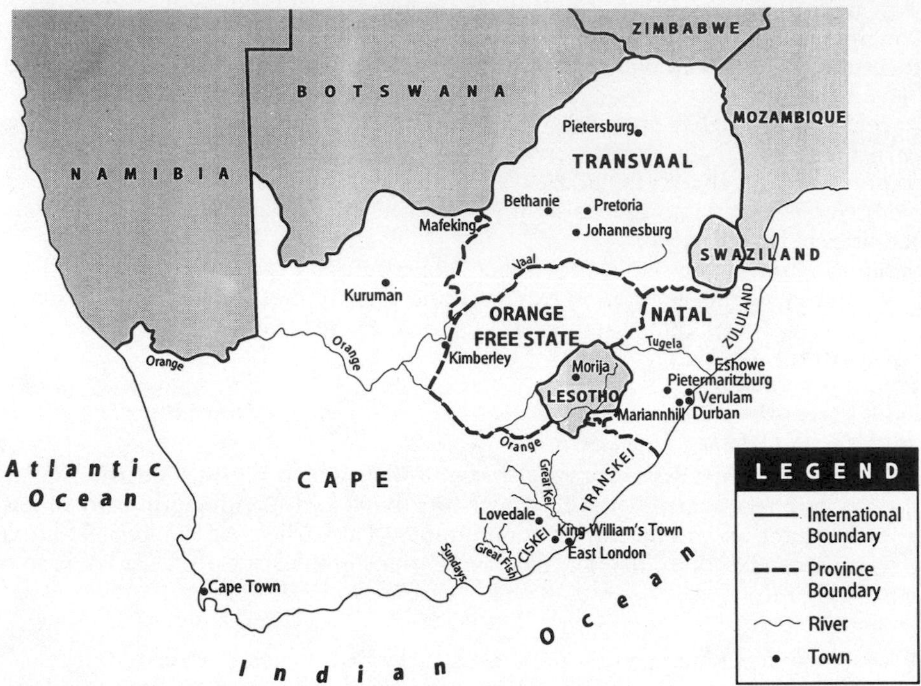

MAP. Cities, towns and villages in South Africa where alternative publications cited in this book were located.

Publication	Date founded	Location (Province)
South African Spectator	1900	Cape Town (Cape)
APO (A[frican] P[olitical] O[rganization])	1909	Cape Town
Educational Journal	1915	Cape Town
South African Clarion	1919	Cape Town
Guardian	1937	Cape Town
Under other titles, including *Advance, New Age, Spark*	1952–63	
Torch	1946	Cape Town
Ilanga lase Natal (Natal Sun)	1903	Durban (Natal)
Indian Opinion	1903	Durban/Phoenix
African Chronicle	1908	Durban
Izindaba Zabantu (People's Topics)	1910	Durban and Mariannhill
Indian Views	1914	Durban
Inkundla ya Bantu (People's Forum)	1938	Durban and Verulam

Publication	Date founded	Location (Province)
Abantu-Batho (The People)	1912	Johannesburg (Transvaal)
Umteteli wa Bantu (Mouthpiece of the People)	1920	Johannesburg
Workers' Herald	1923	Cape Town and Johannesburg
African Leader	1932	Johannesburg
Bantu World Title changed to *World*	1932 1956	Johannesburg
Inkululeko (Freedom) Under three other titles, *International, South African Worker, Umsebenzi* (The Worker)	1939 1915–38	Cape Town and Johannesburg
Fighting Talk	1942	Johannesburg
Drum	1951	Cape Town and Johannesburg
Golden City Post Title changed to *Post*	1955 1960	Johannesburg
Indaba (News)	1862	Lovedale (Cape)
Isigidimi Sama Xosa (The Xhosa Messenger) As a supplement in *Kaffir Express*	1873 1870	Lovedale
Mahoko a Becoana (or *Becwana*) (News for the Bechuana)	1883	Kuruman (Cape)
Imvo Zabantsundu (Native Opinion)	1884	King William's Town (Cape)
Izwi Labantu (Voice of the People)	1897	East London (Cape)
Koranta ea Becoana (Bechuana Gazette)	1901	Mafeking (now Mafikeng) (Cape)
Tsala ea Becoana (Friend of the Bechuana) and *Tsala ea Batho* (People's Friend)	1910 1912	Kimberley (Cape)
Inkanyiso yase Natal (Natal Light)	1889	Pietermaritzburg (Natal)
Ipepa lo Hlanga (Paper of the Nation)	1894(?) 1901(?)	Pietermaritzburg
Colonial Indian News	1901	Pietermaritzburg
Ikwezi le Afrika (Morning Star of Africa)	1928	Eshowe (Natal)
Moshupa (later *Mosupa*) Tsela (The Guide)	1893	Bethanie (Rustenburg) (Transvaal)
Leihlo lo Babathso (Native Eye)	1903	Pietersburg (Transvaal)
Native Advocate	1912(?)	Pretoria (Transvaal)

The Black Petty Bourgeoisie

The concept of the black petty bourgeoisie as a distinct, intermediate class in South Africa's everchanging social formation is not in vogue in the 1990s as it was in the 1970s and 1980s, but it remains a crucial concept in examining the texts of the alternative press. The primary communicators *and* consumers of alternative news and opinion came from this subordinated social class, and at least 8 of the 11 chapters in this book are concerned mainly with their political, economic and social activities.[10]

In the literature on the role of social classes in capitalist cultures, the petty bourgeoisie has always occupied a somewhat precarious position between labor and capital (labor being represented by the working class or the proletariat and capital by the capitalist class or the bourgeoisie in classical marxist terminology). Indeed, the "petty" in "petty bourgeoisie" is used by many contemporary scholars as a deliberate corruption of the French term *petit* or *petite bourgeoisie*, and it has undergone different readings over the years in response to criticism and confusion on the left as to what this class represents. The traditional petty bourgeoisie comprised groups such as petty traders, commodity producers and independent farmers, but this notion of the "middle class" was outmoded even before the emergence of modern capitalism.

While classical marxists perceived the petty bourgeoisie as "a class left over from an earlier social order"–an anachronism that would wither away when members were "progressively forced down into the proletariat"–it was becoming clear even before the end of the nineteenth century that the petty bourgeoisie was expanding rapidly, becoming much more diverse and more autonomous in capitalist social relations. Critical scholars have stressed the shift from manual to mental labor, the growth of nonindustrial occupations and above all the emergence of a new professional-managerial elite within the petty bourgeoisie in the twentieth century.

The petty bourgeoisie, like the middle class it is supposed to embrace, is perceived by marxists and nonmarxists alike as an ambiguous force in modern industrial culture. Some scholars still identify social elements associated with the petty bourgeoisie as mediators of labor, while other scholars identify them as mediators of capital.[11] It could be argued that this book is the story of an aspiring black petty bourgeoisie and its press in South Africa. The texts examined here suggest that elements within this social-class-in-the-making positioned themselves at various points along the labor–capital continuum in the century after conquest.

The petty bourgeoisie was (and is) a structurally ambiguous class in capitalist South Africa. Members were differentiated by "race" or color and segmented further by geography, culture, language, ethnicity, religious persuasion and even gender for much of the period embraced by this study. Although components within the white petty bourgeoisie–mainly (but not exclusively) English-speaking adherents to what is called the liberal tradition in South Africa ("liberal" did not mean that those who held such values were against segregation)–were open to cooperation and sometimes even collaboration with the black petty bourgeoisie, their interests were ultimately dictated by their status in the hierarchy of South Africa's racially stratified society.

Membership in the black petty bourgeoisie was influenced but not predetermined by one's relationship to the shifting mode of capitalist production. The boundaries that separated the black petty bourgeoisie from blacks who labored in white homes, farms, mines and factories or struggled to survive as subsubsistence peasants in the African reserves were never clearly drawn.

Class consciousness was equally difficult to distinguish. Although continuing faith in the capitalist system and in Cape-style liberalism constituted a preferred economic and political discourse for the black petty bourgeoisie inside and outside the Cape between the 1860s and 1930s, for example, the activities of individuals and groups cannot be interpreted simply as a prolonged refomist attempt to gain entry into white middle-class society. Even during this period, alienated segments of the African petty bourgeoisie could find common cause with African peasants or industrial workers in openly challenging the social order, as in the events that occurred on the Witwatersrand (South Africa's industrial heartland, embracing Johannesburg and its environs) in the years immediately following World War I. Self-reliance was also a major theme during the interwar era, and especially in the 1930s many African political activists sought to promote racial and even "tribal" solidarity in an effort to revive the African nationalist movement.

In terms of numbers, the black petty bourgeoisie always constituted an insignificant proportion of the black population. There were wide variations within this class in terms of formal education, occupational status and affluence, and there were disparities in terms of regional and ethnic influence. Xhosa speakers from the eastern Cape, for example, probably formed the most significant component of the African petty bourgeoisie between the 1860s and the 1910s, and Cape Africans were conspicuous as leaders in protest politics inside and outside the Cape until the 1930s. Africans, Coloureds and Indians who aspired to a middle-class lifestyle were effectively separated from each other in their segregated communities, and for the most part this was a male-gendered discourse until the final decades of the apartheid era.

Before the 1940s, the mission-educated community comprised by far the largest component of the African petty bourgeoisie. They saw themselves as a modernizing, upwardly mobile, increasingly urbanized, nonethnic force in the struggle to create a black middle-class culture in South Africa. Their leaders were "organic intellectuals" in the Gramscian sense–thinkers and organizers who sought to concretize the ideas and attitudes of a distinct social class in British South Africa by the beginning of the twentieth century.[12]

Christian values, allegiance to churches recognized by the government, a primary education or at least the ability to read and write in one language (preferably English), individual enterprise, African as opposed to ethnic loyalty–these were cardinal virtues for the minority in town as well as the majority who still lived in the countryside. T. D. Mweli Skota's famous biographical reference guide to the African elite, published in 1930, for example, was saturated with cultural codes inherited from the founding fathers of the African mission church. Skota's "progressive" African, as Tim Couzens suggests, is a man who with luck might possess a royal pedigree, gets involved in his people's welfare and is a hard worker (if he is a farmer, he plows his own fields and works the land in individual tenure). He is a "true, kind-hearted Christian gentleman, respected by Europeans and Africans alike, a good speaker, who does not drink, and who starts as a teacher or interpreter and becomes a clergyman or lawyer."[13]

Between the 1860s and 1930s, the mission-educated petty bourgeoisie in effect organized and controlled African politics at local, regional and national levels. These activists judged themselves to be the harbingers of modernity and the primary mediating force between rulers and ruled. They tried to organize public discourse and provide a public platform for the grievances and aspirations of the majority population, but they remained small in number and very vulnerable to changes that occurred both inside and outside the African community.

Between the 1930s and 1950s, the composition of the African petty bourgeoisie began to change with the development of South Africa's industrializing economy and the increasing demand for black labor. African peasants, the main source of labor, were pushed, as well as pulled, to the cities in search of work. White-owned commercial farms were gradually mechanizing, and African-reserve economies were gradually unraveling–a process that continued into the next generation. The number of peasant families migrating, out of necessity, to the cities (especially to metropolitan areas such as Johannesburg, Cape Town, Durban and Port Elizabeth) rose dramatically during the 1940s and 1950s.

The apartheid state tried vigorously to halt and even reverse the migration of Africans from countryside to town, especially after the National Party succeeded in temporarily blunting black and white opposition to its policies at the beginning of the 1960s, but in the end the state failed. Although the percentage of the African population in designated white urban areas did decrease by 2.6 percent between 1960 and 1980, the urban African population continued to expand in absolute numbers. In 1980, it was estimated at 5.6 million (26.7 percent of the total population), but this did not include millions of Africans living in urban townships that were incorporated into adjacent reserves wherever possible. The real African population in urban areas in 1980 was estimated to be between 33 and 50 percent of the total population, and by the early 1990s the estimate had risen to about 65 percent.[14]

Labor became a crucial site of struggle in the generation after World War II, as the apartheid regime sought to reclassify, redistribute and ultimately relocate the entire black working force in South Africa. In the process of setting up structures to police and modernize the labor-control system, hundreds of thousands of jobs were created for Africans inside and outside the reserves. In addition to this bureaucracy, an equally vast African service industry (from housing, schools and health care to small, independent businesses of every description) developed during the apartheid era. In attempting to decentralize the apartheid system in the 1970s and 1980s, moreover, a major attempt was made to redistribute personal income to privileged segments of the African population and to accommodate their interests and needs.

The impact of these policies on the African petty bourgeoisie can be seen in part by looking at census reports that recorded Africans in certain middle-class occupational categories–professional/technical, managerial/administrative/governmental, clerical/sales and related positions (Table 1).

The percentage of Africans in these categories remained insignificant in comparison with the total African labor force–0.7 percent of the economically active population in 1921, 1.1 percent in 1936, 1.8 percent in 1946, 2.8 percent in 1951, 2.6 percent in 1960, 4.7 percent in 1970 and 10.2 percent in 1980–but the figures are revealing. The number of Africans employed in middle-class jobs grew steadily in the decade or so before the 1950s, declined during the most repressive years of apartheid between the 1950s and mid-1960s, and rose dramatically when the state made a concerted attempt to expand and co-opt the black petty bourgeoisie from the late 1960s and 1970s. Africans came to dominate some professions–like teaching (where they held 43 percent and whites 42 percent of the posts in 1980), ministers of religion (where they held 47 percent and whites 35 percent in 1980) and lower-ranked health services (especially nursing)–as well as clerical/sales and related occupations.[15]

Table 1. *Number of Africans in three middle-class occupation categories, 1921–1980*

Occupations	1921	1936	1946	1951	1960	1970	1980
1.1. Professional/ technical and related	9,756	27,620	48,822	58,910	48,487	91,996	190,089
1.2. Administrative and managerial	—	975	2,737	5,105	5,716	2,306	5,108
1.3. Clerical and Sales	15,057	25,150	34,998	24,407	48,170	174,298	374,697
Totals	24,813	53,745	86,557	88,422	102,373	268,600	569,894

Note: The dash in the first column for Category 1.2 indicates insufficient data.
Sources: *Union statistics for fifty years: Jubilee Issue 1910–1960* (Pretoria, 1960), A-33; Republic of South Africa, Department of Statistics, *Population Census for 1960*, Vol. 8, No. 1 (Occupations), 3 (Table 1); *Population Census for 1970*, Report No. 02-05-04 (Occupations), 1 (Table 1); *Population Census for 1980*, Report No. 02-80-05 (Occupation by statistical region and district), 510. The economically active population was comprised of individuals aged 15 years and above. Jobs were placed under a variety of headings before the job categories themselves were standardized in 1960, so researchers may differ in compiling figures in this table before the 1960 census. Policemen, teachers, clergy (ordained and nonordained), herbalists, prison warders, hospital attendants, nurses and "other professionals" comprised 83 percent of the "professional" category (excluding "entertainment" and "sports"), for example, in the 1946 census. Salespersons and shop assistants, small traders, clerks, hawkers, vendors and other sellers of petty commodities made up 94 percent of the "commercial and financial" category in 1946.

The African petty bourgeoisie was small and relatively easy to track before the 1940s, but it is not so easy to periodize subsequent changes in composition and development. Nevertheless, the African petty bourgeoisie appears to have undergone two major periods of transition, at least in terms of the boundaries dictated by the census data. The first occurred between the 1930s and the 1950s, and the second occurred during the 1970s and 1980s. Each period was characterized by accelerated growth rates in the number of Africans living in town, the number of women, as well as men, employed in South Africa's formal (or industrial capitalist) economic sector, and the number of Africans in designated middle-class occupations and presumably enjoying an improved socioeconomic status. There were also changes in other demographic variables, such as the number of African students in school, especially in postprimary schools. Both periods, moreover, were characterized by significant increases in the number of alternative newspapers and newspaper readers, and in political activities associated with the resistance movement.

The first period is crucial to this book, because it was characterized by a transition in discourse from protest to resistance in African politics. Between the 1930s and the 1950s, there was an unparalleled expansion in the South African economy, especially in manufacturing. As a contribution to the national income, manufacturing had already moved ahead of agriculture by 1930, and it passed mining in 1943. The number of Africans employed in manufacturing, for example, more than doubled, from 151,889 in 1939–40 to 369,055 in 1949–50. The permanent urban African population doubled, from roughly 1.2 million in 1936 to 2.4 million in 1951, and more Africans than whites were living in town by 1946. Africans in designated middle-class occupations increased by an estimated 34,677–a steady though not spectacular growth rate of 64.5 percent–between 1936 and 1951. Nevertheless, women held 31.3 percent of the middle-class jobs by 1951, and they were particularly prominent in the professional/technical category.[16]

The number of Africans seeking postprimary education also grew rapidly. The enrollment of students in segregated African secondary schools (Standards VI–X, roughly equivalent to the eighth through twelfth grades in the United States), for example, soared more than 450 percent in 18 years–from 10,997 in 1935 to 61,132 in 1953, when the Bantu Education Act imposed apartheid on South Africa's primary and secondary school system.[17] African enrollment at the University College of Fort Hare–the only university established for Africans in South Africa before the apartheid era–averaged 82 between 1916 and 1935, 136 between 1936 and 1940, 191 between 1941 and 1945, 284 by the end of the 1940s and 352 by the end of the 1950s, when the Extension of University Education Act imposed apartheid on South Africa's university system.[18]

The missionaries were primarily responsible for African primary and secondary education until the 1953 Bantu Education Act. The provinces subsidized only the teachers' salaries: everything else was subsidized by the mission agencies, and they could no longer bear the financial responsibility of educating so many students. As the debt burden increased, the missionaries cut costs wherever they could, and this triggered an upsurge in student violence, especially during the 1940s. For example, 49 student disturbances (31 of which were regarded as serious by the authorities) were recorded in 28 mission schools between 1937 and 1946, and virtually all the incidents occurred in the boarding (secondary) schools. There was a dramatic increase in serious incidents after World War II, when many veterans returned to school, 20 being recorded between 1945 and 1947. Student agitation in the boarding schools and at Fort Hare helped to fuel the emerging resistance movement.[19]

By 1946, between 250,000 and 500,000 Africans were believed to be reading newspapers and other periodicals. About 21.3 percent of the adult African population was regarded as literate in 1946 and 23.8 percent in 1951, when the first mass-circulation magazines and newspapers targeted at the urban African market were launched in South Africa. In terms of occupation, the literates embraced skilled and semiskilled industrial workers, increasing numbers of students from mission boarding schools and Fort Hare University, self-employed persons in a range of service-related occupations, salaried professionals and members of a steadily expanding government bureaucracy in the urban townships and reserves.[20]

African membership in the petty bourgeoisie during the 1940s and 1950s was still determined in large part by family pedigree, church affiliation (although mission church affiliation was no longer necessary or, in many instances, even desirable), education, occupation, wealth and community status. Nevertheless, African leaders in the African National Congress (ANC, or Congress) and other political pressure groups were now being drawn from a social class that was increasingly literate, better educated (for example, virtually all the leaders of the ANC's Youth League had completed high school and/or had at least some years in a nursing or teacher-training college or university), more urbanized and more diverse in terms of occupation. They were also more secular in social orientation and outlook: the clergy and the organizations they represented did not have the political influence they had had in previous generations. The rejuvenation of the ANC in African national politics during this period was linked inextricably to the rejuvenation of the African petty bourgeoisie in subaltern South Africa.

Contested Issues in Reading Cultural Texts

This book examines a selected group of alternative texts that were produced during the century when South Africa made the transition to a modern industrial culture. The authors have asked certain questions of these texts in an attempt to determine how and why they both reflected and represented South Africa's subject African, Coloured and Indian communities in the ways that they did. We found that the texts could be read in different ways and were by no means static or uniform over time and place, but there were definitely preferred readings.

These preferred readings privileged the black petty bourgeoisie, and this constituency and the community interests it represented provide a focus for most chapters dealing with the alternative press before the 1940s. The remaining chapters examine publications that reflected national interests and more diverse constituencies (in terms of race, class, caste, gender, politics and culture) within the resistance movement between the 1940s and the 1960s.

The petty bourgeois press was never sealed off from the signs and practices of South Africa's peasants and workers–the voiceless majority–but their grievances and aspirations were interpreted in ways that mirrored middle-class sensibilities. Their lived experiences, moreover, constituted a miniscule proportion of the news agenda. The petty bourgeois press also sought to record personalities and events that symbolized the dominant European culture, but these readings of the hegemonic voice were decidedly ambiguous until the apartheid era.

Theoretical Concerns

The contested issues in reading any cultural text revolve around the relationship between language, text and community. Numerous scholars have examined the relationship between language–theories about grammar, about speech acts, about what is meant by what we speak and write–and our experience of the world that language represents. Our sense of self, of who we are and what is real, is determined in the first instance by language, and the language of individuals, as of communities, is made up of many voices.

Hermeneutic scholars, for example, assume that the world and the objects of the world we study always require interpretation in order to convey meaning. Readers come to a text not as the linguistic equivalent of naked apes but as subjects filled with meaning–with "facts," ideas, associations, assumptions, conditions, expectations, memories–and we find that the text is also filled with meaning. The text can reinforce and enhance, or confront and contradict, our existing "horizons of meaning." Ideally, the meanings we bring to the text interact successfully with meanings already in the text that, in turn, are embodied in the community producing the text.[21]

Anchored in the tradition of critical hermeneutics is an approach employed by German social theorist Jürgen Habermas that seems particularly appropriate for this study. He examined the relationship between language, text and community in what he calls the "public sphere"–a term that refers to the "domain in our social life" where "public opinion can be formed."[22] Habermas studied the public languages (including codes of speech and speech acts), gestures, mannerisms, etiquettes, education levels, fashions and other socially bound activities that were employed to gain access to bourgeois life in western Europe between the seventeenth and nineteenth centuries–the beginning of the modern era.

He argues that the bourgeoisie fostered a distinction between "private" and "public" spheres in their social practices and negotiated a public sphere for themselves. The public sphere constituted the nation's citizenry, and, from the beginning, one of the most important components in the creation of a "bourgeois public sphere" was the mass media of communication. The newspaper played a crucial role in developing the language of public debate about what constituted the public issues of the day. "The press remained an institution of the public itself, operating to provide and intensify public discussion, no longer a mere organ for the conveyance of information, but not yet a medium of consumer culture."[23]

By the eighteenth century, in western Europe it had become very important to observe the political language of the bourgeois public sphere, because this was the mode for communicating the world of knowledge. It presumed a world of individuals–unified, centered subjects–who were of a certain social class, because the language of expression in the public sphere emphasized clarity, coherence, organization, evenness, willingness to compromise and a "middle" style of expression appropriate to the emerging middle classes. Once the standards of linguistic correctness were ritualized, the ways one could recognize members of the public sphere were known. Now there was an "objective" measure to verify a person's membership in the public sphere.

Ferdinand de Saussure (1857–1913), the pioneer of modern structural linguistics, argued as Habermas does that social relations are defined primarily by language and that words mean what they do only because as a language community we agree to assign them these meanings. Saussure conceived of language in part as a system of binary signs, in which words, for example, are assigned values in terms of their opposition to other words. Or, to put it another way: the meaning of words is determined by what they are not rather than by what they are.[24] Saussure believed the principles that structure language systems also structure other kinds of communication systems–indeed, all other systems that generate meaning in a given culture. Although his ideas have been supplemented and at least partially supplanted by numerous poststructuralist critics, he has provided us with some enduring insights into the power of language to structure social reality–especially in the public sphere.

The power of the news media, for example, lies precisely in the power to confer meaning on personalities, events and issues that are appropriated for the public sphere. Mass-mediated news–in newspapers, magazines, radio, television and related communication media–is primarily a dichotomous discourse that presumes a certain stability of language. The production of news by definition is a process that seeks to secure fixed readings of the text, and news opinion polls and surveys function mainly to determine whether these preferred readings are understood and accepted by their audiences. The narration of news is grounded in a Saussurean world of binary signs–of life and death, subject and object, male and female, white and black, good and bad, pure and impure, legitimate and illegitimate, sane and insane, normal and abnormal, sacred and profane, skilled and unskilled, capitalism and communism, development and dependency, north and south, metropole and periphery... the dichotomies are endless.

The concept of the bourgeois public sphere–its linguistic and social codes of belief and behavior–is very useful for the present study. South Africa's white commercial press limited the black petty bourgeoisie's access to and participation in the public sphere for most of the century that preceded the end of the apartheid era. In turn, the public sphere in South Africa's altemative press was represented mainly by the black petty bourgeoisie before the 1940s, and they placed similar restrictions on the roles played by black workers and peasants in these publications.

The research presented in this book is essentially a "formal" reading of selected alternative news texts. A formal reading assumes a certain stability of language and specified frames of reference that endure over time and place. But this does not mean the textual analysis should ignore discursive strategies associated with the post-modern project, where the properties of linguistic and social discourse are assumed to be personal, subjective and anchored in local landscapes. These strategies encourage the researcher to be sensitive to obscure, distorted, repressed or concealed readings in the text.

The Russian literary critic Mikhail Bakhtin employed the terms "monologic" and "dialogic" to express the tension between ideological conformity and diversity in cultural texts. Struggles over power are seen to take the form of struggles for control of the symbolic system–or some dimension of it. The monologic voice is the hierarchical authoritarian voice, the privileged language or discourse (anything from a privileged dialect to a privileged social class), the univocal ideological perspective communicated in the text. The dialogic voice is a plurality of discourses, of ideologies–the democratic voice. These are two trajectories of power–one from above, hierarchical and hegemonic, and the other from below, heterogeneous and culturally diverse. For Bakhtin, all cultural texts exhibit tension between the monologic and the dialogic. They operate in a dialectical relationship fraught with struggle. Bakhtin, then, reminds the researcher that the text–in this case, a newspaper–should be read in terms of these conversations.[25]

Scholars in what is called subaltern studies (the study of subordinate, dominated, marginalized or excluded "races," castes, ethnic and linguistic groups, classes, genders, cultures) are concerned with languages, texts, rituals and myths that negotiate and contest power and create space for resistance in everyday life.[26] Subaltern subjects and subject communities can contribute to the monologic narrative structures that sanction obedience, but these structures are also sites of dialogic struggle. This seems to be the case with the texts of South Africa's alternative press.

Methodological Concerns: A Case Study of Six Newspapers

Six newspapers in this study–*Imvo Zabantsundu*, the *Workers' Herald*, *Bantu World*, *Inkundla ya Bantu*, the *Guardian* and *Inkululeko*–were subjected to content analyses in order to provide empirical evidence of a fundamental shift in political rhetoric in the alternative press between the 1920s and 1950s. Switzer was joined in this effort by Ime Ukpanah and Elizabeth Jones, who were graduate students at the University of Houston and the London School of Economics, respectively, when this research was undertaken. Particular stress was placed on how these newspapers organized public dissent and chronicled the transition from petitionary protest to nonviolent resistance outside as well as inside the African nationalist community.[27]

Two primary research questions were posed: (1) How did the alternative press both reflect and represent the African population between the 1920s and 1950s? (2) In what specific ways does the content of these newspapers manifest a shift in discourse from the politics of protest to the politics of resistance?

In responding to these questions, three levels of analysis were established. In Level 1, a random sample of each newspaper was selected for quantitative analysis. The reference base for each story unit (which included the language of communication, the headline and the "news peg" or central theme) was recorded, and each story unit was subjected to three readings before categories were finalized and coding decisions made. First, in reading these stories we made a distinction between "black" and "white" news and entertainment, because we assumed the reference base was conditioned by South Africa's racial order. Second, in reading these stories we made a distinction between political and nonpolitical news and opinion, because we assumed black political responses to South Africa's racial order would be recorded mainly in organized political and trade union activity. Third, in reading these stories we made a distinction between South African and non–South African news, because we assumed black perspectives on political activities outside South Africa might influence black perspectives on political activities inside South Africa.

Four categories–three domestic and one foreign–were then established. Category A news ("Black news of general interest in South Africa") was concerned primarily with the everyday life of the black petty bourgeoisie, where the reference base was not a political or trade union activity. The signs and practices of this emerging social class were inscribed in stories about life at home, at church, at school, at work, at play. Taken together, they comprised a signifying system through which members of this community made sense of, and to some degree came to terms with, their position as a subordinate community in South Africa's racial order. Category B news ("White news in South Africa") was concerned primarily with the political, economic and social activities of those who ruled. The white authoritarian context provided an agenda for negotiation, as well as protest, and to an extent established parameters for what was deemed to be legitimate to discuss and debate. Category C news ("Black political and/or trade union news in South Africa") was concerned primarily with organized political and trade union activities aimed at or intended for the subaltern black population. These stories dealt specifically with the personalities, organizations and issues of a dissident political culture. Category D news ("Foreign news") was concerned primarily with non-South African news, and stories that promoted the domestic political agendas of the African nationalist and socialist press were the focus of interest. (A more detailed description of the categories and the quantitative analysis is provided in the Appendix to this volume.)

In Level 2, specific stories were selected for closer analysis to illustrate how news was handled in the domestic news categories. In Level 3, domestic political and trade union stories that focused primarily on confrontation and consciousness-raising activities, and foreign news stories that focused primarily on socialist activities, were also isolated for closer analysis to test whether a shift in political discourse did occur in these texts during the 1940s and early 1950s.

News percentages in the various categories for the six newspapers are revealing (Table 2). Three of the four African nationalist newspapers–*Imvo Zabantsundu*, *Inkundla ya Bantu* and *Bantu World*–supported the African National Congress and were active in protesting the government's segregationist policies, but they focused primarily on Category A, general interest news (and entertainment) involving the black community. The social activities of the petty bourgeoisie were chronicled mainly in Category A news, and the topics covered were remarkably similar in all African newspapers examined between the 1920s and 1950s. Even the *Workers' Herald*, which also supported the ANC and was active in protest politics as the mouthpiece of the Industrial and Commercial Workers' Union, devoted

Table 2. *News content in six alternative newspapers, 1919–1952 (% of story units)*

Newspaper	Categories[a] A	B	C	D
Imvo Zabantsundu (January 1919–December 1929)	65.9	15.3	16.6	2.2
Workers' Herald (February 1925–December 1928)	27.3	21.3	40.6	10.8
Bantu World (April 1932-December 1939)	78.6	7.1	5.3	9.0
Inkundla ya Bantu (April 1938–November 1951)	53.8	11.6	28.0	6.7
Inkululeko (December 1940–June 1950)	9.8	13.6	47.1	29.5
Guardian (February 1937–May 1952)	15.1	18.2	34.7	32.0

[a]A. Black (multiracial, where applicable) news of general interest in South Africa.
B. White (multiracial, where applicable) news in South Africa.
C. Black (multiracial, where applicable) political and/or trade union news in South Africa.
D. Foreign news.

Note: Percentages are calculated by dividing the number of story units in each category by the total number of story units. "News" refers to all story units, including illustrations and informal advertisements classified as news. Formal advertisements are excluded. See the Appendix for an explanation of the methodology used.

considerably more space to Category A than the socialist press, which had little interest in black community news.

African nationalist and socialist newspapers devoted between 7 and 21 percent of their respective news agendas to Category B, political, economic and social news involving the white community. This was a significant category in establishing the boundaries of permissible dissent, and all the newspapers covered essentially the same types of personalities, events and issues. The discriminatory acts of individuals and organizations in the public and private sector, the segregationist policies of the state and the activities of white-liberal groups (mainly mission, church, welfare and civil rights groups) comprised most of the news in Category B until the apartheid era.

The contrast in political discourse between the African nationalist press and the socialist press can be seen most clearly in stories devoted to Category C, black political and trade union activities (Table 3). Socialist newspapers placed more emphasis on Category C news than African nationalist newspapers in these samples. The *Workers' Herald* was an exception, but 95 percent of the news in this category concerned the Industrial and Commercial Workers' Union (ICU), its officials and its critics.

The depoliticization of the text can be seen most clearly in the white-owned *Bantu World*. Categories B and C combined comprised not much more than 12 percent of the news agenda. As we shall see, this is graphic evidence of what happened to the African nationalist press when it was subordinated to white control and commercialized between the 1930s and the 1950s.

African nationalist press coverage of Subcategory C.1, black political/trade union personalities and organizations, placed much emphasis on stories about African consultative bodies sponsored by white liberal groups or the government. They comprised about 40 percent of the news in this subcategory in *Imvo*, about

Table 3. *Category C news in the alternative press (% of story units)*

	Category[a]		
	C	C.1	C.2
African nationalist newspapers			
Imvo Zabantsundu	16.6	14.0	2.6
Workers' Herald	40.6	36.1	4.5
Bantu World	5.3	4.6	0.7
Inkundla ya Bantu	28.0	18.0	10.0
Socialist Newspapers			
Inkululeko	47.1	27.5	19.6
Guardian	34.7	24.4	10.3

[a]C. Black/multiracial political and trade union news.
C.1 Personalities and organizations.
C.2 Confrontation and consciousness.

33 percent in *Bantu World* and about 24 percent in *Inkundla*. The main consultative bodies covered were the Native Conferences (during the 1920s), Non-European Conferences (1927–34), Joint Councils (1920s–1940s), Natives' Representative Council (from 1937), urban Location Advisory Boards, councils of chiefs, and the local, district and general councils established for rural Africans in the Cape's Ciskei and Transkei reserves (1920s–1950s). In contrast, both socialist newspapers downplayed these stories. They comprised about 5 percent of the news in this subcategory in the *Guardian* and *Inkululeko*.

African nationalist press coverage of independent African political activities focused on the ANC (1920s–1950s), the ICU and its splinter groups (1920s and 1930s), the Non-European Unity Movement, the All-African Convention and allied bodies (mainly 1940s), and local and regional political bodies like the Cape Native Voters' Convention, vigilance and ratepayers' associations (mainly 1920s and 1930s). Coverage was often brief and superficial–notices of meetings, reports of motions presented or resolutions approved. Personal and factional rivalries were sometimes highlighted, but there were few critiques of these organizations, their programs or constituencies.

The *Guardian*, before the 1950s, focused primarily on trade union news, which comprised about 50 percent of the stories in Subcategory C.1. The workers' groups covered during the 1940s were associated mainly with two nonracial coordinating bodies called the South African Trades and Labour Council (launched in 1930) and the Congress of Non-European Trade Unions (launched in 1941), which represented primarily unregistered African unions. As anticipated, our analysis showed that the *Guardian* highlighted the activities of the Communist Party of South Africa (CPSA) and affiliated bodies but downplayed the ANC (only 5.3 percent of Category C.1 news). As anticipated, CPSA's official organ *Inkululeko* focused mainly on party activities, secondly on key left-wing unions like the African Mine Workers' Union, the Garment Workers' Union and the Iron and Steel Workers' Union, and thirdly on black political bodies like the ANC and the South African Indian Congress.

The differences in political discourse between socialist and African nationalist newspapers were particularly noticeable in Subcategory C.2, confrontation or

Table 4. *Category D news in the socialist press (% of story units)*

Newspaper	Category[a] D	D.1	D.2
Inkululeko	29.5	18.7	10.8
Guardian	32.0	21.4	10.6

[a]D. Foreign news.
D.1 International socialism at war and peace.
D.2 Other international.

consciousness. Confrontation stories focused on strikes (and threatened strikes) by students, teachers and various categories of workers, together with boycotts, protest marches and demonstrations initiated by organized political, trade union and community-action groups in the urban and rural areas. Consciousness-raising stories sought in one way or another to challenge the dominant discourse.

Inkululeko was in a class of its own on this topic. No other text analyzed before the 1950s devoted as much space to calls for direct action and appeals for a united front in opposition to the state. Both socialist newspapers, moreover, saw their task as being nothing less than to project an alternative news agenda for South Africa's working classes. The new discourse was the socialist project inside and outside South Africa, which was the main reason why the socialist press placed so much more emphasis on foreign news than the African nationalist press (Table 4).

Category D, foreign news, averaged 31 percent of the news agenda in the *Guardian* and *Inkululeko*, in contrast to 7 percent on average for the four African nationalist newspapers. In the *Guardian*, for example, foreign news was found on virtually every page, and foreign affairs was a topic in at least six weekly columns and on the editorial page during the lifetime of the newspaper.

Stories concerning the trials and tribulations of the international workers' movement before, during and after World War II essentially contextualized South Africa's socialist project within the world socialist arena. Both newspapers linked the fight against fascism abroad with the fight to free black South Africans at home. There was strong support for a two-track approach involving both the workers' front and the battlefront. Even Subcategory D.2, other international news, was linked indirectly to the socialist project.

The quantitative and qualitative analyses clearly point to *Inkululeko* and the *Guardian* as trendsetters in the campaign to represent dissident civil society during the formative years of mass mobilization against the state. The politics of confrontation was finally legitimized in the news agenda. Whereas consciousness raising in the African nationalist press was phrased essentially in negative terms that focused on factionalism in African politics, ethnic conflict and lack of self-reliance, consciousness raising in the socialist press was phrased in positive terms that focused on the world-socialist millennium.

With the banning of the Communist Party in 1950, the *Guardian* and successor publications became leading barometers of dissident news and opinion in what remained of South Africa's altemative press. The *Guardian*'s political agenda during the 1950s and early 1960s would shift dramatically from trade unions to

Table 5. *Formal advertising in six alternative newspapers, 1919–1952 (% of news–advertising units)*

Newspaper	%
Imvo Zabantsundu (January 1919–December 1929)	70.1
Workers' Herald (February 1925–December 1928)	31.5
Bantu World (April 1932–December 1939)	28.1
Inkundla ya Bantu (April 1938–November 1951)	28.6
Inkululeko (December 1940–June 1950)	29.0
Guardian (February 1937–May 1952)	39.3

Note: See Appendix for an explanation of the methodology used.

the ANC and its allies, and to issues of concern to the expanding urban African population in the metropolitan areas.

Advertisers, the vast majority representing white-owned businesses, apparently did not discriminate between the independent African nationalist press, white-owned African nationalist press or the socialist press, and with two exceptions (*Imvo Zabantsundu* and the *Guardian*) the ratio of advertising to news was much the same on average throughout this period (Table 5). The proportion of *Imvo*'s news-advertising agenda devoted to advertising was enormous when compared with the other newspapers examined, and these advertisements were mainly from white-owned businesses. Nevertheless, independent political newspapers were all marginal as business enterprises and relied heavily on volunteers for editorial support, fund-raising and often for transporting and distributing the product. None had anything resembling *Bantu World*'s corporate financial resources, and even the *Guardian*, relatively successful as it was in terms of circulation and advertising, struggled continually to make ends meet.

In our analysis, a somewhat arbitrary but consistent distinction was made between essential and nonessential goods and services advertised by white-owned businesses. We were attempting to measure the relative percentage of advertisements for white-owned and -manufactured luxury consumer items that might be directed specifically at the black petty bourgeoisie. Three newspapers were selected for analysis: the white-owned commercial newspaper, *Bantu World*; the independent African nationalist newspaper, *Inkundla ya Bantu*; and the independent socialist newspaper, the *Guardian* (Table 6).

White businesses dominated the advertising agenda in the three newspapers analyzed, but there was no clear pattern in the type of goods and services favored. Luxury advertisements had the edge in the *Guardian*, which was associated with the Communist Party, whereas *Bantu World*, which was controlled indirectly by the mining industry, favored necessities. Black business advertising (nonessential and essential) was also examined (along with promotional advertising), but *Inkundla* was the only newspaper in which a significant portion of the advertising units was devoted to black businesses (about 33 percent of the advertisements sampled, although the majority of advertisers were Indian rather than African). *Bantu World* was a crusader for economic self-reliance, but in contrast to *Inkundla* this white-owned newspaper had virtually no black advertisers (2.5 percent of the sample).

Table 6. *White business advertising in the alternative press (% of advertising units)*

Category	*Bantu World*	*Inkundla ya Bantu*	*Guardian*
White businesses: Nonessential goods and services	41.6	28.1	53.3
White businesses: Essential goods and services	49.8	21.3	40.9
Total	91.4	49.4	94.2

The Alternative Press, 1860s–1930s

The communities served by the alternative press were transformed by dramatic changes in South Africa's political economy between the 1860s and 1930s. Preindustrial societies everywhere in southern Africa were subjugated to the requirements of an industrial society after huge deposits of diamonds and later gold were discovered (or rediscovered, since various minerals had been mined by Africans for centuries in the precolonial epoch) in the South African interior beginning in the 1860s.

Britain, the major colonial power in southern Africa, sought to gain control of this mineral wealth and was soon inextricably involved in the struggles for power being waged in the South African interior. African kingdoms still independent of settler regimes were either defeated in war (e.g., the Zulu and Pedi in 1879) or otherwise subordinated (e.g., the Tswana and various Xhosa-speaking communities of the eastern Cape) in the last two decades or so of the nineteenth century. British South Africa became a reality with the conquest of the Boer republics in the Transvaal and Orange Free State in the South African War (also known as the Anglo–Boer War) between 1899 and 1902 and the incorporation of the defeated Afrikaners into the unified settler state of South Africa in 1910.

Protest Politics

Protest politics in South Africa in many ways was conditioned by these developments, because the production of minerals under the hegemony of imperial Britain transformed social relations between conqueror and conquered in the subcontinent. The mineral discoveries created an unprecedented demand for a cheap, unskilled and docile labor force to extract the minerals, produce food for the expanding urban population, build the ports and railways, and to erect the factories, businesses and homes for the power brokers of the new South Africa. The migrant African male laborer was the major component in this labor force. For the migrant labor system to work, the mining industry (and other sectors of the capitalist economy) had to control the source, as well as the supply, of labor and the deployment and discipline of laborers once they were recruited. The mining compound initially solved the second problem. Compounds effectively regimented the male workers' lives and prevented them from acting collectively against their employer or from leaving the mines once they had been recruited. The creation of segregated reservations for Africans would resolve the first problem.

In the generation or so between the inauguration of the Union of South Africa in 1910 and the inauguration of the apartheid era in 1948, the segregationist state gradually expanded its power over the majority African population. The 1913 Natives' Land Act, for example, is widely regarded as the single most important piece of segregationist legislation affecting the African peasantry during this period. The measure sought to consolidate the efforts made by the settler colonies to prevent Africans from acquiring land and accumulating capital by curtailing the activities of African tenant producers on white-owned farms and by restricting the bulk of the African population to small tracts of land set apart from the white community. The reserves, as these reservations were called, comprised about 7.1 percent of South Africa's total land acreage at the time, and they were a key migrant labor reservoir for white South Africa.

The Natives (Urban Areas) Act of 1923 (with key amendments in 1930, 1937 and 1945) was intended to control the movement of Africans from rural to urban areas and to provide for the segregation of Africans in town, just as the 1913 Land Act had envisaged for Africans in the countryside. The Native Administration Act of 1927 also offered concrete evidence that long before apartheid the South African state sought to restore "tribal" authority and impose it on the whole of the African population. The chiefs would be reempowered, and customary courts, marriage rites, the lobolo (bride price) system, and other principles of "native law and custom" (as codified by whites) would be standardized throughout the provinces and enforced. The governor general of the Union of South Africa was made the titular political ruler over all Africans: he could rule by proclamation, and his decisions were not subject to challenge by the judiciary. The Native Affairs Department was made the principal agency of social control to repress dissent, promote ethnicity and distance Africans even farther from the rule of law as applied to white South Africa.

A uniform code of African administration in South Africa based on these and numerous other laws and statutes, however, would be possible only when it could be imposed on the Cape as well as the other provinces. The Cape supplied much of South Africa's mine labor and contained (with Natal) most of the land set aside at the time as African reserves. African men in the Cape Colony, however, had access to the franchise, and their right to vote in the Cape had been preserved with the creation of Union in 1910.[28] The Cape African vote was an insignificant factor in all but a few provincial and national parliamentary constituencies after 1910, but Cape Africans were protected to some extent from segregationist policies pursued by governments between 1910 and 1936. Aspects of the Cape liberal tradition, as it was called, were preserved insofar as Cape Africans did not have to carry passes, and they could buy property anywhere in the province. They were not subject to the 1913 Land Act[29] or to other regulations imposed (at least in theory) on Africans in segregated rural and urban locations.

These rights were lost with the Representation of Natives Act and the Native Trust and Land Act of 1936. Cape Africans, like other Africans, were now denied the vote and forbidden to buy land outside the reserves. The 1936 Land Act subjected all Africans in the Cape to the conditions of the 1913 Land Act. The Native Affairs Department was still in charge of day-to-day administration in the reserves, but a new body called the South African Native Trust was created to acquire more land for use as reserves. The Native Trust would be the registered owner of all land not held in freehold in the reserves, which in theory would eventually total about 13.7 percent of South Africa's total acreage. Africans displaced from designated white urban and rural areas would be pushed back to the reserves, but no further attempts would be made to expand these areas to accommodate the African population.

The 1936 Land Act placed more restrictions on African sharecroppers and cash tenants on white farms in an attempt to reduce them to wage labor, and this measure also envisaged a more active role for the central government in conserving reserve land and resettling Africans within these areas. The Native Affairs Department tried initially to promote soil conservation and regulate peasant farming practices in the reserves, but development planning in the mid-1940s shifted to the creation of separate farming and nonfarming villages, and the creation of industries to employ nonfarm workers inside and on the borders of existing African reserves. These policies were not altered substantially under apartheid. The National Party's economic policy for the reserves, which was first articulated in the report of the Tomlinson Commission in 1955, for example, approved a land-use plan that was very similar to the schemes devised by its predecessor the United Party and first introduced in the Ciskei reserve in the eastern Cape during the 1940s.

Once South Africa had a uniform policy that denied African access to the land and the franchise, other parts of the segregationist program–which eventually targeted Coloureds, Indians and even whites as well as Africans–could be enforced more effectively. This was accomplished primarily after the National Party came to power in 1948 to inaugurate the apartheid era.

The boundaries of dissent in South Africa were framed largely by these political and economic realities. The first African protest groups were formed in the eastern Cape in the 1870s and 1880s, and these were followed by African, Coloured and Indian protest groups elsewhere in the Cape, Natal and the other colonies of British South Africa in the years preceding Union in 1910. The South African Native National Congress (SANNC), for example, was formed in January 1912 as a permanent national organization to represent African political interests in South Africa and in the adjacent British protectorates of Bechuanaland, Basutoland and Swaziland. But the SANNC–renamed the African National Congress (ANC, or Congress) in 1923–remained a fragile and deeply fragmented organization, poorly administered and without adequate funding to supervise and coordinate branch activities. Personality conflicts, ethnic differences and tensions among members over the tactics of protest and the suitability of alliances with non-African groups severely weakened its effectiveness even within African political circles until after World War II.

African, Coloured and Indian activists remained isolated from each other in responding to the discriminatory policies of government, and all dissident political groups relied primarily on petitionary protest to make their interests known to the authorities. They employed the same strategies in seeking redress to grievances, used the same political avenues open to them, operated strictly within the narrow legal and legislative frameworks imposed on them by succeeding colonial and post-colonial governments, and continued to cherish British trusteeship. They adhered to the belief–at least in public discourse–that the imperial authority would ultimately intervene if the limited political and civil rights they enjoyed were ever seriously compromised.

Petitionary protest in South Africa, however, was virtually bankrupt by the late 1930s. The fight to retain and even extend limited voting rights for Africans in the Cape to the rest of South Africa had failed after a 10-year civil rights campaign.[30] The loss of the African franchise was a watershed event in the history of black opposition politics, because it symbolized the failure of the aspirant African middle class to gain a place for themselves in the existing political order.

On the eve of World War II, black opposition groups were still in considerable disarray–small and parochial in terms of membership and isolated for the most part from each other. As the established leaders in the protest movement, moreover, the black petty bourgeoisie seemed unable to exercise leadership at a popular, grassroots level in the workplace or in the communities of the disenfranchised population.

Protest Journalism

Chapters 1 through 6 (Part I) are devoted to the independent protest press before World War II. Four chapters focus on newspapers launched by the African petty bourgeoisie, and two focus on newspapers launched by the Indian and Coloured petty bourgeoisie, respectively.

The African protest press was nurtured in African Christian communities that emerged from rural stations and outstations where European and American missionary societies first took root in southern Africa.[31] The heartland of the mission enterprise in South Africa in the first half of the nineteenth century was among the Xhosa and their neighbors west and east of the Great Kei River in the eastern Cape; among Sotho speakers in what is today Lesotho and the southern Orange Free State; among Tswana speakers scattered over a large territory in the northeastern Cape, western Transvaal, Orange Free State and southern Botswana; and among Zulu speakers in Natal, especially below the Tugela (or Thukela) river. (See the Map.)

Although divided by denomination, missionary interpreters of the new cultural order were, in the main, Protestant evangelical Nonconformists caught up in the revivals that had swept through Britain and parts of western Europe and north America and inaugurated a new era in what was perceived to be foreign missions. The pioneer missionary generation, at least, was motivated primarily by ideological conviction, and in this context the mission station was a trojan horse in southern Africa's precolonial cultures. For the missionaries, conversion to Christianity had to be a personal, not a group decision. They were driven by the belief that Christ's Second Coming would not take place until the Gospel was communicated throughout the world. Christians were to be separated from non-Christians, the saved from the unsaved, and Christian culture would be promoted as a superior way of life.

The pioneer missionaries assumed a chiefly role, allocating the land and exhorting their people to believe and behave in ways that conformed to the mission's understanding of a Christian lifestyle. The missionaries to the Xhosa and Zulu, for example, were either passive or active participants in the struggle to undermine and destroy the authority of the African chiefdoms. Only a few were paid government agents, but many reported on the activities of the chiefs in their areas. They also organized and led wartime commando units against independent chiefdoms, helped establish segregated African locations and create the administrative apparatus for taxing Africans who came under colonial jurisdiction, and occasionally acted as de facto recruiters of African labor.

The pioneer missionary generation took over and sanctioned every stage of the life cycle–birth, initiation into manhood and womanhood, marriage, last rites and burial. The mission church's sovereignty was invoked in African Christian homes and in the fields at harvest time, and its temporal base–the church building–was inevitably the biggest and most imposing on the station. Virtually every activity in the life of the Christian community became institutionalized in the mission church. At least for African converts of the pioneer generation, the mission station became their spiritual and often their temporal home.

The strength of the mission stemmed, in part, from its ability to shape the convert's perceptions of reality in such a way that mission authority was legitimated. The missionary's construction of reality was to be accepted as objective reality. Cultural discrimination and the attempt to reconstitute popular oral culture in the mission's image were key themes in developing the first African Christian communities in South Africa. Nonverbal as well as verbal and written modes of communication were employed by the pioneer missionaries in erecting a new cultural order on their stations and outstations.

The mission's success in promoting the new order for its converts depended in part on its monopoly over the written word. Mission communities were centered on the church, school and either possession of or access to a printing press. The preaching and teaching ministry was dependent on the mission's control and manipulation of literate culture. Thus small presses were gradually established to produce a literature in South Africa's major African languages – in particular, Zulu, Xhosa, Sotho and Tswana.

Printing presses were acquired by a number of pioneer mission societies between the 1820s and the 1880s. The Wesleyan Methodists and the Congregationalists, for example, acquired presses on several stations among the Tswana in the interior of South Africa and among the Xhosa-speaking inhabitants of the eastern Cape. The Anglicans acquired presses for several stations in the eastern Cape in the 1860s and 1870s. Missionary societies outside the Cape Colony were also active in publishing. This was especially true in Natal Colony among Zulu missions sponsored by the Congregationalists (American Board), Lutherans (Swedish) and Roman Catholics (Mariannhill Fathers).

The Wesleyan Methodists actually produced the earliest known African newspaper in southern Africa – *Umshumayeli Wendaba* (Publisher of the News) – between July 1837 and April 1841, first in Grahamstown, west of the Fish River, and later at Peddie, east of the Fish River, in what was known as the Ciskei region in the eastern Cape. Written in Xhosa, probably by white missionaries, and published as an irregular quarterly, it contained Christian homilies and devotional items aimed at African converts in these Cape frontier mission communities.

Two significant mission publishing centers emerged during the second half of the nineteenth century, and they played a major role in promoting an indigenous African mission press. The Presbyterians, at Lovedale in the eastern Cape, and the Paris Evangelical Missionary Society, at Morija in colonial Basutoland (Lesotho), became the major Protestant mission publishing centers in southern Africa.[32] Lovedale printed material primarily in English and Xhosa, whereas Morija produced books, pamphlets and serial publications in up to 45 languages for countries throughout sub-Saharan Africa.[33]

A tiny but identifiable African Christian community began to emerge in and around mission stations and outstations in various parts of what is now South Africa between the 1850s and 1880s. The scale of conversions was unprecedented, and apparently all the pioneer missions experienced a rapid growth in African church membership. African preachers, evangelists and teachers, moreover, were responsible for converting the vast majority of new converts. Healing services, prayer meetings, temperance crusades, and mass open-air evangelical revivals continued for many years, especially in mission strongholds like the eastern Cape and southern Natal. African Christians were an organized presence in the countryside and in many towns by the 1880s.

African mission-educated elites formed the nucleus of an aspirant African petty bourgeoisie in all the colonies of British South Africa by the end of the nineteenth century. This pioneer generation typically had at least six years of formal education, and for the most part they were lower-level functionaries in South Africa's nascent industrial economy. They were ordained and unordained ministers and evangelists, primary schoolteachers and journalists, peasant farmers involved to some extent in surplus production, policemen, law agents, magistrates' clerks and court interpreters, semiskilled and even skilled artisans.

African modernizers emerging from the isolation of one or two generations of immersion in mission communities, however, found themselves increasingly alienated and marginalized in the world outside these communities. This world was dominated by white settlers, and it was being transformed economically by the mineral revolution and politically and socially by an ever-expanding segregationist culture. No matter how successful African modernizers were in meeting the "civilized" standards imposed by their conquerors, it was becoming apparent that they would never be accepted on equal terms in the new cultural order.

African entrepreneurs, for example, would never be allowed to gain more than a tenuous foothold in the capitalist economy. African peasants were actually playing a significant role in agricultural production in the Ciskei region between the Fish and Kei rivers in the eastern Cape by the 1860s, but the era of peasant prosperity was over by the end of the 1870s, and only a small minority had benefited from the experience. There were few capitalist farmers left by 1910, and this rough periodization of the rise and fall of an African peasantry in one region would be repeated in other regions of the Cape and South Africa in the late colonial and postcolonial eras. The failure of peasant capitalism would have profound implications for the African nationalist movement, because there would be few other opportunities to gain even partial access to the new economic system.

The modernizing African's potential leadership role in mission churches and schools was also being undermined. Attempts by the settlers to segregate, control and downgrade African education in the Cape Colony, for example, were initiated in the 1860s and accelerated in the 1870s and 1880s. Particularly unsettling was the attitude of mission opinion leaders, such as the influential James Stewart, leader of the prestigious Presbyterian mission at Lovedale in the Ciskei region, where the most famous African secondary school in the Cape was located. He agreed with settler demands that missionaries abandon the effort to promote an elite and concentrate instead on educating as many Africans as possible to the lowest levels of functional literacy.[34]

Mission policy now had to win the approval of the settlers and be in harmony with their interests. In contrast to the pioneer missionary generation, which had sought to "civilize" the African to the level of the "civilized" European, the new missionary generation sought to legitimate an inferior role for African Christians in a racially stratified society. In essence, subordination by race in a segregated society, rather than incorporation of individuals by class in a potentially integrated society, was more acceptable to the mission enterprise in the late colonial period. Even within the mission church, the arbiters of a segregationist culture had begun to limit contact between white and black clergy and separate white and black congregations where they existed.

These developments profoundly influenced Africans writing for the mission press. Their concerns were expressed in newspapers like *Indaba* (the News), produced between August 1862 and February 1865, and *Isigidimi Sama Xosa* (the Xhosa Messenger), produced between July 1873 and December 1888 by the Presbyterian missionaries at Lovedale; *Mahoko a Becoana* or *Mahoko a Becwana* (News for the Bechuana), produced between January 1883 and July 1896 by the London Missionary Society at Kuruman in the northern Cape; and *Inkanyiso yase Natal* (the Natal Light), produced by the Anglicans in Pietermaritzburg, Natal. *Inkanyiso*, launched in April 1889 in Zulu and English, quickly gained a reputation as a protest journal, and it was one of the first mission newspapers to be placed entirely under African control. The Anglicans turned the newspaper over to its African editors in January 1895, and it survived for about 18 months as the first independent organ of African political opinion in Natal Colony.[35]

Some mission publications, then, were no longer restricted to religious matters in attempting to address the grievances of their mission-educated audiences. General-interest news was now printed in English, as well as the vernacular, and articles and letters of protest formed an increasingly important part of the agenda. A few journals, like *Inkanyiso*, apparently were operating beyond the confines of mission censorship.

The most important periodical produced in the first 60 years of the mission press in southern Africa was undoubtedly *Isigidimi*, which was initially a supplement in the *Kaffir Express* (October 1870–June 1873), the Presbyterian mission's flagship journal, edited by James Stewart at Lovedale.[36] *Isigidimi* was launched as an autonomous Xhosa-language mission publication in July 1873. It was to appear as a regular monthly–and at intervals, between 1879 and 1884, as a fortnightly–until its demise in December 1888. Stewart's editorial assistant Elijah Makiwane was placed in charge of the new publication. For eight years he was responsible for the newspaper, the first known African editor of a mission journal in the subcontinent.[37] In 1881, Makiwane, now an ordained minister, was succeeded by John Tengo Jabavu, a teacher and lay preacher who had attended the Wesleyan Methodist's prestige school at Healdtown in the Ciskei and was continuing his studies at Lovedale. William Wellington Gqoba succeeded Jabavu as editor of *Isigidimi* in 1884.

Isigidimi's editors set the tone of the publication. Makiwane became an officer in several pioneer African religious and educational organizations in the region. Gqoba was an accomplished essay writer and poet, and Jabavu soon emerged as the most prominent African political figure in the colony. In addition to the editors, *Isigidimi* had more than 20 named correspondents, representing at least 30 rural settlements and towns in the eastern Cape and in the colony of Natal. The newspaper received contributions from a broad segment of the educated elite, many of whom had written for other publications associated with the Lovedale mission press.

The African editors and contributors to *Isigidimi* were politically conscious and concerned with topical news and opinion of concern to their readers. André Odendaal, one of the first scholars to examine the contents of *Isigidimi*, has shown the extent to which the newspaper acted as a vehicle for mobilizing African public opinion during this period. A sustained, albeit muted, level of protest could be discerned in the news and letters-to-the-editor pages that was to have important implications for the literate African community.[38]

Probably the earliest protest poem published in southern Africa stems from this period. It appeared in *Isigidimi*, and it stands as an icon to an era that would not finally end until after World War II:

Your cattle are gone, my countrymen!
Go rescue them! Go rescue them!
Leave the breechloader alone
And turn to the pen.
Take paper and ink,
For that is your shield.
Your rights are going!
So pick up your pen.
Load it, load it with ink.
Sit on a chair.
Repair not to Hoho.
But fire with your pen.[39]

As editor of *Isigidimi*, Tengo Jabavu sensed that the depths of African protest had hardly been tapped. He not only brought his readers' grievances nearer the surface but also tried to get the newspaper involved in Cape colonial politics by canvassing African voters for white politicians deemed to be sympathetic to African interests. This was too much for Stewart, the paternalistic missionary segregationist who ultimately controlled *Isigidimi*. Jabavu resigned in 1884 and launched his own newspaper less than a year later.

Isigidimi lasted a few more years, but it ceased publication when William Gqoba, the new editor, died in 1888. *Isigidimi*'s demise suggested that mission newspapers and newsletters would not be able to compete with independent African publications unless they communicated more effectively the grievances and aspirations of their readers. From the 1880s the mission press no longer had a captive audience.[40]

Independent Political Newspapers

The first African newspapers independent of missionary control were launched in the Cape. Switzer, in Chapter 1, focuses on the political discourses that were inscribed in these publications between the 1880s and the early years of the postcolonial era after 1910. He begins with the Xhosa and their neighbors in the eastern Cape, where there were two dominant political personalities, two dominant regional political groupings and two dominant newspapers. African divisional rivalries in South Africa were most pronounced in this region, where the first independent African political, economic and cultural organizations in the subcontinent were established in the last four decades of the nineteenth century.

Tengo Jabavu, the patriarch of African politics in the Cape, was the founder and editor of *Imvo Zabantsundu* (Native Opinion), which was launched in King William's Town in November 1884 and is the oldest continuous African newspaper still being published in South Africa today. He was also instrumental in founding several political organizations between the 1880s and 1910s that were known by the generic name Imbumba. Walter Benson Rubusana, an ordained minister, was Jabavu's main political rival, and the political views of Rubusana and his colleagues were represented in a political organization known as the South African Native Congress and its mouthpiece *Izwi Labantu* (the Voice of the People), which was launched in East London in November 1897 and lasted almost 12 years. The editor of *Izwi* for 10 years and Jabavu's main rival as a journalist was Alan Kirkland Soga, a qualified lawyer and a member of one of the most prominent mission-educated families in the region.[41]

Although weekly circulation figures for *Imvo* never rose above 4,000 during the colonial era, it was undoubtedly the most influential African newspaper in South Africa at the end of the nineteenth century. Nevertheless, *Izwi* proved to be a formidable rival during the brief period it was in competition with *Imvo*. Both newspapers must also have had a considerable carry-on readership, because they were read by migrating Xhosa (and apparently by other Africans who read English and/or cognate languages like Zulu) in urban centers far removed from the rural eastern Cape.

Switzer also examines the major Tswana-language protest journals circulating in the northern Cape and parts of the western Transvaal and western Orange Free State, where the leading promoter of African nationalist opinion was undoubtedly Solomon Tshekisho Plaatje, perhaps the most prominent linguist, translator, literary figure and pioneer investigative journalist of his generation. His views were chronicled in *Koranta ea Becoana* (the Bechuana Gazette), which was launched in Mafeking in April 1901 and survived more than six years, and in a newspaper originally entitled *Tsala ea Becoana* (the Friend of the Bechuana) and later *Tsala ea Batho* (the Friend of the People), which was launched in Kimberley in June 1910 and ceased publication in July 1915. Plaatje played a major role in African nationalist politics in the early years of the South African Native National Congress.

Hunt Davis, in Chapter 2, expands the ethnic and geographical boundaries of the African petty bourgeoisie and its press to Natal in his essay on John Langalibalele Dube, the patriarch of African politics in the colony, and Dube's newspaper *llanga Lase Natal* (the Natal Sun), which was launched at Phoenix, outside Durban, in April 1903.[42] Dube was an ordained minister (American Board Mission), but his role in the African nationalist movement did not stem from his status as a member of the clergy. It stemmed from his role as an educator (the founder of a secondary industrial school called Ohlange Institute, which opened in 1901), political leader (the first president general of the South African Native National Congress in 1912) and journalist. Dube and his peers in Natal were confronted by the same issues as their colleagues elsewhere in subaltern South Africa, and these issues shaped the content of his newspaper.

Davis suggests that three themes–race, class and nationalism–dominated the news content of *llanga* during the first 11 years or so of its existence. These were the years when Dube was at the height of his influence as a crusading politician and journalist in Natal. The *kholwa* (meaning "believers"), as members of the African Christian community were designated in Zulu, constituted the new social class in Natal, with definable interests that were not always in harmony with the Zulu majority. As the world views of mission-educated Africans and whites became more disparate, however, some alienated and impoverished *kholwa* sought space for themselves within the confines of a narrow Zulu ethnic nationalism. *Ilanga* promoted these aspirations beginning in the 1930s.

Davis examines four key issues that appeared and reappeared in the pages of *llanga* in the years before World War I. The first issue is encapsulated in the phrase "improving Christianity," which embraced a range of strategies employed by the *kholwa* to gain a more secure place for themselves in colonial society. The second issue concerns the ambiguities in the *kholwa*'s relations with the peasant majority who were not identified with the *kholwa*, which emerges most strikingly during

Ilanga's coverage of the so-called Bambatha Rebellion and its aftermath in Natal between 1906 and 1908. The third issue concerns the role of Africans in the new constitutional framework established when the Union of South Africa was formed in 1910. The fourth issue revolves around the 1913 Natives' Land Act, which had profound implications for members of Natal's *kholwa* community, who still lived and worked for the most part in a rural environment.

Uma Mesthrie, in Chapter 3, examines the class, caste, religious and linguistic divisions, economic divisions, political interests and allegiances within the Indian community in her case study of Mohandas K. Gandhi and his newspaper *Indian Opinion*. The Indians were concentrated in Natal and to a lesser extent in the mining towns of the southern Transvaal. Mesthrie describes their marginalized status and emphasizes their relative isolation from other population groups. The expanding network of Indian traders and the handful of mostly colonial-born lawyers, teachers, clerical workers, interpreters, petty commodity producers and small farmers formed the nucleus of the Indian petty bourgeoisie in South Africa.

They established political protest groups, beginning with the Natal Indian Congress (NIC) in 1894, and protest newspapers like *Colonial Indian News*, which was launched in Pietermaritzburg in May 1901, to represent their interests in the public sphere. *Indian Opinion* was launched in Durban in June 1903, and at least two other significant Indian political journals–African Chronicle (published in Durban from June 1908) and *Indian Views* (published in Durban from July 1914)–were launched during the Gandhi era in South Africa. In the wake of the South African War, the British Indian Association was established in 1903 to protest postwar restrictions on Indians. The focal points of concern were the discriminatory policies of the Transvaal Colony. Gandhi made Johannesburg his home after returning from a visit to India in 1902, and the communal Tolstoy Farm was founded outside Johannesburg in 1906. *Indian Opinion*'s political objectives were linked closely to the NIC and the British Indian Association in the Transvaal.

Mesthrie demonstrates that the history of *Indian Opinion* was closely intertwined with Gandhi's other communal settlement at Phoenix, just outside Durban–the newspaper was published there from December 1904–and with the ideology of *satyagraha*, or passive resistance, which gave impetus to the Indian passive resistance campaigns directed at the Transvaal government between 1906 and 1914. She examines the contradictions in Gandhi's relations with Africans and Coloureds and suggests that the prime objective of *Indian Opinion* and the Phoenix Settlement initially was to establish closer relations with the white community. Gandhi had no interest in establishing a broader alliance with other black political, economic or social groups.

Indians addressed their own grievances through their own organizations. Mesthrie details the role of *Indian Opinion* in mobilizing and organizing the Natal resisters, and the last third of her chapter is concerned with the newspaper, its staff and the Phoenix settlers in the *satyagraha* struggle. After seven years of passive resistance, Gandhi was able to negotiate only a limited settlement on behalf of the Indian community, but he himself emerged a changed man from this experience. When Gandhi returned to India in 1914, he was prepared to lead a mass movement in his homeland's struggle for independence. *Indian Opinion* had also been transformed. It had moved from advocacy to mobilization, from massaging white opinion to resisting white rule, from being the mouthpiece of the Indian merchant elite to being the moral voice of the entire Indian community.

Mohamed Adhikari, in Chapter 4, profiles the Coloured petty bourgeoisie in his examination of the African Political Organization, which was founded in Cape Town in 1902. The acronym of the first major Coloured political group in South Africa was designated as the title of its official mouthpiece, and the *APO* newspaper was launched in May 1909, just in time to protest the 1909 draft of the South Africa Act. The first Cape Town publication aimed at black readers, however, was the *South African Spectator*. (It had sections devoted to Indian news and an occasional column in Xhosa.) The newspaper was launched in December 1900 by the flamboyant Francis Zaccheus Santiago Peregrino, an ardent Pan-Africanist from West Africa who had lived in Britain and the United States before settling in Cape Town. *APO*'s news format and journalistic style were modeled mainly on the *Spectator*. *APO*, however, was intended primarily for Coloured readers, and there were distinct differences in political outlook between the two newspapers.

Under the presidency of Dr. Abdullah Abdurahman, the African Political Organization dominated organized political life in the Cape Coloured community, and by 1910 it had branches throughout southern Africa and several thousand members. *APO* was published at a time when upper-ranked Coloureds–consisting largely of skilled artisans, small traders, clerks, primary schoolteachers and a handful of professionals–were never more united in terms of values, goals and political strategy. As Adhikari asserts, the Coloured petty bourgeoisie at this time "wanted little more than to be judged on merit, to exercise citizenship rights and to win social acceptance within white middle-class society."

APO offers a relatively comprehensive insight into the social and political life of this aspiring, largely English-speaking elite (which rejected Afrikaans, the language used by most working-class Coloureds) during almost 15 years of intermittent publication. Adhikari argues that *APO* was caught between its hatred of racism and the need to mobilize a marginalized community on the basis of an exclusive racial identity. But Coloureds had no economic or political status and never comprised more than 10 percent of South Africa's total population. Thus Coloured political leaders were obliged to use the racial system to their own advantage. *APO* exploited the social Darwinist ideology of the day to position the Coloured community firmly within Western culture, and the newspaper campaigned for a position of relative privilege for Coloureds in South Africa's racially stratified society.

The demoralization of the Coloured elite in the early years of the postcolonial era was reflected in the declining prestige of the African Political Organization and its newspaper *APO*, both of which were virtually dormant by World War I. The war itself generated a revival of sorts as Coloureds eagerly joined the Coloureds-only Cape Corps and looked forward to a peace in which racial barriers would finally be lifted and Coloureds admitted to all levels of national life. Wartime inflation forced *APO* to suspend publication in November 1915, but its views were reflected in the *Educational Journal*, which was launched in Cape Town in May 1915 by Coloured teachers associated with the militant Teachers' League of South Africa.

The Coloured petty bourgeoisie was much more fragmented politically after the war ended, especially when it became apparent that there would be no peace dividend for the Coloured people. *APO* itself was revived in December 1919, eight months after the launching of a newspaper in Cape Town entitled the *South African Clarion*, which was controlled by Coloured supporters of the Afrikaans-speaking National Party in the Cape. The African Political Organization and its newspaper backed the largely English-speaking South African Party, which at least in public was supportive of the Cape liberal tradition.

Political divisions further weakened the marginalized voice of the Coloured community. Although *APO* sought to extend its agenda to embrace workers' concerns in the early 1920s, it did not object strenuously to discriminatory measures that were beginning to undermine the fragile viability of Coloured artisans and limit job mobility. The revived *APO* never gained the vigor or the credibility of the prewar newspaper, and it collapsed in December 1923. The African Political Organization maintained a precarious existence before it too finally collapsed in 1944.

Meanwhile, in the early decades of the twentieth century, the number of African protest newspapers continued to grow, as the African petty bourgeoisie expanded from countryside to town and from their strongholds in the eastern Cape and southern Natal to Johannesburg and other towns in the South African interior. Unfortunately, most of these publications cannot be examined, because very few (and in some cases no) copies have survived. *Leihlo lo Babatsho* (the Native Eye), the first independent African newspaper established in the newly conquered British colony of the Transvaal, lasted about five years, between 1903 and 1908. It was published in English and Pedi and edited by Levi Khomo, a former court interpreter, from Pietersburg in the northern Transvaal. The *Native Advocate* (also cited as the *Advocate*) was launched about 1912 by Alfred Mangena, the second qualified African lawyer to be allowed to practice law in South Africa,[43] and Sefako Mapogo Makgatho, a founder of the Transvaal African Teachers' Association who became ANC president general between 1917 and 1924. The *Advocate* was published in Pretoria as a weekly in English, and probably in various vernacular languages, but it did not survive for more than a year. The newspaper was edited by Cape journalist Alan Kirkland Soga, who apparently had moved to the Transvaal after the collapse of *Izwi Labantu*.

Daniel Simon Letanka (1874–1934), a court interpreter who was also prominent in African nationalist politics in the Transvaal, launched the weekly *Motsoaelle* (the Friend) in Johannesburg in 1910. The newspaper–renamed *Morumioa* (the Messenger) in 1911–was distributed mainly to Tswana and Pedi speakers in the northem Transvaal. Another publication launched by African nationalists in Johannesburg in 1910 was entitled *Umlomo wa Bantu* (Mouthpiece of the People). Saul Msane, a founding member of the Natal Native Congress and ANC secretary general during Makgatho's presidency, helped launch this Xhosa-English weekly. Levi Thomas Mvabaza, a prominent member of the provincial Transvaal Native Organisation before the formation of the South African Native National Congress in 1912, edited the newspaper. *Morumioa* and *Umlomo*, however, were merged to form a new newspaper shortly after Congress was founded.[44]

Abantu-Batho (the People), the ANC's first and only official newspaper before the organization was banned in South Africa in 1960, was launched in 1912 in Johannesburg. It was the inspiration of Pixley ka Isaka Seme (1881–1951), a qualified lawyer, who had spent 12 years studying overseas in the United States and England. Seme and his colleagues from the Transvaal were the real power brokers in the founding of sub-Saharan Africa's oldest African nationalist organization.[45] Seme had become the legal adviser to Swaziland's queen regent, and he was able to secure a gift of £3,000 from her to use to purchase a printing press.

Seme was the first managing director, but production and editorial control soon shifted to Letanka and Mvabasa, the editor-proprietors of *Abantu-Batho*'s immediate predecessors *Morumioa* and *Umlomo*. Mvabasa (d. 1955), a member of two

SANNC protest delegations (to Britain in 1914 and to Britain and Versailles in 1919) eventually succeeded Seme as managing director of the newspaper. *Abantu-Batho* was published in English, Zulu, Xhosa and Sotho/Tswana, and for about two decades it appeared somewhat irregularly as a weekly, monthly or every two months or so, depending on financial constraints. The newspaper apparently had four language editors (each one in charge of a language section) and a managing editor, and these five individuals were also directors of the company.

Virtually the entire ANC hierarchy wrote for *Abantu-Batho* at one time or another. C. Kunene (d. 1916) was the first editor responsible for the Zulu and Xhosa sections, while Letanka was editor of the Sotho/Tswana section throughout the lifetime of the newspaper. Other editors included Saul Msane, Jeremiah W. Dunjwa, R. V. Selope Thema and T. D. Mweli Skota.

Msane (d. ca. 1932) was a member of the 1914 delegation to England protesting the Natives' Land Act. He was employed as a mine compound overseer in Johannesburg–perhaps the highest-ranked job available to an African in the mining industry at the time–and in later life was a mine labor agent in Natal. Msane used *Abantu-Batho* (apparently he edited the Zulu pages for a few years during World War I) to attack Dube's leadership of the ANC and helped bring about his resignation as president general in 1917. Msane, however, broke with militant colleagues in the provincial Transvaal Congress when they supported striking workers after the war. African nationalists were divided over the most appropriate response to take toward industrial strife, and Msane, who was then president of the Transvaal Congress, was obliged to resign in protest. Dunjwa (d. ca. 1935), an organizer of a 1919 Anti-Pass Campaign in the Transvaal, was secretary of the Transvaal Congress and one of the activists who gained control of the newspaper (as editor of the Xhosa section).

Selope Thema (1886–1955) also served as editor of *Abantu-Batho* when he returned to South Africa after traveling to Britain and France with the 1919 protest delegation, but the militant phase of his journalistic career was very brief. Thema would become a leader of the moderate wing in African nationalist politics in the Transvaal during the interwar period. Skota (1890–1976), a subeditor of *Abantu-Batho* in 1912–1913 and an editor in 1928, was a former court interpreter who became a relatively successful businessman, a celebrated biographer and a newspaper entrepreneur.[46] Skota helped launch the Bechuanaland and Griqualand West branch of the ANC. Elected secretary general of Congress in 1923, he played a major role as a mediator in African nationalist politics in the Transvaal before the 1940s.

Prominent contributors to *Abantu-Batho* included people like Davidson Don Tengo ("D. D. T.") Jabavu, Samuel Makama Masabalala, S. E. Krune Mqhayi, S.M. Bennett Ncwana and Zaccheus Richard Mahabane. D.D.T. Jabavu (1885–1959) was the eldest son of Tengo Jabavu and perhaps the most celebrated spokesperson for the moderate African nationalist position outside the Transvaal during the interwar period. Masabalala, a Cape ANC official and trade union leader in Port Elizabeth, joined *Abantu-Batho* in 1929. Mqhayi (1875–1945), the major Xhosa-language writer of his generation, was first christened "Imbongi yeSizwe Jikelele" (Poet of the Race/Nation) by an editor of the newspaper. Ncwana was a veteran Cape journalist who founded and/or edited several African newspapers between the 1920s and 1940s.[47] Mahabane (1881–1970), a Wesleyan Methodist minister, was ANC president general for two terms between 1924 and 1927 and again between 1937 and 1940.

Abantu-Batho gained a considerable audience as a result of the sympathetic coverage it gave to the grievances of African workers mobilizing in Johannesburg and other towns along the Witwatersrand after World War I, but its heyday as a militant protest newspaper seems to have ended in the early 1920s. *Abantu-Batho* was in financial difficulty even before the mid-1920s, and ANC president general Josiah Tshangana Gumede (1927–30) bought a controlling interest in the journal to save it from closure in 1929. *Abantu-Batho* effectively ceased publication in July 1931, a few months after Gumede lost the presidency of Congress to Pixley Seme.[48]

Seme tried to promote a newspaper he had started two years earlier, *Ikwezi le Africa* (the Morning Star of Africa), as the official organ of Congress. But *Ikwezi* (February 1928–October 1932) was published at Eshowe, a rural area in Zululand, Natal. It was simply "out of touch with real Native thought on the problems confronting the Bantu today."[49] *Ikwezi* was absorbed by a new ANC organ entitled the *African Leader* (January 1932–May 1933), which was launched in Johannesburg and printed on *Abantu-Batho*'s old press.

African Leader, published in English, Zulu (*Umholi we Afrika*), Xhosa (*Inkokeli ye Afrika*) and Sotho (*Moetapele oa Afrika*), briefly succeeded *Abantu-Batho* as a mouthpiece for the ANC. Mweli Skota was the editor, and the radical journalist Gilbert Coka resigned from *Bantu World* to join the newspaper.[50] Several ANC figures wrote articles for the English-language section, including Pixley Seme, H. Selby Msimang, Sol Plaatje's son Halley, Joel Nduma, S. H. Mbulawa and others using pseudonyms. *African Leader*, however, lasted only 16 months before it failed – apparently "through sheer bad business management."[51]

A number of other African publications were launched during the interwar period, but again most collapsed after one or two years and few copies survived. Even so, only the Orange Free State of South Africa's four provinces apparently lacked an independent African political journal in the generation after the South African Native National Congress was founded in 1912.

Switzer, in Chapters 5 and 6, chooses three African nationalist newspapers to illustrate various trends in African political journalism during the period between the world wars. The 1920s are represented by *Imvo Zabantsundu* and the *Workers' Herald* and the 1930s by *Bantu World*.

Imvo in the 1920s was more circumscribed in audience and influence than it had been a generation earlier (circulation figures apparently dropped to between 1,000 and 2,000 during the decade), but it was still a leading barometer of African nationalist opinion in South Africa. *Imvo* was representative of the vast majority of African publications in the 1920s in that it was a community newspaper catering largely to the interests of the rural petty bourgeoisie. The *Workers' Herald*, on the other hand, was the official mouthpiece of the Industrial and Commercial Workers' Union, the largest and most influential black trade union movement in South African history before World War II. The newspaper was established initially in Cape Town in May 1923 and moved to Johannesburg in February 1926. The ICU eclipsed the ANC as the leading African political organization during the mid- to late 1920s, and the *Workers' Herald* embraced a national readership that was widely dispersed in town and countryside.

Switzer focuses on the editors, major contributors and the news content of these newspapers, which were recognized organs of moderate and militant nationalist opinion in South Africa at the time. He seeks to isolate the main contradictions in political discourse but concludes that the two texts had much in common. They attacked the political manifestations of white segregationist rule but were virtually silent on the economic and social manifestations. They generally resisted any strategy of protest that promoted racial consciousness and/or solidarity or advocated strikes, boycotts or civil disobedience.

Imvo continued to mediate the interests of the Cape's African voters, whereas the *Workers' Herald* sought to organize a public discourse for its urban and rural working-class constituency. *Imvo* supported the efforts by white and black middle-class liberals to promote class solidarity, which became increasingly urgent as pressure mounted against the African petty bourgeoisie. The *Workers' Herald* sought to break down racial, ethnic and cultural barriers in its efforts to promote worker solidarity, but the black worker was represented as one who aspired to middle-class values. The editors of this trade union newspaper sought to establish a unique African discourse that was not mediated by whites, but no African journalist was prepared to dispense completely with white trusteeship in the 1920s.

Meanwhile, white business and financial interests in postcolonial South Africa, encouraged at least indirectly by the state, were seeking to gain control of the African political press. These efforts actually date back to events following World War I, when mobilizing workers briefly radicalized African politics in the Transvaal. Key officials in Congress–including men like Saul Msane and Sol Plaatje's brother-in-law Isaiah Bud-Mbelle–became increasingly alarmed over the militant posture of *Abantu-Bantu* and sought to involve the Chamber of Mines (the mining industry's coordinating body) in funding a newspaper that would counteract its influence.

In the aftermath of the 1920 African miners' strike, the Native Recruiting Corporation (the subsidiary of South Africa's Chamber of Mines that was responsible for obtaining African mine labor) agreed to establish a rival newspaper. *Umteteli wa Bantu* (Mouthpiece of the People) was launched in May 1920 in a deliberate attempt to wean African writers and readers away from *Abantu-Batho*. The ANC's first president and secretary general, John Dube and Sol Plaatje, appeared initially on the masthead as the editors, but Plaatje had already declined the post, and Dube apparently did as well. Nevertheless, the chamber clearly hoped its newspaper would appeal to moderate African nationalists in the Transvaal and in other regions of South Africa that were recruiting areas for African mine labor.

The contradictions in *Umteteli*'s appeal to the African intelligentsia at this time can be seen in two editorials written in 1920 and 1924. The first editorial was a message of hope–a demand for civil rights that would appeal primarily to the petty bourgeoisie:

> That certain privileges to which all humanity is entitled are withheld from the natives no one can deny, and it is equally positive that those privileges must be granted. The franchise so wantonly disregarded or misused by many Europeans is a valuable gift, and no less to be desired is the right to own property, the right to walk freely in our land untrammelled by Pass Law restrictions and annoyances, and the right of self-government. Industrial equality and the right to progress, free education and a fair chance for our children–these are the things withheld from us.

The second editorial was a message of enlightened self-interest–a direct plea to African liberals to accept the necessity for interracial cooperation under white trusteeship in the pursuit of peaceful change:

> Rather more than four years ago *Umteteli* first appeared to educate white and black and to point out their respective and their common duties. At that time much of the

> Native press was bitterly anti-white in policy...the need for a mediator was felt by a number of farseeing natives, men prominent among their people and gravely concerned for their people's welfare, and it was due to their representations that this paper was launched. We are charged to preach racial amity, to foster a spirit of give and take, to promote the will to cooperate, to emphasize the obligations of black and white to themselves and to each other, and generally to create an atmosphere in which peace and goodwill might thrive.[52]

Umteteli–one of the earliest journals for Africans established by a nonmissionary agent of the dominant culture–carefully selected the events that merited protest and opposed any activity that might pose a threat to the political, economic or social order. Nevertheless, *Umteteli* offered a news agenda that sought to represent the interests of the African nationalist elite, and men like Plaatje and Dube were regular correspondents. The writing staff included Richard Msimang and his brother H. Selby Msimang, two leading officials in the Transvaal ANC during the 1920s, and H. I. E. Dhlomo, who would be heralded as the major African novelist and playwright of his generation. It was a prototype of the captive black commercial publications that gradually replaced the independent African protest press between the 1930s and 1950s.[53]

White-owned *Bantu World* was launched in April 1932 and in little more than a year was installed as the flagship newspaper of Bantu Press, a largely owned subsidiary of the Argus Printing and Publishing Company. Argus, the major white-owned press conglomerate in South Africa, was controlled indirectly by the mining industry. Bantu Press eventually owned or otherwise controlled a chain of black publications extending throughout southern and central Africa. *Bantu World*, under the editorship of Selope Thema (who remained at the helm for 20 years from 1932 to 1952), epitomized the dramatic changes that occurred in the African protest press when it was finally taken over by white representatives of the new industrial order. *Bantu World* (retitled the *World* in January 1956) became a daily in January 1962 and was recast as a tabloid modeled on London's *Daily Mirror*.

The segregationist state was steadily expanding and solidifying its control over the African population during the 1930s, whereas major political organizations like the ANC remained weak and deeply fragmented. Thema and his colleagues on *Bantu World* offered a protest agenda that would not offend those who ruled. Politics were downgraded in favor of social and "human interest" stories, and the newspaper provided a model of the kind of news and entertainment deemed acceptable for Africans in South Africa. Credibility was retained during this decade because *Bantu World* had no competitors, and it was allowed a considerable degree of freedom to attack the government's racial policies. The depoliticization of domestic news was accompanied by repeated appeals urging African unity and self-reliance, and by the promotion of a seemingly endless number of leisure activities designed for readers seeking a vicarious taste of middle-class culture.

The Alternative Press, 1940s–1960s

The alternative press changed dramatically in form and content with the transition to a more militant discourse between the 1940s and 1960s. The new politics of confrontation took various forms, including strikes and other kinds of work stoppages, consumer boycotts, protest marches, noncollaboration with the civil authorities, and various other kinds of nonviolent and at some levels violent acts of resistance.

Petty bourgeois politics gradually faded away in the crusade for full political, economic and social rights for all in South Africa.

Resistance Politics

The most significant political issues during this period concerned the revival of the African National Congress as an effective African nationalist body, the strengthening of relations between Congress and other dissident groups, and the challenges posed by the Communist Party of South Africa, the All-African Convention, the South African Indian Congress and other pressure groups to the leadership of the ANC in an emerging national resistance movement.[54]

The All-African Convention (AAC) was launched in 1935 to mobilize opposition against the impending loss of the African franchise in the Cape. It was controlled essentially by the moderate African nationalist elite until 1943,[55] when a series of events radicalized the AAC and brought it to national prominence. African and Coloured teachers and other salaried professionals, active in various left-wing political discussion groups in and around Cape Town, were galvanized into action when the government set up a separate Coloured Affairs Department (CAD). A national anti-CAD lobby was launched in February 1943, and the AAC and other African, Coloured and Indian opposition groups were urged to affiliate with anti-CAD forces to fight the government's segregationist policies. The AAC, by this time, had been effectively infiltrated by young African and Coloured militants from the Cape Town area in the western Cape and the Ciskei–Transkei regions in the eastern Cape. Activists like Goolam H. Gool and his sister Janub ("Jane") Gool, Isaac Bangani ("I. B.") Tabata and Wycliffe Mlungisi Tsotsi were increasingly frustrated by what they perceived to be a lack of leadership in Congress and other dissident groups.

The anti-CAD coalition and the AAC created a new federal umbrella body called the Non-European Unity Movement (NEUM) in December 1943. A so-called Ten-Point Programme was approved at this conference, a comprehensive bill of rights that established several important precedents in the campaign against the government's discrimination policies. The Unity movement, as it was called, endorsed for the first time a universal franchise for all men and women above the age of 21, and individual rights (including the right to compulsory, free and uniform education for all children to the age of 16) were guaranteed. The manifesto also called for sweeping changes in the laws concerning land ownership, labor, taxation and the legal system.[56]

In December 1944, the All-African Convention joined its allies in the Unity movement in adopting a new strategy of noncollaboration with all government-sponsored consultative bodies servicing blacks. Members henceforth would boycott the various African consultative bodies created by the central government to co-opt the African political elite–the Natives' Representative Council (African members were urged "to resign collectively and immediately"), "Native Representatives" in parliament (whites elected to represent African interests) and all other "segregatory institutions" (including local, district and general councils created for Africans in the Ciskei and Transkei reserves in the eastern Cape, and Location Advisory Boards created for Africans living and working in designated white urban areas) – and seek "Unity with the other sections of the non-Europeans."[57] The AAC was effectively absorbed by the Unity movement, and control of the organization shifted to the militant anti-CAD faction centered in

Cape Town. The Unity movement's strategy of noncollaboration was initially successful in mobilizing protest in the Cape Town metropolitan area and in the villages of peasant communities in the eastern Cape for several years in the late 1940s to early 1950s, but it was rapidly eclipsed by the success of Congress during and after the 1952 Defiance Campaign.[58]

The ANC had perhaps 1,000 members when Alfred Bitini Xuma, a medical practitioner who had received his training in the United States, Hungary and Scotland, was elected president general by one vote in December 1940. In the next nine years, he employed his considerable talents as an administrator to reassert central control over the organization (establishing the administrative headquarters in Johannesburg and requiring members of the executive committee to live within 50 miles of the city), initiate a new, streamlined constitution (eliminating the special privileges given to chiefs and granting women full equality), strengthen financial accountability, set out responsibilities of branches in some detail and cooperate more effectively with sympathetic white, Coloured and Indian protest groups.

The impact of Xuma's reforms, however, was felt mainly in the Transvaal. ANC membership during the 1940s increased more than five times to a high of 5,517 in 1947, and more than half the members lived in this province. ANC membership in the Cape and Natal was no more than 200–300 each in the early 1940s. At times, the only active branch of the Cape Congress was at Cradock in the eastern Cape (which was raided by the police in 1943). Although the numbers increased in both provinces in the mid to late 1940s, overall ANC membership declined to an average of about 4,000 in 1948–49.[59]

Xuma and his colleagues worked hard to recruit younger members, and an ANC Youth League was formally established in Johannesburg with Xuma's blessing in April 1944. Youth Leaguers during the early years were drawn from the same ranks that had produced most of the politicians since the 1880s. They were mainly skilled clerks, teachers and other professionals, an elite trained almost exclusively in mission secondary schools. But they were under 40 years of age, few were clerics, and few, if any, had been educated overseas. The new generation also had fewer illusions about the nature of white rule in South Africa, and they were not so dependent on the tactics of moral suasion that had been characteristic of the African nationalist movement in the past.

The Youth Leaguers were suspicious of alliances with non-African organizations during the 1940s, and their links with dissident African workers' and peasants' groups were fragile at best. Nevertheless, they were convinced Congress could provide the leadership needed to direct a mass movement. Youth League branches had been established in virtually all the major cities and towns of South Africa by the end of the decade.

Six of its leaders were placed on the ANC's executive committee in December 1949–including Nelson Mandela, Oliver Tambo and Walter Sisulu, who was elected secretary general. Xuma was replaced as president general by James Moroka, another physician and a compromise candidate who seemed more acceptable to those in sympathy with Youth League policies of direct action. Congress adopted its own Programme of Action in 1949, originating in large part from a Youth League manifesto drafted a year earlier, that for the first time agreed to employ the strategy of noncollaboration with government bodies–the same strategy implemented by the All-African Convention five years earlier.[60]

The Youth League's rapid rise to power in the ANC and the adoption of the Programme of Action was prompted in part by the National Party's victory in the

1948 whites-only general election that inaugurated the apartheid era. Politically conscious pressure groups of all races began to seek more militant options in the campaign to broaden and democratize the struggle. Sectional protest would gradually give way to various forms of collective resistance.

The Communist Party of South Africa (CPSA) had been rapidly Africanized from the mid-1920s (although whites still dominated the central committee). Black as well as white socialists were still hesitant to accept temporary migrants from the reserves as true representatives of an emerging African proletariat, but a majority in the party soon consisted of African industrial workers. Membership stood at 1,750 in 1928 (of whom 1,600 were Africans) and almost 3,000 in 1929,[61] when a series of events occurred that virtually crippled the party during the next decade.

African trade unions were hard hit by the Great Depression in South Africa (1929–32), and the CPSA was increasingly subjected to more systematic forms of government harassment, especially by Justice Minister (later Defence Minister) Oswald Pirow and the South African police. The CPSA was also fragmented by bitter internal disputes triggered initially by a Communist International resolution in 1928 that the CPSA support a "Native Republic" as the first stage toward an eventual socialist state. Party leaders were hopelessly divided over this question, and membership dropped to 300 or less by 1932.[62]

The growing threat of fascism at home and abroad in the 1930s again prompted the Communist International to urge member organizations to foster "popular front" alliances with antifascist organizations, and in South Africa the CPSA gradually came to accept the necessity of merging the class struggle with a "national liberation movement" that would embrace all classes and all segments of the population. As the *South African Worker*, the party mouthpiece, put it in 1937 with reference to the African National Congress: "The Communist Party of South Africa more than any other organisation realises the necessity for a national movement *and supports every progressive organisation struggling for emancipation of the oppressed and exploited Africans* [italics in the original]."[63]

But the CPSA also faced the Afrikaner nationalists, who were intent on gaining control of the white trade unions, and various paramilitary fascist groups like the Black Shirts, the Grey Shirts and the Ossewa Brandwag [the Oxwagon Guard], who attacked party members and left-wing workers' groups with tacit support from the government. The communists repeatedly sought an alliance with the Labour Party during the 1930s and actually established an all-white "People's Front" in an attempt to combat fascism within the white labor movement. But the dual strategy of simultaneously supporting the African nationalist movement and the white trade union movement did not work. Few black workers joined the party during the later 1930s, and membership stood at only 280 (more than half living in Johannesburg) at the end of the decade.[64]

The party's marginal existence in South Africa's political culture began to improve dramatically with the coming of World War II. Government officials became more conciliatory after the Soviet Union entered the war, and the CPSA was then able to oppose fascism at home and abroad with equal vigor. The party contested elections reserved for whites and blacks at all levels of government but especially in the white municipal councils (winning seats on councils in the major metropolitan areas of Johannesburg, Cape Town, Durban and East London) and the African Advisory Boards (electing members in townships in the Johannesburg metropolitan area, East London and Cape Town). The CPSA became fully involved in organizing black workers in urban areas, and many noncommunist politicians were associated with CPSA groups like the Friends of the Soviet Union (especially during the war years). To a much lesser extent, party activists also helped organize community-action campaigns in the townships and in the reserves (the most notable example being Alpheus Maliba, who worked with peasant dissidents in the Venda area of Zoutpansberg in the northeastern Transvaal).

The CPSA gained considerable credibility within African nationalist circles, and party membership soared to 1,500 in January 1944 and 2,360 in October. The repressive policies of the state slowed recruiting in the later 1940s, but membership stood at an estimated 2,500 in 1950. Whites were still in the majority on the central committee, but blacks constituted 64 percent (Africans 48 percent) of the membership.[65] Three organizers were elected to the ANC national executive committee – John B. Marks and Moses Kotane (the party's general secretary) in 1946 and Dan Tloome in 1949. Edwin Mofutsanyana, editor of the CPSA flagship newspaper *Inkululeko*, also served on the committee during these years. Yusuf Dadoo, Ismail Meer and J. N. Singh, leaders of the Transvaal Indian Congress, were CPSA members, and G. M. Naicker, head of the Natal Indian Congress, was closely associated with party stalwarts. The CPSA had sought to work with Coloured and Indian radicals in establishing a national resistance movement in the 1930s, but organizations such as the National Liberation League (formed in 1935) and the more ambitious Non-European United Front (formed in 1938) did not attract the kind of support that the ANC, the Unity movement and affiliated groups like the All-African Convention were beginning to receive in the 1940s.

ANC leaders were still relatively ambivalent on the question of forming alliances with other resistance groups. Some members, for example, were still affiliated with the AAC after World War II, but all attempts to reconcile differences between the two organizations failed. Although militant Africanists rejected even tentative links with non-African organizations, Congress did begin to make contact with the CPSA and the Transvaal and Natal Indian Congresses during the 1940s. ANC leaders, however, were still reluctant to confront the government. They had little sympathy with the politics of direct action, whether it emanated from workers' groups, community groups or political groups controlled by the petty bourgeoisie.

The timidity of the ANC at this time is revealed in its response to a national Anti-Pass Campaign sponsored by the CPSA toward the end of the war and to the Indian passive resistance campaign between 1946 and 1948. The ANC never went farther than pledging moral solidarity with the Indians, who were protesting legislation limiting Indian land and trading rights in the Transvaal and Natal.[66] When the communists urged a campaign against South Africa's pass laws after massive police raids in April 1943, Congress initially ignored the appeal. Representatives of an estimated 112 protest groups were present at an Anti-Pass conference in Johannesburg organized by the CPSA in November 1943, but the ANC refused to attend. Repeated calls for militant action, including appeals for a national strike, for the burning of passes and for political leaders to accept jail in solidarity with the pass resisters, were rejected by the CPSA and Congress.

Xuma reluctantly agreed to preside at another meeting held in May 1944, where a resolution condemning the pass laws was finally approved. Between 15,000 and 20,000 people joined a parade in downtown Johannesburg on a Sunday afternoon when the city was virtually empty, and a national Anti-Pass signature campaign launched after this demonstration proved to be equally futile. The acting prime minister refused to accept the petition containing the signatures (far fewer than the 1 million promised) when it was finally presented to parliament in June 1945, and the leaders of the Anti-Pass delegation were arrested and fined for leading an unlawful procession.

The ANC did not solidify its ties with non-African protest groups and regain its leadership role in African national politics until the 1952 Defiance Campaign. The ANC and the South African Indian Congress set up a Joint Planning Council in mid-1951 to coordinate a civil disobedience campaign in response to a spate of repressive legislation pushed through parliament after the National Party victory in the 1948 general election. The Group Areas Act, which imposed separate areas for Coloureds, Indians and whites as well as Africans, and the Suppression of Communism Act, which oulawed the CPSA, were enacted in 1950. The Suppression of Communism Act was so broad that it could be used against virtually any individual or organization actively opposed to the ruling National Party.

The Coloured Voters Act, which removed Coloured males from the common voters roll in the Cape as African males had been removed 20 years earlier, and the Bantu Authorities Act, which abolished the Natives' Representative Council and reorganized local government in the African reserves, were passed in 1951. Other measures restricting the movement of Africans in white urban and rural areas, and limiting peasant ownership of livestock and use of the land in African reserves, were tightened up. Legislation such as the Population Registration Act (1950) and bans placed on sexual and other forms of social intercourse between designated racial groups were also protested during the campaign, in addition to numerous local and regional grievances.

The Defiance Campaign was launched in June 1952. It was modeled on the passive resistance campaigns initiated by Mohandas K. Gandhi in South Africa more than a generation earlier. Trained volunteers would deliberately defy designated laws and invite arrest, until all the metropolitan areas were involved in the civil rights struggle. Even militant Africanist-oriented Youth Leaguers could participate, since multiracial groups were formed only in exceptional cases. Each racial group remained separate from the others and opposed legislation directed against that specific group. According to the plan, these efforts would be extended to other urban areas and finally to the rural areas, the white farms and African reserves, but it was never fully implemented.

The campaign was concentrated in the metropolitan areas, and it lasted more than six months before it was abandoned following riots (at least partially inspired by the police) in Port Elizabeth and East London in October and November 1952. The political leadership called a halt to the Defiance Campaign in January 1953, even though rank-and-file volunteers in the Cape and Transvaal favored continuing the boycotts and work stoppages.[67] New legislation provided stiff penalties for those who protested the law and enabled the central govemment to suspend all civil rights by declaring a State of Emergency.

The Defiance Campaign was the most significant example of nonviolent mass action carried out by the ANC and its allies before the 1960 bannings. A permanent Congress-inspired mass movement modeled on the Defiance Campaign, however, required a more effective organization than appeared to be possible at the time. Interpreters of African nationalist politics during this decade, moreover, have stressed that the ANC remained essentially a reformist organization. Congress focused on mass action in the cities and virtually ignored unrest in the rural areas. Civil disobedience in the form of stay-at-home protests was the main tactic used by protesters because it did not involve direct confrontation.

ANC leaders did not indulge in racial rhetoric, and democracy was not perceived simplistically as majority rule. Congress leaders still preferred moral protest to mass mobilization. Their actions were still determined in large part by fears that the resistance movement was not strong enough to confront the state. They continued to hope that white voters would respond to African grievances if they were expressed in nonviolent, nonthreatening terms. They accepted the white liberal view at the time that industrial capitalism and apartheid were incompatible, and they continued to believe political and economic rights would be won if anti-government whites could defeat Afrikaner Nationalists at the polls.

The ANC, however, continued to maintain the links it had forged with other protest groups after the Defiance Campaign. The highlight of the mid-1950s was the creation of the multiracial Congress Alliance between the ANC, South African Indian Congress, South African Coloured People's Organisation (later renamed the Coloured People's Congress), and the white South African Congress of Democrats (most of whom had been members of the Communist Party before it was banned in 1950). The South African Congress of Trade Unions (the successor to the main black umbrella union of the 1940s, the Congress of Non-European Trade Unions) joined the alliance after it was organized in March 1955.

Urban stay-at-home campaigns continued to mobilize opposition in the later 1950s, although popular resistance was manifested in a variety of other forms in the urban and rural areas, sometimes with and sometimes without the aid of the ANC and its allies. Multiracial solidarity was strengthened as the Congress Alliance leadership cadre was decimated by bannings, detentions, and a marathon treason trial for 156 accused that began in 1956 and actually lasted more than four years before all the accused were acquitted.

Africanists within Congress who believed that racial conflict was inevitable became increasingly disenchanted with events following the Defiance Campaign. The issue of collaboration with non-African organizations–in particular, the growing influence of some whites in African politics–was especially unsettling to some Africanists in the Congress Youth League. The ANC's leadership cadre, moreover, were unwilling to implement the policy of noncollaboration approved by Congress in 1949. They were perceived by hard-liners as being too timid and too compromised to provide the dynamic leadership that was needed to mobilize resistance. As the Africanists became more estranged from mainstream African politics, they became more vociferous in their demands. More and more youth who were victims of apartheid, moreover, turned to them for leadership. The key Africanist strongholds were in the Cape peninsula, a haven for tens of thousands of legal and illegal refugees from reserves in the eastern Cape, and in several African townships centering on Johannesburg in the southern Transvaal.

The Africanists broke away from the ANC to form the Pan-Africanist Congress (PAC) in April 1959, and in less than a year PAC leaders claimed a membership of almost 25,000, which rivaled the ANC's paid-up membership at the time. The separation of the Africanists from Congress would have significant implications for the resistance movement, but African divisional politics were almost immediately overtaken by the events of 1960–the Sharpeville-Langa shootings, the banning of Congress and the PAC, and the white referendum that resulted in South Africa becoming a republic and leaving the British Commonwealth.

African, Coloured and Indian activists had remained for the most part divided along community lines. Black political and trade union leaders rarely coordinated their activities, and little had been done to mobilize support from black community-action groups in the urban or rural areas. These factors helped enable the state to seize the moment and attempt to destroy all opposition to its policies. Eight years after the Defiance Campaign, South Africa's main political opposition groups had been banished from South Africa. The government detained nearly 2,000 political activists after declaring a State of Emergency in the country in 1960, and those who escaped this dragnet fled into exile. The resistance movement, however, remained partially on African soil, where it would take root again in the next generation.

Resistance Journalism

Chapters 7 through 11 (Part II) focus on the two decades or so between the 1940s and 1960s. These were formative years in South Africa's emergence as an industrial culture, and these were formative years in the shift in discourse from protest to resistance in South Africa's alternative press. Chapter 7 examines the last major independent African nationalist newspaper launched before the apartheid era; Chapter 8 examines the contributions of black literary journalists working for white-owned commercial publications targeted at black audiences during the 1950s; and Chapters 9, 10 and 11 examine newspapers associated with the socialist project in South Africa.

The African nationalist press was relatively ineffective between the 1940s and the 1960s. *Inkundla ya Bantu* (People's Forum) was the only independent African newspaper with an arguably national audience and the only alternative newspaper that placed a premium on covering the African nationalist movement during this period. Switzer and Ime Ukpanah, in Chapter 7, pull together what is known about *Inkundla*'s proprietors, who were partners in a job-printing and bookbinding venture called Verulam Press that served mainly the African church and the fledgling African business community in southern Natal. They examine *Inkundla* as a business enterprise in terms of its circulation and advertising content, and they critically evaluate the roles played by Govan Mbeki (1938–44) and Jordan Ngubane (1944–51) as editors.

The focal point of Chapter 7 is an analysis of the news (and advertising) content of *Inkundla*. The authors attempt to locate and identify the various strands of a complex political discourse that fully reflected the personal and political idiosyncracies of the editors and the many contradictions within the African nationalist movement. At one level, *Inkundla* functioned as a community newspaper, like *Imvo Zabantsundu* or *llanga lase Natal*. Correspondents were dispersed throughout the eastern Cape and Natal, news reports focused on the everyday activities of the African petty bourgeoisie in both regions, and voices of protest are encoded in these messages. At another level, *Inkundla* functioned as a forum for critics intent on reforming the ANC, and most political news concerned Congress and (from 1944) its youth wing, the Congress Youth League.

Neville Choonoo, in Chapter 8, focuses on the literary journalism of a group of talented writers working for the captive black commercial press, who immortalized the Johannesburg township of Sophiatown in their writings. They would be called the Sophiatown generation, and they worked primarily for *Drum* and the *Golden City Post* in the 1950s and early 1960s. The two publications were owned by James R. A. ("Jim") Bailey, one of the major black press entrepreneurs of this era and son of mining magnate Sir Abe Bailey. Drum set the pace for African journalism during these years, and the magazine's readership eventually extended throughout southern Africa. Two independent editions were produced in West Africa (Ghana and Nigeria) and one in East Africa (Kenya), and distribution agencies were developed in the West Indies, Britain and the United States.

Drum at its height, in the mid to late 1950s, had a larger circulation than any other publication (regardless of language) in Africa. Anthony Sampson, Sylvester Stein and Tom Hopkinson–all British recruits–were the most important editors of *Drum* during the 1950s. They, in turn, worked closely with two legendary African associate editors–Henry ("Mr Drum") Nxumalo (who was murdered in Orlando, Soweto, in 1957) and Can Themba (who died in exile in Swaziland in 1968)–in helping to develop a new breed of black tabloid journalists (and photographers, under the tutelage of Ian Berry). For Nxumalo, Themba, Ezekiel (now Es'kia) ("Zeke") Mphahlele (who was literary editor of *Drum* between 1955 and 1957), Nat Nakasa (who founded and edited with Nadine Gordimer a literary magazine called the *Classic* in 1963), Richard Rive (who was on the editorial board of the literary journal *Contrast*, launched in 1960) and a host of other poets, playwrights, short story writers and novelists, *Drum* was also probably the most important outlet for black creative writing in Africa during this decade.[68]

The Sophiatown generation included people such as Themba, Casey ("Kid") Motsisi, William ("Bloke") Modisane, Nxumalo, Mphahlele, Arthur Maimane, Todd Matshikiza, Peter Abrahams, Lewis Nkosi, Nakasa and Rive. Although bounded by linguistic and social practices associated with the petty bourgeoisie, they were also in some ways transient Gramscian intellectuals who lived in the same segregated, poverty-ridden townships and shared many of the same experiences as ordinary working-class blacks. In contrast to black journalists associated with the political press, however, these journalists were not activists: they were content to observe and record the conditions of life and work in black South Africa.

Their short stories, essays, poems, personality profiles and features represented "a literary renaissance of sorts," according to Choonoo, "that would ring in the appearance of a 'New African' who was not unlike the 'New Negro' of the 1920s Harlem Renaissance." They sought the detached, apolitical stance of the news journalist when focusing on exposés of black township life, and they employed a liberal discourse even when they railed against the liberalism of their white middle-class counterparts. They sought "to penalize white South Africans," as Choonoo puts it, "for their illusions" about Africans, and these whites formed a significant portion of their audience.

The Sophiatown generation has been criticized for being self-indulgent and lacking in political commitment. They wrote for two different, and essentially incompatible, readerships–the African working-class majority, and the white and black liberal middle-class elite–but they reached an audience through the captive black commercial press that was undreamed of in all but a few partisan political newspapers. They perceived the Sophiatown community in their own terms: when Sophiatown became a victim of the Group Areas Act and was finally bulldozed out of existence, Choonoo argues, "they were severed from the very source of their inspiration." The events of the early 1960s drove the resistance movement underground and a majority of the Sophiatown writers into exile. Most of their writings were officially banned by the apartheid regime in the mid-1960s, and the legacy of the Sophiatown generation was not made available to the South African public again until the mid-1980s.

During the 1940s and 1950s, resistance from below–from the mass of the black population still without effective access to political, social and economic networks dominated by the black petty bourgeoisie–was mobilized by trade unions and community organizations in urban and rural areas sometimes far removed from public scrutiny. Switzer begins Chapter 9 with an analysis of these activities to provide a context for studying the texts of the *Guardian* and other newspapers associated with the socialist press.

The *Guardian* (February 1937–May 1952) was a crucial text in the campaign to represent these dissident groups. Switzer profiles the editors and writers, describes the problems in production and distribution, and comments on the advertisers and readers of the newspaper. The focal point of the chapter is a critical assessment of the newspaper's role in chronicling the shift to passive resistance in the 1940s and early 1950s. The news agenda targeted African and multiracial trade unions, the Communist Party and affiliated organizations during these years, and the "*Guardian*'s task was nothing less than to project an alternative news discourse in the workers' struggle for South Africa."

Don Pinnock, in Chapter 10, covers the *Guardian* under its various titles during the 1950s, when African national politics and the Congress Alliance dominated the news agenda. His essay focuses on the writing of Ruth First, who was arguably the most influential investigative journalist during the *Guardian* era. Pinnock examines the main themes in her stories, which offered a unique contemporary perspective on South Africa's resistance movement between the late 1940s and early 1960s, and argues that protest journalism achieved a new dimension of meaning under her tutorship.

He offers four case studies to illustrate First's coverage of alternative news: they concern the plight of black farm workers, African women caught up in the Anti-Pass campaigns, poverty in Johannesburg's African townships and the Alexandra bus boycotts (Alexandra is a black township on the outskirts of Johannesburg). In each case study, First transcended conventional notions of "objective" journalism and asked questions about "how" the story was reported, "how" the reader was positioned to read the story by the writer, and "what" cultural codes were embedded in the text. Pinnock argues that First sought to contextualize her stories to demonstrate "how apartheid cemented in place the class divisions of an emerging industrial capitalist state." First's journalism, as he puts it, "was a probing, dissident perspective, setting ideas and events against one another, sharpening and clarifying differences and thereby intensifying commitment to certain ideologies and discourses. She was to develop ideas that were in advance of, and at times out of step with, the communist, nationalist and liberal thinkers and activists around her."

Elizabeth Jones, in Chapter 11, offers a capsule history of the Communist Party and its press between the 1920s and the Suppression of Communism Act in 1950. She discusses the party's relations with the Comintem and critically examines the main differences in opinion and policy between contending factions that led to purges in the Communist Party of South Africa in the late 1920s and early to mid-1930s. She describes the party's role in the African trade union movement, its links with the main black opposition groups and its role in white and black electoral politics at the local and national levels. She also offers a commentary on the Communist Party press during the interwar period, especially *South African Worker/Umsebenzi* (which appeared in three separate series between July 1926 and March 1938).

The focal point of Jones's essay is her analysis of *Inkululeko* (Freedom) from its founding as a mimeographed newssheet in 1939 to its heyday as the party's flagship newspaper during the mid- to late 1940s. The newspaper was run initially by an editorial board that included prominent blacks in the Communist party, in the ANC and in the trade union movement. Jones profiles unpaid contributors as well as paid members of the editorial and production staff, the most influential editorial figures being Michael Diphuko, Edwin Mofutsanyana and Michael Harmel. About two-thirds of the stories in *Inkululeko* were written in vernacular African languages and the rest in English. Jones carefully documents changes in *Inkululeko*'s format (masthead styles, number of pages and size of headlines), and she examines the visual (use of photographs and photo essays) and verbal (wording of headlines and advertisements) impact of the newspaper during this decade. She also examines various sources of funding, including paid (and unpaid) consumer advertising.

Like other resistance publications, *Inkululeko* operated within a specific economic and political environment, which in the 1940s included a dramatic increase in industrial development and an equally dramatic increase in the number of Africans moving from countryside to town. The newspaper chronicled the events of World War II, the years of protest against low wages, poverty, the pass laws and numerous other acts of discrimination, and the ascent of the National Party to power.

Aside from Communist party activities, *Inkululeko* sought to capitalize on news of political interest to the new urban African constituency. In contrast to the *Guardian*, however, there were virtually no straight news reports, and virtually no sports or entertainment news. *Inkululeko* was in a class by itself in its commitment to confrontation and consciousness-raising stories, but the newspaper often misread or ignored the significance of mainstream events. Jones offers two examples in the 1940s, the Alexandra bus boycotts and the 1946 African miners' strike. She concludes that the Communist Party, unlike the ANC, "had to overcome doubts about its foreign ideology, its subservience to the international communist movement and its history of white elitism." Nevertheless, the newspaper was on target with its largely African audience, because it expressed "the concerns of the African working class... in terms that might advance the struggle as a whole."

Numerous other resistance publications were operating between the 1940s and 1960s, and at least two not examined elsewhere in this book deserve a brief comment here. *Fighting Talk* (January 1942–February 1963) was launched in Johannesburg by the Homefront League of the Springbok Legion. Established in 1941 with a membership of 40,000 (about one-seventh of South Africa's armed forces), the Springbok Legion campaigned for soldiers' rights during and after the war and became a vigorous opponent of the apartheid regime. From 1944, the organization was led by two dedicated communists, Jack Hodgson and Jock Isakowitz.

Fighting Talk, a monthly in English and Afrikaans, was turned into a magazine after the war. The editorial board was expanded in 1954 to include activists from opposition groups that were to form the Congress Alliance in 1955. *Fighting Talk* was an unofficial organ of the Congress Alliance from 1955, until it was forced to cease publication by the apartheid regime in 1963. Most editors were members of the Communist Party. Brian Bunting, for example, edited the newspaper for a brief period before he became editor of the *Guardian*, while Lionel ("Rusty") Bernstein and Ruth First were also editors during the 1950s.[69]

The *Torch* (February 1946–December 1963), a weekly in English and Xhosa, is rarely mentioned in the secondary literature, and most scholars assume that it was read mainly by a small group of Coloured and African radicals living in Cape Town. Rosalynde Ainslie called it "a vituperative, bitter weekly... advocating total withdrawal from white society through boycott," and A. J. Friedgut suggested it was "subject to occasional Trotskyite influences."[70]

The *Torch*, the official organ of the Unity movement, was indeed the first newspaper in South Africa to advocate noncollaboration as a strategy of passive resistance. The first directors of the company that published the *Torch*, as well as the main editor during the turbulent 1950s (Mrs. June Meissenheimer), were Coloured radicals from the Cape Town metropolitan area. Many were influenced by the so-called Trostkyite movement, but in South Africa this term embraced a variety of socialist groups independent of the Communist Party.[71]

The Unity movement preached solidarity with the international workers' movement; it rivaled the ANC as an opposition group in the Cape during the 1940s, and its members were among the first to become actively involved in grassroots community resistance against apartheid. The *Torch*'s approach to opposition politics, its criticism of rival newspapers linked to the Communist Party and the ANC, and the range of nonpolitical and political issues covered set it apart from other opposition newspapers. The *Torch* had a distinct rhetorical style that was employed in analyzing and illustrating the many conflicts and tensions among various players within the anti-apartheid movement.

Although the state attempted to root out and destroy all vestiges of popular resistance during the early 1960s, in less than a decade a small, multifaceted resistance press had reemerged with the Black Consciousness movement. The government gave no priority to African literacy, but the literacy rate of adult Africans was estimated at 35 percent in 1957–58 and about 50 percent in 1970. According to one source, it was between 50 and 60 percent outside the so-called independent African "homelands" (carved out of the old reserves set aside for Africans) in the early 1980s.[72] For the first time in South African history, large numbers of people from all walks of life were able to read these counterhegemonic messages. Numerous grassroots community journals were being produced by the 1980s, and they were linked to other media of mass communication mobilized at the local, regional and national level in the final assault on South Africa's racial order.

Notes

1. See the Appendix for definitions of the terms "black" and "multiracial" as used in this study.
2. In the history of the African press, for example, estimates of carry-on readerships have ranged from 3 to 10 or even more readers for each newspaper purchased.
3. *Union statistics for fifty years: Jubilee issue 1910–1960* (Pretoria, 1960), A-22.
4. According to a survey compiled by the 1950 Press Commission, there were only 36 serial publications aimed at or intended for Africans in South Africa by 1954, and 32 were owned and controlled solely by whites. L. Switzer and D. Switzer, *The black press in South Africa and Lesotho, 1836–1976* (Boston, 1979), 6 (Table 1), 12–13 (Table 2).
5. One of the more bizarre examples of how the press has narrated the past is Vic Alhadeff's *A newspaper history of South Africa* (Cape Town, 1990). This version of white South Africa begins with the 1852 Sand River Convention and the "Birth of the Transvaal Republic." It ends with two graphic events placed unambiguously side by side–the 1983 Pretoria bomb blast and the 1990 release of Nelson Mandela from prison. Alhadeff's attempt to represent South Africa as a series of "events" chronicled in the front pages of various English-language newspapers is now in its third edition.

6. They included Johannesburg's *Rand Daily Mail* and to a lesser extent the *Star*, Bloemfontein's *Friend*, Cape Town's *Cape Times*, Port Elizabeth's *Evening Post*, East London's *Daily Dispatch* and Pietermaritzburg's *Natal Witness*. These newspapers deserve consideration in any future history of South Africa's anti-apartheid press, but they lie outside the parameters of the present study.
7. The English-language press was deemed to be a kind of extraparliamentary opposition, telling the truth about apartheid to South Africans and the outside world in a generation when white opposition parties had virtually collapsed and black opposition parties had been driven into exile. Few English-speaking journalists, however, have actually analyzed the content of the English press, despite scores of reminiscences, biographies and in-house histories. The image of a muckraking, watchdog English "opposition" press defending the civil rights of all who were oppressed was an enduring one during the later decades of the apartheid era. This image – reinforced in the midst of draconian censorship laws, widespread intimidation and sometimes even repression – has been generally accepted by mainstream media and media scholars, outside as well as inside South Africa. E.g., E. Potter, *The press as opposition: The political role of South African newspapers* (London, 1975); R. Pollak, *Up against apartheid: The role and plight of the press in South Africa* (Carbondale, 1981); W. A. Hachten and C. A. Giffard, *The press and apartheid: Repression and propaganda in South Africa* (Madison, 1984); E. McKenzie, "The English-language press and the Anglo American corporation: an assessment," *Kleio* 26 (1994), 98–107.
8. These views are summarized in L. Switzer, "Image and reality: A critique of South Africa's English-language press," *Rhodes University Journalism Review* 10 (July 1995), 17–19. Unfortunately, scholars critical of the English press-as-opposition thesis have focused almost exclusively on the years since the 1976 Soweto uprising, and in most cases they have not analyzed the content of these publications. But cf. L. Switzer, *Media and dependency in South Africa* (Athens, Oh., 1985); K. Tomaselli, R. Tomaselli and J. Muller (eds.), *The press in South Africa* (Chicago, 1987); and G. S. Jackson, *Breaking story: The South African press* (Boulder, 1993), Chaps. 2–3. The struggle to impose meaning on this strand of postcolonial discourse continues in post-apartheid South Africa.
9. Spiraling costs of production forced the editor to drop the chapters and accompanying illustrations covering these decades just before this book went to press. A second volume will consider the resistance press in the last generation before the end of the apartheid era.
10. Alan Cobley offers the best survey of the existing literature and the most detailed description of the political, economic, ethnic, educational and religious consciousness of the African petty bourgeoisie in South Africa before the 1950s. He focuses on the Witwatersrand, as do most other accounts of the African petty bourgeoisie in South Africa. A. Cobley, *Class and consciousness: The black petty bourgeoisie in South Africa, 1924 to 1950* (New York, 1990). A classic but controversial book on the subject is Leo Kuper's *An African bourgeoisie: Race, class and politics in South Africa* (New Haven, 1965). Useful case studies in the history of the African petty bourgeoisie include B. Willan, "Sol Plaatje, De Beers and an old tram shed: Class relations and social control in a South African town, 1918–1919," *Journal of Southern African Studies* 4, 2 (1978), 195–215; P. Bonner, "The Transvaal Native Congress 1917–1920: The radicalisation of the black petty bourgeoisie on the Rand," in S. Marks and R. Rathbone (eds.), *Industrialisation and social change in South Africa* (London, 1982); H. Bradford, "Mass movements and the petty bourgeoisie: The social origins of the ICU leadership 1924–29," *Journal of African History* 25 (1984), 295–310; and G. Baines, "The contradictions of community politics: The African petty bourgeoisie and the New Brighton Advisory Board, c. 1937–1952," *Journal of African History* 35 (1994), 79–l97. For the generation between the 1950s and 1980s, see O. Crankshaw, "Theories of class and the African 'middle class' in South Africa, 1969–1983," *Africa Perspective*, n.s. 1,

1–2 (1986), 3–33; Craig Charney, "Janus in blackface? The African petite bourgeoisie in South Africa, 1945–1985," paper presented to the Southern Africa Research Project, New Haven, Yale University, April 1987. For studies relating to the Indian and Coloured petty bourgeoisie, see Chaps. 3 and 4 of the present volume.

11. For a perceptive discussion of these issues, see P. Walker (ed.), *Between labor and capital* (Boston, 1979). The quotations are from the chapter by B. Ehrenreich and J. Ehrenreich, "The professional-managerial class."

12. For a description of the term "organic intellectual," see A. Gramsci, *Selections from the prison notebooks of Antonio Gramsci*, ed. and trans. Q. Hoare and G. H. Smith (London, 1971), 3 (Editors' Introduction).

13. T. Couzens, *The new African. A study of the life and work of H. I. E. Dhlomo* (Johannesburg, 1985), 5–9ff. See also L. Switzer, *Power and resistance in an African society: The Ciskei Xhosa and the making of South Africa* (Madison, 1993), Chaps. 5–6, 8. Skota's book, *The African yearly register, being an illustrated national biographical dictionary (who's who) of blackfolks in Africa* (1930), is a significant source for the African petty bourgeoisie before the 1930s. It was revised slightly in 1932 and reissued in the mid-1960s.

14. For details, see Switzer, *Power and resistance*, Chap. 10. The Development Bank of South Africa estimated that 65 percent of South Africa's population were "functionally" urbanized in 1993. Ninety percent or more of the whites, Coloureds and Indians (about 25 percent of the total population) were already living in urban areas, so this estimate essentially reflects the growth of the urban African population (Mohamed Adhikari, personal communication).

15. But Africans were still virtually absent from middle- or upper-ranked professional and managerial positions. For details, see Republic of South Africa, Department of Statistics, *Population census for 1970*, Report No. 02-05-04 (Occupations), Table 1 (a comparison between the 1960 and 1970 occupation census for all population groups); *South African labour statistics*, Dl, D6 (1986), Table 2 (employment and unemployment) for 1980; Charney, "Janus in blackface?".

16. For details, see South African Bureau of Statistics, *Urban and rural population of South Africa*, 1904–1960, Report No. 02-02-01, xxxi (Table IV), 5 (Table 1.5), 158 (Table 4.1.5); P. Walshe, *The rise of African nationalism in South Africa: The African National Congress*, 1912–1950 (London, 1970), 300–303. "Urban," during these years, was defined as cities and towns with populations above 500. Urban Africans comprised 18.5 percent of the total African population in 1936 and 27.8 percent in 1951.

17. The total number of Africans enrolled in school was 387,391 in 1935 and 888,757 in 1953. *Union statistics for fifty years*, E-23.

18. Fort Hare was a multiracial university with Coloured, Indian, and even some white (in the early years), as well as African, students. Total enrollment averaged 95 between 1916 (the first graduating class) and 1935, 160 between 1936 and 1940, 238 between 1941 and 1945, 343 in 1949 and 489 in 1959. South Africa's designated white, English-language universities had 139 African students in 1948 and 300 in 1959. (Although they were segregated socially, blacks could enter Cape Town, Natal and Witwatersrand universities until the passing of the 1959 Extension of University Education Act.) Most African university students, however, could only afford to take correspondence courses, so the University of South Africa (which offered degrees by correspondence) experienced the greatest increase in enrollment–from 317 African students in 1948 to 1,252 in 1959. Union of South Africa, *Report of the Commission on Native Education*, UG No. 53/1951 (Pretoria, 1952), 69 (Table 73); Muriel Horrell (comp.), *Bantu education to 1968* (Johannesburg, South African Institute of Race Relations, December 1968), 116–118. I am indebted to Hunt Davis for furnishing this information.

19. J. Hyslop, "Food, authority and politics: student riots in South Africa, 1945–1976," *Africa Perspective*, n.s. 1, 3–4 (1987), 3–41; J. Bolnick, "Preparing the petty bourgeoisie for privilege – Mission school education in the 20's, 30's and 40's,"

paper presented to African Studies seminar, Cape Town, University of Cape Town, 1988. Under the Bantu Education Act of 1953, African schools administered by virtually all missionary agencies were taken over by the central government and transformed into apartheid's version of African education.

20. *Union statistics for fifty years*, A-22; A. J. Friedgut, "The non-European press," in E. Hellmann (ed.), *Handbook on race relations in South Africa* (Cape Town, 1949; rpt. 1975), 489–490.
21. For a useful summary of this position, see W. Outhwaite, "Hans-Georg Gadamer," in Quentin Skinner's *The return of grand theory in the human sciences* (Cambridge, 1985), 21–39.
22. S. Seidman (ed.), *Jürgen Habermas on society and politics: A reader* (Boston, 1989), 231.
23. Ibid., 233–234. The comprehensive account of the emergence and decline of the bourgeois public sphere is contained in J. Habermas, *The structural transformation of the public sphere: An inquiry into a category of bourgeois society*, trans. Thomas Burger with the assistance of Frederick Lawrence (Cambridge, 1989; originally published 1962).
24. Saussure's major work, composed and published after his death by colleagues, was based mainly on student notes of lectures he gave on general linguistics between 1907 and 1911. See F. de Saussure, *Course in general linguistics*, trans. R. Harris (London, 1983). A useful, easy-to-digest summary of his ideas can be found in J. Culler, *Saussure* (Sussex, 1976), esp. Chap. 2.
25. The seminal work is M. M. Bakhtin's, *The dialogic imagination: Four essays*, trans. Caryl Emerson and Michael Holquist (Austin, 1981). See also Michael Holquist, *Dialogism: Bakhtin and his world* (London, 1990).
26. The literature in this field is growing rapidly, and there are now case studies targeting numerous regions in the postcolonial world. A useful summary of the debates in subaltern studies can be found in a recent forum sponsored by the *American Historical Review* (hereafter *AHR*). See G. Prakash, "Subaltern studies as postcolonial criticism," F. E. Mallon, "The promise and dilemma of subaltern studies: Perspectives from Latin American history," and F. Cooper, "Conflict and connection: Rethinking colonial African history," in *AHR* 99, 5 (1994), 1475–1545. See also G. C. Spivak, "The Rani of Sirmur: An essay in reading the archives," in *History and Theory* 24, 3 (1985), 247–272; R. O'Hanlon and D. Washbrook, "After Orientalism: Culture, criticism and politics in the third world," and G. Prakash, "Can the 'subaltern' ride? A reply to O'Hanlon and Washbrook," in *Comparative Studies in Society and History* 34, 1 (1992), 141–184; S. Feierman, "African histories and the dissolution of world history," in R. H. Bates, V. Y. Mudimbe and J. O'Barr (eds.), *Africa and the disciplines* (Chicago, 1993), 167–212.
27. Parts of this section appeared in an earlier format in L. Switzer and E. C. Jones, "Other voices. The ambiguities of resistance in South Africa's resistance press," *South African Historical Journal* 32 (1995), 66–113.
28. The only qualified voters were adult males who owned property or received a wage or salary equivalent to £75 a year and who could write their own name, address and occupation.
29. The Supreme Court ruled in 1916 that the measure should not be applied to the Cape because it would jeopardize African franchise rights.
30. The fight against Hertzog's repeated attempts to abolish the African franchise in the Cape between 1926 and 1936 is analyzed in detail by S. Dubow, *Racial segregation and the origins of apartheid in South Africa, 1919–36* (New York, 1989), esp. Chaps. 5–6; see also Switzer, *Power and resistance*, 272–283.
31. The following information on the mission enterprise and its press is based mainly on L. Switzer, "The African Christian community and its press in Victorian South Africa," *Cahiers d'Etudes africaines* 96, 24–4 (1984), 455–476; idem, *Power and resistance*, Chap. 4. See also N. Etherington, *Preachers, peasants and politics in southeast Africa, 1835–1880: African Christian communities in Natal, Pondoland and Zululand* (London, 1978); J. Comaroff and J. Comaroff, *Of*

revelation and revolution: Christianity, colonialism, and consciousness in South Africa*, vol. 1 (Chicago, 1991), esp. Chaps. 5–7 (on the Tswana).

32. The Roman Catholics also established a major printing and publishing facility in South Africa during the colonial era at Mariannhill, in Natal. Another one was set up at Mazenod, in colonial Basutoland.
33. Cf. R. H. W. Shepherd, *Bantu literature and life* (Lovedale, 1955); J. Zurcher (comp.), *One Hundred Eleven years: Morija printing works* (Morija, 1972).
34. On the educational policies pursued by the missionaries at Lovedale, cf. S. M. Brock, "James Stewart and Lovedale: A reappraisal of missionary attitudes and African response in the eastern Cape, South Africa, 1870–1905," Ph.D. thesis (University of Edinburgh, 1974), Chap. 3; D. E. Burchell, "A history of the Lovedale-missionary institution, 1890–1930," M. A. thesis (University of Natal at Pietermaritzburg, 1979), Chaps. 1–2.
35. *Inkanyiso* claimed 2,500 subscribers in September 1891, which was a very high number for a mission newspaper at the time. It was subtitled "the first native journal in Natal." Switzer and Switzer, *Black press*, 249.
36. The impact of the written word on the developing Christian station communities in southern Africa is exemplified in the Lovedale experience. Lovedale had printing and bookbinding departments (opened in 1861), a retail and wholesale bookstore and the subcontinent's oldest, continuous mission journal. The *Kaffir Express* (October 1870–December 1875) was renamed the *Christian Express* (January 1876–December 1921) and finally the *South African Outlook* (January 1921 to date).
37. On Makiwane, see R. H. Davis, "School vs. blanket and settler: Elijah Makiwane and the leadership of the Cape school community," *African Affairs* 78, 310 (1979), 12–31.
38. For information on the mission press at Lovedale, see A. Odendaal, "African political mobilization in the eastern Cape, 1880–1910," Ph.D. thesis (University of Cambridge, 1983), Chaps. 1–2.
39. "I. W. W. Citashe" (the pseudonym of Isaac Wauchope) in *Isigidimi Sama Xosa*, 1 June 1882. Hoho, in the Amathole Mountains between the Fish and Kei rivers in the eastern Cape, was reputedly the place where Sandile, chief of the Ciskei Xhosa, was killed during the 1877–78 Cape–Xhosa war. It was the ninth and last of a series of wars that had continued for a century in one small region of South Africa. This One Hundred Years' War turned out to be the most protracted period of primary resistance against colonial rule in sub-Saharan Africa. For the translation, see A. S. Gerard, *Four African literatures: Xhosa, Sotho, Zulu, Amharic* (Berkeley and Los Angeles, 1971), 41.
40. The evidence suggests that many mission journals actually de-emphasized secular news in the postcolonial period. *Moshupa Tsela* (the Guide), which was produced originally in Tswana by the Swedish Lutherans in the Transvaal, is a case in point. The first issue of the first series, which apparently ended sometime before World War I, was published in 1893. A November 1896 edition describes *Moshupa* as the "first black newspaper in the South African Republic [Transvaal]," and it was concerned with secular news of general interest to the Tswana as well as religious news. By the second series (which began in 1914), it was a Bible-centered devotional journal. Numerous other African-language, English, Afrikaans and French editions of *Moshupa* (now spelled *Mosupa*) were produced in the third series (which began in 1941), and it became perhaps the major devotional publication in the Protestant mission's African-language press. *Izindaba Zabantu* (People's Topics), the major Roman Catholic journal for Zulu-speaking Christians in Natal and beyond, is another example. It was launched in October 1910 by the Mariannhill Fathers at Mariannhill near Pinetown, Natal. Under the energetic editorship of the Zulu historian Father A. T. Bryant (1910–15), the newspaper established a national reputation as an accurate and sympathetic chronicler of events and issues of concern to the Zulu Catholic community. But *Izindaba* had become more conservative politically and more narrowly denominational by the 1920s. Secular news was de-emphasized and English-language stories virtually dropped

when the newspaper's title was changed to *Umafrika* in December 1928.

41. His father Tiyo Soga (1829–71) was a legendary figure in the African Christian community. He had been a pioneer African missionary and pastor, and a founding father of the African mission church. He wrote for various mission publications and was one of the first in southern Africa to express an African viewpoint in the settler press. He was also a composer of hymns, a translator and a writer. (His translation in 1867 of the first part of *Pilgrim's Progress*, John Bunyan's extended allegory in prose of the search for a Christian utopia, for example, was probably the first book published by an African in the subcontinent.) Tiyo Soga is revered as a saint to this day by African Christians inside and outside the Cape. See D. Williams (ed.), *The journal and selected writings of the Reverend Tiyo Soga* (Cape Town, 1983).

42. The first nonmissionary newspaper in Natal was launched in Pietermaritzburg sometime before *Ilanga* by members of the Natal Native Congress (NNC), the pioneer African political organization in the colony, established in 1900. *Ipepa lo Hlanga* (the Paper of the Nation) came to the notice of the authorities in early 1901, when several letters and commentaries, including one headlined "Vukani Bantu!" ("Rise Up, You People!"), were deemed hostile to whites. This four-page newspaper was produced by the Zulu Printing and Publishing Company, whose proprietors–Chiefs Isaac Mkize and James Mjozi–epitomized the link between politics and religion during this period. They were founding members of the NNC and prominent members of the local Wesleyan Methodist mission church. The editor was Mark Radebe, a graduate of the prestigious mission boarding school at Lovedale in the eastern Cape. He owned a drapery shop in Pietermaritzburg and was also very active in Wesleyan church circles. *Ipepa* seems to have ceased publication, at least initially, at the end of 1901, when the proprietors heeded a warning from the Natal undersecretary for Native affairs and decided not to renew the newspaper's publication license. The Switzers, however, found copies of *Ipepa* between June 1898 and April 1904, and there is evidence that the newspaper was actually published as early as 1894. Cf. S. Marks, *Reluctant rebellion: The 1906–8 disturbances in Natal* (Oxford, 1970), 73; A. Odendaal, *Black protest politics in South Africa to 1912* (Totowa, N.J., 1984), 61; Switzer and Switzer, *Black press*, 44–45.

Another early political organization in Natal was Iliso le Sizwe Esimnyama (Eye of the Black Nation), which was established formally in 1908 and dedicated to uniting the Zulu of Natal and Zululand. According to Shula Marks, it was made up primarily "of Wesleyan Methodist converts and chiefs." Iliso launched a monthly in Zulu entitled *Iso Lesizwe Esimnyama* (also Eye of the Black Nation) in 1918, but apparently it lasted only a few months. The founder-editor was Josiah Gumede, a future president of the ANC. Marks, *Reluctant rebellion*, 363; Switzer and Switzer, *Black press*, 46–47.

43. The first African lawyer to practice in South Africa was a West African named Akilagpa Osabrampa Sawyer. C. Saunders, "Pixley Seme: towards a biography," *South African Historical Journal* 25 (1991), 206 (n. 57).

44. For information on these journals, see Switzer and Switzer, *Black press*, 28 (*African Native Advocate*), 53–54 (*Moromioa, Leihlo lo Babatsho*), 63 (*Umlomo wa Bantu*), 25–26 (*Abantu-Batho*).

45. For details on Seme's life and his role in the ANC, see Saunders, "Pixley Seme."

46. Skota founded at least one newspaper during the 1920s. *African Shield* was published in Kimberley, probably in 1922, and lasted about two years, but no copies have been found in South Africa. Switzer and Switzer, *Black press*, 28.

47. We know little about Ncwana, but he launched the first official organ of the Industrial and Commercial Workers' Union as a monthly in English entitled *Black Man*. The newspaper, published in Cape Town, was subtitled "a journal propagating the interests of workers throughout the African continent," but it lasted only six issues (July–December 1920). Another of his newspapers, entitled the *African Voice*, was published in Cape Town sometime in 1923, but apparently it also lasted only a few issues.

I. B. Nyombolo, a member of the Cape Peninsula Native Association, was associated with Ncwana in the venture, and the *Voice* was probably founded to represent the interests of this pioneer regional civil rights group. Ncwana launched an English-language weekly in Queenstown in 1931 called the *Franchise Gazette*, but the newspaper apparently ceased publication before the end of the year. The *Gazette* was probably established in response to Prime Minister J. B. M. Hertzog's campaign to abolish the Cape African Franchise. Ncwana was also the editor of *Izwi lase Afrika* (the Voice of Africa), a weekly in English and Xhosa published in Cape Town in November 1941. It was the organ of the Cape ANC, but it lasted less than two months before collapsing in January 1942. Ibid., 28 (*African Voice*), 31 (*Black Man*), 37 (*Franchise Gazette*), 48 (*Izwi lase Afrika*).

48. Cobley, *Class and consciousness*, 152–155, 176 (n. 50). Alan Cobley (following Peter Walshe) claims the newspaper did not cease publication in 1931. It was bought by a company called the African and Indian Trading Association Ltd., which had been formed in 1927 and consisted of four main shareholders: two were Indian merchants, K. V. Patel and D. M. Nursoo, and two were ANC officials at the time, Mweli Skota (secretary general) and Henry Reed Ngcayiya (chaplain general). According to Walshe, *Abantu-Batho* was published until 1935, but it served mainly as an advertising medium for "patent medicines." Walshe, *The rise of African nationalism*, 217. According to A. J. Friedgut, the newspaper closed in July 1931 and was "revived" as an advertising news sheet "by a firm of patent medicine vendors" before dying "ignominiously in the 1930s." Friedgut, "The non-European press," 491.

49. *African Leader*, 29 October 1932.

50. Coka was an activist in the independent African trade union movement, an ICU official and later a member of the Communist Party. He wrote briefly for the party organ *Umsebenzi* and also launched the *African Liberator* (September 1935–January/February 1936), but it only lasted three issues. This multilingual publication (English, Zulu, Sotho) was printed by Spes Bona–one of the few African printing companies in existence at the time–in Johannesburg's Alexandra township.

51. E. Roux, *Time longer than rope: A history of the black man's struggle for freedom in South Africa* (Madison, 1964), 350; Switzer and Switzer, *Black press*, 27.

52. *UWB*, 1 May 1920 (cited in Switzer and Switzer, *Black press*, 110); *UWB*, 30 August 1924 (cited in Couzens, *The new African*, 91–92).

53. For information on *Umteteli wa Bantu*, see Switzer and Switzer, *Black press*, 110–111; B. Willan, Sol Plaatje: *South African nationalist*, 1876–1932 (Berkeley and Los Angeles, 1984), 251–253, 302, 315–318. Abner R. Mapanya and Harold T. Kumalo were also among those who edited *Umteteli* between the 1920s and the 1940s, but a white editorial director (and board) actually controlled the newspaper. Political news was de-emphasized in the early 1940s, and the newspaper was completely depoliticized in the early 1950s.

54. Opposition politics during this period has been a popular reference point for South African historians. The most useful general works are Roux, *Time longer than rope*; H. J. Simons and R. E. Simons, *Class and colour in South Africa*, 1850–1950 (Middlesex, 1969); G. M. Gerhart, *Black power in South Africa* (Berkeley and Los Angeles, 1978); and T. Lodge, *Black politics in South Africa since 1945* (London, 1983). On the ANC, see Walshe, *The rise of African nationalism*; F. Meli, *South Africa belongs to us: A history of the ANC* (Bloomington, 1989). On the CPSA during the 1940s, see A. K. Brooks, "From class struggle to national liberation: the Communist Party of South Africa, 1940 to 1950," M.A. thesis (University of Sussex, 1967); D. Fortescue, "The Communist Party of South Africa and the African working class in the 1940s," *International Journal of African Historical Studies* 24, 3 (1991), 481–512.

55. The ANC hierarchy held most of the key posts on the AAC executive committee, and D. D. T. Jabavu served as president of the organization until December 1948. Three presidents general of Congress–A. B. Xuma, Zaccheus Mahabane and James S. Moroka–also served on the AAC's executive committee in the 1930s and 1940s.

56. T. Karis and G. Carter (eds.), *From protest to challenge*, Vol. 2: *Hope and challenge 1935–1952*, Document 65 (AAC and anti-CAD conference statement, 17 December 1943), 352–357.
57. For details, see I. B. Tabata, *The awakening of a people* (Cape Town, 1950; rpt. Nottingham, 1974), 61–67. The anti-CAD coalition had already endorsed these measures at a conference in January 1944. The South African Indian Congress (SAIC) was included in the unity plan, even though its leaders, preoccupied with anti-Indian legislation, did not attend the conference. The conservative merchant group controlling the SAIC backed away after meeting with AAC and anti-CAD leaders in July 1944. When militants succeeded in gaining control of the Indian Congress in 1945, they preferred to align the organization with the ANC.
58. The All-African Convention refused to participate in the Defiance Campaign and thereafter declined rapidly in numbers and influence. The Unity movement probably reached a high point in January 1945 with an estimated 102 federated organizations and almost 60,000 members (mainly in the Cape), but it was virtually a spent force in black politics even in the Cape by the end of the 1950s. Karis and Carter, *Hope and challenge*, 129 (n. 91). African leaders in the AAC were mainly teachers affiliated with the Cape African Teachers' Association, which affiliated with the Unity movement in 1948.
59. The ANC had no more than 1,000 paid-up members in 1940. The 1947 figures show the Transvaal with 2,821 members, Natal with 1,520 members, the Orange Free State with 800 members and the Cape with 376 members. The Transvaal had 60 branches, and the other three provinces combined had 52 branches in 1947. Walshe, *The rise of African nationalism*, 389, 397.
60. Cf. Karis and Carter, *Hope and challenge*, Document 57 ("Basic Policy of the Congress Youth League," manifesto issued in 1948), 323–331; Document 60 (Programme of Action adopted 17 December 1949), 337–339.
61. Simons, *Class and colour*, 406 (for estimates of CPSA membership in 1928 and 1929).
62. For details, see Chap. 11 in the present volume. Brooks, "From class struggle to national liberation," 21 (for estimate of CPSA membership in 1932).
63. *South African Worker*, 6 November 1937, 1. The article was in response to "allegations" that the party was "aiming at capturing the leadership of the African National Congress."
64. Brooks, "From class struggle to national liberation," 25 (for estimate of CPSA membership).
65. Ibid., 26, 32–33, 51–54. Socioeconomic groups that lacked significant representation in the party were "women, workers in heavy industry, peasants, and non-white professional and intellectual groups."
66. The Indian community press was a model of advocacy journalism during this campaign, which lasted, somewhat sporadically, for more than two years. At least five journals mobilized Indian opinion and alerted South Africans in general to the concerns of the Indian community. They provided accurate, more or less continuous, on-the-spot coverage. *The Passive Resister* (July 1946–October 1948) was the official organ of the Transvaal and Natal Passive Resistance Council, which was set up by the South African Indian Congress to coordinate the resistance groups. Indians were exhorted to join the demonstrators, the names of the more than 2,000 detainees were published and their whereabouts in detention made known to readers. Acting alone, however, the Indians had no hope of redressing their grievances. The 1946–48 campaign demonstrated the futility of a resistance movement divided along ethnic lines.
67. ANC membership soared in roughly six months in 1952 from 7,000 to perhaps 100,000, of which 60 percent lived in the Cape. Membership fell to 29,000 in 1953, but it increased rapidly again in the last three years before the organization was banned. Throughout the 1950s, moreover, the number of Congress activists was apparently much larger than the membership lists revealed. Lodge, *Black politics*, 61, 75.
68. A useful summary of the impact *Drum*'s white editors and black associate editors had on the magazine during the 1950s can

be found in D. C. Woodson, "'Pathos, mirth, murder, and sweet abandon': The early life and times of *Drum*," in J. W. Witherell (ed.), *Africana resources and collections: Three decades of development and achievement* (Metuchen, N. J., 1989), 228–246.

69. On *Fighting Talk*, see D. Woodson (comp.), *Decade of discontent: An index to Fighting Talk, 1954–1963* (Madison, 1992).

70. R. Ainslie, *The press in Africa: Communications past and present* (New York, 1966), 53; Friedgut, "The non-European press," 503. Tom Lodge was a bit more positive with his observation that it was "a well produced, if acerbic, newspaper." Lodge, *Black politics*, 87.

71. Several socialist study groups outside the Communist Party were formed in Cape Town during the 1930s and 1940s, but outsiders tended to lump them together under the Trotskyite umbrella. Some did follow the teachings of Leon Trotsky, but others included communists expelled from the party and socialists opposed to Stalinism. Coloured and African teachers were especially active in these study groups. See C. Bundy, "Resistance in the reserves: The A. A. C. and the Transkei," *Africa Perspective*, 22, 1983, 61 (n. 4).

72. *Union statistics for fifty years*, A-22; SAIRR, *Survey of race relations in South Africa 1982* (Johannesburg, 1983), 436–437. According to a BENSO report (Bureau for Economic Research), the adult African literacy rate (15 years and older) was about 67 percent in 1982, excluding the "homelands," where the vast majority of the population was functionally illiterate.

PART I

An Independent Protest Press, 1880s–1930s

CHAPTER 1

The Beginnings of African Protest Journalism at the Cape

Les Switzer

A fledgling African independent press that sought to represent a specifically African political culture first emerged in the Cape during the last two decades of the Cape colonial era. The driving force behind the mobilization of African political opinion, however, seems to have been not so much the pioneer African political, social and economic organizations as the ideas and activities of a few opinion leaders.

The first part of this chapter examines the African protest press in the eastern Cape, a region inhabited by the Xhosa and their immediate neighbors, the Mfengu and Thembu.[1] Two political figures, two regional political groups and two newspapers dominated African nationalist news and opinion for the better part of a generation. The second part of the chapter examines the African protest press in the northern Cape, a region inhabited by the Tswana, where Sol Plaatje and his newspapers were the main arbiters of African nationalist news and opinion.

African Politics and the Press in the eastern Cape

The Cape was the only British settler colony in South Africa that possessed a nonracial franchise. Individual voting rights were restricted to the "civilized" male population, but these rights were enshrined in the 1853 constitution, when the settlers were granted representative government with their own parliament, and in 1872, when African and Coloured voters were able to participate in the political process with the granting of responsible government. This was the political birth of the Cape liberal tradition, as it was called, in South Africa.[2]

African voters in the Cape were mainly but not exclusively mission-educated Christians, who had conformed to the changes wrought by the impact of British colonialism on the eastern Cape. Christianity and formal education were key facilitators of change, and an indigenous African church overriding ethnic and denominational boundaries was in the making by the 1870s. Economic links between white and black modernizers had been firmly established at least a decade earlier, and loose political alliances were being formed by the 1880s.

Settler politicians representing rural and urban constituencies with numbers of African and Coloured voters formed the crucial component of this alliance. Black participation in Cape colonial politics, however, was conditioned in large part by a struggle for supremacy in parliament between the Afrikaners and the English, representing mainly the settlers of Dutch and British origin, between 1872 and 1910. Afrikaners outnumbered English speakers 2 to 1 in the Cape Colony during the

Photo 1. John Tengo Jabavu, founder and editor of *Imvo Zabantsundu* (1884–1921).

Photo 2. Walter Benson Rubusana, a founder of *Izwi Labantu* and Jabavu's main political rival.

Photo 3. Alan Kirkland Soga, editor of *Izwi Labantu* (1899–1909) and the *Native Advocate* (1912?).

Photo 4. Solomon Tshekisho Plaatje, founder and editor of *Koranta ea Becoana* (1901–9), *Tsala ea Becoana* (1910–12) and *Tsala ea Batho* (1912–15).

1880s. The Afrikaner Bond, launched in 1879, was enlarged and reorganized in 1883 to provide an organizational base to unify and direct the Afrikaners' political aspirations.

The rise of Afrikaner nationalism would have a decisive impact on Cape colonial politics during this period. The Bond comprised the largest single political grouping–at least 40 percent of the total in both houses of parliament–between 1884 and 1910. Although Afrikaners never formed a government on their own, J. H. Hofmeyr, leader of the Afrikaner Bond, and his colleagues effectively controlled parliamentary politics by granting and withdrawing support to successive English coalitions in proportion to whether or not they implemented the Bond's policies. English-speaking politicians represented so many conflicting interest groups that it was impossible to forge a single party to challenge the supremacy of the Afrikaner Bond until the late 1890s. In the interim, they sought allies from a variety of sources, including the modernizing African elite.

Africans in the Cape only began registering as voters in large numbers from the 1880s. Whites would always dominate the Cape voters' rolls, but the African vote between 1880 and 1910 was of some significance in 17 constituencies (out of 74 constituencies, for example, in 1891), of which 14 were in the eastern Cape (including the Transkeian territories) and the rest in the northern Cape. To be eligible to vote in the colony, one had to be a male 21 years or older who was accepted as a British subject, owned property valued at £25, or received a wage or salary of £50 a year (or £25 a year plus food and housing). There was no educational test.

Leaders of the mission-educated community aligned themselves with headmen and other persons of authority in the segregated African locations (designated "reserves" after the 1913 Natives' Land Act). They acted as mediators in bringing together African voters and white political candidates, or "friends of the natives," as they were called, who would be sympathetic to their interests. African election committees were organized, and African politicians became increasingly more sophisticated in their understanding of how political power was acquired in a parliamentary democracy. They helped select and tutor liberal-white candidates and ensure that they had access to black voters in the constituencies. African newspapers were mobilized in the effort to gain popular support for electoral politics, and African politicians began to communicate their concerns to an ever-widening audience of white sympathizers.

Jabavu and *Imvo Zabantsundu*

The single most important barometer of African political opinion at the Cape was John Tengo Jabavu (1859–1921). The 25-year-old Methodist lay preacher, teacher and former editor of *Isigidimi* launched *Imvo Zabantsundu* (translated then as "Native Opinion," but today it would be rendered as "Black Opinion") in King William's Town in November 1884, the first newspaper owned and controlled by an African in southern Africa. Jabavu's publication soon eclipsed competing mission journals in offering a more effective platform for the mission-educated African community. It was the beginning of a new era.

Jabavu was immensely powerful during the 1880s and 1890s. He would become the *éminence grise* behind a number of African political, cultural and economic organizations in the eastern Cape, and his newspaper virtually established the agenda for discussion and debate on the options that were available to the African in Cape colonial society. He launched *Imvo* as a journal that was committed to libertarian values but independent of specific political interests. It was to be nonpartisan politically but dedicated to "moderate men within all parties,"[3] which in practice meant all settler politicians opposed to the Afrikaner Bond. Jabavu was certainly aware that English-speaking settlers were no more sympathetic to African interests than Dutch-speaking settlers, but he saw that if the English-Afrikaner split was deliberately exploited, his readers could more easily identify with the issues involved in settler politics. Jabavu also hoped that editorial support for the English liberal platform would lend credence to the popular myth that political differences between the two settler groups represented genuine ideological differences.

Imvo Zabantsundu was a protest journal at two levels. On the one hand, it sought to articulate and unify the interests and needs of the modernizing, mainly Christian African elite. Some idea of the composition of that elite in terms of formal education and occupation can be discerned from a book produced by James Stewart in 1887 in defense of Lovedale Seminary's higher educational policies. More than 2,000 African students (1,520 males and 538 females) had been enrolled in postprimary classes since Lovedale was established in 1841. The subsequent occupations of roughly 70 percent of these students were tracked, and they represented a cross section of the modernizing sector. They included teachers, ordained and nonordained clergy, transport riders and peasant farmers who had acquired land in individual tenure, law agents, police constables, journalists, magistrates' clerks and court interpreters, and semiskilled and skilled craftsmen such as carpenters, blacksmiths, sewing mistresses and dressmakers, telegraph operators, printers, bookbinders, wagon makers, masons, shoemakers, shop clerks, drugstore assistants, small traders and storemen.[4]

Imvo's writers and readers stemmed from the same social strata, but they remained a very small segment of the African population as a whole. *Imvo*'s circulation, for example, probably did not rise above 4,000 before 1910, even though, in addition to the eastern Cape, it was distributed in the colonies of Natal and Basutoland, and in the Afrikaner republics north of the Orange River. One can safely assume that the functional literacy rate even among Africans in the Cape was still very low, probably less than 5 percent. Thus there would be few readers for each newspaper sold, even though there might be many more who heard the news read to them.

Jabavu's links with prestigious mission schools in the Ciskei and Transkei west and east of the Kei River were instrumental in developing a cadre of subscribers to *Imvo*. His brother-in-law Benjamin Sakuba, then secretary of the Native Educational Association (launched in 1880), perhaps the earliest African regional organization in southern Africa that was independent of missionary or settler control, was probably the first subeditor. When he left in 1887 to become a shopkeeper, William D. Soga, a member of one of the region's most respected mission-educated families, replaced him. The subeditors were apparently responsible for the Xhosa columns, where the social history of the African petty bourgeoisie in the eastern Cape would be recorded. Jabavu seems to have concentrated on the English section, especially the editorial page, and focused on topics of political concern to African readers.

White liberals in the Cape parliament, the so-called "friends of the natives" who had a political and often a material interest in cultivating African voters, helped fund the newspaper. Jabavu was the election agent, for example, in a successful campaign to get James Rose-Innes, a prominent settler politician, a seat in the legislative assembly as a representative of the Victoria East district in the 1884 elections. It was Rose-Innes, his brother Richard and some liberal King William's Town merchant-traders, including T. J. Irvine (a former member of the Cape Legislative Assembly), James Weir and William Lord, who furnished the capital and connections to enable Jabavu to launch *Imvo*. Richard Rose-Innes, one of the leading attorneys helping Africans involved in court disputes over registering as voters in the eastern Cape, was the newspaper's first advertising manager. The Mercury Printing Company, which printed the *Mercury*, King William's Town's settler newspaper, agreed to print *Imvo*.

To Jabavu and his contemporaries, legislators and other public figures like the Rose-Innes brothers, John X. Merriman, John Molteno, J. W. Sauer, Thomas Scanlen, Saul Solomon, W. P. Schreiner and Charles Stretch seemed absolutely essential to the democratic process.[5] These "friends of the natives" could make parliamentary politics work on behalf of the African in the colony, and Jabavu became the principal mediator between liberal African and European politicians in the eastern Cape during the later Victorian period.

African politicians would have preferred to retain their links with the British metropole. They wanted indirect rule from London rather than direct rule from Cape Town, and the Colonial Office was bombarded with letters and petitions seeking imperial intervention on issues that ranged from land disputes to discriminatory legislation. British trusteeship became one of the most cherished allegiances of the African petty bourgeoisie. They would continue to rely on imperial intervention on behalf of the African, enshrined in solemn litanies of allegiance to a foreign monarch in a foreign country, until the 1930s.

Jabavu's identification with the liberal tradition also meant that the politics of protest would be conducted strictly within the framework of the colony's segregationist laws. Like Mohandas K. Gandhi, the apostle of Indian passive resistance in Natal, Jabavu was a master publicist who maintained a wide-ranging correspondence with influential lobbyists in and out of parliament in Cape Town and London. He believed in and relied on the tactics of constitutional protest, creating and legitimizing pressure groups, forming delegations and writing petitions to colonial authorities and exploiting the media of mass communication in the form of letters, editorials and news reports in the black and white press.

African modernizers formed a nexus of bonded social and economic as well as political relationships in their pursuit of Victorian middle-class culture. They participated in choral and reading groups, debating societies, sewing and singing groups, and in Victorian-model sports such as tennis, croquet, cricket (where in Port Elizabeth, for example, they more than held their own against white clubs), rugby and even horse racing.[6] Temperance societies and various church-related associations were a powerful social as well as religious force in community life, and these activities were well represented in the columns of *Imvo*. The "old boy" boarding-school networks, moreover, included increasing numbers of educated girls by the 1880s. Intermarriage between mission-educated men and women was now the rule in African Christian communities.

Personal and professional ties cemented in the rural mission communities were re-created among emigrants to the towns. Africans from the Ciskei and southern Transkei began to settle permanently in ports like Port Elizabeth as early as the 1830s and in East London from the beginnings of settlement in the late 1840s, and an urban African petty bourgeoisie from this region could be found in all the settler states of South Africa by the end of the century. Shopkeepers, hoteliers, boarding-house operators, small traders, transport drivers, furniture makers and producers of other commodities, for example, were among the new arrivals, and the social bonds linking mission-educated elites in the countryside were retained even when they moved to urban centers like Cape Town, Johannesburg and Pretoria, far removed from the rural heartland.

The first postconquest organizations in the eastern Cape were created by mission-educated activists in the Ciskei and southern Transkei, and they evolved at three fairly distinct levels. The first groups were formed at mission stations with major educational facilities, for example, Lovedale, Healdtown and St. Matthew's, and they ranged from literary and debating societies to teachers' lobby groups. When students left school, they tended to form "mutual improvement" associations modeled more or less on the clubs they had belonged to in school. More explicit political groups were also launched, and they were the primary catalysts between white candidates and black voters at the local level. Mission-educated Christians, in association with illiterate or semiliterate members of the precolonial ruling elite, organized election committees, registered voters and mobilized opinion. Communication in the rural eastern Cape, however, was slow and cumbersome, and organized political activity was generally uncoordinated. Groups met infrequently, lacking funds and administrative expertise; membership was small, and apparently floating, except at election time.

The first major African political organization to emerge at a regional level in the eastern Cape was called the Imbumba (literally, a "circle"), and four Imbumba were established between 1882 and 1912. The 1882 Imbumba (called Imbumba Yama Nyama, or South African Aborigines Association) was launched mainly by mission-educated teachers in Port Elizabeth, in part to counter the activities of the Afrikaner Bond. The name of the organization was derived from a saying of the early nineteenth-century Christian prophet Ntsikana, who had urged his people, the Xhosa, to be *imbumba yamanyama* (inseparably united). The 1882 Imbumba comprised a cross section of the modernizing elite, but it was restricted mainly to a few towns west of the Fish River. In contrast, the Native Educational Association (NEA) was the strongest regional body in the rural areas. Both groups vied for followers and tried without success to absorb each other's organization. Jabavu was the dominant figure in the NEA during the 1880s, but his efforts to broaden its political base were thwarted toward the end of the decade. The NEA refocused its energy on teachers' concerns, and it was eventually reorganized as the South African Native Teachers' Association in 1906.

The event that served to propel the Imbumba into action under the leadership of Jabavu was the Parliamentary Voters Registration Act of 1887 (known by Xhosa speakers as *tung' umlomo*, or "sewing up of the mouth"). The Cape settlers were determined that Africans in newly acquired territories in the Transkei east of the Kei River would not be eligible for the franchise. Land holding by individual tenure now became the property qualification, and no other form of land holding qualified a man to vote. This measure extended the franchise to the Transkei, but Africans living on communal "tribal" land could not use it to satisfy the property qualification when registering as voters. The 1887 act eliminated about 20,000 voters, most of whom were African. In the eastern Cape, where the African vote was concentrated, about one-third lost the franchise.

Imvo mobilized African opinion to fight the legislation. Meetings were held in African communities throughout the eastern Cape, resolutions were passed and petitions to Cape Town and London were drafted and signed by hundreds of people, many of whom were illiterate. African voters sought legal advice (which initially indicated that the legislation might be unconstitutional) and wrote to liberal sympathizers in the colony and in England in a futile bid to get them to influence the imperial authorities to intervene.

The first truly regional African political body in southern Africa was forged in the Ciskei region in protest against the 1887 Registration Act. The 1887 Imbumba (called Imbumba Eliliso Lomzi Yabantsundu, or the Union of Native Vigilance Associations) was established with affiliated Iliso Lomzis (Vigilance Associations, meaning literally "eyes of the house") at the local level. Existing political groups were converted into these grassroots Iliso Lomzis. They would be coordinated and their activities publicized through the 1887 Imbumba and the medium of Jabavu's newspaper *Imvo*. A permanent executive committee headed by Jabavu was formed in King William's Town, and virtually all its members were Jabavu's close associates.

Despite the 1887 Registration Act, the new Iliso Lomzis succeeded in registering more African voters, and four years later Africans still represented 30 percent of the electorate in 12 constituencies and 20–29 percent in 10 constituencies in the eastern Cape. Consequently, the settlers, especially the Afrikaner Bond, renewed their demands for more legislation restricting the franchise.

The Cape government succeeded in raising the property qualification from £50 to £75 and imposing a basic literacy test (ability to write one's name, address and occupation) in the 1892 Franchise and Ballot Act. Jabavu was forced to stall African protests and accept the legislation, because his liberal allies, James Rose-Innes, Sauer and Merriman, were members of the coalition government (which included members of the Afrikaner Bond) that had initiated the measure.

The 1892 Act had a dramatic impact on black voters: 4,291 Africans and Coloureds in 25 constituencies had lost their voting rights by 1893, whereas only 943 were added to the rolls. Although 1,861 whites also lost the vote in eight constituencies, 6,367 whites gained the vote in 29 constituencies. For the colony as a whole, registered African and Coloured voters dropped from 21,960 to 18,612 between 1891 and 1893, whereas the number of white voters rose from 68,757 to 73,263 during the same period. In subsequent elections, it became increasingly clear that black voters would not offer a serious challenge to white supremacy in the Cape Colony.[7]

Nevertheless, Jabavu remained the reigning power broker in regional African politics. His views were reported widely in the settler press and discussed in parliament, and he was the authentic African voice in African matters as far as white liberals were concerned. Jabavu continued to monitor the legislative records of those who were dependent, at least in part, on African voters, and they continued to seek his support in mobilizing the African vote at election time.

The SANC and *Izwi Labantu*

Jabavu's leadership, however, was being questioned by a number of African political activists in the eastern Cape by the early 1890s. They formed a new organization, called the South African Native Congress (SANC) in King William's Town at the end of December 1891. Like those involved in the Imbumba movement, SANC officials also lived mainly in the Ciskei region, and there were many personal and professional links between members of both political groups. In attendance at the inaugural meeting were 34 delegates from 15 areas in the eastern Cape and 1 delegate from Basutoland. A constitution was approved – a source of considerable concern, because the 1887 Imbumba did not have one – and Thomas Mqanda, a farmer, Methodist lay preacher and headman from Peddie in the Ciskei, was elected president of the executive committee.

The most prominent leader of the SANC, and Jabavu's main political rival during the next two decades, however, was Walter Benson Rubusana (1858–1936). Rubusana was a well-known translator and writer (who produced a 500-page literary and historical work in Xhosa entitled *Zemk' Inkomo Magwalandini* [Preserve your heritage] in 1906) and an ordained Congregational minister, who was raised by the resident missionary at Peelton near King William's Town and educated at Lovedale.

As the African petty bourgeoisie steadily expanded and more and more independent African organizations were created, African politics became more competitive. There is no evidence, however, to suggest that settler politicians were involved in African divisional politics before the late 1890s. Those Africans who supported the SANC did so primarily because they wanted an effective regional organization to represent African interests. Jabavu agreed in principle, as evidenced by the fact that he was the main architect of the 1887 Imbumba, but apparently he could not reconcile himself to the reality of having to share power or prestige with his rivals.

Although Jabavu himself was only in his early thirties, he referred to the organizers of the SANC as "young bloods" who were not yet skilled enough to play a leadership role in African politics.[8] He believed African political interests could best be served by maintaining the small but potent personal power base he had established in the King William's Town Iliso Lomzi and in his newspaper *Imvo*. SANC leaders sought a regional power base that they believed would be less dependent on one person and more representative of African interests.

There were apparently no substantive differences, ideological or otherwise, however, between Jabavu and his rivals. They employed the same strategies in seeking redress to African grievances. They used the same political avenues that were open to them in Cape society and operated strictly within the legal and legislative framework imposed on them by the colonial government. The SANC held conferences in the early to mid-1890s, but its activities were not covered by *Imvo*, and its role in African as well as settler politics was apparently marginal before the late 1890s. The SANC did communicate its views to the Cape authorities, but it could not yet offer a serious challenge to Jabavu as the arbiter of African public opinion in the eastern Cape.

Meanwhile, events were occurring elsewhere in southern Africa that would have a profound impact on settler politics at the Cape. British foreign policy in this corner of the empire was dictated in part by various economic interest groups intent on gaining control over gold deposits discovered in the South African Republic (an independent Afrikaner republic at the time) in the Transvaal.

By 1895, Cecil Rhodes, the Cape's prime minister since 1890 and the wealthiest and most powerful politician in the colony, was ready to embark on a scheme to unify the settler states of the subcontinent under British rule. But his attempt in 1896 to usurp the sovereignty of Afrikaner republicans in the Transvaal by sending his lieutenant Leander Starr Jameson to subdue them was a disaster. Rhodes was forced to resign and the coalition government he had led fell apart. Several independent English liberals–Jabavu's key allies–joined the Afrikaner Bond against Rhodes and his supporters.

The new alignment of forces in settler politics split the liberal alliance. Some English liberals joined former prime minister Sir Gordon Sprigg, a known hardliner in African matters, and his allies in supporting Rhodes. The new coalition launched the South African League, later renamed the Progressive Party, in 1897. The Afrikaners and their English liberal allies began referring to themselves as the South African Party in 1898. Colonial politics would now be organized along party lines, and African politicians were forced to choose between the two parties to ensure continued participation in settler politics.

Jabavu was placed in a most difficult position. He had always believed that an alliance comprised largely of English-speaking lawmakers would best serve African interests. But Rhodes and Sprigg, who had dominated the Cape settler coalition governments of the 1880s and 1890s, were responsible for most of the legislation that had discriminated against Africans. The Afrikaner Bond, which consistently attacked African franchise rights and tried to limit educational advancement, now changed tactics and sought to woo the African vote on behalf of its liberal allies.

Jabavu tried initially to campaign for "friends of the natives" in both parties, but in the end he sided with the Afrikaner Bond, alienating a significant portion of his supporters and ensuring that African voters in future would also be divided along white party political lines. Support from Cape liberals became more tenuous during the 1890s, and Jabavu seems to have become more dependent on the vacillations of his white allies.

SANC officials now embarked on a fund-raising campaign to establish a newspaper that would serve their interests. A private company (Eagle Printing Press Company) was formed, and in November 1897 *Izwi Labantu* (Voice of the People) was launched in East London. Nathaniel Cyril (Kondile) Umhalla, the son of a warrior chief and himself a Xhosa veteran of the last Cape–Xhosa war, and George Tyamzashe, a Lovedale graduate who had started his career as a journalist with *Imvo*, were the first editors. Within 15 months, Umhalla was succeeded by Tiyo Soga's youngest son, Alan Kirkland Soga (1860s?–1938), who virtually ran *Izwi* for the next decade.[9] Richard Kawa, a writer and pioneer political leader who had taught for many years at Healdtown (where one of his students was Tengo Jabavu) replaced Tyamzashe in 1900. Kawa, in turn, was succeeded by J. N. J. Tulwana, another veteran political organizer, and S. E. Krune Mqhayi, the most celebrated Xhosa writer and praise poet of his generation.[10]

Since *Imvo* was now perceived to be an organ of the Afrikaner Bond, the Progressive Party sought another African newspaper that would support its interests. Rhodes offered to help fund the launching of *Izwi*, and it was gratefully accepted. The Progressives continued to provide a subsidy thereafter, but Rhodes and his colleagues had no more success in influencing *Izwi*'s editorial policy than Rose-Innes and Weir, for example, had had with *Imvo*. SANC supporters campaigned for the Progressive Party out of conviction. Like Jabavu, they believed in parliamentary democracy and hoped that Rhodes and his allies would best serve African interests.

Alarmed at the support that the SANC was receiving from the mission-educated community, Jabavu finally called a meeting of the King William's Town Iliso Lomzi and revived the 1887 Imbumba. A conference was held at Indwe in the southern Transkei in July 1898, the first in 11 years, and the delegates who attended declared themselves in favor of campaigning for those "friends of the natives" who had joined the Afrikaner Bond. The revived Imbumba – designated the 1898 Imbumba, to distinguish this organization from its predecessors – met at Pirie, an old Presbyterian mission station near King William's Town, in August 1899, and the delegates drew up a constitution and made plans to organize Imbumba-affiliated Vigilance Associations throughout the eastern Cape.

These efforts were disrupted, however, when the South African War broke out in October 1899. *Imvo* and *Izwi* embarked on their own war of words over African participation in the hostilities. Jabavu assumed a pacifist, antiwar perspective and urged the British to adopt a policy of reconciliation with the Afrikaners. *Izwi* heaped scorn on *Imvo*'s editorial position and trumpeted the support that Africans in the eastern Cape were giving to the British war effort. The merits of Jabavu's independent stand on the war were rejected by his supporters and attacked by his enemies. *Izwi* and other African journals cited the sufferings of the African population in areas controlled by the Afrikaner insurgents, which in the northern Cape included attempts to take away African voting rights, and Jabavu's prestige among African politicians melted away. Many white political allies also disassociated themselves from Jabavu and his newspaper. The press in King William's Town that printed *Imvo* withdrew its contract, and the newspaper was actually banned by the military authorities in August 1901, soon after the British authorities declared martial law in the Cape.

African protest politics in the eastern Cape following the South African War was largely the story of the 1898 Imbumba, the SANC and the personalities who dominated these organizations. Jabavu and several key aides resuscitated *Imvo* in October 1902 but maintained a relatively low profile for several years,[11] whereas the SANC had emerged from the war as the strongest regional political organization in the eastern Cape. The number of branches increased from 18 in 1902 to an estimated 40 in 1908, and there were now several in urban areas outside the eastern Cape, including Cape Town, Kimberley and Johannesburg. Odendaal estimates that the SANC had at least 1,000 members by 1908 with hundreds of other activists linked informally to the organization.[12]

Whites from the former Boer republics temporarily lost the right to vote, and the Progressive Party, with help from SANC electoral agents and *Izwi*, won the 1904 Cape elections.[13] When the voting ban was lifted in 1907, all white males 21 years or older in the Cape, as well as Natal and the former Boer republics, were given unqualified franchise rights. As a result, the South African Party won a landslide victory in the 1908 elections. The SANC maintained its support for the opposition, which was now called the Unionist Party, after an electoral alliance between the Progressives and a group of independents, whereas Jabavu and *Imvo* campaigned for liberal candidates representing the South African Party. John X. Merriman, a staunch defender of the Cape liberal tradition, and now a leader in the South African Party, was elected prime minister in 1908. Merriman led the Cape delegation to a South African National Convention that decided, among other things, the fate of the African franchise in the looming settler state of South Africa. Jabavu, of course, saw these events as a vindication of his decision years earlier to support the Afrikaner Bond.

Only a few Cape constituencies, however, were still affected by the African vote in 1908. More Africans "can read and write," as one *Izwi* correspondent put it in 1908, but they could not meet the franchise qualifications, whereas Africans who owned property were often illiterate.[14] Since the nonracial franchise was no longer perceived as a threat to white rule, nonliberal as well as liberal factions in the Cape parliament were now less hostile to black voters.[15]

The SANC and the Imbumba would remain apart, although individuals often switched sides to support specific issues. The two groups tried but failed in at least five attempts between 1905 and 1911 to reconcile personal and political differences, and these were now compounded by ethnic rivalries. The distinctions among the various African chiefdoms in the precolonial era "created fault lines," as Wallace Mills puts it, "and under pressure the school community tended to fracture along those ethnic fault lines."[16] The Mfengu had responded first to the opportunities available to Africans under the colonial system, so the main lines of division were between the Mfengu and two other Xhosa-speaking communities, the Xhosa and Thembu. Ethnicity became an important factor in the political and religious conflicts dividing the Christian community in the region during the early decades of the new century.[17]

Nevertheless, local Iliso Lomzi affiliates to the 1898 Imbumba or to the SANC were now the grassroots African political organizations inside, and increasingly outside, the eastern Cape. African political activists had been in contact with protest groups outside the region since the 1880s, and within two decades a thin network of African political organizations and journals of opinion had spread to other parts of British South Africa. Xhosa speakers were among the first Africans to join the wage labor force in numbers, and they played a significant role in the development of a specifically African political culture. They were generally the best educated and obtained the better-paying, higher-status jobs. They had the political skills and the most experience in organized politics.

The SANC played an important role in coordinating African political groups outside the eastern Cape immediately after the South Africa War. Xhosa migrants in Cape Town, for example, had formed the Cape Peninsula Native Association, which had links with the SANC. Its president, Thomas Zini, was from Queenstown in the Ciskei. Another Cape Town-based ally was F. Z. S. Peregrino, a West African-born journalist who was editor of the weekly *South African Spectator* and a major political figure in the western Cape Coloured community. Influential supporters in the northern Cape included Sol Plaatje's chief benefactor Silas Molema, a younger brother of Montshiwa, chief of the Tshidi Barolong, the most powerful Tswana chiefdom in Mafeking and the surrounding districts.

Members of the SANC in the Transvaal helped organize the Transvaal Native Congress in 1903, and a Native Press Association (NPA) was formed in King William's Town in 1904 (with Alan Soga as president) in a bid to provide a news agency for the increasing number of black newspapers. All the newspaper editors were facing the same problems by the early 1900s; they often addressed the same issues and quoted with praise or condemnation each other's opinions. Peregrino and Sol Plaatje initiated the idea, which was enthusiastically endorsed by *Izwi*'s Alan Soga and other leaders of the SANC. Editors from as many as 12 black publications joined the organization, but Jabavu refused to cooperate. The NPA survived little more than a year, in large part because it was virtually impossible to coordinate news activities over such a large area, given the available resources.[18]

African political activists in the eastern Cape were initially reluctant to challenge the movement to unify Britain's South African colonies in the years after the South African War. The report of the South African Native Affairs Commission that had urged union was criticized, and the granting of responsible government to the defeated Boers in the Transvaal and the Orange River Colony was condemned, because both had color-bar constitutions that denied blacks basic political and civil rights. The SANC and the 1898 Imbumba joined their counterparts in the northern colonies, petitioning the British prime minister and the House of Commons and making representations to British authorities in South Africa, in a futile bid to block this decision. A public response to the closer-union movement, however, was not made until late in 1907, and the anti-Union campaign was organized mainly by African and Coloured groups outside the eastern Cape.

When the National Convention finally released its draft version of the South Africa Act in February 1909, the Orange River Colony Native Congress called for an African national convention to meet in Bloemfontein. Regional caucuses were quickly convened throughout South Africa to select delegates. Six weeks after the draft act was published, 38 delegates from the four South African colonies, including Rubusana and Alan Soga from the SANC, met in a schoolhouse in Bloemfontein's African location. For the first time in colonial history, the Africans of South Africa were gathering together in a national conference to discuss their mutual grievances and aspirations. The South African Native Convention, as it was called, proposed amendments to the racial provisions of the draft South Africa Act and elected a permanent executive committee. The historic role played by the SANC during this formative period in African national politics was recognized when Rubusana was chosen president and Soga general secretary of the new organization. John L. Dube, the leading African politician in Natal Colony, was elected vice-president.

Jabavu and his followers, however, remained aloof from these proceedings. They refused to attend the Bloemfontein meeting and instead held their own Cape Native Convention in King William's Town in April 1909. Jabavu was elected president of a permanent executive committee, and protest petitions were sent to parliament, which was meeting in Cape Town to debate the draft act, and to the South African National Convention, which was about to reconvene in Bloemfontein. A Native Rights Protection Fund was created, and the resolutions passed at this meeting were sent to other African and Coloured protest groups.

Numerous petitions protesting the proposed act were sent to the governing authorities in South Africa and Britain in 1909, and Jabavu clearly hoped that his Cape Native Convention might join the African Political (later People's) Organization (APO), by far the most important Coloured political force in South Africa at the time, and the South African Native Convention in Bloemfontein in providing the organizational base for coordinating the anti-Union movement. Indeed, the APO appealed to both conventions to form a united front at its own national conference held in Cape Town in April 1909.

The official colonial delegation, however, was proceeding to London to pilot the draft legislation through the imperial parliament, and so the focus of the anti-Union campaign began to shift from South Africa to Britain. Members of the APO, led by Dr. Abdullah Abdurahman, together with white sympathizers met in Cape Town to organize their own overseas protest delegation. William Schreiner, a former Cape prime minister who was regarded by European and African politicians alike as the most sympathetic white spokesman for African political rights, agreed to lead this group, whose members were to be selected by the major African and Coloured political organizations in the four South African colonies and adjacent protectorates.

The anti-Union delegation, which was ready to leave by June 1909, consisted of Schreiner, Jabavu (Cape Native Convention), Rubusana, Daniel Dwanya and Thomas M. Mapikela (the SANC),[19] Abdurahman, D. J. Lenders and Matt J. Fredericks (APO),[20] and J. Gerrans (a Mafeking trader who represented the Tswana chiefs of the Bechuanaland Protectorate in what is today Botswana). The Schreiner group received support from a number of other opinion leaders who were in Britain at this time. Indian organizations in Natal and the Transvaal had sent deputations to London to press for a resolution of various Indian grievances, and Mohandas Gandhi was among these delegates. John Dube was in London, ostensibly to raise funds for Ohlange Institute, the secondary school he had founded near Durban. Protest delegates also conferred with three aspiring lawyers who would later play key roles in African nationalist politics–Alfred Mangena, Richard Msimang and Pixley Seme–and with other students in London, including Tengo Jabavu's eldest son, D. D. T. Jabavu.

As Odendaal suggests, black political activists achieved a hitherto unprecedented degree of solidarity during the anti-Union campaign, and black civil rights became the key issue when the South Africa Act was debated in the British parliament.[21] The protest delegation failed to halt passage of the act, but its members were brimming with optimism when they returned to South Africa. The imperial authorities had been obliged to state publicly that they were not in favor of the color-bar clauses, and the official South African delegation had been obliged to deny publicly that black political and civil rights would be restricted after union.

The South African Native Convention, which had gained considerable credibility during the anti-Union campaign, held its second conference in Bloemfontein in March 1910. Rubusana and Dube were again elected president and vice-president, respectively, of the five-man executive committee. Strenuous efforts were made to unite the various African political organizations in South Africa behind the banner of the Convention and to establish permanent links with the Coloureds in the APO.

Rubusana's political base in the eastern Cape, however, was rapidly unraveling. The biggest blow to the SANC was the loss of its mouthpiece, *Izwi Labantu*, in April 1909. Like all black protest journals, the newspaper had always struggled financially. It was supported initially by Rhodes, and for at least 16 months his deputy, C. P. Crewe, a member of the Cape Legislative Assembly, was in charge of *Izwi*'s financial affairs. But when Rhodes died in 1902, the leaders of his party (now called Unionists) apparently stopped subsidizing the newspaper. Soga's increasingly anticapitalist editorial line may well have contributed to this decision.[22]

Izwi had rivaled and then supplanted *Imvo* as the most militant African protest journal in the eastern Cape. For more than 11 years it had concretized the ideas and attitudes of its readers and translated them into viable political-action programs for the SANC. Rubusana and other members of the executive committee would continue to play an important role as individuals in national politics,[23] but the SANC itself apparently ceased functioning as a political pressure group sometime just before or during World War I.

When the South African Native Convention held its third conference in Johannesburg in May 1911, a spate of segregationist bills was being considered by parliament, a permanent white citizen defense force was being created, and more and more Africans in skilled positions were being replaced by whites. Although the South African Party had triumphed in South Africa's first national election in 1910, it was led by former Boer general Louis Botha, party leader in the Transvaal, rather than the liberal John X. Merriman, party leader in the Cape. Afrikaner republican sentiments, moreover, would soon reemerge with the establishment of the National Party in January 1914 under the leadership of former Boer general Barry Hertzog.

Very little is known about the South African Native Convention's 1911 conference, but in the years immediately preceding union African political activity in British South Africa seems to have shifted decisively from mission-dominated communities in regions like the eastern Cape (and southern Natal) to the southern Transvaal. The executive committee, for example, now included Pixley Seme, who had completed his studies in London and was setting up a law practice in Johannesburg. Alfred Mangena had also returned to South Africa, along with Richard Msimang, and both were prominent in the Transvaal Native Congress.

The pioneer political bodies in the Ciskei region were in various stages of decay. Rubusana and Soga were prominent members of the Convention, but they no longer commanded an organized following. Jabavu remained aloof, as always, from any group he could not dominate. Nevertheless, the leadership in the Transvaal discussed the topic of unity at length, following the 1911 conference, and Seme circulated a proposal that called for a new African national organization to replace the "Bloemfontein Convention."

The South African Native National Congress (SANNC) was formed in January 1912 as a permanent national organization to represent African political interests in the new Union of South Africa and in the adjacent British protectorates. About 60 delegates participated in the four-day conference held in Bloemfontein's African township: the Transvaal had the largest delegation (25), but there were few representatives from Natal (2) or the Cape (6).

The SANNC's influence remained weakest in the eastern Cape, where the African petty bourgeoisie jealously guarded its franchise rights. Neither the SANC nor the 1898 Imbumba had been represented at the inaugural meeting in 1912 (Rubusana was the only person in attendance from the region), and Jabavu was already well advanced on a new scheme to establish his own national organization. While in London, he and 1,000 other delegates from more than 50 countries had attended the inaugural meeting of the United Races Congress, a benevolent association designed to promote international goodwill among peoples of different races and nationalities. Jabavu decided to start a South African branch, and at a conference in King William's Town in May 1911 the Imbumba was reorganized yet again with a new constitution. It was renamed Imbumba Yezizwe Zomzantsi Afrika, or South African Races Congress, in March 1912.

Within the ranks of the 1912 Imbumba were many who had been involved in the earlier Imbumbas initiated in Port Elizabeth in 1882 and in King William's Town in 1887 and 1898. Jabavu himself was at pains to stress the continuity of the Imbumba tradition. The new organization was to be open to all races, in keeping with its aim of promoting a nonracial South Africa. Those who supported the 1912 Imbumba believed that separate, segregated African bodies would isolate and alienate Africans from settler society and thereby further weaken their position in a settler-ruled South African state. Try as they might, however, Jabavu and his lieutenants could not expand the Imbumba's ethnic and geographical support base. It remained essentially an Mfengu organization confined to the Ciskei and southern Transkei. The 1912 Imbumba, like the SANC, apparently collapsed sometime just before or during World War I.

In contrast to Jabavu and his followers, Rubusana, Alan Soga and other prominent members of the SANC seem to have been more sensitive to trends in the African nationalist movement outside the eastern Cape. They made a more effective contribution to the development of a national political discourse, and they identified more positively with the efforts of those who sought to give economic and cultural expression to the independent African. For example, they defended the leaders of separatist churches (many of whom joined the organization) in representations made to the governing authorities, even though the SANC hierarchy remained loyal to mission churches. Jabavu and *Imvo* condemned the separatists as a disaster for those who sought a nonexclusive Christian society at the Cape.

The SANC's unyielding stand in favor of an indigenous African university scheme (a project led by Alan Soga) in the early 1900s, however, strained the credibility of the organization, provoked a schism within the leadership and undoubtedly contributed to its demise. Jabavu opted instead for an alternative plan sponsored by the missionaries at Lovedale. No other issue outside the anti-Union campaign received so much coverage in *Imvo* during these years. When the South African Native College at Fort Hare was finally opened in 1916, in African eyes it was Jabavu's college. Fort Hare was created specifically for Africans, but white, coloured and Indian students were also welcomed. It would be the country's first and only nonracial university for more than two generations.

African Politics and the Press in the northern Cape

The protest press in the northern Cape during the colonial and early postcolonial periods is essentially the story of Sol Plaatje (1876–1932), one of the most prominent African intellectuals of his era in southern Africa. Plaatje belonged to the fourth generation to be in contact with mission culture, and in common with many Christians during the early nineteenth century his family had acquired a European last name, the word plaatje (meaning "flat" in Dutch) apparently conferred on his grandfather by a Dutch-speaking Griqua farmer.[24]

Plaatje was born on an outstation of the Berlin Missionary Society in what is now the Orange Free State, but he spent most of his childhood 50 miles away at Pniel, the Lutheran mission's main station. Pniel was a small enclave in the diamond-digging area that had been designated the British colony of Griqualand West. It was a few miles south of the town of Barkly West and about 17 miles west of Kimberley, the center of the diamond industry. Griqualand West would be incorporated into the Cape Colony in 1880. Plaatje's family – he was one of eight, all-male children – occupied a relatively privileged social and economic position in the life of the Christian community. They were prosperous stock farmers who were intimately involved in church activities, and Plaatje's father and eldest brother held positions of power within the station community.

Plaatje's prowess as a student was quickly recognized, and he was soon being tutored outside the classroom by the resident missionaries Ernst and Elizabeth Westphal. The Westphals were key role models for Plaatje during these formative years. They introduced him to European music (teaching him how to play the piano and violin and giving him voice lessons) and literature and tutored him in German, Dutch and English.[25] Plaatje was appointed a pupil-teacher (at £9 a year) when he was 14 or 15 years old, and he was probably the first African at Pniel to pass the Standard III (equivalent to fifth grade) examination. He may also have had enough private tuition to complete Standard IV, but to the chagrin of his missionary family Plaatje left school at the age of 17 and found a job as a post office telegraph messenger in the diamond-mining town of Kimberley.

Kimberley, in the closing decades of the nineteenth century, was South Africa's leading industrial center and a mecca for the African mission-educated elite. The more or less permanent population was estimated at 20,000 in the early 1890s (not counting several thousand migrant African laborers), and the aspiring African middle-class community (most of whom were Mfengu migrants from the eastern Cape) numbered less than 1,000. Plaatje continued his language studies and began to read the works of Shakespeare. During the $4\frac{1}{2}$ years Plaatje lived in Kimberley, he was very involved in the community's social life, taking part in plays and musical reviews, joining mutual improvement associations, debating societies and sports clubs (even though he did not play a sport).

Plaatje's political consciousness was also raised immeasurably during this formative period. His neighbor, for example, was Gwayi Tyamzashe, one of the first ordained African ministers in the Cape, who had married a white woman and established the Congregational mission's first African congregation in the town about 1872.[26] Tyamzashe and another ordained clergymen, Jonathan Jabavu, a brother of Tengo Jabavu and pastor of the Wesleyan Methodist congregation, were the acknowledged leaders of the mission-educated community. Plaatje's close friend (with whom he shared lodgings) and later his brother-in-law was H. Isaiah Bud-Mbelle (ca. 1870–1947), a staunch educationist and the first African in the Cape to take the civil service examinations and qualify as a court interpreter.[27]

Plaatje's political ideal was Tengo Jabavu: Plaatje actually subbed as editor of *Imvo* for a month in 1911 when Jabavu was in Europe, and their paths would cross on other occasions. Like Jabavu, he sought to cultivate influential "friends of the natives" inside and outside the Cape and canvassed support for liberal candidates during colonial elections. Kimberley was in the constituency of Barkly West, which had one of the highest proportions of African voters in the colony in the 1890s. Cecil Rhodes had represented Barkly West for many years, but Plaatje campaigned for Henry Burton, an independent candidate supported by the Afrikaner Bond, during the crucial 1898 elections that laid the foundations for the Cape's two-party system. Burton was one of those lawyers who represented Africans seeking to protect their civil rights, including the right to vote. Burton's chief advocate in canvassing the African vote was another liberal in whom Plaatje had great confidence, Samuel Cronwright-Schreiner, husband of novelist Olive Schreiner. Rhodes, however, won the hard-fought contest, which turned out to be a case study in African divisional politics at the Cape.

Plaatje had no prospects for advancement in the Kimberley Post Office, but in 1898 he secured a post as a clerk and interpreter in the magistrate's court at Mafeking, where he would spend the next 12 years of his life. With a population of 6,500 (of which about 5,000 were Africans), Mafeking was much smaller than Kimberley. But it had been the capital of British Bechuanaland before the area was annexed to the Cape in 1895; it was a railway junction on the line to Rhodesia, and it was still the administrative headquarters for the Bechuanaland Protectorate (modern Botswana), even though the southern border of the protectorate was 15 miles away. Next to Mafeking, moreover, was a much larger settlement (called Mafikeng, with a population of perhaps 10,000), which was home to the Tshidi Barolong, the paramount Barolong Tswana chiefdom. Taken together, Mafeking was by far the biggest town and marketing center in the region.

The African mission-educated community in Mafeking was a microcosm of the one Plaatje had left in Kimberley. A segregated "Fingo Location," as the name suggests, was populated mainly by Mfengu from the eastern Cape. A separate, segregrated township existed for whites, and there was a Coloured community made up mostly of skilled artisans and employees of the railways and police. Plaatje stayed initially with Silas Molema, who as noted earlier was a member of a leading family within the Tshidi Barolong aristocracy (his father had founded the town) and one of the most influential modernizers in the district. The Molemas were also the first family in the local African Christian community, and Silas Molema was a key intermediary between the Tshidi Barolong and the colonial authorities. It was probably Molema who interceded on Plaatje's behalf to get him the interpreter's job, and it was Molema who would fund Plaatje's first newspaper.

Plaatje's early years at Mafeking were dominated by the South African War. His diary of the seven-month Siege of Mafeking, for example, is the only African account of the attempt by the Boers to capture the town, but it was not published until 1973.[28] Plaatje's official responsibilities expanded dramatically during and after the siege, because he became a conduit in day-to-day affairs between the municipal authorities and the African population. He helped organize the removal of Africans from the town to prevent starvation, and he helped establish a food-rationing program. He also helped conduct a census of the African population, sent out recruits to spy on the Boers and recorded their reports. After the war, he helped draft compensation claims for individual Africans who had suffered losses during the fighting, and for a few years this "educated commoner" actually became the unofficial "tribal secretary" to the Tshidi Barolong.

Plaatje was highly regarded by the local Mafeking magistrate, but job prospects were little better than they had been in Kimberley. Plaatje had already considered the possibility of becoming a journalist, and the window of opportunity was provided by G. N. H. Whales, editor of the *Mafeking Mail*, the local settler newspaper. Whales decided to establish a one-page weekly news supplement in Tswana at the end of August 1901, entitled *Koranta ea Becoana* (the Bechuana Gazette). Since he could not read or write Tswana, it was almost certainly produced by a Tswana, probably Molema and Plaatje. In September 1901 (after 12 issues as a supplement), Whales sold the newssheet to Molema for 25 pounds, on condition that Molema would be liable for any lawsuits that might arise in connection with the new newspaper.

Koranta ea Becoana in Mafeking

Koranta was clearly modeled on its eastern Cape counterpart *Imvo Zabantsundu*. It would be published weekly and written in Tswana and English, and it would be nonpartisan politically and dedicated to topical news and opinion of interest to the African people. With an initial circulation of 500, the one-page newssheet was immediately increased to two pages, news agents were appointed, and for the first time advertisements were solicited. (They were mainly from local white traders, and Whales would receive 20 percent of the advertising revenue.) *Koranta* obtained an immediate financial boost when the resident commissioner of the Bechuanaland Protectorate agreed to place government notices in the newspaper (even though he, like Whales, could not read Tswana), and similar agreements were reached with the imperial and Cape colonial authorities.

Plaatje seems to have been responsible for editing the newspaper from the beginning, and Molema was responsible for funding the project. By February 1902 they had bought their own press (which cost about £1,000), and two months later they had leased a building in Mafeking to house the newspaper's printing and editorial departments. The press, however, had had to be brought from England and transported by rail from Port Elizabeth, so their company, the Bechuana Printing Works, was not opened officially until August 1902, when the new independent and enlarged English-Tswana edition of *Koranta* began production. Plaatje had already quit his job, after eight years in the Cape civil service, to begin his new career as a journalist. He was 25 years old.

Koranta was averaging about eight pages after a few months, although eventually it was increased in page size to a broadsheet and reduced in length to four pages. The newspaper was more or less equally divided between news stories and letters to the editor in Tswana and English, and it sold for 3 pence a copy either by subscription, at the newspaper office itself, or through agents (who, more often than not, doubled as news correspondents) in Tswana-speaking areas in the Cape, Transvaal and the Orange River Colony (as the Free State was called under British rule). Like *Imvo*, it was produced and consumed by a mission-educated elite who knew English (the newspaper was subtitled "Bechuana Gazette" in English), and the most concentrated areas of readership were in the large towns of Johannesburg, Bloemfontein, Kimberley, Mafeking and another Tswana settlement called Thaba Nchu in the Free State.

The printing run may have eventually reached 2,000, but the literacy rate remained low, and *Koranta* never had many more than 1,000 subscribers (including a few whites and blacks who did not read Tswana.) *Koranta* differed from other pioneer African newspapers in one crucial area. Plaatje was now fluent in at least eight European and African languages, and he had managed to set up news exchanges with 61 different publications in various languages by 1904, not only in other parts of the Cape and the main metropolitan centers in southern Africa, but elsewhere in Africa, and also abroad, in Britain, western Europe and the United States.[29]

Koranta's news reports were enriched immensely by these news exchanges, but Plaatje's editorial policy was no different from the policies of his contemporaries. He was critical of Africans who refused to abandon pre-Christian customs and rituals and embrace the moral and material economy of modern culture. As biographer Brian Willan put it, Plaatje sought "to encourage the education and advancement of his people along 'progressive', Christian lines, and to fight, by strictly constitutional methods...for their just rights and fair treatment by the white authorities...to ensure that 'native opinion' became a factor to be taken into account in the political future of the country."[30] As Plaatje himself noted, he did not "hanker after social equality with the white man ... we advise every black man to avoid social contact with whites, and the other races to keep strictly within their boundaries. All we claim is our just dues; we ask for our political recognition as loyal British subjects."[31]

Plaatje's crusading journalism was formulated in facing the issues that confronted Africans at the turn of the century. His Africanist sympathies, for example, were expressed, at least at one level, in every issue of the newspaper with a biblical quotation from the Song of Solomon, which begins: "I am black, but comely, O ye daughters of Jerusalem."[32] Plaatje's ability to mobilize African opinion was revealed initially when white business interests in Mafeking tried but failed to get the British colonial secretary to allow the new Transvaal Colony to annex the Bechuanaland Protectorate and the Mafeking district in the Cape. Plaatje also pressed the Barolong Tswana's war compensation claims, even though the British authorities rejected all such claims by Africans. After the South African War, *Koranta* was very critical of the British administration in the Transvaal and Orange River Colony, where Africans continued to suffer from the police and judicial system, and the pass laws were enforced more vigorously than under the old Boer republics.

Plaatje gradually expanded the newspaper's protest agenda. He campaigned for better treatment of Africans employed in town and in the mines, defended the separatist "Ethiopian" churches and urged that African franchise and civil rights in the Cape be extended throughout British South Africa. A copy of each issue of *Koranta* was given to the Cape colonial authorities, and, like *Imvo,* the newspaper was quoted on occasion in parliament. Members of the 1903–5 South African Native Affairs Commission indicated that they were aware of Plaatje's editorials when they sought to establish a "native policy" for British South Africa, and Willan suggests that by 1905 he had emerged as an "influential public figure" inside and outside the Cape.[33]

Koranta, however, could never hope to be a commercial enterprise. It did not, like *Izwi* (and possibly *Imvo*), receive a subsidy from a white political party, and it could not increase its readership or its advertising because there were not enough literate Tswana-speaking consumers. *Koranta* survived because Silas Molema continued to underwrite the costs of running the newspaper, and Plaatje worked up to 18 hours a day, seven days a week to maintain production. No whites were ever involved in *Koranta* or in the Bechuana Printing Works, but Plaatje and Molema were able to generate enough work to employ three or four permanent African staffers as compositors and printers.

Koranta was having serious financial problems by July 1904, and Molema and Plaatje had to mortgage the printing works to get a loan to keep the newspaper going. Very few copies of *Koranta* dated after December 1904 have been located, but Willan believes the newspaper continued to be published more or less regularly as a weekly until the beginning of 1906. Production was sporadic thereafter, and *Koranta* ceased publication as an independent African newspaper in May or June 1906.

The life of the newspaper in subsequent years is rather cloudy. It was sold back initially to Whales, editor of the *Mafeking Mail*, who announced that *Koranta* would be published again in January 1907. The *South African Spectator*, however, had started publishing special pages in Tswana (Peregrino was very interested in the Tshidi Barolong and a frequent visitor to Mafeking), and there was a possibility that *Koranta* might merge with this newspaper. Willan speculates that relations between Molema and Plaatje had become somewhat strained under the stress of trying to keep *Koranta* alive, and each one sought to find a partner who might revive the newspaper in some form. In any event, *Koranta* was finally bought by the Bechuanaland Press, which produced several country newspapers and had taken over the *Mafeking Mail* when Whales himself got into financial difficulties.

Koranta resumed publication in April 1907, and Plaatje apparently was still the editor. The newspaper appeared sporadically for several months, but it ceased publication, probably in November 1907 when Whales again went bankrupt. This time the printing plant was bought by Molema and Plaatje's lawyer, who revived the newspaper once again in April 1909. Only a few issues, however, were produced. South Africa's first nonmissionary protest journal published for the Tswana people folded for the third and final time at the end of May 1909. Plaatje left Mafeking, heavily in debt, a year later, but he had managed to find a group of African landowners to fund a new newspaper that would be based in Kimberley.

Tsala ea Becoana/Tsala ea Batho in Kimberley

The directors of the syndicate formed to underwrite the costs of launching *Tsala ea Becoana* (the Friend of the Bechuana) were members of the Seleka Barolong branch of the Tswana nation, and they lived in the historic Wesleyan Methodist mission community of Thaba Nchu in the Orange Free State. Some were chiefs and others commoners (one was an ordained minister), but all were men of wealth and standing in the district. They knew Plaatje, and many had been local correspondents or news agents of *Koranta* in Thaba Nchu. Tengo Jabavu was also invited to join the syndicate, and for more than a year the new newspaper was printed with *Imvo* in King William's Town.

Plaatje's involvement in African national politics came about in part because all the members of this group but Jabavu were actively involved in the deliberations of the South African Native Convention and wanted a newspaper that would represent African grievances to a wider audience. The syndicate at Thaba Nchu sought a newspaper that would represent African nationalist interests, just as Africans meeting in Bloemfontein sought a national body to represent African nationalist interests in the looming Union of South Africa.

Tsala ea Becoana was launched as a four-page weekly in Tswana and English in June 1910, and it was aimed at Tswana-speaking Africans in South Africa and the Bechuanaland Protectorate. In terms of makeup, *Tsala* was similar to its predecessor in having letters from readers (often presented as news stories), reports from correspondents, some local, national and international news obtained for the most part through exchanges with other publications, and editorials/commentaries placed on (but not limited to) the editorial page.

The initial focus in the first year of publication was the impending act of union. Unlike most other African activists, Plaatje did not believe British rule would necessarily be more beneficial to Africans than rule by the governing South African Party, and he even argued that the protectorates of Bechuanaland, Basutoland and Swaziland should be attached to South Africa. Plaatje's opinions were based on what he had seen of "arbitrary imperial rule in the Bechuanaland Protectorate," on an enormous respect for the rule of law as it was administered at the Cape, and on a widely shared belief that the Cape liberal tradition would eventually become a South African tradition. Several Cape "friends of the natives" held cabinet posts in Louis Botha's government, including the lawyer Henry Burton, his old colleague from Kimberley and Mafeking days, who became the first minister of Native affairs. As Willan points out, probably no other African had such access or influence with government officials as Plaatje did in the first two years of the new South Africa.[34]

Plaatje also followed the trail blazed by Rubusana and the SANC in seeking to unify the various regional African political organizations in South Africa. He attended the South African Native Conventions in Bloemfontein, helped organize the South African Native National Congress in 1912 and was elected general secretary of the new national political body. Plaatje's credentials for this office were unique. He was fluent in all the major languages used in South Africa, and he was the quintessential watchdog journalist who had monitored the actions of officials concerned with African affairs and kept his readers informed of what they were doing. He had the kind of status that Jabavu had enjoyed before the South African War as a leader of African public opinion among whites as well as blacks, and he was not contaminated by the political and ethnic factionalism of African politicians in the eastern Cape. Thus Plaatje was at the crest of a wave as a public figure.

The bottom fell out, albeit temporarily, when *Tsala ea Becoana* was forced to close down in June 1912. The newspaper had been having periodic financial crises for some time, although apparently they were not publicized. Plaatje had been forced to seek loans from various benefactors, including his brother-in-law Bud-Mbelle, and he himself often did not receive a salary for months at a time. He began writing regularly for the *Pretoria News* and other white newspapers during these years to make ends meet, but the financial burden (and his absence from Kimberley, working on SANNC matters during the early months of 1912) caused the shutdown.

The closure of *Tsala* proved to be brief, because three months later, in September 1912, Plaatje become the editor of a new weekly in English, Tswana and Pedi entitled *Tsala ea Batho* (the Friend of the People). The opportunity to resuscitate *Tsala* came about when Plaatje was able to buy the printing press of a defunct African newspaper in Johannesburg for the minimal price of £200, the money being donated by Africans from Johannesburg who were not Tswana. The newspaper's "new title," in Willan's words, "reflected both the union of Tswana and Pedi peoples" and symbolized the "wider unity" the SANNC was seeking to achieve as a political organization.[35]

Plaatje's political journalism, moreover, achieved a new level of militancy with the passage of the 1913 Natives' Land Act. He now embarked on the greatest crusade of his career. The debate over the Land Act dominated the pages of *Tsala* in 1912 and 1913. When this legislation was enacted in June 1913, it was condemned by every African politician but Jabavu (who was constrained in part by the fact that three *Imvo* shareholders were cabinet ministers in Botha's government). Plaatje organized the assault against the "Plague Act," as he called it, and the SANNC focused all its meager resources on the campaign to overturn the measure. Plaatje's investigative articles of the plight of African tenants evicted from white farms in parts of the Orange Free State were without precedent in the history of the South African press. He also interviewed peasants in parts of the northern Cape, western Transvaal and the eastern Cape, and these reports were carried in white as well as black newspapers. (One of his editorials on the subject was actually read out in parliament.) *Tsala's* circulation had risen to about 4,000 by early 1914, and in Willan's words Plaatje had become "perhaps the most widely-read black journalist of his day."[36]

The SANNC resolved to appeal directly to England over the Land Act, and a five-member protest delegation was organized on the eve of World War I in 1914.[37] John X. Merriman, Prime Minister Louis Botha, and even the governor general, Lord Gladstone, met with the protesters and pressured them not to go to England, but Plaatje stood firm and stiffened the resolve of his colleagues to make the effort. He was the most militant of the delegates, according to Willan, and "the most committed to the deputation's work in England."[38] At the other extreme was SANNC president John Dube (elected in absentia at its inaugural meeting in 1912), who led the deputation but was in doubt about the project from the beginning. Dube returned to South Africa prematurely and then failed to send enough money to get the others home.

The protest delegation, of course, did not succeed in getting the imperial authorities to intervene. But Plaatje's sojourn in England lasted $2\frac{1}{2}$ years, and it was an extraordinary personal achievement. He finished his account of the 1913 Land Act, which was finally published in England in 1916,[39] and embarked on two scholarly projects that would occupy him for the rest of his life. He authored and coauthored (with an English phoneticist) two pioneering works on Tswana language and literature,[40] and he contributed a chapter, entitled "A South African's Homage" to a book on Shakespeare on the three-hundredth anniversary of the playwright's death. Plaatje was the first African to translate Shakespeare's plays into an African language.[41]

While in England, Plaatje also conducted virtually a one-man campaign on behalf of the African people of South Africa. His most significant involvement was with the Brotherhood movement, a religious organization devoted to the task of implementing Christian principles in everyday life. The Brotherhood (there was also a women's organization) was a grassroots enterprise with support groups throughout the country. It attracted primarily the lower middle class but drew support from most Christian denominations and from the major political parties. Half of the 305 meetings Plaatje addressed during his stay in England between 1914 and 1917 were sponsored by the Brotherhood, and the personal contacts he made through the movement would be of considerable importance to him in later years.[42]

Plaatje's extended stay in England, however, proved to be the undoing of *Tsala ea Batho*. His brother-in-law Bud-Mbelle tried to maintain the newspaper, but wartime shortages of ink and paper and an enormous increase in the cost of newsprint (700 percent in less than one year) consumed what little money was available. *Tsala* ceased publication in July 1915, only 14 months after Plaatje left for England, and he did not succeed in reviving the publication when he returned. Plaatje would continue to be heavily involved in the affairs of the SANNC,[43] write for the South African and overseas press, produce pamphlets[44] and publish the first African novel in English by a black African,[45] but he would never again own or edit a newspaper.[46]

African protest newspapers that confronted the new settler state of South Africa after 1910 would remain marginal as commercial enterprises and circumscribed in terms of news coverage, distribution and number of readers. The printed word, however, had become a powerful unifying force for a small portion of the African population, most of whom were now second- and even third-generation Christians.

Although the forms of protest changed as the historical conditions giving rise to protest changed, the symbolic content of protest in the African press remained much the same in the early decades of postcolonial South Africa as it had been during the colonial era. Those who wrote for and read the African protest press represented the beginnings of a new political culture, but it was a marginalized middle-class culture whose roots were still rooted firmly in the African mission-educated community.

Notes

1. The main language of the peoples who occupy the eastern Cape today is Xhosa, which is also the name of one of the major ethnic groups in the region. The Xhosa and the Thembu occupied the area west and east of the Great Kei River (see Map), the historic heartland of the African nationalist movement in South Africa. The origins of the people known collectively as the "Fingo" during the colonial era and rechristened the "Mfengu" by Africanist historians in the 1960s are the subject of considerable debate today. According to the British settler version, they comprised a number of refugee groups who had fled Natal during the destructive military campaigns initiated by Shaka, founder of the Zulu kingdom, between 1817 and 1828. Many settled among the Xhosa, and during the last four Cape–Xhosa wars they were the Cape Colony's main African collaborators. The "Fingo" story has been challenged by a number of historians, who believe it is essentially another story in an African tradition that was invented by Europeans. They believe that most Mfengu were (either) refugees from the interior trying to escape slave and cattle raiders, or impoverished Xhosa captured or displaced during the Cape–Xhosa wars, especially the war of 1834–35. For a brief summary of the various positions, see L. Switzer, *Power and resistance in an African society: The Ciskei Xhosa and the*

making of South Africa (Madison, 1993), 56–60. The Mfengu formed the nucleus of the mission-educated community and the vanguard of a new African modernizing elite in this part of the eastern Cape during the first generation after conquest.

2. This section is based in large part on A. Odendaal, "African political mobilization in the eastern Cape, 1880–1910," Ph.D. thesis (University of Cambridge, 1983), Chaps. 2–4; Switzer, *Power and resistance*, Chaps. 5–6. On the ambiguities of the Cape liberal tradition during the colonial era, cf. M. Legassick, "The rise of modern South African liberalism: Its assumptions and its social base," paper presented at University of London, Institute of Commonwealth Studies (London, 1973); S. Trapido, "'The friends of the natives': Merchants, peasants and the political and ideological structure of liberalism in the Cape, 1854–1910," in S. Marks and A. Atmore (eds.), *Economy and society in pre-industrial South Africa* (London, 1980), 247–274; R. Parry, "'In a sense citizens, but not altogether citizens...': Rhodes, race, and the ideology of segregation at the Cape in the late nineteenth century," *Canadian Journal of African Studies* 17, 3 (1983), 377–391. For the most recent full-length study on the liberal tradition in South African politics, see Paul Rich's *Hope and despair: English-speaking intellectuals and South African politics, 1896–1976* (London, 1993).
3. S. Trapido, "White conflict and non-white participation in the politics of the Cape of Good Hope, 1853–1910," Ph.D. thesis (University of London, 1970), 286 (citing *Imvo Zabantsundu* [*hereafter IZ*], 3 November 1884).
4. J. Stewart (comp.), *Lovedale: Past and present* (Lovedale, 1887), 533–534.
5. For brief biographical sketches of these men, see J. W. deKock et al. (eds.), *Dictionary of South African biography*, James Rose-Innes, vol. 6, 102–103; Merriman and Molteno, vol. 7, 339–341, 496–497; Sauer, Scanlen and Schreiner, vol. 9, 496, 509, 529; Solomon and Stretch, vol. 10, 52–53, 320.
6. On the pursuit of Victorian sports, see A. Odendaal, "South Africa's black Victorians: Sport, race and class in South Africa before union," *Africa Perspective*, n.s. 1, 5, 7–8 (1989), 72–93. Mission-educated Africans in the eastern Cape played the dominant role in introducing and popularizing Western sports to Africans elsewhere in South Africa. They were involved in informal cricket matches in places such as King William's Town by the 1850s, and there were irregular matches between mission schools in the Ciskei region by the 1860s and 1870s. Cricket was the most popular male sport, followed by soccer and rugby (from the 1890s). Sports were essentially segregated by the 1880s, and blacks were developing their own separate (and subordinate) organizations at the provincial and even the national level soon after union in 1910.
7. The foregoing statistics on voting patterns in the Cape Colony are taken from Odendaal, "African political mobilisation," Chap. 3.
8. Ibid., 174 (citing *IZ*, 7 January 1892, 27 July 1898).
9. The impact of the Cape's discriminatory policies on the African petty bourgeoisie during these years is epitomized by the careers of people such as Alan Soga. Educated like his father in Scotland, he became a qualified lawyer and was appointed acting resident magistrate at St. Mark's in the southern Transkei. Soga seemed destined to become South Africa's first African magistrate, but he was abruptly removed from this post and replaced by a European in 1895. Jabavu's brother-in-law Benjamin Sakuba, a court interpreter in King William's Town, was replaced by a European in 1897. S. A. Allen, "Mr. Alan Kirkland Soga," *Colored American Magazine*, February 1904, 114–116. I am indebted to Robert Edgar for sending me this article. See W. G. Mills, "The rift within the lute: Conflict and factionalism in the 'school' community in the Cape colony, 1890–1915," in *The Societies of Southern Africa in the Nineteenth and Twentieth Centuries* (University of London, Institute of Commonwealth Studies, Vol. 15 collected seminar papers, 1990), 34, 39 (n. 41).
10. See P. E. Scott, *Samuel Edward Krune Mqhayi, 1875–1945: A bibliographic survey* (Grahamstown, Rhodes University, Department of African Languages, 1976).
11. *Imvo Zabantsundu* was closed down for 15 months during the South African War and plagued for several years thereafter by

financial problems, but Jabavu apparently was able to buy a press to print the newspaper when it resumed publication. The newspaper did not show a profit until 1905, and within a few years it was in debt again. In 1909 there were so many delinquent accounts that the company publishing *Imvo* was forced to cut circulation in half (from about 4,000 to 2,000 a week) and demand advance payment from subscribers.

12. Odendaal, "African political mobilisation," 202.
13. Jabavu was actually asked by the Afrikaner Bond to be its candidate for Fort Beaufort in the 1904 elections. The offer may have been insincere, as Jabavu's opponents claimed, but in any case he declined.
14. Trapido, "White conflict and non-white participation," 252 (citing *Izwi Labantu,* 16 April 1908).
15. The proportion of African and Coloured voters in the Cape Colony had remained more or less static, at 15–16 percent of the total electorate, between 1892 and 1910. The number of registered African voters, however, steadily declined from 8,117 in 1903 to 6,637 in 1909. Registered Coloured and white voters, respectively, increased from 12,601 and 114,450 in 1903 to 14,394 and 121,336 in 1909. *Report of the South African Native Affairs Commission*, 1903–5, Vol. 1, 93; Cape of Good Hope, 1909 *Statistical Register*, 15. The term "Coloured" in these sources includes the racially designated categories of Chinese, Indian, Malay, Hottentot and "other."
16. Mills, "The rift within the lute" in *The Societies of Southern Africa in the Nineteenth and Twentieth Centuries* (University of London, Institute Commonwealth Studies), 33. Mills suggests that ethnic conflicts surfaced first in the mission churches. As Christian households became poorer, church contributions declined, building programs were curtailed and stipends paid to preachers, evangelists and ordained pastors were cut off or reduced. Ethnic tensions within the churches spilled over into politics at a critical point in time for the struggling petty bourgeoisie.
17. Individual Xhosa and Thembu gradually qualified for the franchise, and by the early 1900s they outnumbered Mfengu on Cape voters' rolls. Africans who were members of the 1898 Imbumba and followed Jabavu in supporting the Afrikaner Bond were mainly Mfengu. Africans who were members of the SANC and supported the Progressive Party were mainly Xhosa and Thembu. Existing political and ethnic differences were also sustained in separate cultural traditions. Veldtman Bikitsha (ca. 1828–1912), the founding father of Mfengu politics in the Transkei, campaigned for a special Mfengu holiday, and Fingo Emancipation Day, as it was called, was celebrated officially on 14 May 1908. Despite claims that the holiday was not meant to antagonize other ethnic groups, meetings were held on that day all over the eastern Cape and as far north as Kimberley. This event provoked the Xhosa, and a parallel campaign was launched to establish a Xhosa day of celebration. Ntsikana Remembrance Day, as it was called, was first celebrated in King William's Town on 10 April, 1909, in honor of the legendary prophet. *Imvo* and the 1898 Imbumba supported Fingo Day, just as *Izwi* and the SANC supported Ntsikana Day.
18. The possibility of resuscitating the NPA was mooted in 1908. Several journals expressed interest (including the Sotho weekly *Naledi ea Lesotho* and the Zulu-English weekly *Ilange lase Natal* as well as *Izwi* and the *Spectator*), but no formal organization emerged from these discussions.
19. Dwanya (d.1922) was a law agent and active politician from the Middledrift District in the Ciskei (eastern Cape), and Mapikela represented the Orange River Colony Native Congress.
20. Lenders was vice-president and Fredericks general secretary of the APO.
21. On the anti-Union campaign, see A. Odendaal, *Black protest politics in South Africa to 1912* (Totowa, N.J., 1984), Chaps. 5–10.
22. On *Izwi*'s tirades against South African capitalism, ibid., 66, 68–69, 81, 95, 153. *Izwi*'s price was cut by half (from 13s. to 6s.6d. a year) in 1906, but there was no significant increase in subscribers. In 1907 the price rose again, and 200 new shares in the publishing company (at £1 each) were

offered to the public. *Izwi*'s paying readership, however, remained small, and the newspaper was never able to gain much advertising support.

23. In the 1910 elections, Rubusana contested the Tembuland seat in the Transkei for the Cape Provincial Council, the highest governmental body accessible to Africans in the new South Africa, and he became the first African member in its history. *Imvo* refused to endorse Rubusana, who was running as an independent, although Rubusana had tried in vain to get Jabavu to contest the Fort Beaufort seat in the Ciskei. Jabavu decided to compete with Rubusana for the Tembuland seat in the 1914 elections, and in the ensuing campaign the African vote was split. Both candidates were defeated, and Cape Africans would never again win a seat in the Cape provincial legislature.
24. This section is based almost entirely on the excellent biography by B. Willan, *Sol Plaatje, South African nationalist, 1876–1932* (Berkeley and Los Angeles, 1984), Chaps. 1–7.
25. When Plaatje was about 11 years old, he seems to have accompanied the Westphals to Kimberley for nine months and attended an English-language Anglican elementary school.
26. Tyamzashe was educated at Lovedale and wrote for several mission newspapers, including *Indaba*. He married Rachel MacKriel, a missionary of Scottish and French descent, and spent several years in the northern Transvaal as a pioneer missionary to the Pedi before returning in failing health to Kimberley, where he died in 1896. George Tyamzashe, one of his sons, has already been mentioned as joint editor of *Izwi* with Nathaniel Umhalla before Alan Soga assumed control of the newspaper about April 1899. Henry Tyamzashe, another son, was editor of the *Workers' Herald*, organ of the Industrial and Commercial Workers' Union, during the mid-late 1920s. See Chapter 5 in the present volume.
27. Bud-Mbelle initiated the call for an indigenous African university that was promoted by the South African Native Congress in the early 1900s. He served as a court interpreter for more than 20 years and was widely regarded as the best at his job in the Cape before he was dismissed abruptly in December 1915, another victim of South Africa's discriminatory job reservation policies.
28. J. Comaroff (ed.), *The Boer War diary of Sol T. Plaatje* (London, 1973).
29. Plaatje corresponded with several African-American newspapers and claimed that *Koranta* was the first African newspaper to publicize the activities of Booker T. Washington, the famous educator from Tuskegee Institute in Alabama. Plaatje's dream of meeting the leaders of black political opinion in North America were realized in an extended trip to Canada and the United States between 1920 and 1922.
30. Willan, *Sol Plaatje*, 112.
31. Ibid., 111 (citing *Koranta*, 13 September 1902).
32. Ibid., 110.
33. Ibid., 123.
34. Ibid., 144–148ff.
35. Ibid., 158.
36. Ibid., 169.
37. The delegation consisted of John Dube (Natal), Walter Rubusana (eastern Cape), Thomas Mapikela (Orange Free State), Saul Msane (Natal and Transvaal) and Plaatje.
38. Willan, *Sol Plaatje*, 182.
39. S. Plaatje, *Native life in South Africa* (London, 1916).
40. Plaatje, *Sechuana proverbs* (London, 1916); D. Jones and S. T. Plaatje, *A Sechuana reader in international phonetic orthography* (London, 1916). Plaatje would become heavily involved in the debate over Tswana orthography – how to render Tswana in written form – in the last years of his life.
41. I. Gollancz (ed.), *A book of homage to Shakespeare* (Oxford, 1916). Plaatje apparently translated five of Shakespeare's plays into Tswana. Two were published, but the manuscripts of the other three have been lost.
42. On the Brotherhood movement, see Willan, *Sol Plaatje*, 201–204ff.
43. Plaatje was asked to assume the presidency of the SANNC when Dube was forced to resign in 1917, but he declined. Plaatje would become somewhat disillusioned with Congress by the early 1920s, and he played only a marginal role in the organization in later years.

44. One of these pamphlets, an exposé of the hypocrisy of white–black sexual relations in South Africa, entitled *The mote and the beam*, reportedly sold more than 18,000 copies in the United States. Willan, *Sol Plaatje*, 269–270.
45. S. Plaatje, *Mhudi: An epic of South African native life a hundred years ago* (Lovedale, 1930). The manuscript was completed in London in 1920, but it took a decade to find a publisher (significantly enough, Lovedale Mission Press). It was republished, with an introduction by Tim Couzens in 1975 (Quagga Press, Johannesburg) and in 1978 (Heinemann, London).
46. Plaatje rejected offers to be the first editor of *Umteteli wa Bantu* (in 1920) and *Bantu World* (probably in early 1932, just before he died). He did agree to be the joint editor of a journal entitled *Our Heritage*, sponsored by an African temperance organization, the Independent Order of True Templars. Plaatje broadened the news agenda considerably from the first issue in June 1931, but only five more were published before it ceased publication in December, six months before his death.

CHAPTER 2

"Qude maniki!"

John L. Dube, Pioneer Editor of *Ilanga lase Natal*

R. Hunt Davis, Jr.

"*Ilanga lase Natal* (the Natal Sun) is a newspaper for the black people in Natal, which will be issued every Sunday."* With this, the first sentence of the lead editorial of his new newspaper, John Langalibalele Dube launched his career as one of South Africa's pioneer African newspaper editors. The date was 10 April 1903. "A newspaper is a blessing," continued the editorial, "since it brings a person, sitting at home, news and other information... A newspaper reports everything that is happening." Therefore, the fledgling editor argued:

> Let us trust the newspaper to keep the people informed about events and to show them ways of improving themselves. We don't believe there is any better way of helping people. Yes, we can do things that are facing us, the way we want to and in a big way. Just look at some people who ask for food from the government. It is a good thing for people to do, but those people do not want to learn how to work with other people. Where is our comradeship? When a person tells you to believe in lies, would you quickly believe him, even if he is one of us, or when a person says here is food would you say he has plenty of it? *Ilanga* promises to show you the right way. The saying, "One who is trustworthy in little things, is also trustworthy in big things" is true. It does not mean that *Ilanga* is going to keep quiet when it sees bad things being done, be it by black or white people. It promises to help people from their suffering. We sit here without knowing that the white people want to bring Chinese people in this country to do their jobs. *Ilanga* wants people to be united. Its aim is to inform people about world news, the government, and everything you have been wanting to know. *Qude maniki* ! (wake up)[1]

John Dube issued his call to the African people of Natal to "wake up." But how did he identify "the people" to whom *Ilanga* was addressed, and why was it necessary to call on them to awaken? The newspaper's editorial columns during the first decade or so provide much of the raw material for answering these questions. Indeed, the answers are embedded in his introductory editorial. Clearly, he conceived of the people in racial terms, contrasting black and white. As already noted, the paper was for "the black people in Natal," who should unite and support a single newspaper. "Can't you see how wise the white people are?" he questioned.

* I am indebted to Mbulaheni Nthangeni for his assistance in translating the original Zulu of this and other Zulu-language articles into English. Suzanne Dacres assisted with research on some of the English-language material in *Ilanga*.

They "read the same newspaper." African people should do the same, for "when it comes to things that are educational and improve us in terms of getting jobs, education, and making us bright, we have to be united, in other words, we should become one bundle."

Dube also defined "the people" in terms of class, the nascent Zulu petty bourgeoisie, or more specifically in terms of the *kholwa* ("believers"), the mission-educated elite of whom Dube was the most prominent member of his day. The *kholwa* were the people who were concerned with "things that are educational and improve us." They were the individuals the editorial chastised for having been taught but not having their knowledge show, "since they just sit there without getting the news which is meant for all those people who are educated." Dube had this audience in mind when he launched his newspaper, which was "going to be a source of information on many issues." The issues of importance were largely those that most concerned the *kholwa*.

A third definition of the people also emerged in the initial editorial. As the second sentence stated, "It has been a long time since our people wanted a newspaper in their own language." In this sense, "our people" meant those who spoke the Zulu language. If there were four newspapers in the Cape Colony written in venacular African languages and they were all doing well, then "What is wrong with us here in Natal and Kwazulu" that there is no newspaper in Zulu? Although *Ilanga* was meant to remedy that situation, it did not in its early years stand for an exclusive Zulu ethnic identity. Rather, it sought to promote both Zulu and wider African identities for the purpose of political action.

The people, variously (and at times rather ambiguously) identified, needed a newspaper for their own edification, uplift and advancement; hence the call "*Qude maniki!*" There was far more to this call, however, than the need for "the people" to become better informed for the purpose of their own advancement. They also needed to awaken to the challenges that white political power and unity posed. The white people of Natal were wise, for they "read the same newspaper" and thus have the same "source of information on many issues," the issues that counted most where their interests were concerned. The colony's Africans needed to do likewise: "A newspaper reports everything that is happening. Just look at the arrival of his excellency [British Colonial Secretary Joseph] Chamberlain from abroad. You did not know how he left and what they were going to do with your chiefs' land." Or again, "We sit here without knowing that the white people want to bring Chinese people in this country to do their [African] jobs."[2] It had become time for Africans to wake up, become united and be vigilant in the face of the issues confronting them under a system of white domination. Dube intended *Ilanga* to be a principal vehicle for uniting "the people," identifying the issues of importance and setting a course of action for them to follow.

John Dube reached the height of his influence in the 11 or so years between the founding of *Ilanga* and the start of World War I.[3] Early in 1900 he had returned from three years of study at the Union Missionary Seminary in Brooklyn, New York, having been ordained by the Congregational Church in 1899. During this second American sojourn (he had previously attended Oberlin College between 1887 and 1892), Dube established good working relationships with Booker T. Washington and other African American and white proponents of industrial education for blacks. As a result, Dube was to adopt the rhetoric of industrial education as his own. For example, in an 1897 commencement address at Hampton Institute in Hampton, Virginia, he noted: "I have come down to Tuskegee and

Hampton to learn something of industrial education, for after working among my people in my own land, I find that the kind of work done at Hampton is the kind of work my people need."[4]

On his return to South Africa, Dube, with funding from a U.S.-based American support committee and from the American Board mission community in Natal, opened the Ohlange Industrial Institute at Phoenix, a rural settlement outside Durban, in August 1901.[5] Ohlange, under African leadership but with an emphasis on black American industrial education, was intended to be nonthreatening to Natal's white community. Two years later Dube founded *Ilanga*, in part to reinforce his essentially Washingtonian message of self-help and practicality to both Africans and colonists in Natal. Although Dube worked assiduously to cultivate the white political support necessary for Ohlange to go about its stated purpose of educating young Africans, the challenge was a daunting one. Not only were most whites in principle opposed to schooling Africans, they considered an independent African school under African leadership to be particularly dangerous.[6]

As if conditions were not already difficult enough for Dube and his school and newspaper, the Bambatha Rebellion of 1906 greatly worsened the situation. When an *Ilanga* editorial entitled "Vukani Bantu"! (Wake up, people!) asked the question, "Where are the peoples' rights?,"[7] in the context of the rebellion, Dube came perilously close to being silenced. The governor, Sir Henry McCallum, compelled Dube to retract the editorial in an apology published in both *Ilanga* and Natal's colonial newspapers. He also lectured Dube, telling him, "'I presume you will acknowledge we are the ruling race'."[8] Dube's political skills and persistence, however, paid off. Within 18 months of his confrontation with Governor McCallum, he was writing to Booker T. Washington to inform him of the opening of a new building at Ohlange. Enclosed with the letter was a newspaper clipping from the *Natal Mercury*, which noted that a number of prominent white Natalians had contributed significantly toward the £1,300 cost of the building and that the new Natal governor, Sir Matthew Nathan, had spoken at the dedication ceremony.[9] For the time being at least, the political future of both Ohlange and *Ilanga* seemed secure.

Dube's success in navigating the difficult and even treacherous waters of Natal politics, along with *Ilanga*'s coverage of the arrest, trial, and imprisonment of the Zulu paramount Dinizulu following the Bambatha Rebellion, made him a household name among colonial politicians and African activists when the four British-ruled colonies of South Africa began to move toward union. He more than any other single African in Natal gave voice, principally through the columns of *Ilanga*, to African concerns and aspirations as South Africa assumed its new constitutional configuration. The formation of the Union of South Africa led in turn to a movement to develop a new African national organization that would supersede existing regional-based African political organizations. The result was the South African Native National Congress, founded in January 1912 (the SANNC was renamed African National Congress, or ANC, in 1923). John Dube was a strong proponent of creating such an organization and, though absent from the inaugural meeting, was named its first president general.

As head of the SANNC, Dube moved from operating within the political milieu of Natal to the much broader and more dynamic political environment of the new Union of South Africa. Having mastered, it would seem, the minefield of Natal politics, he sought to apply his well-honed political skills to the new post. Dube's letter of acceptance to the members of the SANNC outlined his thinking:

Photo 5. John Langalibalele Dube, founder and editor of *Ilanga lase Natal* (1903–15).

> You have asked me to lead, and perchance you would ask me now how I intend to do so. I will show you my frame of mind and my ideal in two words. I take for my motto (and I hope, as faithful and dutiful followers, it will be yours also) "*Festina lente*: Hasten – slowly"; and for my patron saint I select that great and edifying man, Booker Washington. I recognize that the hour is come when we, the Native Races of South Africa, must be up and doing – for God helps those who help themselves. But I recognize, too, the necessity of moving cautiously, of making progress prudently.[10]

This was the style of leadership Dube brought to bear on the first great issue confronting the SANNC, the 1913 Natives' Land Act. "Awaking on Friday morning, June 20, 1913, the South African Native found himself, not actually a slave, but a pariah in the land of his birth."[11] With these few words, SANNC secretary general Sol T. Plaatje summed up the depth of African sentiment against the 1913 act, which would leave them in possession of a mere 7.1 percent of the Union's total land surface. By sending deputations, resolutions and petitions, Congress sought first to prevent passage of the measure and then, once passed, to get its provisions modified. When these efforts failed, the SANNC authorized the delegation, headed by Dube, to travel to England in 1914 to persuade the British government to withhold its assent to the legislation under the provisions of the South Africa Act, which had created the Union. The delegation, too, failed in its efforts, and the outbreak of World War I in August 1914 brought an abrupt end to the SANNC's bid to sway British public opinion against the Land Act.

Ilanga lase Natal was under the editorship of an individual with considerable political influence in Natal and to a lesser extent in South Africa. But Dube's approach, based as it was on accommodation, conciliation and deference to colonial authority, was insufficient when it came to an issue like the control and ownership of South Africa's land resources. A closer examination of *Ilanga* and its editor in the newspaper's first decade or so of existence provides insights into the potential for political maneuver and the boundaries of political dissent for Africans during the crucial formative years of twentieth-century South Africa.

Vigilance and waking up were special words for John Dube during these years. He sought to impart to his fellow *kholwa* a sense of obligation to aspire to a position of parity with white Natalians. Dube and the *kholwa* in general belonged to that category of Africans characterized by Terence Ranger as "the aspirant African *bourgeoisie* [who] sought to make its own that range of attitudes and activities which defined the European middle classes."[12] By the time of the formation of the Union of South Africa in 1910, an aspiring African petty bourgeoisie similar to the *kholwa* were even more fully established in the Cape Colony than in Natal and constituted a significant presence in the Transvaal as well.

The *kholwa,* in the words of Jean and John Comaroff, "were compelled to fight on the linguistic and conceptual terrain of the whites. Imperialism and colonialism alike implied the precedence of European signs and practices." The political language they employed was that of colonialism "with its curious argot of bureaucratic and biblical terms."[13] That such should be the case is not surprising, given the educational background and the material and social aspirations of the *kholwa*. If they wished to make their own the "range of attitudes and activities which defined the European middle classes," they had to adopt the language of the people they knew, the settler petty bourgeoisie. The entire process, then, involved relationships of power. Power, prestige and privilege now rested with the white colonists, and to Dube and the readers of *Ilanga*, the best route to power sharing was the assumption of a European middle-class identity.

The attempt by the African Christian community to carve out for themselves a position within the colonial order, however, was fraught with ambiguities. Shula Marks utilizes the concept of ambiguity in her study of twentieth-century Natal. She views the term as covering "two distinct but related phenomena: ambiguity of meaning and structural ambiguity."[14] Ambiguity of meaning was integral to the operation of the "colonial misunderstanding," in which, as Marks notes, "the words and actions of individuals are both deliberately and accidentally ambiguous."[15] The very meaning of Ohlange school, for example, was ambiguous. Dube had been able to secure the backing of some influential white Natalians for his educational enterprise, but he had done so by arguing that his only purpose was seeing to the welfare of "his people."

Correspondence between Dube and the prominent sugar planter Marshall Campbell illustrates the concept of ambiguity of meaning. Dube, writing in 1909, stated:

> As I told you some few weeks since that I intend to go to England with a view to raise money for our school, I now write you asking for letters of commendation to some of your friends in England. I know you have taken me to task more than once for some of my political writings, I wish to assure you that I have found out by sad experience that politics work against the interest of the work to which I have devoted my life, that of educating my people. I have decided to leave politics severely alone.

Campbell provided Dube with the letter of introduction he had requested, noting in part:

> Mr. Dube is devoting the whole of his time to educational purposes, he has promised that in no way will he meddle with politics in future. His one object in life is to help his own race to a higher standard of life.[16]

The other dimension of ambiguity to which Marks refers, structural ambiguity, concerned the balance of power in colonial society. White domination was certainly the central feature of colonial society, but domination was a matter of gaining to some degree the consent of the Africans, most especially the *kholwa*, as it was not just a matter of force. Dube's relationship with Campbell exemplified this structural ambiguity as well as the ambiguity of meaning. Dube acknowledged that power rested most decidedly with Campbell, but the sugar planters also saw a need to assist Dube and his "race to a higher standard of life."

The attempt to maneuver within the confines of colonial society to advance the position of the aspiring African petty bourgeoisie could be a very frustrating experience. Although there were individual whites like Campbell who could be won over through careful diplomacy, more often than not whites were extremely antipathetic to Africans, whatever their circumstances. *Ilanga* captured the essence of the African's predicament: "Certainly ours is a hard lot, for when we remain in our heathen state, we are blamed and when we follow the white people's customs we are found fault with. What shall we do?"[17] Enmeshed in such contradictions, the *kholwa* were ultimately led to rethink their aspirations.

The Comaroffs again provide a useful insight into how best to interpret the position and actions of Dube and other activists of his generation:

> The Tswana may have learned the political language of colonialism. And they may have conducted themselves according to its practical terms. But the more they were forced to comply with European forms of discourse, the more they came to rely upon, and invoke, the distinction between *sekgoa*, the ways of whites, and *setswana*, Tswana ways...This contrast ... bore witness to the fact that the contradictions between the professed worldview of the mission and the world of material and social inequality in South Africa were to become ever more acute.[18]

Although these contradictions became more readily apparent to Dube in the 1930s,[19] it is also possible to find them expressed in *Ilanga* during its first decade.

The situation for African Christians in Natal and indeed the whole of South Africa in the early years of the new century, then, was ambiguous, and *Ilanga* reflected these ambiguities. By examining some of the key issues that were represented in its pages between the founding of the newspaper and World War I, it is possible to develop a fuller understanding of the concerns of Dube as the editor and of the *kholwa* as a community.

This chapter focuses on four key issues, all of which appear in one form or another in Dube's initial editorial in the first number of *Ilanga*. The first concerns the concept of "improving Christianity,"[20] which embraced the various efforts being made by the aspiring petty bourgeoisie to obtain a more secure place for themselves in colonial society. The second concerns the so-called Bambatha Rebellion in Natal, which brings out some of the ambivalent feelings of the *kholwa* about their own position vis-à-vis the mass of the African people still following precolonial modes of life. The third concerns the formation of the Union of South Africa and the position of Africans within the new constitutional framework. The fourth concerns the

1913 Natives' Land Act, which had profound implications for an emerging middle-class community still tied to a rural environment.

An Improving Christianity

John Dube and his fellow *kholwa* had as one of the principal elements in their social identity their adherence to Christianity. Furthermore, as Tim Keegan has written with reference to the missionized Africans of the interior highveld, it was a "Christianity of a particular kind: a universalist, inclusive, improving Christianity."[21] In a context where the colonists were conspicuous in their identification as Christians, where it was the missionaries among the whites with whom Africans had the greatest interaction, and where Africans were caught up in a situation of great social flux, it is not surprising that a sizeable segment of the African population sought entry into the dominant culture through what appeared to them as a principal identifier of that culture. It was through Christianity that the *kholwa* "sought to make its own that range of attitudes and activities which defined the European [settler] middle classes."[22] This strategy, in turn, meant utilizing the linguistic and conceptual terrain of the colonizers, as the following quotation from a speech Dube presented to an African-American audience at Hampton Institute in 1897 demonstrates:

> My grandmother and her children fled [from Shaka's warriors] to Natal and settled themselves there. It was at the mission station of the Rev. Dan'l Lindley, one of the pioneer missionaries of the American Board. My grandmother was one of the first converts to Christianity, and soon my father was also converted. Then the rest of the dissatisfied tribe came over to this place and asked my father to be their chief, but said he must give up the white man's religion; this my father refused to do. The Zulus are the strongest and most warlike of any African people, and my father would have had a power that England would have found it hard to fight. My father was educated, and became a native preacher. I think it was better than being a king to be Christian, because Christianity is the greatest civilizer in the world. The heathen power that he would have had would not have given his people as much help as he was able to give them by being a Christian.[23]

An integral part of the help that came through Christianity was education. This was especially true in South Africa, where the school was closely tied to the mission. It was through education that Africans would pass from "heathenism" to "civilization." Thus Dube, though himself an ordained minister, concentrated not on the church but the school. The Zulu Christian Industrial School (Ohlange) was the result. As Dube noted in an article designed for a western missionary readership, "The school is proving a great influence for good among the Zulu youths. The bell rings early in the morning, so that the boys at 6 o'clock are ready to begin their work on the farm where they cultivate their own food, or in the shops, where they learn carpentry and make many useful things." The article continued with descriptions of the school's printing department, its gristmill and small blacksmith shop and its orchards, "where our boys have learned to plant fruit trees... [which] promises to be a very useful industry for young Zulus." The boys also learned to do "all the housework connected with the boarding-school," including preparing meals and washing dishes. Classes were held between 9:30 A.M. and 1:30 P.M., and after lunch "the afternoon work is again taken up in farm and in the shops." Dube's "object in respect to the school is to make it practical and capable of turning out first-class Christian agriculturalists ... [since] farming is by far the most important [industry] for our people."[24]

Dube prepared these statements for an overseas audience, and the phrasing carried special connotations for this audience (demonstrating that Dube was able to craft his message to fit his audience). But in their central message concerning "the greatest civilizer in the world," they differed little from his statements to the *kholwa* audience in Natal. Again, his initial editorial in *Ilanga* had spoken of "things that are educational and improve us in terms of getting jobs, education, and making us bright."[25] Nevertheless, there was an added element in the message Dube had for the aspiring African middle class, an emphasis on the respect Christianity secured for its adherents: "In spite of the strong feelings that prejudice the mind of the white man against those of less fortunate colour, we must admit that whenever a Native by education and Christian civilization raises himself to a standard above his fellows, the white man respects and treats him with courtesy and common politeness characteristic of his race."[26]

Respect, courtesy, politeness and proper treatment were much of what the *kholwa* aspired to receive by acquiring the white man's religion and education. African Christians couched their messages to whites in ways that would appeal to white sensibilities and vanities:

> And what duty, pray, has England towards these black-skinned Zulu people? To release them from the dungeons of intellectual darkness in which they have been enchained from the beginning of time; to enkindle the lamp of knowledge and enlightenment in their land; to feed the hungry, to give drink to the thirsty, to clothe the naked–in a word, to take up the White man's burden.[27]

The problem for the African petty bourgeoisie was that although it adopted (at least outwardly) the ways of the whites, the respect it sought was not forthcoming. The *kholwa* called for self-improvement and for whites to do their duty by Africans, but they continued to experience discrimination at all levels of public activity, even as preachers and teachers:

> We hear so much nowadays of restriction to native teachers and preachers in the matter of teaching their own people without a white man... It is a well known fact that each community knows better the need and kind of education their children ought to have... In most cases the success attending the work of Missionaries is due to native workers, because the native, although he may not know as much grammar as the white teachers, still he knows the children. But when such a teacher or preacher who has had training under missionaries goes out to initiate work on his own account, he is suspected of teaching ethiopianism.[28]

Frustration with government-imposed restrictions was accompanied by tension between the *kholwa* and the missionaries. One source of tension was over land, an issue that will be dealt with later in this chapter. As Marks notes, however, there were other sources of tension. *Ilanga* editorials in 1907 and 1908, for instance, "bitterly attacked ... the missionaries ... [for] their general social aloofness, lack of trust for converts, inadequate selection of African officers and failure to defend African interests."[29] All of this contributed to the developing sense that "ours is a hard lot."[30]

The ambiguities of their situation led the *kholwa* into a more critical approach toward the "civilization" they were seeking to enter. They now saw that there was value in some of the "old ways." This point was at the heart of a 1905 *Ilanga* editorial entitled "A Warning to Natives":

> The evils which follow in the train of civilisation are many. It is so easy for us to copy the white man whether he is doing wrong or right. We should be careful what we copy. Drinking in spite of many restrictions here in Natal is getting to be a serious problem amongst the Natives. Stealing used to be punished very severely in the days of Chaka, but it is getting very common amongst our people especially in Cape Colony. Disregard for parental authority or any authority is also seen on every hand. I can count many other things but these are enough.[31]

As with the Tswana and their distinction between *sekgoa* (ways of the whites) and *setswana* (Tswana ways), so too with the Zulu *kholwa* there was emerging an awareness of the more desirable and less desirable features of the two respective cultures. By the 1930s, Dube was telling his people, "We have a lot to learn from the white man and he has a lot to learn from us."[32]

The Rebellion in Natal

The hostile and oppressive climate of early twentieth century Natal erupted into open rebellion against the colonial government in February 1906, a rebellion that was in part engineered by the colonial authorities. Although government troops were able to suppress the rebellion by July, at great cost to African life, unrest continued among Africans for many months. This ultimately led to the arrest of Dinizulu, heir of the last independent Zulu king, Cetshwayo, and to his trial on charges of high treason. He was found guilty, sentenced to prison and died an exile in 1913.[33]

John Dube and his fellow *kholwa* found themselves in an extremely difficult situation. As David Welsh has noted, "In the Natal system the Africans could not win: the traditionalist because of his 'barbarism', and the *kholwa* because of his acceptance of western values and the resulting claim to equal status with whites."[34] Marks further elaborates on the characteristics of this no-win situation in her discussion on the causes of the rebellion, one of which was public flogging:

> In Natal there was little of the lynching and public violence which has characterized so much of race relations in the Southern states of the United States; nevertheless, this form of legalized brutality appears to have constituted an adequate substitute and was, in many ways, probably the outcome of the same psychological factors ... Indiscriminate flogging may have been the final spur prompting into action those Africans who had already watched their cattle confiscated and their kraals destroyed.[35]

It was against such a background of hostility, violence and oppression that Dube sought room to maneuver in order to defend the interests of the *kholwa* community. The catharsis of the rebellion, moreover, may have moderated conditions in the postrebellion aftermath, because the settler authorities became somewhat less hostile to Africans, especially in areas like education. Thus Dube spoke approvingly of the report of the Native Affairs Commission, which the government appointed in the aftermath of the rebellion, in a letter to Booker T. Washington:

> I am sending you ... a copy of the Native Affairs Commission Report ... This Commission has just completed its inquiries in native matters and its comments on the position of native administration will tell you briefly how we have been ruled in the

past. The Commission says of the policies of past Governments that "It was weighed and found wanting."[36]

Ilanga's editor approached the subject of the rebellion by raising and then addressing a number of issues for Africans in general and the *kholwa* in particular. The first of these was the loyalty of the *kholwa*. Harsh as the climate was, the *kholwa* had no reason to rebel. Indeed, the situation for them was quite the opposite. "Fundamentally," writes Marks, "they still identified themselves with the values of the white man, and wished to be received by him as an equal. Armed warfare could not achieve these rights–as Dube pointed out on several occasions in *Ilanga lase Natal*."[37]

Achieving the rights they sought meant both asserting and professing African loyalty to the government. "The loyalty of the natives is beyond dispute," Dube stated publicly.[38] Privately, as in the following comment in a letter to Marshall Campbell, he assured white leaders that he was actively working to maintain order: "Any way I shall inform you of any serious state of affairs, but you may remain assured that so long as I have influence in this district nothing of a serious nature, other than idle rumours, will ever take place."[39]

Although professions of loyalty might reassure whites and provide guidance for Africans, *Ilanga* was not "going to keep quiet when it sees bad things being done."[40] As Dube noted to Booker Washington, "Things had gone so bad that I as one of the leaders of the people felt it my duty to speak the whole truth."[41] Dube did speak out, using as his weapons "words of resistance," by which he meant words that interrogated the linguistic and conceptual terrain of the whites. "Why are you afraid?", he questioned his readers in the editorial "Vukani Bantu!" (the same editorial that almost led to him being silenced): "We must all go with all our grievances and fight for our rights. *Ilanga* is saying to the Zulus that we are not going to fight them with spears, the way to fight the whites is to use words of resistance, the same way they do when they treat us like we are not people but dogs." Dube then listed 14 specific grievances, including taxation without representation, preventing African ministers from preaching, seizing African land, interfering with African education and forcing Africans to carry passes.[42]

One set of grievances related to a central element of *kholwa* identity, their religion. The government interfered with the practice of religion. Dube complained of "The arresting of black people and preachers, who are not allowed to preach at certain locations" and of authorities forbidding "black preachers to conduct marriages for their own people." He said that "our preachers and others" should "be allowed to have permits to collect money on trains, without whites interfering."[43]

These grievances were also linked to the broader issue of colonial opposition to missionaries and missionized Africans. Colonial opposition arose in part out of exaggerated fears, such as the fear of African independent (or "Ethiopian", as the settlers called them) churches, which bordered on hysteria during the rebellion. As Dube noted, all African Christians stood accused of Ethiopianism, whether they rejected the practice or not: "There is no one today who can remove the dust of ethiopianism." What made Ethiopianism objectionable, he argued, was preaching discrimination. It was not Africans who preached such discrimination and separatism but whites. Indeed, it was an Englishman who coined the phrase "Africa is for Africans":

> He has been our demise, because from our point of view he is the one who started bad ethiopianism here in South Africa, by preaching all over the land or sending black

> Americans to preach. We cannot blame these [black Americans] because they do not know us ... We hope that 'the powers that be' can investigate ethiopianism because it is a big problem.[44]

While the imagined Ethiopian threat helped fuel settler opposition to African mission communities, there was also a more deeply ingrained colonial objection to the missionaries and their work. The colonists, claimed Dube, sought to blame the missionaries for the rebellion, but in truth they were using them as scapegoats to excuse their own failure to govern properly:

> The Zulus have been under the English Government for nearly thirty years without ever thinking of rebellion against the government. But ever since a responsible government was granted to Natal, there has been an absence of proper consideration for the natives. The desire on the part of the ruling race to use the natives for their own comfort and aggrandizement has led the natives to resort to armed resistance. The missionaries are blamed on all sides as responsible for this rebellion because they teach the natives that they also are men with souls like white men... If the Europeans wish to know the true cause of native unrest they may find it in their own policy of administration of native affairs. They have debased their national ideals, for instead of national righteousness, they have manifested national selfishness. This makes the missionary's daily example of faithful, unselfish living among the natives a constant rebuke of the colonists. Thus he is placed between two fires–on the one hand, hated by his white neighbors as encouraging the native to be more independent; and on the other hand, suspected by the native as a tool of the oppressors.[45]

As well as defending the missionary role in the midst of the rebellion, Dube could also criticize it. In 1906, for instance, Dube castigated a missionary of the American Zulu Mission for an insensitive sermon related to the events of the rebellion. According to another missionary, the sermon, delivered to an African congregation, seemed to gloat over the colonial victory.[46]

One other issue emerged from the turmoil surrounding the rebellion in Natal–that of the appropriate nature of African leadership. Dube and other *kholwa*, of course, were actively exercising leadership, but the chiefs still held considerable authority under the overall umbrella of the colonial government. One approach of *Ilanga* was to raise the question of having chiefs come from among the ranks of educated people: "The idea of chieftainship not being hereditary will be new to some of our people, and doubtless will cause a good deal of resentment and discontent, but we might as well be prepared for it. In the new order of things the office will be based on utility and fitness, and not upon a predecessor's qualities."[47] At the same time, Dube opposed the government's curbs on chiefly authority. The "Vukani Bantu!" editorial, for example, called for "Chiefs to be given more powers to rule their people."[48] Thus there clearly was some ambivalence about the position of the chiefs. Were they to come from among the ranks of the *kholwa,* or were they representatives of a distinctly African heritage?

On the question of respect for the institution of the chiefship, however, there was no ambivalence, and such respect readily translated into the wider issue of African self-respect. Thus there was real anger in the pages of *Ilanga* over the arrest and trial of Dinizulu in the last stages of the rebellion:

> You should come into contact with the real Zulu in Durban and you would there see the bitterness. I saw an educated native boy buying a paper containing a picture of him [Dinizulu] being marched by the soldiers which the boy was showing the natives. A young Zuluman looked at the picture again and again and then the tears streamed; he beat his breast and walked on.[49]

Africans and the Union

Fundamental to the rebellion was the underlying question of the place of Africans in colonial Natal society. The "Vukani Bantu!" editorial framed the issue very effectively in the first of its list of 14 itemized complaints, protesting against "Taxation, even though we do not have any say on this, and no voice in parliament."[50] In short, were Africans to be citizens of the state in which they lived, or were they to remain rightless subjects of a state run by and for whites? The political debate leading to the formation of the Union of South Africa brought such issues to the forefront. What was to be the place of Africans in the new constitutional arrangement?

For Dube, the principal issue was the vote, and he approached it from a decidedly *kholwa* perspective. From its inception, *Ilanga* had held forth the standard of "civilization" as the gauge for measuring African preparedness for full citizenship: "we...feel that a man's political freedom should be measured only by his lack of civilization."[51] Furthermore, Africans had "natural rights to a place in the legislature of our country."[52] It was this set of arguments that Dube employed as his contribution to discussions on the proposed unification of South Africa:

> There is but one specie of solution left for Statesmen to adopt in South Africa, and that is the one briefly enunciated by the Hon. C. J. Rhodes and that is "that every civilized man shall have equal parliamentary rights throughout South Africa." Then it follows that a full definition of the term "civilized" must be given, and that must include all men; a graded civilization would not do, it would merely advertise a new kind of political aberration, and as the world's political market has plenty of that on show without any positive demand being made for it, it will be well not to add to that supply. Given these two factors (a) that all civilized men shall have equal political rights, and (b) that the term "civilized" is properly defined, the rest of the operation can safely be left to develop, simply because the broad principle of equity is complied with. Would any hurt to South Africa arise of that?[53]

In the end, white settler interests were too entrenched for arguments like "No taxation without representation" and "equal rights for every civilized man" to prevail on behalf of the African petty bourgeoisie. Only in the Cape did Africans retain access to the franchise, but even Cape African voters could not elect one of their own to parliament, since membership was limited to white males. Having lost his battle for the vote, Dube was reduced to dire predictions of an uneasy future for the new Union of South Africa. The constitutional arrangement "will leave a festering sore...and create disaffection and disloyalty among a large section of its population."[54] "Are we Africans," observed *Ilanga*, "to view that abominable folly as one of the triumph of civilization?"[55] The answer was clearly no, and the future was to demonstrate the accuracy of Dube's prediction. Africans would resist the constitutional order in a long and difficult struggle that lasted more than eight decades.

Dispossession

As Dube and *Ilanga* predicted, exclusion from parliament led to a further diminution of African rights. Formation of the Union meant that political authority now rested firmly and unambiguously in the hands of white male South Africans. All political discourse of any real significance took place within their ranks. Passage of the 1913 Natives' Land Act, for example, became a test case for the newly formed South African Native National Congress, to see if it possessed any significant political clout on issues of such consequence. The outcome, not surprisingly, was that Congress lacked any such clout.

Adequate access to land was absolutely crucial to African economic and social well-being in the new South Africa. For somewhat different reasons, control over land was also of vital importance to white interests. And within these two sets of interests, African and white, there were varying subsets of interests. The *kholwa*, for example, were still a rural-based community and regarded land as a key to any ongoing success they might enjoy. "Farming," as Dube noted in his *Missionary Review of the World* article, "is by far the most important [industry] for our people."[56] As Manning Marable has written, "Dube's program of self improvement rested upon the precondition of ready access of lands which the educated Kholwa could purchase."[57]

Dube had long been attentive to any limitations on access to land. For example, the Mission Reserve Act of 1903 was a matter of considerable apprehension. Missionary administration of reserve land in Natal entitled the missionaries to a 50 percent share of the £3 tax on inhabitants.[58] Dube and other *kholwa* were highly suspicious of this arrangement, and it eventually led to rather bitter attacks in the columns of *Ilanga* about missionary decisions on land allotments in areas under their control.[59] The "Vukani Bantu!" editorial succinctly summed up the matter by noting that the grievance was one of "the 'cutting' of land belonging to Zulus and giving it to the whites."[60] The introduction of legislation that ultimately led to the enactment of the 1913 Natives' Land Act produced great consternation."The very suggestion that Natives be prohibited from renting or leasing land except under degrading conditions," *Ilanga* noted, "fills us with anxiety and foreboding."[61]

Dube's arsenal of weapons to use against the proposed act was very limited. The futility of rebellion was evident to all, given the events of 1906 and 1907. Africans had yet to formulate and develop a strategy of confrontation, such as the use of strikes, boycotts and other forms of mass protest. The constitutional arrangements for the Union had, with the partial exception of the Cape's African voters, denied Africans basic citizenship rights. This left the use of persuasion as the only tactic available to Africans. One approach was to appeal to the imagined sense of justice among whites: "It [the act] strikes at the root of the elementary rights and liberties as free-born men, as members of the common brotherhood of the human family."[62] Another was to argue that such legislation was ultimately inimical to white interests: "the salvation of the Natives and the welfare of South Africa depends vitally upon Natives becoming tillers of the soil."[63]

The language Dube utilized in the struggle against the 1913 Land Act was clearly the language of colonialism. He was fighting on "the linguistic and conceptual terrain of the whites," as the Comaroffs would phrase it. In postcolonial white South Africa, however, such persuasion had lost most of its force. It was much more suitable to the metropolitan political discourse. Having learned one set of European cultural codes, the *kholwa* now found themselves in an environment where another set was operating. Under such circumstances, defeat was inevitable. Although there was an element of ambiguity in the act, in that its provisions did not apply to the Cape, for the *kholwa* it meant that they could no longer as a community hope to find economic security and social stability on the land.

"Qude maniki!"

The formation of the Union of South Africa and the passage of the 1913 Land Act demonstrated the limits of Dube's "qude maniki!" approach to politics. In the setting of Natal as a separate, British-ruled colony, there was some room for maneuver, even though Dube charged the British with having "cruelly abandoned" the Africans' "natural right to a place in the legislature of our country... when it gave Representative Government to Natal [1893] and again when it annexed Zululand to Natal [1897]."[64]

Great Britain still remained the final arbiter of political discourse in the colony. When Natal's Governor Nathan spoke at the opening ceremonies for the Ohlange School's industrial department in 1908, for example, he was providing direct political support for Dube and his education enterprise. His statement, "I have had a great deal of experience in other parts of Africa of industrial schools for natives, and in every case I have observed they have done good,"[65] was in effect an open endorsement of improving Christianity. Dube and his fellow *kholwa* had mastered the political discourse as this was represented by Governor Nathan's presence at the Ohlange celebration. They could even put to their own use the ambiguities of power that the rebellion posed for a small settler population in the midst of an overwhelming African majority. Protestations of loyalty, in such tenuous circumstances, proved helpful to furthering the *kholwa* cause. In short, observing the codes and rituals of colonial discourse did have some payoff, limited though it may have been.

With the changed circumstances of the Union, however, Dube's "Qude maniki!" approach was incapable of further advancing the cause of Natal's aspiring African petty bourgeoisie or even of defending the advances they had made. In the new South Africa they were losing the rather tenuous foothold they had managed to obtain for themselves. In large part this was owing to the final shift in the locus of power away from metropolitan Britain and into the hands of white colonial interests. Changing power relationships had changed the nature of the political discourse, so the *kholwa* community had to learn anew the appropriate linguistic and conceptual terrain on which they had to fight. This was ultimately the achievement of a new generation, the generation that was born during the era of World War I.

Notes

1. *Ilanga lase Natal* (hereafter *ILN*), 10 April 1903. Unless otherwise noted, quotations of the introduction in subsequent paragraphs also come from the same editorial, entitled "Ilanga lase Natal."
2. Shortages of indigenous African labor in the gold mines during and immediately after the South African War forced the Chamber of Mines to recruit labor from other parts of Africa and other parts of the British Empire. More than 63,000 indentured laborers from northern China were recruited to work on mines in the Witwatersrand in 1904–5. They supplied up to 35 percent of the unskilled mine labor for several years, but most of them had been sent back to China by 1910.
3. For full details of Dube's life, see Manning Marable, "African nationalist: The life of John Langalibalele Dube," Ph.D. thesis (University of Maryland, 1976). See also R. Hunt Davis, Jr., "John L. Dube: A South African exponent of Booker T. Washington, "*Journal of African Studies* 2,4 (1975–76), 497–528; S. Marks, "The ambiguities of dependence: John L. Dube of Natal," *Journal of Southern African Studies*, 1,2(1975), 162–180; S. Marks,

The ambiguities of dependence in South Africa: Class, nationalism, and the state in twentieth-century Natal (Baltimore, 1986), 42–73. A concise biographical sketch appears in T. Karis and G. M. Carter (eds.), *From protest to challenge: A documentary history of African politics in South Africa, 1882–1964*, Vol. 4, *Political profiles* by G. M. Gerhart and T. Karis (Stanford, 1972–77), 24–26.

4. " 'Need of industrial education in Africa,' speech by Mr. John Dube, a Zulu missionary," *Southern Workman*, 27, 7 (July 1897), 141–142.
5. Marable, "African nationalist," 122, writes that Ohlange opened on 8 August 1900, but he seems to have misread his source. "Statement No. 3 'Concerning the Rev. John L. Dube and his wife, and their work in Natal, South Africa,' by the American Committee," dated November 1901, notes that "We are able now to state that the Industrial School was formally opened in August last. The exercises were held during the annual meeting of the African Congregational churches at Inanda, and one day of the conference (Friday, August 8th) was devoted to the school opening." See Mrs. Bryan Horton, secretary, American Committee, to Booker T. Washington, 26 June 1903, Container 261, Booker T. Washington Papers (hereafter BTW Papers), Library of Congress.
6. See, for example, D. Welsh, *The roots of segregation: Native policy in Natal (1845–1910)* (Cape Town, 1971), 268–272.
7. *ILN*, 4 May 1906.
8. S. Marks, *Reluctant rebellion: The 1906–08 disturbances in Natal* (Oxford, 1970), 333.
9. Dube to Booker T. Washington, 30 November 1907, Container 346, BTW Papers.
10. Published letter, Dube to Chiefs and Gentlemen of the South African Native Congress, 2 February 1912, MSS Brit. Emp. S19, D2/3, papers of the British and Foreign Anti-Slavery and Aborigines Protection Society (hereafter APS Papers), Rhodes House Library, Oxford University.
11. Sol T. Plaatje, *Native life in South Africa* (London, 1916; rpt., New York, 1969), 17.
12. Terence Ranger, "The invention of tradition in colonial Africa," in E. Hobsbawm and T. Ranger (eds.), *The invention of tradition* (Cambridge, 1983), 237.
13. J. Comaroff and J. Comaroff, *Of revelation and revolution: Christianity, colonialism, and consciousness in South Africa*, Vol. 1 (Chicago, 1991), 307.
14. Marks, *The ambiguities of dependence in South Africa*, vii.
15. Ibid., 1.
16. John L. Dube to Marshall Campbell, 10 June 1909, and Marshall Campbell, "To Whom It May Concern," 3 July 1909, in Marshall Campbell, Letter Container 8, Killie Campbell Africana Library, University of Natal, Durban.
17. Welsh, The *Roots of segregation*, 295 (citing *ILN*, 19 February 1908).
18. Comaroff and Comaroff, *Of revelation*, 308.
19. See, for instance, Marks's essay "John Dube and the ambiguities of nationalism" in her *Ambiguities of dependence*, 42–73.
20. I have borrowed the term from Tim Keegan, *Facing the storm: Portraits of black lives in rural South Africa* (Athens, Oh., 1988), 77.
21. Ibid.
22. Ranger, "The Invention of tradition," 237.
23. Dube, "Need of industrial education in Africa," 142.
24. John L. Dube, "Practical Christianity among the Zulus," *Missionary Review of the World*, n.s. 20 (1907), 370–373.
25. *ILN*, 10 April 1903.
26. *ILN*, 29 May 1903.
27. John L. Dube, "The Zulu's appeal for light" [1909], 5, in APS Papers, MSS Brit. Empire S.22, G191.
28. *ILN*, 10 November 1905. Turn-of-the-century colonial South Africa viewed "Ethiopianism," or the wish for African independence in religious matters, as a major menace, comparable to the communist-inspired "red scares" of later eras. In this editorial, Dube was directly addressing his own personal circumstances as principal of Ohlange as well as the more general situation facing the *kholwa*. For more details on the restrictions the Natal government imposed on educated Africans as a result of its fear of Ethiopianism, see Welsh, *Roots of segregation*, 253–258.
29. Marks, "The ambiguities of dependence," 173.

30. *ILN*, 19 February 1908.
31. *ILN*, 27 October 1905. For further discussion of a defense of "traditionalism," see Welsh, *The Roots of segregation*, 298–299.
32. From transcript of a speech by John L. Dube, 27 March 1934, as quoted in Marks, *The Ambiguities of dependence*, 44.
33. For a comprehensive account of the rebellion, see Marks, *Reluctant rebellion*.
34. Welsh, *The Roots of segregation*, 322.
35. Marks, *Reluctant rebellion*, 239.
36. Dube to Washington, 21 September 1907, Container 346, BTW Papers.
37. Marks, *Reluctant rebellion* 332. For specific examples, see *ILN* for 23 February and 2 March 1906, as noted by Marks in n. 5.
38. Marable, "African nationalist," 212 (citing *Natal Mercury*, 1 June 1906, "Further Native Views").
39. Dube to Campbell, n.d. [1906], item 746, in Carol Botha (comp.), *A catalogue of manuscripts and papers in the Killie Campbell Africana collection relating to the African peoples* (Johanesburg, 1967).
40. *ILN*, 10 April 1903.
41. Dube to Washington, 21 September 1907, Container 346, BTW Papers.
42. *ILN*, 4 May 1906.
43. Ibid.
44. "Ubutopia", *ILN*, 16 March 1906. The "Englishman" was undoubtedly Joseph Booth. For Booth, see Marks, *Reluctant rebellion*, 60.
45. John L. Dube, "Zulus and the missionary outlook in Natal," *Missionary Review of the World*, n.s. 20 (1907), 205.
46. See Marks, *Reluctant rebellion*, 358, nn. 2–3, for citations.
47. Welsh, *The Roots of segregation*, 287 (citing *ILN*, 22 November 1907).
48. *ILN*, 4 May 1906.
49. Marks, *Reluctant rebellion*, 361, n. 4 (citing *ILN*, 27 December 1907).
50. *ILN*, 4 May 1906.
51. *ILN*, 29 May 1903.
52. *ILN*, 19 February 1909.
53. *ILN*, 26 February 1909.
54. *ILN*, 12 March 1909.
55. *ILN*, 5 March 1909.
56. Dube, "Practical Christianity," 372.
57. Marable, "African nationalist," 210.
58. The Mission Reserve Act continued the policy, first established in legislation in 1895, of government control over mission lands. African residents were taxed £3 annually. For further information, see Marks, *Reluctant rebellion*, 77–78.
59. Ibid., 75, n. 1 (citing *ILN*, 15 November 1907 and 20 March 1908).
60. *ILN*, 4 May 1908.
61. *ILN*, 4 April 1913.
62. *ILN*, 23 May 1913.
63. *ILN*, 4 April 1913.
64. *ILN*, 19 February 1909.
65. *Christian Express*, March 1908.

CHAPTER 3

From Advocacy to Mobilization

Indian Opinion, 1903–1914

Uma Shashikant Mesthrie

When Mohandas Karamchand Gandhi left South Africa in 1914 after a period of 21 years in South African Indian politics, he left behind a newspaper, *Indian Opinion*; a communal settlement at Phoenix, just outside Durban; and an ideology of resistance, *satyagraha*.* The histories of all three are closely intertwined, and these interconnections are the focus of this chapter. The South African experience transformed Gandhi, and this transformation was reflected in *Indian Opinion*'s political objectives, its political strategies and its class and racial biases.

Historical Background

Indians first came to Natal in 1860 as a result of the demand by white sugarcane planters for a regular and stable supply of labor.[1] Although most laborers, bonded by contract, worked on sugar estates, up-country farms and wattle tree plantations, some were employed to construct railways and work in the coal mines. A much smaller percentage were employed as cooks, waiters, washermen, coachmen and hospital orderlies. By 1911, when the importation of indentured labor was discontinued, 152,184 indentured workers had come to Natal.

Indentured Indians had a number of options open to them once their contracts had expired. They could reindenture, remain in the colony as free Indians or take advantage of free passage to India. More than half the indentured population elected to remain in the colony. From here many spread out to the Kimberley diamond fields and to the Transvaal. The formerly indentured in Natal sought employment in the agricultural and industrial sectors, but many became independent market gardeners, hawkers and fishermen. A few opened modest provision stores. Some 45 years after the arrival of the first indentured workers, a small group of colonial-borns in Natal, descendants of the indentured workers, were employed as lawyers, civil servants, accountants, teachers, bookkeepers, clerks, interpreters, petty entrepreneurs and small farmers. This comprised the nucleus of the Indian petty bourgeoisie in South Africa.

*Drafts of this paper were presented in 1990 at the Southern African Research Program, Yale University, where much of the research was also undertaken, and in 1991 at a conference entitled "A Century of the Resistance Press in South Africa," held at the University of the Western Cape. I would particularly like to thank Chris Lowe for his very useful comments as well as James Hunt, Les Switzer and Christopher Saunders.

A second stream of migrants followed on the heels of the indentured laborers, the "passenger Indians" (mainly Indians paying their own passage), who came under the colony's ordinary immigration laws. Some were Christian Indians from India and Mauritius–teachers, interpreters, catechists and traders.[2] But most new migrants were Gujerati traders from areas on the western coast of India, such as Surat and Bombay, together with a few from Mauritius. These merchants soon appeared in the Transvaal, the Orange Free State and the Cape Colony. Ten years after the arrival of the first merchant in 1875, they owned 60 stores in Durban and 20 branches elsewhere in Natal, Transvaal and the Orange Free State. By 1904 there were 1,225 Indian traders in Natal and 581 in the Transvaal.[3] The total Asian population in South Africa by 1904 was 122,734, of which 100,918 (82.2 percent) were in Natal, 11,321 in the Transvaal, 10,242 in the Cape and 253 in the Orange Free State.[4]

Numerous restrictions were placed on Indians, wherever they settled. The most severe were imposed in the Orange Free State, which had the effect of closing off the Afrikaner republic to Indians except for a handful who remained in menial jobs. An 1885 law denied Indians the right to buy or rent property there. Five years later, Indians were not permitted to settle in the Free State for longer than two months without permission or to pursue business of any kind.[5] In the Transvaal, Law 3 (1885) denied Indians citizenship rights and the right to own property, except in special areas to be set aside for them. A registration fee of £25 (later reduced to £3) had to be paid by all Indians.[6]

Indentured laborers, who had left India mainly to escape poverty, found themselves captives within a system that was open to abuse by employers. Bound by contract, they lacked the freedom to negotiate better working and living conditions. Following the grant of responsible government to Natal in 1893, the white settler government enacted a series of anti-Indian acts. A £3 tax was imposed on all formerly indentured Indians to discourage the growth of a free Indian population, to maintain the indentured laborer in a permanent state of bondage or to encourage his return to India under the free passage provided by the law. In addition, Indians were deprived of the franchise. The growth of the Indian trader class was inhibited by a strict licensing policy and by immigration legislation that required a literacy test in a European language.[7]

As Indian commercial interests became the target of white hostility in Natal and the two Afrikaner republics, Indian political activity was stimulated. This began in the form of petitions to the British and Indian governments by various committees. Ultimately, a formal political organization, the Natal Indian Congress (NIC) was launched in 1894. At the end of that year, the NIC had 222 members, the main group consisting of merchants and a smaller group consisting of clerical workers.[8] Its organizing secretary was Mohandas Gandhi, a lawyer who had first come to Natal in 1893 to assist an Indian firm in a legal matter, whose legal training and proficiency in both Gujerati and English were invaluable to the NIC.

The idea of putting out an Indian newspaper was first discussed in 1896 and 1897 by the NIC and its supporters. Such a newspaper, it was hoped, would develop better relations between whites and Indians, provide information about India and Indians and investigate the grievances of Indians in colonial South Africa. But Gandhi was not able to purchase the special type faces needed to print in the various Indian languages or find suitable technical personnel when he visited India in 1896.[9]

The first Indian newspaper in South Africa was actually published by P. S. Aiyar, a journalist from Madras who had settled in Natal. An initial attempt in 1898 to establish a newspaper entitled the *Indian World* was unsuccessful,[10] but in May 1901 the first issue of the *Colonial Indian News* was published from Pietermaritzburg. Initially it appeared only in English, but by August news stories were also being produced in Tamil. The *Colonial Indian News*, in its early issues,[11] reflected the interests of formerly indentured and colonial-born Indians. It provided Natal with parliamentary news and also focused on educational issues as well as Indian labor issues. Information about the prices of market vegetables, for example, was a regular feature. Tamil general dealers, fruit and vegetable dealers and others such as tailors in Pietermaritzburg and Durban advertised their services. A few wealthy Muslim merchants, such as Amod Bayat and M. C. Anglia, also bought advertising space. This early effort at publishing was a modest one: a single issue often consisted of only four pages: two pages of advertisements, one English news page and one Tamil news page. After two years it began to appear irregularly, and it seems to have closed in 1903, possibly owing to limited readership and financial difficulties.[12]

The effort to establish *Indian Opinion* must be placed against the background of a revitalization of Indian politics in South Africa after 1902. When the NIC's constitutional protests failed to prevent most of the discriminatory legislation of the 1890s, its political activity declined. Only a handful of individuals was involved in NIC activities by 1900, and Gandhi returned to India in the following year.[13] A new phase of political activity, however, opened in the wake of the South African War (1899–1902).

The Afrikaner republics were now brought under British rule, and this gave hope to British Indians. In the years leading up to the war, the British government, through its high commissioner in South Africa, Lord Alfred Milner, and the British agent in the South African Republic (Transvaal), W. Conyngham-Greene, took up the cause of British Indians and succeeded in preventing the Afrikaner government from implementing its laws restricting Indian trade and residence. British Indians, then, expected vastly improved conditions when British colonial rule was established in the Transvaal. Once it became a Crown colony, however, Milner's primary objective was to resuscitate the gold-mining industry and gain the support of local whites. Undoing the former republic's anti-Indian laws would have earned him the hostility of whites who were organizing themselves into vigilante groups against Indian competition. During the war, many Transvaal Indians had moved to Natal or to India, but with the conclusion of hostilities they began to pour back into the Transvaal. The British reacted by making conditions for reentry difficult. In addition, they began to implement the former republic's law to segregate Indians in locations.[14]

In December 1902, Joseph Chamberlain, the British colonial secretary, visited South Africa. This provided Indians with the opportunity to put forward the case for a more liberal policy in the Transvaal. Indian politicians calculated that if they were successful in the Transvaal, a liberal order might eventually also spread to Natal.

Thus the Transvaal became the center of Indian political activity. Gandhi returned to South Africa in 1902 and made Johannesburg his base. The British Indian Association (BIA) was established in 1903 as the main political organization and soon found itself working to prevent new restrictions on Indians. On 8 April 1903, the new Transvaal government indicated its commitment to segregating Indian shopkeepers into bazaars, and in Natal there were tendencies toward a similar program. The need for an Indian newspaper to publicize these issues became urgent.

Establishing *Indian Opinion*

Three individuals were closely involved in founding *Indian Opinion*. Madanjit Viyavaharik, a former Bombay school teacher, was the owner of the International Printing Press in Grey Street, Durban. The press had been established in 1898 with some encouragement from Gandhi.[15] It undertook the printing of wedding cards, visiting cards, business cards, letterheads, circulars, receipt books, delivery books and other orders such as bookbinding and the production of rubber stamps.[16]

Madanjit was to be *Indian Opinion*'s proprietor, and the first references to *Indian Opinion* speak of the newspaper as "Madanjit's paper."[17] His task was to secure a publishing license, get the necessary type faces to print in Hindi, Gujerati and Tamil as well as English, secure the support of prominent Indian merchants and traders, sell advertising space and solicit customers.[18]

Mansukhlal Hiralal Nazar, who was associated with the newspaper from its planning stages, was the joint secretary of the NIC. He was originally from Surat, India, and had gone to London with his brothers to establish a business. From there he came to Natal in 1896, where he took an active role in the NIC. He had an office in Mercury Lane, Durban, from which he conducted business as an agent for other commercial firms.[19] The correspondence between Nazar and Gandhi[20] indicates that Nazar did all the worrying and planning. He defined the objectives of the newspaper and isolated the subjects to be covered in the first issue. He also supervised the translation of articles into the Indian languages. Nazar spent almost a month planning articles, discarding and rearranging them for the first issue of the newspaper.

Although Nazar was sophisticated, politically astute and quite knowledgeable about current news topics, he relied on Gandhi, who was still in Johannesburg, to do most of the serious writing. Since the 1890s, Gandhi had become adept at drawing up memorandums and petitions. He had also written prolifically to newspapers, both in India and South Africa, about issues affecting Indians in South Africa.[21] Reflecting some anxiety about his dependence on Gandhi to write for *Indian Opinion*, Nazar initially suggested the subjects of several leading articles to him but later wrote him a letter stressing that news topics should come "*from you*."[22]

The production of *Indian Opinion* was difficult in the beginning. The special types required for each of the three Indian languages made the enterprise expensive. Nazar, for instance, was told by the Gujerati compositor not to use too many words with the Gujerati letter *a*, because stock was limited.[23] The editor, who was not literate in Tamil, had to explain the spirit of the English articles to translators who were not wholly proficient in English.[24] It was also important to get Gandhi to send his articles in time for the translators and typesetters to meet edition deadlines. Nazar urged Gandhi to send in material "early" and warned: "if the matter is not in hand at the right time, the men in the press may revolt."[25]

The staff worked well into the night for several days to produce the first issue of *Indian Opinion*, dated 4 June 1903 but only made available to the public two days later.[26] A single issue sold for 3d. A yearly subscription was available to readers in Natal for 12s. 6d. and to readers outside Natal for 17s.

Nazar, who refused any money for his work as editor, told Gandhi the first issue should state very clearly that *Indian Opinion* was being published "for a *cause*, not for profit." He believed each issue of the newspaper should contain an account of disabilities that British Indians endured in South Africa.[27] The policy of the newspaper, Madanjit declared on the first page of *Indian Opinion*, was to advocate "the cause of British Indians in this subcontinent." Although it would focus on the rights that Indians should have, it aimed also "to bring about a proper understanding" between the Indian and white communities. Indians needed to be educated about their own failings, and whites needed the veil of prejudice and ignorance to be lifted. The newspaper thus aimed to give whites "an idea of Indian thought and aspirations." Both groups, it was hoped, would find the newspaper useful as an "advertising medium."[28]

Gandhi perceived *Indian Opinion* as having an imperial objective.[29] The newspaper would inform whites about matters "which should not be ignored by true Imperialists."[30] The imperial ideal, Gandhi believed, embraced values such as justice, fairness, equality and liberty and was truly color-blind. The treatment of Indians in the colonies was an aberration that had to be rectified. To this end, *Indian Opinion* sought to popularize the proclamation of 1858, issued by Queen Victoria after the mutiny of Indian sepoys in 1857. This proclamation, which promised equality of treatment and opportunity to all British subjects irrespective of "race or creed," was "the Magna Charta of the British Indians."[31]

The objectives of *Indian Opinion* were couched in moderate terms to secure white approval. The editorial in the first issue noted that Indians suffered "undeserved and unjust" disabilities, but it emphasized "there is nothing in our programme but a desire to promote harmony and good will between the different sections of the *one* mighty Empire."[32] Later editorials declared: "We have unfailing faith in British Justice,"[33] and "We have abiding faith in the mercy of the Almighty God, and we have firm faith in the British Constitution."[34] It was by "well sustained continuous and temperate constitutional effort" that Indians should seek redress of their grievances, an editorial declared in 1904.[35]

Gandhi observed in 1905 that the newspaper "often tones down the feelings of the Indian community."[36] *Indian Opinion* published favorable comments on its efforts from prominent whites in Natal and the Transvaal. M. Chamney, who occupied the post of protector of Asiatics in the Transvaal, commended *Indian Opinion* for its "moderation" and "spirit of Loyalty."[37] One wonders whether Nazar and Gandhi had been aware of the fate of the African newspaper *Ipepa lo Hlanga*. Its publishers chose to suspend publication after incurring the wrath of the Natal government for articles deemed to be seditious and for giving the call "Vukani Bantu!" (Rise up, you people!).[38] Sir John Robinson, a former prime minister of Natal colony, advised Nazar to remain "*moderate* and dignified."[39]

Given Nazar and Gandhi's close ties to the Natal Indian Congress and the British Indian Association, it is understandable that *Indian Opinion*'s political objectives were closely linked to these organizations. NIC and BIA meetings, petitions and correspondence were often reproduced in *Indian Opinion*. Their strategy encompassed constitutional protest, primarily in the form of petitions to authorities and prominent people in the colonies, and in Britain and India. To this end, more than 500 complimentary copies of each issue of *Indian Opinion* were distributed in South Africa, India and Britain. The two Indian political organizations paid for the cost of distributing these complimentary copies,[40] but the journal soon found itself in serious financial difficulty. A radical restructuring of operations was necessary by 1904.

Founding of Phoenix Settlement

Indian Opinion proprietor Madanjit Viyavaharik was in the Transvaal in 1904 soliciting support for the newspaper, and he decided to stay there and do volunteer work in connection with an outbreak of plague. As someone was needed in Durban to manage the printing press and the newspaper, Gandhi offered the job to an Englishman named Albert West, whom he had met at a vegetarian restaurant in Johannesburg. West, originally from Louth in Lincolnshire, operated his own printing press in Johannesburg. He accepted the offer for a salary of £10 a month plus a share of any profits, but soon after arriving in Durban he found that the newspaper was in financial chaos and wrote to Gandhi: "The books are not in order. There are heavy arrears to be recovered, but one cannot make head or tail of them."[41]

Gandhi, with a flourishing law practice in Johannesburg,[42] had borne most of the newspaper's financial costs. But, as the editor noted, "the Paper continued octopus-like, to devour all it received and wanted more . . . Although this journal supplied a real want, what may be termed a commercial demand had yet to be created. In other words, the paper had not only to find its matter but its readers also."[43]

The newspaper had only 887 subscribers at the end of 1904.[44] Although Natal had a sizable Indian population, the vast majority were indentured workers. The literacy rate for the Indian population was 12.9 percent.[45] Subscribers were mainly traders and the very small group of professionals and clerks. Although there were some 25,000 Gujeratis in Natal and the other colonies,[46] *Indian Opinion* clearly reached only a small proportion of the Indian population.

The newspaper, moreover, made for rather dull reading. It chronicled grievances and published parliamentary debates, and the activities of Indian political organizations and news stories culled from other newspapers. The vernacular columns did contain reports of local social and cultural activities,[47] but in general entertainment and recreational activities were not a priority. Foreign news focused on India with an occasional reference to other international events. The fact that *Indian Opinion* was published in four languages further limited its potential audience: a Tamil speaker, for example, might be able to read only 25 percent of the newspaper.

If the list of paid subscribers was bound to be short, *Indian Opinion* could find revenue from selling advertising space. Madanjit advertised the services of his own printing press and urged fellow businessmen to advertise in *Indian Opinion.* One promotional advertisement noted, "Business Bad?" In that case, "Let people know you are in existence. You cannot expect to get business if you simply sit in your shop and wait for people to walk in and buy."[48] Businessmen, he said, would also benefit as advertisers in a newspaper that circulated throughout South Africa, England and India. Advertisements were translated, on request, into any of the Indian languages at no extra charge.[49] The proprietor also advertised for agents to sell advertising space.[50]

Some of the most prominent Indian commercial firms in Natal and the Transvaal did buy advertising space. White employers also advertised to secure Indian labor, and a shipping company advertised the departure dates for ships to India. But despite Madanjit's efforts, advertising sales could not carry the newspaper. Apart from the cost of printing, regular monthly salaries had to be budgeted for the staff of the printing press, who now numbered about 13.[51] The staff drew salaries that varied from £8 to £18 a month per person.[52]

The critical financial position of the newspaper required a drastic solution. Gandhi made his way to Durban in the latter half of 1904. As he boarded the train for the 24-hour trip to Durban, he was given a book to read by a Jewish journalist who had befriended him after initially seeing him at a vegetarian restaurant.

The friend was 22-year-old Henry Saloman Polak, and the book was John Ruskin's *Unto This Last.* Gandhi had recently pondered the value of farming, and the book reinforced this interest. He isolated three principles that Ruskin had highlighted:

1. That the good of the individual is contained in the good of all.
2. That a lawyer's work has the same value as the barber's inasmuch as all have the same right of earning their livelihood from their work.
3. That a life of labour, i.e. the life of the tiller of the soil and the handicraftsman, is the life worth living.[53]

These principles provided the key to saving *Indian Opinion.*

Gandhi's proposal was that the newspaper should be located on a farm, where all workers would labor in the press as well as cultivate the land. All would draw the same salary of £3 a month, with profits to be shared at the end of the year.[54] The benefits to management were clear, since the scheme relieved it of worrying about finding large sums of money every month to meet the payroll. There were three incentives to the workers: "an ideal to work for in the shape of *Indian Opinion;* perfectly healthy surroundings to live in, and an immediate prospect of earning a piece of land on the most advantageous terms; and a direct tangible interest and participation in the scheme."[55] Gandhi noted that this experiment "may mark a revolution in business methods."[56]

To put the plan into operation, Gandhi bought 100 acres of land in a rural setting for £1,000. The plot, 14 miles out of Durban, was to be called the Phoenix Settlement, after the nearby railway station. Madanjit did not approve of the plan to move the press to Phoenix, but by this time he was so indebted to Gandhi financially that he was only the nominal proprietor. Gandhi in fact had become the full owner of *Indian Opinion* by October 1904.[57] Madanjit soon sailed for India. A few years later he returned to publishing, putting out an English weekly entitled *United Burma* in Rangoon.[58]

Gandhi supervised the removal of the press to Phoenix. The first task was to build a structure to house it. Parsee Rustomjee, a wealthy merchant and Gandhi's friend, provided old, used corrugated iron sheets and other building materials. Indian carpenters and masons who had worked with Gandhi in the ambulance corps during the South African War constructed the press building. Within a month, it was erected. "Four wagons, with a span of sixteen oxen each, were lined up early in Grey Street," and by nightfall the 64 oxen and their drivers bearing the press had reached their destination. West bought an engine to power it, but he also built a printing machine that could be operated manually. The first number of *Indian Opinion* from Phoenix was issued on 24 December 1904.[59]

Once the press building was completed, houses for the settlers had to be built. Nazar, no doubt wishing to continue his own commercial interests in Durban, did not become a settler at Phoenix but retained his post as editor.[60] Only two members of the original *Indian Opinion* staff in Durban apparently received full salaries once the press was moved to Phoenix.[61] Three members of the original staff–Sam Govindswami Raju, Chhaganlal Gandhi and the Englishman West–settled in Phoenix. The settlers drew a monthly allowance of £3, expected a share of the profits and had the option of owning 2 acres of land at Phoenix.

Raju had first worked as a messenger for the railways and then as a "kitchen boy" for a white woman in Umkomaas on the southern coast of Natal. He then met

Madanjit and took a job with the International Printing Press. He was somewhat puzzled by Gandhi's new scheme: "He could understand a wage but not a share in profits, particularly when he believed that there were no profits."[62] But he could not say no to Gandhi, and the promise of land was no doubt a major incentive.

Chhaganlal was a nephew of Gandhi's from India, who had come to South Africa in 1903. He and West were to be the joint managers of the International Printing Press.[63] While at Phoenix, Chhaganlal looked after the Gujerati section of the newspaper, saw to the accounts, collected amounts due and visited the Durban office of the newspaper to secure advertisements as well as job-work for the press.[64] His brother Maganlal, who had come to South Africa with Gandhi in 1902 and then joined a relative to operate a store in Tongaat, gave up that business and also moved to Phoenix.[65] The brothers were joined by their wives and children, and Gandhi's wife and sons also settled there.

Apart from West, other whites also became settlers. They shared with Gandhi a faith in the British Empire, an interest in ethical, moral and religious issues, and a willingness to experiment in dietary changes and nature cure treatments. Several closed down their own commercial enterprises to join the Phoenix community. Herbert Kitchin, an electrical contractor who had met Gandhi in the ambulance corps in the South African War, edited the newspaper for a while after Nazar died in January 1906. Kitchin's relationship with the other settlers and with Gandhi became troubled throughout 1905 and 1906, although the specifics of the discord are not quite clear. He handed in his resignation in February 1906 and eventually left the settlement later that year, because he disagreed with Gandhi on the adoption of passive resistance as a strategy.[66]

Polak resigned his position as journalist for the *Transvaal Critic* to work for Gandhi. He and his wife became settlers for awhile, but from 1906 he was based essentially in Johannesburg, where he served his articles in Gandhi's office and was admitted as an attorney of the Supreme Court.[67] Polak became editor of the newspaper after Kitchin resigned, and he held this post until 1916.[68] Other white settlers also stayed for short periods. These included A. J. Bean, about whom not much is known except that he was one of the first settlers, and John Cordes, a German who had been in Rhodesia for some time and joined the scheme in 1907. He left the settlement three years later.[69] West apparently lived longer at Phoenix than any other white settler during the Gandhi era.

Although Gandhi was the full owner of *Indian Opinion* and Phoenix, he stayed there only occasionally. He maintained Johannesburg as his base of operations, from which he monitored everyday activities in Phoenix. Gandhi wished, as he once noted, to be informed about everything that happened in the settlement: "Changes like recruitment, dismissal, etc., must not be made without my approval."[70] After Nazar's death, Chhaganlal even sent Gandhi all the letters to the editor, until Gandhi issued some general guidelines on publishing letters.[71]

As Gandhi and Polak shared the same office and for some time even the same house, they worked closely to produce articles for *Indian Opinion*. It is likely that the editors wrote many editorials, but Gandhi also wrote editorials and was a regular contributor to the Gujerati section.[72]

Although there was a division of labor in the press, all the settlers were expected to try their hands at composing.[73] On the night before the newspaper was issued, most settlers stayed awake and helped print and bundle copies that had to be posted. A communal spirit developed as the home and workplace fused into one. As Polak's wife Millie recalled,

> It was indeed a busy and happy band of workers at the machine. Everyone seemed to feel a quiet excitement in getting the paper out to time, and however late we all worked, no one grumbled or felt aggrieved. Seldom were the last papers finished and folded before midnight and often much later. Then ... goodnights would be exchanged, and each would go his own way absolutely tired out, but content.[74]

A Restricted Vision

The settlers at Phoenix could see a few huts occupied by Africans in the near distance and often heard the voices of Africans making their way to and from the railway station.[75] Just over a mile or so away was another settlement built around John Dube's Ohlange Institute (founded in 1901). Dube, the editor of *Ilanga lase Natal,* ran an industrial school modeled on Booker T. Washington's Tuskegee Institute, and there was some contact between the two settlements.[76]

The objectives of *Indian Opinion* and Phoenix Settlement clearly underlined the importance of closer relations between white and Indian, and Gandhi succeeded in drawing around him a band of loyal white supporters, but his political vision was restricted when it came to Africans and Coloureds. Although there were a few Zulu laborers at Phoenix, no African became a settler. In 1906, Gandhi wrote to Chhaganlal: "I believe it would be better, in so far as it is possible to have Indians working with us instead of Kaffirs."[77]

Because Gandhi controlled *Indian Opinion* and the newspaper represented the interests of the NIC and the BIA, their political position with respect to other blacks is important in understanding the policy of the journal. One of the main emphases of Indian politics in this period was to protest against any legislation that sought to place Indians in the same category as Africans. Soon after it was founded, the NIC drew up a petition against the Natal government's plans to disenfranchise Indians. The NIC noted that "the Bill would rank the Indian lower than the rawest Native."[78] After spending three years in Natal, Gandhi observed:

> Ours is one continual struggle against a degradation sought to be inflicted upon us by the Europeans, who desire to degrade us to the level of the raw Kaffir whose occupation is hunting, and whose sole ambition is to collect a certain number of cattle to buy a wife with and, then, pass his life in indolence and nakedness.[79]

In 1906 he noted that "sharp distinctions ... undoubtedly exist between British Indians and the Kaffir races in South Africa."[80]

The NIC asked the Natal authorities to provide three entrances, instead of two, to segregated public buildings such as the Post Office, so that Indians could be separated from Africans.[81] When whites clamored for segregated facilities in the Transvaal, Gandhi asked that Indians be separated from Africans. In 1904, Gandhi complained about "this mixing of the Kaffirs with the Indians" in the Johannesburg location.[82] When Gandhi and other passive resisters were forced to wear prison clothes marked "N" for "Natives" and had to share prison cells with Africans during the *satyagraha* struggle in the Transvaal, he was very unhappy, although he regarded this as an opportunity to learn more about Africans.[83]

The policy of *Indian Opinion* reflected these separatist goals. An editorial in *Indian Opinion* admitted that it was not "within the purview of this journal" to advocate the cause of Africans and Coloureds.[84] A very blunt editorial in 1905, which could have been written by Nazar, lamented the fact that Indians and Africans had been classed together in a bill to control firearms:

Photo 6. Mohandas Karamchand Gandhi, founder of *Indian Opinion*, as a young man in 1906.

Photo 7. Madanjit Viyavaharik, first proprietor of *Indian Opinion* (1903–4).

Photo 8. Mansukhlal Hiralal Nazar, editor of *Indian Opinion* (1903–6).

Photo 9. Henry Saloman Polak, editor of *Indian Opinion* (1906–16).

Photo 10. Rev. Joseph J. Doke, acting editor of *Indian Opinion* when Polak was in India.

Photo 11. Albert H. West, joint manager of *Indian Opinion*.

Photo 12. Manilal Gandhi, longest-serving editor of *Indian Opinion* (1918–56).

> Evidently the framers of the Bill have associated the Asiatics almost instinctively with the Natives, and it is that attitude of mind against which we have always firmly and respectfully protested . . . justice will never be done to the Asiatic unless he is treated as apart from the Native. The Native question is a big question in South Africa. The Native population is very large. The Native civilization is totally different from the Asiatic or the European. The Native, being the son of the soil, has the right to fair treatment, but being what he is, perhaps some legislation, which may be of a restrictive character, is necessary.[85]

Indian Opinion's attempts to understand black resistance were quite limited. On the Bambatha Rebellion of 1906, for example, the newspaper commented: "It is not for us to say whether the revolt of the Kaffirs is justified or not. We are in Natal by virtue of British power. Our very existence depends upon it. It is therefore our duty to render whatever help we can."[86] Gandhi and others organized a volunteer corps to aid the Natal government. White settlers, who were outnumbered by Indians in Natal,[87] feared Indian dominance, and this effort would demonstrate Indian loyalty and a willingness to do their share of work for the empire.

Although *Indian Opinion* shied away from making common cause with other blacks, the newspaper did carry articles on the grievances of Africans and Coloureds. Some of these grievances Indians shared, such as the footpath regulations (which prohibited all blacks from walking on the pavements) or discrimination on the trains. When an African named Magato was ejected from the first-class coach of a train, *Indian Opinion* devoted one and a half pages to the incident.[88] A landmark judicial decision in the Transvaal recognizing the right of Africans to purchase land there received much publicity and comment.[89] When white teachers in the Cape tried to exclude African and Coloured teachers from their teachers' association, an item on this from *Imvo Zabantzundu* was reprinted.[90] *Indian Opinion* called Walter Rubusana's election to the Cape Provincial Council in 1910, shortly after the four colonies became the Union of South Africa, "an event of great importance." The newspaper also commented that it was a great "anomaly" that blacks like Rubusana could not sit in the South African parliament.[91]

The activities of Dr. Abdurahman's African Political Organization (founded in 1902) and its newspaper *APO* (founded in 1909) were news items in *Indian Opinion.*[92] An extract from Dube's speech as the first president of the South African Native National Congress (founded in 1912) was also printed in the newspaper.[93] The resistance of African women in the Orange Free State against the pass laws in 1913 received front-page coverage.[94] The passage of the Land Act of 1913, which initially relegated only 7.1 percent of South Africa's land to Africans, was regarded as a serious "act of confiscation."[95]

African accomplishments were also commented on in *Indian Opinion*, particularly when Indians could learn from these examples. Shortly before Phoenix was purchased by Gandhi, an article on missionary activities at Mariannhill (a Roman Catholic monastery run by the Trappist order) near Pinetown was published in *Indian Opinion.* Here Africans were trained to become printers, blacksmiths, carpenters, saddlers and shoemakers.[96] *Indian Opinion* praised the ideals of Booker T. Washington and Dube, who was described as "our friend and neighbor" and was commended for his work at Ohlange.[97] An article from *Ilanga lase Natal* that sermonized about the value of manual labor, in particular cultivation of the land, was reprinted. The editor of *Indian Opinion* advised that colonial-born Indians, who were moving from the countryside to the towns in search of desk jobs, would be better advised to remain on the land and work with their hands.[98]

War on Women

Photo 13. Publicizing the cause of the resisters and their families in *Indian Opinion*.

Although Gandhi's autobiographical recollections reveal nothing about his contact with African elites (and considerable ignorance about Africans in general),[99] articles in *Indian Opinion* suggested some knowledge of their activities. As Gandhi became more enamored with embracing poverty and glorified the value of manual work, he wrote from Tolstoy Farm, the communal settlement he established in 1909 outside Johannesburg, "I regard the Kaffirs, with whom I constantly work these days, as superior to us. What they do in their ignorance we have to do knowingly, in outward appearance we should look just like the Kaffirs."[100] He explained his preference for traveling third class on trains as a desire to experience some of the hardships that Africans endured.[101]

Despite these statements, Gandhi remained firmly convinced that Indians had nothing to gain from a broader alliance with other black organizations. When W. P. Schreiner led a joint African and Coloured deputation to London in 1909 to protest the draft bill to establish the Union of South Africa, Gandhi also led an Indian deputation to the imperial capital. The Indians, however, were concerned only with matters related to the *satyagraha* struggle. Although Gandhi had some contact with Schreiner and Abdurahman and sympathized with the deputation's cause, the interests of the Indian deputation were pursued separately.[102]

Gandhi argued that the different black communities could "give strength to the other in urging their common rights,"[103] but in several articles in *Indian Opinion* he explained his aversion to any formal alliances. He recognized that blacks shared many common grievances with Indians, but he felt their political paths had to be different. Although Gandhi certainly had ethnocentric biases, the reasons he advanced for maintaining separate political identities were strategic. Africans, he argued, had "a better right" to South Africa than the newly arrived Indian settlers because this was their mother country. Whereas Africans and Coloureds asked for political rights, Indians could not even aspire to make these demands, as their "civil rights are so insecure that all their energies must of necessity be devoted to conserving or seeking to acquire them." If Indians wished to improve their *political* position, they had to rely on appeals to the British secretary of state for India and base their claims to equal treatment on the promise of Queen Victoria's proclamation of 1858.[104] This restricted vision, solidly rooted in what was deemed to be in the best political interests of an insecure minority group, remained the policy of *Indian Opinion* for more than a generation.

Elitism, Community and National Identity

Indians in South Africa constituted quite a heterogeneous group. Gandhi referred to "religious antagonisms" (among Hindus, Muslims, Christians and Parsis), "provincial distinctions" (among Bengalis, Madrasis, Gujeratis, Punjabis and others), and caste distinctions (among Brahmins, Kshatriyas, Vaishyas and Shudras).[105] Although he did not refer to class distinctions, these were implicit in the articles and news reports. By and large the Indian merchant came from the western coast of India, was Muslim and spoke Gujerati. Two-thirds of the indentured laborers came from the south of India and spoke Tamil. The rest came from districts in northeastern India and spoke Hindi (or related dialects such as Bhojpuri) and Urdu. The majority of workers were Hindu. Gandhi observed that "Indians from Bombay are often rude to those hailing from Calcutta and Madras and indifferent to their feelings. The term *colcha* [coolie] has still not gone out of use in our language." The Indians who came from India, Gandhi noted, also had a low regard for the colonial-born Indian.[106]

The editor boldly declared in *Indian Opinion*'s first year of publication: "We are not, and ought not to be, Tamils or Calcutta men, Mohamedans or Hindus, Brahmans or Banyas, but simply and solely British Indians."[107] In 1906 Gandhi said that perhaps the main purpose of *Indian Opinion* was to work to remove these distinctions.[108] The newspaper was printed in three Indian languages to avoid charges of sectionalism, and it covered news about Indians in South Africa's other British colonies in the hope of forging a common identity. Unity among Indians became even more important as the Union of South Africa loomed. *Indian Opinion* focused on the idea of "one community" that was determined to defend its "national honour."[109]

Nevertheless, *Indian Opinion*'s ideal of serving all Indians equally was difficult to achieve in practice. From the beginning, production of the Hindi and Tamil columns had been a considerable burden. Neither the management nor Gandhi knew Tamil, and in January 1906, when a Tamil member of staff named Pillay resigned, a decision was taken to discontinue the Tamil and Hindi sections. It was too difficult to find suitable compositors and editors who were fluent in these languages.[110]

Gandhi regretted the decision and tried to master the Tamil language himself so that one day the columns might be resumed. Meanwhile, the number of Gujerati pages increased dramatically. An edition of 28 pages in 1905 had 10 pages of advertisements; 3 news pages each, in Tamil and Hindi; 5 in Gujerati; and 7 in English. An edition in 1906 had 12 pages in Gujerati and up to 8 pages in the English section. Thus *Indian Opinion* had little appeal for Tamil and Hindi speakers. Colonial-born Indians who could read English were also not attracted to buy the newspaper. Joseph Royeppen, a barrister who had qualified in England and was a descendant of indentured workers, explained to Gandhi in 1912 why the newspaper had failed the youth. His letter is indicative of what colonial-born Indians thought about the newspaper at the time: "As it is I hardly ever see a boy with *Indian Opinion* in his hand simply because there is nothing specially for him there to raise his curiosity, interest or criticism. He only knows that 20 out of 24 pages are Gujerati and he wants to know what all that Gujerati stuff is about!"[111]

The problem with *Indian Opinion* was that its founders were motivated by a distinct sense of purpose that had little consideration for what readers might want. Colonial-born Indians were beginning to seek their own identity independently of the NIC through a variety of organizations, including the Natal Indian Patriotic Union (NIPU, founded in 1908), the Colonial Born Indian Association (CBIA, founded in 1911), and the South African Indian Committee (founded in 1911). P. S. Aiyar, who was a founding official of both the NIPU and the Indian Committee, began a Tamil-English weekly, the *African Chronicle*, in 1908. A Tamil reader wrote that *African Chronicle* satisfied "a long felt want" and was welcomed by "Indian farmers, hawkers and fruiterers."[112] The *African Chronicle* carried much news about sports and social activities. It included a regular column on education and physical culture, a column on humor and for a while a special column for women.

Historian Jay Naidoo has observed that Gandhi's "bias by upbringing, tradition and culture was with the trader class."[113] This is equally true of Nazar, Chhaganlal and Maganlal Gandhi. Maureen Swan argues that at least until 1906 Gandhi was "simply a representative of the merchant class."[114] *Indian Opinion*, then, was largely a newspaper written by an elite for an elite, which was mainly the Gujerati commercial class. This elite bias was sometimes presented in ways that contrasted sharply with the ideal of "one community," especially in the early years of the newspaper. In 1905 the editor lamented that all Indians were "classed indiscriminately [by whites] as 'Coolies' or 'Arabs.' " There were in fact, two main classes, the editor noted, the trading class and the indentured laborers, who were of "low caste."[115]

But *Indian Opinion* did comment about the plight of indentured laborers. The annual report of the Protector of Indian Immigrants, an official whose duty was to see to the welfare of indentured workers, was always given publicity, and *Indian Opinion* from time to time took this official to task for failing to do his job.[116] The newspaper reported numerous cases of workers being ill-treated by their employers and having no recourse to justice. An editorial asked, "Is *all* well on the estates?"[117] The editor demanded an investigation into the high suicide rate among indentured workers, "which was a public scandal of first class dimensions."[118]

Indian Opinion finally initiated a campaign to bring the immigration of indentured laborers to an end, as it was an "evil" system.[119] The editor noted: "No attempt is made to raise the poor Indian in the scale of civic life. They are used more like beasts of burden, to be got rid of as soon as they are unfit for work ... and they are called upon to pay, as the price of their freedom, an annual tax of three pounds."[120] In 1907, the editor concluded in a strongly worded editorial exposing the inhumanity of the system, "One thing is certain – the indenture system must be ended; there is no possibility of mending it. We call upon all humane men and women to join in the crusade against a system that extorts so gruesome a toll from its wretched victims, and that threatens to undermine the moral fabric of the whole Colony. This is a national work."[121] Four years later, in 1911, after Polak had done much lobbying in India, the campaign bore results, and it was front-page news in *Indian Opinion*: "Thank God! Indentured Labour to be stopped in July."[122]

On closer analysis, however, the anti–indentured worker campaign reveals how important the issue was to elite interests. As Gandhi explained, "Natal cannot be allowed to draw upon India for a supply of indentured labour when she refuses to treat the resident Indian population with justice and decency."[123] When the Indian government refused Milner's request for Indian labor for the Transvaal after the South African War, *Indian Opinion* applauded the decision. "And why should the Indian Government go out of its way to accommodate a government which is callous in all ideas of justice in treating the resident Indian population with fairness?"[124] Indentured labor could be used as a bargaining chip to improve the position of the Indian elite in South Africa.

The main cause for the growing anti-Indian feeling among white settlers in Natal was their fear of being overwhelmed by Indians. If large-scale immigration were terminated, according to *Indian Opinion*, the population ratios would be in rough balance, "and there would be hardly any opposition to the Indian trader, or to Indian enterprise in general."[125] Thus Gandhi explained to Gujerati readers how the fates of indentured laborers and free Indians were linked. The system exploited the indentured, and its ending would lead to "an immediate improvement in the condition of Indians now settled in South Africa."[126]

The *African Chronicle* did not campaign for the termination of indentured immigration, arguing that it was more important to see that workers were not ill-treated.[127] From 1908 onwards, through the NIPU, colonial-borns had protested the £3 tax that was a special burden to former indentured workers. In 1911 the *African Chronicle* launched a vigorous campaign for the abolition of this tax. The NIC and Gandhi responded.[128] Gandhi had noted in 1905 that the tax was a grave injustice but added, "one has to reconcile oneself to the situation."[129] He had shifted his position by 1909 and was urging "the business community" to agitate for the abolition of the £3 tax.[130] Polak and Maganlal Gandhi attended meetings held by the NIPU, and on one such occasion in 1908 Polak argued that those affected should embark on passive resistance and not pay the tax.[131] But it was not until 1913 that Gandhi adopted the £3 tax as a political issue. This belated action was to have a dramatic impact on the *satyagraha* struggle that had begun in the Transvaal in 1906.

Mobilizing Resisters

In 1906 the Transvaal government passed the Asiatic Law Amendment Ordinance, but this was disallowed by the British government after organized protests by the

BIA and by a deputation to London. In 1907, the Transvaal received self-government and reenacted the 1906 ordinance. This time the British government (which in theory could still disallow the measure but in practice rarely intervened to block the legislative efforts of self-governing colonies) gave its assent.

Act 2 (1907) provided that all Asians in the Transvaal–men, women and children more than 8 years of age–had to take out certificates of registration. They had to supply their full details of residence and occupation and give their finger and thumb impressions. The certificate had to be carried at all times, and failure to comply with this pass law could result in a fine, a term of imprisonment or deportation.

In September 1906 the BIA resolved it would never submit to such legislation. Members took an oath in the name of God to resist the law if passed. When the legislation became effective in July 1907, the resistance campaign began, and it lasted seven years. The movement broadened to incorporate additional issues during these years. The Immigration Restriction Act of 1907 in the Transvaal, which sought to exclude new Indian immigrants (even those who could pass the education test) was taken up in 1908. Two new issues were raised in 1913, when the South African government refused to recognize marriages solemnized according to Indian rites and refused to honor its promise (in 1912) to repeal the £3 tax.[132]

The number of resisters was subject to considerable flux during this seven-year campaign. Between July and November 1907, when the objective was to defeat the registration of Indians, there was overwhelming support. Only 545 Indians registered out of the eligible 7,000. In November the first arrests were made, and by the end of January 1908 some 2,000 Indians as well as Chinese[133] had been jailed.

The campaign resumed in August 1908 (after negotiations with the government failed), and an attempt was made to expand the struggle beyond the Transvaal. But only 13 Indians from Natal responded to the call to challenge Transvaal's immigration laws. By the end of 1908, some 1,500 sentences had been passed on Transvaal Indians–mainly hawkers–who continued to refuse to register. When the government began to auction the goods of traders to settle their fines and deport resisters to India, support for the campaign dwindled. Only 100 dedicated resisters were left by 1910. In fact, 97 percent of those eligible to register had done so by 1909.[134]

The battle was resumed again in 1913 as women and workers responded to the Indian marriage and the £3 tax issues and became resisters. As more than 65 percent of the Indian work force in Natal were under second or third terms of indenture, no doubt because of an inability to pay the tax, the movement found its mass following. By the end of October 1913, between 4,000 and 5,000 northern Natal coal miners were on strike, and they were joined by 15,000 workers from the Natal coastal sugar estates. Gandhi led at least 2,000 men, women and children on a march from the town of Newcastle toward the Transvaal.

The passive resistance leaders were arrested and imprisoned. There was chaos in Natal as the strike brought industries and farm operations to a standstill. The coal mine compounds were turned into jails for the striking workers, and mounted police assaulted and drove workers on the sugar estates back to work. As news of police brutality spread, the viceroy of India protested against the South African government's handling of the situation. The campaign was suspended in January 1914 as the South African government and Gandhi began to negotiate a settlement. The £3 tax was then abolished and Indian marriages recognized.[135]

Although Gandhi became the chief director of the movement and its chief resister, all the staff of *Indian Opinion* were closely involved in these activities. Polak was not only editor of the newspaper, but from 1906 he was also the assistant secretary of the BIA. Once he was admitted as an attorney of the Transvaal Supreme Court in 1908, he represented the resisters in court. When the movement was in dire financial straits in 1909, Polak traveled to India to raise the funds that saved both the movement and *Indian Opinion.*[136] Polak also published a book in India on the grievances of Indians in South Africa.[137] He made another journey to India in 1911–12, addressing mass meetings in every major center to arouse public opinion in support of the struggle in South Africa.[138] On the eve of leaving for a third trip to India in November 1913, Polak discussed the situation with Gandhi, who was then leading the Natal workers' march into the Transvaal. Polak became involved in the march and was subsequently arrested. He told the court he was "an Englishman, a Jew, and a member of the legal profession," and he could not simply watch while Indians suffered injustices.[139]

During Polak's absence in India, Rev. Joseph Doke served as acting editor. Doke, originally from Chudleigh in Devonshire, had come out to the Cape as a Baptist minister. In 1907 he moved from Grahamstown, where he had spent the previous four years, to Johannesburg and soon established contact with Gandhi. In 1908 he rescued and nursed Gandhi after the latter had been attacked by an angry Indian who opposed Gandhi's compromise settlement with the government. Doke wrote the first biography of Gandhi, and this was published in 1909. It helped to give publicity both to Gandhi and the *satyagraha* struggle.[140] Both Doke and Polak served on a committee that was formed in 1908 by whites who supported the resisters.[141]

When Gandhi moved from Johannesburg to Phoenix in early 1913, the staff of *Indian Opinion* and the Phoenix settlers became more directly involved in the struggle. Kasturba, Kashiben and Santokben, the wives of Gandhi and his nephews Chhaganlal and Maganlal, respectively, became women *satyagrahis* and went to prison. Chhaganlal himself became a resister, while West and Maganlal were left to run *Indian Opinion.*[142]

Indentured workers descended on Phoenix from the surrounding sugar estates, once the strike spread. Some of them had been flogged by angry managers. West, who was acting editor, was arrested for harboring these workers. *Indian Opinion* publicized the case of Soorzai, a worker who died after such a beating. West became personally involved in this case and took the manager of the Phoenix Wattle Estates (for whom Soorzai had worked) to court for threatening him.[143] Maganlal Gandhi, who was one of the few adults left at Phoenix, ensured that stories were written and the newspaper printed and distributed. He also took on the burden of looking after the children of the *satyagrahis* who remained at the settlement.[144]

Indian Opinion played a very significant role throughout the course of the passive resistance campaign. At one level, it highlighted the major issues, chronicled the activities of the resisters, and brought Indian grievances to the notice of influential people in Britain and India. At another level, it became an active agent in mobilizing and organizing resistance.

As soon as Gandhi read the draft ordinance providing for registration in 1906, he translated it into Gujerati, and this translation was printed in *Indian Opinion.*[145] From then on, the newspaper urged its readers to resist the law. The editor gave the call "To the Gaol!" once the law received imperial assent in 1907.[146] Editorials asserted that resistance was "bravery" and "a duty." Although resistance involved "self-sacrifice," it also meant retaining "self-respect." Avoiding imprisonment would be an act of cowardice, entail loss of honor and "be a sin against God," since Indians had taken a pledge in 1906 to resist the law.[147]

In a regular column he wrote from Johannesburg, Gandhi urged his readers: "The more we suffer, the earlier we shall be free."[148] When Indian marriages became an issue, *Indian Opinion* declared that the matter "demands, on the part of the Indians, sacrifice of their all–their businesses, their money, their ease." They must prepare to become "once more His Majesty's guests in his gaols in South Africa."[149] Editorials in 1913 also called for resistance against the £3 tax, "The Blood Money."[150]

A poem by Narmadashankar, a Gujerati poet in India, was printed in May 1907 to encourage readers to resist:

> Forward ye all to battle, the bugles sound
> Raise the cry and take the plunge, for victory's around.
> By plunging in and savouring success is strength found.
> Raise the cry and take the plunge, for victory's around.

The poet referred to acts such as Columbus's discovery of the New World and Martin Luther's defiance of the Roman Catholic Church as examples of courage.[151] Another poem sought to convince readers that although one could regain lost wealth, loss of honor could never be recovered. Cowardice would bring eternal disgrace.[152]

Indian Opinion offered numerous examples to its readers of contemporary passive resistance outside the Indian community. One of the earliest editorials on the subject referred to the ongoing passive resistance of the Nonconformist churches in England against a government tax.[153] The English suffragette movement was also cited in Gandhi's column: "The more they are repressed, the more resistance they offer. Many of them have been to Gaol. They have borne being kicked and stoned by base and cowardly men."[154] Closer to home, Gandhi commented on a white miners' strike in the Transvaal in 1907: "for the sake of what they believe to be their right, they have girded up their loins against the authorities and the fabulously rich mine-owners ... it is their spirit and daring that we are to think of and emulate."[155] In 1913, when the *satyagraha* campaign sought the inclusion of Indian women as resisters, the front page of *Indian Opinion* hailed "Native Women's Brave Stand" against the pass laws in the Orange Free State.[156]

Gandhi also cited role models from Western antiquity. He translated Plato's life of Socrates into Gujerati, and this was serialized in *Indian Opinion* in 1908. Socrates was hailed as a "Soldier of Truth," who remained steadfast throughout his trial by Athenian officials and chose death as the most honorable option.[157] Gandhi also drew on the ancient Hindu epic, the *Ramayana*. The hero Rama (representing good) first sent a messenger, Angada, on a peace mission to the evil Ravana before declaring war on him. Ravana was thus given the opportunity of doing the right thing: "What Rama did with Ravana, the Indian community has done with the Transvaal Government ... However much Angada [the BIA] tried, he could not make Ravana understand. And in the end, Ravana was defeated because he was in the wrong."[158]

James Hunt has suggested that Gandhi "sought to reinforce the Indian community by building a spiritual community of legitimizing authorities for their unusual course of action."[159] To this end, extracts from the works of the New England transcendentalist Henry David Thoreau, the Russian author Leo Tolstoy, the Italian nationalist Joseph Mazzini and the American abolitionist William Lloyd Garrison were published in *Indian Opinion.* These works emphasized the importance of fighting for the just cause.[160]

Thoreau's essay *On the Duty of Civil Disobedience* was quoted with approval for urging the citizenry to disregard the law if it conflicted with one's conscience and sense of what was right: "I think that we should be men first and subjects afterwards. It is not desirable to cultivate a respect for the law, so much as for the right... Under a government which imprisons any unjustly, the true place for a just man is also prison."[161] Mazzini's work *On the Duties of Man* provided a similar justification for breaking the law: "God is the sole lawgiver to the human race. His law is the sole law you are bound to obey. Human laws are only good and valid in so far as they conform to, explain, and apply the law of God. They are evil whensoever they contrast with or oppose it, it is then not only your right, but your duty to disobey and abolish them."[162]

Gandhi employed Thoreau's observation that "what is well done is done for ever," no matter how small the numbers involved,[163] to stress the virtues of individual commitment to his readers: "In satyagraha, the victory of a single member may be taken to mean the victory of all, but the defeat of the side as a whole does not spell defeat for the person who has not himself yielded. For instance, in the Transvaal fight, even if a majority of Indians were to submit to the obnoxious Act, he who remains unyielding will be victorious indeed, for the fact remains that he has not yielded."[164]

Indian Opinion also sought to involve its readers in the search for "legitimizing authorities." In June 1907 the newspaper offered a prize of £1 to the reader who submitted the best poem in Gujerati, Hindi or Urdu that would examine why Indians should remain committed to going to jail. The poem should give examples of courage.[165] A few months later, readers were invited to compete for a prize of £10 by submitting an essay on the subject of "The Ethics of Passive Resistance." The essay should draw on the works of Thoreau and Tolstoy and provide examples.[166] Gandhi became unhappy with the term "passive resistance," because it seemed to imply weakness, so he invited readers to invent a specifically Indian word. This competition yielded the word *satyagraha*, meaning "the force of truth," or "soulforce."[167]

Apart from educating readers about the ideology of the movement, the newspaper also provided practical assistance to resisters. They were told exactly what they would encounter once they became resisters and how they should respond. They were advised to tell the courts that they wished to go to jail, and they should not pay their fines. To give courage to the fainthearted, Gandhi ruled out the possibility of every Indian being arrested and jailed by the government.[168]

One tactic that *Indian Opinion* used to mobilize resisters, particularly in 1907 and 1908, was to reward acts of courage with publicity. Using combative language, the journal followed the progress of the Permit Office (nicknamed the "Plague Office"),[169] which traveled to different centers to register Indians. The names of resisters and volunteers who picketed the Permit Office were listed at length in *Indian Opinion.* To stir up some competition and also to illustrate widespread support for the campaign, resisters were listed by caste, religion and place of origin in India. For instance, *Indian Opinion* noted that among those arrested and given orders to leave the Transvaal were "4 Surti Mahomedans, 1 Memon Mahomedan, 2 Pathans, 3 Madrassis, 3 Bannias, 1 Lohana, 1 Brahman, 2 Desais, 1 Calcutta, 1 Parsi, 1 Punjabi, and 3 Chinese."[170]

Specific acts of courage were noted, as in the case of S. M. David, a court interpreter who was prepared to risk his government-paid job by not registering.[171] The first hero of the movement was Ram Sundar Pundit, a priest in Germiston who was the first to be arrested for not having a permit. He chose to go to jail rather than pay the fine.[172] Other prominent members of the Indian community who served several jail sentences and made financial sacrifices were Parsee Rustomjee, A. M. Cachalia, Sorabji Shapurji Adajania, Imam Abdul Kadir Bawazeer, Joseph Royeppen and C. K. T. Thambi Naidoo. The newspaper praised their efforts and published their photographs.[173]

Indian Opinion condemned collaborators. Those who applied for registration certificates, the "title-deed of slavery," were labeled "black sheep" or "blacklegs." Because they gave their finger and thumb impressions, they were also called "piano-players."[174] In addition, *Indian Opinion* exposed traders who arranged with the Permit Office to register secretly at night.[175] But those who repented were given the chance to apologize in the newspaper.[176]

Although Gandhi later regretted the coercive propaganda of the 1907–8 campaigns, he considered it necessary at that stage.[177] As his ideas on *satyagraha* became more refined, coercion ceased to be a feature in the newspaper. When merchants eventually deserted the movement, Gandhi simply noted in 1909, "In a tyrannical state, only those who subserve its purposes can be happy or grow prosperous." Those who accumulated wealth in these circumstances were "accomplices in ... tyranny."[178]

Gandhi continually wrote about his experiences in jail. Readers were told that they might have to perform hard labor and food would be restricted. There were no luxuries and comforts in jail, but Gandhi said "happiness and misery are states of the mind." He argued that while the "body is held in bondage ... the soul grows more free."[179] Gandhi eventually recognized that not all had the capacity to go to jail. Readers of *Indian Opinion* were informed that the special qualities of a *satyagrahi* were a love for the truth, fearlessness, a disregard for wealth, comforts and good food, a willingness to lessen family attachments and an overall trust in God.[180] As he prepared readers for the campaign in 1913, Gandhi suggested other ways they could support the movement. Money could be donated, meetings could be held and the government could be besieged with telegrams and letters. Those who remained out of jail could look after the interests of prisoners.[181]

According to Gandhi, "Satyagraha would probably have been impossible without *Indian Opinion*."[182] The newspaper did play an important role in the 1907 and 1908 campaigns. By October 1907 the Gujerati section had expanded from 12 to 16 pages.[183] The English columns explained why Indians were resisting, and they were directed at white readers. The Gujerati columns offered guidelines for resisters in the campaign and were less guarded. Gandhi's Gujerati column "Letter from Johannesburg" was longer than the English column giving news from Johannesburg. There was considerable demand for the newspaper in the Transvaal. Gandhi increased Transvaal's weekly order of 100 copies to 350 in 1907,[184] and *Indian Opinion*'s total subscriber list in that year climbed to 1,100.[185] Gandhi said that at the peak of the struggle (he did not give a date) the number of subscribers rose to 3,500,[186] but this represented only a small fraction of the newspaper's audience: "The paper generally reached Johannesburg on Sunday morning. I know of many, whose first occupation after they received the paper would be to read the Gujerati section through from beginning to end. One of the company would read it, and the rest would surround him and listen."[187] He estimated that for each subscriber there were at least 10 others who read the newspaper.[188]

Gujerati traders, according to Swan, supported the 1907 campaign because there was a sound "economic rationale" behind the movement's ideology. Gandhi emphasized that the government's registration plans would ruin the traders' vested interests. They withdrew their support for resistance in 1908, once the government linked the failure to register with the nonrenewal of trading licences.[189] Gandhi's subsequent appeals for resistance on moral grounds failed to mobilize this class in any significant way.

Although the number of Gujerati resisters dwindled, it was the Tamil community in the Transvaal (mainly hawkers) who became the backbone of the movement. *Indian Opinion* continued to provide detailed news in Gujerati but did not cater to a potential Tamil audience, despite Gandhi's efforts to learn the language. The *African Chronicle*, which supported Gandhi's passive resistance campaign in the Transvaal, helped by translating one of Gandhi's English speeches into Tamil in 1909 and sent copies to the BIA for distribution in the Transvaal.[190] It was only in December 1913 that *Indian Opinion* supplied news in Hindi and Tamil in recognition of the role these speakers had played in the struggle. And the effort lasted only four months.

The newspaper was only one element in the total strategy of mobilization. The BIA held mass meetings, and pickets who monitored the Permit Office ensured that the antiregistration drive of 1907 was effective. The band of *satyagrahis* who visited the coal mines and urged workers to strike served as the catalyst for workers on the sugar estates who went on strike in 1913. They were responding to years of hardship and economic frustration, not solely to the campaign against the £3 tax.

The newspaper's strategy of creating heroic figures sometimes backfired. Resister Ram Sundar, for example, could not face a second term in prison and deserted the movement by leaving the Transvaal. *Indian Opinion* demonized the hero Sundar as an example to readers: "We... need to retain the image of Ram Sundar before our eyes. With that image before us, we should pray constantly 'O Khuda-Ishwar, save us from Ram Sundar's fate... Keep us on the right path till the end.'"[191]

Other *satyagrahis* died in circumstances that could have frightened off potential resisters. Sammy Nagappan, aged 18, for example, died shortly after his discharge from prison.[192] A. Naryansamy was deported to India: he tried to return to South Africa but died on a ship after no port would allow him to disembark.[193] Valliamaha Moodaliar, aged 16, died after a prolonged illness in jail, where she had served three months with hard labor.[194]

Indian Opinion would not allow its readers to forget these resisters and held them up as perfect *satyagrahis*. In an editorial entitled "Legalised Murder," the newspaper cited Naryansamy's death as a model for others: "But there is a feeling of joy, too, for we feel that Naryansamy has died well. He has died as befits a true soldier–he has died fighting for the principles he held so dear."[195] As the newspaper emphasized the value of suffering, loss of wealth and even death, its capacity to mobilize resisters–particularly in 1909 and 1910–shrank. The newspaper did indeed serve the *satyagraha* struggle, but there were limits to its role as a mobilizer of public opinion.

Although *Indian Opinion* greeted the end of *satyagraha* on a positive note,[196] an alternative position was taken by its Indian rivals–*African Chronicle*, which (at least until 1911) had been supportive of Gandhi,[197] and a new Gujerati-English newspaper entitled *Indian Views*, which was launched by M. C. Anglia in Durban on 3 July 1914. Both newspapers were very critical of the limited settlement negotiated by Gandhi after seven years of struggle.[198] *Indian Opinion* thus reflected one point of view–Gandhi's view–and played a key role in portraying him as a successful leader.

Transformations

Gandhi emerged from the *satyagraha* experience a changed man. He had arrived in South Africa as a young barrister togged in the finest of Western attire. Not quite articulate and lacking confidence, he had become a sophisticated political organizer. His constituency was initially the commercial class, but by 1913 he had adopted the clothing of an Indian laborer–and he was undoubtedly the leader of a mass movement.

One recent biographer stresses the emergence of Gandhi as "a deeply religious man" whose inner world had been totally transformed. He had developed a vision of man "as a spiritual being created to find fulfillment in a lifelong pursuit of truth."[199] Out of his South African experiences, the outer shell of what became known as Gandhism had emerged. He had taken his vow of celibacy in 1906, experimented in diet and nature cure treatments, established two communal settlements at Phoenix and Tolstoy Farm and forged the *satyagraha* movement. In 1909 he had written *Indian Home Rule*, which was a critique of the materialistic values of Western civilization and a guide on how to win Indian independence.

Indian Opinion remained constant in its determination to advocate a cause and its devotion to achieving harmonious relations between white and Indian. But it started off as "Madanjit's paper" and ended up as "Gandhi's journal."[200] It was very anxious to secure white approval in the beginning, but within a few years it was advocating a special brand of resistance against white rule. It moved from simply advocating a cause to mobilizing resisters. It had always carried articles on religious, ethical and moral issues, but by 1910 the goal of morally uplifting its audience was a major credo.

Indian Opinion had been virtually dependent on the Indian commercial class for support in the beginning, but the newspaper gradually became more independent. This is reflected in its advertising policy. Financial stability was ignored as the *satyagraha* struggle progressed. The newspaper was saved in 1909 only after funds were raised in India.[201] Gandhi had stopped practicing as a lawyer by 1910 and had no regular source of income. At this stage, however, the newspaper announced that it would be very selective about the advertisements that it would accept. No advertisements for liquor, patent medicines or cigarettes or for anything that would "injure our fellows, both morally and physically" would be published. The printing press also stopped taking on job work from January 1910.[202] Finally in an extraordinary decision for a newspaper, *Indian Opinion* announced a ban on all advertisements in 1912.[203]

Gandhi explained that the staff of the press spent much time taking on job work and flattering advertisers who could be easily offended. The newspaper's objective was to increase its "capacity for public service."[204] Advertising space now was filled with books for sale at the International Printing Press, and many of these had been influential in the development of Gandhi's intellectual thought. *Indian Opinion* would rely henceforth on subscribers to pay its way. At the same time, the subscription fee was reduced in accordance with downsizing the newspaper after advertisements were dropped and mailing costs consequently lowered.[205]

Gandhi also relinquished his ownership of Phoenix Settlement and *Indian Opinion.* A new title deed in 1912 gave control of the settlement and the newspaper to a board of trustees.[206] Gandhi left for India in 1914, taking with him many Indian settlers from Phoenix. The task of continuing *Indian Opinion* was left to Polak, West and later Gandhi's son Manilal.[207] Gandhi's apprenticeship with *Indian Opinion*, however, would serve him well when new political journals (like *Young India, Navajivan* and *Harijan)*[208] were launched to advance his political goals in a bigger cause–the liberation of India.

Notes

1. The following discussion on indentured labor is drawn from J. B. Brain, "Indentured and free Indians in the economy of colonial Natal," in B. Guest and J. M. Sellers (eds.), *Enterprise and exploitation in a Victorian colony: Aspects of the economic and social history of colonial Natal* (Pietermaritzburg, 1985), 210–226; Y. S. Meer et al., *Documents of indentured labour in Natal 1851–1917* (Durban, 1980); M. Swan, *Gandhi: The South African experience* (Johannesburg, 1985), 1, 3–4, 10–12, 19–21.
2. J. B. Brain, *Christian Indians in Natal, 1860–1911: An historical and statistical study* (Cape Town, 1983), 8.
3. Swan, *Gandhi,* 5.
4. B. Pachai, *The international aspects of the South African Indian question, 1860–1971* (Cape Town, 1971), 69. Although most Asians in Natal were Indians, in the Transvaal there were a number of Chinese as well.
5. H. J. van Aswegen, "The Orange Free State experience," in B. Pachai (ed.), *South Africa's Indians: the evolution of a minority* (Washington, D.C.,1979), 186–187, 195–198.
6. B. Pillay, *British Indians in the Transvaal: Trade, politics and Imperial relations, 1885–1906* (London, 1976), 11, 16–17.
7. Pachai, *International aspects,* 8–12; S. Bhana, "Indian trade and trader in colonial Natal," in Guest and Sellers, *Enterprise and exploitation*, 246–248.
8. Swan, *Gandhi,* 38–52.
9. Pyarelal, *Mahatma Gandhi*, Vol. 3: *The birth of satyagraha: From petitioning to passive resistance* (Ahmedabad, 1986), 64–66.
10. Ibid., 66–67.
11. I consulted only the 1901–1902 issues.
12. Swan, *Gandhi*, 57.
13. Ibid., 55, 61–69.
14. The discussion of prewar and postwar politics in the Transvaal is based largely on Pillay, *British Indians*, 57–105; Swan, *Gandhi,* 79–111; and S. Bhana and J. D. Hunt (eds.), *Gandhi's editor: The letters of M. H. Nazar, 1902–1903* (New Delhi, 1989), 11, 32, 63, 82, 101, 105.
15. See Pyarelal, *Gandhi*, Vol. 2, *The discovery of satyagraha: On the threshold* (Bombay, 1980), 192–194.
16. *Indian Opinion* (hereafter *IO*), 4 June 1903 (advertisement for International Printing Press).
17. Bhana and Hunt, *Gandhi's editor*, 53, Nazar to Gandhi, 13 March 1903.
18. Ibid., 65, 76, Nazar to Atmaram Maharaj, 15 April 1903, and Nazar to Gandhi, 7 May 1903.
19. Ibid., 2–5.
20. Ibid., esp. 58, 60–61, 65, 75–77, 79–80, 82–84, 86–100, 105, 108, 111–114. These letters were written between 1 April and 12 June 1903.
21. See S. N. Bhattacharya, *Mahatma Gandhi: The journalist* (Bombay, 1965), 1–5.
22. Bhana and Hunt, *Gandhi's editor,* 88–91, Nazar to Gandhi, 16 and 18 May 1903.
23. Ibid., 112, Nazar to Gandhi, 11 June 1903.
24. Ibid., 94, Nazar to Gandhi, 22 May 1903.
25. Ibid., 111–114, Nazar to Gandhi, 11 and 12 June 1903.
26. Ibid., 107–108, Nazar to Gandhi, 4 and 6 June 1903.
27. Ibid., 62, 80, 109, Nazar to Gandhi, 9 April, 9 May, 8 June 1903.
28. *IO*, 4 June 1903.

29. *Mahatma Gandhi, Collected works* (*hereafter CWMG*),Vol. 4, 1903–5 (New Delhi, 1969), 340, Gandhi to J. Stuart, 19 January 1905.
30. *IO*, 4 June 1903.
31. *IO*, 9 July 1903, 27 May 1905 (editorials); J. Naidoo, *Tracking down historical myths: Eight South African cases* (Johannesburg, 1989), 145–147; J. Brown, *Gandhi: Prisoner of hope* (New Haven, 1989), 63–64.
32. *IO*, 4 June 1903 (editorial).
33. *IO*, 11 June 1903 (editorial).
34. *IO*, 7 January 1904 (editorial).
35. *IO*, 21 January 1904 (editorial).
36. *CWMG*, Vol. 4, 340, Gandhi to Stuart,19 January 1905.
37. *IO*, 25 March 1905. See also 4, 11 February 1905.
38. A. Odendaal, *Vukani Bantu: The beginnings of black protest politics in South Africa to 1912* (Cape Town, 1984), 61.
39. Bhana and Hunt, *Gandhi's editor*, 112, Nazar to Gandhi, 11 June 1903.
40. *IO*, 24 December 1904 (editorial).
41. *Mahatma Gandhi, Selected Works*, Vol. 2, *An autobiography, or the story of my experiments with truth* (Ahmedabad, 1968), 438–439, 444.
42. In 1903, he employed six clerks and a typist. Pyarelal, *Gandhi*, Vol. 3, 431.
43. *IO*, 24 December 1904 (editorial).
44. *CWMG*, Vol. 5, *1905–6*, 289 [*IO*, 28 April 1906 (Gujerati; hereafter *G*)].
45. R. A. Huttenback, *Gandhi in South Africa: British imperialism and the Indian question, 1860–1914* (Ithaca, 1971), 37–38.
46. *CWMG*, Vol. 5, 290 [*IO*, 28 April 1906 (G)].
47. A comparative content analysis of the four languages used in *Indian Opinion* has yet to be made. The Documentation Centre for Indians at the University of Durban-Westville, however, has indexed the subject titles of the Gujerati section. Although the list is not exhaustive, it does indicate that *Indian Opinion* carried news about local religious festivities and other cultural events of interest to the Gujerati-speaking community.
48. *IO*, 4 June 1904.
49. *IO*, 7 May 1904.
50. *IO*, 30 April 1904.
51. These included two men known only as Oliver and Orchard, who did the job work; a Cape Coloured named Mannering and two English compositors from Mauritius and St. Helena whose names are not known. Kababhai and Virji Damodar composed the Gujerati and Hindi sections, while a man named Moothoo composed the Tamil section. Sam Govindswami Raju was in charge of the machine and binding sections. Pyarelal, *Gandhi*, Vol. 3, 434, 441.
52. P. Gandhi, *My Childhood with Gandhiji* (Ahmedabad, 1957), 35–36.
53. Gandhi, *Autobiography*, 444–446.
54. Ibid., 447.
55. *IO*, 24 December 1904 (editorial).
56. *CWMG*, Vol. 4, 340, Gandhi to Stuart, 19 January 1905.
57. Gandhi, *Selected Works, Vol. 5*, Gandhi to Gokhale, 13 January 1905; *CWMG*, Vol. 5, 289 [*IO* 28 April 1906 (G)].
58. *CWMG*, Vol. 6, *1906–7*, 303.
59. Pyarelal, *Gandhi*, Vol.3, 436–437.
60. Bhana and Hunt, *Gandhi's editor*, 5.
61. P. Gandhi, *Childhood with Gandhiji*, 36.
62. F. Meer, *Portrait of Indian South Africans* (Durban, 1969), 56.
63. See *IO*, 4 July 1908.
64. See *CWMG*, Vol. 5, 189, Gandhi to Chhaganlal, 13, 18 February 1906.
65. P. Gandhi, *Childhood with Gandhiji*, 33–35.
66. See *CWMG*, Vol. 5, 125–126, 199, Gandhi to Chhaganlal, 6 November 1905, 22 February 1906; Pyarelal, *Gandhi*, Vol. 3, 440–441. Kitchin committed suicide in 1915.
67. See M. G. Polak, *Mr. Gandhi: The man* (London, 1931), 17–19, 47–54, 67–70; A. West, "In the early days with Gandhi," *Illustrated Weekly of India*, 10 October 1965, 33.
68. B. Pachai, "The history of *Indian Opinion*: Its origin, development and contribution to South African history, 1903–1914," in *Archives year book for South African history* (1961), 28.
69. James D. Hunt, "Experiments in forming a community of service: The evolution of Gandhi's first ashrams, Phoenix and Tolstoy farms," in K. S. L. Rao and H. O. Thompson (eds.), *World problems and human responsibility: Gandhian perspectives* (New York, 1988), 182.
70. *CWMG*, Vol. 5, 88, Gandhi to Chhaganlal, 5 October 1905.

71. Ibid., 197, Gandhi to Chhaganlal, 19 February 1906. He advised that letters about local news events and "all letters against us" be published.
72. Some of these unsigned articles have been identified and translated, and they are published in *CWMG*.
73. Gandhi, *Autobiography*, 454.
74. Polak, *Gandhi*, 54.
75. Ibid., 49; P. Gandhi, *Childhood with Gandhiji*, 37.
76. See *IO*, 1 May 1909; J. D. Hunt, "Gandhi and the black people of South Africa," *Gandhi Marg*, April–June 1989, 17.
77. *CWMG*, Vol. 5, 196, Gandhi to Chhaganlal, 18 February 1906.
78. *CWMG*, Vol. 1, 1884–96, 124.
79. Hunt, "Gandhi and the black people," 10.
80. Naidoo, *Historical myths*, 134–135.
81. P. F. Power, "Gandhi in South Africa," *Journal of Modern African Studies* 7, 3, (1969), 445.
82. Swan, *Gandhi*, 112–113.
83. See, for instance, *CWMG*, Vol. 8, *1908*, 134–135 [*IO*, 7 March 1908 (G)].
84. *IO*, 4 February 1905 (editorial).
85. *IO*, 25 March 1905 (editorial).
86. *CWMG*, Vol 5, 282 [*IO* 14 April 1906 (G)].
87. Indians constituted 9.1 percent, whites 8.8 percent and Africans 82.1 percent of Natal's population in 1904. Meer et al., *Documents*, 16.
88. *IO*, 23 March 1912.
89. *IO*, 15 April 1905 (G), 29 July 1905 (G), 12 August 1905 (G).
90. *IO*, 29 April 1905.
91. *CWMG*, Vol. 10, *1909–11* [*IO*, 24 September 1910].
92. See *IO*, 6 May 1905, 31 March 1906, 29 May 1909 (editorial).
93. *IO*, 10 February 1912.
94. *IO*, 2 August 1913.
95. *IO*, 30 August 1913.
96. *IO*, 8 October 1904.
97. *IO*, 30 November 1907 (editorial), 6 March 1909 (editorial), 10 February 1912.
98. *IO*, 8 June 1912 (editorial).
99. He wrote that Africans were the descendants of African-American slaves who had returned to Africa. See M. K. Gandhi, *Satyagraha in South Africa*, 2nd ed. (Ahmedabad, 1950), 7.
100. *CWMG*, Vol. 10, 308, Gandhi to Maganlal, 21 August 1910.
101. Ibid., 183, Gandhi to M. P. Fancy, 16 March 1910.
102. Odendaal, *Vukani Bantu*, 213–220.
103. *CWMG*, Vol. 5, 241–242 [*IO*, 24 March 1906].
104. See *CWMG*, Vol. 5, 241–243 [*IO*, 24 March 1906 (G)]; *CWMG*, Vol. 7, *1907*, 125 [*IO* 27 July 1907 (G)]; *IO*, 29 May 1909 (editorial).
105. *CWMG*, Vol. 12, *1913–14*, 482, Gandhi's letter to Indians in South Africa, July 1914.
106. Ibid.
107. Quoted in Bhana and Hunt, *Gandhi's editor*, 6.
108. *CWMG*, Vol. 5, 1905–6, 289–290 [*IO*, 28 April 1906 (G)].
109. *IO*, 12 September 1908 (editorial), 6 March 1909 (editorial).
110. *CWMG*, Vol. 5, 174, Gandhi to Nazar, 5 January 1906; 183 [*IO*, 3 February 1906].
111. Joseph Royeppen to Gandhi, 6 August 1912. I am grateful to James Hunt for providing me with a copy of this letter.
112. *African Chronicle*, 4 July 1908 (letter from Aambalavanen).
113. Naidoo, *Historical myths*, 136.
114. Swan, *Gandhi*, 109.
115. *IO*, 14 January 1905 (editorial).
116. *IO*, 21 July 1906 (editorial).
117. *IO*, 15 September 1906 (editorial).
118. *CWMG*,Vol. 4, 205 [*IO*, 4 June 1904]; *IO*, 18 August 1906.
119. *CWMG*,Vol. 7, *1907*, 43 [*IO*, 15 June 1907 (G)].
120. *IO*, 18 November 1905 (editorial).
121. *IO*, 23 November 1907 (editorial). See also 5 March 1910 (editorial): "We must make it clear that we ask for a stoppage of indentured labour for its own sake and because we consider that it is detrimental to the moral well-being of those who indenture."
122. *IO*, 7 January 1911.
123. *CWMG*, Vol. 6, 254, Gandhi to private secretary to the secretary for the colonies, 1 December 1906.
124. *IO*, 11 February 1904 (editorial).
125. *IO*, 9 July 1903 (editorial); also *IO*, 11 June 1903 (editorial).
126. *CWMG*, Vol. 10, 178–189 [*IO*, 12 March 1910 (G)]; also 201 [*IO*, 2 April 1910 (G)].
127. *African Chronicle*, 5 March 1910 (editorial).
128. Swan, *Gandhi*, 193–196, 211–216.

129. *CWMG*, Vol. 4, 417 [*IO*, 22 April 1905 (G)].
130 *CWMG*, Vol. 10, 99–100 [*IO*, 11 December 1909 (G)]. See also *IO*, 30 December 1911 (editorial).
131. *IO*, 12 September 1908.
132. See Pachai, *International aspects*, 31–62.
133. There were about 1,000 Chinese in the Transvaal, and their leaders worked with Indian leaders to ensure the success of the antiregistration campaign. Chinese resisters continued to court prison up to 1911. See Hunt, "Gandhi and the black people," 11–12.
134. This section is heavily indebted to Swan, *Gandhi*, 141–143, 173–174, 226.
135. Ibid., 243–256; M. Swan, "The 1913 Natal Indian strike," *Journal of Southern African Studies*, 10, 2 (1984), 239–258.
136. *IO*, 12 September 1908, 3 July 1909.
137. It was entitled *Indians of South Africa: Helots within the empire* (Madras, 1909).
138. *IO*, 10 August 1912 (editorial).
139. *IO*, 26 November 1913.
140. See *IO*, 23 August 1913; J. J. Doke, *M. K. Gandhi: An Indian patriot in South Africa* (London, 1909), and W. E. Cursons, *Joseph Doke: The missionary-hearted* (Johannesburg, 1929). Thanks to Christopher Saunders for loaning me a copy of Cursons' book.
141. The committee's main organizer was William Hosken, who had mining investments in the Transvaal.
142. See P. Gandhi, *Childhood with Gandhiji*, 125–131, 134–137, 152.
143. See *IO*, 26 November, 3 December, 17 December 1913; 14, 21 January 1914.
144. P. Gandhi, *Childhood with Gandhiji*, 152–153.
145. Gandhi, *Satyagraha*, 91.
146. *IO*, 11 May 1907 (editorial).
147. See *IO*, 15 September 1906, 30 March, 6 April, 11, 18 May 1907 (editorials).
148. *CWMG*, Vol. 9, *1908–9*, 6 [*IO*, 5 September 1908 (G)].
149. *IO*, 22 March, 12 April 1913 (editorials).
150. *IO*, 7 June, 19 July, 13, 24 September 1913 (editorials).
151. *CWMG*, Vol. 6, 480–481 [*IO*, 18 May 1907 (G)].
152. Ibid., 492–494 [*IO*, 25 May 1907 (G)].
153. *IO*, 15 September 1906 (editorial). The possible influence of this movement on *satyagraha* has been explored in J. D. Hunt, *Gandhi and the nonconformists: Encounters in South Africa* (New Delhi, 1986).
154. *CWMG*, Vol. 7, 453 [*IO*, 28 December 1907 (G)].
155. Ibid., 10–11.
156. *IO*, 2 August 1913. See also issue of 5 July 1913.
157. *IO*, 16 November 1907; *CWMG*, Vol. 8, 172–174, 185–187, 196–199, 212–214, 217–221, 227–229. The series appeared in Gujerati between April and May 1908.
158. *CWMG*, Vol. 7, 63–64 [*IO*, 29 June 1907 (G)].
159. J. D. Hunt, "Thoreau and Gandhi: A re-evaluation of the legacy," *Gandhi Marg*, 14 , 3 (1970), 328.
160. See *IO*, 5, 19 March 1910 for quotations from Tolstoy and Garrison.
161. *IO*, 26 October 1907.
162. *IO*, 20 February 1909.
163. *IO*, 26 October 1907.
164. *CWMG*, Vol. 9, 224–225 [*IO*, 29 May 1909 (G)].
165. *CWMG*, Vol. 7, 5 [*IO*, 1 June 1907 (G)]. There were 20 entries, and the winner was Ambaram Mangalji Thakar, president of the Natal Sanathan Dharma Sabha (see *CWMG*, Vol. 7, 48–49).
166. *IO*, 9 November 1907. But there were only four entries. The winner was M. S. Maurice, a Christian Indian from Cape Town (see *IO*, 25 January 1908).
167. Although there were a number of suggestions from readers, Gandhi favored his nephew Maganlal's suggestion of *sadagraha*, which he then modified to *satyagraha* (see *CWMG*, Vol. 8, 22–23, 131–132 [*IO*, 11 January, 7 March 1908 (G)].
168. *IO*, 18 May 1907; *CWMG*, Vol. 6, 393, 485–488, 495–497 [*IO*, 6 April 1907 (G); *IO*, 18, 25 May 1907 (G)]; Vol. 7, 390–392 [*IO*, 30 November 1907 (G)].
169. *CWMG*, *Vol.* 7, 250–254 [*IO*, 28 September 1907 (G)].
170. *IO*, 4 January 1908.
171. *IO*, 20 July 1907.
172. *CWMG*, Vol. 7, 363, 378 [*IO*, 16, 23 November 1907 (G)].
173. See for instance *IO*, 25 July, 1 August and 8 August 1908; *CWMG*, Vol. 7, 119–120 [*IO*, 27 July 1907 (G)]; Vol. 8, 472 [*IO*, 22 August 1908 (G)]; Vol. 9, 35 [*IO*, 12 September 1908 (G)]; 155–156 [*IO*, 23 January 1909]; 176 [*IO*, 30 January 1909 (G)].

174. *CWMG*, Vol. 7, 134–135, 250–252, 315 [*IO*, 3 August, 28 September, 26 October 1907 (G)].
175. *CWMG*, Vol. 7, e.g., 134–135 [*IO*, 3 August 1907 with reference to a Mr. Khamisa (G)].
176. See *IO*, 30 November 1907 (letter from S. Halloo).
177. *CWMG*, Vol. 7, 155 [*IO*, 10 August 1907 (G)].
178. *CWMG*, Vol. 9, 160, 226 [*IO*, 23 January, 29 May 1909 (G)].
179. See *CWMG*, Vol. 8, 119, 134 [*IO*, 7 March 1908]; Vol. 9, 182–183 [*IO*, 30 January 1909].
180. *CWMG*, Vol. 9, 225–227 [*IO*, 29 May 1909 (G)]; 236–237 [*IO*, 5 June 1909 (G)].
181. *IO*, 20 September 1913 (editorial); *CWMG*, Vol. 12, 196–197 [*IO*, 20 September 1913 (G)].
182. Gandhi, *Autobiography*, 426.
183. *CWMG*, Vol. 7, 277 [*IO*, 12 October 1907 (G)].
184. *CWMG*, Vol. 6, 380–381, Gandhi to Chhaganlal, 25 March 1907; Vol. 7, 40, Gandhi to Chhaganlal, 12 June 1907.
185. *CWMG*, Vol. 7, 277 [*IO*, 12 October 1907 (G)].
186. Gandhi, *Satyagraha*, 133.
187. Ibid.
188. *CWMG*, Vol. 10, 7 [*IO*, 22 November 1909 (G)].
189. M. Swan, "Ideology in organized Indian politics, 1891–1948," in S. Marks and S. Trapido (eds.), *The politics of race, class and nationalism in twentieth century South Africa* (London, 1987), 195–196.
190. *IO*, 13 March 1909.
191. *CWMG*, Vol. 8, 3–4 [*IO*, 4 January 1908 (G)].
192. *IO*, 10 July 1909.
193. *IO*, 22 October 1910.
194. *IO*, 25 February 1914.
195. *IO*, 22 October 1910 (editorial).
196. See *IO*, 8 July 1914 (editorial).
197. There are numerous editorials commenting favorably on Gandhi's leadership between 1908 and 1910. Although there was some tension between the two newspapers in 1911 over the veracity of a news item about the ill-treatment of an indentured woman, it was only from April 1913 that Aiyar became viciously anti-Gandhi. He disagreed in particular with Gandhi's acceptance of the closed-door immigration policy, regarded passive resistance as a failed strategy and objected to indentured Indians striking in 1913.
198. See *Indian Views*, 17 July 1914 (editorial); *African Chronicle*, 20 June 1914 (editorial).
199. Brown, *Gandhi*, 30, 74.
200. Pachai, "History of the *Indian Opinion*," 3.
201. Swan, *Gandhi*, 226.
202. See *IO*, 8 January 1910. The *African Chronicle*, in contrast, carried advertisements for Castle Ale and Castle Lager and advertised the services of bars or taverns.
203. *CWMG*, Vol. 11, *1911–13*, 329–330 [*IO*, 14 September 1912 (G)].
204. Ibid.; Gandhi, *Satyagraha*, 133–134.
205. *IO*, 28 September 1912 (editorial). The yearly subscription rate was lowered from 15 to 14 shillings in Natal and from 17 to 14 shillings elsewhere in South Africa and 15 shillings outside South Africa.
206. *IO*, 14 September 1912.
207. Manilal took over the editorship from West in 1918 and continued in this position until his death in 1956. The newspaper ceased publication in 1962.
208. His journalism in these publications is discussed in Bhattacharya, *Gandhi: The journalist*.

CHAPTER 4

Voice of the Coloured Elite

APO, 1909–1923

Mohamed Adhikari

The African Political Organization, founded in Cape Town in 1902, was the first substantive Coloured political pressure group in the Cape Colony.* Seven years later, during the wave of protests that preceded the establishment of the Union of South Africa in 1910, the APO launched a newspaper entitled *APO*, the acronym of the organization, to represent the interests and concerns of the Coloured community in British South Africa.[1]

The APO took the decision to publish a newspaper at its seventh yearly conference in April 1909 as part of a protest campaign against the clauses of the 1909 draft South Africa Act, which denied blacks the franchise outside the Cape and deprived blacks within the colony of the right to be elected to the proposed Union parliament.[2] The first issue of the *APO*, on 24 May 1909, justified its existence on the grounds that the Coloured community needed a medium to voice its opinions and promote its interests. Claiming that no other newspaper dared to champion "our just claims to political equality with whites," it accused the white commercial press of promoting only the "rights of property for the few who have it, rather than the broad rights of humanity," and of acting "on the assumption that South Africa belongs to the whites ... by right of conquest."[3]

A quarto-sized fortnightly, published on alternate Saturdays, the *APO* normally consisted of 16 pages. The newspaper was bilingual, with an English section that took up at least three-quarters of the space and a Dutch section confined to the back pages. Editorials and the more important articles appeared in both languages. The *APO* was not really a commercial newspaper, and it did not attempt to provide systematic coverage of local or international news. As the fortnightly mouthpiece of a political organization representing the Coloured community, the *APO* was more in the nature of a political journal.

The *APO* was not the first Cape Town newspaper aimed specifically at black readers. This honor belongs to the *South African Spectator*, which was founded and edited by Francis Zaccheus Santiago Peregrino, one of the more colorful Cape Town characters at the time. Peregrino was born in Accra (in what is now Ghana) in 1851 and educated in England. He emigrated to the United States while in his late thirties, and in Albany, New York, he set up a newspaper for African Americans called the *Spectator*, which he edited during the 1890s. After attending the first Pan-

* I would like to thank Christopher Saunders for his helpful comments on an earlier draft of this chapter and to acknowledge financial aid from the University of Cape Town.

African Congress in London in July 1900, he decided to come to Cape Town to spread the gospel of Pan-Africanism to southern Africa. He believed a British victory in the South African War was inevitable, and it would lead to an era of freedom and prosperity for black people in the region. In December 1900, within a few weeks after arriving in Cape Town, he started publishing the *South African Spectator*.[4] The newspaper seems to have appeared sporadically for the next eight years, but only 44 issues, spanning the period January 1901 to December 1902, have survived.[5]

The *South African Spectator* probably set a precedent for the *APO*. Peregrino demonstrated the financial feasibility and the political merit of publications aimed at the Coloured community. Notwithstanding substantive differences in political outlook, the *APO* copied the format of the *South African Spectator* and borrowed many of its journalistic practices.

The APO sought to speak on behalf of the Coloured people as a whole, but in reality it represented the interests of the emergent Coloured petty bourgeoisie. APO's newspaper reflected the *Weltanschauung* of this social group, which formed an elite within the Coloured community. The Coloured petty bourgeoisie in the early decades of the new century was more united in its political aims and social aspirations than it would be after World War I. The APO completely dominated Coloured politics, and it had a national network of branches with several thousand members by the time of Union in 1910.[6] Contemporary Coloured political organizations, such as Peregrino's Coloured Men's Political and Protectorate Association, his Coloured People's Vigilance Society and the South African Coloured Union under the leadership of James Curry, drew negligible support

For nearly 20 years, informal open-air political meetings, called "Stone Meetings," were also held on Sunday mornings in the vicinity of a large boulder on the lower slopes of Table Mountain above District Six. These meetings helped to foster political education within the Coloured community and establish a forum for the debate of political issues. The APO was one of the organizations that emerged from the Stone Meetings.[7]

The APO had no serious political rival until the Afrikaanse Nasionale Bond (ANB) was launched in 1925. The APO, however, remained far more popular than the ANB, which was organized in part by leading Cape nationalists to influence Cape Coloureds to support the National Party. The APO was finally eclipsed by the National Liberation League, which represented a radical political movement that had emerged within the Coloured community during the 1930s.

The *APO* newspaper throughout its life was regarded as the authentic voice of the Coloured petty bourgeoisie and reflected the social and political concerns of its readership. This Coloured elite consisted largely of artisans, small retail traders, clerks, teachers and a handful of professionals. They were conditioned by the assumptions and premises of Western middle-class culture, and they shared on the whole its values and social practices. Despite some rhetoric about the need to cultivate Coloured race pride, the aspirations of this social group were almost entirely assimilationist. The Coloured elite wanted little more than to be judged on merit, to exercise citizenship rights and to win social acceptance within white middle-class society. They did not wish to make fundamental changes in the social order, except for the abolition of institutionalized racial discrimination. The *APO* therefore continually reiterated the sentiment that "it is not race or color but civilization which is the test of man's capacity for political rights."[8]

Photo 14. Francis Zaccheus Santiago Peregrino, founder and editor of the *South African Spectator* (1900–08?).

Photo 15. Dr. Abdullah Abdurahman, APO president and the *APO* newspaper's main editorial writer and commentator.

Photo 16. Matt J. Fredericks, APO general secretary and editor of the *APO* newspaper.

The *APO* newspaper sought to further the objectives of the APO organization, which were defined in its constitution as follows:

1. The promotion of unity between the Coloured races of British South Africa.
2. The attainment of better and higher education for the children of these races.
3. The registration of the names of all the Coloured men who have the necessary qualifications as Parliamentary voters on the Voters' List.
4. The defence of the social, political and civil rights of the Coloured races.
5. The general advancement of the Coloured races in British South Africa.[9]

News Agenda

The *APO* covered society, sports and cultural events, but news concerned with Coloured politics, education and socioeconomic conditions dominated the newspaper. The APO's political positions were argued at length, and the newspaper sought to educate its readers politically in covering local and national issues of concern to the Coloured community. The *APO* focused on Coloured education, in the belief that education was an essential prerequisite to being assimilated into the dominant society, and the newspaper sought to improve socioeconomic conditions by inspiring a self-help work ethic within the Coloured community.

A column entitled "Straatpraatjes" (literally "street talk" or in this context "street gossip") was a regular feature in the newspaper between 1909 and 1922. Published under the pseudonym of "Piet Uithalder," *uithalder* meaning "smart" or "quick-witted," it was probably written by Dr. Abdullah Abdurahman, president of the APO throughout the period under review.[10] "Straatpraatjes" was a satirical political column that lampooned APO's opponents and passed caustic comment on topical issues, but it was more than political commentary. It was written in the local Cape Dutch dialect commonly spoken among working-class Coloureds, a forerunner of what South Africans today refer to as *kombuis Afrikaans*, an amalgam of English, Dutch and Cape Dutch. Thus Piet describes, for example, the reception he and his fictitious friend Stoffel Francis received on their return to Cape Town with the 1909 APO delegation to London protesting the draft Act of Union: "Welkom thuis, welkom thuis, Mr. Uithalder en Mijnheer Stoffel, en die gentlemans en ladies van die Kaap het my so gehandshake dat my en Stoffel sij arm glad seer was" (Welcome home, welcome home, Mr. Uithalder and Mr. Stoffel, and the gentlemen and ladies of the Cape shook our hands with such vigour that our arms were quite sore.)[11]

The conversations between Piet Uithalder and his friend Stoffel reveal much about the popular culture of Cape Town's Coloured community. Uithalder comments about such diverse matters as his visits to Stone Meetings, picnics at Camps Bay, drinking, dancing, shopping and playing popular games such as *pan pan* and *klawerjas*. The column was written in a lively, humorous vein and in language readily accessible to the readership of the newspaper. Although the APO leadership viewed the language of "Straatpraatjes" as "uncultured" and "uncivilised," it proved to be an extremely effective medium for ridiculing political opponents.

The bilingualism of the *APO* reflected the main social cleavage within the Coloured community, because the use of English and Cape Dutch broadly corresponded with the major class differences in that community. Whereas most Coloureds spoke the vernacular featured in "Straatpraatjes," the upwardly mobile elite tended to speak English. But virtually all English-speaking Coloureds were familiar with the Cape Dutch dialect, because they retained intimate links with the working-class population through family ties, friendships and daily contact.

English had far greater prestige among Coloureds, because it was an international language with a rich literature and was spoken by the elite within white society at the Cape. Identified as the language of "culture," "civilisation" and "progress," it was also associated with the grandeur of the British Empire. By the same token, English was associated with the rhetoric of liberalism, fair-mindedness and racial tolerance of British rule at the Cape and elsewhere in British colonial culture. Coloureds generally regarded proficiency in English as essential for social and occupational advancement. Thus *APO* urged Coloureds

> to perfect themselves in English–the language which inspires the noblest thoughts of freedom and liberty, the language that has the finest literature on earth, and is the most universally useful of all languages. Let everyone of them–the young people in particular–at once drop the habit as far as possible, of expressing themselves in the barbarous Cape Dutch that is too often heard.[12]

Cape Dutch, especially the version spoken within the Coloured community, was derided as a "Cape patois." The *APO* scorned the emergent Afrikaans language as "a vulgar patois fit only for the kitchen," because it lacked a formal grammar or significant literature. The newspaper deplored "the height of impudence" that would claim for the Afrikaans language "the same rights as for the language of Shelley, Milton and Tennyson."[13] Within the Coloured elite, Cape Dutch-cum-Afrikaans was generally associated with the boorishness and racism of white Afrikaners. Being the language of the Coloured laboring poor, Afrikaans was also taken to be a badge of lower-classedness within the Coloured community. Cape Dutch-speaking parents who had ambitions for their children insisted that they be instructed in English at school, even though it was not their mother tongue.[14]

Thus most Coloureds spoke Cape Dutch, but about 75 percent of the *APO* was written in English. APO leaders published part of their newspaper in Dutch because they sought to represent the Coloured population as a whole and wanted to communicate their political messages to potential constituents. The language bias in *APO* was a measure of the newspaper's class bias as it attempted to reify the values and aspirations of the Coloured petty bourgeoisie, the perceived representatives of English bourgeois culture.

Matt Fredericks, general secretary of the APO, was editor of the newspaper, but Abdurahman exercised the greatest influence on editorial content. As the preeminent APO leader, he dominated the organization for the entire 35 years of his presidency, from 1905 to his death in 1940. *APO* was produced largely by Fredericks, Abdurahman and a close circle of associates.[15] Abdurahman wrote most of the editorials, and Fredericks was Abdurahman's closest collaborator within the APO. Fredericks had organized the "coup" that paved the way for Abdurahman's ascent to the presidency in 1905, when it appeared that rivalry between then president William Collins and vice-president John Tobin would tear the organization apart. There was a large measure of truth in contemporary quips that the acronym of the organization stood for "Abdurahman's Political Organization" and the acronym of its newspaper stood for "Abdurahman's Political Opinion." The rival Coloured newspaper *South African Clarion* mockingly interpreted it as "die Apie se oë" (literally "eyes of the monkey"), which was a reference to Abdurahman.[16]

Political Impotence

The Jameson Raid (1896) and the South African War (1899–1902) initially boosted hopes that Coloureds might be assimilated into the dominant culture. Their vote could be of significance, given the balance of power between the polarized English and Afrikaner communities, and Coloured activists hoped to exploit this schism. They viewed the South African War, in particular, as an opportunity for Coloureds to demonstrate their allegiance to the British Empire. Coloured expectations were further heightened by Sir Alfred Milner, British high commissioner for South Africa, who cited the disfranchisement of Coloureds as a reason for British intervention in the Transvaal.[17] But Britain's victory did not usher in a new era. The Treaty of Vereeniging in 1902 granted the vanquished Boers a generous peace that effectively ruled out the enfranchisement of blacks in the former Boer republics and precipitated the founding of APO.[18]

The extent of Coloured marginality was also brought home to APO's leaders in several campaigns against discrimination during the early 1900s. Coloured activists together with a handful of white-liberal allies, for example, had failed in 1905 to have the provisions of the Cape's School Board Act extended to Coloureds. This act had introduced a program to provide all white children with compulsory public education to Standard IV (sixth grade) or 14 years of age. The APO also sent a delegation to London in 1906 that failed to persuade the British government to modify the discriminatory franchise to be granted to the Transvaal and the Orange River Colony when they attained responsible government in 1907 and 1908, respectively. This was followed by the unsuccessful joint Coloured and African delegation to London in 1909 to protest the draft South Africa Act, the clearest demonstration yet of the political impotence of the Coloured community.

The newspaper, in the first year of its existence, was devoted largely to campaigning against the 1909 draft South Africa Act. The impending Union of South Africa was characterized as "The Great Betrayal."[19] Much publicity was given to the protest delegation, which was led by W. P. Schreiner, a noted liberal and former prime minister of the Cape. The Coloured delegates were Abdurahman, Matt Fredericks and D. J. Lenders, an APO stalwart from Kimberley. Union Day itself was described by *APO* as a day of "mourning," "humiliation" and "prayer" for the Coloured people of South Africa.[20]

The APO had come into being at a time when the embattled Coloured elite was confronted by the rising tide of segregationism, and the newspaper reflected the elite's struggle to defend its civil rights. But APO's political tactics had not protected Coloured interests in the Cape Colony, and South Africa after 1910 was much less sympathetic to Coloured aspirations, whether they were promoted by the Coloured elite or their main white allies, the Cape liberals. In response, the APO shifted from political activism to a more cautious, incremental strategy in pursuit of immediate, attainable social goals, a change of agenda that was noticeable in APO's newspaper as early as mid-1911. APO also changed its name to the African People's Organization in 1919, the new title reflecting the organization's commitment to the social advancement of the Coloured community.

Coloureds at no stage formed more than 10 percent of South Africa's population, and they never had significant economic or political power. With few choices open to them and little room in which to maneuver, Coloured politicians tended to be pragmatic and opportunistic. They succeeded in holding the middle ground between the dominant white and the numerically preponderant Africans during this period by claiming blood ties with Europeans and claiming to be culturally more advanced than Africans. The intermediate position of Coloureds in the dominant culture, however, generated numerous contradictions within the Coloured community, especially within the tiny fraction–no more than 5 percent of the Coloured population by World War I–that comprised the Coloured petty bourgeoisie.

The most striking of these ambiguities was the tension between the discourse of nonracism and the practice of Coloured separatism, which was clearly manifest within the organizational life of the APO and its newspaper. During the decades straddling the turn of the century, the Coloured petty bourgeoisie faced a predicament common to most racially defined, subordinate elites. Although many Coloureds were acquiring the material means to sustain a middle-class lifestyle, their political and civil rights were eroding. Coloured assimilationist overtures were rejected by whites, and Coloureds were increasingly subjected to racial discrimination. They were unable to assert themselves politically or gain access to middle-class social or professional networks to any meaningful extent. No matter how much Coloureds achieved individually, as a community they were branded as socially inferior by whites and accorded second-class citizenship.

The leaders of the Coloured elite were faced with a moral and political dilemma. They embraced nonracial politics, but as a marginal community they felt they had little option but to mobilize separately on the basis of their racial identity. The potential advantage of being relatively privileged vis-à vis Africans in South Africa also provided the Coloured elite with an incentive for cultivating Coloured separatism. White privilege, moreover, served to encourage racial exclusivity within the Coloured community by heightening their group consciousness and prompting them to rally together in defense of their rights.

These contradictions were clearly evident in *APO*. Although the credo on the newspaper's editorial page noted that APO itself would "advocate a policy of justice and equality for all men in South Africa," the newspaper advocated Coloured separatism and in many ways accepted South Africa's ruling racial hierarchy. *APO* displayed much sympathy for Africans, but it was careful to demarcate Africans as a separate group that should minister to its own needs. On occasion, the *APO* also used the more pejorative term "Kafir" (also spelled "Kaffir") when referring to Africans. Notwithstanding APO's name,[21] the organization was established only for Coloured people and for the advancement of the Coloured community. Although Africans were not prevented from joining, the handful who did were identified as "Natives."[22]

APO's editorial policy on the issue of black solidarity contrasted sharply with that of its predecessor, the *South African Spectator*. Peregrino, true to the Pan-Africanist ideal, tried to get Coloureds and Africans to recognize their common interests as black people. The *Spectator* denounced Coloureds who felt they were superior to Africans and dismissed South African usage of the term "Coloured" as a "vague, meaningless and indefinite appellation."[23] Peregrino used the term to refer to blacks generally. As he explained, "It is distinctly understood that the term Coloured is used here to embrace all who are not known as white."[24] It was largely because of Peregrino's advocacy of black unity that he and the various political associations he formed found little acceptance within the Coloured political elite.

Although it is difficult to determine why Peregrino was not involved in the founding of the APO–he may have been ostricized by his peers, or he may have decided not to become involved in a separatist project–his absence does indicate the degree to which he was alienated from the Coloured community. The *Spectator* was read by the Coloured elite (especially in Cape Town), but Peregrino was regarded as an outsider, and his reputedly arrogant manner and abrasiveness no doubt contributed to his estrangement from this group. No proponent of black political unity in South Africa, however, was going to find favor with the Coloured petty bourgeoisie at this juncture. Peregrino remained a political adversary of the APO until his death in 1919.

> The *APO* newspaper characterized Coloureds essentially as black or brown Europeans: Everyone is well aware that in South Africa there is a large population of Coloured people as opposed to natives. Their number is estimated at about half a million. They are the product of civilization–in its most repellent manifestation according to some. They are of varying degrees of admixture. Their complexions vary from the black skin of the Kafir to a light tint that hardly discloses any trace of the Negro ... and their mode of life conforms with the best European model.[25]

The APO preferred to wage a separate campaign against racism, but it did not rule out cooperation with African political organizations to combat the most blatant forms of racial discrimination.[26] Thus Abdurahman noted in his presidential address to the 1910 APO conference: "We have a deep interest in the native races of South Africa, and the Union Act of South Africa puts us all into one fold but it is my duty as President of the APO ... to deal with the rights and duties of the Coloured people of South Africa as distinguished from the native races."[27]

African-American Role Models

The APO reconciled the contradiction between its rejection of racism and its acceptance of an inferior status for Coloureds by adopting a political philosophy heavily influenced by African-American academic and educator Booker T. Washington (1856–1915), perhaps the most influential black advocate of accommodation in the segregationist society of his day.[28] Washington reasoned that blacks could best elevate themselves by working hard, acquiring practical training (especially in agriculture), improving their educational qualifications and observing strictly the Christian moral code. If blacks could achieve economic self-sufficiency and demonstrate they were responsible citizens, they would win the respect of whites. Through self-interest and an innate sense of justice, whites eventually would accord them full civil rights.[29]

This strategy seemed eminently sensible to the Coloured petty bourgeoisie in the early decades of the twentieth century. It would break down white prejudice and in time win blacks social acceptance and civil equality within the dominant society.[30] Although APO leaders were apprehensive about the immediate future,[31] they viewed the history of the Coloured people as a steady march of progress from a dark past of slavery and savagery to a hopeful present, where the most advanced members of their "race" had a just claim to full equality with whites. Recent political reverses were temporary setbacks. Liberal values would be reasserted, South Africa would evolve toward a meritocratic society, and Coloureds would continue their social and political advancement. By demonstrating their "rise in the scale of civilization," Coloureds in time would overcome white racial prejudice and win full political and civil rights.[32]

This partly explains why the mouthpiece of the APO was prepared to relinquish its political activism and concentrate on the socioeconomic advancement of the

Coloured community. Contemplating the most effective way for Coloureds to gain "full political freedom and privileges," the newspaper endorsed the opinion that "we have to better ourselves, improve our education, mode of living and environment, seek to become proficient in our callings and trades...we shall be required to prove that we are worthy of these and other rights which we claim as loyal British subjects."[33]

APO's Coloured separatism, however, did not preclude it from seeking cooperation with other black groups. Its newspaper showed some interest in Gandhi's ideas about passive resistance and even set up an Indian Passive Resistance Fund to show solidarity with Indians and their political objectives.[34] The *APO* also supported African political initiatives. The founding of the South African Native National Congress (SANNC) in 1912 was welcomed "as one of the most important events that has ever happened in South Africa," because it "has transformed them [the 'Native races'] from a congeries of warring atoms into a united nation."[35] Executive members of the two organizations met for discussions soon after the inauguration of SANNC, when a delegation was sent to Cape Town to protest the Native Squatting Bill, a forerunner to the 1913 Land Act. The two groups resolved to meet together and to cooperate on matters of mutual concern, but there was no true collaboration until 1927, when Abdurahman convened the first of a series of Non-European Conferences to protest the National Party's segregationist policies.[36]

Although Washington's pragmatic approach remained dominant within the APO during this period, a younger generation of educated and politicized Coloureds found the assertive and self-confident ideology of W. E. B. Du Bois (1868–1963) more attractive.[37] Du Bois was a noted African-American scholar, journalist and intellectual whose central concern was to organize blacks for collective action against the social injustices they suffered. The dominant theme in his philosophy, strongly assimilationist until the 1930s, was the need for black people to take pride in their racial and cultural distinctiveness and reject white stereotypes of people of color.[38]

Those influenced by Du Bois felt that Coloureds were too diffident and too dependent on whites in matters relating to the welfare of their community. Coloureds needed to build self-confidence and take the initiative in uplifting their people. Exhortations to develop a positive self-image and an affirmative group identity or "race pride" became more frequent in the pages of the *APO* after 1910. Colouredness was promoted as a positive and desirable quality. In a lecture to APO's Cape Town branch in 1911, Harold Cressy, a leading Coloured teacher, complained of South African blacks relying on whites to be their spokesmen and to act on their behalf: "In America, no people make a greater study of the Negro than the Negro himself. The same cannot be said of the Coloured and Native races of South Africa...They have so little race pride and lack national feeling. Consequently they have taken little or no interest in questions that affect their welfare as a race."[39]

Politicized Coloureds were remarkably receptive to the ideas and strategies of the African-American petty bourgeoisie. This was partly because black Americans appeared to be making real strides in their struggle for civil equality. The African Methodist Episcopal (AME) Church, an independent African-American church, had operated in South Africa since 1896 and had served as a conduit for these ideas. The church had considerable influence within the Coloured elite, and several AME churchmen were intimately involved in Coloured politics. William Collins, first president of the APO, for example, was a lay preacher in the church, and Dr. Francis

Gow of the church's Bethel Institute, in Cape Town's District Six, was elected APO president in 1942.

APO leaders were also identifying with subordinated blacks in other parts of the world. The *APO* painted a somewhat exaggerated and romanticized picture of the achievements of Indians, Chinese and Africans in Africa and the Caribbean, but it also described how Africans and Asians were being exploited by whites in the British, Portuguese and Belgian colonies.[40] Although Coloureds and most other black peoples were believed to be "backward" compared with whites, *APO* did not regard this inferiority as inherent or permanent. The superiority of whites was assumed to be the result of certain historical and environmental conditions that had allowed the Europeans to outpace the rest of humanity. The *APO* endorsed the opinion that "the Negro, given the environment, the education, and the opportunity of the white man, will behave, think, and live in much the same way as the average white man."[41]

Coloured leaders especially admired the Japanese, perceived to be a "brown race" like the Coloureds, who had transformed themselves from an insular, tradition-bound society into a world power within a few decades. The warships that occasionally arrived at Table Bay symbolized Japanese power and technological advancement. A party of prominent Coloureds (led by the Abdurahman family), for example, was entertained aboard the Japanese training ship, the *Taisei Maru*, in 1910.[42] Coloured attitudes toward the Japanese are revealed in J. R. Strydom's report of the arrival of a Japanese warship in Cape Town harbor in 1922. Strydom, a prominent Coloured teacher, enthused about these "little yellow men...the silent Japanese," who could have been role models for the Coloured community:

> The wonderful little Japs...those little, narrow-eyed, high-cheekboned and determined looking sons of the Land of the Rising Sun [who had]...rapidly risen to one of the most exalted and powerful positions in the civilized world...We saw them associating with our most distinguished and autocratic citizens on a footing of exact equality, and I believe it did our hearts good to see it all. Hopes were refreshed and revived...Some saw our future in a different light and new possibilities appeared on the horizon, for here we saw the members of a race not quite dissimilar from ours in variegation of origin and the circumstances that attended their progress...in the civilized world.[43]

Education: A Key to the Future

After politics, the newspaper's most important priority was education. It appeared self-evident to the Coloured elite that an improvement in educational opportunity was essential for social and economic advancement, and eventual assimilation into white middle-class society.[44] Education held the promise of higher social status and an escape from manual labor, and the *APO* placed great importance on education for the Coloured community. Abdurahman himself was cited as a living example of the power of education to elevate the individual. Descended from grandparents who were manumitted slaves, he had risen above the obscurity of his lowly birth in Wellington in 1872 to a position of social eminence in Cape society. He had gained entrance to the elite Marist Brothers school and the South African College in Cape Town. His subsequent qualification as a medical doctor at Glasgow University in 1893, and his election to the Cape Town City Council in 1904, the APO presidency in 1905 and the Cape Provincial Council in 1914 were attributed to his superior education by *APO* and the Coloured community.[45] An editorial succinctly summed up the attitude of the Coloured elite to education: "Knowledge is power, no matter what may be the nature of it ... [Education] is the greatest uplifting power in the world and by means of it more will be accomplished than by any other means at our disposal."[46]

Confronted with a segregated and highly inequitable school system, one of the main aims of the *APO* was to reform Coloured education. A dual education system that mirrored the racial divide within Cape society had emerged during the nineteenth century. Mission schools set up by the churches for the poorer sector of the population had come to be reserved largely for blacks, whereas public schools under the control of the Education Department were reserved almost exclusively for whites. As noted earlier, the Cape parliament, in 1905, promulgated the School Board Act that formally segregated the educational system and provided all white children with compulsory public schooling.[47] Education would now be employed to bolster white supremacy and ensure the effective exploitation of black labor.[48]

Since the churches received limited government aid and the communities they served were poor, in most cases mission schools were vastly inferior to public schools, which were almost entirely funded by the state and reserved for whites. Mission school buildings were dilapidated and accommodations makeshift, classrooms crowded and unhealthy, furniture and equipment scarce. Many students were undernourished and in poor health. It was not uncommon to find several classes sharing a single room, pupils sitting in pews or on the floor and many unable to afford bare necessities such as books, slates or pencils. Few mission schools went beyond standard IV (sixth grade), and more than two-thirds of all pupils at mission schools were in substandard levels A and B (first and second grade). Most Coloured children received only a smattering of the three R's, therefore remaining functionally illiterate, and a substantial portion did not attend school at all.[49]

Under no illusions about the exploitative nature of the educational system,[50] the *APO* accused whites of using differentiated schools to maintain Coloureds as "drudges and labourers" and as "a means of ministering to their ease and pleasure."[51] The newspaper did not hesitate to attack the educational authorities: "The Coloured races are manual drudges. The black people are the descendants of Ham according to their ideas. They were meant to be the hewers of wood and the drawers of water through all eternity ... Any education that would give a being a thought beyond his station in life is accursed in their eyes."[52]

Although prepared to acknowledge the debt that Coloureds owed the churches for providing them with education, the *APO* did not mince words about the quality of mission schooling. The newspaper censured churches for trying to perpetuate an outdated and flawed educational system and continually urged the state to take full responsibility for Coloured schooling.[53] *APO* opposition to church control of Coloured education was also reinforced by the realization that Coloureds were subsidizing white education by paying rates, taxes and their own school fees.[54] The *APO* seethed at what it regarded as the shameless exploitation of Coloured teachers. In an article entitled "The Sweating of Our Coloured Teachers," the newspaper angrily denounced both the Cape Education Department and the churches: "The pay of our mission school teachers is indeed a disgrace, and it is difficult to see how a civilized government can tolerate such a state of affairs...How ministers of religion can have the audacity to ask publicly for the services of any individual at such wages and at the same time preach happiness, contentment and honesty is difficult to understand."[55]

As far as APO and the Coloured elite were concerned, the teachers had a particularly important role to play in the Coloured community.[56] As the *APO* put it, "[The teacher's] work is of the highest calling. The influence he wields in shaping the minds of those under his care and largely making their characters what they are forever to be, is seldom recognized."[57] The teachers formed the only substantial professional group within the Coloured community, and they were very conscious of their elite status. They tended to appropriate for themselves the primary role in leading the Coloureds forward to "civilization" and their rightful place in society.[58]

But the *APO* also acknowledged that Coloured teachers were poorly equipped for this responsibility. Whereas the ordinary teacher lacked "self-assertiveness and push and insistence on his social and economic worth," Coloured teachers in particular were ill-paid, badly trained, overworked and browbeaten by those in authority over them.[59] The mouthpiece of the APO saw the need for a Coloured teachers' association to organize the profession for collective action to improve their working conditions and to complement the political work of the APO: "The APO is the wide-awake watchdog of the Coloured man's interests ... and it is time that our teachers performed a share and discharged the much needed and specialized function of the wide-awake watchdog of the Coloured child's education."[60]

The APO and its newspaper played a decisive role in the formation of the first Coloured teachers' association, the Teachers' League of South Africa (TLSA), in Cape Town in June 1913. Although Harold Cressy, a prominent APO member, has been given credit as its founding father, the TLSA in fact was established by a group of teachers attached to the APO, under the influence of Abdurahman.[61] Whereas Cressy may have been the main organizer of the inaugural conference, Abdurahman was clearly instrumental in galvanizing teachers to join the organization. As the *Educational Journal*, the official organ of the TLSA, conceded in its obituary to Abdurahman, "It was he who influenced and guided the late Harold Cressy in the organisation of a Teachers' Union."[62]

The *APO* itself played an important part in the founding of the TLSA. The initial impulse to establish a Coloured teachers' association came in the form of an anonymous letter to the newspaper in July 1912 proposing the formation of a Coloured teachers' association to improve the "burdensome lot" of the Coloured mission school teacher. The merits of the proposal were discussed in the following issues of the *APO*, and reports concerning the planning and preliminary arrangements for the inaugural conference were publicized in the newspaper.[63] The role of the *APO* in this regard should not be underestimated, since several prior attempts to establish a Coloured teachers' association had failed owing to lack of organization.[64]

In addition to education, the Coloured petty bourgeoisie called for social programs to be initiated by the state and by the Coloureds themselves. *APO*'s abiding interest in the social welfare of the Coloured people reflected the elitism of the APO and the seriousness with which the organization assumed the mantle of leadership within the Coloured community. The Coloured petty bourgeoisie believed it had a moral obligation to uplift the Coloured laboring poor. Consequently, the *APO* commented at length on the social problems afflicting most members of the Coloured community.

The newspaper was most consistently concerned with the prevalence of "drink, dagga [marijuana] and dice" among the Coloured laboring classes. Alcoholism, in particular, was believed to be destroying family life. The high incidence of criminal behavior and disease as well as the continued poverty of Coloureds were to a large degree attributed to excessive drinking. To "respectable" Coloureds alcoholism was the most conspicuous and humiliating mark of Coloured social degradation. They were embarrassed by the drunken behavior of their working-class brethren, and they regarded alcoholism as a real impediment to the acceptance of "advanced" Coloureds into white middle-class society. The tot system[65] and vested interests in the liquor industry were blamed for the "drink curse" that hung over the Coloured commmunity. The *APO*'s crusade against alcoholism also reflected Abdurahman's concerns as a medical doctor as well as his convictions as a Muslim, for whom the consumption of alcohol was taboo.[66]

Anxiety was also expressed about the high incidence of *dagga* smoking among poorer Coloureds. A correspondent to the *Educational Journal*, for example, complained that whereas "only the lowest type of Coloured man" once smoked *dagga* ("in fact the Hottentots alone fell victim to it"), the habit was spreading to the "respectable classes" and even to whites.[67] *APO* also came out periodically against other "social evils" in the coloured community such as prostitution and gambling, the plight of homeless children living on the streets, the high infant mortality rate, juvenile delinquency, the absence of public facilities to care for retarded children and adults and to fight disease, the shortage of housing, and the harmful effects of poor working conditions.

The *APO*'s desire to raise the social condition of the Coloured masses was derived in part from the perception within the Coloured petty bourgeoisie that "progressive" and "respectable" Coloureds would not be distinguished from Coloured workers in the minds of whites. Coloured politicians assigned themselves the task of establishing middle-class standards for the entire community, so that there would be no justification for discriminating against the Coloured elite.

The Declining Years of the *APO* Newspaper

The enthusiasm that had sustained the newspaper during the early years of its life, however, gradually evaporated from 1911 onward. The membership of the APO itself had been shrinking after Union, and the association had become virtually dormant as a political pressure group by 1914. The newspaper was deeply in debt as a result of declining circulation and private news agents defaulting on payments for newspapers they had sold. The demoralization of the Coloured elite in the aftermath of Union, moreover, was reflected in *APO* news reports, which were repetitious and banal in tone and lacked originality.

The APO and its newspaper received a temporary reprieve with the coming of World War I. *APO* suddenly had access to exciting news stories that could be obtained with little cost. The attitude of the newspaper to the conflict was determined largely by the perception within the Coloured petty bourgeoisie that the Allied forces would triumph and white racial prejudice would be blunted in the postwar era. APO leaders proclaimed that the contribution of Coloureds to the war effort would be recognized and rewarded with the gradual lifting of racial barriers and with Coloureds in time being fully integrated into all aspects of national life.[68] *APO* helped to recruit volunteers for the Cape Corps, which was created to allow Coloureds to serve during the war. The Coloured petty bourgeoisie took great pride in the Cape Corps, and several APO leaders either served on the Cape Corps Comforts Committee or helped with fund-raising efforts.[69] Abe Desmore, a prominent APO member and a leading Coloured intellectual in the first half of the twentieth century, volunteered for service and wrote a book about his experiences.[70] Echoing the feelings of the Coloured elite, Desmore described the

Cape Corps as the answer to the "prayer of the Coloured community to be allowed to do their share in the toils of the Great War."[71]

Income from sales, advertising revenue and donations from APO branches, however, had barely covered operating expenses, even when the newspaper's circulation was at its height. Wartime inflation appeared to be the final straw,[72] and *APO* was forced to suspend publication in November 1915.

The views of the Coloured petty bourgeoisie during the war can be gauged from reading the *Educational Journal*, which was launched in May 1915 by the Teachers' League and was in a very real sense an associate publication of the *APO* newspaper. The *Journal* proclaimed in its first issue: "we look forward with calm confidence to the triumph of British might and British right. We are prouder than ever of being subjects of the glorious British Empire."[73] The expectations of the Coloured petty bourgeoisie as the war drew to a close were evident in the way the *Journal* reported a speech by Justice Frederick George Gardiner (who later became the first attorney general of the Cape Province) at a memorial service for Cape Corps members who had fallen in the East African campaign. Entitling the article "For the Empire and Right," the *Journal* savored his praise for Coloureds having "nobly answered the call [to enlist] in a way that must have shamed some of the young White men ... [and for helping to] bring home to those of European parentage a sense of duty." Gardner struck a deep chord within the Coloured elite when he extolled the Cape Corps for having fought "to free the world of slavery ... for the cause of humanity and civilization and ... the claim of Coloured people to be civilized."[74]

War's end, however, did not herald a new era for the Coloured people. APO in response resurrected its newspaper in August 1919 and organized the first party conference since 1913.[75] The postwar years witnessed a brief return to political protest. Immediately after the war, for example, the APO appealed to the British government not to place German South-West Africa under South African control until Coloured political rights had been restored, but this request was brushed aside by the colonial secretary. The APO sent a similar appeal to the Peace Conference in Paris in March 1919, but it was also ignored, and South Africa's racial franchise was extended to South-West Africa.[76]

Despite these and other disappointments, the *APO* remained optimistic that the Coloured petty bourgeoisie at least could achieve civil equality. The years between the end of World War I and the demise of the newspaper in 1923 predated the legislative onslaught on black political and civil rights. As late as 1920, the *Educational Journal* was confident that "the leavening effect of the South [the Cape liberal tradition] is slowly having its effect on the North."[77] The Coloured middle class, moreover, was growing in size and gaining confidence in its ability to sustain the economic standards required to achieve white middle-class respectability.

Cape Coloureds were becoming increasingly politicized and able to meet the franchise qualifications, and the Coloured vote was a growing force in the politics of the western Cape. The black (African, Coloured, Indian) vote had grown from about 15 percent of the Cape electorate in 1910 to 21 percent by 1921, while the Coloured share of the electorate had grown from about 9.5 percent to 14 percent during the same period.[78] Coloureds constituted about 26 percent of the electorate in nine Cape peninsular seats and 44 percent of the Woodstock (Cape Town) constituency by 1915.[79] The Coloured vote was also becoming significant in the larger towns of the western Cape.[80]

Coloured political leaders were also drawing encouragement from white opposition to the South African government, as evidenced by the 1914 revolt and the 1922 Rand Rebellion. They hoped that white rebelliousness would serve as a foil for Coloured patriotism, and Coloureds by comparison would be perceived as responsible, law-abiding citizens worthy of full acceptance into the dominant society. By condemning the extremist tactics of white workers, APO invited direct comparison between "respectable" Coloureds and the fractious white working class.[81]

Given its constituency, the *APO* had little choice but to persist with a news agenda that combined economic and social enterprise with a cautious, pragmatic approach to the struggle for political rights. For example, at APO's yearly conference in 1923, the year its newspaper ceased publication, two very successful self-help ventures aimed at harnassing the savings generated within the Coloured community were launched. The APO Burial Society and the APO Building Society outlived the parent organization and are still in existence today.[82]

The revival of APO's mouthpiece was prompted by the appearance of the weekly *South African Clarion*, which was launched in April 1919. This newspaper was controlled by Coloured supporters of the National Party and opposed the APO, which had supported the Unionists and later the South African Party.[83] Coloured National Party supporters came together in October 1919 at the instigation of J. B. M. Hertzog, the future prime minister, and leading Cape Nationalists to form the United Afrikaner League (UAL). UAL supporters, who were given assurances by Hertzog that Coloureds would receive better treatment in a future Nationalist government, began canvassing support for the National Party within the Coloured community. This initiative was probably orchestrated by Cape Nationalist leaders, who had received an object lesson in the significance of the Coloured vote in the western Cape during the 1915 general election, when the South African Party won most of the seats. They were determined to gain the support of Coloured voters in the upcoming 1921 election.[84]

Gavin Lewis's characterization of the *Clarion* as "the mouthpiece of the Cape Nationalists" is clearly justified. The *Clarion* denied any party political affiliation at first and tried to create a semblance of political impartiality, but by August 1919 it was openly supporting the National Party.[85] Although the UAL later used the *Clarion* to publicize its political views and attack the APO, the newspaper was more in the nature of what Lewis calls "a propaganda bulletin for the Cape National Party." The *Clarion* was funded by the National Party and printed on *Die Burger*'s presses, and it went so far as to promote the idea of Cape Coloureds being placed on a separate voters' roll, a proposal that even the UAL found unacceptable.[86] The *Clarion* tried to manipulate the UAL to serve Nationalist political interests, and attacked Abdurahman and the *APO* for being the pawns of foreign mining capitalists and biased in favor of the English and their political parties. The newspaper stressed the cultural and historical ties between Coloureds and white Afrikaners and urged Coloureds to support the Nationalists, because they would advance Coloured interests.[87]

The *Clarion* made little headway, because the UAL, its main advocate, had minimal credibility within the Coloured community. The idea of placing Coloureds on a separate voters' roll, for example, found no support whatsoever within the community. Abdurahman and the APO made strenuous efforts to counter the propaganda of the *Clarion* by pointing to the inherent racism of Nationalist policies. *APO* warned Coloured voters repeatedly that the overtures of the

National Party (and the Labour Party) consisted of empty promises and were nothing but a cynical attempt to manipulate them politically.[88] The APO was vindicated when the *Clarion* abruptly ceased publication after the 1921 general election. The UAL collapsed about the same time, but most members resurfaced in the Afrikaanse Nasionale Bond when it was established in 1925.

A noteworthy feature of the resuscitated *APO* newspaper was its concern with Coloured labor and employment issues. This interest stemmed from the APO's abortive attempt to organize Coloured workers under the umbrella of the APO Federation of Labour Unions, which was launched at the 1919 conference. The APO's foray into labor organization was symptomatic of the upsurge in labor unrest in the postwar years. The APO saw the growing militancy of Coloured workers as an opportunity to expand support. Except for some municipal workers and a few branches of the newly established South African Workmen's Cooperative Union under the leadership of Charles Meyer, however, few workers could be persuaded to join the Federation. Skilled Coloureds organized in small craft unions preferred to affiliate with the Cape Federation of Labour Unions, which organized white as well as black artisans, while unskilled black workers joined the Industrial and Commercial Workers Union. The APO Federation of Trade Unions collapsed almost immediately, and an attempt to revive it at the APO's 1920 conference also failed.[89]

Meanwhile, a sustained attack on the economic position of skilled and semiskilled black workers was mounted by the state in the early 1920s. The Juvenile Affairs Act of 1921 and the Apprenticeship Act of 1922, for example, were intended to encourage more white youths to enter skilled trades. Since the Juvenile Affairs Act applied only to those subject to compulsory education, whites were virtually the only ones who benefited from it. The measure regulated the Juvenile Affairs Board, whose main function was to find suitable employment for white youths. A parallel but subordinate Juvenile Advisory Board, staffed by voluntary workers, was set up for Coloureds. The *APO* was initially optimistic about the potential of the Advisory board for serving Coloured interests, and prominent APO members like Abdurahman, Stephen Reagon and C. J. Carelse agreed to serve as members of the Board's executive committee.[90]

The Apprenticeship Act also made devious use of the compulsory education regulations to give an advantage to whites in the competition for employment. It set a minimum educational requirement of Standard VI (eighth grade) for entrance into an apprenticeship for specified trades. Since passing Standard VI by this time was a minimum condition for complying with the compulsory education regulations, most white youths would qualify for an apprenticeship. Very few Coloureds had the economic resources to gain more than two years of formal education, and few mission schools went beyond Standard IV (sixth grade).[91] Thus the vast majority of Coloureds did not qualify for apprenticeship programs. Coloured artisans believed the necessary skills could be passed on from tradesman to apprentice through on-the-job training. In fact, it was fairly common for an artisan to train his son in the trade, and these skills would be retained in the family for several generations. Many skilled but poorly educated Coloured tradesmen feared their children would be unable to follow in their footsteps with the passing of the Apprenticeship Act.[92]

The APO and its newspaper did not object as vociferously as one might have expected to these discriminatory measures. Many, in the early 1920s, hoped Coloured education would be reformed and Standard VI placed within reach of most Coloured youth. Thus the Juvenile Advisory Board could be turned to the advantage of Coloureds. It took several years of futile effort to convince Coloured activists that meaningful reform of Coloured education would not happen and that they would not be able to use the Advisory Board to their advantage. It was only from the late 1920s, when Coloureds started experiencing severe restrictions to occupational mobility, that the political elite protested more vigorously against this legislation.

The revived *APO* never regained the vigor it displayed in the early years of its existence. The newspaper switched from an irregular fortnightly to a monthly in October 1920, but the quality of the reportage continued to decline as increasing financial problems and falling circulation sapped the morale of its staff. *APO* ceased publication in December 1923, while the APO as an organization maintained a precarious existence for two decades, until it finally collapsed in 1944.

Nevertheless, the *APO* was by far the most important Coloured newspaper before the advent of a commercial Coloured press in the 1930s.[93] *APO* reflected primarily the lived experiences of the petty bourgeoisie, and as the mouthpiece of the APO it epitomized the spirit of social assimilation and political accommodation that characterized black protest politics during this era. The newspaper also sought to represent a range of issues affecting the Coloured population at a time when Coloured voices were rarely recorded. *APO* provided a window into a community that would remain on the margins of South Africa's resistance movement for many years to come.

Notes

1. The term "Coloured" in South Africa refers to a phenotypically diverse community descended largely from imported slaves, indigenous Khoisan and other "free" blacks assimilated to Cape colonial society. Coloureds are also partly descended from European settlers, and are identified as a "mixed race," a distinct intermediate group in South Africa's racial hierarchy.
2. L. M. Thompson, *The unification of South Africa, 1902–1910* (London, 1961), 305–306, 340–341.
3. *APO*, 24 May 1909, 4; 4 June 1910, 6, 10.
4. C. Saunders, "F. Z. S. Peregrino and the *South African Spectator*," *Quarterly Bulletin of the South African Library* 32, 3 (1977–78), 81–90.
5. For a list of the surviving issues of the *South African Spectator*, see Saunders, "Peregrino," 81. For the claim that the *South African Spectator* was probably still appearing as late as 1908, see B. Willan, "Correspondence," *Quarterly Bulletin of the South African Library* 33, 1 (1978), 34–36.
6. But it is doubtful that APO membership had reached 20,000, as claimed at the time by its newspaper and by some contemporary scholars. Cf. *APO*, 14 January 1911, 9, and G. Lewis, *Between the wire and the wall: A history of South African "Coloured" politics* (Cape Town, 1987), 30. It is possible the organization attracted these numbers for a short while during the protest campaign against Union, but the evidence suggests that membership was in the region of about 5,000 and the circulation of *APO* about 4,000 in early 1911. *APO*, 14 January 1911, 9, 11. Specific figures are not available, but it is clear from the text that APO membership, and consequently the newspaper's readership, declined in subsequent years.
7. John Tobin, a local café owner, convened the Stone Meetings in May 1901, and they drew considerable interest initially from Coloureds and from white politicians who were courting their support. Tobin himself broke with the APO in 1905, but he continued to convene sporadic meetings to publicize his pro-Afrikaner sympathies

until at least the late 1910s. His views after 1905 had little impact on the Coloured petty bourgeoisie or on the community as a whole.

8. R. E. van der Ross, "A political and social history of the Cape Coloured people, 1880–1970," 4 vols., 902 pages, typescript (Manuscripts and Archives Division, University of Cape Town, 1973), 484.
9. *APO*, 25 February 1911, 10.
10. Although the identity of Piet Uithalder was never revealed by the *APO* itself, the rival *South African Clarion*, which included former APO stalwarts like N. R. Veldsman and J. A. Poggenpoel, identified Abdurahman as the author of "Straatpraatjes." See *Clarion*, 17 January 1920, 9.
11. *APO*, 11 September 1909, 14.
12. *APO*, 13 August 1910, 5.
13. *APO*, 8 April 1911, 3.
14. *APO*, e.g., 13 August 1910, 5; 8 April 1911, 3; 6 May 1911, 5; 13 January 1912, 6; 10 August 1912, 8; *Educational Journal*, July 1917, 7; June 1918, 6; September 1918, 2–3.
15. *APO*, 4 June 1910, 6.
16. *Clarion*, 17 January 1920, 9.
17. J. S. Marais, *The Cape Coloured people, 1652–1937* (Johannesburg, 1957), 275–276; Lewis, *Wire and wall*, 15.
18. Marais, *Cape Coloured*, 275–277; Lewis, "The reaction of the Cape 'Coloureds' to segregation," Ph.D. thesis (Queens University, 1984), 27–29, 40; S. Trapido, " 'The friends of the natives': Merchants, peasants and the political and ideological structure of liberalism at the Cape," in S. Marks and A. Atmore (eds.), *Economy and society in pre-industrial South Africa* (London, 1980), 256; Thompson, *Unification*, 11–12. Britain's willingness to sacrifice black political rights in order to appease the Boers was confirmed when blacks were excluded from the municipal franchise of the Transvaal and the Orange River Colony in 1903.
19. See esp. *APO*, 24 May 1909, 2–4; 5 June 1909, 2–4; 17 July 1909, 7; 14 August 1909, 5; 11 September 1909, 5–7; 9 April 1910, 5–8.
20. *APO*, 7 May 1910, 8–9; 4 June 1910, 8.
21. The term "African," in this instance, was meant to denote the geographical location of the organization and in a vague way to imply international solidarity with black people. It was not intended to express a desire for political unity with Africans in South Africa.
22. For example, when reporting a meeting of the Cape Town branch, the newspaper identified a Mr. Zini who participated in the discussion as "a native from Queenstown." *APO*, 4 November 1911, 7.
23. *SAS*, 4 May 1901, 4.
24. *SAS*, 18 May 1901, 8.
25. *APO*, 24 May 1909, 5.
26. Lewis, "Reaction," 149–150; Marais, *Cape Coloured*, 257, 278-289; *APO*, 14 August 1909, 5–6; 9 April 1909, 8.
27. *APO*, 9 April 1910, 7.
28. *APO*, 12 February 1910, 9–10; 12 March 1910, 9–10; 24 September 1910, 2; 22 April 1911, 8; 22 Oct 1910, 10; 3 June 1911, 10; 17 June 1911, 9; 7 October 1911, 14; 18 May 1912, 5–6.
29. A. Meier, *Negro thought in America* (Ann Arbor, 1966), Chap. 7; L. Harlan, *Booker T. Washington: The making of a black leader* (New York, 1972), esp. Chap. 11; A. Taylor, *Travail and triumph: Black life and culture in the south since the Civil War* (Westport, Conn., 1976), 54–55.
30. *APO*, e.g., 31 July 1909, 5; 12 February 1910, 5; 10 September 1910, 5; 22 October 1910, 10; 5 November 1910, 10.
31. *APO*, e.g., 8 April 1911, 5–7; 6 December 1913, 7–8.
32 *Educational Journal*, December 1917, 7; November 1920, 4; August 1922, 6; J. Rhoda, "A contribution toward the study of education among the Cape Coloured people," B.Ed. thesis (University of Cape Town, 1929), 2ff., 59; R. E. van der Ross, *Myths and attitudes: An inside look at the Coloured people* (Cape Town, 1979), 75.
33. *APO*, 31 July 1909, 4; 3 December 1910, 10.
34. *APO*, 4 December 1909, 7; 3 December 1910, 11; 24 December 1910, 2–4; 6 May 1911, 9; 6 December 1913, 5; 12 September 1919, 7; 30 October 1920, 10; 1 July 1922, 11; 2 September 1922, 11.
35. *APO*, 24 February 1912, 5.
36. Lewis, *Wire and wall*, 79.
37. Trapido, *Merchants*, 257; *APO*, 8 October 1910, 7–8; 24 December 1910, 7–8; 26 August 1911, 9; 4 May 1912, 11; 1 June 1912, 7–9.

38. M. Weinberg (ed.), *W. E. B. Du Bois: A reader* (New York, 1970), xi–xvii; Meier, *Negro thought*, Chap. 9; see also D. L. Lewis, *W. E. B. DuBois: Biography of a race, 1868–1919*, Vol. 1 (New York, 1993).
39. *APO*, 25 March 1911, 7.
40. *APO*, 12 March 1910, 8; 26 March 1910, 3, 5, 8–9; 7 May 1910, 11; 24 September 1910, 3–4; 17 June 1911, 7–9; 23 September 1911, 7, 10; 13 January 1912, 3–4; 6 March 1912, 7; 6 April 1912, 9–10; 20 April 1912, 7; 1 June, 1912, 7–9; 7 November 1919, 6; 2 October 1920, 2.
41. *APO*, 12 February 1910, 5.
42. *APO*, 7 May 1910, 11; 24 September 1910, 4; 22 October 1910, 11; 6 May 1911, 4; 13 January 1912, 3–4; 12 June 1920, 4; 2 December 1922, 11.
43. *Educational Journal,* March 1922, 3–4.
44. *APO*, 4 June 1910, 8; 3 October 1910, 3; 28 January 1911, 5; 21 December 1912, 2–4; S. Trapido, "The origin and development of the African Political Organization," in *Institute for Commonwealth Studies: Collected Seminar Papers* (London, 1969–70), 97; Trapido, "White conflict and non-white participation in the politics of the Cape of Good Hope," Ph.D. thesis (University of London, 1970), 425.
45. J. W. de Kock et al. (eds.), *Dictionary of South African biography*, Vol. 1 (Cape Town, 1968), 1–3 (Abdullah Abdurahman); E. L. Maurice, "The development of policy in regard to the education of the Coloured pupils at the Cape, 1880–1940," Ph.D. thesis (University of Cape Town, 1966), App. E; H. J. Simons and R. E. Simons, *Class and colour in South Africa, 1850–1950* (London, 1983), 117–120. See also *Sun,* 1 March 1940–14 June 1940 for a series of biographical articles on Abdurahman.
46. *APO*, 2 July 1910, 6.
47. Compulsory education was first provided to the age of 14, or Std. IV (sixth grade), and subsequently raised to 15, or Std. V, in 1917 and 16, or Std. VI, in 1919.
48. Cf. *Education Commission Report*, 1879–80 (G.75-1880), 2; *Superintendent General of Education Report*, 1882, 13; *SGE Special Report*, 1890 (G.6a-1890), 3–4; *Report of the Select Committee on the Three Education Bills*, 1896, (C.1-1896), 79–86.
49. Cf. Maurice, "Development of policy," 23ff.; *APO*, 12 July 1913, 4, 7; 1 August 1919, 3; *Cape Times,* 7 September 1921; *SGE Report,* 1913, statistical index, 43a; Cape Archives Depot, Cape Town, *Records of the Cape Provincial Administration, Department of Education*, PAE, Vol. 1903, SF/C5/27, Inspector Charles to S.G.E., 7 October 1919.
50. *APO*, 19 June 1909, 6-7. See also *APO,* 17 July 1909, 5–6; Van der Ross, *History,* 466.
51. A. Abdurahman, *The education bill* (Cape Town, 1905); *APO,* 28 January 1911, 5.
52. *APO*, 19 June 1909, 6.
53. *APO*, 29 July 1911, 7–8; 21 October 1911, 5–6; 13 July 1912, 6; 27 July 1912, 6; 5 April 1913, 7; 18 April 1914, 7; van der Ross, "History", 466.
54. *APO*, 7 October 1911, 10; 1 June 1912, 5; 26 June 1915, 4–5; Maurice, "Development of policy," 311.
55. *APO*, 27 July 1911, 7–8.
56. *APO*, 2 July 1910, 6; M. Adhikari, "The origin and founding of the Teachers' League of South Africa," B.A. honours thesis (University of Cape Town, 1981), 43–45, 75ff.
57. *APO*, 2 July 1910, 6.
58. Van der Ross, "History," 702. M. Adhikari, "The Teachers' League of South Africa, 1913–1940," M.A. thesis (University of Cape Town, 1986), Chap. 5.
59. *APO*, 2 July 1910, 6.
60. *APO*, 27 July 1912, 6.
61. M. Adhikari, *Let us live for our children: The Teachers' League of South Africa, 1913–1940* (Cape Town, 1992), Chap. 1.
62. *Educational Journal,* February 1940, 5.
63. *APO*, 13 July 1912, 7; 27 July 1912, 6–7; 10 August 1912, 5–6; 24 August 1912, 5–6; 7 September 1912, 10; 12 July 1913, 7–8.
64. Adhikari, *Let us live for our children*, 20, 22, 24.
65. The "tot system" was a practice in which white employers, especially farmers, paid black employees part of their wages in daily rations of cheap wine. These employers used alcoholic addiction to control labor and maintain a docile and dependent workforce.
66. *APO*, 9 October 1909, 7; 9 April 1910, 8; 5 November 1910, 5; 7 October 1911, 15;

16 November 1912, 15; 8 February 1913, 5–6, 10; 20 March 1920, 3; 2 October 1920, 3.

67. *Educational Journal,* October 1917, 4.
68. *APO*, 3 October 1914, 4; 17 October, 1914, 4; 31 October 1914, 4; 14 November 1914, 5, 7; Cf. Van der Ross, *Myths*, 76; Lewis, *Reaction* , 208ff. J. D. Shingler, "Education and the political order in South Africa," Ph. D. thesis (Yale University, 1976), 11–12.
69. *APO*, 5 September 1914, 3–7; 19 September, 1914, 7; *Educational Journal,* May 1915, 4-5; April 1917, 4; July 1917, 8; December 1917, 7.
70. A. Desmore, *With the second Cape Corps through central Africa* (Cape Town, 1920).
71. Ibid., 5.
72. See R. McGregor, *McGregor's who owns whom: The investor's handbook* (Cape Town, 1990). The rear foldout contains an index and the annual percentage changes of the purchasing power of the rand or its equivalent for the period 1910 to 1989.
73. *Educational Journal,* May 1915, 4.
74. *Educational Journal,* December 1917, 7.
75. M. Simons claims that the newspaper was reconstituted with financial aid from the Unionist Party but offers no evidence to substantiate this claim. M. Simons, "Organized Coloured political movements," in H. W. van der Merwe and C. J. Groenewald (eds.), *Occupational and social change among Coloured people in South Africa* (Cape Town, 1976), 212.
76. *APO*, 1 August 1919, 10–12.
77. *Educational Journal,* December 1920, 3.
78. *Union Year Book*, No. 23, 1946 (G.P. 53895-1947), Chap. 2, 46–47; L. M. Thompson, *The Cape Coloured franchise* (Johannesburg, 1949), 55.
79. *Cape Times,* 19 October 1915, 6; T. Shifrin, "New deal for Coloured people: A study of National Party policies toward the Coloured people, 1924–1929," B. A. honours thesis (University of Cape Town, 1962), 10; *APO,* 1 August 1919, 5.
80. Lewis, *Wire and wall* , 21, 84, 128–131; R. E. van der Ross, *The rise and decline of apartheid: A study of political movements among the Coloured people of South Africa, 1880–1985* (Cape Town, 1986), 72–78.
81. *APO,* 28 January 1922, 5; 25 March 1922, 9–11; *Educational Journal,* April 1922, 5.
82. *APO,* 1 August 1919, 4–5; 15 August 1919, 8; 12 September 1919, 12; 3 April 1920, 4; 15 May 1920, 3; 28 January 1922, 2; 22 April 1922, 5; 1 July 1922, 5; 21 April 1923, 9; 22 December 1923, 1, 3, 6.
83. After Union, the APO supported the Unionist Party, by and large the successor to the Progressive Party of the former Cape parliament. The Unionists were supported by the Cape liberals, so Coloured activists believed this was the party that would most likely protect Coloured civil rights. After the Unionist Party disbanded in 1920 and most of its members joined the South African Party, the APO transferred its electoral support to these candidates.
84. *Clarion,* 25 October 1919, 11; 1 November 1919, 9.
85. *Clarion,* 23 August 1919, 6.
86. Lewis, *Wire and wall* , 122–125.
87. *Clarion,* e.g., 3 May 1919, 7–8; 10 May 1919, 11; 23 August 1919, 6; 13 September 1919, 14; 25 October 1919, 7, 11; 1 November 1919, 6; 13 December 1919, 6–7; 21 February 1920, 4; 13 March 1920, 4–5.
88. *APO,* 7 November 1919, 8–9; 22 November 1919, 8-9; 30 December 1919, 6; 17 January 1920, 5, 11; 31 January 1920, 4; 28 February 1920, 7; 20 March 1920, 3.
89. *APO,* 29 August 1919, 5–6; 12 September 1919, 3; 26 September 1919, 3, 6; 6 December 1919, 4; 21 August 1920, 11; Lewis, *Wire and wall* , 94–101.
90. *APO,* 31 January 1920, 11; 17 April 1920, 6; 19 May 1923, 9.
91. In 1922 only 1.5 percent of pupils in Coloured schools were beyond Standard V (seventh grade). See *SGE Report*, 1922, 168.
92. Rhoda, "A contribution toward the study of education among the Cape Coloured people," 47.
93. The *Sun* was established in August 1932 and the *Cape Standard* in May 1936.

CHAPTER 5

Moderate and Militant Voices in the African Nationalist Press during the 1920s

Les Switzer

The African petty bourgeoisie became more impoverished and more fragmented in the generation after 1910.* As the new South African state steadily expanded its power over the black population and discrimination and oppression at all levels intensified, these mediators of African political and civil rights found themselves increasingly marginalized. More and more lower-ranked Africans on the fringes of the middle class descended into the ranks of the proletariat, but salaried white-collar workers fared little better. Pay scales, living and working conditions were so poor that even Africans positioned in the highest ranks of the professional elite had little opportunity to emulate the lifestyles of their white counterparts. It is not surprising that alienated segments of the African petty bourgeoisie from time to time found common cause with unorganized industrial workers and peasants in openly challenging South Africa's social order.

Such a challenge occurred in the years immediately following World War I. In town, soaring food prices, low wages and job discrimination temporarily galvanized African workers, especially in the Johannesburg area, where a wave of wildcat strikes and boycotts appeared to threaten civil order. Members of the South African Native National Congress were divided over the most appropriate response to take toward industrial strife, and mobilizing workers briefly radicalized African politics in the Transvaal.[1] In the countryside, fluctuating grain prices, prolonged drought, and plant and animal diseases posed an immediate threat to food and stock production in the reserves, while outbreaks of smallpox, typhoid, cholera and the dreaded Spanish influenza epidemic of 1918–19 had a devastating impact on the malnourished African peasantry.[2]

The ruling South African Party, under the leadership of Jan Smuts since 1919, responded in part by creating an all-white Native Affairs Commission under the 1920 Native Affairs Act to advise the authorities on matters involving Africans living outside as well as inside the reserves. Another consultative body, made up of government-approved Africans from the urban and rural areas, met once a year in a Natives' Conference to discuss matters deemed to be relevant to Africans. Individual land tenure and local government in the African reserves would be

*I am grateful to Catherine Nawa-Gwamanda, a South African living in Houston, for her work in translating and coding the Xhosa-language stories in the *Imvo Zabantsundu* sample. I am also grateful to Ime Ukpanah for acting as a coder in the quantitative analysis of the *Workers' Herald*.

extended beyond the few districts in the eastern Cape that had implemented such measures under the 1894 Glen Grey Act. Africans in town would be given a forum for discussion in local government with the establishment of Location Advisory Boards. These measures signaled a desire on the part of the central government to employ moderate African nationalists as intermediaries in the ongoing process of organizing African opinion to conform to the demands of the new political dispensation.

The process of co-optation in the cities had already begun during the war, when white "friends of the natives," the guardians of the Cape liberal tradition in postcolonial South Africa, with the backing of mining capital, began forming welfare associations in a bid to improve African living standards. Following the end of hostilities, a number of social and recreational facilities for Africans were established that became cultural venues for the parties, contests, concerts, film shows, speeches, debates and meetings targeted specifically at the urban African petty bourgeoisie. Parallel cultural organizations were created for Africans already segregated in other activities: the Pathfinders and Wayfarers, for example, would duplicate the Boy Scouts and Girl Guides.

The "friends of the natives" established clinics and child-care centers, night schools, libraries and reading rooms, literary, debating and drama groups; sports, games and film shows were even introduced in the mining compounds housing African workers.[3] These activities were centered on the Witwatersrand (or Rand), an Afrikaans term that means literally "Ridge of the White Waters." In the 1920s, the Rand was a crescent-shaped constellation of towns in the southern Transvaal, with Johannesburg at its center, that stretched for 60 miles across the largest goldfield in the world. It was, and would remain, the industrial heartland of southern Africa.

The Joint Council movement was the most important political response by white liberals to African grievances during the 1920s and 1930s.[4] The first Joint Council was organized in Johannesburg in 1921, a year after an African mine workers' strike on the Witwatersrand, and there were 26 Joint Councils in the major cities and towns of South Africa by 1930 and about 40 by 1935. The agents of co-optation comprised a cross section of the white-liberal petty bourgeoisie. Clergy were most represented, and it was the Dutch Reformed Church, for example, that took the lead in organizing European–Bantu conferences in 1923 and 1927 in conjunction with the Joint Councils. But university academics, teachers, lawyers, journalists, businessmen, and even municipal officials and government civil servants joined the councils and were involved in their activities. Supplementing the councils were a variety of other interracial mission, church and student welfare-cum-civil rights groups.

Although membership fees were kept low for black members in an attempt to ensure racial parity, it was clear from the beginning that white members would provide the leadership in the Joint Councils. They had the time and money, the contacts with white officialdom and the experience in white party politics. Above all, they were committed to redirecting the liberal discourse toward an accommodation with the government's segregationist policies.[5]

These policies expanded dramatically in the aftermath of the Rand Rebellion, the confrontation in 1922 between capital and white labor on the Witwatersrand that resulted in the death of more than 200 people (including about 30 blacks, who were killed by white mobs). Striking white mine workers had formed commandos and threatened to take over Johannesburg and adjacent mining towns, and Smuts had employed armed and mounted troops, heavy artillery and even planes to suppress them. A Nationalist-Labour coalition government, under the leadership of J. B. M. Hertzog, came to power two years later with overwhelming support from alienated white workers and low-ranked members of the white middle class. Succeeding governments would enact a series of legislative measures in the next 15 years to protect the status of white workers at the expense of their black counterparts. Hertzog and his allies would attempt to proletarianize and retribalize the entire African population in pursuit of these interests and reduce all Africans to the lowest levels of wage labor.

The African petty bourgeoisie was now clearly in danger of being pushed wholesale into the ranks of the working poor and unemployed. Some segments continued to accept white trusteeship as the best guarantee that their existing rights and privileges would be safeguarded. The South African Native National Congress (SANNC), renamed the African National Congress (ANC, or Congress) in 1923, was a political haven for moderate nationalists, but Congress in the 1920s and 1930s was fragmented by numerous internal conflicts, poorly administered and without financial resources. Nevertheless, some branches (notably the Cape Western Congress) had important links with working-class groups, and President General Josiah Gumede would provide a more militant agenda for the organization during his stormy tenure (1927–30).

Alienated nationalists found other alternatives in a burgeoning African trade union movement epitomized by the Industrial and Commercial Workers' Union (ICU) and the Communist Party of South Africa (CPSA), which resolved in 1924 to concentrate on organizing black workers, in African-American expressions of black unity and independence, and in millenarian religious movements operating mainly in the countryside. The African nationalist movement embraced most of these strategies in a complex and sometimes volatile mix of discourses that would have important implications for protest politics during this period.

Case Study of *Imvo Zabantsundu* and *Workers' Herald*

This case study examines the narrative structures of two independent African nationalist newspapers in the 1920s, a turbulent decade in South African history. *Imvo Zabantsundu* and the *Workers' Herald* were recognized organs of moderate and militant political opinion, respectively, and it was assumed that these newspapers would seek to represent the divergent interests and concerns of their respective audiences.[6]

Imvo under the Editorship of the Jabavu Family

Imvo Zabantsundu (Native Opinion), still published by the Jabavu family in King William's Town, continued to provide news and opinion that was primarily of interest to the aspirant middle-class sector in the eastern Cape. *Imvo* is of particular interest to this study because most subscribers were voters, the only Africans who had even qualified franchise rights in South Africa. African and Coloured franchise holders constituted at their peak in 1921 about 20.8 percent of the Cape vote. A record 16,481 African voters (7.6 percent of the Cape vote) were recorded in 1927, but the African electorate declined steadily thereafter under pressure from the central government. An estimated 10,453 of 14,912 African voters in the province in 1926, 70 percent of the Cape voting community, resided in *Imvo*'s prime circulation area in the eastern Cape.[7] The voters were a fragile elite – socially isolated, increasingly destabilized and extremely conscious of their vulnerability. They were relatively insignificant in numbers and increasingly differentiated as regards occupation, education and affluence. In an ever-expanding culture of poverty, lower-ranked members with little education and low incomes were hardly distinguishable from the African majority, especially in the African reserves.

The mission-educated families who had dominated African middle-class political and social life in the eastern Cape in the late colonial period continued to do so in the generation after 1910. John Tengo Jabavu, the pioneer figure in Cape African politics, would be followed by his eldest son Davidson Don Tengo Jabavu, one of the most prominent mediators of moderate African nationalist opinion in South Africa during the interwar period. His personal piety and lifelong allegiance to the church coupled with his compelling belief in the power of the written word gave him a status within the mission-educated community that few others could emulate. As a leading proponent of white trusteeship, he was closely associated with groups like the Joint Councils and Native Welfare Societies that had been established by white liberals for Africans. Working with organizations like the Ciskeian Missionary Council, an attempt was made to provide these amenities for Africans in the eastern Cape.[8]

Jabavu family members also played a prominent role in the government advisory bodies for Africans established during the interwar period, and they were a driving force in the development of independent African political, economic and cultural organizations in the region. D. D. T. Jabavu himself was the standard-bearer for African nationalists in relations with the central government. As a member of the government-sponsored Native Conferences, for example, he was often their representative when legislation affecting Africans was contemplated. His advice was regularly sought by legislative committees and commissions of inquiry during the 1920s when considering such topics as the pass laws (Godley Committee in 1920), residence in urban areas (Native [Urban Areas] Act of 1923), wages and living conditions (Economic and Wage Commission of 1925–26).

Jabavu and APO leader Dr. Abdul Abdurahman, still the most prominent spokesperson for Coloured rights in the Cape, organized four Non-European Conferences between 1927 and 1934 that for the first time brought together leading members of the African, Coloured and Indian petty bourgeoisie to discuss Hertzog's segregationist policies. No permanent body was formed, and the Indians remained on the periphery of proceedings, but it set a precedent for the future. The African liberal tradition in the eastern Cape would eventually coalesce with the All-African Convention in 1935.

The African mission-educated community maintained control over most African political bodies in the eastern Cape in the 1920s and 1930s. Although the key organizations during the colonial period – the various Imbumba and the South African Native Congress – had ceased functioning during World War I, new ones were established soon after the war ended in 1918. They included the Bantu Union; the Ciskei Native Convention and the Cape Native Voters' Convention; the ANC's eastern Cape branch, headquartered at Cradock; and various branches of the ICU. These regional organizations were linked to local political networks, or Vigilance Associations (Iliso Lomzis); to groups representing farmers, teachers, students and other special interests; and to the government-sponsored Location Advisory Boards in town, and local and district councils (and regional councils in the case of the Transkei and eventually the Ciskei) in the African reserves.

Tengo Jabavu himself seems to have been increasingly disenchanted with organized African politics in the waning years of his life. He had already antagonized segments of the Cape voting community by backing the Afrikaner Bond during the 1898 Cape colonial election, by refusing to join the SANNC in 1912, by accepting the 1913 Natives' Land Act and by splitting the African vote in the 1914 Cape provincial election. His tirades against African nationalists in the northern provinces after 1912 were equaled only by his denunciation of the Afrikaner nationalists, and these issues dominated *Imvo*'s editorial pages after World War I.

Tengo Jabavu's attitude to the SANNC at this time was epitomized in *Imvo* editorials and news reports covering the African protest delegation to London and Paris in 1918–19. As noted in earlier chapters, African nationalists had been organizing overseas deputations since the late nineteenth century. They protested the impending Act of Union in 1909, and the SANNC continued to protest after Union in 1910 in an effort to bring outside pressure to bear on the South African government. A delegation in 1914 had appealed to King George V and the British parliament to annul the 1913 Natives' Land Act, and at the conclusion of World War I another overseas delegation to London sought to petition the monarch to intervene on behalf of his African subjects. The deputation also crossed the channel in an unsuccessful bid to present African grievances to delegates meeting in Versailles to decide the fate of Germany and its allies.

Editorial-page articles in *Imvo* positioned the "Dutch Nationalists" next to the "Native Nationalists" and condemned both for "desiring to go to the Peace Conference with internal and local grievances, which anybody with any common sense would tell them are unfit subjects for such a gathering." The decision to send a SANNC delegation was "perfectly ridiculous and puerile," and the delegates were "embarked on a fools' errand." They were "loud-mouthed agitators" who represented "a minority of the Natives, the best part of whom realise that they are members of the Union of South Africa ... if they have grievances–and nobody denies that they have–they are domestic questions not for outsiders to arrange a settlement."[9]

Tengo Jabavu's fear of "Hertzog's escapades"[10] was equaled only by his fear of militant African nationalists who sought to confront those who ruled. Strikes by Africans in Johannesburg in 1918, for example, were covered only from the official point of view: "Native labourers" were warned to avoid being the "tools" of "certain white agitators" and advised "when in trouble to come to the Government, their Father." A riot in April 1920 by "irresponsible youths" at Lovedale, the prestigious mission school in the eastern Cape that Jabavu's sons had attended, had done "incalculable harm to Native education."[11]

Alexander Macaulay ("Mac") Jabavu inherited this legacy when he took over as editor of the newspaper after the death of his father in September 1921. He had qualified as a primary school teacher at Lovedale and lived for several years in Kimberley, where he became active in sports, music (as a singer and piano player) and other cultural activities in the life of the local African middle-class community. Like D. D. T. Jabavu, his elder brother, Alexander was an officer in the Cape Native Voters' Convention and other independent African organizations at the regional level, and a prominent figure on numerous government advisory bodies–a founder-member of the Location Advisory Boards' Congress of South Africa (established in 1928); the Ciskei General Council, or Bunga (established in 1934);[12] and the Natives' Representative Council (he represented the Cape rural areas outside Transkei from 1937 to 1942), which was created as a national forum for Africans after the promulgation of the 1936 Representation of Natives Act abolishing the Cape African franchise. The Jabavu family would lose control of *Imvo* to the Argus Company in 1934, although Alexander stayed on as editor until 1940. He resigned apparently because of ill health but remained active in regional politics until his death in 1946.

Imvo was probably more circumscribed in content in the 1920s than it had been a generation earlier when literate African culture was in its infancy. The newspaper's circulation is unknown, but apparently it had declined from a high of 4,000 during the colonial era to perhaps 2,000 by the beginning of the 1920s.[13] The "carry-on readership"–those who had access to the newspaper after it was purchased–may have been 5 to 10 times this figure. Xhosa speakers were still the most widely dispersed ethnic group in South Africa, and there was always a significant pool of potential readers in metropolitan areas outside the eastern Cape. *Imvo* increased in size from six to eight pages after the war and remained at eight pages throughout the 1920s. It was essentially a Xhosa-language publication with one of the two editorial pages in English.

Workers' Herald under the Editorships of James Thaele and Henry Tyamzashe

By far the most militant of the independent African journals during the 1920s, in terms of political rhetoric, was the *Workers' Herald*, an irregular monthly in four languages (English, Xhosa, Sotho and Zulu) launched in May 1923. It was the official mouthpiece of the Industrial and Commercial Workers' Union, which was founded in Cape Town in 1919 under the charismatic leadership of Clements Kadalie, a former schoolteacher from colonial Nyasaland (Malawi). Kadalie teamed up initially with H. Selby Msimang, the leader of a workers' organization in Bloemfontein, but a conference held in the city in July 1920 failed to unite the two groups. Msimang was elected president of a new Industrial and Commercial Coloured and Native Workers' (Amalgamated) Union of Africa (ICWU), and Kadalie withdrew with his followers to Cape Town. The ICU rapidly expanded its activities in the Cape Province, and the trade union was renamed the Industrial and Commercial Workers' Union of Africa. The ICU would remain essentially a Cape trade union until its headquarters was moved to Johannesburg in 1925.[14]

ICU organizers in the Cape during the early 1920s included men like Samuel Masabalala, the founder of Port Elizabeth's trade union movement. Masabalala had been jailed in October 1920 during a campaign to mount a general strike over low wages; police fired on the crowd demanding his release, and a night of rioting ensued in which 24 people were killed. The incident had reverberations throughout the region and beyond. Kadalie and Masabalala joined forces, and within a few years the rural eastern Cape was a major center of ICU activity.

One of Kadalie's lieutenants in the western Cape was the flamboyant James Thaele, who had spent about 10 years studying in the United States and acquired two undergraduate degrees (one in theology) from Lincoln University in Pennsylvania, the alma mater of a number of Africans from South Africa during the first half of the twentieth century. Thaele became a follower of Marcus Garvey and his Africanist-oriented Universal Negro Improvement Association before returning to South Africa in the early 1920s.[15] Thaele aligned himself with the ICU in Cape Town, and he also helped organize a local branch of the ANC. The Cape Western Congress, as it was called, soon became a dominant force in the recruitment of

Photo 17. Alexander Macaulay (Mac) Jabavu, editor of *Imvo Zabantsundu* (1921–40).

Photo 18. Clements Kadalie, leader of the ICU and titular editor of the *Workers' Herald*.

Photo 19. James M. Thaele, editor of the *Workers' Herald* (1923–25).

Photo 20. Henry Daniel David Tyamzashe, editor of the *Workers' Herald* (1925–28).

African and Coloured workers in the wine districts of the southwestern Cape. Thaele and his followers remained in the Cape when the ICU made the move to Johannesburg.

The trade union rapidly developed into a populist movement in the mid- to late 1920s and eclipsed Congress as the most influential African political organization in South Africa. The ICU was effectively controlled by officials recruited from the upper ranks of the petty bourgeoisie, but most new members were tenants and laborers on white-owned farms and peasants from the segregated African reserves. Although membership in the union soared to perhaps 100,000 in 1927, the ICU leadership could not accommodate the complex and often contradictory needs of its urban and rural constituents. Personality conflicts, organizational weaknesses, factional disputes, allegations of mismanagement and misuse of funds, and the personal extravagances of Kadalie and other officials also helped undermine confidence in the union. Kadalie himself resigned from the ICU after a series of confrontations with William Ballinger, a British trade union organizer who had arrived in South Africa in June 1928 to advise the union at Kadalie's request. By the early months of 1929 it was in an irreversible state of disintegration, and by the end of the year three main splinter groups had emerged in East London, Johannesburg and Durban.

The ICU organ *Workers' Herald* was edited by Kadalie in name only. The newspaper was actually run by a "subeditor," and there were two in its lifetime between May 1923 and December 1928. Thaele seems to have edited the *Workers' Herald* for the first two years of its existence in Cape Town, but the internal evidence suggests that only 10 issues were produced. The subeditor from May 1925 was Henry Daniel David Tyamzashe (1880–1951), the son of Gwayi Tyamzashe, a prominent leader in the Cape mission church.[16] Educated at Lovedale, he qualified as a journeyman printer in 1902. Tyamzashe practiced his trade for several years in Lovedale, the adjacent town of Alice and in East London before moving to Mafeking in the northern Cape, where he worked briefly as a printer for Solomon Plaatje on his newspaper *Koranta ea Becoana* (the Bechuana Gazette). Tyamzashe then found work as a printer with various white-owned newspapers in the northern and eastern Cape (Dordrecht and Uitenhage) and Natal (Pietermaritzburg) before moving to Johannesburg in the early 1920s to work on the Chamber of Mines' African newspaper *Umteteli wa Bantu*.

Tyamzashe was a member of an exclusive group of qualified black artisans, eagerly employed and just as eagerly exploited by white businessmen, at a time when the state was beginning to enact job reservation laws to eliminate all skilled black workers. He was also a freelance journalist and writer, contributing news articles, essays, poems and even short stories to various publications. "Being a man of working-class principle," Tyamzashe said he resigned from *Umteteli* because "he soon discovered the exploitation going on by the Chamber of Mines."[17] He found work early in 1925 as a foreman in an Indian-owned printing firm but was fired shortly thereafter when the white Typographical Union discovered he was working as a printer and insisted he be paid the prevailing union wage. Tyamzashe, who had become a member of the ICU in April 1925, successfully sued his former employer and obtained wages owed him for wrongful dismissal. Kadalie, who had assisted Tyamzashe in the court case, then offered him the job as subeditor of the ICU newspaper.

Although Tyamzashe was one of Kadalie's key lieutenants, he does not seem to have played much of a role in trade union activities. As Transvaal provincial secretary for a few months in 1926, for example, Tyamzashe was apparently a poor orator and an ineffectual organizer, and he was designated from August 1926 as the ICU's "Complaints and Research Secretary," a position apparently created specifically for him.[18] Nevertheless, he retained his power base in the ICU through his position on the newspaper and his friendship with Kadalie. Between May and October 1927, for example, A. W. G. Champion, secretary of the largest and wealthiest branch of the ICU in Natal, took charge of the union during one of Kadalie's periodic trips overseas.[19] Champion immediately clashed with Tyamzashe, who later wrote: "He [Champion] installed himself editor of the paper and 'ORDERED' the writer to publish every bit of clotted nonsense that flew from his erratic pen."[20] The ICU's National Council, however, apparently backed Tyamzashe and placed him in temporary charge of the head office in Johannesburg.

Tyamzashe's editorship was challenged again a year later when Ballinger was brought in as the ICU adviser. Soon after his arrival at the end of June 1928 (the newspaper was not published in June or July), Ballinger took over as business manager, severing the newspaper's administrative ties with the ICU hierarchy and changing its format from broadsheet to tabloid (August 1928). Tyamzashe later wrote that Ballinger "edited it himself, without consulting me. I took exception to that–and told him so."[21] Tyamzashe remained as the subeditor, but only five issues of the *Workers' Herald* were published as a tabloid. The newspaper collapsed when Tyamzashe was fired for insubordination and expelled from the ICU in January 1929.

The *Workers' Herald* under Tyamzashe was published regularly as a monthly, six-column broadsheet in Cape Town and Johannesburg (from February 1926). The newspaper increased from four to eight pages in April 1925, and it continued as an eight-page newspaper when the format was changed to a three-column tabloid between August and December 1928.[22] Circulation rose to perhaps 27,000 in May 1927 (judging by membership figures for the ICU), the highest circulation ever recorded for an alternative newspaper before the mid-1940s. Tyamzashe was the principal writer[23] and de facto editor for a crucial $3\frac{1}{2}$ years of the trade union's existence. His reports of the ICU's yearly conferences, for example, are apparently the only ones that have survived.

With the fragmentation of the ICU in the late 1920s, several newspapers or newsletters were started by dissident union leaders. Champion established *Udibi Lwase Afrika* (African Mixtures) as the organ of the ICU Yase Natal in 1928. Ballinger tried to resurrect the official ICU newspaper under a new title, calling it the *Workers' Herald: The Voice of African Labour*, in 1929, but only two issues (September, November 1929) have been recovered. Kadalie resigned from the ICU in February 1929 and launched the Independent ICU the following month in Johannesburg with Tyamzashe and other close associates.[24] Kadalie, like his rivals, tried to start a new publication, initially entitled *Weekly Newsletter* and then *New Africa* (edited by Tyamzashe), but none of the ICU journals that followed the *Workers' Herald* lasted even one year.

News Agenda

The quantitative analysis clearly revealed contrasting moderate and militant discourses in the African nationalist press during the 1920s (especially Categories A and C) (Figure 1).

Figure 1. Domestic and foreign news in *Imvo Zabantsundu* and *Workers' Herald* (in %). Percentages are calculated by dividing the number of story units in each category by the total number of story units. News refers to all story units, including illustrations and informal advertisements classified as news. Formal advertisements are excluded. *Imvo Zabantsundu* (IZ) had 535 story units, and *Workers' Herald* (WH) had 1,222 story units.

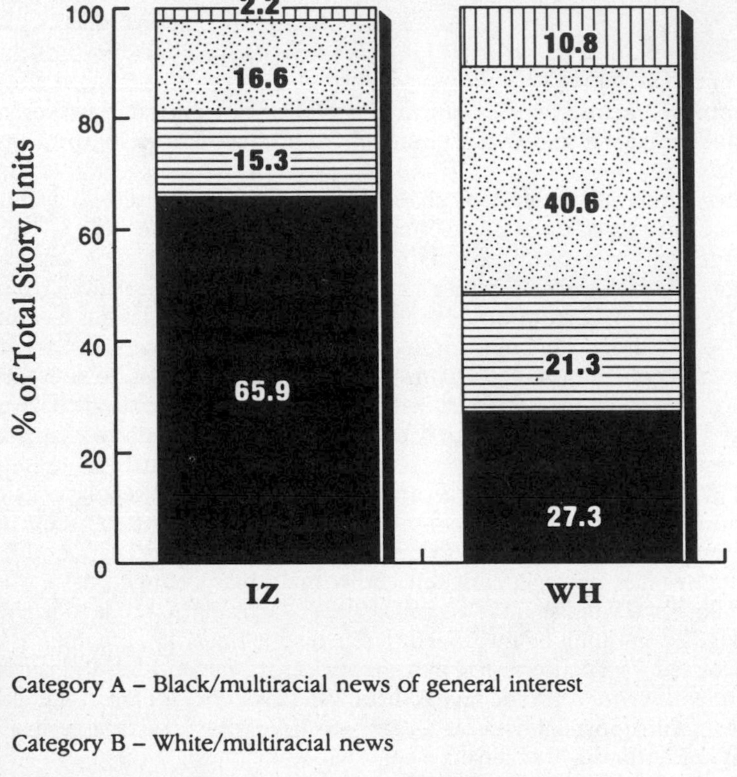

Category A – Black/multiracial news of general interest

Category B – White/multiracial news

Category C – Black/multiracial political and trade union news

Category D – Foreign news

General-interest News

Imvo, under Alexander Jabavu, continued to feature news and entertainment that depicted the vocational and leisure-time activities of the African petty bourgeoisie in the eastern Cape. The *Workers' Herald*, on the other hand, contained a much smaller percentage of Category A, Black general-interest news (Table 7). Category A stories consisted mainly of African community news. *Imvo* focused on church and school activities and society news, which together formed about 45 percent of the newshole. Alexander Jabavu had been trained initially as a teacher by the Presbyterian missionaries at Lovedale, and education retained its status in the news agenda. Tengo Jabavu himself had complained on *Imvo*'s thirty-sixth anniversary in 1920 that the newspaper "is not what it should be by reason of the backwardness of its people educationally and otherwise."[25]

Table 7. *Categories A and D news in* Imvo Zabantsundu *and* Workers' Herald *(% of story units)*

Category	Imvo Zabantsundu	Workers' Herald
A. Black/multiracial news of general interest	65.9 (352 units)	27.3 (334 units)
A.1 Education and religion	10.1	2.6
A.2 Society	35.0	1.9
A.3 Sports	2.6	2.1
A.4 Living conditions in urban areas	1.3	5.5
A.5 Living conditions in rural areas	4.9	0.5
A.6 Independent economic activities	7.9	0.2
A.7 Crime and accidents	2.8	4.1
A.8 Other: Promotional and miscellaneous[a]	1.3	10.4
D. Foreign news	2.2 (12 units)	10.8 (132 units)

[a] "Miscellaneous" includes jokes, homilies, apologies and advertisements disguised as news.

School news (A.1) included reports about teachers' associations and conferences, teachers' promotions, examination results, new courses, school fees and other miscellaneous activities relating to teachers, pupils and schools. News about the South African Native College at Fort Hare featured regularly in the editorial pages. Religious news (A.1) included notices of church meetings and the activities of the clergy as well as devotional articles and occasional essays of concern to African Christians. In religious matters, *Imvo* favored churches that were recognized by the government. Little coverage was given to the activities of independent, nonapproved churches.

Society news (A.2) consisted of the births, marriages, deaths and the everyday activities of the petty bourgeoisie at work and play. This was essentially personality news, and it included regular features such as "Abantu" (People) and "Izinto Ngezinto" (meaning "This and That," or miscellaneous events), which effectively chronicled the leisure activities – dances, beauty contests, fund-raisers, farewells and reunions, teas, dinners, parties, receptions, concerts, speeches and meetings – of the mission-educated community. News concerned with death, a solemn but celebrated event in Christian as well as non-Christian circles, comprised a significant number of the stories in this sample subcategory. Items included death notices, tributes to the dead, funerals and memorial services, the reading of wills and lists of persons who helped the bereaved, often in a column entitled "Imibulelo" (meaning "In gratitude" or "With thanks").

One of the few social activities of the petty bourgeoisie that was de-emphasized during this period was sports news (A.3). Although African cricket, rugby and tennis clubs in South Africa, for example, were formed initially in the last half of the nineteenth century by the African Christian community in the eastern Cape, organized sports played a major role in the African press only from the 1950s, with commercial publications like *Drum* and *Golden City Post*.

News stories in two subcategories focused on living and working conditions in the urban (A.4) and rural (A.5) areas. *Imvo* rarely commented on the urban areas except on the subject of industrial workers, and this was usually mentioned in connection with support for the ICU.[26] A number of stories, however, focused on problems ordinary Africans were facing on white-owned farms, especially in the reserves. Low wages, discrimination in employment, the plight of migrant workers and the methods of labor recruiters were topics discussed from time to time on the English-language editorial page.[27] Regional weather reports also chronicled drought conditions that persisted in parts of the eastern Cape throughout the 1920s. Although the 1918–19 influenza epidemic received considerable coverage, public health news in general was rare unless there were local outbreaks of communicable diseases (smallpox, typhus and typhoid in the test sample). Almost 9 of every 10 Africans living in *Imvo*'s main circulation area–the Ciskei region–were classified as rural in the 1920s, but there were few stories on subjects like soil erosion, land conservation and improving farming methods.[28]

The subcategory Independent economic activities (A.6) included articles on meetings of farmers' associations, notices of land auctions and a regular column on agricultural prices ("Market Trends"). Employment opportunities were also sometimes disguised as news stories, an established custom in the African press. Although jobs for laborers were included in these inventories, *Imvo* focused mainly on vacancies for salaried professionals (teachers and nurses) and skilled tradesmen (cobblers, carpenters and compositors) representing the vocational aspirations of the petty bourgeoisie.

The subcategory Crime (A.7) included stories on nonpolitical crimes committed by whites as well as blacks, but crimes committed by blacks against blacks were apparently downplayed. Discrimination between white and black in the administration of justice merited the most coverage. Editorials and letters to the editor–punctuated by headlines like "South African Justice!", "Yet Another Native Shot!", "Injustices to Natives!", "Fine for the White, Gaol for the Black," "Perverted Justice!", "European's Brutal Assault"–angrily contested these events.[29]

As anticipated, Category D (Foreign news) was virtually ignored in this community newspaper. The test sample consisted primarily of personality profiles featuring the British royal family, Anglo American politicians and the activities of African Americans in the United States, and occasional articles about political unrest in Ireland.

Although *Imvo*'s news agenda was heavily weighted in favor of nonpolitical activities, these social practices were nevertheless infused with the language of protest. The protesters included church groups–even those associated with the Jabavu family's denominational favorites, the Wesleyan Methodist and Presbyterian mission churches–ministers' fraternal organizations, the autonomous Eastern Grand Temple of the Independent Order of True Templars (the main temperance organization) and especially the teachers' and farmers' associations.

The Cape Native Teachers' Association (CNTA), made up of Africans west of the Kei River, and the Transkei Native Teachers' Association, for Africans east of the Kei River, amalgamated in December 1924 under the leadership of D. D. T. Jabavu. He was a founder and president of both the CNTA and the umbrella organization, the South African Federation of Native Teachers, organized in 1922. Although the teachers fought mainly for higher salaries and better working conditions, they protested a wide range of discriminatory measures against Africans. These grievances, published in *Imvo* and other African newspapers and sometimes forwarded to the governing authorities, formed an important part of the protest agenda during this period.[30]

Imvo devoted considerable space to the activities of the Native Farmers' Association (NFA), which was launched in 1918 by a group of progressive farmers from the districts of Victoria East and King William's Town (which then included the future districts of Keiskammahoek and Middledrift) in the Ciskei region.[31] Attendance at their quarterly meetings reached 285 in 1920, but it seems to have declined to between 80 and 150 for the rest of the decade.[32] Members were primarily interested in developing their land as commercial farms, and they made repeated attempts to gain access to capital and technical expertise through the Land Bank (which Africans themselves partially subsidized) and the Department of Agriculture: "The Natives [i.e., farmers] have not asked to be spoonfed like the whites, but have said ... 'we, in all humility, ask you to help us to help ourselves.'"[33]

NFA officials were also involved in more overt forms of political protest. They attacked the 1917 Native Affairs Administration Bill and the subsequent Cape Natives' Land Committee proposals[34] and, according to *Imvo*, helped persuade the Smuts government to insert the provision for local councils in African reserves in the 1920 Native Affairs Act. They condemned the mine contract system and the methods of labor recruiters; they issued reports in 1920 citing the brutality of white farmers and the desperate plight of African farm laborers that were published in the white as well as the black press.[35]

The NFA also provided intermittent reports of deteriorating conditions for Africans living in rural Ciskei and southern Transkei.[36] In 1919, for example, the farmers sent a memorandum to the secretary for Native affairs offering evidence concerning the "alarming rapidity with which poverty is growing and pressing upon the Natives in our districts [the Ciskei] ... Never in their history, not even in Nongqause [the cattle-killing events of 1856–57] ... have the Native people generally been faced with such a serious economic crisis as they are today."[37] The NFA sought to represent the interests and concerns of peasant householders who were restricted to subeconomic plots and had virtually no access to formal education or guidance from trained agriculturists: "We would wish that our white friends would not always think of us as a mere reservoir for the supply of cheap labour on their estates. We too have our own ambitions, rightful ambitions, for progress in education and advancement in agriculture and other pursuits of life."[38]

The NFA was instrumental in organizing the South African Native Farmers' Congress in July 1926. At this time, there were at least 33 aspiring commercial African farmers' groups in South Africa, with a membership of roughly 1,400. Colonial Basutoland (Lesotho), Transvaal and Natal were represented in the umbrella organization, but most of the farmers came from the eastern Cape. Like the teachers, the South African Native Farmers' Congress and its affiliates played an important role in the wider political arena.[39]

The quantitative analysis revealed that the *Workers' Herald,* as expected, devoted relatively little space to general interest news (A). The most significant subcategory was actually concerned with news promoting the ICU and its newspaper, product testimonials and advertisements disguised as news (A.8). These messages were not technically news stories, but every issue carried appeals urging readers to recruit members for the ICU, pay their union dues, support the Kadalie defense fund, buy the ICU newspaper, purchase ICU-sponsored diaries, reports, pamphlets and books or attend ICU lectures, dances and other social activities (in Johannesburg, they were held in "Workers' Hall," a building leased by the ICU in September 1925 in the city's "working class quarters").[40] As the newspaper proclaimed in December 1926; "it has championed the cause of the oppressed peoples of Africa ... In dealing with political, industrial and social matters it surpasses any

African Native paper in this continent for its frankness and fearlessness. It is, in fact, the most radical paper in South Africa."[41]

Vendors were urged to return unsold copies of the newspaper; readers were advised (repeatedly) when the ICU headquarters in Johannesburg moved to a new building; correspondents were occasionally admonished for improper remarks or poor English;[42] and requests from the ICU's head office in Johannesburg to branch secretaries were noted. There were also stories unabashedly publicizing the activities of proprietors who supported the trade union–shopkeepers, traders, pharmacists, booksellers.[43] The newspaper was also pockmarked with short advertising homilies on health matters–temperance, constipation, bowel complaints, cough complaints, bad breath, teething children, appendicitis, rheumatism and dysentery–sometimes with and sometimes without mentioning a brand name.[44]

In contrast to *Imvo*, there was very little school or church news (A.1) or society news (A.2). Sports stories (A.3) were devoted almost exclusively to boxing, Tyamzashe himself having boxed as a student at Lovedale. The sports editor most of the time seems to have been "Jolly" Jack Bernard, a white American and an honorary member of the ICU who owned a bookshop in Johannesburg and was the "sole agent" for the *Workers' Herald* and the black American newspaper *Negro World* in South Africa.[45] Black boxers were eulogized, and Bernard's sports column was a veritable history of the black boxing fraternity in the United States, Europe and the Caribbean region. Discrimination against black boxers inside and outside South Africa featured regularly in the boxing column.[46] Crime themes (A.7 in the *Workers' Herald* consisted almost entirely of crime stories) were much the same as they were in *Imvo*–acts of violence and discrimination against Africans by South Africa's criminal justice system as recorded in letters to the editor, news stories and in editorial commentaries.[47] The stories, usually tagged with provocative headlines,[48] were sometimes grouped together under a column entitled "Black Man's Burden."

As anticipated, *Workers' Herald* devoted some space to African living conditions in the urban areas but virtually none to the conditions the majority of its readers were facing on farms and in the reserves.[49] None of the urban stories were in-depth reports, but they covered a wide range of activities, most of them centering on Johannesburg and the Witwatersrand. In an account about the alleged "lawlessness of Natives on the Rand," for example, the newspaper noted that the authorities provided "no place of recreation" for blacks and advised: "We are in accord with those who say that lawlessness must be put down with a firm hand; but lawlessness is sometimes inspired by lawless laws."[50] In response to complaints about the high birth rate and unemployment among Africans and Coloureds, the newspaper noted: "Not a single sign, not a half-kind word is breathed, either from pulpit or press on behalf of the millions of starving Natives, in the towns and in the country districts."[51]

Stories about everyday life in town embraced such activities as employers who mistreated or refused to pay their employees,[52] workers injured on the job and miners dying from "phthisis" (tuberculosis or other lung diseases) who were sent back to the reserves with little or no compensation,[53] shopkeepers who were "in the habit of cheating Natives,"[54] white nurses who went on strike because they had to work with an African doctor,[55] inadequate hospital care,[56] public vaccination measures that focused only on blacks,[57] the remains of Africans removed from "the old Native graveyard, near the Germiston location" to make way for factories,[58] missing persons,[59] the high crime rate,[60] the refusal to appoint Africans as court interpreters,[61] inadequate transportation[62] and lack of pensions for the elderly.[63] The newspaper "from time to time" would criticize the "bullying attitude of a certain type of policeman" and "the tactlessness and impatience of certain young constables."[64] There were also several reports concerned with housing and other basic amenities, and with municipal regulations directed at Africans in segregated mining compounds and locations.[65]

The *Workers' Herald* contained very few news reports of African economic activity (A.6), but the African entrepreneur was not displaced in the ICU's priorities:

> It is our firm belief that in the years to come all avenues of business, dependent or independent, will be closed to the black man...At the present time in this country (thank God) there is still a small opening in which the black man could exploit his business acumen. Why not then take time by the forelock and make wholesale propositions of these openings?...All that is needed is sacrifice, honesty, and a true spirit of loyalty to one another.[66]

The newspaper in fact was an important advertising venue for the struggling black tradesman–self-employed tailors, saddlers, shoemakers, bootmakers and cobblers, printers, picture framers, plumbers, carpenters and blacksmiths–who were still finding work in Johannesburg and other urban areas during the 1920s. Page 1 was all advertising until February 1926, and self-employment advertisements dominated the page: "I am a blackman. My Trade is Bootmaking. I can Sole and Heel a Pair of Boots or Shoes Equal to any Whiteman in South Africa. Give me a Trial."

The advertising copy of African craftsmen frequently called for support on racial grounds–with bold type, capital letters and exclamation marks: "Why do your tailoring with other Races?"; "THE AFRICAN TAILOR!!!"; "WE ARE BLACK WORKERS/PLEASE SUPPORT US"; "Fellow Workers Support a Blackman and be proud of it;" "GIVE THIS BLACKWORKER A TRIAL"; "SUPPORT A BLACKMAN." Advertising copy would also sometimes note: "We are fervent supporters of the I.C.U. You should support those who support you." These advertisements comprised about one-third of the advertising on English-language pages between February 1925 and January 1926, but thereafter self-employment advertisements were placed on the vernacular pages. Racial designations were gradually abandoned, and advertisments from black entrepreneurs had virtually disappeared from the newspaper by 1927.[67]

In commenting on news outside South Africa (Category D), the *Workers' Herald* concentrated on the European-dominated International Federation of Trade Unions (IFTU handouts were an important source of foreign news stories), the British Trade Union Congress and especially Britain's Independent Labour Party, which had sponsored Ballinger as the ICU adviser and supported the activities of the trade union. The newspaper regularly reproduced reports from foreign English-language news sources that mentioned Kadalie or the ICU. News outside South Africa, however, was rarely covered unless it was related to ICU activities. Only a few stories were concerned with European colonialism, such as one headlined, "How British Imperialism Rules in Africa":

> there is wholesale massacre of the African under British Imperialism, throughout its possessions, and this wanton massacre is carried on in this day-light of much boosted democracy. Wherever the British flag flies the Africans have been cynically massacred in heaps, and it is a wonder that the blacks have survived in spite of this manslaughter.[68]

The "American Negro" featured prominently in an irregular column entitled "Bookshelf," which was produced by a white liberal-segregationist sympathizer who exercised some influence on Kadalie and other ICU officials during the 1920s. Ethelreda Lewis, a British/South African writer whose interest in the ICU was motivated by a crude form of racial paternalism toward those of "darker blood,"[69] wrote most of these columns, under the pen name "Reader."

Lewis projected a subordinate, trivialized image of the African American as a role model for African readers of the *Workers' Herald* :

> There are a number of facts which would strongly support the theory that the Negroes are constitutionally no more lazy than other people. As longshoremen... as workers in fertilizer and tobacco factories or for construction companies... as cooks... waiters in private homes, in hotels... And, when it comes to cake-walks and dances, no other race can even equal them for spirited action and endurance... They may not respond as sensitively to stimulation, nor to the same kind of stimulation as the white man, but wherever the conditions are favourable they display both energy and thrift.

She quotes a white American officer in World War I:

> If I were to join the army again, I should like to serve with coloured troops. They are so cheerful and willing, and they march so well. They enjoy the theatrical effect of their drill... What a simple loveable people are these dark-skinned brothers of ours!... I should like to have the power to raise a body of Negro troops... that would shed great glory on their race.[70]

These carefully selected portraits of African Americans–"The negro's great gift, as we see by his works in America, no less than by the uneducated African, is Rhythm"[71]–were typical of white-liberal stereotypes served up to black South Africans at the time:

> this great army of black workers [during World War I] always sang...Their own hospitals were full of... "crooning singers" ... And where did the American Negro get his good voice and his instinct for expressing everything in music? From his ancestral tribes on the West Coast of Africa, where, just as natives show us here to-day, manual labor is often lightened by the rhythm and beauty of song.[72]

White Authoritarian Context

At least three other whites, in addition to Lewis, became contributors to the *Workers' Herald* in 1928, the last year of the newspaper's existence. Winifred Holtby, a "definitely negrophile" British journalist and novelist, wrote the occasional "Bookshelf" or separate book review column, under her own name. H. N. Brailsford, a British socialist and former editor of the *New Leader* (London), was the probable author of articles summarizing coverage of South Africa in the foreign press, and Norman Leys, a medical practitioner and the author of a book on Kenya, who was "a devoted friend of the Africans," wrote an occasional column entitled "Hygiene."[73] Despite the rhetoric against white liberals in the newspaper, Kadalie believed that these writers would give the ICU more credibility in white-dominated political and trade union circles. The *Workers' Herald* eventually suggested that whites be recruited to campaign for parliamentary elections as ICU representatives: "Natives are at present disqualified from entering Parliament but there is nothing to prevent the ICU, in conjunction with kindred Native organisations, from placing Europeans... in native constituencies, nominating them for

Table 8. *Category B news in* Imvo Zabantsundu *and* Workers' Herald (*% of story units*)

Category	*Imvo Zabantsundu*	*Workers' Herald*
B. White/multiracial news	15.3 (82 units)	21.3 (260 units)
B.1 Political, legislative and administrative	11.0	11.8
B.2 Economic and social	4.3	9.5

office and making every endeavour to secure their return to the Union Parliament as direct representatives of Native interests."[74]

The activities of the dominant groups in South African society (Category B, White/multiracial news) were obviously of considerable concern to African journalists. The political, economic and social institutions of those who ruled provided an agenda for negotiation as well as protest (Table 8).

Imvo tried to be a newspaper of record, and government statutes, bills and acts, published mainly in Xhosa, appeared in every issue analyzed in the test sample. The newspaper also published reports of parliamentary committees, commissions and debates, chronicled election results and the activities of local MPs (sometimes in an irregular feature entitled "E Palamente") of interest to African voters.

As Tengo Jabavu had done in the Cape colonial period, his sons continued to organize the African vote for the white party that was deemed to be most sympathetic to African interests (Subcategory B.1). *Imvo* had supported the largely English-speaking South African Party, which was backed by the white liberal establishment, since 1910. Speeches by party leader Jan Smuts were generally recorded with approval, but National Party as well as local South African Party candidates received considerable coverage during election campaigns.[75]

Nevertheless, by the early 1920s many African nationalists were becoming disillusioned with white trusteeship. The shift in editorial policy on white party politics was already apparent by the end of 1921: Smuts was "so pre-occupied with making this a white man's country that he finds no time even to address a Native meeting in his political tours."[76] *Imvo*, well aware of the "degree of desperation" in the grievances of Africans from the northern provinces, complained that under the Smuts government "Native policy" was "drifting."[77] The prime minister was censured for refusing to appoint a separate, full time minister of Native affairs[78] and for selecting a new secretary for Native affairs (Major J. F. Herbst) "without even pretending to ascertain the feeling of the leaders of Native opinion."[79]

The newspaper maintained its watchdog stance over discriminatory legislation such as the Native Education Tax Bill, which the Smuts government had introduced in response to the teachers' demand for higher wages. The bill would "tax the Native heavily to appease the hungry teachers and thus bring a class conflict among the Natives themselves... It is difficult for us to imagine a more iniquitous and monstrously inconsistent proposal."[80] This measure was enacted, in an amended form, by Smuts's successor. The Native Tax Act of 1925 raised the base tax from 10 shillings to 30 shillings a year, a crippling burden, as *Imvo* often noted, to African peasants in rural areas like the eastern Cape.[81]

The Smuts government was also under fire for not implementing local-government councils as envisaged under the 1920 Native Affairs Act. The few white-style village management boards created for Africans under the 1909

Mission Stations Act were withdrawn in 1920 on the promise that local councils would be provided. Africans living in the segregated reserves paid taxes to white-controlled local governing bodies, the divisional councils, but received virtually no benefits in return; hence they wanted councils, so that they could control their own tax money. *Imvo* crusaded for years to obtain local councils and a general council for the Ciskei region, for example, despite fears on the part of many voters that they might lose their citizenship rights if they accepted these institutions.[82]

A Native commissioner for the Ciskei was appointed in 1922, but *Imvo* complained bitterly that his "attitude" was "consistently one of opposition" to instituting local councils. The newspaper attacked him for trying to undermine the credibility of local mission-educated organizers by pitting "the intellectuals against the illiterate" and replacing rural leaders "of standing and influence" with "inferiors."[83] When the powers of African councils were reduced in 1926, new local governing bodies were established in seven Ciskeian districts in the next six years. The United Transkeian Territories General Council was created in 1931 and the Ciskei General Council in 1934. Outside the Ciskei and Transkei, however, no other local or general councils for Africans in the reserves were created until these areas were reorganized under Bantu Authorities in the apartheid era.

Although African political activists in the eastern Cape were disillusioned with the Smuts government, he was deemed the lesser evil in white party politics.[84] The formation of Hertzog's Nationalist coalition government in June 1924 was a blow to the African voting community, and newspapers like *Imvo* became increasingly vitriolic in attacking his policies during the mid- to late 1920s. Hertzog himself was labeled "the greatest enemy of Native political rights we know of... a compound of German Prussianism and Dutch Afrikanerdom leading an anti-Native host of Northern Boer farmers."[85] Veteran journalist Bennett Ncwana, for example, wrote a series of articles for *Imvo*'s English-language editorial page in 1925–26, which, among other things, detailed the plight of African laborers and condemned government officials for the way they treated chiefs and headmen in the reserves. He attacked the missionary as "the forerunner of European domination in all parts of the world," denounced the "farcical" Natives' Conference and called for "passive resistance" against the state's segregationist policies.[86]

Imvo's lead editorials, written presumably by Alexander Jabavu, dealt with the same themes. He wrote disparagingly of the Native Affairs Commission: "We have never been enamoured of this Commission nor have we ever been able to see what good it has done for the Natives."[87] He noted the "shortcomings of European civilisation in the elements of Christianity," rejected claims by Hertzog that "educated Natives looked down upon uneducated Natives as being beneath them"[88] and accused the government of being the "greatest offender" in the campaign to "stir up racial hatred between whites and blacks."[89]

The newspaper was particularly successful in rallying public opinion against Hertzog's campaign to disenfranchise the Cape's African voters. Hertzog revealed the plan in November 1925 in a speech to his constituents in the small town of Smithfield in the Orange Free State, 17 months after the election that had brought the National Party to power. African voters actually won a temporary reprieve when the House of Assembly rejected his "Native Bills" at their first reading in March 1927 and referred them to a select committee of parliament. Revised versions were sent to parliament in January 1929 and again in February 1930, but again they failed to gain the necessary majority. The bills were referred to a new interparty select committee (whose meetings were closed to the public), which deliberated for another five years before its recommendations were presented to parliament. The Representation of Natives Act abolishing the Cape African franchise was not passed until 1936.

The draconian Native Administration Act of 1927 posed a more immediate threat to the voting community, because, among other things, it gave the governor general (represented in practice by the minister of Native affairs and the Native Affairs Department) the power to investigate all individual land titles that did not conform to the 1894 Glen Grey Act and "proclaim" them invalid. Since those who held land under the Glen Grey system did not qualify for the franchise, Africans forced "to adopt the suicidal course of the Glen Grey system" could be deprived of their voting rights. Refusal to submit would "render thousands of occupiers homeless," because the Native Affairs Department would simply allot the land to landless followers of collaborative chiefs and headmen. Africans in the Ciskei region were hardest hit, since they held most of the individual quit-rent and freehold titles that had been allotted to Africans in South Africa before the passing of the 1894 act. The Native Affairs Department was soon "feverishly introducing" the Glen Grey system of land tenure in the nine Ciskeian districts where there were Africans who had individual tenure rights.[90] The issue became a cause celebre for *Imvo* and the Cape voters at the end of the decade. Protest meetings forced the newly appointed minister of Native affairs, E. G. Jansen, to come to King William's Town to discuss the matter, and a case (*Rex v. Ndobe*) was eventually pursued on appeal up to the Supreme Court.[91]

Imvo attacked "the mentality... of the ruling classes in insisting on passing legislation with the sole object of 'hurting the soul' of the Native people by making them aliens in the country of their birth."[92] One leading article cited "the demon of white supremacy" as "a democracy only of white skin peoples of the world, and its philosophy is that of brazon spoliation and the violation of human rights of all peoples whose colour is black... As sure as the sun is shining, the black man will not for ever be the bottom dog."[93]

The targets of protest against white authoritarian rule in the *Workers' Herald* remained pretty consistent throughout this period. When Smuts used the ICU to frighten white voters, he was depicted as an unprincipled politician: "A public man like General Smuts who can stoop to such gross exaggerations is certainly a political danger–not only to South Africa but to the whole world... a man who is intellectually and spiritually unfit to become a leader and statesman."[94] ICU leaders had found temporary solace in the segregationist rhetoric of Hertzog,[95] but initial support for the Nationalist–Labour coalition soon turned to condemnation: "The Pact Government leaves a trail behind it as bloody as that of its predecessor, and a record of cruelty and injustice just as black."[96] Tyamzashe wrote an "Open Letter" to Hertzog in which he declared: "one can hardly come to any other conclusion than that you and your colleagues have concerned yourselves more with the suppression of Native advancement than with anything else."[97] After four years under the Nationalists, the *Workers' Herald* concluded:

> We have learnt that the substitution of one capitalist government for another can bring no benefits to the worker, and this is a lesson well worth learning. The Smuts Government was a government of, by and for the industrial capitalists. The Hertzog Government is one of rural capitalists, of big land-owners and farmers which, true to type, is more thoroughly conservative and more blatantly opposed to working-class interests than the more progressive governments of urban exploiters.[98]

The newspaper was particularly scathing in its comments on the Labour Party. The "hypocrisy of our 'White' South African Labour Party"[99] was condemned as a betrayal of the workers' movement. Kadalie claimed that the ICU had joined "our fellow white workers ... to rid South Africa of one common enemy, General Smuts and his Corner House Government" in the 1924 election, but "our poor miserable Labourites, ignominious in its [*sic*] intellectual outlook, assists capitalism in South Africa to keep the workers of this country divided. When will [the members of the Labour Party] ... relieve themselves of this foolish dogma of a 'white South Africa?' ... the sooner the whole lot of them join the Nationalist or the Chamber of Mines Party–the S.A.P.'s–the better for the Labour Movement in South Africa and the world at large."[100] The ICU tried to affiliate formally with the white-controlled South African Trades Union Congress, but the application was rejected in January 1928. It was "a blessing in disguise," the *Workers' Herald* declared: "There is not the slightest doubt that they have advertised to the world now their prejudice and hang-dog principles."[101]

The *Workers' Herald* was as outspoken as *Imvo* in its attacks on the state's repressive legislative and administrative apparatus. "Passes are Badges of Oppression," as one homily put it, "no matter how they are administered."[102] Most Africans, the newspaper declared, regarded the officials of the Native Affairs Department as "mere tax collectors,"[103] and Hertzog's "infamous Segregation Bills" were "capitalistic" in design and intended "to further the exploitation of seven million workers in South Africa."[104] The ICU's response was to call for a "National Assembly" representing all Africans to draft a "People's Charter for Freedom and No Surrender!"[105] The newspaper did support one segregationist measure, providing "justice is carried out without bias or race prejudice," during these years. It was the Immorality Bill, prohibiting sexual contact between white and black: "For years and years white rogues have been playing ducks and drakes with the flower of African womanhood."[106]

The trade union newspaper virtually ignored the various government commissions and committees of inquiry that were appointed during the 1920s. One exception was the 1925 Economic and Wage Commission, singled out for extended comment because the trade union submitted a memorandum to the commission and ICU officials gave evidence "in an honest, fearless and frank manner." The newspaper claimed that its testimony would "eclipse all previous attempts to lay the Native case before a Government Commission," but the verdict of history has been somewhat less charitable.[107]

As with other African journals during the interwar period, coverage of white economic and social practices (B.2) by the two newspapers was relatively low. White-owned mines, factories and farms were not included in the news agenda, unless the subject concerned African labor. White churches, schools, sports groups and even the activities of white missionary agencies were generally ignored, unless they were deemed to play a direct role in African social life. Nevertheless, mission and nonmission "friends of the natives" were regular contributors to *Imvo*, as they had been in the past, and white liberals retained their status as role models for the mission-educated elite.[108] Articles on *Imvo*'s English-language editorial page publicizing the activities of white churches, welfare societies and other white-dominated institutions favoring interracial dialogue were sometimes reprinted in Xhosa on the news pages. News reports and letters to the editor occasionally cited the activities of white missionaries and school administrators or expressed gratitude in citing the rare instances where whites praised or provided aid to blacks.[109]

The economic and social mechanisms that structured consent, however, did not guarantee consent. Alternative readings were scattered throughout the *Imvo* sample. A white missionary, for example, was criticized for trying to justify the beating of African women by their husbands in so-called traditional "tribal" households. A news report noted that the Cape Education Department deplored the actions of another missionary who tried to force a teacher to join the mission denomination that operated the school by threatening dismissal. Even the principal of Fort Hare was attacked for a statement referring to the "cruelty" of Sandile, a prominent Xhosa chief during the nineteenth century Cape–Xhosa wars.[110] The newspaper noted that the entrance to a Dutch Reformed Church chapel contained the following notice, which it reprinted without comment: "Kaffirs, dogs and cats, not admitted."[111] It reported that a prisoner in Johannesburg asked a judge to change his sentence from three months to four, because convicts preferred staying in jail and being fed to going hungry in the outside world.[112] Correspondents complained about the word "Native" and urged that Africans refer to themselves as Africans.[113]

The language praising white benefactors, moreover, was often tinged with irony. *Imvo* thanked the Department of Railways for an act of generosity but noted: "It is not often that Natives of the Union have cause for spontaneously thanking a Government Department."[114] Financier and philanthropist Percy Molteno was cited as a "noble example" because he had "amassed his wealth out of Native labour" and was "returning some of it for the benefit of the Native. Unfortunately he is not typical of his fellow magnates who disburse their surplus funds strictly for the advantage of Europeans."[115]

The *Workers' Herald*, despite the efforts of advisers like Ethelreda Lewis, generally attacked multiracial bodies sponsored by white liberals. The Joint Councils, which did not court Kadalie, were "an incompetent, ignorant and indifferent body,"[116] and the Bantu Men's Social Centre, a leading cultural venue for Africans in Johannesburg sponsored by white missionaries, was "composed of run-aways from Native wrath."[117] The newspaper deliberately separated white church and missionary leaders from the Gospel message. Africans were urged to leave mission churches and "patronize your own [i.e., independent African] churches," even though church activities were barely part of the news agenda. Missionaries were "unmitigated hypocrites and humbugs," and "the so-called missionary spirit" was "pregnant with capitalistic and racial animosity." The Anglican dean of Johannesburg, for example, was characterized as the "lord dean of capitalism."[118] Nevertheless, "True religion" [i.e., Christianity] was "one of the planks in the platform of the ICU."[119]

The Chamber of Mines and its Native Recruiting Corporation were occasionally censured for their treatment of African mine workers, and the recruiting of migrant labor for the mines was "a system which we strongly condemn."[120] But most criticism directed at the mining industry, as we shall see, was reserved for Africans who wrote for the Chamber of Mines' African newspaper *Umteteli wa Bantu*. The ICU newspaper devoted very little space to the economy or to white (or multiracial) trade unions that represented the workers. On occasion, however, Tyamzashe commented on white workers in a manner that was all too rare in the alternative press:

> If it comes to "the push" and the Native worker is done without, South Africa will simply "stink," because the white "won't works" have already become an almost

unbearable burden to the State and a public danger to the country. Their forefathers taught them that honest hard toil was "kafirs' work." We have on many occasions watched white relief gangs in action on municipal and other works, and the way many of them loaf about is enough to turn the laziest ass green with envy.[121]

Black Politics and Trade Unions

Contrasting moderate and militant discourses in African nationalist newspapers during the 1920s were found not in news stories protesting white authoritarian rule but in news stories concerned with black politics. Category C was clearly a priority for the *Workers' Herald* but not for *Imvo Zabantsundu* (Table 9).

Imvo devoted only slightly more coverage to black politics than it did to white politics, and both categories (B and C) combined constituted only about one-third of the news story units. Stories about government-sponsored consultative bodies for Africans, moreover, comprised about 40 percent, and independent black political and trade union organizations about 60 percent, of the story units in subcategory C.1 (Personalities and organizations). Natives' Conferences, interracial meetings sponsored by the Joint Councils and the Dutch Reformed Church, and also councils of chiefs, local-government boards and the Transkei Bunga were covered in 9 issues, ANC politics in 7 issues, local/regional politics in 4 issues and ICU politics in 4 issues of the 22-issue test sample. Political coverage was often brief and superficial, consisting of notices of meetings, suggestions for agendas or lists of resolutions approved. Most speeches, meetings and conferences were representative of the voting elite, and almost every story cited the names of those in attendance.

Nevertheless, *Imvo* was far more upbeat in its coverage of black political organizations under Alexander Jabavu than it had been under his father after World War I. The various voters' groups created to protect the Cape African franchise were regularly publicized in the journal, especially in the vernacular pages.[122] The Cape Native Voters' Convention (CNVC), which became the key regional body in the 10-year crusade against Hertzog's attempt to disenfranchise the Cape voters, attracted most of the active African politicians in the province. Delegates generally met once or twice a year–in places such as King William's Town, Kimberley and Queenstown in the eastern Cape–issuing resolutions, petitioning parliament, mobilizing protest delegations and interviewing officials at the local, provincial and national level. Attendance at meetings during the mid- to late 1920s apparently varied from 100 to 200 to more than 3,000, depending on the severity of segregationist legislation directed against the Cape voting community or their allies in the northern provinces.[123] Regional organizations already in existence associated themselves with the CNVC, and their officials became leaders in the new organization.[124]

Although the Jabavu brothers apparently never joined the African National Congress, they attended branch meetings at Cradock and elsewhere, and *Imvo* always supported the organization. The Congress was particularly admired for attempting to redress grievances through the courts. It was time-consuming and very costly, and there were few lasting victories, but *Imvo* was meticulous in recording these events.[125] When Smuts described a SANNC protest delegation, in 1923, "as mere intellectuals who did not represent all the Natives," *Imvo* replied that the organization was "unrivalled" in the northern provinces; SANNC and Bantu Union were "true representatives" of the African population.[126]

Table 9. *Category C news in* Imvo Zabantsundu *and* Workers' Herald *(% of story units)*

Category	Imvo Zabantsundu	Workers' Herald
C. Black/multiracial political and trade union news	16.6 (89 units)	40.6 (496 units)
C.1 Personalities and organizations	14.0	36.1
C.2 Confrontation and consciousness	2.6	4.5

The ICU, which organized its East London branch in 1922, also merited special treatment, especially when Alexander Jabavu joined the trade union in 1924 and was elected senior vice-president a year later.[127] *Imvo* supported the "wise words" of Kadalie, and the South African government was urged to expand African representation in the Natives' Conference to include men like Kadalie.[128] In January 1924, D. D. T. Jabavu gave the opening address at the ICU's annual conference, which was held in East London, and he "stressed the wisdom of the use of moderate language and sane objects in a movement destined to play a great part in the upliftment of Native labourers."[129] The attempt by whites to highlight the communists' role in the ICU was regarded by at least one reader as a scare tactic designed to hinder the organization of African labor.[130] Kadalie was "immensely popular" in the eastern Cape, "by reason of his dashing personality and fearless language in expressing the woes of his downtrodden people." His speeches were "strong, brave and outspoken but never seditious nor calculated to arouse anarchy." The ICU constituted an important element in *Imvo*'s political agenda, even though editorials did on occasion criticize Kadalie for his "provocative" and "intemperate" remarks and cautioned that in "politics he lacks judgement and has made mistakes."[131]

Imvo's more positive response to African politics under the editorship of Alexander Jabavu was revealed in other areas as well. The triumphs and tribulations of leading members of the African-American Pan-Africanist movement, for example, were the subject of numerous news reports in the English and Xhosa-language editorial pages during the early 1920s.[132] The major news personalities were two Americans, Harvard-educated W. E. B. Du Bois, editor of the National Association for the Advancement of Colored People's newspaper *Crisis* and a leading member of the so-called Harlem Renaissance, and Jamaican immigrant Marcus Garvey, a black nationalist who advocated a separatist alternative for the diaspora with his "Back to Africa" movement.

Articles and letters to the editor on the activities of Garveyites in the eastern Cape in the mid- to late 1920s, however, attest to the ambivalent response accorded these messages. *Imvo* published a series on the English editorial page by "A South African in America" (a correspondent named Theodore M. Kakaza, who was clearly sympathetic to Garveyism),[133] and the newspaper supported a suggestion made by Garvey himself to the CNVC in 1929 to send a South African delegate to a U.S. conference sponsored by the Universal Negro Improvement Association. The topic was debated in the vernacular pages as well, and the leader in this debate (one Alex Njaba) claimed that there was "no evidence that the majority of your readers were against Garveyism."[134] But *Imvo* also criticized the ANC for using Garvey's slogan "Africa for the Africans." Some readers were very critical of the articles by Kakaza (for example, Bennett Mdledle, secretary of the Cape African Teachers' Association, argued that Garveyism "does not appeal to a large section of the enlightened

Natives"), and *Imvo* acknowledged: "The term 'Garveyism' is a bugbear to some of our people in this part of the world."[135]

About 60 percent of the *Workers' Herald* news agenda was devoted to the ICU, if one includes promotional messages (A.8) and foreign news (D) involving the trade union. As anticipated, news coverage of personalities and organizations (C.1) focused almost exclusively on ICU policies and achievements, including branch activities and national council decisions, reports of demonstrations and resolutions passed at mass meetings.[136] Related themes dealt with the growth of the ICU in South Africa, southern Rhodesia (Zimbabwe) and Nyasaland (Malawi) or advocated support for the ICU. At least 20 percent of these stories focused on Kadalie. The cult of personality within the organization was especially evident in stories dealing with his activities and achievements. Kadalie "inspired enthusiasm among the rank and file" everywhere he went,[137] it was said, and the packaging of Kadalie as a success story formed a crucial component in the newspaper's coverage of the ICU.[138] A "National Secretary's Defence Fund" was established, for example, when the Native Affairs Department tried to limit his movements outside the Cape in 1926 and actually banned him from entering Natal. The authorities feared this "proletarian ambassador," the newspaper declared, who would "mobilise all African workers in a short space of time against the Government's segregation policy."[139] The *Star*, a leading white-owned newspaper with "no high opinion of Mr. Kadalie's judgment," was cited to suggest how liberal whites responded to the government's continued refusal to exempt him from the pass laws: "If the Minister [of Native Affairs] takes pleasure in the thought that he is inflicting some sort of personal humiliation on Kadalie by keeping him on the level of the kitchen boy or the Native labourer, he must be a very crude person indeed."[140]

Several upper-echelon ICU officials were also ANC officials, but there was relatively little coverage of the Congress in the *Workers' Herald*. The ICU's attitude toward its rival can be seen in a comment on S. M. Makgatho, the former ANC president general (1917–24) and perennial leader of Congress in the Transvaal, who announced his retirement "from all political fields" in June 1926: "we would have liked to see also that all the other old political school of thought should follow the example of Mr. Makgatho, and give the young bloods a chance to face uncompromisingly the bitter struggle ahead."[141] The ICU criticized the 1926 ANC congress for allowing so many whites to speak "who had no sympathy whatever with the black man" and for being "overrun with ministers," and two years later the ICU criticized the ANC for alleged links with the communists.[142] Nevertheless, the ANC's December 1925 congress, for example, was heralded as an "extraordinary session ... the most representative Convention staged in this country for many years."[143] The ICU advocated "collaboration" with the ANC from time to time, and in 1928 the two bodies resolved "to work together in future,"[144] but it was too late: by the end of the year the ICU was hopelessly fragmented and no longer a force in African politics.

The *Workers' Herald* rarely dealt with government-sponsored bodies like the Native Conferences or with other black or multiracial political organizations, unless the trade union and its leaders were under attack. Broadsides against real or imagined ICU critics, however, comprised more than 5 percent of the total news agenda. In sharp contrast to *Imvo*, the ICU journal continually attacked African nationalists who were deemed to be cooperating too enthusiastically with the ruling authorities, the "Silent murderer of black colour, usually of the educated class."[145]

Two groups were singled out, for example, in an article entitled "Who Are the Enemies Of Our Race?" in 1925. The first group was "the selfish lot of [black] leaders...who merely accumulate money for their own advantage and maintenance, regardless of their people." The second group, named the "good boys," were the main enemy. These were "blood-suckers" who "endeavour to destroy (for the benefit of their white capitalistic gods) all...that are for the uplifting and upbuilding...of our race." They had "betrayed their own blood."[146] They were to be found among the "servile contributors" who wrote for the Chamber of Mines newspaper, *Umteteli*, in those "run-aways" who belonged to Johannesburg's Bantu Men's Social Centre, and in the "mob of political hypocrites" affiliated with the Joint Councils.[147] One of the two "ears" on the *Workers' Herald* masthead during these years read: "*The Herald* exposés the 'good boys' as tools of imperialistic hypocrisy."[148]

In retrospect, it seems surprising that the *Workers' Herald* virtually ignored *Abantu-Batho*, the ANC's chief mouthpiece in the Transvaal during the 1920s. *Umteteli*, however, was singled out for attack time and time again: "In its fury our contemporary allowed its capitalistic zeal to outpace its discretion, although we doubt whether the word 'discretion' could be found in the vocabulary of this mining 'mouthpiece.'"[149] Other targets of criticism included chiefs ("paid government servants"), clergymen ("raving lunatics" and "dummies," when they got into politics), ANC members who relied too much on "prayer" and "reading of the Bible,"[150] and a variety of "political renegades."[151]

Members of the Communist Party who were also members of the ICU's executive committee–James ("Jimmy") LaGuma, John Gomas and E. J. ("Eddie") Khaile–contributed to the *Workers' Herald* and provided much of the radical working-class rhetoric in 1925 and 1926. "There will be no peace, not until the workers triumph," Gomas proclaimed: "We must prepare ourselves to work for the betterment of the entire exploited people of the world."[152] Russia was projected as the role model for the ICU: "Our motto has been given to us by Karl Marx: 'Workers of the world, unite!' Yes, let us unite for the purpose of attacking capitalism throughout, and substitute the present system of society with a Socialistic Commonwealth on the Russian model."[153] When the communists were expelled from the ICU in December 1926, the *Workers' Herald* claimed that CPSA leaders had been "prying deeper and deeper into the internal affairs of the Union [ICU]"[154] and had misinterpreted Communism:

> The term "Communism" has a sweet meaning, but the way it is interpreted by the party of that ilk in South Africa brings to my vision nothing but fire, brimstone and hell!...I am at one with the aspirations of the Communist Party (if they are sincere) to strive for the emancipation of the Workers, but that issue is not going to be realized if the workers seek to enforce it with pick-handles and guns.[155]

Nevertheless, "comrade" continued to be the accepted mode of address, and terms such as "capitalism," "imperialism," "socialism" and the "proletariat" remained key sign words in news stories and editorials.[156]

Much use was also made of biblical allusion. The flight of the Jews from ancient Egypt, as depicted in Exodus , for example, was "a social document...'The Story of an ancient labour movement'." And Moses was "the labour leader who freed the slaves...His heart beat true to his own class."[157] The pharaohs of Egypt were compared to the Pharaohs of South Africa: "The modern Pharaohs are strenuously bent to fetch us back to the house of bondage. They have hired our kith and kin to fetch us back to Egypt. This is a time of crisis. Once again there rings the ancient challenge 'Wherefore criest thou unto me? Speak unto the children of Israel, that they go forward.'"[158] The phrase "MENE, MENE, TEKEL, UPHARSIN," from the prophet Daniel, was used on a number of occasions in editorials and essays to refer to the end of white rule in South Africa and in Africa.[159] Jesus "challenged the existing order" and was "the greatest agitator ever known to mankind."[160] He and his apostles "seemed to have practised a rough and ready Communism... Some say the present headquarters of his Party are in Moscow."[161]

Normally, one issue was devoted to the ICU's yearly congresses, which were minuted in the style of a Hansard debate by Tyamzashe. Only a few names, virtually all members of ICU's National Council, appear in this record out of the many who attended these conferences. Most delegates, branch officers from the rural areas, were not fluent in English, which was the medium of communication for the petty bourgeoisie. All speeches were made in English and then translated into Xhosa (or Zulu) and Sotho. News reports frequently referred to the educational gap that separated the ICU leadership from the mass of mainly rural members, and in practice very few working-class members seem to have participated in public debates.

Three levels of political rhetoric within the union hierarchy were identified by Tyamzashe at the 1926 congress:

> There was first of all the "Moderates," whose policy it was to face facts, and to deliberate soberly and moderately on them. Then there were the "Die Hards," whose policy was that "Nay was Nay and Yea was Yea." Lastly came the "Ginger Group," composed of all the young bloods; their policy was "Direct Action."[162]

The "Moderates," who "had their way" in 1926, generally represented the Cape liberal tradition, and they included men like Alexander Jabavu, John Mzaza and Theo Lujiza, who had helped launch the ICU in East London, and James Dippa, ICU provincial secretary for the eastern Cape. Champion, the Natal ICU leader, was regarded as a "Die Hard," along with Alex Maduna, ICU provincial secretary for the Orange Free State, CPSA members James LaGuma, an ICU leader in the western Cape, and Eddie Khaile, the ICU's financial secretary. The "Ginger" group included leading ICU members in the Orange Free State like John Mancoe and Keable 'Mote, CPSA members T. S. Thibedi, a veteran of several socialist factions (International Socialist League and the Industrial Workers of Africa) and Thomas Mbeki, the ICU's provincial secretary for the Transvaal.

Alliances, however, shifted continually. John Gomas, the outspoken Coloured CPSA member from Cape Town, fluctuated as a Die Hard and Ginger in the *Workers' Herald*, while Die Hard LaGuma was sometimes designated a Ginger, and Die Hard Champion on occasion was identified as a Moderate. There was much emphasis on parliamentary decorum and on Kadalie's influence as chairman in the recorded sessions:

> The proceedings throughout were conducted in a most orderly manner... At times six or seven "young bloods" [i.e., Gingers] were on their feet at the same time; but, according to strict Parliamentary procedure, the member who "caught" the eye of the Chairman first was permitted to speak, and in not a single instance are we aware that the Chairman's ruling was questioned or disobeyed.[163]

The Gingers were tolerated, indeed admired, but they had little power. Tyamzashe explained their junior role at the 1927 congress:

> The Ginger group were again present in strong force, but to their credit it must be said that their debates this year were on a higher scale than last year. Little Comrade Thomas Mbeki... was the hero of the Congress. Calm in his debates, of small stature and young in years, he swayed the house with his clear stentorian voice. This comrade is a "coming man" in the industrial and political affairs of non-Europeans.[164]

Confrontation and Consciousness

Perhaps the most interesting example of the limits of political protest in the African nationalist press during the 1920s was in news that confronted the social order (C.2). The *Workers' Herald* advocated class consciousness, but few stories in either newspaper advocated racial solidarity. Although the *Workers' Herald* cultivated "race consciousness" and supported the Garvey movement when Thaele was the de facto editor,[165] the newspaper under Tyamzashe frequently condemned black as well as white nationalists: "The government accuses us of being racialists, but I say that the government itself is preaching racialism the same as Marcus Garvey in America. He preaches 'Africa for the Africans' and the Pact government says 'Africa for the whites.'"[166] Events concerned with strikes, boycotts or civil disobedience in any form actually constituted less than 0.5 percent of both newsholes.

Only a few direct-action stories were recorded in the *Imvo* sample, and they are revealing of the normative framework within which the protest movement operated in the eastern Cape. When violence erupted in Port Elizabeth during the October 1920 strike, for example, the newspaper was generally critical of the protesting workers. Tengo Jabavu sympathized with his old adversary Walter Rubusana of the defunct South African Native Congress, who had been called in by local officials to urge a halt to the strike and was assaulted for his efforts. The report of the commission investigating the riots was reprinted in full.[167]

Millenarianism, which had formed part of the African reaction to conquest since the nineteenth century Cape-Xhosa wars, was a particularly potent focal point of popular resistance in the eastern Cape. A prophet figure by the name of Enoch Josiah Mgijima and his followers, who were called "Israelites," provided the most dramatic example during the 1920s.[168] They confronted the state at Bulhoek in the Mfengu location of Kamastone (about 25 miles from present-day Queenstown) in May 1921. An 800-man police contingent drawn from all parts of the country and equipped with rifles, machine guns and artillery – the largest peacetime force ever assembled up to that time in South Africa – was pitted against a group of white-robed warriors armed with spears, knives and "knobkerries" (sticks). When the shooting finally stopped, at least 183 Israelites were dead and 100 wounded, while 1 policeman suffered a stab wound.

The Israelites represented a new stage in the transition to a fully Africanist political and ecclesiastical tradition. Unlike millenarian prophets during the wars of conquest, they embraced Christianity and were more broadly African. Unlike the Ethiopian separatists of the late colonial era, they were not orthodox Christian reformists. Israelites stopped paying taxes and refused to recognize the authority of the government over their church. Particularly interesting was Mgijima's success in attracting farm laborers, landless peasants and converts from the non-Christian community. As the Israelites embraced more Africans from the most alienated sections of the peasantry, church leaders apparently moved farther away from conventional Christian doctrines and rituals. Mgijima and his contemporaries, moreover, accepted chiefs and other precolonial ruling figures when they were not used against their churches. A restored and rejuvenated chiefly authority was more acceptable to millenarians like Mgijima than the authority of mission-educated politicians.

Tengo Jabavu was critical of the Israelites even before the Bulhoek incident: "These people are fanatics. The best course seems to be for the Government to sell them a farm where they can go on with their worship forever and not trouble other people."[169] *Imvo* relied on official reports of the massacre and exonerated the government of any wrongdoing: "That the people were demented there remains no room to doubt; and no inquiry, however searching, can reveal anything... There are always elements ag'in the Government. These are irresponsible... At the bottom it is a political movement identified with worship. The main object being to drive the whiteman from the country."[170] D. D. T. Jabavu described Mgijima as an example of "an untrained intellect, the undisciplined mind," who "failed in the end to adapt his religion to the conditions imposed by Government." Mgijima's followers were "unsophisticated rustics" who accepted his prophecies "with typical innocence and gullibility."[171]

Imvo unquestionably expressed the feelings of the voting community in steadfastly refusing to recognize any political action that was not identified with the petty bourgeoisie. The focal point of opposition to Hertzog's "Native Bills" was the Cape African franchise. The other measures, including the Land Bill, were "of little consequence."[172] *Imvo* rarely acknowledged divisions between so-called Red and School communities–those Africans who did not, and those who did, conform to Western cultural norms–in the eastern Cape. "Reds" were always referred to in quotation marks on the English-language editorial page, and only two clashes, one of which was publicized initially by Presbyterian missionaries, were recorded in the test sample.[173]

Popular resistance, apart from petitionary protest as legitimized by the petty bourgeoisie, was condemned. Elias Wellington Buthelezi, a Zulu born near Melmoth in Natal about 1895, is another religious figure worth mentioning at this point, because his career illustrates how millenarian messages, Africanist-oriented separatist churches, African-American images (generally derived from the Garveyites) and local grievances could be fused to broaden the discourse of popular resistance in the rural areas. Buthelezi and his "Wellingtonites" appeared and reappeared all over the eastern Cape during the 1920s–throughout the Transkei and surrounding areas, from East Griqualand and Herschel to Queenstown, King William's Town and Komgha in the Ciskei.[174]

The mission-educated community felt particularly threatened by Buthelezi. *Imvo* published a series of articles written by a white missionary on the "pernicious doctrines" of the Wellingtonites,[175] and the newspaper almost visibly breathed a sigh of relief when they apparently failed to establish a permanent center in the Ciskei. As D. D. T. Jabavu put it, "imposters of the type of Wellington would cut no ice with Ciskei Natives, thanks to the [Ciskei Native] Convention, where the educated men led their backward fellow citizens on lines of economic wisdom and loyalty to authority."[176] Joseph Fanana, a spokesman for dissidents at Herschel before Buthelezi's arrival, was classed with Mgijima as the kind of "so-called leader of the unintelligent people... who suspect everything that leads to better educational facilities, progress and civilisation."[177]

The *Workers' Herald* sought to represent the interests of workers and peasants, but it never advocated the strike weapon. In July 1927, for example, Tyamzashe urged more than 400 contract laborers who had staged a wildcat strike at the

Kazerne railway goods depot in Johannesburg to go back to work: "The reasonable attitude of the ICU officials at the recent Kazerne strike should prove to the Government that they are not dealing with a lot of hotheads, but that they are dealing with men who are anxious to assist both employer and employed."[178] In a revealing response to a complaint by Edward Roux, a CPSA member at the time, who claimed the trade union had "scarcely conducted any strikes in its whole existence," Tyamzashe wrote:

> the duties of a real trade union is [*sic*] not to 'look for' or 'manufacture' strikes, but to endeavour to overcome circumstances that may lead to strikes. The strike weapon is only used as a last resort, and no employee or employer should be proud of a strike because it means that there is something rotten somewhere, either on the side of the employers or the employees.

Tyamzashe was "glad to say" the ICU had used the "strike weapon" only three times "since its formation in 1919."[179]

As expected, there were many more consciousness-raising stories in the *Workers' Herald* than in *Imvo*. Six-column homilies in bold (often capital) letters, for example, appeared at the top of many newspaper pages in 1926:

- Comrades! When you get into a tight place and everything goes against you until it seems that you cannot hold on a minute longer, never give up then, for that is just the place and time that the tide will turn.

- COMRADES: Down with Pass Laws and Segregation Policy: Onward with Proletarian March towards Economic Freedom.[180]

The ICU was a nonracial union – it even had a few white members[181] – and the newspaper would remain committed to workers' solidarity at the national and international level:

- Never in the history of South Africa has a non-European organisation been able to marshal within its ranks all non-European labour. Here you have an army of workers, Native Africans, Coloureds and Indians, who know each other as "Comrades in arms." No more do the members of the regiment call themselves Zulus, Ama-Xosa, Basuto, Coloureds, or Indians. They have been taught to know themselves as the working class of South Africa.[182]
- The attitude of some of the South African white workers, those who place race prejudice before class interests, was quite incomprehensible to the European workers... The African workers must establish close unity with the European workers. International working class unity is the slogan of the day.[183]

The newspaper continued to express the hope that the schism between white and black workers in South Africa was a "temporal" (temporary) problem:

> We think that in this move for a civilised standard of life, both black and white workers should join hands and approach the greedy capitalists with a united front. Only in this manner can the working classes of South Africa hope to eliminate exploitation. But so long as the working classes are divided, so long will they form a stepping stone for capitalism.[184]

The problem, of course, was the racist attitudes of the white working class: "When 'O When' will our White fellow workers realise that Industrialised Capitalism, in its forward march, knows neither Colour nor Creed."[185]

A Preferred Reading

The differences in political rhetoric employed by moderate and militant wings of the African nationalist movement during the interwar period are revealed, at least to some extent, in these alternative newspapers. *Imvo*, with no competitors in its main circulation area, was more representative of mainstream trends in journalism that emphasized factual reportage (focusing on events rather than issues and featuring primarily what happened and who was involved) and sought to be nonpartisan in terms of the news agenda. *Imvo* was essentially a community newspaper specializing in news of general interest to the mission-educated community in the eastern Cape. The *Workers' Herald,* on the other hand, was competing with *Umteteli* (and possibly *Abantu-Batho*) as a national newspaper and focusing on partisan news of concern to ICU members throughout southern Africa. Both publications attacked the political, legislature and administrative manifestations of white authoritarian rule with vigor (B.1) but were relatively silent on the economic and social manifestations (B.2). Wages and working conditions of African miners, factory and farm laborers, and the living conditions of Africans in town and countryside, moreover, received relatively scant coverage (A.4, A.5).

Both newspapers generally resisted any strategy of protest that promoted racial consciousness or solidarity or that advocated strikes, boycotts or civil disobedience (C.2). *Imvo* for the most part continued to modulate its protests in the interests of the Cape's African voters, and the *Workers' Herald* sought to enlist support from urban workers and peasants. *Imvo* tried to speak with moral authority on behalf of the African Christian community, and its news reports were framed in relatively didactic and dispassionate terms. Even when indignant, the language of protest was measured and restrained under Alexander Jabavu's editorship. The stories in the *Workers' Herald* were far more colorful and aggressive in tone, but in the English section, at least, they were apparently written far above the reading comprehension levels of an African working-class audience.[186]

Imvo supported the ongoing efforts of white and black middle-class liberals to promote class solidarity, and a considerable portion of the news agenda was devoted to individuals and organizations committed to constitutional reform of the existing political system. The newspaper acted as a conduit for these concerns, which became more urgent as pressure mounted against the African petty bourgeoisie. As the protest movement expanded, the Jabavu family increasingly stressed the need for African unity and for solidarity with Coloureds and Indians as victims of white discrimination.[187] "The unskilled Native labourer," as one editorial put it, "is beginning to realise that his salvation ... lies in group action and group ideals." The Msimang and Kadalie factions in the ICU-inspired labor movement were urged to unite "to save the position of the unskilled labourer." And all Africans were urged to "work for racist [i.e., racial] unity within and racial cooperation without."[188]

The *Workers' Herald* also sought to break down ethnic and cultural barriers between African, Coloured, Indian and white workers in the ongoing effort to promote working-class solidarity, and the newspaper also adhered strictly to the legal and social boundaries of the political order. The word "constitutional," for example, was used to express the ICU's abhorrence of extraconstitutional methods in bringing about change: "We believe in persistent agitation on constitutional lines ... Constitutional pressure carries more weight than mob law, and we shall always denounce those human sharks who attempt to lead the peaceful Native community over the precipice."[189]

Tyamzashe himself did not claim equality with whites,[190] and this view prevailed in the *Workers' Herald*. Both Thaele and Tyamzashe were attempting to establish a singular African discourse that was not mediated by whites–this was the substance of their diatribes against the "good boys" of *Umteteli* and other white-controlled publications aimed at an African audience[191]–but in the 1920s no African journalist was prepared to dispense completely with white trusteeship. "I hope," as one writer put it, "Native leaders will make it a point to see that nothing is done to hurt the feelings of the white people."[192] As expressed in an editorial entitled "Future of the European," "the white people will remain the leaders for many years to come, but that leadership will only be maintained if they LEAD and NOT DRIVE the native; if they maintain a high standard of morals and a real sense of justice...Unless high morals among the Europeans is [*sic*] upheld, their doom is sealed."[193] Whites attended and addressed delegates at ICU conferences and were well received. Although white clergy were usually pilloried in the newspaper, those few who were sympathetic to the ICU were invariably given the opportunity to air their views.[194]

The *Workers' Herald* sought to represent the African worker as one who aspired to middle-class values: "The Native of today wants the right and privilege of earning his livelihood according to his ability, devoid of color prejudice, and to live a standard of life as becoming a civilised man."[195] The Native Affairs Department was continually attacked for linking "a certain class of lawless Native" with "Native intellectuals or Native organisations."[196] The most advertised commodity in the newspaper when it was published in Cape Town, for example, was "Percine,"a "Hair Straightener and Beautifier" that "actually straightens the hair similar to a European." In addition to conventional advertisements, various bold-type, multicolumn Percine messages were placed at the bottom of virtually every page. Some examples: "The Unsophisticated Say, 'I Was Born With Curly Hair, Why Straighten It,'" and on the next page, "Percine Syndicate Say, 'So Were You Born Without Clothes.'" "Why Let Your Hair Remain in Its Aboriginal State When Percine Is Available." "Possibly There Is a Slight Suspicion of Colour Which Is Accentuated by Frizzy Hair," and on the next page, "Percine (Afric) Removes That Suspicion."[197]

Health-care products dominated *Imvo*'s advertising hole during the 1920s. The advertisers were a small group of white chemists (pharmicists) and shopkeepers, who sought to exploit a market that was made up largely of impoverished peasants in one of South Africa's most depressed rural areas. They advertised essentially the same products, in the form of pills, syrups and powders, week after week. Most illustrations used in these advertisements depicted whites, and when drawings of Africans were used they were often gross caricatures. One multicolumn line drawing for a pill advertisement that featured regularly on the front page of the newspaper during the early 1920s depicted a pith-helmeted, uniformed white man (complete with an African manservant holding the reins of his horse) dispensing medicine to seminaked Africans in front of a grass hut.[198]

These medicines promised to cure every conceivable ailment. Chamberlain's powder (also advertised in the *Workers' Herald*), for example, was offered on successive pages of the same edition as a remedy for different ailments ranging from bad breath, constipation and colic to cholera, and even as a liniment for golfers! There were "life blood" tonics and "blood, brain and nerve" tonics, and mixtures to cleanse "witchcraft poisoning" and increase "fertility and virility."[199] The African market must have been pretty competitive, for these advertisements made increasing use of photographs and other illustrations (conspicuously absent from the news pages), bolder and larger type, prizes and even celebrity endorsements: D. D. T. Jabavu, for example, featured in one claiming a cure for epilepsy.[200]

Although segregation was condemned in principle, white officials were often urged to distinguish "between civilised and uncivilised Natives."[201] The ICU had "no objection to the establishment of decent non-European townships,"[202] and said that "a sympathetic Location Inspector, and one who knows the Natives, could do a great deal of good in advising local authorities as to what class of rooms or dormitories would suit decent Natives."[203]

Both newspapers were primarily concerned with sustaining the values of a social class whose survival was now at stake. This meant that the language of protest was essentially reformist: the desirable course of action was to challenge the dominant political order without jeopardizing the existing rights and privileges of the dominated African political elites. In this respect, it is significant that *Imvo* cited all of the major organs of African political opinion–*Abantu-Batho*, *Workers' Herald*, *Ilanga lase Natal* and *Umteteli wa Bantu*–as "responsible" newspapers that reflected the interests and needs of the African population.[204] Journalists of the alternative press could contemplate no other viable alternative for themselves and their constituents in South Africa during the 1920s.

Notes

1. E.g., F. A. Johnstone, "The I.W.A. on the Rand: Socialist organising among black workers on the Rand, 1917–1918," and P. L. Bonner, "The 1920 black mineworkers' strike: A preliminary account," in B. Bozzoli (comp.), *Labour, townships and protest: Studies in the social history of the Witwatersrand* (Johannesburg, 1979), 248–297. See also earlier references to the African petty bourgeoisie in the present volume, especially in the Introduction.
2. South Africa's per capita death rate during this epidemic was one of the highest in the world. At least 300,000 people are believed to have died: most victims were rural blacks, and the death toll was highest in the Cape. These losses influenced the demographic profile of the African population for virtually an entire generation. H. Phillips, "South Africa's worst demographic disaster: The Spanish influenza epidemic of 1918," *South African Historical Journal* 20 (1988), 57–73.
3. E.g., T. Couzens, *The new African: A study of the life and work of H.I.E. Dhlomo* (Johannesburg, 1985), Chap. 3.
4. On the Joint Councils, see B. Hirson, "Tuskegee, the Joint Councils, and the All African Convention," in *The Societies in Southern Africa in the Ninteenth and Twentieth Centuries*, University of London, Institute of Commonwealth Studies, Vol. 10 (London, October 1978–June 1979), 65–76; P. B. Rich, *White power and the liberal conscience: Racial segregation and South African liberalism, 1921–60* (Johannesburg, 1984), Chap. 1.
5. On the ambiguities of the liberal tradition during this period, see Rich, *White power and the liberal conscience*, Chaps. 1–3; idem, "The appeals of Tuskegee: James Henderson, Lovedale, and the fortunes of South African liberalism, 1906–1930," *International Journal of African Historical Studies* 20 (1987), 271–292; idem, *Hope and despair: English-speaking intellectuals and South African politics, 1896–1976* (London, 1993), Chaps. 1–3.
6. Parts of this case study appeared in earlier formats in L. Switzer, "The ambiguities of protest in South Africa: Rural politics and the press during the 1920s," *International Journal of African Historical Studies*, 23, 1 (1990), 87–109; idem, "Moderation and militancy in African nationalist newspapers during the 1920s," in K. Tomaselli and P. E. Louw (eds.), *The alternative press in South Africa* (Bellville, South Africa, 1991), 33–76; *idem*, *Power and resistance in an African society: The Ciskei*

Xhosa and the making of South Africa (Madison, 1993), Chap. 8. Several sections were expanded, and the newspapers themselves were subjected to new content analyses in preparing this chapter. Newspaper references specify page numbers but not the languages of non-English stories. All stories cited from the *Workers' Herald* (hereafter *WH*) and the editorial page (usually page 5) from *Imvo Zabantsundu* (hereafter *IZ*) were in English.

7. The African vote was no longer a significant factor in provincial politics, except in a few constituencies. By 1936, only 10 of the 61 electoral districts in the Cape had more than 450 African voters, and 9 were in the eastern Cape. V. Klein, "African responses in the eastern Cape to Hertzog's Representation of Natives in Parliament Bill, 1926–1936," University of Cape Town, B.A. Honours thesis (Cape Town, 1978); 20, Apps. A and B.
8. The Ciskeian Missionary Council eventually included officials from the Cape Education Department and Native Affairs Department, members of mission churches and prestigious secondary schools, representatives of Native Welfare Societies and Students' Christian Associations, and councillors from local or district councils and the Ciskei General Council in the African reserve. Ciskeian Missionary Council, Minutes, October 1925–November 1951. Cory library, Rhodes University (Grahams Town, South Africa).
9. Tengo Jabavu's broadsides would provoke considerable debate on the English-language editorial page, for example, in 1918–19. *IZ*, 24 December 1918, 5; 7, 14, 28 January 1919, 5; 4, 18 February 1919, 5; 18 March 1919, 5; 20, 27 May 1919, 5; 17 June 1919, 5; 26 August 1919, 5; 14 October 1919, 5; 9 December 1919, 6.
10. Hertzog was depicted as one who "looked upon the Convention [i.e., the Act of Union] so solemnly signed and sealed in 1910 as a mere scrap of paper that could be torn up at the first opportunity." *IZ*, 31 (misnumbered 21) October 1919, 5.
11. *IZ*, 19, 26 November 1919, 5; 3 December 1919, 5; 27 April 1920, 5; 4 May 1920, 5.
12. He was also the most prominent member of the Tamacha (King William's Town) local council during his lifetime. Local councils established for Africans in the Ciskei and Transkei reserves were created originally under Cape colonial rule with the 1894 Glen Grey Act.
13. Imvo Company Limited had operated for many years at a loss; debts totaled £5,060 when Tengo Jabavu died. *IZ*, 11 October 1921, 5; 15 November 1921, 5.
14. On the ICU, see P. L. Wickins, *The Industrial and Commercial Workers' Union of Africa* (Cape Town, 1978); H. Bradford, *A taste of freedom: The ICU in rural South Africa, 1924–1930* (New Haven 1987). On *Imvo*'s reaction to the abortive trade union unity conference in Bloemfontein, see *IZ*, 2 August 1921, 5: "All the stock grievances were ransacked, and a long boohoo pronounced on them" by these "self-advertising associations."
15. On the Garveyites in South Africa, see R.A. Hill and G.A. Pirio, "'Africa for the Africans': The Garvey movement in South Africa, 1920–1940," in S. Marks and S. Trapido (eds.), *The politics of race, class and nationalism in twentieth century South Africa* (London, 1987), 209–253.
16. On Gwayi Tyamzashe, see Chapter 1 in this volume. Henry was the second oldest of eight children. After his father's death in Kimberley in 1896, the family was sent to live with relatives in the Ciskei region in the eastern Cape. On Henry's early life, see J. Richards, "The *Workers' Herald*, May 1925–December 1928," Rhodes University, B.A. honours thesis (Grahamstown, 1979), Chap. 2.
17. *WH*, June 1926, 3.
18. *WH*, e.g., August 1926, 2; Wickins, *Industrial and Commercial Workers' Union of Africa*, 106, 146. Tyamzashe retained his position on the ICU National Council as "deputy councillor for Rhodesia." Richards, "*Workers' Herald*," 13 (citing Tyamzashe's unpublished autobiography).
19. Kadalie embarked on an extended tour of Britain and other European countries to visit various trade union bodies and to attend a conference of the International Federation of Trade Unions–a European-dominated body–in Geneva.
20. Richards, "*Workers' Herald*," 14 (citing Tyamzashe's unpublished autobiography).
21. Ibid., 17 (citing Tyamzashe's unpublished autobiography].

22. The September issue was 10 pages.
23. Tyamzashe was fluent in Afrikaans as well as English, and the newspaper was apparently unique in the African press during the 1920s for its translations of news reports from Afrikaans-language publications, but he was not fluent in any African language. He often wrote under the pseudonym "Oupa" ("Grandpa," in Afrikaans), the nickname given to him by Kadalie's personal secretary Abe Phoofolo, a regular contributor to the *Workers' Herald*.
24. The Independent ICU found a permanent home in East London and the rural hinterland of the Ciskei and southern Transkei. On the Independent ICU, see W. Beinart and C. Bundy, "The union, the nation and the talking crow," in W. Beinart & C. Bundy, *Hidden struggles in rural South Africa* (London, 1987), Chap. 8.
25. *IZ*, 2 November 1920, 5.
26. For example, James M. Dippa, an ICU organizer from Port Elizabeth, attacked "the white man's law which has branded the Native worker an out-cast" in an article entitled "The Native Worker ."*IZ*, 26 October 1926, 5; see also 5 August 1924, 5 ("The Poor Blacks"), 10 November 1925, 5 ("The Rand Native Wages" and "N.R.C. and Native Labour"), 9 March 1926, 5 ("The Cost of Living for the Natives"), 30 November 1926, 5 ("A Serious Social Problem").
27. *IZ*, e.g., 5 August 1924, 5; 10 November 1925, 5; 9 March 1926, 5; 11 May 1926, 5; 26 October 1926, 5; 30 November 1926, 5.
28. Rural Africans living in the 14 magisterial districts of the Ciskei (including Herschel District, which was classified as part of the Ciskei reserve) constituted 86.2 percent of the region's population in 1911 and 1921 and 84.5 percent in 1936. *Census* return, UG 15-1923 (1919 and 1921), UG 21-1938 (1936).
29. *IZ*, e.g., 28 June 1921, 5; 5 July 1921, 5; 17 October 1922, 5; 16 October 1923, 5; 29 January 1924, 5; 29 April 1924, 5; 7, 14, 21 October 1924, 5; 2 December 1924, 5; 24 March 1925, 5; 6 July 1926, 5; 25 October 1927, 5; 2 October 1928, 5; 12 November 1929, 5.
30. *IZ*, e.g., 10, 17 January 1922, 5; 5 September 1922, 5; 4 September 1923, 5; 30 October 1923, 5; 15 January 1924, 5; 19 August 1924, 5; 24 March 1925, 5; 2, 9, 16 June 1925, 5; 6 July 1926, 5; 14 September 1926, 5; 5 October 1926, 5; 23 July 1929, 5.
31. James East, an African-American Baptist missionary stationed at Middledrift, played a major role in launching the NFA. (Personal communication from Robert Edgar.)
32. *IZ*, e.g., 30 March 1920, 5; 12 June 1923, 5; 9 December 1924, 5; 15 September 1925, 5; 26 September 1926, 5; 13 December 1927, 5; 9 April 1929, 5.
33. *IZ*, e.g., 15 April 1924, 5; see also 13 May 1919, 5; 16 September 1919, 5; 22 June 1920, 5; 30 August 1921, 5; 6 September 1921, 5; 7 November 1922, 5; 6 November 1923, 5; 4, 18 March 1924, 5; 17 June 1924, 5; 15 July 1924, 5; 22 September 1925, 5.
34. The Native Affairs Administration bill sought to consolidate reserve administration under the central government and implement the proposals of the Natives' Land Commission, appointed in 1916, that additional land be "released" for African occupation (especially in the Transvaal and Orange Free State, where there were very few reserves). The bill was dropped and provincial committees appointed to review the commission's findings. The Cape Natives' Land Committee completed its report in 1918.
35. *IZ*, 30 September 1919, 5; 25 November 1919, 5; 9, 30 March 1920, 5; 6 December 1921, 5.
36. *IZ*, e.g., 22, 29 July 1919, 5; 9, 16 December 1919, 5; 31 March 1928, 5.
37. *IZ*, 9 December 1919, 5.
38. *IZ*, 9 September 1919, 5. On rare occasions, the newspaper highlighted success stories: e.g., 7 October 1919, 5 ("How I Succeeded as a Farmer").
39. *IZ*, 1 April 1924, 5; 13, 27 July 1926, 5. D. D. T. Jabavu was organizing secretary of the NFA and secretary-treasurer of the Native Farmers' Congress during the 1920s.
40. *WH*, e.g., December 1925, 6.
41. *WH*, February 1926, 1.
42. *WH*, e.g., January 1926, 6 (To a Durban reader: "We tried to sub-edit your communication but the further we went into your wearisome effusion, the more hopeless the task became. Try and express your views

in the vernacular"); December 1926, 3 ("Answers to Correspondents ... we do not necessarily place our columns open to premature or immature expositions").

43. Sometimes with the admonition "Do not buy from those firms who do not advertise in this journal." *WH*, e.g., August 1927, 5.
44. Most health problems, however, would be cured with "Chamberlain's Tablets": *WH*, e.g., October 1926, 3 ("Bad Taste in the Mouth" and "Bowel Complaint in Children"); November 1926, 3–4 ("For a Lame Back" and "How the Trouble Starts"); December 1926, 2 ("Constipation"); February 1927, 1 ("Are You Going on a Journey?" and "Operations Averted").
45. *WH*, September 1927, 1.
46. *WH*, e.g., March 1926, 6 ("The Negro Race Holding Their Own with Europeans in the Boxing Ring"); May 1926, 5 ("Bill Richmond, Ex-Slave, One-Time Champion of England"); December 1926, 5 ("Records of Famous Black Boxers"); April 1927, 5 ("Great American Negro Boxers").
47. *WH*, e.g., December 1925, 4 (In a story entitled "The Black Page of Infamy," a white sympathizer is quoted: " 'the conviction and execution of a white for a black murder is, I fear, unheard of in the land'"; June 1926, 4 ("Native Woman Marched 15 miles to Gaol"); July 1926, 4 ("White Man Charged with Shooting Native ... It is very very seldom that a white man pays the extreme penalty of the law for murdering a black man in this country").
48. *WH*, e.g., July 1926, 4 ("A 'Black Ringhals' in the Grass! And a 'White Ringhals' With a Gun" and "Capitalist Cussedness"); October 1926, 1 (" 'Tickling' a Native with Knife"), 4 ("A Flogging Missionary"); October 1927, 3 ("Jury System Scandal" and "An Incorrigible Rogue"); February 1928, 5 ("Justice under Capitalism!" and "A Bad Character").
49. Only a few letters to the editor were concerned with this question, but they are interesting precursors to the farm labor exposés that appeared in publications like the *Guardian* and *Drum*. One correspondent provided a detailed, factual interview with a 20-year-old African farm laborer on living conditions in the Orange Free State's Vrede District "to educate those who still harbour the foolish notion that the white man is the friend of the native." *WH*, November 1926, 4. A Coloured correspondent offered readers another factual account of what it was like to be the child of a farm worker in the western Cape: "There is no doubt that South African farmers treat their employees exactly like slaves and serfs." *WH*, January 1927, 4.
50. *WH*, November 1926, 1, 4. Tyamzashe frequently responded to stories in the white Johannesburg press about "Native lawlessness." A *Rand Daily Mail* reporter, for example, was praised for investigating "some of the causes" of "lawlessness" and attacked for ignoring low wages, the pass laws and "one-sided liquor laws." Although the newspaper condemned home-made liquor (dubbed "skokiaan") and "shebeens" (illegal African drinking establishments) as a scourge of urban African life, the "illicit liquor traffic" was the result of laws that discriminated against Africans. *WH*, October 1925, 3; November 1926, 4; December 1926, 5. On another occasion, the *Mail* was attacked for publishing "some of the most misleading and grossly incorrect reports ... about the behaviour of Natives on the Rand." *WH*, January 1927, 1.
51. *WH*, December 1925, 4.
52. *WH*, March 1926, 1 ("some Native female servants are treated worse than dogs by their European mistresses"); October 1926, 4 (about employers who break contracts with their workers "whenever they please" and "not infrequently refuse to pay them for work actually done").
53. *WH*, October 1925, 2; January 1927, 5; July 1927, 2 (editorial).
54. *WH*, July 1927, 4.
55. The case involved nurses at a hospital in Mafeking: "The action of the matron and her nurses is a blot on the dignity and humanity of the whole medical and nursing fraternity." *WH*, June 1927, 1; August 1927, 5.
56. *WH*, e.g., December 1925, 3 (Indian dies from "a large bed sore" in S. A. Railways and Harbours Native and Indian Hospital).
57. *WH*, e.g., June 1926, 3 (smallpox); July 1926, 4 (no smallpox).
58. *WH*, August 1927, 4 (headline: "The Way of the Capitalist Press").
59. *WH*, e.g., October 1925, 6; April 1927, 3.

60. *WH*, e.g., October 1925, 2 (warning "first-time visitors" about crime in Johannesburg).
61. *WH*, e.g., September 1926, 3.
62. *WH*, e.g., January 1927, 4 (referring to second-class compartments on trains).
63. *WH*, e.g., August 1926, 6 (railroad workers).
64. *WH*, October 1926, 4; April 1927, 3. On the daily harassment of Africans by the police and other authorities, see *WH*, October 1925, 3 (a policemen in Johannesburg is defined as one who "smacked" Africans "in the mouth"); January 1926, 6 (correspondence between the ICU and Johannesburg police concerning the treatment of Africans); July 1926, 4 ("In the locations Natives are often unduly harassed and hounded down for nothing whatsoever"); September 1926, 4 ("vagrancy"); March 1927, 3 (Africans forced to appear before the authorities simply to "give a satisfactory account" about what they were doing]; March 1928, 4 (harassment of young boys and older "vagrants").
65. *WH*, October 1925, 5–6 (conditions in Bloemfontein); January 1926, 6 (conditions on the Rand); June 1926, 4 (requesting an African as superintendent of Germiston location); September 1926, 6 (page misnumbered 4–commenting on one Rand location rule that would admit only African couples with marriage certificates); October 1926, 3 (holding public meetings in locations without permits), 7 (too many white bureaucrats in African locations); March 1927, 5 (conditions in East London); March 1928, 4 (married Africans in mine compounds); December 1928, 3 (plea to standardize municipal regulations for locations and make them known to African residents).
66. *WH*, October 1927, 2 (editorial: "Help Yourself").
67. *WH*, e.g., October 1925, 1; November 1925, 1; December 1925, 1; January 1926, 1; August 1926, 2. Black self-employment advertisements comprised about 17.6 percent of the advertising items between February 1925 and December 1928.
68. *WH*, May 1926, 5. The article was actually repeating part of a story originally published in the September 1925 issue (now lost) and providing readers with "fresh information" to support "our indictment with regard to British Imperialism in Africa."
69. *WH*, February 1927, 5.
70. *WH*, July 1927, 4.
71. *WH*, August 1928, 2.
72. *WH*, March 1927, 5. Lewis occasionally called for contributions from readers ("We wish to be the first to find a true Bantu poet"), but none were deemed suitable for her column. Three poems, for example, were apparently submitted for the October 1928 issue. Two were condemned as "purely doggerel propaganda" and the third as "propaganda." The "Bookshelf" was "meant to be a rest and refreshment from political strife." *WH*, September 1928, 2; October 1928, 2.
73. *WH*, December 1927, 2 (editorial: "Our Future"). Lewis, a militant anticommunist and a staunch member of the Unionist Party and later of the South African Party, and Holtby, a self-styled pacifist and a member of Britain's Independent Labour Party, were two of three significant female voices in a white-liberal discourse that sought to control the ICU's political–trade union agenda during these years. Mabel Palmer, another influential figure in this group, was a prominent British feminist and social critic who spent much of her life working on behalf of Africans and Indians in Natal. For brief pen sketches of these women, see Wickins, *The Industrial and Commercial Workers' Union of Africa*, 103–106ff.; Bradford, *A taste of freedom*, 20, 173, 182, 184, 315 (n. 44), 316 (n. 58); S. Marks (ed.), *Not either an experimental doll: The separate worlds of three South African women* (Bloomington, 1987), 2–8 (Mabel Palmer).
74. *WH*, May 1928, 1.
75. *IZ*, e.g., 15 February 1921, 5. Editorial comment on the 1920 general election: "May the S.A. Party live forever."
76. *IZ*, 14 November 1922, 5.
77. *IZ*, 24 April 1923, 5; 31 July 1923, 5.
78. *IZ*, e.g., 6 February 1923, 5; 5 June 1923, 5 ("Wanted: A Minister for Native Affairs").
79. *IZ*, 27 March 1923, 5. On the role of Herbst in the NAD, see S. Dubow, "Holding 'a just balance between white and black': The Native Affairs Department in South Africa, c.1920–33," *Journal of*

Southern African Studies 12, 2 (1986), 228–230.

80. *IZ*, 6 February 1923, 5; 22 July 1924, 5.
81. *IZ*, e.g., 4 August 1925, 5; 23 February 1926, 5; 3 August 1926, 5; 10 January 1928, 5; 7 February 1928, 5; 23 October 1928, 5; 12 November 1929, 5.
82. *IZ*, e.g., 2 May 1922, 5; 25 July 1922, 5; 24 April 1923, 5; 8 May 1923, 5; 26 June 1923, 5; 17, 24 July 1923, 5; 14, 28 August 1923, 5; 30 October 1923, 5; 19 February 1924, 5; 1, 8 April 1924, 5; 8 July 1924, 5; 26 May 1925, 5; 9 February 1926, 5; 1 February 1927, 5; 18 October 1927, 5; 20 December 1927, 5; 7 May 1929, 5; 4 June 1929, 5.
83. *IZ*, 14 April 1925, 5; 12 August 1925, 5; 9 February 1926, 5; 15 June 1926, 5.
84. *IZ*, e.g. 6 May 1924, 5; 24 June 1924, 5.
85. *IZ*, 22, 29 June 1926, 5.
86. *IZ*, cf. 13 January 1925, 5; 10, 17 February 1925, 5; 10, 17 March 1925, 5; 7, 28 April 1925, 5; 12, 19 May 1925, 5; 30 June 1925, 5; 4, 13 August 1925, 5; 22 September 1925, 5; 1, 15 December 1925, 5; 12 January 1926, 5; 6 April 1926, 5.
87. *IZ*, 30 November 1926, 5.
88. *IZ*, 22 September 1925, 5.
89. *IZ*, 11 May 1926, 5.
90. *IZ*, 22 January 1929, 5; 12 February 1929, 5; 2, 23, 30 April 1929, 5; 7 May 1929, 5; 16, 30 July 1929, 5; 6, 27 August 1929, 5; 3 September 1929, 5.
91. The case was dismissed because the courts could not overturn a governor general's proclamation. The judges urged parliament to "address" the "grievances" of the landholders, but nothing was done. *IZ*, cf. 15 October 1929, 4–5, 8; 22 October 1929, 4–5; 19, 26 November 1929, 4–5; 10 December 1929, 4–5; 14 January 1930, 5; 18 February 1930, 4–5, 8; 11 March 1930, 4–5; 22 April 1930, 2, 5; 8 July 1930, 4–5, 8.
92. *IZ*, 16 April 1929, 5.
93. *IZ*, 23 June 1925, 5.
94. *WH*, October 1927, 4.
95. *WH*, e.g., February 1925, 1: "General Hertzog was a peaceable man. He was a fine fellow, and a better man than Smuts, a soldier who always wanted trouble" (citing a speech by Kadalie).
96. *WH*, March 1926, 3 (article by Thomas Mbeki).
97. *WH*, August 1926, 4.
98. *WH*, May 1928, 1. See also November 1928, 2 (editorial comment: Hertzog was "a political weakling").
99. *WH*, November 1926, 3 (headline: "The S.A. Labour Party's Hypocrisy: Coloured Workers in the Cape Beware!").
100. *WH*, September 1926, 1, 4. See also October 1927, 3 (headline: "The Natives and The S.A. Labour Party").
101. *WH*, January 1928, 1, 2 (editorial); see also March 1928, 1 (headline: "The Triumph of Race Hatred"), 5 (comment: "The S.A.L.P. is doomed to failure"); October 1928, 1, 3 (ICU tries to work with the Trades Union Congress in settling a strike by African workers at Onderstepoort, the country's main veterinary research station).
102. *WH*, February 1926, 2.
103. *WH*, February 1926, 2. See also September 1926, 2 (editorial: "Native Affairs Department Slapped in the Face").
104. *WH*, June 1926, 1; see also February 1927, 4 and March 1927, 4 (headline: "Prime Minister's Native Bills Analysed").
105. The call was not taken up by the ANC. *WH*, February 1926, 2 (editorial: "The Dawn of African Revolution").
106. *WH*, January 1926, 3; see also *IZ*, 10 October 1922, 5 (At a meeting in Queenstown, women urged the ANC to make representations to the government to ban "white men from having children with native women").
107. *WH*, October 1925, 3; cf. March 1926, 4 (advertising an ICU pamphlet summarizing the information presented to the commission; the advertisement was carried in several issues of the newspaper). Wickens concludes: "Although it is clear that the ICU speakers were forthright and unintimidated by the Commission, one is forced to admit that their evidence was not impressive ... It was their vagueness and lack of preparation that vitiated their testimony." Wickens, *The Industrial and Commercial Workers' Union of Africa*, 92.
108. *IZ*, e.g. 17 August 1926, 5 (John X. Merriman obituary).
109. *IZ*, e.g., 16 March 1920, 4 (letter from a Benoni reader praising the government for providing food to the Transkei); 18 May 1926, 1 (Africans should be grateful

to the Chamber of Mines for paying to have miners buried and for raising mine wages); 15 March 1927, 5 (pension after 20 years' service for African workers at Fort Beaufort mental asylum in the eastern Cape).

110. *IZ*, 11 February 1919, 2, 5; 22 May 1923, 5.
111. *IZ*, 17 June 1924, 6.
112. *IZ*, 9 September 1924, 8.
113. *IZ*, 5, 19 March 1929, 5. "African" replaced "Native" in the titles of virtually all independent African organizations in South Africa during the 1930s.
114. *IZ*, 12 September 1922, 5.
115. *IZ*, 22 August 1922, 5.
116. *WH*, October 1927, 2.
117. *WH*, October 1925, 3.
118. *WH*, April 1925, 7 (headline: "Non-Co-Operation with White Churches"); August 1926, 6 (headline: "Victimised by Missionaries"); October 1926, 3 (headline: "Hypocrisy in Church. Capitalism Camouflaged").
119. *WH*, January 1926, 2.
120. *WH*, e.g., July 1926, 2 (editorial: "The N[ative] R[ecruiting] C[orporation] Popes").
121. *WH*, August 1926, 3. See also March 1927, 2 (editorial: "The white man is mad! On the one hand he maintains that the Native could never draw up on a level with him. On the other hand he imposes iniquitous laws and admits that this is done for fear of Native competition. Such mentality is the mentality of a lunatic. But a lunatic has been known to run at large for a considerable time before his insanity is detected").
122. *IZ*, e.g., Bantu Union in the first 6 months of 1923: 6 February 1923, 6; 13 February 1923, 3, 6–7; 20 February 1923, 8; 6 March 1923, 6; 27 March 1923, 6; 3 April 1923, 2; 10 April 1923, 2, 4; 17 April 1923, 6; 24 April 1923, 6; 1 May 1923, 7; 8 May 1923, 7–8; 5 June 1923, 4, 6.
123. On the CNVC, see *IZ*, e.g., 3, 10 June 1924, 5; 23, 30 December 1924, 5; 22, 29 December 1925, 5; 26 January 1926, 5; 23 March 1926, 5; 25 May 1926, 5; 3 August 1926, 5; 28 December 1926, 5; 3, 10 January 1928, 5; 25 September 1928, 5; 8 January 1929, 5; 26 February 1929, 5; 11 June 1929, 5.
124. Meshach Pelem and Elijah Makalima of Bantu Union, for example, were the first vice-presidents of the CNVC, and Bennett Ncwana of the Ciskei Native Voters' Association was the first organizing secretary. D. D. T. Jabavu replaced Elijah Mdolomba, a senior Cape ANC official during the interwar period, as president of the organization in 1929. Other activists during the 1920s and 1930s included Alexander Jabavu, the editor of *Imvo*, who was secretary-treasurer; A. Frank Pendla, a court interpreter, businessman and one-time postmaster of Port Elizabeth's African township of New Brighton, who unsuccessfully contested one of the city's provincial council seats in 1929; and Richard H. Godlo, a key moderate in African nationalist politics in the eastern Cape between the 1920s and the 1940s.
125. *Imvo* noted Congress's "admirable methodological moderation and constitutional procedure" in winning poll tax test cases against the Transvaal provincial authorities. *IZ*, e.g., 30 May 1922, 5; 4 July 1922, 5; 28 November 1922, 5; 9 February 1926, 5.
126. *IZ*, 3 July 1923, 5; see also 13 July 1926, 5 (re ANC and Hertzog).
127. *WH*, April 1927, 1 (photo/caption of Jabavu).
128. *IZ*, e.g., 9 May 1922, 5; 14 August 1923, 5.
129. *IZ*, 22 January 1924, 5.
130. *IZ*, 9 September 1924, 5.
131. *IZ*, e.g., 20 January 1925, 5; 13, 20 April 1926, 5; 26 January 1926, 5; 11 May 1926, 5; see also 17 January 1928, 5; 17 April 1928, 5; 30 October 1928, 5.
132. *IZ*, e.g., 27 September 1921, 5; 20 December 1921, 5; 24, 31 January 1922, 5; 21 March 1922, 5; 20 June 1922, 5; 27 June 1922, 4; 28 November 1922, 5.
133. Kakaza was a Xhosa, born in the eastern Cape, who qualified as a medical doctor in the United States and practiced for some years in Buffalo, N.Y. He befriended Sol Plaatje on his visit to America in 1920. B. Willan, *South African nationalist, 1876–1932* (Berkeley and Los Angeles, 1984), 264.
134. *IZ*, 5, 12 February 1929, 5; 11, 18, 25 June 1929, 5; 9, 16 July 1929, 5; 13 August 1929, 5; 10 September 1929, 5.

135. *IZ*, 23 October 1928, 5; 20 November 1928, 5; 12 February 1929, 5; 27 August 1929, 5; 5 November 1929, 5.
136. On the ICU's achievements, for example, see *WH*, February 1927, 3 (headline: "Workers of Africa! Listen! Read! Digest!").
137. *WH*, March 1927, 1.
138. *WH*, e.g., July 1927, 1 (Kadalie's account of "How I Left South Africa"); August 1927, 1, 3 (headline: "ICU National Secretary Tells the World the Truth"), 4 (headline: "African Ambassador in Europe: Eulogised by Swedish Labour Party"); September 1927, 1 (headline: "Clements Kadalie's Speech at the Paris Congress"), 6 (Kadalie's account of his reception in London and Geneva); December 1927, 1 (headline: "National Secretary's Work Eulogised in England").
139. *WH*, May 1926, 1. Kadalie was sometimes depicted in Christ-like terms, as in *WH*, November 1926, 3 (headline: "Like a Sheep before His Slaughterers").
140. *WH*, September 1927, 3.
141. *WH*, August 1926, 3 (headline: "At Last").
142. *WH*, February 1926, 3; March 1928, 2.
143. *WH*, January 1926, 6.
144. *WH*, May 1928, 2 (editorial: "Birth of a New Nation").
145. *WH*, April 1925, 2.
146. *WH*, April 1925, 7. This article was written by S. M. Stanley Silwana, secretary of the ICU's Cape Town branch, who also contributed to *Imvo*.
147. *WH*, October 1925, 3.
148. When Ballinger assumed control of the newspaper, this "ear" was modified to read: "The Herald exposes Political and Industrial Hypocrisy. It constructively criticises." *WH*, August 1928, 1.
149. *WH*, November 1925, 2 (editorial: "*Umteteli's* Wrath").
150. *WH*, e.g., February 1926, 3 (headline: "Bloemfontein [i.e., ANC] Convention"); January 1927, 2 (editorial: "Dupes"); August 1927, 3 (headline: "Why the Natives Lost Their Land and Became Helots"); September 1927, 2 (editorial: "The ICU").
151. These included Transvaal ANC leaders such as H. Selby Msimang, R. V. Selope Thema (future editor of *Bantu World*) and the Natal leader John L. Dube. Some of them, like Bennett Ncwana, had been contributors to the ICU newspaper. *WH*, e.g., January 1926, 2 (editorial: "Forgetfulness and Lethargy"); October 1927, 2 (editorial: "Lauding Two Political Jackanapes"), 5 (page no. illegible) (headlines: "Is It War to the Knife?" and "To Bennett Ncwana").
152. *WH*, October 1925, 5 (headline: "Africans Know Your Power); see also *WH*, July 1926, 4 (headline: "Who are the Communards?" by John Gomas: "We are at war with an old, trained, victorious ruling class, of whose strategical and manoeuvring tactics we are very ignorant. In this case we have got a lot to learn of our unrealised power and of the manner in which our oppressors are conducting the fight against us").
153. *WH*, February 1926, 1.
154. *WH*, January 1927, 2 (headline: "ICU Manifesto. Bunting & Co., Political Murderers"). The Communist Party claimed that its members were expelled from the ICU because they insisted on "a more active and forthright policy, stricter control of finance, and a curb on the National Secretary's [Kadalie] power." Wickins, *Industrial and Commercial Workers' Union of Africa*, 107.
155. *WH*, November 1928, 3 (headline: "Communists' Futile Attempt to Capture ICU").
156. *WH*, e.g., May 1928, 1 (headline: "Manifesto Urging International Unity"... "We are confident that the rank and file desire it. Let them make their voices heard. Let them raise again with overwhelming force, the historic appeal of Karl Marx–Workers of the World Unite!").
157. *WH*, February 1925, 3 (headline: "Ancient Leadership Becomes Our Object Lesson").
158. *WH*, October 1925, 2 (editorial: "Strike off the Fetters!!").
159. *WH*, e.g., January 1926, 2; September 1926, 2. The citation is from Daniel 5. 25–28. The words were written by a disembodied hand (i.e., the hand of God) on the wall of King Belshazzar's palace during the period of the Jewish exile in Babylon. Daniel interpreted the message as follows: "mene. God has numbered

the days of your kingdom and brought it to an end; tekel: you have been weighed in the balance and found wanting; u-pharsin: and your kingdom has been divided and given to the Medes and Persians" (translation: *The New English Bible*).

160. *WH*, December 1925, 2.
161. *WH*, March 1926, 4 (headline: "Executed for Sedition"–a story lifted from the British journal *Workers' Weekly*); see also article entitled "The Eve of Struggle" by T. W. Keable 'Mote on the same page: "I would like to warn some young leaders that they must respect Christianity. The natives must not be given thought for atheism!"
162. *WH*, April 1926, 4.
163. *WH*, May 1927, 1.
164. Ibid. Mbeki, the "Chief Whip of the 'Ginger Group,'" was only 20 years old when he succeeded Tyamzashe as Transvaal provincial secretary. *WH*, May 1926, 1 (photo/caption of Mbeki). See also an article entitled "The Awakening of a People" by Mbeki on page 3: "A spirit of class consciousness is now taking root in the African proletariat... the exploited masses of this country are determined to take their place as one of the 'iron battalions' of the international proletariat." ANC president general Rev. Zaccheus Mahabane (1924–27) told delegates to a special ICU congress in Kimberley in 1928 that "extremists... are a blessing in disguise sometimes." *WH*, January 1928, 3.
165. *WH*, February 1925, 2 (headline: "Chats to the People"); April 1925, 1 (subscription advertisement: "Are You a Race Man? If so... [buy the] Race Journal *The Workers Herald* "). Thaele probably solicited a full-page advertisement on Garvey that appeared in March 1926 and was datelined New York City. *WH*, March 1926, 5.
166. *WH*, September 1926, 4 (citing speech by Kadalie); see also June 1926, 5 ("Thaele... now spends his time stirring up racial feeling among the Natives... He has been publicly disowned by the Industrial and Commercial Workers' Union").
167. *IZ*, 26 October 1920, 5; 2 November 1920, 5; 7 December 1920, 1. One other strike, in which two persons died, was recorded in the test sample. No explanation was given as to who went on strike, what caused the strike or why these deaths occurred. *IZ*, 16 March 1920, 2.
168. On the Israelites, see R. R. Edgar, "The fifth seal: Enoch Mgijima, the Israelites and the Bullhoek [*sic*] massacre, 1921," Ph.D. thesis (University of California at Los Angeles, 1977); idem, "The prophet motive: Enoch Mgijima, the Israelites and the background to the Bullhoek [sic] massacre," *International Journal of African Historical Studies* 15 (1982), 401–422; idem, *Because they chose the plan of God: The story of The Bulhoek massacre* (Johannesburg, 1988).
169. *IZ*, 3 May 1921, 5. The Israelites rejected a delegation of moderate African political leaders led by Tengo Jabavu and Meshach Pelem (of Bantu Union), which was sent to mediate in the dispute on the government's behalf in December 1920.
170. *IZ*, 31 May 1921, 5.
171. *IZ*, 21 December 1920, 4–5; 10, 17, 24, 31 May 1921, 5; 7, 21 June 1921, 5; 19 July 1921, 3; *Christian Express*, 1 July 1921, 105–106.
172. *IZ*, 26 September 1926, 5.
173. During the 1918–19 influenza crisis, alienated Red householders in the Victoria East District refused to cooperate with missionaries and student volunteers from Lovedale and Fort Hare who had been sent to help them. There was also one news report of a fight between Red and School youths in Port Elizabeth. *IZ*, 21 January 1919, 5; 16 May 1922, 8; *Christian Express*, 2 December 1918, 185–186.
174. On the Wellingtonites, see R. R. Edgar, "Garveyism in Africa: Dr. Wellington and the 'American movement' in the Transkei, 1925–40," in *The Societies in Southern Africa in the Nineteenth and Twentieth Centuries* (London, University of London, Institute of Commonwealth Studies, October 1974–May 1975), Vol. 6; idem, "African educational protest in South Africa: The American school movement in the Transkei in the 1920s," in P. Kallaway (ed.), *Apartheid and education: The education of black South Africans* (Johannesburg, 1984), 184–191; W. Beinart, "*Amafelandawonye*

(the Die-Hards): Popular protest and women's movements in Herschel district in the 1920s," in Beinart and Bundy, *Hidden struggles*, Chap. 7.

175. *IZ*, e.g., 23 October 1928, 5; 20 November 1928, 5; 12 February 1929, 5.
176. *IZ*, 29 January 1929, 5; see also 15 January 1929, 5; 14 May 1929, 5. The *Workers' Herald* told readers that if they saw Wellington Buthelezi they should "kick him on the chin because he is an impostor." *WH*, September 1927, 1.
177. *IZ*, 11 April 1922, 5.
178. *WH*, July 1927, 2. The Kazerne strikers ignored Tyamzashe's advice and were fired. As Wickens puts it, "The episode showed the ICU in a poor light... Many members must have wondered what was to be gained from paying subscriptions to such an organization." Wickins, *Industrial and Commercial Workers' Union of Africa*, 145–146.
179. *WH*, November 1928, 3 (headline: "Communists' Futile Attempt to Capture ICU"). This was reemphasized when Ballinger took control of the newspaper: "all avenues of peaceful settlement, and negotiation, must be exhausted before extreme measures are sanctioned." August 1928, 2 (editorial).
180. *WH*, e.g., February 1926, 2, 4–5; May 1926, 2.
181. The ICU constitution would not allow whites to "hold office in the organisation," but at least one did, a communist who was on the executive committee of the ICU branch in Pietermaritzburg, Natal. *WH*, August 1926, 4.
182. *WH*, e.g., July 1926, 1 (headline: "The Struggle Has Begun").
183. *WH*, May 1926, 6 (headline: "Workers of Europe Welcome Progress of African Workers"). See also editorial entitled "Support British Workers" on page 2 of the same issue.
184. *WH*, March 1926, 2 (editorial: "Civilised Standard"); see also 4 ("The Eve of Struggle" by T. W. Keable 'Mote: "none of us White and Black must ever forget that we ought to fight as a class against the common foe–capitalism").
185. *WH*, August 1928, 3.
186. R. Gunning's American-oriented "fog index" was applied to the English-language section of the ICU newspaper as a measure of credibility. J. Richards chose one newspaper for each year of Tyamzashe's tenure as subeditor (1925–28). She calculated the fog index of one editorial and one front-page article (except for the October 1925 edition, where she chose a page 2 story, since page 1 was still being used only for advertising). There were no consistent differences in readability scores between the editorials and articles. Six of the eight news items selected would have required at least some American college-level education to be easily understood (fog indices of 13, 14, 15, 14, 13, 19). The remaining two would have been understood by an American high school student (fog indices of 12 and 10). Richards, "*Workers' Herald* ," 62–63; R. Gunning, *The technique of clear writing* (New York, 1968).
187. Consciousness raising at this level was contained in poems, essays and letters to the editor as well as editorials and news reports. *IZ*, e.g., 13 November 1923, 5; 25 March 1924, 5; 17 June 1924, 3, 5.
188. *IZ*, 5 August 1924, 5 ("The Release of Maritz"); 17 March 1925, 5 ("Native Industrial Labour").
189. *WH*, January 1927, 2 (editorial: "Dupes"). When the communists were expelled from the ICU, the issue was used to demonstrate to the government that the trade union was not a "seditious" organization. Parliament was debating the Prevention of Disorders bill, popularly known as the Sedition bill, in a bid to curb speeches, meetings and publications deemed to be inflammatory. For example, note the story (headline: "The Dismissed ICU Officals") on page 4 of this issue: "We consider this article almost the most important statement ever made relative to non-European trade unionism... Communists, White and Black, never lost an opportunity of opposing constitutional methods. Their chief aim is to bring about strife and trouble in the country. It is, says Mr. Kadalie, the desire of himself and other leaders of Native industrialists that their efforts towards betterment should be strictly constitutional... it is good to know that the constitutionalists... have won the day."

190. In a letter to the *Christian Express* (September 1921), Tyamzashe wrote: "There is no desire on the part of any section of the Native population to do anything unconstitutional... Let it be clearly understood that we do not claim equality with the European... We want Justice and the 'right to live.'"
191. Thaele criticized the news in *Umteteli*, for example, because the newspaper's editorial director was white: "As long as we have our opinions expressed by the white people so long shall we remain helpless." *WH*, April 1925, 4.
192. *WH*, February 1926, 5 (the author–probably Tyamzashe–used the pseudonym "Old Boy").
193. *WH*, November 1926, 2.
194. *WH*, e.g. October 1927, 4 ("The Church and the ICU... The ICU must have Christ"); May 1928, 3 (proceedings of the ICU's eighth congress).
195. *WH*, June 1926, 2 (headline: "Let Us Stand Together and Fight for Freedom" by A. J. Phoofolo).
196. *WH*, e.g., October 1926, 2 (editorial).
197. *WH*, e.g., November 1925, 1–8; December 1925, 1–8; January 1926, 1–8.
198. Other advertisements featured "Kaffir" books and a "Kaffir" Bible. *IZ*, e.g., 23 May 1922, 7; 9 September 1924, 5.
199. *IZ*, e.g., 15 December 1925, 18 May 1926, 15 March 1927.
200. *IZ*, 17 June 1924, 7.
201. *WH*, November 1926, 1; see also January 1926, 6 ("Segregation on the Rand... rough Natives of the Amalaita or liquor-selling class should not be mingled with decent and law-abiding people in the Native Townships").
202. *WH*, May 1926, 3.
203. *WH*, September 1926, 6 (misnumbered 4), headline: "Native Housing on the Rand."
204. *IZ*, e.g., 27 March 1923, 5; 4 March 1924, 5; 5 August 1924, 5.

CHAPTER 6

Bantu World and the Origins of a Captive African Commercial Press

Les Switzer

Very few independent African journals survived the Great Depression between 1929 and 1932. As the potential market for African consumers expanded, and the state increased its efforts to institutionalize segregation and retribalize the Africans, white business interests moved in to take over surviving African publications and develop a captive black commercial press.*

Bertram F. G. Paver, a failed farmer and advertising salesman, founded Bantu Press (Pty) Ltd. and launched *Bantu World* as a national weekly newspaper in April 1932.[1] Paver was a liberal segregationist, who wanted to "provide the Native people with a platform for fair comment and the presentation of their needs and aspirations."[2] He made an effort to attract black investors, and by the end of 1932 more than one-half of the 38 shareholders in the company were African. R. V. Selope Thema, who was to be the editor of *Bantu World* for the first 20 years of its existence, and Isaiah Bud-Mbelle, who had promoted the Chamber of Mines' African newspaper *Umteteli wa Bantu*, were on the board of directors.[3]

The credo espoused by Paver and his supporters had distinct commercial and cultural implications that were made manifest in the very first issue of the newspaper. One story headlined "Old Customs Lose Appeal For Natives," was subtitled "Emancipation of Black Man Has Important Bearing on Union's National Life and Commercial Prosperity." The story claimed that Africans had £30 million to spend a year:

> The Native's standard of living is rising, his wants are multiplying and commodities, but a short time back considered luxuries, are to-day in demand as necessities... Native women...are rapidly adopting European dress, and a promising market is developing for hats, coats, shoes and stockings as well as for the more intimate articles of feminine wearing apparel. Commodities such as tea, coffee, cocoa, sugar, jam, tinned foodstuffs, fruit drinks, paraffin oil, candles and matches are being consumed in quantities. Not content with emulating the European example in food and clothing, the Native has embraced the same sporting and recreational activities...the popularity of gramophones and other musical instruments is increasing rapidly...the segregation policy of municipal authorities has led to the adoption of European methods of locomotion [citing "Native" buses, taxis, bicycles and personal cars]...Apart from money held in trust for him by European employers...thousands of pounds are deposited in Post Office savings banks, commercial banks, building societies and life

*I am grateful to Ime Ukpanah for acting as a coder in the quantitative analysis of *Bantu World*.

> insurance associations...The Native has become a cash purchaser who buys wisely and well... as a consumer his custom has become a valuable aid to increased turnover and increased profits.

A "before" and "after" photograph accompanied the story with the following caption:

> YESTERDAY: He lived in semi-barbarism, eating his "mealiepap" with a wooden spoon out of a clay pot.
> TO-DAY: He lives the life of a civilised man, taking tea at a well appointed Bantu club.[4]

About 14 months later, *Bantu World* was taken over by the Argus Printing and Publishing Company, the largest white-owned press conglomerate in South Africa, which in turn was controlled by the mining industry. The African (and most of the white) shareholders of Bantu Press were bought out, and Thema and Bud-Mbelle were removed from the board of directors. Argus now had majority control of Bantu Press, which would be used to gain control of the independent African press.[5]

Bantu Press owned 10 African weekly newspapers by 1945, and 2 more had been added by 1950. The company distributed and syndicated stories and helped underwrite the cost of newsprint. Bantu Press also controlled the printing, distribution and advertising for 12 nonnewspaper periodicals in 11 languages. Circulation figures for its African publications totaled 113,000 by March 1946. *Bantu World* circulation had also climbed to 24,000 a week: the newspaper's promoters claimed each issue was read by at least five literate adults, who in turn shared its contents with illiterate friends and household members.

By the 1950s, Bantu Press either owned or otherwise controlled most African general-interest news and entertainment journals, as well as the main African religious, educational and other cultural journals, in South Africa. According to a press commission set up by the National Party in 1950, the number of African newspapers had been reduced to seven by 1954, and they were owned and controlled solely by whites. *Bantu World* accounted for about 25 percent of African newspaper circulation. Bantu Press, moreover, now had a chain of black newspapers, newsletters and magazines extending throughout southern and central Africa. Alongside Bantu Press, white entrepreneurs like James Bailey were creating role models for a black tabloid press, and the major Afrikaans press groups, aided by the state, were gaining a monopoly over the black magazine and photocomic market.[6]

Bantu World, then, helped shape the form as well as the content of South Africa's captive black press in the generation after 1932. Although white advertisers had been involved in the independent black press from the beginning, *Bantu World* attracted corporate business and financial interests that provided the newspaper with a relatively new and stable source of income.

Bantu World developed rapidly as a business enterprise and had full-fledged editorial, advertising, accounting, printing and circulation departments. At the same time, the newspaper became a resource center for training Africans in the skills needed to run a successful business–printers and truck drivers, typists, clerks, sales and advertising personnel as well as journalists.

Case Study of *Bantu World*

Bantu World in the 1930s was an arbiter of taste in urban African politics and culture and by far the most important medium of mass communication for the literate African community. As the flagship of Bantu Press, the newspaper provided a model of what was deemed permissible and relevant for Africans to buy and read. Indeed, it had virtually no competitors for two decades. Only *Bantu World* and the Chamber of Mines newspaper *Umteteli wa Bantu* were regarded as national publications. *Bantu World* circulated mainly in the Transvaal (in Johannesburg and other towns on the Witwatersrand) and Swaziland, and *Umteteli* also circulated mainly in the Transvaal's urban areas, and in the home areas of South Africa's migrant mine workers in the Orange Free State and the Ciskei and Transkei reserves in the eastern Cape.

The Editorship of R. V. Selope Thema

Editor Selope Thema played an important role in making the newspaper a credible organ of African news and opinion during the 1930s. He was apparently free to pursue his own policies, and his African staff controlled the content of the newspaper without overt interference from white management. Social control in the newsroom did not have to be communicated officially, because Thema, like other editors of Bantu Press publications, conformed to the policies of the newspaper's proprietors.[7] The political views of white liberals like J. D. Rheinallt–Jones and Howard Pim,[8] who had helped Paver launch the newspaper, were never really challenged by black liberals like Thema, who controlled African nationalist politics during the interwar period.[9]

The rhetorical practices of the African petty bourgeoisie during the interwar period are vividly illustrated in Thema's unpublished autobiography, which he wrote about 1935.[10] It is a literary work cast deliberately in the public sphere. As Jane Starfield suggests, "the growth of African Nationalism was the central plot" and Thema and his companions "the central characters." Thema claimed the role of omniscient narrator who spoke on behalf of his people–the subject is "I" and the community is generally a distant "they" in this memoir–but he "remains an observer, not a participant in their struggle." Thema seeks to represent a middle-class community that has not yet come into being. Consequently, his autobiography "contains all the conventions of ambiguity between the actual and the imagined community."[11]

Thema was urged to write his life story by two of the most prominent liberal segregationists of his generation, Rheinallt–Jones and Charles T. Loram.[12] Like other members of the African petty bourgeoisie at this time, Thema depicts his life as a morality play. The narrative he constructs for himself, from his birth in a Pedi village near Pietersburg in the northern Transvaal "in a hut and in a heathen family surrounded by the invisible gods of my fathers"[13] to his appointment as editor of *Bantu World*, forms a strand in a master narrative depicting the "journey" of his people from "barbarism" to "civilisation."[14]

Thema was determined to redress the distortions and omissions of South African history as represented by the historians of the dominant culture:

> There was nothing that our ancestors did which was not severely criticised and stigmatised as barbarous and cruel...Their [white historians of South Africa] primary object seems to have been to impress the world with the wickedness and cruelty of the African race, and to enhance the prestige of the white race.[15]

His favorite subject in school was history, and one of the first history books he read was of England before the Roman conquest:

> It opened the eyes of my mind and made me see the British people as they were before the Roman invasion of Great Britain. They were people who painted themselves, who lived in huts and who used skins of animals for garments [read the Africans in their precolonial state]...I saw how England advanced stage by stage; how it was invaded first by the Romans and secondly by warlike tribes from the north of Europe; how these tribes [read the Afrikaner Boers] deprived the Native Britons of their lands and drove them to the mountainous part of the country, now known as Wales; how in turn these tribes were conquered by the Normans under William the Conqueror [read the English]; and how Saint Augustine and other missionaries from Rome brought the light of Christian civilisation to the heathen inhabitants of Great Britain [read the missionaries in South Africa], whose religion was no better than the religion of my ancestors. To me this was a wonderful discovery, a discovery which was destined to change my outlook on life. For as I read this history I discovered the parallel between it and that of my people. I saw that white people...came out of conditions similar to those under which my people were living, that they were Christianised in the same way as my people, and that they rose from barbarism to civilisation...I came to the conclusion that the African people also shall rise from obscurity to the heights of civilisation. I have maintained this belief ever since.[16]

Britain was the perfect historical metaphor for Thema's South Africa.

The signposts in Thema's life and in the life of his people are clearly delineated in his autobiography. Thema's birth in February 1886 coincides with several "great events," including the founding of Johannesburg.[17] Two years later, the "Boers" force Thema and his people to leave "our homes, lands, the graves of our fathers and the pots of our gods" and resettle in a location that eventually formed part of the Pedi reserve.[18] Thema stemmed from a line of healers – his paternal and maternal grandfathers were both "medicine men" – and he was expected to follow in their footsteps after he entered the men's lodge [the *bogwera*], "a college where every man was a teacher, and where every boy was taught men's way of life."[19] Thus Thema establishes his credentials as a man of the people, but he does not dwell on these experiences.

Thema first encounters "the White man's God" as a herd boy on an Afrikaner farm where regular prayer meetings were held,[20] and when he enters a church for the first time a few years later "to me it was the greatest day of my life."[21] Thema accepts Christianity and is allowed to attend the local mission school, but the South African War intervenes, and he is "commandeered" to work on an Afrikaner farm (in the vicinity of Pietersburg) until British forces capture the area. He is employed by the British (at £1 a month) and is discharged at the end of 1901.[22] He goes to Pretoria and finds work as a domestic, in which capacity he learns some English and becomes a "nurse boy" to two white English children, who "could not tolerate any injustice being done to me." This experience convinces him "there is no inherent prejudice against racial differences."[23] He then finds work with the Imperial Military Railway pharmacy in Pretoria before returning to his village and reentering the mission school. Thema passes Standard III (fifth grade) in 1903 and is finally baptized, adopting the Christian names Richard and Victor,[24] and becoming a full member of the church. Thema is asked to establish a new school in a nearby village; he passes Standard IV (sixth grade) and is admitted to Lovedale to continue his studies in 1906 at the age of 20.

Thema spent the next four years at Lovedale. He was one of 20 students who passed the School Higher Examination (equivalent to the Junior Certificate, or at least the tenth grade) in 1909 and was admitted to the matriculation class. Lovedale proved to be the turning point in his life: "Lovedale not only gave me book educa-

Photo 21. Richard Victor Selope Thema, editor of *Bantu World* (1932–52).

tion,[25] and taught me the dignity of labour,[26] but it also taught me how to be [a] useful citizen of South Africa."[27]

His role model was Booker T. Washington (1856–1915), principal of Tuskegee Institute, the African-American college in Alabama. For those who favored accommodation with the dominant segregationist culture, Washington was one of the most influential interpreters of the captive black experience of his generation: "I wanted to be like him in every respect. I wanted to be a great orator as he was, to be able to speak before European audiences on behalf of my people as he did on behalf of the Negroes in the United States. This became the burning passion of my life." Thema did not finish the matriculation course, but "when I left Lovedale at the end of 1910 I had ceased to think as a barbarous boy and was already grappling with the problems of civilised life."[28]

Thema returned to the Transvaal and found work initially as a clerk in a miners' recruiting depot, the Pietersburg office of the Native Recruiting Corporation. He moved to Johannesburg in 1915 to work in the law office of attorney Richard W. Msimang, a founder-member of the South African Native National Congress (SANNC), and formally joined the organization the same year. The SANNC was controlled by the leadership in the Transvaal, and Thema, already an accomplished public speaker and debater, was soon promoted to the post of secretary of the Transvaal branch. While Sol Plaatje was in England during World War I, Thema subbed for him as SANNC secretary general. He was then appointed corresponding secretary (having already established something of a reputation in the African press as a news correspondent), and he was a member of the abortive 1919 protest delegation to London and to the Peace Conference at Versailles. He also received some tuition in journalism from a London correspondence college, which he would put to good use on his return to South Africa.

In his autobiography, however, Thema rewrote crucial parts of this phase of his life. As noted in Chapter 5, South Africa between 1917 and 1921 was faced with a major challenge from desperate but disorganized African workers in town and countryside. Thema and other activists saw these years as a turning point in the history of the African nationalist movement, but they were divided over the extent to which they should support the workers. They were also divided by personal loyalties and ambitions, and they had differing perceptions of how their own class interests could be preserved in the postcolonial order.

Starfield cites two examples to illustrate how Thema essentially sanitized his role in African nationalist politics during these years because it did not conform to the image he created for himself and the imagined African middle-class community as editor of *Bantu World*. The first example concerns an incident that occurred in 1917, when Thema was inadvertently embroiled in a factional dispute that pitted the Transvaal leadership against John Dube, SANNC president general, and his supporters in Natal. As corresponding secretary, Thema provided reports of SANNC activities to numerous supporters outside as well as inside South Africa. John Harris, secretary of the London-based Anti-Slavery and Aborigines' Protection Society, used a distorted version of a confidential letter Thema had written to him about the 1913 Natives' Land Act to enlist the support of SANNC officials who might favor the case for segregation. The letter caused an uproar during the SANNC's annual meeting in 1917, and it was used as a pretext to force Dube's resignation.Thema felt duty-bound to resign as well, even though the anti-Dube faction assured him he was not at fault and should not resign. This event, "so crucial to his own life and to the history of Congress," is ignored in his autobiography.[29]

The second instance occurred over the next few years, when Thema sought to align himself with SANNC members who wanted the organization to participate actively in the protest movement on the side of the workers. Thema himself was apparently an editor of *Abantu-Batho* for a brief period shortly after World War I, and as a journalist he highlighted the struggles on the Witwatersrand. He singled out the 1918 sanitation workers' strike, the 1919 Anti-Pass Campaign and the 1920 African miners' strike as the "Campaign against European organised terrorism" and claimed he became "one of the fiercest racialists that the Bantu race has produced." He supported the "God of our Chiefs" and denounced the kind of Christianity that oppressed blacks. He backed the "radicals" controlling *Abantu-Batho* in their attacks on missionaries, who had taught Africans to ignore life on earth in favor of the heavenly kingdom, and he condemned the exploitation of Africans by "the European Capitalists." Fifteen years or so later, however, Thema chose to interpret these events as a warning of what could happen if whites saw African leaders only as "fanatics" and did not negotiate with "reasonable men." As he put it, "the two races are destined to live side by side ... as equal partners."[30]

Thema had already distanced himself from militant nationalists when he joined the Johannesburg Joint Council at its first meeting in 1921, and the SANNC's anti-Council faction forced him to resign as secretary of the Transvaal branch. He distanced himself even farther from militant discourse, when he was appointed superintendent of the Bantu Men's Social Centre in 1924, shortly after it was established in downtown Johannesburg with the aid of the American Board Mission. Thema would remain in charge of this cultural bastion of the educated African elite until he was appointed editor of *Bantu World*.

Thema's detractors referred to him as the "darling of the European liberals,"[31] but Thema himself was morally committed to what he called the "stern realities" of racial cooperation.[32] He corresponded with numerous white-controlled civil rights groups lobbying on behalf of Africans inside and outside South Africa, promoted the agenda of the Joint Council movement, and participated in conferences between 1923 and 1936 for Europeans and Africans sponsored initially by the Dutch Reformed Church and later by the South African Institute of Race Relations. Thema was also active in various African consultative bodies sponsored by the central government–in the Native Conferences, initiated after the 1920 Native Affairs Act, and in the urban African township Advisory Boards.

Like D. D. T. Jabavu, his friend and counterpart in the eastern Cape, Thema was the consummate, self-styled "moderate" spokesman of African nationalist aspirations. The Cape African franchise, for example, was "a sacred right on which there can be no compromise," because "sooner or later this franchise will be extended to us [educated Africans in the Transvaal]."[33] Thema was a crusading journalist at this level, and he campaigned vigorously against Prime Minister J. B. M. Hertzog's attempts between 1926 and 1936 to eliminate the Cape's African voters. When the Representation of Natives Bill denying the vote to Cape Africans was finally passed in April 1936, however, Thema embraced the national African consultative body created as a substitute for the Cape franchise. He was elected to the Natives' Representative Council (NRC) to represent rural Transvaal and Orange Free State in 1937, and he remained an influential member until the NRC was dissolved by the apartheid regime in 1951.

As a protest journalist, Thema believed the educated modernizers were "the spokesmen of their inarticulate people."[34] The targets of protest in *Bantu World*, often featured in front-page stories, were mainly government policies that provoked racial confrontation (by promoting white unity and narrow Afrikaner nationalism) and undermined the increasingly fragile position of the African petty bourgeoisie. In his first few months as editor, for example, Thema attacked police brutality and job reservation for whites,[35] and he deplored the pass laws and other discriminatory legislation that made criminals of Africans.[36] He condemned slum conditions in the municipal townships that were forcing children to turn to crime,[37] described the plight of the unemployed,[38] and complained about inferior education and poor housing for Africans.[39]

Thema was fearful of government measures to retribalize Africans, because he believed they were directed against the petty bourgeoisie. The "new" African, he wrote in 1927, ignored "tribal wars and feuds" and talked instead "about the whiteman's oppressive rule." In condemning an amendment to the 1927 Native Administration Act, he wrote in 1935:

> The Government wants to preserve tribal organisation, not because it wants to prevent the disintegration of Bantu life, but because tribal organisation ensures control and enables the white race to impose its will upon our race. The underlying principle of the Native Administration Act of 1927 is to maintain this tribal organisation in order to force those Africans who have outgrown the tribal environment back into the conditions of the past.[40]

Thema continued to play a major role in African national politics during the 1930s. He was a key figure, for example, in ousting left-wing sympathizer Josiah Gumede as ANC president general in 1930, and he retained his status as a kind of *eminence grise* in the ANC's Transvaal hierarchy during the tenure of Pixley Seme (1930–37). Thema remained on the ANC's national executive committee until 1949. *Bantu World* regularly covered Congress activities and occasionally even used front-page leads to inform readers of the organization's past triumphs.[41]

Thema, however, was increasingly out of step in the campaign to broaden and democratize the struggle for African rights in the 1940s. Ever fearful of communist influence and opposed to cooperation with Indian militants, he had become increasingly critical of the ANC by the end of the decade. Thema formed a splinter group called the National Minded Bloc and together with his followers left Congress in 1950. He refused to support the Defiance Campaign and retired as editor of *Bantu World* in 1952.[42]

News Agenda

Bantu World expanded rapidly as a general-interest weekly under Thema's editorship. Between April and December 1932, the five-column broadsheet increased from 8 to 10 to 12, and occasionally 14, pages. It reached 18 pages for the first time in April 1933, and for the next two and one-half years the newspaper ranged in length from 16 to 18 pages. In November 1935 *Bantu World* reached 20 pages, apparently the most pages of any African newspaper in southern Africa at that time. It remained more or less a 20-page newspaper until World War II, when the shortage of newsprint forced Bantu Press to reduce the sizes of its publications. *Bantu World* stories were written mainly in five languages–English, Xhosa, Zulu, Sotho and Tswana–with occasional news articles and commentaries in Afrikaans (especially in the early years), Venda and Tsonga (or Thonga). In a typical 20-page newspaper, 7 pages were produced in vernacular languages and the rest in English.[43]

Bantu World sought to cultivate an image of itself that would appeal to those white-liberal segregationists who sought a place for the "civilized" (and urbanized) African in the new industrial South Africa. Page 1 of the newspaper on its third birthday, for example, was a promotional page. *Bantu World* was expanding rapidly in size, and its permanent staff had increased from 9 to 20 (together with 5 part-time staffers).

The newspaper declared its popularity was conditioned by its "community service" and its "well organised news service." *Bantu World* had demonstrated "to European business men" that there was "a fertile but undeveloped market in their midst." It was also "making them realise that the payment of more wages to African workers is a safe investment for the expansion of industry and commerce." A birthday greeting from the *Pretoria News* that is quoted with approval is very revealing of the newspaper's editorial policy during the 1930s:

> In the pages of *Bantu World*, we are able to catch a glimpse of the black races as they struggle from barbarism to civilisation, from ignorance to knowledge, from an Africa that has been theirs from the dawn of history to an Africa remoulded by... Western Europe–a hand of culture, but a hand that can chastise ... the surprising quality about this journal... is its restraint. A conscious effort is obviously being made to put the right emphasis on the varied news it publishes; and in this way hysteria is avoided and a sense of proportion developed.[44]

Figure 2. Domestic and foreign news in *Bantu World* (in %). Percentages are calculated by dividing the number of story units in each category by the total number of story units. News refers to all story units, including illustrations and informal advertisements classified as news. Formal advertisements are excluded. *Bantu World* had 1, 554 story units.

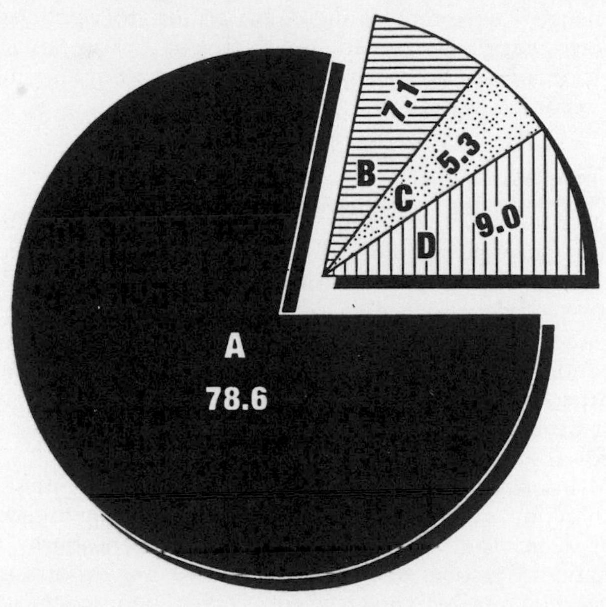

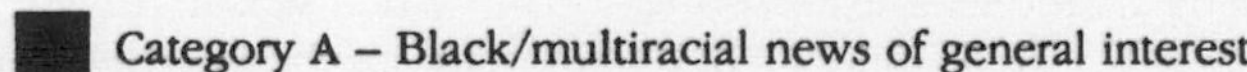

The vernacular-language as well as the English-language sections usually contained a formal editorial page. Each section also contained miscellaneous letters to the editor and regional news, mainly from urban centers outside Johannesburg. Two English-language pages were concerned with sports, although sports news could also be found on the vernacular pages. Normally, four pages in English were devoted to women, two pages in English to regional news (entitled "News from Different Centres"), and one page in English to news personalities, who were mainly from Johannesburg (entitled "People in the News This Week"). Page 1 was always in English and, like the English and vernacular editorial pages, it featured the major overseas stories together with domestic news of immediate concern to the urban African population. There was also at least one page of school news in

English. The back page was devoted to miscellaneous world, local crime and political news in English.

The profile of *Bantu World*'s news agenda in the 1930s is similar to *Imvo Zabantsundu*'s news agenda in the 1920s, the dominant theme being nonpartisan news of general interest to Africans. But in contrast to the other newspapers subjected to quantitative analyses between the 1920s and 1950s, *Bantu World* deemphasized negative news that highlighted discriminatory policies and activities. Even less coverage was given to black political activities in the 1930s–a particularly depressing decade in the history of the African nationalist movement. The news agenda is recorded in the graph in Figure 2.

General-interest News

Bantu World focused unabashedly on the cultural concerns and leisure-time activities of the African petty bourgeoisie (Table 10). The life cycles of the petty bourgeoisie were recorded essentially in society news (A. 2). *Bantu World* was saturated with reports of dances, beauty contests and other competitions, fund-raisers, farewells and reunions, exhibitions, teas, dinners, parties, receptions, concerts, speeches and meetings. The births, confirmations, baptisms and weddings of the petty bourgeoisie were celebrated, and the sick, hospitalized, infirm and especially the dead were mourned in notices of bereavement, testimonials, eulogies, funerals and memorial services.

Factual information was secondary to the personalities involved–who was visiting, thanking, seen with, doing what with, spending time with whom; who had arrived or departed (often from the "city"–Johannesburg), who was attending what function. Personal success stories were an important feature of society news–who won a prize, who received a degree, who was appointed, promoted or ordained to what position in business or the professions. News about events was inextricably linked to the individuals and organizations involved in society news. Stories generally focused on the barest essentials–on "who" was involved, "when" and "where" the event occurred, and "what" happened. Gossip, rumor and even the occasional scandal pervaded these reports. As society news was exploited–the number of society stories in this sample rose from 14 in 1932 to 90 in 1938–more stories were written in English and displayed prominently in the newspaper.

Personality stories dominated vernacular and English-language news and entertainment pages. As in rural community newspapers like *Imvo Zabantsundu*, the new middle class–clergymen, lawyers, court interpreters, school administrators, teachers, students, nurses, educated chiefs and headmen, clerks, traders, commercial farmers, skilled craftsmen, journalists, business men (and women, covered in the women's pages)–dominated the who's who stories. Sports figures, artists, musicians, singers, poets, playwrights and novelists shared the limelight with policemen, members of urban African Advisory Boards and those elected to the Natives' Representative Council (from 1937). Individuals who represented working-class pursuits–factory operatives, miners, subsubsistence peasants and rural laborers, gardeners, domestics–were almost never mentioned, except occasionally in crime or accident reports.

Bantu World was adept at recording the many clubs and societies established by the petty bourgeoisie in the cities and listing the members of these organizations. At the same time, *Bantu World* sought to ensure that both communicators and consumers identified with the newspaper. There were stories about writers, reporters,

Table 10. *Categories A and D news in* Bantu World (% *of story units*)

Category	%
A. Black/multiracial news of general interest (1,221 units)	78.6
A.1 Education and religion	13.1
A.2 Society	43.7
A.3 Sports	10.2
A.4 Living conditions in urban areas	4.4
A.5 Living conditions in rural areas	0.6
A.6 Independent economic activities	2.0
A.7 Crime and accidents	3.5
A.8 Other: Promotional and miscellaneous[a]	1.1
D. Foreign news (139 units)	9.0

[a] "Miscellaneous" includes a table of contents column, homilies, some public notices and advertisements disguised as news.

editors and other staffers who worked for or distributed the publication, notices about personalities who visited the newspaper's offices, prizes for competitions sponsored by the newspaper and thank-you notes to readers for their support. The newspaper's "liberal" credentials and its "objectivity" were outlined in a seven-point credo that was printed on the editorial page of the first issue and frequently reprinted in subsequent issues during the 1930s.[45]

The proprietors of *Bantu World* were among the first to recognize that African women were a crucial source of potential readers for the black commercial press. The number of pages devoted to "women's activities" rose from one in 1932 to two in 1933 to four in 1935. Although the women's supplement was entitled "Marching Forward," most of the news in this subcategory was what one would expect of a society in which the normative framework featured women as decorative objects and homemakers submissive to their husbands.

Articles aimed at women were concerned with cooking recipes, household hints (making and repairing clothes and curtains, cleaning blankets and linen, economizing in the kitchen), health and home remedies, personal etiquette (stressing good behavior and cleanliness), safety (especially from fires, poisons and weapons), child rearing, love and marriage. Advice was a major theme in the letters and stories in the women's pages. Marriage, of course, was a fixture of legitimacy for women inside and outside the home, and anything that might jeopardize the prospect of getting married and bearing children was condemned. Women were told to strive to maintain a Christian home (the Christian family was sanctified in the newspaper), and working women were told that they had a primary responsibility to cook and to clean for their working husbands. Angry letters to the women's editor sometimes urged drastic alternatives (such as a return to polygamy) as preferable to allowing urban women to be independent of men.[46]

Male–female relationships were a perennial topic of discussion and debate. Indeed, the women's pages sometimes seemed to project an image of women that revolved solely around love relationships with men. Women were urged to remain silent, for example, in men's company and not to argue with them. Readers suggested that women avoid going to dances (despite the fact that elsewhere the newspaper carried numerous stories on dance competitions) and avoid trying to "befriend" men, because they might be sexually exploited and "good boys" would lose interest in them.

The only society news that deviated slightly from the stereotypical image of the petty bourgeoisie at play, however, was found in the women's pages and in news devoted to African language, literature and history. Readers sometimes complained that there was too much advice to the lovelorn in the newspaper. There were a number of letters testifying to the fact that women were mistreated by men and not encouraged to participate in social activities or allowed to improve themselves, especially outside the home. "Over the Tea Cups," a regular humor and advice column that featured the characters "Arabelle" and "Isabelle," often departed from the norm,[47] and there were a number of success stories concerning women who had made names for themselves independently of men. *Bantu World*, moreover, was one of the first African newspapers to publish (albeit irregularly) African divorce cases during this period.

Like other black newspapers, *Bantu World* contained poetry, short stories, plays, essays, occasional musical compositions and drawings by African artists. The contradictory images of the new urban African elites projected by the newspaper could be discerned to some extent in the literary works published during the 1930s and 1940s. Those writing for *Bantu World* were mainly freelancers, but some were employed full time as staff reporters and editors. Along with Selope Thema (who used at least two pseudonyms – "Wayfarer" and "Scrutator" – when his columns appeared in the newspaper), many became household names in African politics, literature and journalism. They included Stanley Silwana, Jameson G. Coka, Guybon Sinxo (editor of the Xhosa section), T. D. Mweli Skota, P. D. Segale, Jacob N. Nhlapo (future editor of the *World*), Obed S. Mooki (who used the pseudonym "Isaiah"), S. E. Krune Mqhayi (the most important Xhosa literary figure at the time), Henry D. Tyamzashe (former editor of the *Workers' Herald*), Godfrey R. Z. Kuzwayo (who used the pseudonym "Gossip Pen"), B. W. Vilikazi, Solomon L. Sidzumo, A. C. Jordan, Jordan Ngubane (future editor of *Inkundla ya Bantu*), Peter Abrahams, Fezile Teka (who used the pseudonym "Paupers and Gems") and Henry Nxumalo (the future "Mr Drum" of *Drum* magazine).

R. R. R. Dhlomo, assistant editor of *Bantu World* from 1933, was also editor of the women's pages in the 1930s and undoubtedly the author of "Over the Tea Cups" as well as a regular editorial-page column that contained some of the finest examples of informal or familiar essay writing in African literature. "R. Roamer Esq," or more commonly "R. Roamer," the pseudonym Dhlomo used, was the all-knowing chronicler of the African experience in South Africa. Through the eyes of his two principal characters, "Joshua" and "Jeremiah," he might offer a bitingly satirical view of what it meant to be black in a white world, comment in a wry manner on the subtleties of betting on horses or complain about increases in the bus fare.

Dhlomo was also a prominent member of Bantu Press's stable of African editors during the 1930s and 1940s. Formerly assistant editor of *Ilanga lase Natal*, taken over along with *Imvo Zabantsundu* by Bantu Press in 1934, he was to return as editor of *Ilanga* in 1943. Dhlomo was one of 15 African journalists employed by *Bantu World* in the later 1930s.[48] The assistant editor's brother, Herbert (H. I. E.) Dhlomo, probably the most prominent African literary figure writing in English during this generation, joined the staff in 1935. His description of the African journalist who worked for the white-controlled African press is revealing:

> The African journalist in most cases is under-paid, over-worked, is hampered with irritating restrictions, and is not free to speak out loud and bold. Our journalists must be and are bilingual – they must write in English and Vernacular every week. They are reporters, subeditors, Editors, proof-readers all in one. They are expected to write on every topical subject under the sun for there is no division of work.[49]

Herbert later followed his brother to *Ilanga*, where he was assistant editor in the 1940s.

The urban African's cultural heritage – the attempt to recover and develop an authentic African history and literature – was perhaps the most important, potentially deviant discourse communicated by these literary journalists. Readers occasionally objected to English surnames,[50] complained that the press never used African names in accident reports[51] or criticized the use of the term "Bantu."[52] Africans who used hair straighteners and skin lighteners were also attacked by at least one reader.[53]

Although *Bantu World* continued to extol the virtues of Western culture, readers were also urged not to reject all precolonial customs. Poems as well as folk stories recalling the past were frequently published, particularly on the vernacular pages. A series entitled "History of the Bantu" was produced for several years, and there were numerous articles, profiles, essays, reviews and editorials in the test sample that sought to highlight the achievements of African culture.[54] One article, for example, might report a claim that Great Zimbabwe was built by Africans,[55] while an editorial might admonish Zulu readers to preserve their language.[56] The newspaper sometimes offered literature prizes for aspiring African writers, occasionally reprinted material written in English by non-South African (notably African-American) writers, and supported the efforts of Lovedale and other mission presses in their attempts to publish works by African writers.

Bantu World was undoubtedly the first black newspaper to highlight sports news (A.3), although African sports did not really play a significant role in the black press until popular commercial publications began to dominate the market from the 1950s. Stories generally consisted of team schedules, results of matches and notices of meetings. The African petty bourgeoisie were involved in a surprising number of sports during the 1930s, and virtually all were organized with their own segregated unions, associations or leagues. Soccer was the top sports item in the sample, followed by tennis. Other sports features included baseball, cricket, golf, athletics, boxing, rugby, basketball, cycling, women's and men's hockey, horse racing and draughts.

Religious and educational news content (A.1) in *Bantu World* was much the same as it was in other community-oriented African newspapers. Educational stories dealt with examination results, degrees, diplomas and certificates awarded or recognized, job vacancies for teachers, new appointments and promotions of teachers and administrative staff, and notices of new courses being offered at various mission schools. Lists of teachers and the courses they taught together with the addresses of secondary schools were occasionally compiled for the benefit of parents with school-age children, undoubtedly a majority of *Bantu World's* readers. But criticism of teachers' wages and working conditions, for example, was generally downplayed in favor of occasional articles citing the lack of farm schools and the problem of unqualified teachers.

Religious news consisted of notices of church services, meetings and conferences (full reports of these proceedings were rarely given) and miscellaneous activities of selected clergymen. This subcategory was dominated by the major mission-sponsored churches–Anglican, Lutheran, Methodist, Presbyterian, Congregational, Baptist, Salvation Army, Roman Catholic–and various lay (including temperance) organizations sponsored by these churches, together with independent African and African-American denominations (especially the African Methodist Episcopal Church) approved by the government. Nonapproved separatist churches rarely featured in these stories; when they did, they were usually criticized. An editorial in Zulu, for example, cited the "more than 500 independent churches" in South Africa and condemned the fact that "some have no more than 12 members, some meet in homes, and some are a disgrace, with uneducated, poor 'bishops' and 'presidents.'" The writer urged these churches to unite.[57] *Bantu World* also carried letters urging African political leaders not to ignore God, "the source of wisdom."[58]

Living conditions in the segregated urban African townships (A.4) merited a number of stories in the newspaper. There were reports in this sample about children's health problems[59] and outbreaks of typhoid and bubonic plague.[60] There were reports about the lack of land,[61] segregated schools[62] and government moves to take over African education,[63] poor wages,[64] jobless whites who obtained black jobs,[65] high taxes,[66] high rents,[67] high doctors' fees[68] and other comments from the African townships that were sometimes grouped together in a column or page labeled "People's Point of View."[69]

The everyday experiences of jobless Africans trying to survive in designated white urban areas, however, were virtually ignored, and the concept of segregation itself was not subject to criticism. The front page of the first issue, for example, featured two stories–the lead story having a banner headline that read "BUILDING A GREAT BANTU CITY." The stories concerned the building of Orlando African township outside Johannesburg. Many thousands were now living in Johannesburg's "shanties," where "different tribes" and "different classes" mixed together. They would be moved to a "city" with "modern conveniences" for 80,000 people. The story did not indicate where the "slum districts" were located or whether they could have been rebuilt, and there were no comments from residents who would be removed to Orlando.[70]

Bantu World devoted virtually no space to news concerned with the living conditions of Africans in rural areas (A.5). Although South Africa experienced one of the worst droughts in its history in the 1930s, the topic was rarely mentioned in this sample except indirectly in rainfall reports buried in the vernacular regional news sections. The problems faced by migrants, peasants in the reserves and agricultural workers on white-owned farms were almost completely ignored.[71]

Thema sought to promote the African entrepreneur, and in his writings he proclaimed the virtues of self-discipline and individual enterprise. *Bantu World* supported African business organizations like the Bantu Business League and the Bantu Traders' Association,[72] and cited the activities of progressive African farmers.[73] Much independent African entrepreneurial activity (A.6), however, seemed to be predicated on the goodwill of white benefactors. As one reader, a farmer, put it: "If we try to help ourselves, the white people will surely help us."[74]

News about crime and accidents (A.7) constituted another relatively minor subcategory. *Bantu World* was the principal forerunner of the African tabloid press in South Africa, but in the 1930s the newspaper did not exploit this type of news. Nevertheless, crimes were recorded, along with car and bus crashes, fires and mining accidents. These stories were usually placed on the vernacular regional news pages, but bizarre or violent crimes, and accidents involving many deaths, were often placed on the English-language back page to attract more readers.

Foreign news (D) was relatively well covered in *Bantu World*. Western Europe was the most favored region, followed by Africa, East Asia, North America and the Middle East. There were no stories about Latin America in the sample. As expected, Britain (including Ireland) was by far the most important single source of foreign news. British politics, parliamentary activities, elections, strikes and, of course, the royal family were regularly featured.[75] In addition, most soft news in *Bantu World* – unusual, human interest stories not necessarily linked to ongoing events – were taken from British or North American sources. The newspaper supported the League of Nations and in the late 1930s provided broad coverage of events leading to World War II.

African news from other parts of Africa was almost exclusively divided between the social activities of African elites in nearby Swaziland (who had kinship and other ties with Africans living in the Transvaal) and the Italian invasion of Ethiopia, the symbol of independent Africa to many black South Africans and the subject of numerous letters and articles (in English and vernacular languages) on page 1 as well as the inside pages of the newspaper between 1935 and 1939. In a similar vein, the Japanese invasion of China dominated East Asian news. Only 19 of 139 foreign news stories were concerned with North America and the Middle East. Single themes again dominated both subcategories – race relations, the achievements of African Americans[76] and conflicts between Jewish immigrants and Muslims in Palestine.

White Authoritarian Context

The depoliticization of domestic news in *Bantu World* can be discerned in the quantity of news devoted to those who ruled South Africa (Table 11).

The political, legislative and administrative framework of white rule (B. 1) generally provided the targets and dictated the limits of permissible dissent. The most frequently reported stories in this subcategory were about individuals and institutions representative of the prevailing political order. Consensus news and opinion included the actions of government ministers, beginning with the prime minister; municipal officials, insofar as they were involved with African affairs; and prominent members of parliament. This weekly catalogue was supplemented by occasional government proclamations, reports of commissions and committees of inquiry, census data, election results and notices of government appointments. But the main trends in white party politics, especially the growing conflict with Afrikaner nationalist extremists, were ignored.

Bantu World's credibility with its audience was maintained in part because it was allowed a considerable degree of deviance in attacking selected government policies during the 1930s. As noted earlier, Thema lashed out at segregationist legislation that made criminals of Africans and weakened their ability to compete economically, and he campaigned vigorously against Hertzog's assault on the African franchise in the Cape. The newspaper frequently carried letters from readers and recorded the speeches of white and black liberals condemning these and other discriminatory acts of government. Government reports were also occasionally attacked.[77] *Bantu World* sometimes included news items about individual whites, particularly when they got into trouble, even when blacks did not feature in these stories.[78] The police were consistently cited for harassment, brutality, unjustified arrests and occasionally even corruption.[79]

Bantu World did not express reservations editorially about white liberals who sought to represent African interests in white power politics, and only one reader

Table 11. *Category B news in* Bantu World (*% of story units*)

Category	%
B. White/multiracial news (111 units)	7.1
B.1 Political, legislative and administrative	5.9
B.2 Economic and social	1.2

did so in this sample.[80] Numerous editorials, however, communicated readers' grievances against the government. Editorials blamed white laws for "lawlessness among the natives"[81] and for creating interracial strife.[82] The Natal Native Law Code was attacked,[83] and the government's treatment of Africans,[84] and its attempts to segregate Indians and Coloureds,[85] were deplored.

The economic and social framework of white rule (B.2) was virtually ignored in *Bantu World*, as it was in other alternative newspapers during the interwar period. In the aftermath of the Great Depression, for example, there was only one story in this sample on the South African economy.[86] But the activities of white missionaries, mission churches and various multiracial bodies like the South African Institute of Race Relations (SAIRR) and the Joint Councils formed part of the dominant discourse in *Bantu World*. Virtually all the articles, letters and editorials in this subcategory were about white-sponsored groups and institutions – the SAIRR, the National Union of South African Students, the Rotary Clubs and the Bantu Men's Social Centre – seeking to foster better race relations or promote multiracial social activities.

These were the stories where whites praised, helped or showed concern for blacks in terms of perceived economic and/or cultural interests and needs. The many supplements generated by *Bantu World* were often used to promote a positive image of race relations, as in the following publicity announcement for the supplement *Bantu Weekly Reader*:

> THIS WEEK'S NEWS tells you about Bantus who have no work and no food to eat ... Then there are some people who have no FOOD in ZULULAND. White people are helping them, giving them many, many bags of corn ... At a place called Reitz in the Free State many Bantus have no food, and they had to eat roots. But the white people have also sent them many, many bags of corn.[87]

The newspaper cited statements by white officials who had positive things to say about blacks or who were seeking to promote "goodwill" between the races. Most of these articles and letters were printed in English.[88] White-sponsored social organizations seeking to promote dialogue between the races were not criticised in this sample. And only one story referred to the experiences of most Africans that most whites in reality were vehemently opposed to social interaction.[89]

Black Politics and Trade Unions

Coverage of black politics and trade unions (C) in this sample was actually slightly less than coverage of white politics (B) – the two categories combined comprised only 16.5 percent of the total news agenda – and it was a revealing foretaste of exactly how the captive commercial black press would deal with black political and trade union activities in the next generation (Table 12). Stories about government-

Table 12. *Category C news in* Bantu World (*% of story units*)

Category	%
C. Black/multiracial political and trade union news (83 units)	5.3
C.1 Personalities and organizations	4.6
C.2 Confrontation and consciousness	0.7

appointed advisory bodies, together with their appointed or elected members, and stories about independent political organizations each comprised roughly one-third of the stories in Subcategory C.1 (Personalities and organizations). Only four articles and/or letters in this sample focused on militant political or trade union organizations.[90] Most stories in this subcategory were brief, superficial news reports – notices of meetings, suggestions for agenda, reports of resolutions approved, or occasional tales of personal and factional rivalries. Only four editorials in the sample highlighted black political organizations.[91]

Subcategory C.2 (Confrontation and consciousness) had the least number of story units in the six newspapers subjected to a quantitative analysis. There was no news of any kind that mentioned or advocated strikes, boycotts or other forms of civil disobedience. Few stories even queried the effectiveness of petitionary protest, which was still the most popular political strategy of the African petty bourgeoisie during this period.[92]

The only other significant and potentially deviant political discourse involved stories projecting African solidarity and self-reliance. Eight editorials – more than any other except those editorials protesting aspects of white authoritarian rule – as well as articles and letters were devoted to this topic. Zulu stories, in particular, called for Zulu unity as a step toward African unity. Africans were urged to work hard to improve themselves,[93] promote African political, economic and cultural organizations and activities[94] and, above all, eliminate "tribal" differences and unite.[95]

Commercial Advertising

Although *Bantu World* was the flagship of an emerging black commercial press, advertisements as units of measurement represented not much more than one-quarter of the news-advertising agenda during the 1930s (Table 13).

Goods and services advertised in *Bantu World* during the 1930s were generated mainly by white entrepreneurs. Most advertisements were one column, but numerous businesses (especially department stores) provided displays ranging in size from two to five columns. Occasionally, these stores offered full-page advertisements. The illustrations used in these advertisements depicted blacks (especially in the African-language pages) as well as whites, but English was the preferred language. Only a few self-employed Africans – such as signpainters, shoemakers, real estate agents and photographers – offered their services in the *Bantu World* sample, far fewer than in other African newspapers between the 1920s and 1940s.

A somewhat arbitrary but consistent classification was made between essential and nonessential goods and services in *Bantu World* in an attempt to measure the relative percentage of luxury consumer advertising that might have been directed

Table 13. *Formal advertising content in* Bantu World (*% of advertising units*)

Category	%
White businesses: Essential goods and services	49.8
White businesses: Nonessential goods and services	41.6
Black goods and services (essential and nonessential)	2.5
Promotional	6.1

Note: Bantu World had 608 advertising units, or 28.1 percent of the news-advertising units.

specifically at the urban African petty bourgeoisie. Food, clothing and furniture were categorized as essential items, along with plowing and gardening tools, bicycles, tea and primus stoves, even though some of these goods might have been targeted for more affluent audiences. Cosmetics – hair straighteners, hair and skin creams, razors and razor blades, shaving equipment, toothpastes, dyes and soaps – comprised the largest single nonessential subcategory. Educational services – focusing on the secondary schools, Fort Hare and to a lesser extent the correspondence colleges and Bible institutes – were also significant luxury items. All the major, mainly mission, secondary schools – including Lovedale, Healdtown, Adams, Inanda, Edendale, Tiger Kloof, Kilnerton, Mariannhill, Ohlange, St Peter's, St Matthew's and Morija (in colonial Basutoland) – advertised in *Bantu World*. Other educational advertisements included those for books and bookshops, for writing pads and pencils, and for service groups sponsored by white liberals such as the Helping Hand for Native Girls.

Alcoholic drink, tobacco and entertainment – three significant items in the captive black commercial press from the 1950s – formed a relatively insignificant proportion of the *Bantu World* advertising agenda in the 1930s. There were virtually no advertisements for beer, whiskey, brandy, wine or cane spirits—a necessity, since Africans were not allowed to buy, sell or drink so-called "European" manufactured beer and liquor at the time. Manufactured cigarettes (and snuff) were advertised, but the tobacco industry only began to target the African market in this newspaper from the late 1930s.[96]

Bantu World in some ways was a trend setter in the shift from an elite to a mass audience. Other African newspapers in the 1930s, owned by white entrepreneurs, were also beginning to concentrate on social news (mainly education) and leisure activities (mainly sports and society news), and to de-emphasize partisan political news. A few newspapers were already beginning to experiment with pictorial journalism, foreshadowing the tabloid press of the post-1950 generation.

The first illustrated newspaper for African readers in South Africa, for example, was reputedly *Umlindi we Nyanga* (the Monthly Watchman), which was launched as a Xhosa-English monthly in 1934 by a company in East London that manufactured goods for the African market in the eastern Cape. *Umlindi*, in its original series (month unkown, 1934–June 1941), was little more than an advertising vehicle for the company's products. Richard H. Godlo, however, was the editor during the 1930s, and Godlo's presence lent considerable prestige to the newspaper. Godlo was one of the most active political figures in the eastern Cape during this generation – the principal founder and long-time president of the South

African Congress of Advisory Boards (established in 1928), an All-African Congress official during the 1930s, a member of the Natives' Representative Council (representing the Cape urban areas) between 1936 and 1951, and a member of the ANC's national executive committee during the 1940s.

Umlindi was revived in Johannesburg after World War II as an African pictorial magazine, and it was published in four languages (English/Zulu/Sotho/Xhosa) under a white editor. In the new series (October 1945–September 1952), *Umlindi* consisted mainly of noncontroversial news photographs, drawings and cartoons with long captions, pen sketches of African leaders, Bible stories in comic book form, English lessons, and occasional agricultural, health and sports notes.[97]

Although *Bantu World* catered largely to the upper-ranked petty bourgeoisie during the 1930s, there were signs that the captive African commercial press was developing a style of sourcing and packaging news, entertainment and even advertising that also appealed to lower-ranked readers. By 1946 the African literacy rate had increased to 21.3 percent of the adult African population, and it was probably even higher in key urban areas like Johannesburg. Social stratification in the potential readership was discernible to observers like A. J. Friedgut, writing in the 1940s. He noted two distinct categories of readers in addition to the intelligentsia:[98]

- readers with relatively less formal education and lower incomes. These included primary schoolteachers; petty-commodity producers of goods and services; lower-level clergy (preachers and evangelists), especially from independent African churches; office workers; and semiskilled industrial workers.
- readers with little formal education, who could not read English. These were essentially semiliterate, low-income rural and urban dwellers, including some peasants, laborers on white farms and in government offices, who might read a vernacular language and thus have access to the African press. These readers were the ones who would most likely communicate mass-media messages to illiterate listeners.

Bantu World and its imitators did not have to compete with the independent African political press for these readers, because there were virtually no publications of this kind left by the mid-1930s. The few dissident journals that did survive were associated mainly with the socialist press. These newspapers would initiate a new era in protest journalism beginning in the 1940s and chart the transition to the popular resistance press of the 1950s and beyond.

Notes

1. Parts of this case study appeared in an earlier format in L. Switzer, "*Bantu World* and the origins of a captive African commercial press in South Africa," *Journal of Southern African Studies* 14, 3 (1988), 351–370. A new section on editor Selope Thema has been added, other sections expanded, and *Bantu World* itself subjected to a new content analysis. *Bantu World* citations will specify page numbers, languages and editorials. Stories not designated by language are in English.
2. Quoted in L. Switzer and D. Switzer, *The black press in South Africa and Lesotho, 1876–1976* (Boston, 1979).
3. Paver originally offered the editorship to Bud-Mbelle's brother-in-law Sol Plaatje, but he turned it down, just as he had done 12 years earlier in the case of *Umteteli wa Bantu*. B. Willan, *Sol Plaatje, South African nationalist, 1876–1932* (Berkeley and Los Angeles, 1984), 380.
4. *BW*, 9 April 1932, 3. Other stories on this page cited African interests in world news

and African achievements in medicine, law, literature and music.

5. The dilemma faced by African newspaper proprietors who sought to remain independent of Bantu Press is illustrated by *Valdezia Bulletin*, a registered monthly in English and Tsonga (or Thonga) founded in 1931. The journal was initially aimed at students attending school in the village of Valdezia, near Louis Trichardt in the northern Transvaal, the first station established by the Swiss Mission in South Africa. Editors Daniel C. Marivate, E. A. Tlakula and A. E. Mpapele sought to provide news and entertainment of general interest to their readers, and the *Valdezia Bulletin* became a thriving community newspaper. Independent of missionary control, it was printed initially by Spes Bona – an African-owned printing works – in Alexandra township, Johannesburg. But Spes Bona apparently failed, and the editors turned to Bantu Press for assistance. Bantu Press, however, wanted to control the publication. The editors, faced with mounting financial problems, closed down the newspaper in 1937 rather than submit. M. C. Bill to author, 9 August 1983. See also Switzer and Switzer, *Black press*, 109.
6. On Bantu Press, see T. Couzens, "A short history of *The World* and other black South African newspapers," *Inspan* 1,1 (1978), 69–92; Switzer and Switzer, *Black press*, 7–9, 121–124.
7. Paver told Couzens, in an interview in December 1975: "I liked Thema's personality... He was a politician but he was about the most balanced of a whole crowd of, well, what one might call the intelligentsia of that day and they were very thin on the ground, you know, there were damned few... I didn't interfere with the editorial... They had to do the editorials and so the policy was a cooperative one. We used to have meetings and when I had new reporters I would brief them... There was a lot of goodwill and faith... I couldn't presume to put a blue pencil through what was said. It had to be done by my personality... and I had to say to them, 'Well, you know you'll have Native Affairs officials who are proficient in your own languages reading this.' " Couzens, "A short history of *The World*."
8. Rheinallt – Jones and Pim were leading promoters of African middle-class culture in Johannesburg during the interwar period. Rheinallt – Jones was a key organizer in the Joint Council movement, a founding father of the South African Institute of Race Relations and one of the Native Representatives in the Senate (representing African voters in the Transvaal and the Orange Free State from 1937 to 1942). Pim, an accountant who worked for the Chamber of Mines, was an art patron and a city councillor. Paver also consulted William Ballinger, the British trade union organizer and ill-fated adviser to Clements Kadalie and his Industrial and Commercial Workers' Union. Ballinger's brand of advocacy journalism, however, was too militant for the founder of *Bantu World*. P. Walshe, *The rise of African nationalism in South Africa: The African National Congress, 1912–1952* (Berkeley and Los Angeles, 1971), 218.
9. Even so, white "advisers" and "editorial directors" were appointed from the 1940s to oversee Bantu Press publications. H. J. E. Dumbrell, director of education in the Bechuanaland Protectorate (Botswana) and an editorial adviser for two African journals, was appointed "director of adult education" for all Bantu Press publications in 1946. His responsibilities ranged "from presenting information about health and agricultural methods to expository accounts of international affairs, from giving facts about the political status of the African to encouraging the development of literature among Bantu adults and the artistic talents of Bantu children." By the 1950s, apparently all journals owned by Bantu Press had white editorial directors, and many employed white journalists in the newsroom. Interviews with black and white journalists conducted in the 1970s, and the author's own experiences as a journalist on the *World*, however, suggest that in practice African journalists still exercised considerable control over the news agenda. A. J. Friedgut, "The non-European press" in E. Hellmann (ed.), *Handbook on race relations in South Africa* (Cape Town, 1949), 497.
10. R. V. S. Thema, "From Cattle-herding to the Editor's Chair," unpublished typescript, ca. 1935. Photocopy obtained from

the library of the University of the Witwatersrand (Johannesburg).

11. J. Starfield, "'Not quite history': The autobiographies of H. Selby Msimang and R. V. Selope Thema and the writing of South African history," *Social Dynamics* 14, 2 (1988), 21, 23–25.
12. Loram was a member of the Native Affairs Commission during the 1920s and chief inspector of Native Education in Natal.
13. Thema, "From Cattle-herding," Chap. 1 ("Ushered into the World"), 16. Cited hereafter by chapter and page.
14. The subtitle "Out of Darkness" is written on the first page of Thema's autobiography. Chap. 1 ("Ushered into the World"), 1.
15. Chap. 6 ("The Veil Is Lifted"), 24, 28.
16. Chap. 5 ("Back to School"), 32–36.
17. Chap. 1 ("Ushered into the World"), 6–7.
18. Chap. 2 ("My Boyhood"), 3–4, 8.
19. Chap. 2 ("My Boyhood"), 24–25, 33–34.
20. Chap. 2 ("My Boyhood"), 26–32.
21. Chap. 3 ("Pinched into School"), 8.
22. Chap. 4 ("War Intervenes"), 10, 15.
23. Chap. 4 ("War Intervenes"), 21–22.
24. "The only names in the Bible that would have suited my taste and satisfied my ambition were those of Moses and David but there were already too many persons by those names...I remembered reading the story of Richard, the Lion-hearted, one of the leaders of the Crusaders against the forces of Islam, and remembered also the name of Victor Emmanuel King of Italy. I discovered that Richard meant strong-hearted and Victor, the conqueror...I adopted them on the day of my baptism as my own, including the family name of Selope. Chap. 5 ("Back to School"), 23–25.
25. In addition to academic subjects, Thema took shorthand, typing and photography, three skills that were to be useful in his journalistic career.
26. Thema received a book prize (*With the Boers in the Transvaal*) for his efforts in "road-making, tree-planting and bridge-making" at Lovedale. Chap. 6 ("The Veil is lifted"), 50–51.
27. Chap. 6 ("The Veil Is lifted"), 52.
28. Chap. 6 ("The Veil Is lifted"), 4, 54–55.
29. Starfield, "Not quite history," 26. The incident is recounted in Willan, *Sol Plaatje*, 211–214.
30. Quoted in Starfield, "Not quite history," 18, 29–30.
31. This was the view of another African journalist in Johannesburg, Edwin Mofutsanyana, a prominent member of the Communist Party and editor of its newspaper *Inkululeko* during the 1940s. Starfield, "Not quite history," 17 (citing an unpublished interview conducted by historian Robert Edgar with Mofutsanyana, n.d.).
32. Quoted in Walshe, *The rise of African nationalism*, 144.
33. *South African Outlook*, September 1928.
34. Walshe, *The rise of African nationalism*, 241.
35. *BW*, 7 May 1932,1, 8.
36. *BW*, 4 June 1931, 1; 12 November 1932,1.
37. *BW*, 14 May 1932, 1.
38. *BW*, 30 July 1932, 1.
39. *BW*, 14 June 1932, 1; 18 June 1932, 1.
40. T. J. Couzens, *The new African: A study of the life and work of H. I. E. Dhlomo* (Johannesburg, 1985), 137 (citing *BW*, 27 April 1935). Thema accused the government of rejecting "trusteeship" in favor "of keeping the African in his proper place as a hewer of wood and drawer of water for the white race." *BW*, 27 April 1935, 8 (editorial: "The Proposed Native Bills").
41. *BW*, e.g. 13, 20 January 1934, 1.
42. Thema's credibility as editor apparently declined during the 1940s. Like his successors, Jacob M. Nhlapo and M. T. Moerane, he grew disillusioned with politics and became actively involved in the Moral Re-Armament movement (cf. *BW*, 15 July 1939, 18). A heavy drinker in his later years, Thema died at 69 in September 1955. *BW*, 24 September 1955, 4 (obituary).
43. Two pages were generally in Zulu, two in Xhosa and three in Sotho/Tswana.
44. *BW*, 13 April 1935, 1. See also *BW*, 20 April 1935, 1 (headline in capital letters: "European Businessmen Should Explore South Africa's Ever Growing Home Market").
45. *Bantu World* was "independent of party politics" and in favor of "instilling racial self-help and self-respect, thereby promoting harmonious race relationships and the maintenance of inter-racial goodwill and cooperation." It would "print without

prejudice or bias all the news that will be interesting and instructive to the Bantu peoples." It would "encourage the development of the Bantu as an agricultural people" and "foster the growth of Bantu arts and crafts, literature and music." It would cater "to the needs of semi-literates as well as to the most highly advanced." Controversial points were qualified in an editorial below the credo. Although the newspaper sought "to give every man an equal chance," this did not mean "equality for all in the sense of equality of possessions or capacities" or "equality of opportunity in the sense of the same opportunity for all." *Bantu World* would not ignore "the interests and the just claims of the Europeans." The editorial page in the first issue also included a set of journalistic guidelines entitled "The Journalist's Creed" in English and Afrikaans. *BW*, 9 April 1932, 4.

46. *BW*, e.g., 4 March 1939, 6 (Xhosa).
47. *BW*, e.g., 11 March 1939, 9: Women were urged not to marry just for the sake of being married.
48. *BW*, 8 April 1939, 8.
49. Quoted in Couzens, *The new African*, 275.
50. *BW*, e.g., 4 March 1939, 6 (Xhosa).
51. *BW*, e.g., 20 June 1936, 16.
52. *BW*, e.g., 25 April 1936, 16.
53. *BW*, 4 March 1939, 5.
54. *BW*, e.g., 11 June 1932, 3 (Xhosa); 12 November 1932, 3; 28 January 1933, 11; 3 November 1934, 7 (Xhosa); 2 February 1935, 3 (Zulu); 20 July 1935,1 (re S.E.K. Mqhayi), 6 (Zulu); 25 April 1936, 6 (Xhosa); 22 January 1938, 6 (Zulu); 6 August 1938, 2 (Xhosa).
55. *BW*, 20 June 1936, 1.
56. *BW*, 20 July 1935, 6 (Zulu).
57. *BW*, 22 January 1938, 6 (Zulu). See also *BW*, 15 January 1938, 8 (English editorial).
58. *BW*, e.g., 30 June 1934. 8.
59. *BW*, e.g., 10 June 1933, 6, 7 (Zulu), 10.
60. *BW*, e.g., 3 November 1934, 5 (typhoid story in Xhosa), 2 February 1935, 1 (bubonic plague).
61. *BW*, e.g., 11 June 1932, 7 (Xhosa); 2 February 1935, 4 (Zulu); 4 March 1939, 4 (English editorial).
62. *BW*, 11 June 1932, 1.
63. *BW*, 11 March 1939, 1.
64. *BW*, 20 July 1935, 8 (English editorial), 16.
65. *BW*, 2 February 1935, 5 (Xhosa).
66. *BW*, 3 November 1934, 7 (Xhosa).
67. *BW*, 6 August 1938, 6 (Zulu).
68. *BW*, 27 March 1937, 4.
69. *BW*, e.g., 20 June 1936, 16. For complaints in the vernacular about living conditions, see *BW*, 10 June 1933, 4 (Xhosa); 2 February 1935, 5 (Xhosa editorial); 25 April 1936, 2 (Zulu).
70. *BW*, 9 April 1932, 1.
71. Three articles only in the sample were related in some way to the reserves. *BW*, 12 November 1932, 5 (two Zulu articles: one article urged reserve residents to write to *Bantu World* to keep migrant relatives informed of events in the rural areas; another article urged African businessmen to provide jobs for "hungry" people in Natal); 6 August 1938, 7 (reserve residents in Natal complained that they were forced to reduce their cattle herds and compensated with baby formula and bags of maize – article in Zulu).
72. *BW*, e.g., 12 November 1932, 5 (Zulu), 6; 12 November 1932, 6; 12 February 1938, 8 (English editorial). Natal's political leader John Dube and the editor of his newspaper, Ngazana Lutuli, were president and secretary of the Bantu Business League (which was apparently limited to Natal Province), and Selope Thema helped launch an African National Business Men's League in Johannesburg, but most attempts by African entrepreneurs to generate capital during the 1930s were unsuccessful. Walshe, *The rise of African nationalism*, 147.
73. *BW*, e.g., 30 June 1934, 7, 9. But the focus of these and other articles on farmers was on the "wonderful work undertaken by the Department of Native Affairs on behalf of Bantu welfare."
74. *BW*, 12 November 1932, 6; see also 30 June 1934, 7; 3 November 1934, 5 (Xhosa).
75. Although Britain was criticized on one occasion when it appeared to be sympathetic to Hertzog's attempt to gain control of the protectorates in southern Africa (*BW*, 20 June 1936, 8 – English editorial), British political and cultural traditions were revered. Virtually every page in the newspaper, for example, had an article mourning the death of King George V (*BW*, 25 January 1936, 1 February 1936),

and other major events in the life of the monarchy during these years merited front-page treatment (*BW*, e.g., 12 December 1936, 8 May 1937). The governor general was still regarded as "the Supreme Chief of the African people" and "the connecting link between the races" (*BW*, 5 June 1937, 8 – English editorial).

76. A series on the role of African Americans in American history, for example, was launched in 1939 (*BW*, 11 March 1939, 4). The African American who possessed the cardinal virtue of self-reliance was an important role model for men like Thema – an "elder brother" from whom the African might receive "guidance and inspiration." Couzens, *The new African*, 118, n. 49.
77. *BW*, e.g., 11 June 1932, 8 (Native Economic Commission – in Zulu).
78. *BW*, e.g., 11 June 1932, 3 (white man fined for beating up black servant, white woman imprisoned for living with black man – two articles in Xhosa); 12 November 1932, 13 (court case involving Stellenbosch Dutch Reformed Church minister); 10 July 1937, 6 (white doctors threaten to strike – article in Zulu).
79. *BW*, e.g., 3 November 1934, 6 (Xhosa); 25 April 1936, 1, 3 (Zulu); 20 June 1936, 2 (Zulu); 10 July 1937, 7 (Zulu). Police "terrorism" was cited in one editorial, for example, calling for an inquiry into the role of police in the illicit African liquor trade. *BW*, 25 April 1936, 8.
80. *BW*, 27 March 1937, 16.
81. *BW*, 2 February 1935, 8.
82. *BW*, 27 March 1937, 8.
83. *BW*, 28 January 1933, 5 (Zulu).
84. *BW*, 20 June 1936, 6 (Xhosa).
85. *BW*, 11 March 1939, 4.
86. *BW*, 10 June 1933, 1 (South Africa's commercial banks lower interest rates on fixed deposits).
87. *BW*, 16 April 1932, 5.
88. *BW*, e.g., 11 June 1932, 4 (International Confederation of Students); 12 November 1932, 11 (government irrigation schemes for jobless blacks); 10 June 1933, 8; 10 July 1937, 20 (NUSAS); 30 June 1934, 1 (SAIRR on race relations); 30 June 1934, 2 (white farmers willing to teach black farmers); 3 November 1934, 1, 8 (Anglican bishop says blacks need and deserve the best of Western culture – English editorial); 3 November 1934, 1 (minister of education says racial segregation not possible), 8 (two articles: blacks should follow white example in farming, professional and business pursuits; praise for a company that helped build latrines and roads in a black township); 2 February 1935, 2 (white town council decides not to cut black wages), 9 (white girls are happy to work in Indian shops); 20 July 1935, 8 (Africans have always been loyal to government); 20 June 1936, 20; 22 January 1938, 5; 6 August 1938, 2 (municipalities are building and upgrading black townships – articles in English and Xhosa); 11 March 1939, 1 (Johannesburg Joint Council opposes govemment bid to take over African education).
89. *BW*, 6 August 1938, 6 (some whites express "outrage" over a multiracial concert held in Johannesburg – article in Zulu).
90. They were inspired by Coloured radicals and/or the Communist Party – the National Liberation League, Non-European United Front and the Council of Non-European Trade Unions. *BW*, 27 March 1937, 2 (Xhosa editorial); 6 August 1938, 5; 11 March 1939, 20; 6 August 1938, 20.
91. *BW*, 20 June 1938, 2 (AAC urges Hertzog to compromise on his "Native Bills" – in Zulu); 10 July 1937, 6 (NRC – in Zulu), 22 January 1938, 8 (NRC – in English); 27 March 1939, 2 (National Liberation League – in Xhosa).
92. Letter writers occasionally complained about members of urban Advisory Boards who did not represent the people (e.g., 4 March 1939, 7 – in Xhosa) or about political leaders who lacked "leadership qualities" (e.g., 30 June 1934, 6 – in Xhosa). One writer urged educated Africans to remain in the rural areas (10 June 1933, 9).
93. *BW*, e.g., 12 November 1932, 4 (Xhosa editorial), 5 (Zulu editorial); 2 February 1935, 3 (Zulu editorial).
94. *BW*, e.g., 11 June 1932, 2, 7 (Zulu); 10 June 1935, 5 (Xhosa editorial); 27 March 1937, 6 (Zulu editorial).
95. *BW*, e.g., 28 January 1933, 6 (English editorial); 3 November 1934, 3 (Zulu editorial); 25 April 1936, 3 (Zulu); 10 July 1937 8 (English editorial); 22 January 1938, 6 (Zulu editorial).
96. Luxury goods advertised also included sewing machines, carpets, gramophones

and records, second-hand cars, petrol (gasoline), musical instruments, cameras, air guns and pellets, pressure cookers, tires, heating irons, wax polishes and window cleaners. In addition to mission secondary schools, luxury service advertisements featured Post Office savings accounts, hotels and theaters (open to Africans), land sales, car-rental agencies and service garages.

97. Another forerunner of the tabloid journalism era was *Umthunywa* (the Messenger), an English-Xhosa weekly produced in Umtata (Transkei) by a white editor (William H. Hutcheson) in association with the local white newspaper, the *Territorial News*. It focused on personalities and developments in the Transkei and East Griqualand. *Umthunywa* was printed and distributed by Bantu Press from 1940 and eventually sold to the Argus Company, which closed it down in July 1966. Switzer and Switzer, *Black press*, 119–120.

98. *Union statistics for fifty years*, A-22; Friedgut, "The non-European press," 487, 489.

PART II
From Protest to Resistance, 1940s–1960s

CHAPTER 7

Under Siege

Inkundla ya Bantu and the African Nationalist Movement, 1938–1951

Les Switzer and Ime Ukpanah

The African nationalist press remained weak and relatively powerless during the crucial years of political transition between the loss of the Cape African franchise in 1936 and the banning of the main African nationalist organizations in 1960.* The few independent African political journals that survived were marginal as commercial enterprises and circumscribed in news coverage, distribution and number of readers.

Inkundla ya Bantu (People's Forum) was the only independent African nationalist journal that played a significant national role in the alternative press during these years.[1] It was launched in April 1938 as a moderate African nationalist community newspaper distributed mainly in the port cities and adjacent rural areas of the eastern Cape, including the Ciskei and Transkei reserves, and southern Natal. It ceased publication about five months before its fourteenth birthday in November 1951–and seven months before the launching of the Defiance Campaign.

Inkundla first appeared as a monthly, under an English title, *Territorial Magazine*, but in June 1940 it was given the Zulu/Xhosa title *Inkundla ya Bantu*, a change in name that was welcomed by readers.[2] The new title was translated as "Bantu Forum"–"Bantu" meaning literally "people" but conveying the sense of humanness or humanity, and "forum ... a Latin word meaning a public place." The significance of the change was carefully explained to *Inkundla* readers:

> At the forum ... the masses of men and women used to gather to hear great speeches and not only hear them but express their own opinion. The parallel of this in African society is the "Inkundla." ... Decisions made at such a "Inkundla" [a village council] were ... the embodiment of the people's soul ... It is the desire of the proprietors that as the policy of the paper is independent and seeks to bring to the foreground the African interests as the African people desire them given prominence, the African public will co-operate in making this paper the real "Inkundla" whose decisions reflect African opinion.[3]

Inkundla was an African nationalist newspaper dedicated solely to the African National Congress (ANC, or Congress). As the editor put it in 1941,

*We are most grateful to Catherine Nawa-Gwamanda for the thorough job she did as a translator and coder in the content analysis of *Inkundla*.

> The African National Congress is the mouth-piece of the African people of the Union of South Africa. It stands for racial unity and mutual helpfulness and for the improvement of the African people politically, economically, socially, educationally and industrially ... *Inkundla ya Bantu* is in agreement with this policy.[4]

The political orientation of *Inkundla* was just as clear five years later. "Apart from numerous small missionary journals, there are only four Bantu papers of consequence outside the [white-owned] Bantu Press group: *Umteteli wa Bantu*, *Inkululeko*, *Inkundla ya Bantu* and *Umlindi*." The only newspapers of political consequence were *Inkululeko*, the Communist Party organ, and *Inkundla*, which "supports the African National Congress."[5]

This chapter focuses on the political discourses in *Inkundla ya Bantu*. The first section describes the founding of the newspaper, discusses its proprietors and editors, and outlines its political objectives. The second section examines the circulation and advertising content. The third section analyzes the news content in an attempt to locate and identify the various strands of a complex political agenda that reflected numerous contradictions in the ANC and in its relations with various other opposition groups at the local, regional and national level during this turbulent period.

Case Study of *Inkundla ya Bantu*

Inkundla's proprietors were two Xhosa-speaking entrepreneurs from Mpondoland, in the Transkei, who had migrated to Natal and settled in Verulam, about 17 miles north of Durban along the coast, apparently sometime in the mid-1930s. Paul Knox Bonga and Phillip Goduka Katamzi were printers and compositors who probably learned the trade at Lovedale, the prestigious Presbyterian mission school in the eastern Cape. They formed a partnership and launched Verulam Press as a job-printing and bookbinding venture serving mainly the African community in southern Natal.[6] Their clientele comprised church groups, tradesmen, shopkeepers and other would-be commercial entrepreneurs, but Verulam Press was always fragile as a business enterprise.

The proprietors decided to publish a newspaper – intially to advertise the services of Verulam Press – but more capital was needed. The solution was to bring in more partners. Cuthbert Paul Motsemme, a Tswana originally from Thaba 'Nchu in the Orange Free State who had become a successful herbalist and owned a mail-order business in Durban, was recruited at the beginning of the 1940s. Motsemme became responsible for advertising and apparently was the newspaper's most effective fund-raiser. He lived at Verulam and was one of Bonga and Katamzi's neighbors. Roseberry Tandwefika Bokwe (1900–63), a Xhosa-speaking friend of Motsemme's, was recruited in the mid-1940s. Bokwe was a well-known educator (headmaster of Ohlange Institute, 1922–27),[7] who had later qualified as a physician. His practice was in Middledrift in the Ciskei region, where he was eventually appointed district surgeon, one of the few Africans ever to hold this post in South Africa. Bokwe was responsible for distributing *Inkundla* in the eastern Cape. Cleopas M. Xaba, a Zulu who was pastor of the separatist Zulu Congregational Church in Doornfontein (Johannesburg), was recruited about the same time as Bokwe, and he helped to distribute copies of the newspaper on the Witwatersrand.

Soon after Motsemme joined Verulam Press, it became a limited liability company.[8] Since the shareholders were based in the eastern Cape, Johannesburg and southern Natal, the newspaper was read mainly in these regions of South Africa. *Inkundla* was especially strong in African communities along the coast and the immediate hinterland between Port Elizabeth in the eastern Cape and southern Natal below the Tugela River, if one is to judge by the datelines of the stories and the languages used.

Verulam Press had separate editorial, circulation and accounting, printing and bookbinding departments, and there was a business manager in addition to the editor. Bonga and Katamzi were responsible for the printing and bookbinding department, which had the most paid workers (employing seven Xhosa men in the printing department alone during the mid- to late 1940s),[9] and Motsemme was the business manager for both Verulam Press and *Inkundla*. Katamzi was also initially in charge of the newspaper's circulation and accounting department, but this was soon turned over to Motsemme's wife, Daisy Motsemme.

The Editorship of Govan Mbeki (1938–1944)

The political editor of *Inkundla* was Govan Archibald Mvunyelina Mbeki, who was born in July 1910 in the village of Mpukane in the Nqamakwe district in the southern Transkei.[10] His parents were Mfengu, his father a Christian convert and a headman for more than 20 years. He was dismissed from office the year of Mbeki's birth, but the family was relatively prosperous by rural African standards. They were staunch Wesleyan Methodists, and Mbeki was raised in a pious Christian household that distanced itself from the "customs and traditions" of pre-Christian culture.

Mbeki was educated at Healdtown, the most prestigious Methodist mission secondary school in the eastern Cape, and entered Fort Hare Native College on scholarship in 1931. He remained at Fort Hare for more than five years, spending the first two taking matriculation subjects (Fort Hare at the time still had high school courses for those without the matriculation certificate) and the next three studying for a B.A. in Political Studies (Administration) and Psychology as well as the College Diploma in Education. Mbeki became a political activist at Fort Hare (joining the ANC in 1935), where he was also first introduced to marxism through contact with people like Max Yergan and Edward ("Eddie") Roux.[11] Mbeki, however, did not join the Communist Party until 1953, three years after it was banned in South Africa.

Mbeki received his degree in 1937 and spent the next three years teaching, initially in Durban, where he first met the proprietors of Verulam Press.[12] Bonga and Katamzi offered him the editorship of *Inkundla*. Mbeki was to be given "all the freedom to express your ideas – all we [the proprietors] are interested in is that the paper should be there, so that it advertises our services."[13] Mbeki was "writing the leaders, the sub-leaders and other articles" by June 1938,[14] and apparently he was responsible for changing the name of the newspaper to *Inkundla ya Bantu*.

Mbeki returned to the Transkei late in 1939 to teach at Clarkebury Institution, a mission-run teacher-training college, but was fired within a few months for his political activities. He obtained a trading license (one of the first Africans in the Transkei to get one) and opened up a cooperative trading store early in 1940 in a village a few miles from Idutywa in the southern Transkei. Mbeki and his wife Epainette (née Moerane) spent the next 12 years of their lives living and working among the impoverished peasants in the South African government's showpiece African reserve.

None of the major political opposition groups – Congress, the All-African Convention (AAC) or the Communist Party – had much of a following in the Transkei at this time, and Mbeki was a pioneer in working through existing community organizations – including teachers' associations, credit cooperative societies, farmers' unions, vigilance associations and women's groups – to reestablish an oppositional political culture in the region. Mbeki was also secretary of two major regional political bodies – the Transkei African Voters' Association (TAVA), launched originally in the 1930s in defense of the Cape African franchise, and the Transkei Organised Bodies (TOB), a more radical citizen-action group that Mbeki had helped to launch in February 1943 – and in the same year he was elected to the United Transkeian General Council, or Bunga, representing the district of Idutywa.

Inkundla played a major role in Mbeki's "political project," as Colin Bundy puts it.[15] Between 1939 and 1941, for example, Mbeki sought in vain to get ANC president general A. B. Xuma to pay greater attention to the "working classes" and endorse *Inkundla* as the official organ of Congress:

> The foremost duty in which Dr. Xuma should throw his whole weight is arousal of interest in both professional and working classes in ... the consolidation of a national organisation. He has to draw the professional classes into better understanding of the working classes and their conditions. To do that he will himself have to acquire full knowledge of such conditions, sympathise with them and make the struggle for the general advancement of their lot his goal. [Xuma would need] a newspaper that will further his policy – that is absolutely essential ... We hope he will pull us to himself.[16]

Mbeki also used the newspaper to promote the political agendas of the TAVA, the TOB and other local opposition groups. Peasant resistance to the government's conservation measures in rural Transkei was given coverage in *Inkundla*, and in 1946 half the Bunga members lost their council seats because they had supported the government's so-called Rehabilitation scheme. In addition, Mbeki (who represented the eastern Cape on the Anti-Pass Council) worked hard to raise support in the Transkei for the abortive national Anti-Pass Campaign initiated by the Communist Party in November 1943 and for the equally abortive Natives' Representative Council (NRC) boycott campaign initiated by the ANC at its annual conference in December 1946. The 1946 decision was effectively overturned at the 1947 conference, when communist and moderate nationalist members combined to outvote Youth League members in a resolution that confirmed Congress would contest the 1948 NRC elections.[17]

Mbeki was very representative of the "new Africanism" of his generation, even though he was not in sympathy with the Congress Youth League's Africanist ideology. The quest for African solidarity that would bridge class and ethnic differences, for African economic independence, for African political alliances that would not require alliances with non-Africans was a common theme in African nationalist rhetoric and in *Inkundla* in the 1930s and 1940s. Mbeki claimed the moral high ground for the newspaper that served African interests first. In 1941 he wrote:

> *Inkundla* ... is chained to no petty political, economic, social nor religious group. It primarily owes its allegiance to the African people. Its duty is to state the cause of the African people, interpret their feelings, guide them in moments of doubt, and defend them tooth and nail in critical moments. Without wavering in the least we have done this since the first birthday of this paper.[18]

Photo 22. Govan Archibald Mvunyelina Mbeki was the consummate journalist-activist as political editor of *Inkundla ya Bantu* (1939–43), a member of the *Guardian*'s editorial board and editor–branch manager of the Port Elizabeth office during the *New Age* era.

Inkundla launched a series of feature articles in the same year entitled "Gallery of African Heroes, Past and Present" that would be devoted to portraying "African men and women who in their lifetime devoted their attention to the advancement of the African cause." Readers were urged to contribute to this "African People's History in the Making," and an "African Heroes' Fund" was established to pay for the cost of publishing a photograph with each profile. Among those who were honored with a profile in *Inkundla* was D. D. T. Jabavu, the most prominent African liberal in the Cape of his generation.[19]

Bundy's characterization of Mbeki's years as editor of *Inkundla*, however, leaves a number of questions unanswered. Although Mbeki was cited on a few occasions as the editor of specific features (such as the "Gallery of African Heroes") or as the editor of the editorial page, the text itself indicates that the overall editor of *Inkundla* resided in Verulam (Natal), where the newspaper was published.[20] Bundy notes that Mbeki served as editor until May 1943, but the circumstances of his departure are cloudy.[21] The proprietors apparently waited more than a year, moreover, to appoint a new editor. The languages used (as well as the datelines of stories)

Table 14. *Languages used in news stories and advertising in* Inkundla ya Bantu, *April 1938–June 1944*

	English		Zulu		Xhosa	
Year (no. issues)	Stories	Ads	Stories	Ads	Stories	Ads
1938 (2)	19	3	75	4	11	1
1939 (2)	15	6	37	11	43	7
1940 (2)	28	4	45	11	52	5
1941 (2)	59	13	16	5	20	0
1942 (2)	34	11	24	3	58	0
1943 (2)	52	5	15	3	34	1
1944 (2)	57	17	12	3	10	0
Total no.	264	59	224	40	228	14
Total %	36.9	52.2	31.3	35.4	31.8	12.4

also suggest that Xhosa – the indigenous language of most Africans living in the Transkei region – did not dominate the news and advertising agenda during Mbeki's editorship (Table 14).

Mbeki was undoubtedly *Inkundla*'s political editor before Jordan Ngubane assumed control, writing most, if not all, of the editorial-page articles, but his editorial duties, in all probability, did not extend to the rest of the newspaper.[22] Despite Mbeki's tenure, moreover, circulation remained small, and there was little advertising in the newspaper.

It would appear that *Inkundla* was actually edited by Katamzi at Verulam. Of Katamzi, however, we know virtually nothing. He was a lay preacher (along with Bonga) in the Methodist Church and active in church affairs. We know he wrote and/or edited Xhosa-language news reports and commentaries in *Inkundla* when Ngubane was the editor. Katamazi was involved in African divisional politics in Natal, but apparently he was not committed to any particular point of view. "I never knew precisely where Katamzi stood," as Ngubane later put it, "but I could always talk him into taking a particular position."[23] Katamzi remained nominally responsible for *Inkundla* throughout the lifetime of the newspaper.

The Editorship of Jordan Ngubane (1944–1951)

Jordan Kush Ngubane was first offered the editorship of *Inkundla* in November 1943, but he did not assume the post officially until about June 1944.[24] Ngubane was the only paid editorial employee and the only full-time journalist, and he would claim many years later that there were no major disputes with the directors of Verulam Press during his tenure: "Verulam Press was not able to pay me the salary they said I deserved, [so] they gave me a free hand in the running of *Inkundla*." He was closer in "political thinking" to Motsemme than to Katamzi or the other directors. Motsemme was active in Location Advisory Board politics and was associated with the founding of the Congress Youth League in Natal. He was also the host of numerous political discussion groups Ngubane had attended in Durban

Photo 23. Jordan Kush Ngubane, editor of *Inkundla ya Bantu* (1944–51), served as a political officer in the KwaZulu "homeland" government from 1979 to his death in 1985.

in the late 1930s, and it was Motsemme who convinced him to take up the editorship of *Inkundla*.[25]

Ngubane was born in November 1917 and raised in a rural village called Ntwebebe near Ladysmith, Natal. His mother was illiterate, but his father, a police constable, had "some schooling and could write a little."[26] When Jordan, the eldest of four children, was 10 years old, his father bought two small plots of land and built a house. The family was moderately affluent by rural African standards: "We were comfortable as landowners. For black people. Most of our neighbors were poor."

Jordan's father, rather than his mother, was the dominant influence in his early life. An "honest, very just" man who "stood no nonsense," he was the son of tenant laborers on a white farm, and he "hated the experience to his death." He was determined that his children would not "go and work for white people," and Jordan never forgot this admonition. His father refused to go to church, and Jordan would regard himself in later years as "an agnostic." He would remark toward the end of his life that white missionaries were primarily responsible for "robbing the African of his rights."

Jordan's father was determined to give his children an education – "to raise us," as Jordan later put it, "to the black middle class ... the landowning class." Jordan proved to be an adept pupil at primary school, and he entered Adams College, a prestigious male secondary school founded by the American Board Mission for Africans in Natal, in 1933 at the age of 16. One of his fellow students was Anton Lembede, the intellectual driving force behind the Congress Youth League (CYL) in the early to mid-1940s. Among his teachers were Albert Lutuli and Z. K. Matthews, who became prominent ANC leaders in Natal and the Cape, respectively, during the 1940s. The principal of Adams was Edgar Brookes, a distinguished academic and liberal statesman, who was elected to parliament in 1937 as the Senate's Native Representative for Natal's African population, a position he retained for the next 15 years.[27] Ironically enough, Ngubane admired and looked up to Brookes, for whom he often translated at meetings with Zulu constituents, and the two remained in contact until Ngubane fled South Africa 25 years later.

Jordan had wanted to read law, but in his final year of study for the matriculation certificate (roughly equivalent then to the first year of an American university) his father died, and he decided to take a correspondence course in journalism. He also began contributing articles to *Ilanga lase Natal*, the Zulu-English newspaper in Durban. It was now owned by Bantu Press but still controlled by John L. Dube, the founding father of African politics in Natal, who invited young Jordan to join the staff as assistant editor when he graduated from Adams in 1938. *Ilanga*'s editor was Ngazana Lutuli, one of Albert Lutuli's uncles, and Jordan became well acquainted with the family, particularly with his former teacher. This friendship would become a factor in the careers of both men in the 1940s.

As assistant editor of *Ilanga*, Ngubane's primary responsibility was to cover African politics in Natal. The two dominant African political factions were headed by Dube (1871–1946)[28] and trade unionist and former Natal ICU leader A. W. G. Champion (1893–1975),[29] but their rivalry had essentially brought the nationalist movement in the province to a standstill by the early 1930s. Ngubane was among those reformers seeking to break the stalemate, but his first attempts proved unsuccessful. In 1939, Ngubane and a young teacher (and future editor of *Bantu World*) named Manasseh Tebatso ("M. T.") Moerane launched the National Union of African Youth to "challenge and destroy Championism and Dubeism and ultimately bring together the like-minded young men and women in the other provinces."[30] The Natal Education Department, however, soon pressured Moerane into withdrawing from the organization, and Ngubane could not afford to carry on alone for fear of antagonizing Dube, who was, after all, his *de facto* employer. The organization held only a few meetings and attracted perhaps "a dozen" people before it disbanded.[31]

After two years as assistant editor of *Ilanga*, Bantu Press sent Ngubane to Johannesburg in 1941 as assistant editor of *Bantu World*. Ngubane joined the Transvaal African Congress, but apparently there is no record of his political activities in the Transvaal until 1943, when he got involved in the formation of the Youth League. He was in contact with Anton Lembede, who had also moved to Johannesburg and joined Pixley Seme's law firm as a junior partner, and other young activists who would form the core of the new organization. Ngubane helped write the Congress Youth League's 1944 Manifesto, which set out the CYL's political objectives. Looking back on those years, Ngubane recalled "a militancy and urgency about the mood of my generation which had been absent in Natal... As the circle in which I moved in Johannesburg widened, I realized that the ferment in me was in everybody else."[32]

As a journalist with *Bantu World*, however, Ngubane was obliged to be careful about how he represented the ferment within African nationalist circles. Phrases like "white domination," "oppression" and "confrontation," for example, were apparently taboo. Bantu Press policy was designed to "discourage thinking on the fundamentals of conflict," according to Ngubane, who believed editor Selope Thema was "little more than a glorified clerk" and he himself "a leader-goat channelling African thought in the direction of accepting oppression."[33] The opportunity to join *Inkundla* as editor in mid-1944 came at the right time both for Ngubane (who apparently took a pay cut in accepting the position) and for the Congress Youth League.

In reading *Inkundla,* one finds no evidence that it was ever the official organ either of the ANC or the CYL, but, as we shall see, the proportion of news devoted to African nationalist politics did increase during Ngubane's tenure. He introduced two new political columns, entitled "What the People Say" and "Comment on Events,"[34] and *Inkundla* was an ardent mouthpiece for African nationalist news and opinion under his editorship.

Ngubane's perspective on the founding of the CYL is significant, because it served to highlight a role he would celebrate throughout his newspaper career:

> We wanted to re-organize the ANC; to destroy the hold of the Old Guard; to direct the thinking of our people in the direction of self-confidence and positive action. We wanted to teach them that emancipation would not be brought about by anybody other than themselves. We wanted to prepare them for the great sacrifices that would lie ahead of all of us. We desperately wanted them to feel that they belonged together... We wanted to interpret our people to themselves... We wanted to be sure that we lay [*sic*] the right foundations for a society where our people would be free to determine their lives.[35]

This is vintage Ngubane, the omniscient narrator who speaks of his peers as "we" and "our people" as "them." Kathy Eales has characterized him as the epitome of the petty bourgeois intellectual, a political liberal at heart, who commented on rather than participated in events. Ngubane himself later admitted: "While I wanted to oppose white domination, I had no desire to play a leading role. My real ambition was to be involved in a mind-versus-mind clash with the whites and beat them on that plane."[36]

The Congress Youth League actually represented several different, and ultimately contradictory, visions of the future in the mid- to late 1940s and early 1950s. The Africanist wing was represented by people like CYL president Anton Lembede (until his untimely death in 1947) and his successor Ashby Peter ("A. P.") Mda. Ngubane gave Lembede and likeminded associates considerable space to air their views in *Inkundla,*[37] but Lembede's brand of racial nationalism (even cooperation with Coloureds and Indians was "a fantastic dream")[38] was downplayed in the newspaper. African nationalism, Ngubane argued, was the cultural environment that would allow the individual to reach his or her fullest potential. Lembede was criticized for his "fanatical nationalism and his narrow conception of the South African nationhood" that focused on Africans only as a people rather than as individuals.[39] Ngubane believed that "every South African must be free to derive the maximum benefits from human civilisation and be free to make his fullest contribution to the welfare of the community."[40] Africans "accept all human beings as individual masterpieces of the Supreme Artist," he declared, and "want the greatest possible acquaintance with good things from other cultures," so long as African cultural advances are not "given an inferior place."[41]

The views of CYL members who moved essentially to the left in advocating links with the Communist Party of South Africa (CPSA) and a stronger commitment to the socialist alternative were also downplayed in *Inkundla*. They would include people like V. J. G. ("Joe") Matthews, eldest son of Cape ANC leader Z. K. Matthews, and a founder-member of the Fort Hare branch and a national CYL official in the early to mid- 1950s; William Nkomo, a left-wing student activist while in medical school at the University of the Witwatersrand during the 1940s and a founder-member of the CYL in the Transvaal; Godfrey M. Pitje, CYL president between 1949 and 1951; David W. Bopape, Youth League official in the Transvaal and a CPSA activist during the 1940s; and Massabalala ("M. B.") Yengwa, Youth League leader in Natal.

Eales believes Ngubane rejected the socialist alternative essentially because it threatened the economic position of the African petty bourgeoisie,[42] and this is confirmed by a reading of *Inkundla*. The communists were like the Afrikaner nationalists, Ngubane believed, in setting limits to individual rights. The communists "want to keep us a proletariat community while the other racial groups become the ruling hierarchy." Individual Africans would be limited "in the exercise of the God-given talents."[43]

Ngubane was actually more representative of the African elite of the previous generation than he was of the majority of Youth Leaguers in the 1940s. He did not advocate a South Africa for the Africans but a "united South Africa ... composed of Africans, Coloureds, Europeans and Indians, all finally equal under the law."[44] *Inkundla*, according to the credo that appeared on the editorial page during Ngubane's tenure, was "an independent, wholly African, non-party organ, serving the ideal of a Greater South Africa, where merit and not colour shall be the criterion of all values."[45]

Ngubane tended to view white racism as a problem that could be resolved if individuals were placed in the right "environment":

> We believe that Europeans, like every other human group, are more or less the product of their environment. Those who have been exposed to enlightening forces tend to come nearer the full appreciation of the human personality and those who have not been exposed to these civilizing influences cling to the jungle creed of "My race, right or wrong."[46]

White South Africans could still choose between "democratic rights" for all or "Fascism" for the few, but in the end democracy would triumph:

> Ultimately Africans will get democratic rights either as a result of a liberal outlook among White South Africans or after a series of upheavals. The static conditions can no longer continue. It is up to White South Africa to choose whether to pander to a Fascist outlook or whether it will take the course of progress towards a democratic South Africa with equal rights to all its people.[47]

It is little wonder, then, that many prominent members of the Youth League did not believe *Inkundla* represented their interests. Indeed, the newspaper carried very little news about Youth League activities between 1944 and 1946, and Ngubane was often critical of CYL policies in subsequent years.[48] Mda, Youth League president in 1948, said in a letter to Pitje:

> I hope the Youth Leaguers realize that we do not necessarily identify ourselves with all the views of the *Inkundla*. The *Inkundla* is not a Youth League paper, and it does not always express genuinely African Nationalistic views. Nonetheless, we urge the

> Leaguers to subscribe individually to the "*Inkundla*", because it is the only paper owned by Africans, and also because it gives publicity to the Youth League and it gives a wide platform to the forces of African Nationalism.[49]

Ngubane himself complained in a letter to Pitje, who would succeed Mda as president of the Youth League in December 1949, that members "simply make no use of [*Inkundla*] at all."[50] And Pitje would comment many years later: "I had never thought of *Inkundla* as a Youth League paper until Mda drew my attention to it... We were encouraged to think of it as the best available medium in which we could express ourselves."[51]

The Youth League, moreover, had already begun to moderate its ethnic Africanist ideology after Lembede's death in 1947 and especially after the National Party's election victory in 1948. A majority within the CYL would shift toward an accommodation with mainstream moderates in the ANC hierarchy, with non-African activists and with political opposition groups outside the ANC. One result, as noted in an earlier chapter, was the election of several African communists and Youth Leaguers to the ANC executive committee and the adoption of the CYL-crafted Programme of Action in 1949.

The gulf between Lembede-style Africanists and the left-wing majority within the Youth League had become virtually unbridgeable by the early 1950s. Joe Matthews in 1953, for example, would attack "those forces which under the cloak of protecting 'the sacred principle of African nationalism' have taken a right-wing reactionary path, hampered the mass struggles, sought to cut off contact with the masses, and maintain the League as a body in the air, periodically issuing political statements."[52] Prominent Youth Leaguers were now working seriously with the communists in developing new strategies of mass action. As Nelson Mandela, who succeeded Pitje as CYL national president in 1951, would observe years later:

> for many decades communists were the only political group in South Africa who were prepared to treat Africans as human beings and their equals; who were prepared to eat with us; talk with us, live with us and work with us. They were the only political group which was prepared to work with the Africans for the attainment of political rights and a stake in society. Because of this, there are many Africans who, today, tend to equate freedom with Communism.[53]

These shifts in CYL policies and activities in the late 1940s and early 1950s were not covered in any detail in *Inkundla*, in large part, it seems, because Ngubane was preoccupied with the byzantine world of African divisional politics in Natal. Indeed, Ngubane's involvement in these factional disputes may well have weakened the newspaper's effectiveness as a mobilizer of African political opinion at the national level. Ngubane claimed in later years that he had two main objectives when he took up the editorship. The first was to destroy the credibility of the old political elite–in particular, the faction led by Abner S. Mtimkulu,[54] who had long been Dube's deputy and was acting president of the Natal Native (now called African) Congress during the elder statesman's final years–and reintegrate the Natal Congress into the national movement with the help of the Youth League. The second was to break out of the Dube-Champion stalemate and promote Chief Albert Lutuli's candidacy as head of the ANC in Natal.[55]

There were numerous contradictions, however, between Ngubane's stated objectives many years after these events and the extent to which these objectives were articulated in *Inkundla*'s coverage of Natal politics between 1944 and 1951. On the one hand, Ngubane had to tread warily in attacking Mtimkulu, because *Inkundla*'s proprietors (Bonga, Katamzi and Motsemme) supported him just as they had supported Dube. On the other hand, before Ngubane became editor *Inkundla* had also supported Champion and had continually urged the two leaders to settle their differences.[56] The newspaper did not endorse Champion as its candidate for the presidency until a few months before he defeated Mtimkulu in the Natal Congress election of April 1945.

Ngubane later claimed that he persuaded Lutuli not to contest the election and that he told his superiors *Inkundla* should support Champion in order to give him "a platform from which he could discredit himself."[57] Eales argues that Ngubane "constructed this elaborate alibi ... to substantiate his claim that he had master-minded Lutuli's elevation to political prominence, and further, to dissociate himself from an embarrassingly conservative former president of the Natal Congress [Champion]." She concludes that Lutuli never intended to contest the April 1945 election; *Inkundla* played no significant role "in elevating Lutuli to political prominence in the late 1940s" and was not a significant factor in Lutuli's victory over Champion in the May 1951 Natal Congress election.[58]

The analysis of *Inkundla* during these years can confirm only the first part of Eales's reconstruction. Ngubane did indeed promote Champion unabashedly for the Natal Congress presidency in the 1945 elections, and there was no interest in Lutuli as an opposition candidate. But *Inkundla* also sought to position Lutuli as a political leader as early as 1946, and the newspaper apparently did play an important role in mobilizing support for Lutuli in the May 1951 Natal Congress election that catapulted the chief to national prominence in the ANC.

The Natal Youth League was launched in May 1944 with M. T. Moerane as president. Ngubane was on the provincial executive committee along with people like H. I. E. Dhlomo (the leading African novelist and playwright of his generation), Selby Ngcobo (a prominent figure in Natal educational and academic circles) and Congress Mbata (a schoolteacher and CYL national secretary briefly under Lembede).[59] Moerane was forced to resign in July–once again, his status as a government teacher was deemed to be incompatible with his holding a "political" office[60]–and he was succeeded by Dhlomo, the committee's secretary. *Inkundla*, however, seldom referred to the activities of the Natal CYL in subsequent years.

Champion and Dhlomo, "in defiance of the ... Natal African Congress,"[61] then established a Durban branch of the ANC. Xuma, who hoped to reestablish links with the Natal ANC and had trouble dealing with Dube, recognized Champion as the official organizer of Congress in Natal. Ngubane described Xuma's gesture as a "virtual vote of no-confidence" in the Dube faction. The "balance of power" had shifted to Champion, but the issue of control over the Natal Congress was "merely academic." The real issue was how to unify African politics in the province: "The duty before responsible men and women in Natal," as Ngubane put it, "is to see how best the two wings may be united to work as one strong body." Xuma then visited Durban in October 1944, apologized for endorsing Champion and echoed Ngubane in urging the two sides to cooperate with one another.[62]

Ngubane, however, joined the Durban branch in January 1945 and aligned himself officially with the Champion faction.[63] *Inkundla* declared that Champion's victory in the forthcoming Natal Congress election was "almost a certainty." The newspaper campaigned for the former trade union leader in the ensuing months: Champion was supported by "all congressmen who [were] anxious to forget the quarrels of the past and work for a united Congress, [and Champion was] strong enough to champion the people's cause." Champion was duly elected president of the Natal Congress in April 1945, and Ngubane, Dhlomo and Albert Lutuli were among those elected to the provincial executive committee. Xuma officially recognized Champion as president of the Natal Congress, and ANC membership in the province rose sharply, from 250 at the time when Champion was elected to 700 by the end of the year. Xuma visited Natal twice in 1946, prompting Ngubane to remark that the Natal ANC was enjoying an "unprecedented political peace."[64]

The peace, however, was soon tested when Dube finally died in 1946 and his seat on the NRC became vacant. Lutuli defeated ANC veteran Selby Msimang, an ally of Champion's, by a large margin in the subsequent by-election. Ngubane now began to position himself and *Inkundla* behind Lutuli and against Champion and Dube's successor Mtimkulu. He declared that "in a few years Lutuli would be Natal Keyman No. 1." Lutuli was "the embodiment of the policies of cooperation," a man of "very balanced judgement, broad sympathies and unimpeachable character," a "strict constitutionalist" who believed in "the democratic method of organised opinion as the only bulwark against further oppressive policies."[65] Following his NRC victory, Lutuli was appointed in February 1947 to the Native Education Advisory Board for Natal. On this occasion, *Inkundla* again declared that "Chief Lutuli is one of our coming leaders."[66]

Articles critical of Champion began to appear in the newspaper in the late 1940s.[67] Champion, who had vehemently opposed the CYL during the mid- to late 1940s, refused to accept the 1949 Programme of Action and provoked young militants in Natal by attacking the Youth Leaguers publicly as "enemies of Congress." Ngubane condemned Champion in the early months of 1950, for example, for trying to preserve the Natal Congress as "the private club of his good boys," for rejecting "any approach" that was "different from his" and for criticizing the 1949 Programme merely because it was "inimical to his infallible person." The Natal CYL saw little merit in "meeting government officials to have tea," like the "Championists." The Youth Leaguers were concerned with "organizing the people."[68]

Inkundla's attacks on Champion increased dramatically in the early months of 1951. His dislike of the CYL was "uncompromising Zuluistic hatred," and in a detailed criticism of the "tyranny of Championism," Ngubane pondered on how "strange" it was that a "political philosophy [could] cripple a people's life, stunt its spiritual growth, and make life empty for otherwise useful people." Instead of being a "team man," Champion "postulated that the will of the leader was supreme." Ngubane accused Champion of being "an old fashion isolationist," who did not understand "African nationalism."[69] Lutuli triumphed in the May 1951 Natal Congress election, and *Inkundla* continued to support his presidency until it ceased publication six months later.

The Programme of Action adopted by the ANC in December 1949 had called for the establishment of a national newspaper,[70] and the proprietors of Verulam Press in 1950 pressed Congress to adopt *Inkundla* as its official organ. But Congress did not have the financial resources, and by this time the newspaper was experiencing financial problems of its own. Verulam Press apparently had accumulated debts that could not be repaid, and the shareholders were finally forced to close down *Inkundla* in November 1951.[71]

Ngubane, who suffered from chronic asthma, had moved to a smallholding he had purchased at Rosetta (near Mooi River, Natal) in 1947 and edited *Inkundla* from there until the newspaper collapsed. He apparently spent the rest of the 1950s and early 1960s raising poultry at Rosetta.

Believing the communists had taken over the Youth League and now dominated the ANC, Ngubane became increasingly disenchanted with Lutuli and with Congress politics in general during the 1950s.[72] He rejected the Freedom Charter when it was drafted by the ANC and its allies in 1955 and sought new political alliances. First, he identified himself with policies advocated by white liberals like his old mentor Edgar Brookes, and he joined the multiracial Liberal Party in 1955. He was elected its national vice-president in 1958 and represented the party at conferences inside and outside South Africa.[73] Then he renewed his links with the Africanist wing of the African nationalist movement. He attended the inaugural convention of the Pan-Africanist Congress in April 1959, and, according to Gail Gerhart and Tom Karis, he became an advocate of the PAC position in later years.[74]

Ngubane's position in apartheid South Africa, however, was becoming untenable by the early 1960s. He was served with a banning order in 1963–incredibly enough, because he was deemed to be promoting hostility between the races and furthering the aims of communism–and in the same year he went into self-imposed exile. Ngubane settled first in Swaziland but in 1969 moved to the United States, where he lived for 10 years. He returned to South Africa in April 1979, having now adopted the credo of ethnic nationalism, and was appointed political officer in Gatsha Buthelezi's KwaZulu government. He remained a staunch supporter of Buthelezi and the Inkatha movement until his death in Ulundi (Zululand) two months before his sixty-ninth birthday in September 1985.[75]

Circulation and Advertising

In contrast to other alternative newspapers at the time, *Inkundla* was sold mainly by subscription. According to Ngubane, street sales even in places like Durban "were not very successful."[76] The subscription rate was 3 s. 6 d. a year between 1938 and 1943 (monthly), 7 s. 6 d. a year between 1944 and 1947 (fortnightly), and 11 s. a year (6 s. for six months) between 1947 and 1951 (weekly and fortnightly). These rates would have been high for lower-or even middle-ranked members of the African petty bourgeoisie, and they were also high when compared with the socialist press in the 1940s.[77]

Nevertheless, circulation had reached about 7,000 by October 1946, and *Inkundla* was the only African nationalist publication at the time with an arguably national readership. Circulation statistics for African newspapers are rare and unreliable, but in the history of the independent African political press this figure is second only to that for the ICU organ in the 1920s, the *Workers' Herald*.[78]

Advertising in *Inkundla* was insignificant until Ngubane was appointed editor in mid-1944, and the newspaper became at least nominally associated with the ANC Youth League. Under his editorship, the proportion of advertising in the newspaper increased dramatically (Table 15).

As with *Bantu World* and the *Guardian*, in the analysis of *Inkundla* an attempt was made to measure the relative percentage of consumer advertising intended for the black petty bourgeoisie by making an arbitrary but consistent distinction between essential and nonessential goods and services promoted by white entrepreneurs. Goods and services promoted by black (African, Coloured, Indian) entrepreneurs (irrespective of whether the items advertised were essential or nonessential) and promotional advertisements were enumerated in separate categories (Table 16).

Table 15. *Advertising as a proportion of news–advertising units in* Inkundla ya Bantu *before and during Ngubane's editorship*

	Ad units	% of total ad units
Before: 1938–June 1944	113	13.6
During: July 1944–November 1951	537	37.3

Table 16. *Formal advertising content in* Inkundla ya Bantu (% *of advertising units*)

Category	%
White businesses: Nonessential goods and services	28.2
White businesses: Essential goods and services	21.2
Black goods and services (essential and nonessential)	33.1
Promotional	17.5

Note: Inkundla ya Bantu had 650 advertising units, or 28.6% of the news–advertising units.

Food, clothing (including shoes and boots) and furniture of all kinds in *Inkundla* were classified as essential, even though some goods, such as wedding dresses and veils, tuxedos and other luxury clothes, were targeted at an elite. Health and health supplements (mainly for infants and children), in the form of pills, tonics, elixirs and powders, were also regarded as essential, as were bicycles, tools and household goods and various miscellaneous items (like matches and polishers) deemed to be necessities. Nonessential goods included musical instruments, watches, jewelery, books, stationery, cameras, gramophones and used cars.

Although white advertising constituted about 50 percent of the advertising units in the test sample, the number devoted to nonessentials was only about 7 percent more than the number devoted to essentials in the test sample. *Inkundla* did not seem to attract white advertisers, moreover, as moderate African nationalist newspapers like *Imvo Zabantsundu* had done in the 1920s or as even militant nonpartisan socialist newspapers like the *Guardian* did in the 1940s. There were only a few services for either essential or nonessential goods (e.g., car repair garages, dry-cleaning establishments, pharmacists and insurance companies). There were few cigarette advertisements, a surprising omission, given the fact that cigarette advertisements were a major source of white advertising in other alternative newspapers in the 1940s and 1950s. Even though white entrepreneurs had a virtual monopoly on the production of African-style beer outside the reserves, apperently no advertisements for beer were carried. Church groups were Verulam Press's main customers, Bonga, Katamzi and Motsemme were devout Methodists, and one or more may have been involved in the African temperance movement.[79]

Inkundla's advertising content clearly served as a vehicle for the black petty bourgeoisie. No other African newspaper examined before the apartheid era devoted such a large percentage of advertising units to the struggling black entrepreneur. Despite Ngubane's well-known antipathy to Indians and the strident African nationalist tone of many of the newspaper's editorials and essays, it is interesting to note that in the test sample a majority of these advertisers were Indian. The huge growth in this subcategory, moreover, occurred under Ngubane's editorship.

Real estate agents, undertakers, tailors, shoemakers and cobblers, bootmakers, printers (including Verulam Press), signwriters, picture framers, hairdressers, owners of restaurants, dry-cleaning firms, shoe and furniture stores, tobacco sellers, herbalists, grocers, mail-order merchants, general store owners, hawkers, and even songwriters and the owners of an Indian cinema advertised in *Inkundla*. Whereas white advertisers were selling used cars, black advertisers were urging readers to come to them to learn how to drive a car. In the vernacular pages, in particular, there were advertisements for livestock sales and land sales, notices about African credit and cooperative societies and agricultural shows (especially in the Transkei and Zululand), and occasionally even classified advertisements, such as the following from Shaka's Kraal (near Stanger, on Natal's northern coast): "All those with wife problems should contact Bethlehem Home... Satisfaction guaranteed!"[80]

News Agenda

Inkundla was the last major independent African political journal established before the apartheid era. The newspaper appeared as a monthly between April 1938 (the publication date is missing from most monthly editions) and 30 December 1943, as a fortnightly between 17 January 1944 and 13 February 1947, as a weekly between 20 February 1947 and 15 April 1950, and as an irregular fortnightly again between 15 April 1950 and 3 November 1951. *Inkundla* averaged eight pages an issue between 1938 and 1944, and six to eight pages an issue (depending on the size and number of advertisements) between 1945 and 1949. The newspaper was essentially six pages for the last two years of its life. *Inkundla* started as a three-column newspaper and changed to four columns in November 1943, just before it became a fortnightly. The newspaper shifted from four to six columns in October 1945 and remained at six columns until November 1951.

Sotho was added after Ngubane took over as editor, but English was clearly the dominant medium of communication in news stories, and especially advertising copy, between 1944 and 1951(Table 17).

News stories in English comprised an average of 52 percent of the news items and advertisements in English an average of 80 percent of the advertising items in the July 1944–November 1951 test sample. News stories in Zulu comprised an average of 26 percent and news stories in Xhosa an average of 20 percent of the news items. Whereas Zulu advertisements comprised an average of almost 14 percent of the advertising items, only an average of about 4 percent were in Xhosa during this period.

Ngubane himself later claimed that he promoted English over vernacular stories because he thought it would attract the kind of African readers he was seeking – the "serious young person," especially at university, who was "politically conscious." He believed most *Inkundla* readers, when he was editor, were "young members of the Youth League." Ngubane wrote political commentaries in Zulu, as well as English, using the pseudonym "Khanyisa" (sometimes spelled "Kanyisa"). When he attacked the political views of specific personalities, he used the "secret" pseudonym "Peregrine of the Crossroads," and when he wrote general news stories he often employed the pseudonym "Twana."[81]

Table 17. *Languages used in news stories and advertising in* Inkundla ya Bantu, *July 1944–November 1951*

	English		Zulu		Xhosa		Sotho	
Year (no. issues)	Stories	Ads	Stories	Ads	Stories	Ads	Stories	Ads
1944 (1)	42	7	8	2	12	0	3	0
1945 (3)	72	14	27	2	16	3	0	0
1946 (4)	102	69	27	12	22	3	0	0
1947 (4)	88	97	31	13	51	8	8	8
1948 (4)	69	97	46	23	16	1	0	1
1949 (4)	45	81	21	10	25	3	0	0
1950 (3)	27	38	60	10	27	2	0	0
1951 (3)	29	27	18	2	12	0	0	1
Total no.	474	430	238	74	181	20	11	13
Total %	52.4	80.1	26.3	13.8	20.0	3.7	1.2	2.4

Like the other African nationalist newspapers subjected to quantitative analyses, *Inkundla*'s news agenda clearly favored Category A, general-interest news, over all other categories (Figure 3).

Ngubane claimed toward the end of his life that as editor he had increased *Inkundla*'s political content dramatically and achieved a personal goal of employing the newspaper "as the communications medium which would put the Youth League on the political map."[82] The content analysis, however, paints a more ambiguous picture (Figure 4). During Ngubane's tenure as editor, Category A, general-interest news, did decline as a proportion of the news agenda by almost 20 percent, and Category C, political and trade union news, rose by almost 10 percent, but general-interest news remained the dominant news category. As anticipated, Category B, white political, economic and social news, and Category D, foreign news, formed a relatively small portion of the news agenda. Thus there were significant shifts in the percentages of two news categories (A and C), but the ranking of the categories themselves did not change.

General-interest News

Inkundla was arguably a community newspaper for most readers. The vernacular pages, in particular, were full of general-interest news reports from correspondents in places like Port Elizabeth and the nearby African township of New Brighton, Port Alfred and Rhini (Grahamstown), west of the Fish River; East London, Queenstown, Fort Beaufort, Lovedale and Alice in the Ciskei region; Umtata, Idutywa, Xalanga, Mount Ayliff, St. John's, Maclear, Mount Frere, Palmerton, Tsomo, Lusikisiki, Bizana, Umzimkhulu and several other settlements in the Transkei; Matatiele and Kokstad in Natal–East Griqualand; Pietermaritzburg and the nearby African community of Edendale, as well as Ladysmith and several smaller settlements in southern Natal; and as far north as Nqutu and Nongoma in Natal–Zululand. *Inkundla* also had correspondents in Amanzimtoti (Adams College), Inanda, Tongaat, Stanger and other towns along the Natal coast, in addition to those reporting from Durban and Verulam.

Figure 3. Domestic and foreign news in *Inkundla ya Bantu* (in %). Percentages are calculated by dividing the number of story units in each category by the total number of story units. News refers to all story units, including illustrations and informal advertisements classified as news. Formal advertisements are excluded. *Inkundla ya Bantu* had 1,620 story units.

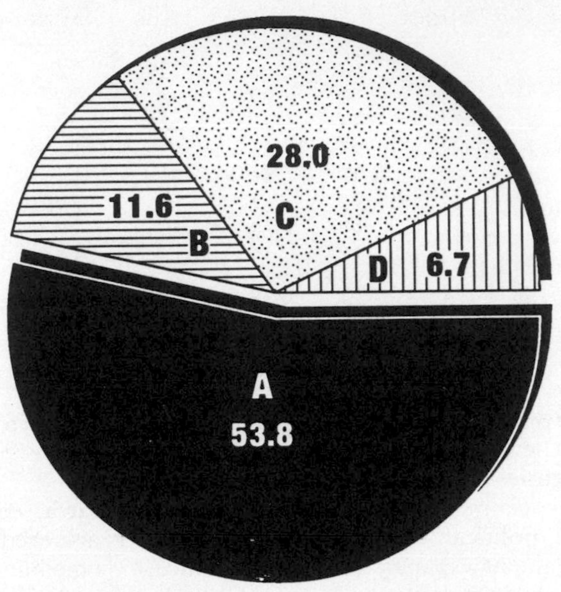

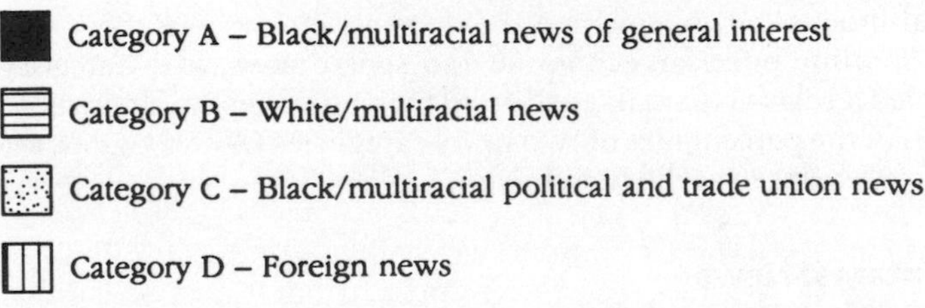

These reports focused in the main on the everyday activities of the local petty bourgeoisie, and Category A reflected their interests and concerns (Table 18).

In many respects, *Inkundla*'s general-interest news profile during the 1940s was a reflection of *Imvo Zabantsundu*'s general-interest news profile during the 1920s. The life cycles of the petty bourgeoisie were recorded essentially in their school and church activities (A.1) and in other social activities (A.2). Educational news was a dominant feature, which is understandable when it is remembered that teachers comprised the largest component in the Youth League.[83] There were reports about teachers' associations and conferences, teachers' promotions, examination results, new courses, school fees, student bursaries (grants and scholarships), notices providing information about mission boarding schools and various types of correspondence courses (such as a regular notice in the later 1940s for a home economics course). Numerous stories highlighted African achievements in tertiary

Figure 4. News in *Inkundla ya Bantu* before and during Ngubane's editorship (in %). Part 1, Before Ngubane's editorship, April 1938–June 1944; Part 2, During Ngubane's editorship, July 1944–November 1951. Percentages are calculated by dividing the number of story units in each category by the total number of story units. News refers to all story units, including illustrations and informal advertisements classified as news. Formal advertisements are excluded. *Inkundla* before Ngubane's editorship had 716 story units. *Inkundla* during Ngubane's editorship had 904 story units.

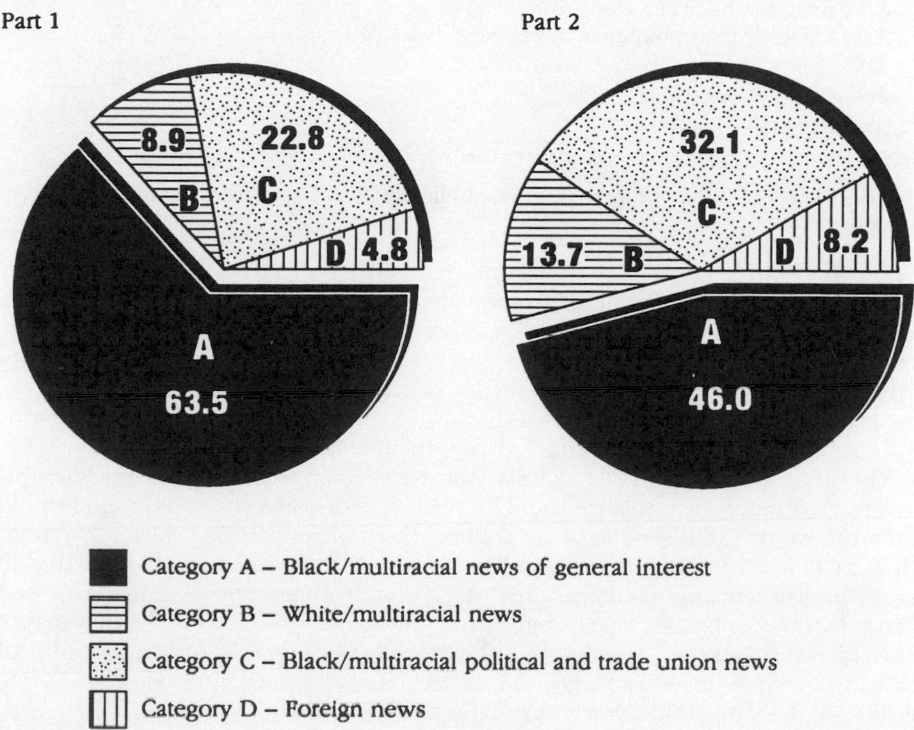

education: Natal University College was a regular news item in the mid- to late 1940s, and correspondents noted "with pride... the ever-increasing numbers of Africans attaining University education."[84] Activities considered detrimental to the social status of the mission-educated elite were also criticized.[85]

Religious news included church (and temperance) events, the activities of clergy and prominent lay members, dedications of various kinds, and services celebrating events in the religious calendar, such as Christmas and Easter. The church, as one writer put it, had a "divine mandate" to lead South Africa.[86] Mission and mainstream separatist churches recognized by the government – such as the African Methodist Episcopal Church, Presbyterian Church of Africa, Bantu Methodist Church and Zulu Congregational Church – received extensive coverage, whereas unrecognized separatist churches – such as the many Zionist churches – received little coverage. Nevertheless, Africans were urged to get involved in independent churches, because they were a training ground for leadership and a forum for discussion on all issues affecting African life.[87]

Table 18. *Categories A and D news in* Inkundla ya Bantu *(% of story units)*

Category	%
A. Black/multiracial news of general interest (871 units)	53.8
A.1 Education and religion	9.0
A.2 Society	27.5
A.3 Sports	1.7
A.4 Living conditions in urban areas	3.0
A.5 Living conditions in rural areas	2.8
A.6 Independent economic activities	3.3
A.7 Crime and accidents	0.8
A.8 Other: Promotional and miscellaneous[a]	5.7
D. Foreign news (108 units)	6.7

[a] "Miscellaneous" includes homilies, a few public notices and advertisements disguised as news.

Society news was essentially news about the personalities, activities and achievements of the petty bourgeoisie–dances, beauty contests, fund-raisers, school reunions and farewells, parties, receptions, art exhibits, concerts and school eisteddfods, speeches and meetings, births, baptisms, weddings and accounts of the dead in the form of death notices, lists of the bereaved, tributes to the dead, funerals and memorial services, and even a few reports of suicides.[88]

The activities of women's *zenzele* (self-help) groups and *manyano* (church) groups were regularly publicized, and there were occasional columns on household hints for women, but women were subordinated at numerous levels in the text. Most newsworthy activity revolved around men, and women rarely appeared in social news except as homemakers and caregivers. In an interview Ngubane himself stated, without a hint of irony, that only "young men" wrote for the newspaper when he was the editor.[89] The absence of women in photographs of African political leaders, for example, was so obvious that it elicited comments in *Inkundla*. As one writer put it, "The nation deserves to know and see them."[90]

Nevertheless, general-interest news stories painted a rich tapestry of ordinary African life in the urban and rural areas, especially the African reserves. There were several reports comparing various ethnic groups, mainly in the Xhosa-speaking eastern Cape and in Zulu-speaking Natal, in the test sample. The activities of various royal lineages (especially the Zulu royal family) were covered, chiefs were praised and criticized, events of the precolonial and conquest period were commemorated. Calls to modernize various customs and rituals–such as *lobola* (brideprice), female initiation rites, social etiquette for women, inheritance laws or beliefs such as witchcraft[91]–invariably triggered vigorous discussion, especially in the vernacular pages.

The voices of protest were embedded in the structures of these narratives. The plight of African teachers, faced with overcrowded classrooms, breakdowns in discipline, severe shortages in food for students and in essential equipment for the schools, low wages, poor job mobility and the declining status of teachers in the community, was the subject of numerous complaints. *Inkundla* regularly covered the meetings of the Cape African Teachers' Association, one of the more militant of the teachers' bodies during this period, even though CATA affiliated with the All-African Convention in 1948 and became part of the Unity movement.[92]

Mission-educated Africans, by the 1930s and 1940s, were very ambivalent in their support of mission churches, condemning denominational rivalries that threatened the schools as well as the churches. These concerns were expressed mainly in the vernacular by correspondents in the various communities served by *Inkundla*: "They stuff our children with religion and very little else... Their thinking is controlled and limited... we need to take control of the education of our children."[93] In an article entitled "Interested but Dishonest," for example, the missionaries were even blamed for the low wages paid to skilled African workers:

> Most of the Natives learnt their trades in the missionary schools or Colleges, but... missionary propaganda is the very body which keeps low the wages of the Bantus in the Union. They claim to know all our needs. Their representation about the African state of living is claimed as correct by the Authorities. The Native must be a Christian, but if a person's income is below the living standard, how can he be expected to be a faithful Christian?[94]

Rivalry among mission denominations generated many letters to the editor. Correspondents appealed for church unity – for one African church, led by Africans, to fight hunger, disease and illiteracy – and for funds to support independent African schools.[95] The African church's subordinate position in the social order was an underlying theme in this correspondence: "Why are our people from the traditional to the most educated more afraid and respectful of the white people than they are of God?"[96] The impact of the early apartheid regime on the churches, moreover, was not lost on *Inkundla*'s readers: "The new Boer government has stepped up the surveillance and persecution of Independent Churches. It is time for the ministers to band together and fight the system."[97]

There was very little sports news (A.3) until the last year or so of the newspaper's existence, despite the fact that organized sports in African communities were developing rapidly during the 1940s and 1950s. Sports stories focused mainly on soccer and boxing, followed by cricket and rugby, the last two restricted to the eastern Cape in terms of news coverage. Crime and accidents (A.7), common news categories in the commercial press, were virtually ignored. The newspaper's attitude towards crime, especially in the early years of apartheid, can be gauged from the following comment on jails in rural areas: "The government is making sure that wherever an African is a jail is not far away."[98]

Two potentially major subcategories – Living and working conditions in urban and rural areas (A.4, A.5) – formed a surprisingly small portion of general-interest news in this sample. The ANC did not have a Programme of Action for the workers and peasants, although some Youth League branches attempted to provide one in the early 1950s in places such as East London, Port Elizabeth and the adjacent Ciskei reserve.[99]

Inkundla's coverage of African conditions in urban areas was more noticeable in the years when Ngubane was editor. Complaints from local correspondents focused on topics such as public transportation, public health (e.g., the high incidence of tuberculosis in African areas located in or near cities such as Durban, Port Elizabeth and East London), poor wages, everyday harrassment by the police and numerous other white authority figures,[100] lack of housing (some coverage of the growth of squatter communities in Johannesburg, Durban and East London)[101] and the lack of opportunity to buy land. A continual source of irritation was the virtual absence of amenities in the segregated African townships – lack of roads, street lights, public sanitation facilities, recreation facilities and the presence of the beerhall problem.[102] Readers also protested whenever a government official at the local or national level raised the issue of forcing African women to carry passes, a threat that was eventually carried out when the pass laws were extended to include African women in 1952.[103]

Inkundla's coverage of African conditions in rural areas tended to focus on the eastern Cape (especially the Transkei) and Natal–Zululand. Drought (which occurred intermittently throughout the 1940s), poor harvests and lack of food, the diseases of an impoverished peasantry, factional fighting, lack of land and disputes over reserve boundaries (in the Cape and Natal) and appeals for aid were common themes in these news reports. When there was rain, the readers expressed their thanks to God. When the government, on rare occasions, sent in food, they thanked the government.[104] Attempts by the Native Affairs Department to limit livestock and control land use in the African reserves received a mixed review in *Inkundla*. Although overstocking was acknowledged, the measures were not "impartial," because they did not apply to whites or the African elite. They applied only to the African poor, who would become "even poorer" when they were forced to give up what little stock they had.[105]

Inkundla rhetoric stressed self-reliance and economic independence, but African entrepreneurs (A.6) received relatively little space in the news agenda. Nevertheless, there were articles about the importance of starting African businesses and supporting African businessmen as "the Indians support one another."[106] African goods and services were promoted in news reports as well as advertising. Stories on this topic from correspondents in rural areas were concerned mainly with African farmers' associations, cooperative credit societies, agricultural shows, handicraft demonstrations, stock sales and land sales (in the reserves where Africans were allowed to buy land).[107] Stories on this topic from correspondents in urban areas were concerned mainly with informal-sector activities, since Africans were virtually denied access to South Africa's formal economic sector. They included public transportation (owners of buses and taxis), food, clothing and furniture. (There was an extensive network of African traders, shopkeepers, petty-commodity producers and sellers in cities like Durban and Johannesburg by the 1940s.)

Stories promoting the newspaper itself (A.8) comprised more than 5 percent of the news agenda. *Inkundla* was filled with notices to correspondents, appeals for subscribers and advertisers, calls to "Support Your Own Newspaper" in various languages, letters from readers praising the newspaper and offering birthday greetings, and also stories celebrating newspaper anniversaries: "*Inkundla ya Bantu* is the paper you can call your own because it is owned by Africans, edited by Africans and printed by Africans and depends for its growth on African support." Ngubane himself was very conscious of the role that *Inkundla* played in the African community:

- The functions of a paper owned entirely by the African people go far beyond giving and interpreting news; they cover the difficult job of having to give directions for courses of development and also, as far as possible, to lead opinion, in the hope that in the course of time the people will see their problems in their proper perspective and in that way find good and effective solutions to them.

- We want to do all in our power reasonably to enable those who do not see eye to eye with us to have their point of view given the widest publicity possible in this journal because permanent settlements can be arrived at only when both sides of any question are presented.[108]

Educated Africans were criticized on several occasions, especially in the vernacular pages, for ignoring the African press: "Our literate people would rather read a White newspaper than ours ... Our papers are our forum. That is where we share our thoughts as a race. Wise up! Being literate does not make you less African!"[109]

Although foreign news (D) occupied a relatively insignificant niche in the news agenda, the major events of the period were covered in the vernacular as well as English. News about World War II was intermittent in the test sample and focused mainly on African interests – whether African men would be allowed to bear arms; care packages put together for African soldiers by African women's groups; money collected from Africans for the war effort; accounts by African soldiers of what they had seen and experienced in North Africa, the Middle East or Europe. British politics and the British royal family, U.S. politics, the American president and the African-American community, Pan-African activities, Cold War conflicts[110] and the twilight of the European colonial era[111] were common foreign news themes.

Many stories were written with a South African angle. In colonial Rhodesia, as in South Africa, for example, whites allegedly did not want Indians in their residential areas.[112] The creation of the Jewish state of Palestine was a story with special implications for the Africans of South Africa:

> the Jews have been given Palestine but their problems persist. They cannot occupy their land because the English are fighting them. The Arabs and Moslems are shooting at them. Here in South Africa they are accused of being communists and tricky merchants. We have a lot in common with the Jews. In parliament they are always on our side. We need to form strong ties with Jews and fight together for freedom. It is in our national interest.[113]

Reports of mutual slaughter of Muslims and Hindus after the partitioning of India was another story with implications for the African community:

> Indians are killing one another but according to eyewitnesses the carnage is nowhere near the numbers reported in White papers ... No matter how few the deaths in India [however] they are still significant because they remind us of our own situation. They [Indians] have religious reasons, we have tribal. Let India be a lesson.[114]

The visit by King George VI and his family to South Africa in early 1947 was a cause for great rejoicing among many Africans, who still viewed the British sovereign as their ultimate protector.[115] Another news event in 1947 was the trip by Xuma and other members of a protest group to the headquarters of the United Nations in New York City, where the world body was alerted for the first time to the grievances of the black population in South Africa.

White Authoritarian Context

The boundaries of public discourse in *Inkundla*, as in other protest newspapers, were ultimately established by the ruling culture. Dissent in part was framed in reaction and response to white political, economic and social events (Table 19).

There were relatively few stories concerned directly with European affairs in *Inkundla*, but news involving those who ruled South Africa was what one might

Table 19. *Category B news in* Inkundla ya Bantu (*% of story units*)

Category	%
B. White/multiracial news (188 units)	11.6
B.1 Political, legislative and administrative	8.3
B.2 Economic and social	3.3

expect in an African protest newspaper. There was coverage of the parliamentary crisis that split the United Party over South Africa's entry into World War II on the side of Britain and her allies and brought Smuts to power. *Inkundla* supported South Africa's war efforts:

> As no other war known to human history, it is a struggle against the law of the jungle ... If Germany wins then the freedom of the individual as we know it, or even as an ideal to which all subject races are aspiring, will disappear ... If the Allies win, then peace on earth and good will among all men of all races will be possible.[116]

But this support was not without qualification. *Inkundla* criticized African leaders, for example, for public statements lauding these war efforts: "Our own problems are as fierce as those on the European Western Front. Sometimes there is wisdom in silence."[117]

Inkundla supported the United Party during the war because it feared Afrikaner nationalism and hoped Prime Minister Smuts would "protect the African from the like of [J. B. M.] Hertzog, [Daniel F.] Malan and [Nicolaas C.] Havenga," the leaders of the National Party.[118] Smuts had also indicated to African political leaders that he would respond to at least some of their grievances. Thus *Inkundla* was generally sympathetic to Smuts when covering his speeches, recording cabinet reshuffles and reporting on debates in parliament on matters important to Africans. The newspaper carried an irregular Zulu column during these years called "Ezokotha Ebandla" (Fireside Chat), presumably modeled on the U.S. radio talks made famous by President Roosevelt. It focused on domestic politics from an African point of view.[119]

White trusteeship, the ideology of the ruling United Party and its English-speaking supporters, however, was no longer acceptable to African nationalists in the 1940s. Smuts had described the promise of ultimate equality under trusteeship "as the only Christian approach to the thorny question of black and white relationships,"[120] but *Inkundla* saw it as "slavery for which a philosophy is being sought." Ngubane spoke for his generation in demanding an end to this rhetoric: "Trusteeship means that the white race has undertaken to guide the African people on their path to full and equal citizenship. In practice, however, it emerges as a cunning doctrine invented to act as a good cloak for the domination of the African people."[121]

The honeymoon for Smuts was over, at least for some readers, even before the war ended: "Now that the war is almost over, the government has turned with a vengeance to the business of controlling the African."[122] Xhosa readers were told, in September 1945, "It's time for the African to take matters into their own hands ... Fight for your rights because nobody else will."[123] Less than a year later the mood remained somber: "Peace has broken out everywhere except in South Africa where the Government is preparing fresh assaults on what is left of our civil rights."[124]

Inkundla's attitude to the "liberal" English-speaking whites in Natal was always ambivalent. Zulu readers were told: "It is a myth and untruth that the English speaking Natal Whites treat Africans more humanely than Boers."[125] When the specter of a South African republic first loomed, after the National Party came to power in 1948, Ngubane toyed with the idea, even though his comments were probably not in harmony with the sentiments of the majority of his readers. The statement was directed at English-speaking South Africans, who "seem to fear that the British Link is preventing South Africa from becoming a Nazi State":

> The Crown might stand for ... precious things sentimentally to the English-speaking South African. But it does not stand for precious things in so far as the overwhelming majority of Afrikaners as well as Africans go. On the contrary, it might very well symbolise their humiliation. In these circumstances, why should they not, in their own country, be free from the tyranny of (even) symbols? ... The English minority has for a long time forced its own sentiments on the majority of the population ... it has done exactly what it accuses the Nationalists of doing now ... If Dr. Malan [the prime minister] wants a Republic, at least on this issue ... he will find for once that the majority of his countrymen of all races are with him.[126]

Nevertheless, the "Boers" (the term *Inkundla* and other black protest newspapers usually used when referring to members of the National Party) were attacked much more vehemently than English-speaking whites. As one Zulu writer put it in 1940, "There is nothing as annoying to an African as listening to the Boers ... discussing ways of getting rid of Africans."[127] When the National Party under Malan came to power in 1948, the English and vernacular news pages were full of stories of the government's "segregation" plans, of the expanding apartheid bureaucracy at the local level and of the way "separate development" was being justified in the Afrikaans churches and press and in government circles.[128] The leaders of the apartheid regime were compared with the Nazis: "Hitler started war hoping that at the end of hostilities he will have peace and all the land and respect he craved. Afrikaners are doing the same thing ... with the hope of achieving peace at the end. We know that in the end it's not going to work."[129]

Inkundla's tone became more urgent as the legislative framework of *apartheid* unfolded: "There is widespread panic in our community ... Boers can do and say what they want with Africans, but Africans dare not complain."[130] On the eve of a new parliamentary session under the Malan government in 1951, the newspaper's mood was somber: "We are watching with apprehension what is in store for us."[131]

The economic and social framework of white authoritarian rule (B.2) was virtually ignored in *Inkundla*, as it was in other protest newspapers. There were very few stories on the South African economy in the test sample. White-owned mines, factories and farms were not included in the news agenda except on rare occasions, usually when the focus of the story was on African labor or when African land was taken over by whites.[132] White churches, schools, sporting groups and even the activities of white missionary agencies were also ignored unless they played a direct role in African life, as in the case of mission-controlled education. Unlike the African press during the interwar period, *Inkundla* carried few stories about white liberal organizations involved in interracial dialogue of any kind.[133]

Black Politics and Trade Unions

There was certainly no dearth of stories concerned with black politics and trade unions (Category C) in *Inkundla* over the lifetime of the newspaper (Table 20). The only other African nationalist newspaper in this study with a higher percentage of Category C news stories was the ICU newspaper *Workers' Herald,* with 40.6 percent, although most political news in that newspaper was concerned with the trade union and its leaders.[134] *Inkundla* was also one of the few African nationalist newspapers before the bannings in 1960 to place some stress on confrontation and consciousness raising in opposing white rule in South Africa.

Ngubane's claim that the newspaper became a more militant ANC mouthpiece under his editorship has some validity, as the quantitative analysis revealed when focusing on coverage of Category C, political and trade union news, before and during Ngubane's editoriship (Table 21). The portion of the news agenda devoted to the ANC and allied bodies rose about 10 percent under Ngubane's tenure, while the portion devoted to African political bodies sponsored and controlled by the government fell about 8 percent. The explanation lies at least partly in the fact that a majority of this news was concerned with Transkei politics until 1944, and in addition to Mbeki it seems there were more correspondents from this region than from Natal. Thus *Inkundla* under Mbeki contained more news on the Transkei Bunga, for example, on local/district councils and on chiefs in the Transkei. The central government's African policy in the rural areas before the apartheid era, from land tenure and conservation schemes to local government, also focused on the Ciskei and Transkei reserves, which were front-runners in rural resistance politics during the 1940s.

The speeches and election campaigns of white Native Representatives like Margaret Ballinger (who represented Africans in the eastern Cape in the House of Assembly) and Edgar Brookes were a staple in the vernacular as well as the English-language pages of the newspaper under both the Mbeki and Ngubane editorships.[135] Even more important were Africans competing for seats and commenting on the Natives' Representative Council. In fact, the NRC boycott dispute was a highlight of political news in 1947. Even though Ngubane did not support those who wanted to boycott the NRC, he and other commentators were very critical of its activities. The NRC was now perceived to be ineffective and without power to make a difference in the lives of the African people.[136]

The rebirth of the African trade union movement in South Africa was evident in *Inkundla*'s coverage of black as opposed to white-dominated multiracial unions. As one Xhosa correspondent put it; "Whites could never have the interest of the Black worker at heart... A wolf cannot look after the lambs."[137] Bundy suggests that the mobilization of workers in trade unions formed a significant theme in Mbeki's writings during the early 1940s,[138] but stories concerned with this topic comprised an insignificant portion of the news agenda during the years of his editorship. The percentage of trade union stories was actually higher when Ngubane was editor, prompted in large part by labor unrest during the mid- to late 1940s.

> When workers have organised themselves and "strike" for better wages or employment conditions, they do so with the intention of making their employer accede to their demands because if he does not, the stoppage of work will bring about a loss in profits. As employers fear nothing on earth [so much] as a falling-off in profits, the well-organised strike remains the only effective weapon in the hands of the worker. In other words by exerting organised pressure on the employer, the workers make him suffer loss until he is compelled to give in to their demands.[139]

Table 20. *Category C news in* Inkundla ya Bantu *(% of story units)*

Category	%
C. Black/multiracial political and trade union news (453 units)	28.0
C.1 Personalities and organizations	18.0
C.2 Confrontation and consciousness	10.0

Table 21. *Category C news in* Inkundla ya Bantu *before and during Ngubane's editorship (% of Category C)*

	Before: 1938–1944 (163 story units)	During: 1944–1951 (290 story units)
C.1 Personalities and organizations	61.4	66.2
C.1.1 Government-controlled groups	27.0	19.3
C.1.2 ANC and allied groups	24.5	34.8
C.1.3 NEUM, AAC and allied groups	7.4	3.1
C.1.4 Other political groups (e.g., SAIC, NIC, CPSA, ADP) and trade unions	2.5	9.0
C.2 Confrontation and consciousness	38.6	33.8
C.2.1 Consciousness	38.0	17.2
C.2.2 Confrontation	0.6	16.6

Confontation and Consciousness

Inkundla's news agenda placed far more emphasis on the crucial C.2 subcategory, confrontation and consciousness, than that of any other African nationalist newspaper subjected to a content analysis. Before 1944, *Inkundla* focused almost entirely on consciousness-raising in the form of appeals for self-reliance and unity.[140] These appeals were voiced on all kinds of occasions but especially at ethnic anniversaries or commemorative events recalling the past like Dingaans Day, Ntsikana Remembrance Day, Fingo Emancipation Day and Mendi Memorial Day. Correspondents continually condemned the factionalism of African politics and urged reconciliation. They called on Africans to forget tribal differences and work together for the "unity of the race." They commented on the "poverty of leadership" in African political bodies, and they sought to raise a national moral consciousness. They questioned the need to privilege "white values" over "African values." They urged Africans to patronize black businesses and strive for economic independence. They pleaded for African Christian unity, but they also urged their readers to join independent African churches.[141]

The calls for unity extended to other population groups in South Africa,[142] but even before the creation of the Congress Youth League they did not go unchallenged. As one correspondent (using the pseudonym "Inkspot") wrote in 1943:

> Fellow-Africans, let us paddle our own canoe! I am not against collaboration with other sections of the Non-Europeans on issues of common interest but let us build up our own organisations first and foremost. Let us exact the respect of other sections through our own united and solid front. The prospects of a Non-European front are remote and are only possible after we have consolidated our own position.[143]

Confrontational news stories, about strikes, boycotts and attempts at civil disobedience by various protest groups, increased dramatically during Ngubane's editorship. Unrest in mission schools in the reserves, especially after World War II, were the subject of numerous news stories and commentaries in *Inkundla*.[144]

The mounting sense of urgency during the 1940s was reflected in other forms of confrontation as well, including strikes and various types of work stoppages on the docks and in the factories of the main cities, the test sample featuring Durban, Port Elizabeth and East London.[145] *Inkundla* in the mid- to late 1940s also provided intermittent coverage of unrest in squatter communities in Johannesburg and Durban, pass law protests, bus boycotts in Johannesburg (focusing on the African township community of Alexandra) and Port Elizabeth, boycotts in the reserves (especially the Transkei), and riots in various towns and cities.[146]

The most disturbing, and destructive, race riots in South Africa during the 1940s were generated by poor living conditions in the sprawling Durban slum of Cato Manor, where enraged and impoverished Zulu householders went on a rampage against Indian slumlords and shopkeepers in January 1949.[147] The ambivalent reaction of *Inkundla* to these riots reflected the ambivalent reactions of rank and file members and leaders of the ANC and the Youth League to the Indian community in Natal.

Ngubane was deeply suspicious of Indian intentions and had remarked in 1947: "the Indian community as a whole is interested only in making money out of us and... when it has done this, it avoids doing anything tangible to help the African march to a better life."[148] But he condemned the riots, and the tone used to censure the African "mobs" was similar to the tone used by the Jabavus in condemning Enoch Mgijima and the Israelites in 1920:

> Left without a leader and without the guidance of a trained mind, they expressed themselves in the only way open to desperate and betrayed men – violence... What is more, who can swear that the mobs that turn against the Indians yesterday will not turn against the so called [African] intellectuals tomorrow?... Since it endangers everybody, even the innocent, no words must be minced in condemning it [the rioting].[149]

The riots helped trigger a subordinate discourse in *Inkundla*, restricted mainly to vernacular letters to the editor, supporting the government's apartheid policies as an alternative to grinding poverty and discrimination. Stories began to appear in the newspaper urging the government to separate Africans and Indians: "Indians despise Africans and Africans keep patronising their businesses. This lop-sided relationship should be ended once and for all. We should ask the government to intervene and separate us. 'When your sons do not get along, one leaves the home.'"[150]

These correspondents were in the minority, but they were now asking readers to think the unthinkable – to accept apartheid and live "their own lives away from White domination."[151] Some moderate African nationalists were in agreement with the National Party on this point. Although *Inkundla* criticized the activities of men like H. N. P. Ngwenya, Richard G. Baloyi and S. M. Bennett Ncwana,[152] their views were given coverage. Ncwana, for example, actually contributed a column to the newspaper for several months in 1951.[153]

Correspondents in *Inkundla*'s vernacular pages, in particular, became increasingly despondent about the African nationalist movement in the mid- to late 1940s. Long, soul-searching articles were written on why Africans had not been able to liberate themselves.[154] Many commentators were now critical of African leadership: "White leaders are working together and our leaders are back-stabbing one another. Some of them are doing nothing whilst others run to the government to show Whites what 'good boys they are.'"[155]

African leaders were sometimes compared unfavorably with "Boer" leaders. One writer declared that the "Boers" had "a language of their own that unites them," that Afrikaans-language newspapers focused only on issues that would "build them up" and that a policy of uplift ensured that the "least of them" ultimately would be "the most important." In contrast, "the opposite was true" of African leaders. They could not unite their people, and they were "pre-occupied with petty jealousy."[156] Africans were "masters in the art of self-defeatism. 'Whites are smarter than us'. 'Indians are more prosperous than we are'. 'We are incapable of taking care of our affairs'. Alcoholism, preoccupation with mundane affairs of the flesh, and incapacitating cultural habits. We have to overcome all these negative beliefs about ourselves."[157]

The dominant discourse in *Inkundla*, however, remained bitterly anti-apartheid, both before and after the National Party victory in 1948. When *Bantu World*'s offices were burned by white extremists in 1944, for example, one writer raised the battle cry of racial war: "With the war coming to an end the African has got to be prepared for the onslaught by Whites. It is imperative that Africans come together and fight like those European nations who risked all to defeat Hitler."[158] Even moderates like Cape ANC leader James Calata were now finding common cause with the Africanists. "Africa is our homeland," he declared in 1949, "and, while we do not deny any human being of any race, colour or creed the right to become an African or a South African, nevertheless we maintain that we are the real South Africans."[159]

Opposition to apartheid moved Ngubane to declare: "[National Party leader] Malan [has succeeded] in making African national unity a living reality... Government without desiring it turns out to be [the] best ally in welding the African people into one political striking force."[160] Commentators writing in Zulu and Xhosa were also optimistic that "separate development" would "galvanize all the people opposed to this idea," and there would be "unity" within the African nationalist movement.[161] In the early 1950s, however, it was not to be. African nationalists remained divided, and in future Africans would join together with non-Africans in a broader resistance movement to end apartheid in South Africa.

Notes

1. *Inkundla* (hereafter *IYB*) references specify page numbers and languages. All stories not designated by language are in English. *Inkundla* had no rivals, but there were a few vocal newsletters that represented Africanist perspectives within Congress during the 1950s, including the *Voice* (later *the Voice of Africa*), the *Africanist*, the *African Lodestar* (all three produced in Orlando Township, Johannesburg) and a bulletin called *Bureau of African Nationalism* (East London). See L. Switzer and D.

Switzer, *Black press in South Africa and Lesotho, 1836–1976* (Boston, 1979), 28 (*African Lodestar*), 29 (*Africanist*), 64 (*Voice*).
2. *IYB*, e.g., March 1940, 1 (Xhosa supplement): reader asks why African newspapers should have English titles; August 1940, 7 (Xhosa).
3. *IYB*, May 1940, 3.
4. *IYB*, August 1941, 2.
5. *IYB*, 1st fortnight, September 1946, 3. It is interesting that *Inkundla* ignored the *Guardian*, which focused on trade union activities during the 1940s.
6. Information on Verulam Press and its proprietors was obtained mainly from an interview with Jordan Ngubane conducted by Les Switzer in July 1982.
7. As noted in Chap. 2, John Dube established the secondary school, the only independent African school of its kind in South Africa, at Verulam in August 1901.
8. According to Ngubane, each man paid about £250 to become a shareholder in the company. The newspaper also received occasional donations from white as well as black readers, particularly in Johannesburg, but "no white ever financed the paper." Les Switzer interview with Ngubane, July 1982.
9. Much of the printing equipment was located and purchased with the aid of a Mr. Godfrey, a mechanic from the island of Mauritius who "passed as a Coloured in Durban," according to Ngubane, and "kept the machines going at Verulam Press." Ibid.
10. Colin Bundy is writing a biography of Mbeki, and the following paragraphs are based primarily on two papers he gave at Yale University's Southern African Research Program in April and December 1992. C. Bundy, "Breaking the midnight slumber: Govan Mbeki and Transkeian politics in the 1940s," and "Schooled for life? The childhood and education of Govan Mbeki." On Mbeki's editorship of *Inkundla,* see also Switzer and Switzer, *Black press*, 43–44; K. Eales, "Jordan Ngubane, *Inkundla ya Bantu* and the African National Congress Youth League, 1944–1951," B. A. Honours thesis (Pietermaritzburg, University of Natal, 1984), 21.
11. Bundy, "Schooled for life?" 31–35. Roux, then a member of the Communist Party, was on honeymoon in the Ciskei in 1933 and spoke at several outdoor meetings near Fort Hare that Mbeki attended. Yergan was an African American who spent 14 years in South Africa between 1922 and 1936. He lived on the Fort Hare campus and was heavily influenced by what he saw and heard about communism on a visit to the Soviet Union in 1934. On Yergan, see D. Anthony, "Max Yergan in South Africa: From evangelical pan-Africanist to revolutionary socialist," *African Studies Review* 34, 2 (1977), 27–56.
12. Mbeki was about to launch himself as a perceptive writer on current events with *Transkei in the Making*, which was first published in 1939 in Durban in eight installments in a liberal English-language monthly entitled *New Outlook*. This pioneer news magazine lasted two years, between April 1937 and April 1939. (A new series was started in August 1939, but only one issue was produced.) Switzer and Switzer, *Black press*, 112–113. *Transkei in the Making* was reproduced as a booklet by Verulam Press and advertised for several years in *Inkundla* during the early to mid- 1940s.
13. Bundy, "Breaking the midnight slumber," 12 (citing a published interview with Mbeki in 1990).
14. Ibid., 13 (citing letter from Mbeki to A. B. Xuma in May 1940).
15. Ibid., 29.
16. *IYB*, February 1941, l.
17. Mbeki was critical of the ANC's failure to follow through on the NRC boycott decision. "We have already lost face in the Anti-Pass Campaign which was just dropped when we were working up the people [in the Transkei] ... That should not happen again in this affair [the NRC boycott] unless we must risk a setback for a decade or more." Bundy, "Breaking the midnight slumber," 34 (citing letter from Mbeki to A. B. Xuma in June 1947).
18. *IYB*, April 1941, 2. Mbeki wrote in an editorial a year earlier: "Our duty has always been, ever is, and shall always be to the African people first." *IYB*, July 1940, 2.
19. *IYB*, March 1941, 1–2; April 1941, 5; June 1941, 4. The profiles were submitted by various contributors to a five-man

committee of African teachers from the Orange Free State, Transvaal, Natal, Ciskei and Transkei. See also *IYB*, 1 May 1941, 3; August 1941, 6; December 1941, 4.

20. *IYB*, e.g., March 1941, 1–2; April 1941, 5.
21. Mbeki resigned as editor of *Inkundla* in 1943, according to Kathy Eales, to enter the Transkei Bunga. Eales, "Jordan Ngubane," 21. Mbeki told Bundy he left the newspaper "because he was too radical for the publishers." Colin Bundy, personal communication.
22. Ngubane claimed in an interview that Mbeki had been a contributor but never the editor of *Inkundla*. Ngubane's antipathy to the Communist Party and anyone associated with the socialist project, however, is well known. Les Switzer interview with Ngubane, July 1982. Mbeki returned as *Inkundla*'s "contributing editor," according to Bundy, for about four years between 1945 and 1949. Bundy, "Breaking the midnight slumber."
23. Katamzi's flexibility was apparently in contrast to the firm opinions of Bonga, a "right-wing Methodist" who thought political faction fighting was "un-Christian" and would not support "views that tended to offend the established order." Bonga's occasional contributions to *Inkundla* dealt with religious topics. Les Switzer interview with Ngubane, July 1982; *IYB*, e.g., February 1939, 7 ("The Call to Preach").
24. Les Switzer interview with Ngubane, July 1982. Ngubane had been contributing articles to *Inkundla* since 1942 under various pseudonyms: *IYB*, e.g., 30 January 1942, 3 (as "Khanyisa" or "Kanyisa"); 30 September 1943, 2 (as "Twana"). Ngubane was not officially identified in the newspaper as the editor until 25 February 1948, at which time he was also listed on the editorial page masthead as a director of Verulam Press along with Katamzi, Motsemme, Bokwe and a J. N. Jacobs. These individuals apparently managed the press between 1948 and 1951. There is no further reference to Bonga, who died in late 1947 or early 1948, and Xaba, the church leader from Johannesburg, is also missing from this roster. The identity of Jacobs remains unknown.
25. Les Switzer interview with Ngubane, July 1982.
26. Unless otherwise indicated, the following quotations are taken from the Ngubane interview.
27. Brookes also had been editor of the short-lived *New Outlook*, which first published Mbeki's *Transkei in the Making*.
28. On Dube's early career as a clergyman, educator, journalist and politician, see Chap. 2. Dube, a product of the American Board Mission, was the first president of the South African Native National Congress (SANNC, later renamed the African National Congress, or ANC) in 1912. Although forced to resign the presidency in 1917, he retained control of the Natal Native Congress until 1945, a year before he died. Dube's image in Natal's white community changed dramatically during this period, from that of a radical who needed "to be watched" to that of a "revered elder statesman" who represented "responsible native opinion." He was supported by upper-ranked members of Natal's petty bourgeoisie, who continued to work within existing segregationist structures to gain political concessions. A Justice Department bulletin not surprisingly described Natal's African petty bourgeoisie in the 1930s as "steady and law-abiding" and the conservative Natal Native Congress as "doing considerable good among the Natives." Quoted in E. Roux, *Time longer than rope: A history of the black man's struggle for freedom in South Africa* (Madison, 1964), 251–252; quoted in S. Marks, *The ambiguities of dependence in South Africa: Class, nationalism, and the state in twentieth-century Natal* (Baltimore, 1986), 44.
29. Allison Wessels George Champion was a product of the American Board Mission, like Dube, but he was suspended from the mission school at Amanzimtoti before completing Standard 7 (ninth grade) for participating in a student protest. He helped organize and was the first president of the Native Mine Clerks Association in 1920. He joined the ICU in 1925 and was Clements Kadalie's point man in Natal. The Natal ICU under Champion had become a formidable political machine by 1928, when he was suspended as Natal ICU secretary for allegedly mismanaging

union funds. Champion retained his political power base in Natal, but his image in African politics inside and outside the province in later years was decidedly more conservative than it had been in the 1920s. He served as a pillar of the old-guard establishment on the ANC executive committee for 14 years (1937–51) but resigned from Congress following his defeat in the 1951 Natal Congress presidential election. He remained an influential figure in local government politics, in the affairs of the Zulu royal family and in KwaZulu politics in the 1950s and 1960s. T. Karis and G. Carter (eds.), *From protest to challenge*, Vol. 4: *Political profiles, 1882–1964,* by G. M. Gerhart and T. Karis (Stanford, 1977), 18–19; Marks, *Ambiguities of dependence*, Chap. 3. On the ICU, see Chap. 5 in the present volume.

30. Eales, "Jordan Ngubane," 16 (citing Ngubane).
31. Ibid., 17 (citing Ngubane). Peter Walshe cites several attempts to found similar youth groups outside Natal during these years but apparently they were all short-lived. P. Walshe, *The rise of African nationalism in South Africa: The African National Congress, 1912–1952* (Berkeley and Los Angeles, 1971), 351–352.
32. Eales, "Jordan Ngubane," 17 (citing Ngubane). For descriptions of the early years of the CYL, see Karis and Carter, *From protest to challenge*, Vol. 2: *Hope and challenge, 1935–1952*, by T. Karis, 98–107; G. Gerhart, *Black power in South Africa* (Berkeley and Los Angeles, 1978), Chap. 3.
33. Eales, "Jordan Ngubane," 20 (citing Ngubane).
34. The column of readers' comments entitled "What the People Say" appeared regularly from 1944. It often contained the following introductory paragraph: "In these columns our readers may express themselves freely on any subject under the sun so long as they are tolerant, brief and to the point." *IYB*, e.g., 17 October 1944, 2; 26 March 1949, 4. The column entitled "Comment on Events" (by "Khanyisa") was launched in 1947. *IYB*, e.g., 10 July 1947, 5 ("Transkei Boycott and After").
35. Eales, "Jordan Ngubane," 18 (citing Ngubane).
36. Ibid., 19 (citing Ngubane).
37. *IYB*, e.g., 2nd fortnight, October 1945, 2; 2nd fortnight, May 1946, 2; 27 February 1947, 5.
38. Gerhart, *Black power*, 76 (citing Lembede in 1943).
39. *IYB*, 13 March 1947, 5.
40. *IYB*, 26 June 1947, 5.
41. *IYB*, 3 March 1948, 6; 10 April 1947, 3. See also Gerhart, *Black power*, 71.
42. Eales, "Jordan Ngubane," 110.
43. *IYB*, 10 December 1949, 4; 7 August, 1948, 6. See also 17 February 1944, 4 ("The African will always suffer from the prejudice of the dominant whites, whether they are capitalistic or communistic"); 17 May 1945, 3 ("Many Africans are loath to identify themselves with the African National Congress as controlled by the Communist Party, especially the Transvaal branch"); 10 December 1949, 4 ("The Communists do not believe in self-determination for anybody other than themselves").
44. *IYB*, 17 May 1945, 2.
45. *IYB*, e.g., 17 September 1947, 6. Ngubane applauded people like Z. K. Matthews, who were spokesmen for "responsible African nationalism... co-operation between Black and White is the only way out." *IYB*, 5 March 1949, 3.
46. *IYB*, 29 May 1947, 5.
47. *IYB*, 31 May 1945, 3.
48. Ngubane, for example, called on the CYL to "come down to the people and do some solid work" like teaching literacy classes in the "shantytowns." He attacked the lack of a "spirit of self-sacrifice" by Congress or the CYL, without which they could not "inspire people with the zeal to sacrifice themselves" in the struggle. *IYB*, 8 May 1947, 5; 31 July 1947, 5 ("Kanyisa").
49. Eales, "Jordan Ngubane," 114 (citing letter from A. P. Mda to G. M. Pitje, 8 November 1948).
50. Ibid. (citing letter from J. K. Ngubane to G. M. Pitje, 26 October 1949).
51. Ibid. (citing Eales's interview with G. M. Pitje in November 1983).
52. T. Lodge, *Black politics in South Africa since 1945* (Johannesburg, 1983), 80. (Matthews was elected CYL national secretary in 1951.)
53. Karis and Carter, *From protest to challenge*, Vol. 3: *Challenge and violence, 1953–1964*, by T. Karis and G. M. Gerhart (Stanford, 1977), Document 75

(Statement during the Rivonia Trial), 789. But the CYL opposed links with whites in the early 1950s. As Joe Matthews put it in 1951; "The racialist propaganda amongst the whites and their desire to maintain what they imagine to be a profitable situation makes it utterly unthinkable that there can be a political alignment that favours a liberal white group. In any case the political immorality, cowardice and vacillation of the so-called progressives amongst the whites render them utterly useless as a force against fascism." Quoted in Walshe, *The rise of African nationalism*, 349.

54. Mtimkulu was ordained as a minister in the Wesleyan Methodist Church, but he left the mission to become president of the independent Bantu Methodist Church. He served as the ANC's senior chaplain for a time and was a participant in numerous activities promoted by the moderate nationalist hierarchy during the interwar period. A brief profile of Mtimkulu is contained in Gerhart and Karis, *Political Profiles*, 106.

55. Eales, "Jordan Ngubane," e.g., 57 (citing G. M. Carter's interview with Ngubane in March 1964). Albert John Mvumbi Lutuli (1898–1967) was trained initially as a primary school teacher and later graduated from Adams College, where he also taught for many years. Lutuli was a dedicated Christian, a one-time lay preacher in the Wesleyan Methodist mission church, who in 1935 became chief of the Umvoti Mission Reserve community centered at Groutville (a town on the coast north of Durban). Lutuli was ANC president general for $14\frac{1}{2}$ years, retaining the post even after Congress was banned in 1960. He was awarded the Nobel Peace Prize in 1960. For a pensketch of his political career, see, Gerhart and Karis, *Political Profiles*, 60–63.

56. *Territorial Magazine,* e.g., November 1938, 5; *IYB,* e.g., November 1942, 1; December 1942, 3; 30 June 1943, 3.

57. Eales, "Jordan Ngubane," 77 (citing Ngubane).

58. Ibid., 75–82. Eales presented this argument as a counter to the assessment by Gerhart and Karis of Ngubane's achievements in Natal politics during these years. Cf. Gerhart and Karis, *Political Profiles*, 115.

59. *IYB,* 31 May 1944, 1. Brief profiles of Ngcobo and Mbata can be found in Gerhart and Karis, *Political Profiles*, 82–83 (Mbata), 112 (Ngcobo). On Dhlomo, see T. Couzens, *The new African: A study of the life and work of H. I. E. Dhlomo* (Johannesburg, 1985).

60. Couzens, *The new African*, 262. Moerane was also forced to state publicly that he had convened the Natal CYL's inaugural meeting "on the assurance that it was to be a non-political mass organization whose aim was to encourage Youth to play their part in the social upliftment of the African people." Eales, "Jordan Ngubane," 25 (citing *Ilanga lase Natal,* 1 July 1944).

61. *IYB,* 31 July 1944, 2.

62. *IYB,* 31 August 1944, 2; 18 September 1944, 2; 17 October 1944, 2–4.

63. *IYB,* 31 January 1945, 3.

64. *IYB,* 17 April 1945, 1; 31 July 1945, 1; 2nd fortnight, May 1946, 2. Walshe, *Rise of African nationalism*, 394.

65. *IYB,* 2nd fortnight, July 1946, 2.

66. *IYB,* 3 April 1947, 5.

67. *IYB,* e.g., 11 June 1949, 5; 19 March 1949, 5–6.

68. *IYB,* 22 April 1950, 6; 13 May 1950, 6.

69. *IYB,* 14 April 1951, 3; 19 May 1951, 2; Eales, "Jordan Ngubane," 72 (citing Ngubane).

70. T. Karis, *Hope and challenge,* Document 60 (1949 Programme of Action statement), 338.

71. Eales, "Jordan Ngubane," 114–115 (citing Ngubane). According to Ngubane, the government's Industrial Council monitored news content and summoned the directors on several occasions to defend the newspaper's editorial policies. He claimed that the Industrial Council virtually forced Verulam Press out of business by insisting that its printers be paid white journeyman's wages. Whereas *Bantu World* and other "reliable" black publications were not forced to pay these wages, the Industrial Council rejected repeated appeals for exemption from Verulam Press because they "didn't like our [*Inkundla*'s] politics." Les Switzer interview with Ngubane, July 1982.

72. Ngubane's bitter attacks on the ANC and its leadership and Albert Lutuli's point-by-point responses, for example, found an outlet in *Indian Opinion* for several months in

1956. Ruth First commented in *Fighting Talk*: "Ngubane has now reached the point where to defend his own isolated position he is prepared to storm Congress with any shell he can grasp and he seems past caring that he and the [Afrikaner] Nationalists are bombarding the same freedom movement." Cf. *Indian Opinion,* 17 February, 24 February, 2 March 1956 ("Dr Xuma and the ANC" and "Congress and Its Difficulties" by Jordan K. Ngubane); 29 June, 6 July, 13 July, 20 July 1956 ("A Reply to Mr. Jordan K. Ngubane's Attacks" by Albert J. Lutuli); 6 July, 13 July, 27 July, 3 August, 7 August 1956 ("Comments on Mr. Luthuli's Reply" by Jordan K. Ngubane); *Fighting Talk,* August 1956, 2 ("From the Sidelines" by Ruth First). I am indebted to Dorothy Woodson for sending me this correspondence.

73. Ngubane claimed in later years that he was not close to any of his white liberal colleagues – he found most of them to be "racist" – except Patrick Duncan, editor of the party organ *Contact* and perhaps the most militant of the Liberal Party's key officials. Les Switzer interview with Ngubane, July 1982.
74. Gerhart and Karis, *Political profiles*, 115.
75. Bernice M. Wardell-Ngubane to Switzer 22 October 1993.
76. Les Switzer interview with Ngubane, July 1982.
77. As noted in previous chapters, the weekly newspapers *Inkululeko* and *Guardian* both sold for a penny a copy – "4 s. 4 d." a year during this decade.
78. The circulation figure is taken from A. J. Friedgut, "The non-European press," in E. Hellmann (ed.), *Handbook on race relations in South Africa* (Oxford, 1949; rpt, New York, 1975), 499. For the *Workers' Herald*, see Chap. 5 in the present volume. The ICU newspaper apparently reached a peak of 27,000 in May 1927.
79. Les Switzer interview with Ngubane, July 1982.
80. *IYB,* 5 September 1942, 2 (Xhosa).
81. Les Switzer interview with Ngubane, July 1982.
82. Ibid.; Eales, "Jordan Ngubane," 21 (citing Ngubane).
83. Lodge, *Black politics,* 24.
84. *IYB,* 30 September 1946, 5 (Xhosa); see also 21 January 1950, 1 (Zulu) regarding African medical students. When Africans did comparatively well in the 1945 matriculation examinations, for example, one writer commented: "African teachers are more effective in our schools than white ones." *IYB,* 2nd fortnight, January 1946, 3 (Xhosa).
85. The secretary of the Natal Teachers' Union, for example, was condemned when he wore "tribal attire" during a celebration (Dingaan's Day). The author was embarrassed, because "whites were present." *IYB,* November 1938, 1 (Zulu).
86. *IYB,* October 1941, 8 (Xhosa).
87. *IYB,* e.g. April 1942, 8 (Xhosa – review of a book by D. D. T. Jabavu, who had once been a major apologist in the eastern Cape for the mission church tradition); 28 May 1949, 2 (Zulu – praising the Zionist church leader S. G. Shange).
88. ANC members were prominently featured in stories about the dead. *IYB,* e.g., 30 June 1951, 4.
89. Les Switzer interview with Ngubane, July 1982.
90. *IYB,* 17 May 1945, 8 (Zulu). In a story about South Africa's white hospitals using the Lamaze method of natural childbirth, another writer commented: "God knows when African women will experience it." *IYB,* 24 March 1948, 1 (Zulu).
91. On witchcraft: "There has never been evidence to prove the existence of this supernatural power yet the lives of innocent people have been destroyed. It is time to shed this aspect of our past and move on." *IYB,* 13 January 1951, 2 (Xhosa).
92. This support was maintained to the last issue. *IYB,* 3 November 1951, 4 ("A Clarion Call to African Teachers").
93. *IYB,* 5 June 1947, 2 (Zulu); see also May 1938, 1 (Zulu); 17 September 1947, 3 (Zulu). There was even some criticism of the educated elite. One writer, for example, commented bitterly on a "plot of the educated Africans to give scholarships to their children only irrespective of their performance ... that is why we keep turning out mediocre leadership. Opportunity is given to those who do not deserve it." *IYB,* March 1944, 6 (Xhosa). The story is headlined "The Plot of the Unscrupulous."
94. *IYB*, August 1940, 2.

95. *IYB*, e.g., May 1941, 8 (Xhosa–two story items).
96. *IYB*, June 1939, 2 (Xhosa).
97. *IYB*, 13 November 1948, 1 (Zulu). See also 15 April 1950, 4 (Xhosa): "The Church has become a part of the apartheid machinery."
98. *IYB*, 21 January 1950, 1 (Zulu).
99. On this region, see L. Switzer, *Power and resistance in an African society: The Ciskei Xhosa and the making of South Africa* (Madison, 1993), Chap. 9.
100. *IYB*, e.g., 16 January 1946, 3 (Zulu) on medical examinations for African female employees: "Africans should rise up against the injustice and humiliation of subjecting our women to mandatory medical examination of their genitals."
101. *IYB*, e.g., 30 May 1946, 6 (Zulu); 17 September 1947, 3 (Zulu).
102. Readers were very critical of municipal beerhalls. *IYB*, e.g., 27 February 1947, 3 (Zulu): "People of all ages, particularly the elderly, are subjected to all sorts of abuse just for a drink."
103. *IYB*, e.g., 29 April 1950, 1 (Zulu), 6 (English); 13 January 1951, 1 (Zulu).
104. There were also stories critical of the government's food-distribution efforts. *IYB*, e.g., 27 February 1947, 3 (Zulu): "Whites get preference and Indians give to other Indians and the African population is left out."
105. *IYB*, e.g., October 1941, 8 (Xhosa).
106. *IYB*, e.g., 30 May 1946, 6 (Zulu), 13 November 1948, 8 (Zulu).
107. Only a few economic activities involving women were found in the test sample. *IYB*, e.g., 10 July 1947, 6 (Xhosa) regarding the Bantu Women's Home Improvement Association.
108. *IYB*, 1 May 1947, 5; 3 July 1947, 5.
109. *IYB*, 27 February 1947, 2 (Zulu); cf. 30 November 1944, 8 (Xhosa): "*Inkundla*... has a role and access that individuals do not have. It is imperative for Africans to support *Inkundla* before they buy White papers. 'Charity begins at home.'"
110. The foreign policy of the Americans, British and French in the early years of the Cold War were sometimes depicted as their "Banding together against Russia." *IYB*, e.g., 17 July 1948, 1 (Zulu).
111. "Everybody is getting their independence," as one writer put it, with reference to Egypt, Iran and India. "Africans, where is yours?" *IYB*, 30 May 1946, 4 (Xhosa).
112. *IYB*, 21 January 1948, 1 (Zulu).
113. *IYB*, 27 February 1947, 2 (Zulu).
114. *IYB*, 5 June 1947, 2 (Zulu). Another writer in a story on the same page perceived independence in India on these terms as an "English Plot."
115. Africans, Coloureds and Indians would seek to use the opportunity to present their grievances, whereas "the Boers" would stay away from the ceremonies. Readers complained that government officials were going to put Africans on display for the king: "We do not want to be displayed as exotic natives doing traditional dances! If they [the government] present these uneducated people, it may make their case for our oppression." *IYB*, e.g., 27 February 1946, 3 (Zulu); 30 September 1946, 6 (Zulu).
116. *IYB*, April 1940, 1.
117. *IYB*, November 1939, 2.
118. *IYB*, e.g. May 1941, 7 (Xhosa). *Inkundla* did attack the Labour Party on occasion for "betraying African workers." *IYB*, e.g., March 1944, 2.
119. *IYB*, e.g., 31 July 1945, 5 (Zulu): "What Boers are saying."
120. *IYB*, 28 February 1942, 2.
121. *IYB*, 28 February 1942, 2; 31 August 1944, 6.
122. *IYB*, 30 November 1944, 8 (Xhosa).
123. *IYB*, 29 September 1945, 3 (Xhosa).
124. *IYB*, 30 May 1946, 4 (Xhosa).
125. *IYB*, 29 September 1945, 6 (Zulu).
126. *IYB*, 9 April 1949, 5; see also editorial on 2 July 1949, 4, entitled "Warning to some Englishmen: If the English want to insulate themselves from the rest of South Africa, they are free to please themselves. But we, for our part, are for the Greater South Africa unto the death."
127. *IYB*, March 1940, 3 (Zulu); see also 16 January 1946, 3 (Xhosa).
128. *IYb*, e.g. 17 July 1948, 1 (Zulu), 8 (Zulu); 29 April 1950, 1 (Zulu), 3 (Zulu headline: "Apartheid Is Failing").
129. *IYB*, 29 April 1950, 2 (Zulu); see also *IYB*, 13 August 1949, 3 (English): apartheid regime is attacked as the

"agent of Communism" at a Cape African Teachers' Association conference.

130. *IYB*, 30 April 1949, 1 (Zulu).
131. *IYB*, 13 January 1951, 1 (Zulu).
132. *IYB*, e.g., 21 January 1948, 1 (Zulu).
133. The Joint Councils (founded mainly in the 1920s and early 1930s), for example, were still operating in the 1940s, and many ANC leaders were still involved in their activities. Other white-dominated, multiracial organizations included the South African Institute of Race Relations (founded in 1929), National Union of South African Students (founded in 1924), which was active mainly in English-language universities, the Students' Christian Association and various other church-sponsored groups. See Chaps. 5–6 in the present volume.
134. See Chap. 5 in the present volume.
135. On the Native Representatives, *IYB*, e.g., November 1938, 3 (Zulu) re Native Representatives for Zulu population; October 1941, 7 (Xhosa) re Margaret Ballinger; April 1942, 1, 5, 7 (Xhosa) re D. M. Buchanan; September 1942, 1, 4 (Xhosa) re W. Campbell, 2 (Xhosa) re Neil J. Boss; January 1944, 1; 17 May 1945, 8 (Zulu) re Edgar Brookes.
136. On the NRC, *IYB*, e.g., 30 May 1946, 4 (Xhosa); 2nd fortnight, January 1946, 4 (Zulu); 22 May 1947, 3; 10 July 1947, 2 (Xhosa); 24 July 1947, 1; 22 October 1947, 6; 12 November 1947, 1; 19 November 1947, 6. Ngubane tried to get Mbeki to soften his boycott position and even urged him to stand for an NRC seat on the "pro-boycott ticket" that had been adopted by Congress at its 1947 conference. Bundy, "Breaking the midnight slumber," 35.
137. *IYB*, 2 January 1946, 3 (Xhosa supplement).
138. Bundy, "Breaking the midnight slumber," 21–22 (citing *IYB*, November 1939, October 1940, December 1940).
139. *IYB*, 17 April 1944, 6 (by "Twana"); see also 31 May 1944, 3 (by "Kanyisa," a strike by Indian teachers at Sastri College in Durban); 31 July 1944, 1.
140. The coders did not find one story that could be defined as confrontational in the test sample until the March 1944 issue.
141. *IYB*, e.g., June 1939, 2 (Xhosa); August 1940, 4 (Zulu); May 1941, 8 (Xhosa); April 1942, 5 (Zulu); April 1943, 1 (Xhosa supplement).
142. The Non-European Unity Front, launched in 1939, for example, was endorsed enthusiastically: "Any struggle whose purpose or any act whose result is the bringing closer together of these three groups [Africans, Coloureds and Indians] should be welcomed by all." *IYB*, September 1940, 2; see also June 1941, 2; July 1941, 2.
143. *IYB*, 30 October 1943, 1. Ngubane wrote in January 1944: "As long as the African people are not welded into a compact organised group, they will never realise their national aspirations. When they meet with other Non-European groups, they will be an unwieldly encumbrance, serving the purpose of stepping stones for the better organised groups." *IYB*, 31 January 1944, 4.
144. *IYB*, e.g., 17 May 1945, 2–3; 31 July 1945, 6 (Zulu); 5 June 1947, 3 (Zulu); 21 January 1950, 4. On unrest in the mission schools, see the Introduction to the present volume.
145. *IYB*, e.g., 30 November 1944, 7–8 (Zulu); 17 September 1945, 6 (Zulu); 2 January 1946, 1, 6; 30 May 1946, 3, 4 (Xhosa), 6 (Zulu); 5 June 1947, 1, 4 (Sotho); 24 March 1948, 1 (Zulu); 17 July 1948, 4; 29 April 1950, 3 (Zulu).
146. The 1949 Port Elizabeth boycott coverage, for example, featured poems dedicated to the boycotters and the slogans they used. *IYB*, e.g., 28 May 1949, 6 (Xhosa). On the squatter movement, *IYB*, e.g., 2 January 1946, 1. On pass law protests, *IYB*, e.g., 30 November 1944, 6; 31 July 1945, 6 (Zulu). On boycotts in town and countryside, *IYB*, e.g., 30 November 1944, 3; 5 June 1947, 5; 10 July 1947, 7; 13 August 1949, 5; 28 May 1949, 4, 6 (Xhosa); 15 April 1950, 6. On beer riots in Johannesburg, 29 April 1950, 8 (Zulu).
147. The Cato Manor riots generated continued discussion and debate in *Inkundla* until the newspaper ceased publication almost three years later. *IYB*, e.g., 10 January 1949, 1 (Zulu), 1 (Xhosa), 2–3; 30 April 1949, 1 (Zulu), 4, 6; 16 June 1951, 1 (Zulu), 3.
148. *IYB*, 20 February 1947, 2. Ngubane's antipathy toward the Indian community

was well established in the pages of *Inkundla* before the riots. E.g., 10 December 1947, 5; 9 June 1948, 6.

149. *IYB*, 19 March 1949, 6. On the Israelites, see Chap. 5 in the present volume.
150. *IYB*, 13 August 1949, 2 (Zulu).
151. *IYB*, 13 August 1949, 1 (Zulu).
152. *IYB*, e.g., 28 May 1949, 4. Ngwenya was an ANC official in Natal. Baloyi was a well-to-do businessman from Alexandra Township in Johannesburg, a member of the NRC (1937–42) and a Congress official in the Transvaal in the 1930s and 1940s. Ncwana was a veteran Cape journalist and political activist in the 1920s and 1930s (on Ncwana, see Chap. 5 in the present volume).
153. *IYB*, e.g. 14 April 1951, 4; 19 May 1951, 4; 26 May 1951, 5.
154. "Africans have left their traditions," as one writer put it, "and that which defines them as a people." *IYB*, 21 January 1950, 3 (Xhosa).
155. *IYB*, 17 July 1948, 1 (Zulu). See also *IYB*, 28 May 1949, 3 (English editorial): "African Nationalism: Is It a Misnomer?" This editorial actually appeared three times in the newspaper; see also 23 April 1949, 4; 29 April 1951, 3 (Xhosa).
156. *IYB*, 15 April 1950, 4 (Xhosa); 29 April 1950, 3 (Zulu): Infighting was "the downfall of the Zulus."
157. *IYB*, 24 March 1948, 8 (Zulu supplement).
158. *IYB*, 30 November 1944, 7 (Zulu).
159. Walshe, *The rise of African nationalism*, 358 (citing *Bantu World*, 3 July 1949).
160. *IYB*, 9 June 1948, 6.
161. *IYB*, e.g., 13 August 1949, 1 (Zulu).

CHAPTER 8

The Sophiatown Generation

Black Literary Journalism during the 1950s

R. Neville Choonoo

In the history of African literature in South Africa, no literary generation is currently enjoying a more wistful revival than that of the 1950s: the Sophiatown generation. This was one of the most turbulent decades in modern South African history. The 1950s witnessed the passing of key apartheid laws, the ruthless expansion and implementation of pass regulations, the reorganization of the reserves, the first forced removals of Africans from the cities, widespread bannings, detentions and the marathon Treason Trial, the 1952 Defiance Campaign and the banning of the the African National Congress (ANC) and the Pan-Africanist Congress, the massacre at Sharpeville and the imposition of a State of Emergency in 1960.

Drum and the *Golden City Post*

Altogether, about a dozen African literary journalists from the 1950s have captured our attention. They launched their careers in two of the most popular publications serving the black community in South Africa at the time, *Drum* and the *Golden City Post*. The Johannesburg township of Sophiatown was immortalized in their writings. Their exposés and short stories as well as their later autobiographies reveal not only their protest against white injustice but also, ironically, their growing alienation as intellectuals who would never find a personal place in any community, black or white. This lost generation of urban African writers and journalists assumed the role of detached apostates, criticizing the state, the meager black and white liberal opposition and the rootlessness of the African working class. By the end of the 1950s, embittered and overwhelmed by state tyranny, they chose or were driven into exile and their works banished.

But if it was a decade of defeat, it was also a "fabulous decade," as Lewis Nkosi, one of these writers, called it. If this generation failed to effect a literary renaissance, they failed flamboyantly. Protesting beneath the gaze of the grand wizards of apartheid–Malan, Strydom and Verwoerd–they were indeed minstrels in a horror show.[1] Naively, but with much swagger, they mocked and indulged in a society that they both loved and hated. Where the state tried to evict and retribalize urban Africans, they promoted the popular culture of these segregated township dwellers. Where the state communicated racial divisiveness, they promoted the common concerns of those living in the unique melting pot that was Sophiatown. However brief and contradictory, the exuberance of this protest era merits a return visit.

Drum (original series, March 1951–April 1965) and the *Golden City Post* (original series, March 1955–January 1960) were launched in part in response to an emerging urban African culture that was virtually unrepresented in either the captive black commercial or the alternative political press at the time. Both *Drum* and the *Golden City Post* were guardedly sympathetic to ANC policies, although Congress itself had little interest in these publications. The African journalists themselves shied away from political membership. Unlike their counterparts in the political press, they chose to be independent, nonpartisan observers of the absurdity of life in South Africa. At the same time, they remained (like Congress) locked in the politics of moderation and of liberal middle-class values and debate.

African "protest writing" of the 1950s was relatively moderate in tone, especially if one compares this output with the strident literary expression of Black Consciousness writers during the 1970s and 1980s. A few of the literary journalists of the 1950s – for example, H. I. E. (Herbert Isaac Ernest) Dhlomo (b. 1903) – belonged to the generation before World War I, but most were born during the interwar years. These included Ezekiel (now Es'kia) Mphahlele (b. 1919), Peter Abrahams (b. 1919), Henry Nxumalo (b. 1920s), William ("Bloke") Modisane (b. 1923), Todd Matshikiza (b. 1924), Can Themba (b. 1924), Richard Rive (b. 1931), Moses Karabo ("Casey") Motsisi (b. 1932), Arthur Maimane (b. 1932), Lewis Nkosi (b. 1936) and Nat Nakasa (b. 1937). Dhlomo, Nakasa, Themba, Modisane, Matshikiza, Motsisi, Nxumalo and Rive are dead. Mphahlele returned to South Africa in 1977 after many years of self-exile in the United States. Maimane has returned as well, but Abrahams and Nkosi still live outside South Africa.

Many of these writers received a formal education at elite mission schools (like St. Peter's College in Johannesburg and Adams College in Natal) and at the University College of Fort Hare before the state took over Fort Hare and the mission schools during the 1950s. Urban-born and anglicized, these writers were self-conscious representatives of South Africa's expanding black petty bourgeoisie. In the black townships, however, they lived alongside a mass-migrant working-class population whose lives they were to write about as journalists and fiction writers in *Drum* and the *Golden City Post*. At different times in the 1950s they all lived in Sophiatown. It was the fast-paced life of Johannesburg and its African townships that informed the writing of the Sophiatown generation.

These writers were anything but a homogenous group. Each brought to his work a distinctive style and posture that endeared him to his readers. Todd Matshikiza, a famous musician and composer, wrote regular features and record reviews, using a distinctive combination of American, British and South African slang that came to be called "Matshikese." Arthur Maimane wrote a sports column and a series of crime stories in which his lone detective protagonist, Chester Morena, heroically fights crime like a Sam Spade of Johannesburg. Casey Motsisi wrote a series of vignettes that romanticized the hustler figure in the townships. Can Themba wrote about shebeen culture, defending and glorifying the life of the underdog, an image that he self-consciously and recklessly cultivated.[2] Nat Nakasa, Es'kia Mphahlele and Bloke Modisane wrote many short pieces that offered an impression of daily life for the average Sophiatownian. Themba, Mphahlele and Modisane were most drawn to the short story form, and in their reportage they often employed fictional techniques to dramatize life in the townships.

As young men who had come to maturity during the 1940s, they were not impressed with the conservative literary credentials of their predecessors. As Lewis Nkosi observed: "The evidence of their writing was not the least encouraging.

When we turned to their literature our sense of outrage was sharpened. A great deal of this writing, stimulated as it was by missionary endeavor, was purposefully Christian and aggressively crusading: the rest was simply eccentric or unacceptably romantic."[3]

Many Sophiatown writers were intent on breaking away from the past and creating a new voice. They would lead a literary renaissance of sorts that would ring in the appearance of a "New African," who would be not unlike the "New Negro" of the 1920s Harlem Renaissance.[4]

Drum and the *Golden City Post* provided these writers with a platform during the 1950s, from which they honed their skills as writers and cultivated a wide black readership. As Nkosi recalled: "for me journalism had never been more than an interesting place where one might be given a chance, if one was lucky, to write a good story once a week ... I was in the newspaper business for many things, but the most important was to learn to use the language."[5]

These writers were also very conscious of another audience, the white liberals. One of the most celebrated novels in South Africa, *Cry the Beloved Country*, was published in 1948. The novel, written by arch white-liberal Alan Paton, was serialized in the early issues of *Drum*. It dramatized the kind of rural African figure that African writers had come to detest, the docile African country preacher, Stephen Kumalo, awkward and hesitant before the white man and his ways. Nkosi writes:

> We thought we discerned in Stephen Kumalo's naivete and simple-minded goodwill, white South Africa's subconscious desire to survive the blind tragedy that was bound to engulf the country sooner or later; for if the African (or anyone else for that matter) was as fundamentally good and forgiving as Stephen Kumalo was conceived by Paton to be, then the white South Africans might yet escape the penalty which they would be required to pay.[6]

In championing the outlaws of Sophiatown as heroes, some African journalists emphasized the young, brazen, urban African personality over the passive rural types created by novelists like Paton.

In attempting to direct their protest against white liberals, however, African writers found themselves in the contradictory position of writing piercing criticisms of white ignorance while at the same time sharing with them common middle-class values. Even though whites in general did not read African publications, many Sophiatown writers found they were attracting a white rather than a black audience in seeking to penalize white South Africans for their illusions.[7]

Sophiatown and the Black Writer

The 237 acres of land known as Sophiatown were purchased in 1897 by a developer, H. Tobiansky, who named the area after his wife Sophia. Because of poor drainage and its proximity to the municipal sewerage plant, Sophiatown was not attractive to whites, and by 1910 Tobiansky was selling lots to anyone who could afford to buy them. Most of these would-be plotholders were African, but the government exempted Sophiatown from the Urban Areas Act (the burgeoning manufacturing industry on the Witwatersrand needed permanent black labor) and tolerated it as a freehold urban location. African families from the slum yards and outlying areas flocked to Sophiatown, which was located about 3 miles west of the center of white Johannesburg. There were 12,000 residents in 1928 and 28,500 in

1937: as scores of thousands of African laborers poured into Johannesburg in the next decade, the population rose to about 40,000 in the early 1950s.[8]

In contrast to the racially segregated character of South African life, Sophiatown remained a stubborn collage of people of color, African working class in the main but with a discernible African middle-class elite and numerous Coloured, Indian and white families (many of them traders). There was no "geography of class," as one might find in white suburbia.[9] Miriam Tali, a contemporary South African writer who lived in Sophiatown, looked back on these years with a mixture of pride and nostalgia:

> Sophiatown. The beloved Sophiatown. As students we used to refer to it proudly as the "center of the metropolis." And who could dispute it? The most talented African men and women from all walks of life–in spite of the hardships they had to encounter–came from Sophiatown. The best musicians, scholars, educationists, singers, artists, doctors, lawyers, clergymen.[10]

The imagined community, however, contained a sobering reality. As Paul Gready put it:

> Sophiatown's elastic housing capacity expanded to accommodate tenants and subtenants in backyard shacks, to the extent that by 1950 there were on average over eight families per stand. Thus the magnetism of Sophiatown produced a situation of potentially explosive overcrowding accentuated by poverty which condemned over 80% of African families to living on incomes below the poverty datum line. However the relative security of freehold tenure also encouraged... [an "emotional"] commitment to the area... What had been mere "space" became stained with the sentiments of its inhabitants to become an intensely personal "place."[11]

Such a reality stimulated a distinct subcultural mix that embraced, among other things, criminal activities, shebeen life, musical and literary expression, and aspects of American popular culture.

The African-American Influence

The importation of African-American political and cultural traditions into a black South African milieu dates back to at least the 1880s. The migration of thousands of rural African Americans into major American cities at the turn of the century and the subsequent experience of ghettoization, poverty and racial segregation somewhat paralleled the experience of black South Africans. Moreover, the literary, musical and political traditions of African Americans had a direct influence on black South African writers, musicians and politicians. In literature, concepts like the "talented tenth" and the "New Negro" of the Harlem Renaissance found eager disciples among black writers in South Africa like H. I. E. Dhlomo, Peter Abrahams and others of the Sophiatown generation. African-American writers like Langston Hughes (who was published by *Drum*), Richard Wright, Ralph Ellison and James Baldwin were role models for aspiring South African writers. The popularity of musicians like Duke Ellington, singers like Lena Horne, and boxers like Jack Johnson and Joe Louis was an urban African response to the domination of white cultural models in South Africa. Nat Nakasa wrote triumphantly:

> Gone is my image of the Superman. And it is looking to see how the image was destroyed over the years which now intrigues me. It is a process which is going on in the lives of all black men in the world today. For some of us, it began when Joe Louis

> knocked out Max Schmelling in the late thirties. In one blow, Joe Louis proved that the black man can also make the grade if allowed to compete on the basis of fair play. So did Louis Armstrong and Nat Cole.[12]

Here one detects not only the strain of African protest typical of the 1950s ("if we only had the chance") but also the myth that African Americans had succeeded because of "fair play."

The Americanization of urban black culture was accelerated primarily by an increase in American investment in a booming postwar South African economy. American consumer goods, movies, jazz records, comics, pulp novels, hats, shoes and the like were cheap and appealed to both township masses and the African elite. *Drum* and the *Golden City Post* widely advertised such goods, and some of the short stories they printed exploited an American idiom to attract readers. Arthur Maimane, for example, serialized a story headlined "The Chief Meets the Blackmailers" in the *Golden City Post* during its first year of publication. In one episode, the black detective Chester Moreno is being threatened by some tough henchmen, who demand he leave town:

> "We got orders, Buster, so don't try to get hurt. Orders is orders, ain't it?" He says in a thin, soft and menacing voice. "I wouldn't know, Johnny" I tell him getting some of my confidence back, "I never worked for a hoodlum." "The boss ... says for you to lay off this job if you know what's good for you ... and if you don't lay off and try to make Durban tonight, you'll find one helluva reception committee waiting to give you the lead-shoe swim. And don't forget it!" the big guy says, moving forward as the spokesman retreats.[13]

Maimane's debt to writers like Peter Cheyney and Damon Runyon and American movies is clearly evident. As Maimane himself admitted: "I never had any journalistic training. I went into journalism straight from school. Everything I knew about journalism, I learned from Hollywood."[14]

The "tsotsi" (young criminal) figure in the *Drum* pieces by Casey Motsisi, Todd Matshikiza, Can Themba and Arthur Maimane was often presented as a slick young outlaw who constantly lived on the edge. Invariably, he is portrayed as an Americanized African, as in the writing of Casey Motsisi. Motsisi's column "On the Beat" appeared monthly in *Drum* until June 1962. These short, humorous sketches were based on a township hustler type affectionately called the "Kid," whose last name changed, from story to story, depending on the context. "Kid Chance" took too many chances, "Kid Toothless" was always in trouble and got his teeth busted now and again. The Kid, no doubt based on real-life figures in the township, frequently hustled the author himself for money or liquor. In the sketch "Kid Hangover," the author is invited to a midnight party thrown by the Kid that the narrator is not too happy about attending. Motsisi writes:

> But I guess I'll have to go to this here midnite party 'cause the bizaro who's throwing it happens to be my pal with the name of Kid Hangover. And besides I reckon he'll need the boodle he charges guests since he's been out of a job for a mile of a time and spending the better part of it in the jailhouse on account he didn't square up with the maintenance of his two bambinos – not that he's wedded.[15]

Todd Matshikiza's inventive prose "Matshikese" evoked an American influence as well. In a tribute to Father Trevor Huddleston, a much-loved defender of black causes, Matshikiza wrote: "They've written songs of thanks an' tribute askin' him to hang on. They've hung epithets of slime on him an' jes' 'bout skinned him an' ate him up raw ... They've had heart attacks an' headaches an' toothaches an' bellyfuls of this Huddleston bloke."[16] A jazz critic himself for *Drum* and *Golden City Post*, Matshikiza incorporated the dialect of the American South into a South African idiom that portrayed Huddleston as something of an abolitionist hero.

White-Liberal Capital and the African Press

Although white-liberal politicians in the 1950s still perceived themselves as trustees of African political concerns, white-liberal industrialists professed a desire to join the African literary elite to meet the consumer needs of the new urban African. In their exposés and short stories in *Drum* and the *Golden City Post*, and later in their autobiographies, African writers were active participants in marketing the promise of upward mobility to their working-class readers. Such a partnership occasionally drew strong criticism from the writers, but it offered them a platform from which to launch their professional careers in a country that was intent on destroying all such platforms.

The relentless efforts by white management in the early 1950s to capitalize on African consumer interests through the African commercial press had never been attempted before on such a large scale. By 1956, when *Bantu World* changed its format and its name to *World* to attract a wider readership, competition from newly established, flashier publications like *Zonk!* and *Drum* and the *Golden City Post* had already reaped most of the harvest. But a persistent question remained, even for latterday entrepreneurs: How would they continue to exploit African consumers, whose cheap labor was essential but whose pockets were poor? Apartheid legislation constrained economic progress for working-class readers, who were enticed by these publications but could not indulge in the goods and services advertised.

Although they were essentially Johannesburg publications, *Drum* and the *Golden City Post* (the common African expression for Johannesburg is Egoli, the golden city) enjoyed a very wide readership throughout South Africa and beyond during the 1950s. *Drum* was launched in Cape Town by entrepreneur Jim Bailey and various partners as a magazine called *African Drum*.[17] The first issues featured stories about idyllic rural life and tribal traditions, but its readers were not interested: "Ag, why do you dish out that stuff man?" said one concerned reader. "Tribal Music! Tribal History! Chiefs! We don't care about chiefs! Give us jazz and film stars, man! We want Duke Ellington, Satchmo, and hot dames! Yes, brother, anything American."[18] The magazine was moved to Johannesburg in October 1951 and retitled *Drum* in February 1952. Under the tutelage of British journalist Anthony Sampson and his successors, the magazine was repackaged for urban Africans, and it was a huge success in various editions throughout sub-Saharan Africa.

Drum became a glossy pictorial laced with photos of pinup girls and sensational stories about famous African personalities, all of which were interspersed with screaming advertisements for items such as skin-lightening creams and other cheap American consumer goods. Tucked in among the advertisements were the journalistic pieces and short stories that were to launch the literary careers of the Sophiatown writers. *Drum* sales rose from 20,710, in 1951, to 60,024 in 1953, to 73,657 in 1955, making it the largest-circulation magazine in Africa in any language.[19]

The *Golden City Post* was a Sunday tabloid newspaper, modeled after the style of the British *Daily Mirror* and published by Bailey from March 1955. It had three separate editions, aimed respectively at Africans, Coloureds and Indians. Although it represented itself as a defender of the oppressed working class, in reality the newspaper displayed the same interest in middle-class consumerism as its magazine counterpart. In fact, it exploited racial and class stratification by sensationalizing the injustices of apartheid with stories about illegal interracial sex, reports of Coloureds "passing" as whites, gang warfare and numerous instances of rape.

Drum and the *Golden City Post* were overtly sexist publications that depicted women as sex objects and mindless consumers of cheap household goods. The editorial policy of *Drum* was clear:

> The cover girl must be happy and good looking – preferably aged 15 to 18 so that she appeals to young readers. Every second or third cover girl should be Coloured, preferably Africanish. The cover must be bright and striking and this depends on the use of a model who is not static – movement is an important part of the cover's appeal. The girl must be doing something cheerfully.[20]

Nevertheless, the Sophiatown generation did include a few women writers, most notably Bessie Head (b. 1937), who wrote occasionally for *Drum* and later established a considerable reputation as a novelist and short story writer in Botswana.

The *Golden City Post* attempted to create a brawny, macho image by publishing headline stories about prostitution, adultery and the behavior of "bad girls." Beneath a crusading morality, the newspaper used every opportunity to exploit sexual innuendo. A success story that praised a black academic who had written a master's thesis on educational training for Indian girls, for example, was given the headline, "Father of 8 Wrote on Girls."[21] In August 1956, a week before the historic ANC women's protest against passes in Pretoria, the newspaper had been asked to appeal to male readers to assume domestic responsibilities while their wives attended the demonstration. Reporter Henry Nxumalo took the occasion to jibe playfully at female readers by declaring that men might handle such responsibilities better than women. In urging women to attend the demonstration, he added: "So come on, girls. But please don't decide to march against me – instead of Pretoria next Thursday."[22] In one way or another, many Sophiatown writers trivialized women in their writings, a phenomenon that needs to be examined in more detail than has been done here.

Within months of its appearance, the *Golden City Post* reached the 70,000 sales mark and became the first black newspaper to achieve a circulation of more than 100,000.[23] Despite the popularity of both publications, Bailey faced the problem of poor management and of competition from larger companies such as the Argus Company and the Bantu News Agency. *Drum* folded as an independent magazine, appearing as a fortnightly supplement in the *Golden City Post* (now entitled the *Post*) between May 1965 and March 1968. The journalism of the Sophiatown generation was already a memory when *Drum* was revived as an independent magazine in April 1968 and the *Post* sold to Argus in November 1971.[24]

The Dialectic between Exposés and Short Stories

The success of *Drum* and the *Golden City Post* in the 1950s can be attributed to three things: the rise in the literacy rate of an urban black working class, the com-

Photo 24. Henry Nxumalo, "Mr Drum" of *Drum* magazine, was one of the best known of the tabloid exposé journalists of the 1950s. He also covered sports for the *Guardian.*

mercialization of the publications themselves and the exposés and stories of the Sophiatown writers. Between 1951 and 1958, *Drum* published more than 90 stories and "opinion pieces," in which writer-reporters used the conventions of the short story form to capture the charged atmosphere of the urban townships.

It was a series of political exposés by *Drum*'s first reporter, Henry Nxumalo, that helped boost the sales of the magazine between 1952 and 1954. Nxumalo's role as roving reporter and his daring investigation of the ill-treatment of African farm workers and prisoners made him popular among township readers. But such probing, analytical reports were more the exception than the rule. The reader was exposed to the horrors of apartheid, but there were only a few news exposés in *Drum* during the 1950s. African journalists seldom questioned the fundamental structures of the apartheid system or paid much attention to making African working-class readers conscious of these structures. Instead, they protested against racism on moral grounds and called for cooperation and harmony between white and black. Can Themba, in his *Golden City Post* columns, for example, frequently expressed a personal disgust with whites who alienated him. Thus he wrote in his column "Us," in response to the Sophiatown evictions: "Everyday I am made to feel in some way or another that I don't belong to South Africa...We, non-Europeans feel cut off from the world and from other racial groups."[25]

The *Golden City Post* showed no interest in the kind of investigative reports highlighted in *Drum* beyond its coverage of gang violence.[26] Arthur Maimane, for example, ran a serialized exposé on gang warfare in the township of Evaton, near Johannesburg. He concluded that African crime was an aberration that must be stamped out. In calling for police protection, one editorial declared: "Let us call for the police to concentrate on real crime instead of petty technical offenses, and let us support them wholeheartily when they do this big and vital job."[27] In the same edition, however, there was no reference, except for a small photograph, to the historic women's protest in Pretoria against passbooks.

Journalists on both publications were writing to two different, and essentially incompatible, audiences – the working-class African, and the liberal-white and black petty bourgeois elite. For working-class readers, they wrote short, entertaining stories in which they championed the resilient survivors of apartheid – the tsotsi, the detective crime buster, the shebeen queens and their customers. For petty bourgeois readers, in particular white readers, they sought to use their stories to stir protest against the conditions wrought by apartheid. In essence, these literary journalists wrote stories to appeal to readers who sought to escape the reality of pain, but at the same time they sought to stir the consciences of readers who needed to be made aware of the pain.

Michael Chapman argues that the *Drum* stories should be seen "in terms of a social and political process rather than simply as 'artistic' products...which utilize story-telling conventions of atmosphere, dialogue and character presentation in the service of social exposés and factual reportage."[28] David Maughan Brown disagrees, suggesting that such a distinction between art and journalism is questionable: "Where *Drum* is concerned the 'creative writers' as often as not were the journalists," and their writing "often employed language indistinguishable from that of the journalism."[29] *Drum*'s policy did stress the use of a particular journalistic style: "The important feature should be written in the simplest of English. Almost all adjectives should be cut out...If the story is built up out of details, the narrative carries you along with it."[30] Maughan Brown prefers to label these stories "nonfiction" stories. Nick Visser suggests that *Drum* writers were precursors to a mode of literary journalism that was labeled the "New Journalism" by American writers such as Tom Wolfe in the 1960s.[31]

Sophiatown journalists were compelled to subordinate themselves to the material and to present it on its own terms. The creative writer, on the other hand, was supposed to get the reader to see life on the writer's terms. Creative writing allows readers to escape into a vision other than their own, in the hope that they will return with a greater understanding of the real world. As Ronald Weber describes the process:

> [New Journalism] tries to draw together, or draw closer, the conflicting worlds of journalism and literature. It carries over into traditional journalism a variety of literary techniques and attitudes – the most important of which being the artist's need to drag everything back to his cave, to stamp everything, character, events, language, with the imprint of his person.[32]

Dwight Macdonald refers to this synthetic product as "parajournalism," which exploits "the factual authority of journalism and the atmospheric license of fiction."[33] Thus the aim of parajournalism is not

> to convey information (even though the information may be totally accurate) but create entertainment. Its tendency to personalize issues and events and, depending on how much literary apparatus is warmed up, to dramatize situations through novelistic scene setting and character building makes for interesting reading but dubious history.[34]

The blend of journalism and creative writing can be seen in the following examples by *Drum* writers Can Themba and Nat Nakasa. In a story entitled "The Dube Train," Themba describes an incident in a busy Dube Township train coach, in which a young woman is physically harassed by a tsotsi. The story opens with the narrator sitting on the commuter train to Johannesburg on a Monday morning. He feels depressed and nauseated and is resentful of his fellow passengers, whom he describes as "sour-smelling humanity." He is impatient with the "hostile life" and the "shoving savagery of the crowds," who are "dull," "dreary," "undramatic." A young woman walks into the car and sits next to him. When the train stops at a later station, a tsotsi bounces into the car. "I knew the type," the author says, setting the reader up for the action. The tsotsi verbally humiliates the young woman. The narrator expresses his personal lack of concern and directs the reader's attention to the wonder of bridge construction outside his window, declaring: "After the drab, chocolate-box houses of the township, monotonously identical row upon row, this gash of man's imposition upon nature never fails to intrigue me."[35] He bemoans the drabness of township houses but does not link this observation with the construction of the bridge, which is perceived only in terms of man's conquest of nature – and all the while a crime is about to be committed right next to him. The tsotsi viciously slaps the woman sending her flying over the author's lap. Another woman loudly berates the other men in the car for their inaction, but they, like the narrator, are understandably afraid of the tsotsi. The narrator observes, again in a detached manner, that "The men winced" – as if he himself were not part of the crowd. The tsotsi pulls out a knife and stabs one man, who manages, nonetheless, to hurl the tsotsi out the window. Themba ends the story: "it was just another incident in the morning Dube train," and the crowd is "greedily relishing the thrilling episode."[36]

This story by Can Themba highlights the problem of anonymous crime in the townships, which was caused in part by the government's indifference to the conditions of life in these communities.The author poses a social problem through narrative and positions himself as the objective, disinterested observer while he educates the reader about his version of the truth: thuggery is a problem, and African people (like the government) are too indifferent to care.

Nat Nakasa's exposé, "Must we ride ... to disaster?" appeared in *Drum* and, like Themba's story, deals with the problem of crime on an overcrowded train. This news story also opens with the author standing on the Dube platform, gazing at the rushing crowds. In trying to enter one of the cars, he is suddenly flung into it by the shoving of those behind him. Nakasa writes: "I couldn't help wondering anxiously what would happen if a train like the 'five-to-seven' were ever to be involved in an accident. There I was pinned to the door by the other passengers."[37] Nakasa includes the dialogue of the passengers, some angry, some complacent. Then the account shifts abruptly from Nakasa's personal discomfort and his opinions about train travel to a meeting he has with a white Public Relations officer of the South African Railways, who rejects the questions Nakasa asks him. Nakasa's literary introduction, then, is followed by the factual argument with the official regarding the problem of overcrowding.

Like the short story, the exposé is appropriating techniques of dialogue and of reflection from the author's point of view. In another piece for *Drum*, Nakasa composed a personality profile of Ezekial Dhlamani, a legendary boxer known as "King Kong," whose life story became the subject of a famous black musical of that name. Nakasa turns the profile into a dramatic real-life story, complete with far-fetched anecdotes about the "King." The story moves into slick melodrama when the "protagonist," at the height of his popularity, runs afoul of the law:

> But the big conflict–with the law and with himself–was still ahead. It is a night in 1956 at the Polly Centre Hall. The king was out with his only known girl, Maria Miya. King suspected that the girl had been unfaithful to him for some time. So when a misunderstanding came up between them, King stabbed her to death. While a shocked crowd muttered around, King himself ordered them to "Call the police." The police came to find the giant standing in the hall, a knife in his hand. "Drop that knife," the police ordered. King refused. They warned that they would take action if he did not drop the knife. King still said "No."[38]

Nakasa is deft at drawing out the classic tragedy here in his dramatic use of dialogue and in his emphasizing of a by-now clichéd thematic pattern: big tough boxer is putty in the hands of his only girlfriend, whom he kills out of blind jealousy. Nakasa conflates the myth with the real event to make his profile a more gripping tale. The blurred nature of journalism and fiction writing would see its full flowering in short stories and autobiographies written long after the writers of *Drum* left the magazine.

The Politics of the Sophiatown Generation

Despite the fact that the 1950s was one of the most politically turbulent decades in the history of South Africa, the Sophiatown writers were virtually silent on political events. Apart from Bloke Modisane and Es'kia Mphahlele, who showed some interest and sympathy for the nationalist ideals of the Pan-Africanist Congress, few writers made any serious reckoning, on paper, with the major struggles of the decade. Some writers, like Can Themba, claimed to be uninterested in politics and opted for a cultural no-man's-land, where they would be out of the line of fire: "The conflict between the opposed forces seems inevitable: the (roughly) white nationalism poised before the (not too roughly) black nationalism. The dilemma is so complete."[39]

Paul Gready points out that "many writers, torn between the desire to be objective and the inevitable frustration of their daily lives, adopted variations on a political confusion characterized by individualism, cynicism, and a lack of direction."[40] Modisane later complained, in his autobiography *Blame Me on History*: "Although I felt a mental accord with Pan-Africanists I retained my political alienation, I was exhausted by South African politics; everywhere I turned there was politics and there were flies and there were the attitudes of our country."[41] To be sure, these writers had much to fear. "Mr Drum" Henry Nxumalo, for example, was murdered in 1956 during his investigative reporting of illegal abortions in Johannesburg's Western Native Townships.[42] The white editors of *Drum* also were wary of overt political commentary, although they were loathe to use scissors on their own copy.

By and large, the absence of political analysis in the stories of the Sophiatown writers can be attributed mainly to their desire to market a myth to their preferred audience, white-liberal readers. In an interview, Richard Rive pointed out that *Drum* was

> basically a kind of protest writing... The black character [was] a passive recipient of all kinds of victimization... The Drum approach was towards a sympathetic readership, essentially white, who would have a conscience and have the power to effect change... I would suggest that most of the people who read the short stories in *Drum* were white.[43]

Gready describes the contradictions in the protest writers of the Sophiatown generation:

> Despite the Sophiatown authors' criticisms of certain forms of liberalism, many, like their literary predecessors, couched their protest in liberal terms; for example by perceiving Afrikaners as the main enemy, and advocating the benefits of missionary vis-à-vis "Bantu Education" without fully acknowledging the psychological and social tensions caused by the former, which they personified.[44]

The Sophiatown writers were a middle-class literary vanguard. They perceived Sophiatown and its largely working-class inhabitants in terms of their own distinct and personal relationship to this community. Modisane, for example, saw Sophiatown as being "like our nice-time parties or the sound of the penny whistle, a mounting compulsion to joyousness, but always with the hint of pain."[45] Maughan Brown questions this "pathology of compulsive joyousness" and what he sees as the writer's creation of a Sophiatown myth concerning

> [the] stoicism and capacity for endurance of black people, commingled with myths about their energy and "rhythm." In colonial and ex-colonial societies the explicatory powers of Black and White Minstrels, Coons and the perpetually smiling and everlasting comical Sambo are always waiting in the wings to be drawn on in the absence of firmly grounded psycho-social and historical analyses.[46]

Functioning as a kind of bohemian subculture within Sophiatown, these writers depicted the community as they would a bullied drunk, laughing at her oppressor, too numb to feel the pain, too late in the night to want to complain. By day, they wrote about the precarious and self-indulgent life of Sophiatowners. By night, they imbibed this experience themselves. The shebeen, for example, became a frequent motif in the exposés and stories of Themba, Nkosi and Nakasa. A "noble" institution technically prohibited in South Africa, it offered homely warmth and communal hospitality and the beloved "hooch" itself. But the shebeen owners not only defied the law; they saw through it as well, and created a temporary haven for their white and black middle-class customers, who appreciated what was being offered. As Nakasa put it: "They [the shebeens] are not like the municipal bar lounges with their business atmosphere and the inevitable high fencing which gives them the look of cages."[47]

This class coexistence was not without its problems. African intellectuals were sometimes regarded with suspicion by their less privileged white and black neighbors. Modisane writes:

> There is a resentment–almost as deep-rooted as the prejudice itself–against the educated African, not so much because he is allegedly cheeky, but that he fails to conform to the stereotype image of the black man sanctified and cherished with jealous

intensity by the white man; such a native must – as a desperate necessity – be humiliated into submission. The educated African is resented equally by the blacks because he speaks English, which is one of the symbols of white supremacy, he is resentfully called a Situation, something not belonging to either, but tactfully situated between white oppression and black rebellion.[48]

Conclusion

Between 1955 and 1959, Sophiatown became the victim of the Group Areas Act and was mercilessly bulldozed, its residents denied freehold rights anywhere else. Local ANC officials disagreed with the national executive committee about the strategy for opposing these removals. Local ANC leaders called for residents to resort to violence if necessary, whereas official ANC policy advocated civil disobedience and nonviolence. But Don Mattera, a contemporary South African writer and resident of Sophiatown, recalls:

> Most of the strikes, boycotts and other anti-government incidents preceded or coincided with the removal of Sophiatown. Elated by the success of the bus boycotts and the potato boycott, the ANC anticipated greater victories because the people were directly involved. Through the removals, the ANC and its many allies gambled on an uprising which would spark national insurrection and eventually result in the overthrow of the Nationalist Government.[49]

The protests were soon crushed by the government, and the intended revolution was aborted. The ANC's elitist leadership had not cultivated a popular front strong enough to withstand government pressure. There was little resistance to removals on the part of the tenants; many preferred the promise of better housing in Meadowlands, a segregated African township, over the squalid conditions of over-crowding they had endured in Sophiatown.[50] In February 1955, about 2,000 armed police in 80 trucks moved in to evict Sophiatown's residents. The evictions were completed in 1959, and one of the historic townships in South Africa was demolished, only to be rebuilt as the white suburb of Triomf (Afrikaans for Triumph).

For this generation of writers, the destruction of Sophiatown, like the destruction of District Six, its counterpart in Cape Town, was a tragedy of incalculable dimensions. Myth or reality, they were severed from the very source of their inspiration. Anguished and alienated, they perceived the destruction as a metaphor for the betrayal of an intellectual tradition. In a series of autobiographies, they used the event as catalyst for reflecting on their relationship with white and black liberals, with political movements and with South Africa in general.

On the broad political front, the anticommunist bias of the Pan-Africanist Congress attracted some *Drum* writers like Themba and Modisane. But the events of the early 1960s that drove the resistance movement underground also drove the majority of the Sophiatown writers – people like Mphahlele, Modisane, Themba, Matshikiza, Nakasa and Nkosi – into exile. In April 1966, Justice Minister John Vorster used an amended version of the 1950 Suppression of Communism Act to effectively banish all these writers and their writings. The bannings were not lifted until the mid-1980s, when the legacy of the Sophiatown generation was finally made available to a generation of South Africans deprived of this rich literary heritage.

Notes

1. G. Addison, "Drum beat: An examination of *Drum*," *Speak* 1, 4 (1978), 8.
2. E.g., C. Themba, *The will to die* (London, 1978), Intro. (Lewis Nkosi).
3. L. Nkosi, *Home and exile* (London, 1963), 4.
4. T. Couzens, *The new African* (Johannesburg, 1985), Chap. 3.
5. Nkosi, *Home and exile*, 139.
6. Ibid., 4.
7. K. Sole, "Continuity and change in black South African literature," in B. Bozzoli (ed.), *Labor, townships and protest* (Johannesburg, 1979), 160.
8. D. Coplan, *In township tonight* (London, 1985), 143; T. Lodge, *Black politics in South Africa since 1945* (New York, 1983), Chap. 4.
9. Lodge, *Black politics*, 92.
10. M. Tali, *Muriel at metropolitan* (Johannesburg, 1975), 70.
11. P. Gready, "The Sophiatown writers of the fifties: The unreal realities of their world," *Journal of Southern African Studies* 16,1 (1990), 142.
12. N. Nakasa, "Breaking down the old Sophiatown image," in E. Patel (ed.), *The world of Nat Nakasa* (Johannesburg, 1975), 69.
13. A. Maimane, *Golden City Post* (hereafter *GCP*), 21 August 1955, 12.
14. I. S. Manoim, "The black press (1945–1963): The growth of the black mass media and their role as ideological disseminators," M.A. thesis (Johannesburg: University of the Witwatersrand, 1983), 32 (interview with Maimane).
15. C. Motsisi, "Kid Hangover," in M. Mutloatse (ed.), *Casey and Co* (Johannesburg, 1983), 14.
16. T. Matshikiza, "Tribute to Father T. Huddleston," *Drum*, February 1956.
17. Jim Bailey (the sole owner by June 1954) promoted the magazine initially as his personal "plaything." Manoim, "The black press," 86.
18. A. Sampson, *Drum, an African adventure and afterwards* (London, 1983), 20.
19. Manoim, "The black press," 83 (citing Bailey).
20. Quoted in Manoim, 127.
21. *GCP*, August 1956, 4 (editorial).
22. H. Nxumalo, *GCP*, August 1956.
23. Manoim, "The black press," 91.
24. M. Chapman (ed.), *The Drum decade: Stories from the 1950s* (Pietermaritzburg, 1989), Preface vii; L. Switzer and D. Switzer, *Black press in South Africa and Lesotho*, 1836–1976 (Boston, 1979), 102–103, 115–116.
25. C. Themba, *GCP*, August 1956.
26. The policies of *GCP*'s politically indifferent editor, Cecil Eprile, may have accounted in part for the lack of investigative exposés. Manoim, "The black press," 194.
27. *GCP*, August 1956, 4 (editorial).
28. Chapman, *The Drum decade*, Preface vii.
29. D. M. Brown, "The anthology as reliquary?," *Current writing* 1 (1989), 19.
30. Quoted in Manoim, "The black press," 129.
31. N. Visser, "South Africa: The renaissance that failed," *Journal of Commonwealth Literature* 11, 1 (1976), 42–57.
32. R. Weber (ed.), *The reporter as artist: A look at the new journalism controversy* (New York, 1974), 23.
33. D. Macdonald, "Parajournalism, or Tom Wolfe and his magic writing machine," in Weber, *The reporter as artist*, 223.
34. Weber, *The reporter as artist*, 24.
35. C. Themba, "The Dube train," in E. Patel (ed.), *The world of Can Themba* (Johannesburg, 1985), 37.
36. Ibid., 39.
37. N. Nakasa, "Must we ride ... to disaster?" in Patel, *The world of Nat Nakasa*, 35.
38. N. Nakasa, "The life and death of King Kong," in Patel, *The world of Nat Nakasa*, 96.
39. C. Themba, "The bottom of the bottle," in *The will to die* , 115.
40. Gready, "The Sophiatown writers," 153.
41. B. Modisane, *Blame me on history* (London, 1963), 249.
42. Chapman, *The Drum decade*, 188.
43. R. Rive, from an interview conducted by Abraham de Vries, in *Current Writing* 1 (1989), 45.
44. Gready, "The Sophiatown writers," 152.
45. Modisane, *Blame me*, 9.
46. Brown, "The anthology," 7.
47. N. Nakasa, "... And so the shebeen lives on," in Patel, *The world of Nat Nakasa*, 58.
48. Modisane, *Blame me*, 44.
49. D. Mattera, *Gone with the twilight* (Johannesburg, 1987), 138.
50. Lodge, *Black Politics*, 109.

CHAPTER 9

Socialism and the Resistance Movement

The Life and Times of the *Guardian*, 1937–1952

Les Switzer

> This is the credo of the *Guardian*. The *Guardian* will fight tooth and nail for the preservation of that modicum of democracy which persists in South Africa. It will fight to make political democracy coterminous with economic democracy for we hold that the one is incomplete without the other. To that end it pledges its support to all those groups and individuals who share its outlook. The *Guardian* is for the under-dog. It is the paper of those whose work with hand and brain keep this country going. In this sense it is the paper of the working-class.[1]

The contours of resistance in South Africa were shaped in large part by structural changes in the developing industrial economy following the outbreak of World War I.* Scholars working on South Africa's labor movement in recent years have argued that trade unions were organized primarily in response to the way capital organized labor, and the limits of trade union bargaining power were essentially set by developments within the labor process.[2]

*I am most grateful to James Zug, who is working on a full-length study of the *Guardian* newspapers, for reading a draft of this chapter, filling in numerous biographical gaps and allowing me to cite his own research in telling the *Guardian* story. I owe an immense debt to *Guardian* editor Brian Bunting and to his colleagues Ray (Alexander) Simons, Naomi (Shapiro) Barnett and Len Lee-Warden for their assistance. Brian read the manuscript twice, and his valuable comments were incorporated in the final revision. In addition, I want to thank Don Pinnock for sharing some of his interview notes with me, and Jonathan Hook, a graduate student in history at the University of Houston, for locating some quotes used in this chapter, acting as a coder in the final stage of the content analysis and contributing to the initial draft of the section dealing with the socialist project.

As elsewhere in the industrial world, the craft skills of South African workers were replaced by machines, and they were made subject to machines. New workers (drawn mainly from subordinated sectors of the white and black population) with little or no experience in craft trades were also recruited. So-called scientific management techniques were increasingly exploited by industrial employers and the central govemment to separate mental from manual labor, fragment jobs and de-skill job categories, and in numerous other ways to standardize and police the system of work and thereby transform the labor process.[3]

The Trade Union Movement

The white-dominated, largely English-speaking craft guilds that had traditionally controlled the trade union movement in South Africa were gradually undermined as machine technology was introduced and the industrial work force reorganized between the 1920s and 1940s.[4] A new division of labor distinguishing between semiskilled and unskilled machine operatives was developed, and the new urban work force was drawn in large part from agriculturalists (white as well as black) driven off the land. Local capital and local technology were now available to assist in mechanizing production, and the tariff policies of successive coalition governments between 1924 and 1939 offered protection for local capitalists. The newly urbanized work force also offered an expanding market for locally produced goods.

Private and public companies replaced individual owners initially in highly competitive consumer products industries that did not require too much capital or technology to mechanize production and reorganize the workplace. The leather and footwear, clothing and furniture industries (and to a lesser extent the laundry, rope and canvas industries) were the first to experience this transformation in the 1920s. They were followed by the textile, food and canning, sweet (candy) and tobacco industries in the 1930s.

Manufacturing had become the most significant contributor to the national income even before the end of World War II. The need for African industrial workers in particular had increased dramatically, especially during the war years, when the labor pool contracted as hundreds of thousands of black and white South Africans were serving in the armed forces. Africans employed in private industry apart from the mines, for example, increased rapidly from 54,856 in 1932–33 to 215,582 in 1945–46.[5]

The heart of mining and industrial activity in South Africa was the gold-laden Witwatersrand in the southern Transvaal. New mineral discoveries, beginning in the early 1930s, extended the Rand southward to Klerksdorp and Vereeniging on the borders of the Orange Free State. A majority of the country's white and African industrial work force were employed on the Rand, and Johannesburg was the center of the trade union movement.

White females (including juveniles) and black males – the cheapest sources of labor available – formed the bulk of the new industrial work force. "Industrial unions," as they were called, were gradually established from the 1920s to organize workers in newly mechanized industries and in the distributive trade. (A Reef Native Trade Assistants' Union, for example, was organized in 1926.) The process of mechanization, job fragmentation and de-skilling in the consumer products sector was so rapid that the craft unions in these industries were also forced to open their ranks to semiskilled workers. Thus tailors, cabinetmakers and other skilled workers abandoned exclusive craft unionism in favor of open industrial unions.

The Garment Workers' Union, under its charismatic leader E. S. ("Solly") Sachs, was the largest and by far the most powerful of the militant open industrial unions before the 1950s.

Industrial unions had none of the credentials of the older craft unions, and most recognized that their bargaining power was based on strength of numbers. The organizers of these unions were mainly socialists sympathetic to the possibility of a nonracial (and nongendered) alliance of workers, and under their leadership a South African Trade Union Congress (TUC) to coordinate the activities of the new industrial unions was organized in 1924. The TUC was initially reluctant to recruit African workers and refused to allign itself, for example, with the Industrial and Commercial Workers' Union (ICU), the largest black trade union in South Africa at the time. Nevertheless, members of the Communist Party of South Africa (CPSA) and other socialist groups began organizing African workers (for example, CPSA members Benjamin Weinbren and T. W. Thibedi helped set up an independent South African Federation of Non-European Trade Unions in March 1928). Faced with this competition, the TUC also began urging its affiliated unions to enroll all employees regardless of racial origin or at least to establish segregated "parallel" branches for persons of color.

The growth of South Africa's industrial labor unions came to a temporary halt with the onset of the Great Depression and the splintering of the ICU into several irreconciliable groups in 1929–30. The Federation of Non-European Trade Unions also collapsed, but in 1930 the TUC, together with the Cape Federation of Labour Unions, voted to establish a new, specifically nonracial body called the South African Trades and Labour Council (TLC).

Between 1930 and 1948, South Africa's nonracial trade union movement in the industrial heartland of the Transvaal was largely in the hands of the TLC and its affiliated unions.[6] Between 1934 and 1939, trade union membership, generated largely by the industrial unions, more than doubled from 126,000 to 264,000, and between 1937 and 1947 the number of unions affiliated with the TLC increased from 32 to 117.[7]

Coloureds and Indians, as well as whites, were members of industrial and even some craft unions, but few Africans were represented. No more than six African unions were affiliated with the TLC in any one year, but the trade union body did provide financial and legal aid to individual African unions. Several industrial and craft unions, moreover, established parallel African branches, and there was cooperation between TLC committees and African unions at the local level and within specific industries where there was still little if any distinction between black and white workers.

These linkages were maintained in the 1930s and 1940s, despite the historic compromise between capital and white labor following a so-called revolt by white miners on the Witwatersrand in 1922 and the formation of a National-Labour coalition, or "Pact," government in 1924.[8] The Industrial Conciliation Act of 1924 was negotiated at the expense of African industrial workers. White trade unions were formally recognized by the government, and industrial councils were created to set up collective bargaining procedures, resolve disputes involving issues such as wages and working conditions, and to administer health and insurance benefits and apprenticeship programs. Africans were not considered "employees" under the act, and therefore they were excluded from its provisions, a status that applied to African workers in nonindustrial categories as well. Coloureds and Indians could join registered unions, so they had little incentive to join all-black unions until so-called "mixed" unions were effectively banned during the apartheid era in an amendment to this legislation in 1956.[9]

African unions were not illegal, but they were not recognized by the government and therefore had no legal standing. Most workers did not earn enough money, moreover, to pay union membership dues. Africans were restricted from entering the urban areas–pass laws favored only young, able-bodied males–and they had few rights when they got there. Collective bargaining was limited for African industrial workers and virtually illegal for non-industrial workers. Africans could only qualify for certain job categories in certain regions of the country, and all strike action was forbidden.

The most difficult African workers to organize were miners, domestics and farm laborers, but they constituted the vast majority of the employed or employable African work force (about two-thirds of the adult male population, for example, in 1937), and they were the most vulnerable to exploitation. An African Mine Workers' Union was established in August 1941 under the leadership of a committee drawn from liberal groups like the South African Institute of Race Relations (SAIRR) and left-wing groups like the CPSA (7 of the 15 members were communists, including party stalwarts Edwin Mofutsanyana, Gaur Radebe, Eli Weinberg and J. B. Marks, who was elected head of the union in December 1942). Attempts to organize nonindustrial workers, however, largely failed during this period. Apart from these three job categories, the potential number of African industrial workers who could be organized was perhaps 218,000 in 1936 and 341,000 in 1945–46.[10]

The second phase of the independent African trade union movement on the Witwatersrand (the first phase began in World War I and ended with the Great Depression) was initiated in the mid-1930s mainly by dissidents from the CPSA such as Max Gordon, a self-proclaimed Trotskyite who was also associated with the SAIRR, and Gana Makabeni, a former organizer for the ICU and the Communist Party (expelled from the CPSA in 1932). By 1940, a Non-European Coordinating Committee sponsored by Makabeni had 11 unions with 2,670 members, and a Joint Committee of African Trade Unions sponsored by Gordon had 7 unions with 16,000–20,000 members. The two committees combined to form the Council of Non-European Trade Unions (CNETU) in 1941, and membership rose dramatically during the war years.

The CNETU was the most important coordinating body representing primarily unregistered African unions in South Africa. Cordial relations were maintained with the nonracial TLC, and unions affiliated with the CNETU were established outside the Rand, especially in the Cape. By 1945, the coordinating body claimed 158,000 members organized in 119 unions (about half of which were located on the Rand).

African trade unions achieved some victories before and during World War II–even though African workers did not qualify as employees–because they were able to get the Labour Department and a sympathetic Wage Board[11] to enforce legal minimum wages and obtain a hearing for workers cheated out of wages by their employers. Several registered industrial unions (operating mainly in the food and canning, garment, textile and distributive trades) also began admitting Africans as members–especially women, who could claim full trade union rights because of a loophole in the Industrial Conciliation Act–and a degree of solidarity was achieved between registered and unregistered unions in confrontations with management during the war.

Although African workers were forbidden to strike, there was a dramatic increase in unorganized as well as organized work stoppages by Africans on the Rand and in port cities such as Cape Town, Port Elizabeth, East London and Durban during the war.[12] The African National Congress (ANC, or Congress), the CPSA (after the German invasion of the Soviet Union in 1941) and virtually every other organized protest group, however, rejected the tactics of direct action in the interest of maintaining the war effort. Grievances other than wages–and African workers complained about working conditions, seeing fellow workers forced out of jobs, lack of overtime pay and the refusal to recognize their trade unions–were rarely recognized as legitimate even by African political leaders at this time.

The United Party government under Jan Smuts (1939–48) tried a carrot-and-stick approach to contain the African trade union movement. Allied defeats in the early years of the war and the activities of several pro-Nazi groups in South Africa convinced many leaders in government and industry that they should respond more positively to African trade union demands. The minister of labour had expressed support for some kind of recognition for African unions as early as 1939, and this was reinforced in a government report (the Smit Report) three years later.

Various economic interests (represented primarily by commerce and manufacturing), and their advocates within the ruling United Party, were also beginning to think that productivity would be enhanced if a permanent African labor force enjoying an improved standard of living was housed in the cities. Such views were in conflict with other economic interests (represented primarily by mining and agriculture), and their advocates within the opposition National Party, who could not compete with secondary industry in attracting workers and continued to rely heavily on migrant labor. The prime minister himself publicly endorsed the principles enshrined in the 1941 Atlantic Charter, which had outlined the postwar aims of the allies and anticipated the United Nations. His minister of Native affairs also told members of the Natives' Representative Council in December 1942 that the "Freedoms" expressed in the charter were applicable to Africans in South Africa. Smuts in a widely reported speech at an SAIRR meeting in March 1942 declared that "segregation has fallen on evil days."[13]

The pass laws controlling African migration to the cities were temporarily relaxed during the early years of the war, Africans in some economic sectors (mainly manufacturing) succeeded in gaining significant wage increases, and the 1941 Workman's Compensation Act offered limited benefits to African workers. The Old Age Pensions Act (1926) and Blind Persons Act (1936) were amended to include Africans in 1944, and unemployment (for those earning less than £78 a year) and disability grants were extended to Africans two years later.

Wage increases and social welfare benefits for Africans, however, remained glaringly unequal and discriminatory. The authorities formally outlawed strikes by Africans (War Measure 145 of 1942), and a measure prohibiting meetings of more than 20 persons on ground "proclaimed" off-limits by the authorities (Proclamation 201 of 1939) was reinforced with specific reference to property owned by mining companies (War Measure 1425 of 1944). The pass laws were also tightened up again toward the end of the war. Although the Smuts govemment had accepted in principle that African workers could organize unions and participate marginally in the collective bargaining process, an Industrial Conciliation (Natives) Bill introduced in 1947 would have granted only limited recognition to African unions and placed restrictions on their activities. The bill was dropped when it received little support from industry and was rejected by the TLC and most independent African trade unions.

The decade's major confrontation between African labor and the state ended in disaster for the workers, their leaders and the unions, when the Smuts government brutally repressed a strike by 70,000-100,000 miners in Johannesburg in August 1946 (for details, see Chapter 11). The miners had not consulted the CNETU (or the ANC or any other organized African political body), but virtually all African trade union activity on the Rand was doomed in the aftermath of the strike. The CNETU had been undermined by faction fights[14] and allegations of corruption throughout its history, but the miners' strike effectively destroyed the organization. African workers' solidarity had received a stunning setback at a crucial point in its history.

State Intervention in the Workplace

Attempts to mechanize production and reorganize labor had received increasing support from the central govemment since the 1920s. A racially exclusive work force developed in certain key industries, beginning with mining, where large-scale de-skilling and job reorganization first took place. Other industries requiring a lot of capital–such as railways and steel (beginning with ISCOR, the parastatal Iron and Steel Corporation, created in 1928)–were even more dependent on the state. White wage earners in these economic sectors were progressively removed from productive work and made supervisors over subordinated African workers. The white workers were to accept mechanization and be responsible for policing the workplace, and in return they would be effectively promoted to the lower ranks of the middle class. The most powerful of the government-protected, white industrial unions during this period were the Mineworkers' Union and the Iron and Steel Trades Association.

Craft unions in the relatively low-paid consumer products sector had been undermined by the new division of labor, but they relied on trade union action rather than the government to secure their members' interests. As noted earlier, they supported the TLC's nonracial policies and allied themselves to the industrial unions. Other craft unions, especially in the metal and engineering industries, were able to slow down efforts to transform the production process. Local entrepreneurs did not have the capital or machine technology to invest in these industries unless the state intervened, and a mass market for these goods was not created until the armaments industry was developed with the coming of World War II. The Amalgamated Engineering Union was the largest of the skilled craft unions in these industries.

Labor historian Jon Lewis argues that capital's struggle to reorganize the production process did not succeed in transforming most sectors of the industrial economy until the end of World War II. With considerable support from management in the private and public sectors, however, craft unions after 1945 began to employ a strategy of racial exclusion in order to reestablish themselves as "pseudo craft unions" and maintain their privileged position. Apprenticeship programs and various other training schemes were expanded to absorb as many unskilled and semiskilled whites as possible. Skilled whites, especially in the militant industrial unions, were promoted to supervisory positions or given other white collar jobs.

Most work involving production was preserved for persons of color at low wages. By 1950, blacks were performing an estimated 16 percent of all skilled, 66 percent of all semiskilled and 98 percent of all unskilled industrial work.[15] Management arbitrarily classified production jobs designated for blacks as unskilled or semiskilled and reduced the wage gap between them. The militancy of white workers in the trade union movement was blunted as the division of labor was redefined along racial lines. Whites became even more of a privileged caste as registered white trade unions increasingly alligned themselves with white management in the new economic order.

The reorganization of labor along racial lines had a decisive impact on registered trade unions and on the nonracial tradition of the TLC, their main coordinating body. Leadership of the TLC had always been in the hands of more conservative craft unions, who generally supported the United Party and sought to blunt the activities of the more militant, nonracial industrial unions. The National Party, moreover, was adept at exploiting tensions within the white labor movement over relations with African workers.

The uneasy alliance between craft and industrial unions within the TLC began to unravel in the later 1940s. The first white splinter group to leave (the steel unions and several other craft unions in the Pretoria area) did so in 1947 over the issue of allowing unregistered African trade unions to affiliate with the TLC. The white miners' unions broke away in 1948, but the TLC was not really crippled until the mainly English-speaking craft unions left in 1950. The militant nonracial wing of the TLC finally gained control of the executive committee in 1948, but the coordinating body was already breaking up as large numbers of white workers aligned themselves with the National Party and its policy of establishing a racial hierarchy of segregated unions. Facing mounting pressure from the newly elected apartheid government, left-wing trade unionists were detained, served with banning orders or otherwise forced into exile. Defections continued, and membership in the TLC declined from 184,000 to 82,000 between 1947 and 1952.[16]

In an attempt to unite the country's mixed craft and industrial unions, the TLC and several regional coordinating bodies dominated by the craft unions voted to exclude African unions altogether and form a new South African Trade Union Council (SATUC) in 1955. Some mixed unions rejected the SATUC and with surviving African unions that had been affiliated to the CNETU and other groups they formed the South African Congress of Trade Unions (SACTU) in 1955. There were now five trade union coordinating bodies (two white, two mixed and one open to all racial groups) and a growing number of unaffiliated unions in South Africa, and all of them were increasingly vulnerable to pressure from the state. The National Party's labor strategy between the 1950s and 1970s largely succeeded in meeting the conflicting demands of mining, agricultural and industrial capital for workers, separating white workers from black workers and neutralizing the independent African trade union movement.

Community Mobilization

Historian and political activist Baruch Hirson has distinguished between the struggles organized by African community-action groups and the struggles organized by urban African trade unions and African political pressure groups like the ANC during the 1930s and 1940s. Whereas the workers had their own unions and confronted white employers along class lines, community-action groups had members from all segments of the population, including the petty bourgeoisie. Class priorities tended to merge in issues that affected everyone in the community. Hirson argues that organized political and labor groups failed to work together with community groups until the 1950s. Even then, popular resistance at the community level, especially in the rural areas, was relegated to the fringes of the resistance movement.[17]

The transition from peasant to proletarian was a slow, uneven and, for Africans especially, a very painful process. The number of Africans resident in the rural areas who were migrating out of necessity to the cities rose steadily during the 1920s and 1930s and dramatically during the 1940s and 1950s. The reserves could no longer feed the resident population, and survival in these areas was an increasingly precarious enterprise. The authorities put pressure on impoverished householders to limit livestock and participate in schemes to "rehabilitate" the reserves, but their efforts met with increasing resistance from the later 1940s. The development of mechanized commercial agriculture in the designated white farming areas during and after the war also forced many semiautonomous black farm workers (some of whom were still sharecroppers and leasehold tenants) off the land and into the cities.

Protest groups at the community level mobilized over specific concerns but did not seek to confront the conditions in town and countryside that gave rise to these concerns. For example, they did not protest residential segregation, but they did protest poor and insufficient housing, water and sanitation facilities, arbitrary evictions from makeshift homes, high bus fares and inadequate public transport, police harassment and attempts to criminalize certain entrepreneurial activities (such as selling petty commodities, brewing beer, and operating lodging houses and taverns or shebeens).

Social links between town and countryside were retained at all class levels and even reinforced through language, kinship and age group loyalties in the segregated urban townships. Informal organizations originating in the villages were reestablished in the cities for mutual aid and protection, and ethnic affiliation could be used to obtain housing and preferential employment in some economic sectors (such as mining). Conflicts originating in the urban townships migrated to the villages, just as conflicts associated with rural "tribal" life migrated to the cities.

New allegiances were also formed between disparate groups within the urban population. Shopkeepers, clerks and upper-ranked professionals participated in community protest campaigns along with alienated domestics, industrial workers and members of criminal gangs. Those who aspired to middle-class status, however, remained timid in the face of militant action and retreated when confrontation threatened to turn to violence. As Hirson suggests, the demoralized petty bourgeoisie played at best a secondary role in township struggles before the 1950s.

Community-action groups were very active in the cities. Popular resistance in the Johannesburg metropolitan area, for example, was highlighted by a series of bus boycotts between 1940 and 1945 organized by residents of the African freehold township of Alexandra, and by a squatters' rights movement between 1944 and 1947 motivated in large part by the desperate housing shortage. But there was also mounting unrest in the countryside. The Ciskei and parts of the Transkei reserves in the eastern Cape remained focal points of popular resistance between the 1940s and 1960s, and in the interior there were confrontations between peasant groups and government authorities in the Zoutpansberg (Venda) and Sekhukuniland (Lebowa) reserves in the northem Transvaal and in the Witzieshoek (Basotho Qwa Qwa) reserve in the Orange Free State.

Case Study of the *Guardian*

The socialist press played the key role in chronicling the struggles of dissident political, trade union and community-action groups between the mid-1930s and early 1960s, and the most influential socialist journal during this period was the *Guardian*, an English-language weekly. The Guardian was the inspiration of a group of left-wing activists living in the Cape Town metropolitan area. Many were associated with Cape Town's Left Book Club, a discussion group "for progressive people who met and discussed world and South African problems." They believed a newspaper was needed for "workers and people who were anxious to fight against fascism and for democracy and... workers' rights."[18]

Members of the Left Book Club organized an informal subcommittee to explore the possibility of establishing such a newspaper. It consisted of veteran trade unionists William ("Comrade Bill") Andrews (South African Trades and Labour Council), James ("Jimmy") Emmerich (Cape Town Tram and Omnibus Workers' Union), John Gomas and James ("Jimmy") La Guma (who, with Zainunnissa ["Cissie"] Gool, had launched the National Liberation League); academic Harold Baldry and his wife Carina Pearson; and Cape ANC official Thomas Ngwenya. George Sacks, a medical doctor, and his wife Betty Radford, a journalist, were also on the subcommittee along with an anti-Nazi by the name of Arthur Trommer, who had escaped Hitler's Germany and was a journeyman compositor and typesetter; and printer Charles Stewart, owner of the Stewart Printing Company, who was sympathetic to left-wing causes. Stewart printed the *Guardian* for the first 10 years of its existence.[19]

The subcommittee sought financial backing initially for a newspaper that would promote working-class issues. There was an immediate response, according to Ray Alexander (Simons), "from the trade unionists, artists, journalists, academics and professionals." Donations were also received from various business enterprises, in particular a pharmaceutical company owned by two brothers named Eric and Norman Flegg, who played an important role in helping to finance the newspaper during the 1940s.[20]

The subcommittee turned itself into an editorial board, which was made up initially of Radford, Baldry, Gomas, Ngwenya, Emmerich, Andrews and two other (unknown) trade unionists. The newspaper was published every Thursday in Cape Town, and the editorial board met every Friday to plan the contents for the following week. An editorial conference for the Cape Town news staff was also held every Monday. Radford was appointed editor, and Pearson was placed in charge of circulation, but many others also helped produce the newspaper. Virtually all editorial and administrative staffers, in the early years at least, were unpaid.[21]

The *Guardian* was a trade union newspaper supported by "all organisations of the workers–the Trade Unions, the Labour and Socialist parties."[22] It was launched as the *Cape Guardian* in Cape Town in February 1937, but in June the title was shortened to the *Guardian*. Editions appeared every week under this title until May 1952, a month before the Defiance Campaign, when it was banned by the authorities. Editors and contributors were frequently forced to defend themselves in court and subjected to police raids and other forms of harrassment; some were jailed and eventually forced into exile. The *Guardian* maintained production for 26 years by continually changing its title. Three titles were banned during the lifetime of the newspaper, and individual issues were banned on at least two occasions; one, during the 1960 State of Emergency, effectively silenced the weekly for several months.[23]

It was finally forced to cease publication in March 1963, "when the producers were forbidden on pain of imprisonment to take any part in editing, writing or publishing any journal whatsoever."[24]

This case study focuses on the *Guardian* during the 15 years it appeared under the *Guardian* title, describing the editors and writers, readers and advertisers, and the news agenda. Special attention is paid to domestic political and trade union news and foreign news in order to assess the newspaper's role in chronicling the transition to nonviolent resistance and in representing the socialist project as the goal of the resistance movement during these years.

Editors and Writers

The *Guardian* was a national newspaper with offices in the three major metropolitan areas during the 1940s–Cape Town, Johannesburg (opened in August 1941 in the same building housing *Inkululeko*'s offices) and Durban (opened in March 1942)–and it was also distributed outside South Africa.[25] Another office was opened in Port Elizabeth early in 1953. The *Guardian* boasted two editions by August 1945, a northern edition for the Transvaal and Natal, and a southern edition for the Cape. The front and back pages, including some advertisements, were changed in each edition to cater to local news, sports and entertainment.[26]

The *Guardian* was organized very much like an established commercial newspaper with a managing editor, business manager, circulation manager and other departmental heads. It also looked like a commercial newspaper of the 1940s and 1950s, employing the standard vertical layout of the day, and the main story was usually accompanied by a banner-size headline that stretched across two or more columns below the masthead. Unlike most other socialist publications, the *Guardian* offered factual news reports as well as labeled opinion pieces and features on designated pages. The back page generally consisted of sports, social events and miscellaneous news stories. The newspaper varied in width from five to seven columns and in length from 6 to 8 pages (although the first issue and on occasion other issues had as many as 12 pages). In addition, there were numerous special supplements, ranging from 2 to 6 pages in length. In the five-column tabloid format, advertisements were generally large (two columns in width, except for designated "adlets," and at least 4 or 5 inches deep), and they anchored the lower right- and/or left-hand columns of most pages.[27]

The *Guardian* was registered in Betty Radford's name in March 1937, and for the first eight years of its existence she was the sole owner/proprietor and managing editor. But increasing pressure from government and private industry during the war years–news cables from London, for example, were censored and the newspaper itself was sued by four gold-mining houses over an article on miners' wages published in August 1943–compromised the newspaper's legal standing. The *Guardian* was placed under the control of a registered company, the Guardian Newspaper (Pty) Ltd., in November 1945 with its own board of directors, many of whom were liberal establishment figures. The *Guardian* "retained its legal independence," as Bunting put it, which proved crucial to the survival of the newspaper when the CPSA was banned in 1950.[28]

The *Guardian* during the first four years or so of its existence was produced essentially by Betty Radford, Carina Pearson and their husbands George Sacks and Harold Baldry. Radford (1906–75) was born in England and migrated to South Africa in 1931. The only professional journalist on the newspaper at the time, she had previously worked as a reporter for the *Cape Times* and had eventually been made editor of the weekly women's page. Radford and husband George Sacks, a prominent Cape Town surgeon, and their companions were members of Cape Town's white elite, left-wing community during the 1940s, most of whom were far removed from the realities of black *or* white working-class life. Radford herself has been described as a kind of socialist socialite on display with her "clipped English accent, patrician mannerisms, smart clothes and jewelry, [and] the footmen at her grand Oranjezicht home below Table Mountain where she dressed each evening for dinner."[29]

None were Communist Party members initially, but Radford, Carina and their husbands finally joined the CPSA in May or June 1941, probably just before the Germans attacked the Soviet Union. In fact, the *Guardian* offices in Cape Town were a few blocks from the party's headquarters, which had been moved from faction-ridden Johannesburg to Cape Town in January 1939. Radford herself was elected as a CPSA candidate to the Cape Town City Council in 1943, and she was a member of the CPSA's central committee between 1946 and 1948. Her husband George Sacks would become editor of *Freedom*, a Communist Party journal devoted mainly to socialist theory, which was also published in Cape Town.

Radford never received a salary during the 11.7 years she served as editor of the newspaper. She monitored the news operation very carefully, and in addition to administrative duties she wrote general news stories and a regular miscellaneous news column (entitled "Topical"). Harold T. ("Jack") Simons, a lecturer in African law and administration at the University of Cape Town and the sole Communist Party member when he was elected to the editorial board in November 1937, wrote most of the editorials until 1947.[30]

A massive police swoop on left-wing groups throughout the country following the 1946 African miners' strike apparently placed a severe emotional strain on Radford, who had been sick with tick-bite fever for several months preceding the strike. The offices of the *Guardian* were raided, documents confiscated, and Radford herself was arrested on charges of sedition. The charges against her were dropped after a preliminary hearing in August 1947, but she remained in poor health. After losing a bid for reelection to the Cape Town City Council in 1947, Radford took a leave of absence from the *Guardian* for almost three months. She returned to the newspaper in February 1948, but she complained of the "gruelling and harassing job" and resigned six months later. Radford continued writing her "Topical" column until about March 1949, but by then she was very disillusioned as an activist. She also resigned from the Communist Party (along with Carina Pearson), and she retired from politics altogether during her remaining years in South Africa.[31]

Brian Bunting (born 1920), a veteran of World War II who was appointed assistant editor in 1946, succeeded Radford as managing editor in September 1948.[32] The *Guardian* became much more militant in its coverage of left-wing politics under Bunting's editorship. He retained this post for 15 turbulent years, despite receiving a personal banning order in 1952, being detained in the 1960 emergency and placed under house arrest in 1962. The title of the newspaper was changed five times during his tenure – *Clarion* (May–August 1952), *People's World* (August–October 1952), *Advance* (November 1952–October 1954), *New Age* (October 1954–April 1962, August–November 1962) and *Spark* (December 1962–March 1963).[33] Bunting was virtually forced to leave South Africa in 1963, after he was barred from working as a journalist.[34]

Bunting, the son of a founding father of the Communist Party (see Chapter 11), was among the new-breed protest joumalists who had worked on commercial

Photo 25. Betty Radford (Sacks), editor of the *Guardian* (1937–48).

Photo 26. Brian Percy Bunting, editor of the *Guardian* and successor newspapers (1948–63).

Photo 27. Fred Carneson served for almost two decades as a staff writer, acting editor, distributor and eventually business manager of the *Guardian*.

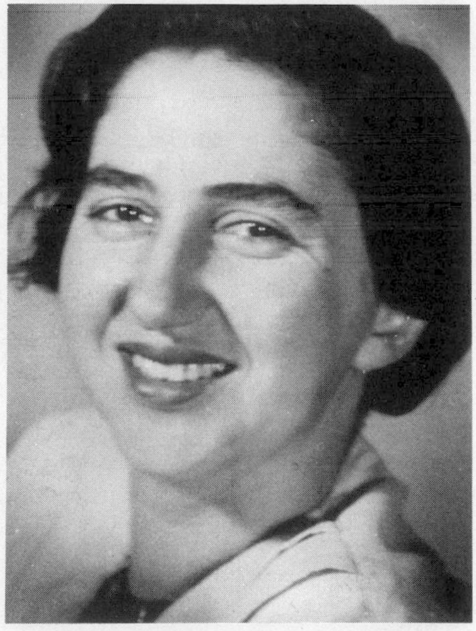

Photo 28. Naomi Shapiro (Barnett), a permanent staff reporter, photoghrapher and acting editor of the *Guardian* when Bunting was away from Cape town.

newspapers (he had been a subeditor on the *Rand Daily Mail* and *Sunday Times*). Like Radford, he brought a professional expertise that was invaluable to the *Guardian* and other alternative newspapers during the 1950s. He was also an official in the Springbok Legion, the militant servicemen's organization established to fight fascism inside as well as outside South Africa, and for a brief period after returning from the war he was editor of its journal *Fighting Talk*. Bunting was elected to the CPSA's Johannesburg district committee in 1946 and to the party's central committee in 1948.

Bunting, like other CPSA recruits who worked on the newspaper, participated in parliamentary politics insofar as it was possible for a party member to do so in South Africa during the 1940s. Sam Kahn, also a member of the party's central committee (1949–50) and an unpaid legal adviser and contributor to the *Guardian*, had been elected to the House of Assembly representing the African population in the western Cape in November 1948.[35] As a communist he was expelled from parliament three years later, but Bunting found a loophole in the 1950 Communism Act and was elected a Native Representative to succeed Kahn in November 1952.

Bunting, in turn, was expelled from parliament 11 months later. Trade unionist Ray Alexander (Simons), who had also been a member of the party's central committee in the 1940s, was elected to replace Bunting in 1954, but she was not allowed to take her seat in parliament. Len Lee-Warden, the *Guardian*'s printer during the 1950s and early 1960s, replaced Alexander. Lee-Warden had never joined the Communist Party, and he was allowed to enter parliament (when he was not in detention) until the office of Native Representative was abolished in 1960.[36]

Fred Carneson, a member of the party's central committee in the last four years before the party was banned in South Africa, was elected to the Cape Provincial Council in 1949, but he would also be expelled because of his communist affiliation. Carneson played a prominent role in the newspaper during Bunting's editorship, as a staff writer, acting editor (for example, in the 11 months Bunting was in parliament) and business manager.[37]

Africans, Coloureds and Indians were involved in editorial activities in the Cape Town, Johannesburg and Durban offices of the *Guardian* from the beginning, but few had by-lines in the newspaper before the 1950s. Jellico Ntshona, for example, was one of these anonymous contributors. He and his wife helped with bookkeeping and clerical jobs and wrote articles on occasion. Henry Nxumalo covered sports for more than three years, between September 1947 and roughly January 1951, when he left to join *Drum* magazine, flagship of the commercial African tabloids in the 1950s and 1960s. As "Mr Drum," Nxumalo would become a household name in African journalism with his investigative exposés.

The first editor-manager of the Port Elizabeth branch office when it was established in 1953 was Gladstone Tshume, a local ANC and Communist Party activist who had been banned the previous year. Tshume was succeeded by Govan Mbeki, the former editor of *Inkundla ya Bantu* and a key figure in both the ANC and the underground Communist Party after 1950. Mbeki was a member of the *Guardian*'s board of directors from 1946 and head of the Port Elizabeth bureau for *New Age* between 1955 and 1962. Like his counterpart M. P. Naicker in Durban, Mbeki became a celebrated journalist in the *New Age* era. He reorganized the Port Elizabeth office and expanded its coverage of events in the eastern Cape. His investigative articles on unrest in the Transkei, for example, are regarded as a primary source of information on conditions in the reserve during these years.

The most prominent Indian writer under the *Guardian* title (and the third full-time member of staff following Radford and Pearson) was Harry Allimuthu

("H. A.") Naidoo, who had entered activist politics as a trade union organizer representing Natal's sugarcane workers. Naidoo joined the CPSA in the mid-1930s and served on its central committee between 1945 and 1950, while he was working on the newspaper in Cape Town. He was also active in Indian politics and an ardent supporter of closer relations between the ANC and the South African Indian Congress (SAIC). Naidoo represented the South African Resistance Council in the first South African protest delegation to the United Nations in 1946.[38] He left South Africa in 1951 shortly after the CPSA was forced to disband.

A number of prominent Indians in Durban wrote and/or collected funds for the newspaper during the 1950s, including SAIC leaders G. M. ("Monty") Naicker and Yusuf Dadoo, George Seedat, Ismael Meer, J. N. Singh and M. P. Naicker of the Natal Indian Congress. Dawood Seedat, a trade unionist and CPSA leader in Durban for more than 20 years, was an editor and branch manager of the Durban office in the early- to mid-1950s. Marimuthu Pragalathan ("M. P.") Naicker took over in 1956, and in the next seven years he transformed the Durban bureau. He hired a number of talented people, reorganized news production practices and established the newspaper as a key mediator in resistance politics in the Natal region.

There were literally dozens of people who contributed articles to the *Guardian* between 1937 and 1952. They included members of the South African Labour Party like C. F. Miles Cadman, Duncan Burnside and M. J. van den Berg, and trade unionists like Isaac ("Issie") Wolfson (Tailoring Workers' Union), E. S. ("Solly") Sachs and Anna Scheepers (Garment Workers' Union). "Comrade Bill" Andrews, a revered figure in trade union circles and a founding father of the Communist Party in South Africa (d. 1950), was head of the board of directors of the *Guardian* as a registered company and a regular correspondent to the newspaper. He became the *Guardian*'s "industrial" editor in March 1943 and wrote a weekly column on trade union news for almost a year.[39] Various left-wing commentators and activists from Britain also sent in contributions during the *Guardian* era. They included people such as John Strachey (a leading British politician and author of books on socialism), John Galloway and Eric Cook (who operated a news service and was the *Guardian*'s London correspondent for some years), Derek Kartun (another contributor from London) and Ivor Montagu (a prominent peace activist).

Other South African contributors included Pearson's husband Harold Baldry, a lecturer in Classics at the University of Cape Town, who wrote a long-running, full-page column on foreign news under the name "Vigilator"; Radford's husband George Sacks; Glyn Thomas, a Witwatersrand University registrar and a prominent publicist in the Medical Aid for Russia campaign during World War II; Harry Bloom, lawyer, author and librettist for the musical *King Kong*, who wrote under the pen name "Walter Storm"; R. K. ("Jack") Cope, noted novelist and biographer, who worked part time for the newspaper for two years beginning in 1952 and wrote a regular feature entitled "Art and the People"; Michael Harmel, who wrote a column entitled "By the Way," using the pseudonym "Alan Doyle"; and Victor Clapham, the newspaper's political cartoonist and an activist in the Springbok Legion.

Eddie Roux wrote a series of essays entitled "1652–And All That" in January–April 1952 that was one of the first left-wing attempts at a revisionist history of South Africa. Hyman Basner wrote a parliamentary column for the 1947 session, and Sam Kahn continued with his "In Parliament and Out" column for more than three years. A flock of new political activists–people like Lionel Forman (who was editor for a short while after the *Guardian* was banned in 1952),

Photo 29. Harry Allimuthu ("H. A.") Naidoo, the most prominent Indian staff writer on the *Guardian* before it was banned, with his wife Pauline Podbrey.

Tennyson Makiwane and Alex La Guma–joined the newspaper in the post-*Guardian* era.[40]

Female journalists played a significant role, and in the early years when Radford was editor, women sometimes comprised a majority of the news staff. They were also prominent in fund-raising support committees set up in the metropolitan areas, and they worked in a variety of administrative positions, a rare event in the life of the alternative as well as the mainstream press at the time. The administrative staff included women such as Winnie Kramer (future wife of Yusuf Dadoo), who joined the Johannesburg office as bookkeeper in 1946 and stayed until 1960 (leaving during the State of Emergency). Marjorie Till was bookkeeper in Cape Town during the 1940s. Amy Thornton subbed as a reporter and was responsible for the Cape Town office filing system for six years or so before the newspaper finally ceased publication in 1963. The wives of male staffers–people such as Sonia Bunting, Sarah Carneson and Leslie Schermbrucker (in Johannesburg)–were also actively involved in producing the newspaper.[41]

Among those women who wrote for the *Guardian* in Cape Town were Pearson, the circulation manager (who wrote an advice column on cooking using the pseudonym "Hannah"), Gail Hardy (a qualified health worker), Marjorie Willett (one of Radford's nieces, who wrote a fashion feature), Petronella van Heerden (a gynecologist with a big medical practice in Cape Town, and a militant antifascist and supporter of the Republican cause during the Spanish Civil War), Rona Worrall

(Johannesburg correspondent for the *Guardian* in the early to mid-1940s), and Christine Cash (a British-trained journalist and the chief reporter in Cape Town when Radford was editor). Margaret Ballinger, the most noted of the Native Representatives in the House of Assembly (representing Africans from the Cape Eastern District), occasionally aired her views in the *Guardian* and received much coverage in the newspaper. The same was true of Cissie Gool, a prominent political figure in Cape Town's Coloured community. She was a Communist Party member and a Cape Town city councillor representing District Six.

Naomi Shapiro (Barnett) started off as Radford's secretary and clerk in 1946, but she received training in journalism from Cash and others and was soon getting stories on her own. She helped cover the Defiance Campaign and became one of the *Guardian*'s top investigative journalists in the Cape Town office. According to Bunting, she was "a first-class reporter and photographer," as well as acting editor when he was away from Cape Town.[42] Mary Butcher (wife of activist Ben Turok) joined the Cape Town staff as a reporter in March 1953 and stayed several years. Ray Alexander (Simons), who started writing for the *Guardian* from 1943, contributed a regular column for five years between 1953 and 1958. Vera Poonen, an activist from England who married George Poonen, a leading Indian trade unionist in Durban during the 1940s, was the first editor-manager of the Durban branch office. She was succeeded by Jacqueline Lax (Arenstein), wife of Rowley Arenstein, a leader in the Congress of Democrats in the 1950s.

Ruth First, who became editor and manager of the *Guardian*'s Johannesburg office shortly after the 1946 African miners' strike, was the most celebrated of the women journalists. (Her role in the resistance press especially during the turbulent 1950s is assessed in Chapter 10.) First's colleagues in Johannesburg included Tennyson Makiwane, Joe Gqabi and Robert Resha, sports editor during the 1950s. Ivan Schermbrucker was business manager and Arnold Selby circulation manager.[43] Michael Harmel, a Johannesburg correspondent for the CPSA mouthpiece *Inkululeko* and for the *Guardian* from virtually the first issue, acted as branch editor when First was away from the office.

Circulation and Advertising

In terms of readership, the *Guardian* was unquestionably the most successful newspaper in the history of the alternative press before the 1980s. Circulation jumped from 1,000 to 4,000 in the first year of publication, soared to 8,000 in 1939 and 12,000 in 1940. Circulation had more than doubled to 25,000 by January 1942, and it stood at 42,500 in July 1943. According to Brian Bunting, newspaper circulation topped 55,000 during the 1943 general election, and the Simons placed the *Guardian*'s circulation at 50,000 in 1945. This figure dropped slightly after World War II (it was reputedly 46,000 in 1947), and the slide was more dramatic in the early years of the Cold War, apparently reaching a low point of 19,000 in 1950.[44] Circulation increased dramatically during the 1952 Defiance Campaign but decreased again in the mid-1950s. As Bunting put it, "the circulation of the paper would go up and down with the politics." Nevertheless, the carry-on readership was a major point in trying to sell advertising space. The longest-lasting successor publication *New Age*, for example, had a circulation of about 30,000 in 1958, but the readership was conservatively estimated at 100,000.[45]

The *Guardian* had subscribers, but apparently it relied mainly on street sales because commercial distributors would rarely handle this newspaper or any other

Photo 30. A "Defend the *Guardian*" protest meeting. Speaking at the podium is Dr. Yusuf Dadoo (South African Indian Congress, Communist Party and ANC). Seated on Dadoo's right is Ruth First and an unidentified man. Seated on Dadoo's left is Moses Kotane (Communist Party and ANC) and James Phillips (a noted singer, trade unionist, and activist in the Communist Party, ANC and Coloured People's Organisation in the 1940s and 1950s). Seated alone in the front row, right, underneath the sign "The *Guardian* Speaks for the People," is Joe Slovo (Communist Party, Congress of Democrats, ANC).

publication associated with the alternative press. Virtually everyone connected to the *Guardian* in the Cape Town metropolitan area was involved in its distribution. "Sympathetic café proprietors," according to Ray Alexander, sold the *Guardian* to their customers, and trade unionists "took bundles of papers to sell amongst their workers." They hawked it "house to house" every week in Cape Town Coloured working-class areas such as District Six, Woodstock, the docks and Salt River.[46] As Fred Carneson explained, these individuals "were political comrades and colleagues who kept us in touch with what was going on in the [African and Coloured] communities." He described his own experiences selling the newspaper door to door:

> I'd knock... and they'd open the door. I'd walk through to the kitchen, there would be my money on the mantle-shelf there. I'd take my money, and we'd sit down, maybe have a cup of tea or something, and talk. And then you'd pick up all sorts of stories from the people themselves... they'd raise personal problems with you. And you'd try and sort it out because next week you know you're going to go back there again... That used to happen to a lot of our sellers. We used to take up the personal problems of the people and win their confidence and respect that way... You'd also learn a hell of a lot about where the shoe was pinching. And then there were the straight political

Photo 31. Hawking the *Guardian* in 1940. African newspaper sellers were on the front line in confrontations with the police.

Photo 32. Hawking *New Age* in the 1950s.

Vorster Murders "SPARK"

SPARK

New Series. Vol. 1 No. 22 PRICE 5c March 28, 1963

WE SAY GOODBYE BUT WE'LL BE BACK

VORSTER HAS STRANGLED "SPARK" AND THIS IS THE LAST ISSUE OF "THE PAPER" AS YOU OUR READERS HAV E GOT TO KNOW IT EACH WEEK. Three sets of bannings, two of which take effect on April 1, have made it absolutely impossible for us to continue. A full statement is inside on page 2.

So now we say goodbye. We have tried everything, believe us, but this is the end of the road. We hope that others can to some extent fill the gap, until the day comes when we re-appear in a free South Africa. **Then we promise to be yet bigger and brighter, and to come out not weekly, but every day.**

- Thank you for your magnificent support during all this time.
- Thank you to the five great journalists who have helped us make our mark in South Africa and through the world.

Goodbye, until we meet again. **WE'LL BE BACK!**

★ FRED CARNESON ★

★ GOVAN MBEKI ★

★ M. P. NAICKER ★

★ BRIAN BUNTING ★

★ RUTH FIRST ★

Photo 33. The final issue of *Spark*, 28 March 1963. After twenty-six turbulent years, the *Guardian* under its various titles was forced to cease publication forever.

> talks–Group Areas Act, what it means, what's this law going to mean to us. We used to never take it for granted that ordinary people knew the bloody ins and outs of the law like we do, or pending legislation. They don't. So they'd ask you, and you'd point to an article and explain to them ... From that point of view, too, selling the newspaper was a very useful form of political activity.[47]

"Distribution was a form of training for activists," as Thecla Schreuders put it, "and demonstrates how the newspaper was used as an organizing tool. It was an important communication link between organisations and their base."[48] When Carina Pearson resigned as circulation manager in 1946, for example, she was replaced by "Sergeant John" Morley, a one-eyed veteran of both the British and South African armies. Morley had hawked the *Guardian* to South African soldiers in north Africa and played a key role in the formation of the Springbok Legion in 1941 . After the war, he helped organize and politicize hungry black women and their families in Cape Town, who were seeking to establish food committees. Fifty-nine of these food banks were in operation by November 1947. The food crisis had abated by 1948, so Morley established a Christmas club that sold various types of commodities at wholesale prices to the needy. Each parcel contained a year's subscription to the *Guardian*, and all profits from the sale of these parcels went to the newspaper.[49]

There were a number of dedicated, full-time African (as well as Coloured and Indian) hawkers who sold the newspaper in the black townships of Cape Town, Johannesburg and Durban during the 1940s and 1950s. Some were Communist Party members–the two best known in Cape Town being Joe Motloheloa and Jack Masiyane–and others were ANC activists–they included Looksmart Solwandle Ngudle, Greenwood Ngotyana, Zoli Malindi and Douglas Manqina (who hawked the Cape Town *Guardian* for about 20 years). African newspaper sellers in particular were on the front line, as it were, in confrontations with the police.[50]

The *Guardian* sold for only a penny (one pence) until 1950,[51] so advertisements must have played an important role in helping to fund the newspaper. The "smalls," or classified section, offers some insight into the coalition of interests that comprised the political Left in South Africa during these years. Every edition carried notices of meetings, lectures, pageants, concerts, dances, plays, exhibits and other social events sponsored by branches of various socialist groups and workers' organizations. These notices were often grouped under a "What's On" column on the last page.

The organizations advertised included the Communist Party, Young Communist League, Springbok Legion (or its various support groups, such as the Cape Town Home Front League), People's Club, Left Book Club (which had discussion groups in five major cities–Johannesburg, Pretoria, Cape Town, Durban, Port Elizabeth and East London–on the eve of World War II), Progressive Music Society, Friends of the Soviet Union, Medical Aid for Russia Fund, trade union correspondence schools such as the International Correspondence Schools in Cape Town and the Union College in Johannesburg ("The Largest Institution of its kind in South Africa will train you in any of [the following] Trades or Professions"), and the *Guardian* League (which raised funds to support the newspaper).[52] The *Guardian* drew much of its inspiration for an alternative society from these organizations and from the insights of ordinary people who communicated their experiences in various forms through the newspaper.

Although the *Guardian* was perceived as a trade union newspaper, commercial advertisements in this sample were not aimed at working-class readers. Virtually

Table 22. *Formal advertising content in the* Guardian (*% of advertising units*)

Category	%
White businesses: nonessential goods and services	53.3
White businesses: essential goods and servises	40.9
Black goods and services (essential and nonessential), and Promotional[a]	5.8

[a]The two categories were combined. Some miscellaneous items, mainly for government services, war bonds, and war-related appeals for food and medical aid, were placed in the Promotional category.
Note: The *Guardian* had 1,230 advertising units, or 39.3% of the news – advertising units.

all the advertisers in the test sample, moreover, were white-owned businesses, and the illustrations used in their advertisements depicted whites (Table 22).

Nonessential manufactured goods included gargles, perfumes and other cosmetics, soft drinks, alcoholic beverages (a strip advertisement for Lion Beer, for example, was featured at the bottom of page 1 for several years in the mid-1940s), cigarettes and cigars, jewelry, radios, typewriters, stationery, watches, clocks and cars. Nonessential services included restaurants, hotels, dry-cleaning establishments, insurance companies, opticians, real estate agencies, various educational and other cultural enterprises (schools and school materials, bookshops and books, cinemas and theaters), sports and photographers. Essential goods included health and health supplements, certain kinds of personal items (like tobacco for pipes and paper for hand-made cigarettes), tools and household goods (including workers' tools, plowing and gardening tools, sewing goods, bicycles, stoves, matches, pest control and cleaning agents), and all food, clothing and furniture.

Consumer advertising in the *Guardian* was aimed effectively at higher-paid white workers and more generally at the white petty bourgeoisie. Even the advertisements for goods classified as "essential" featured luxury items–mahogany furniture, inner-spring mattresses, hand-tailored shirts, suits and dresses, sports clothes, evening gowns and tuxedos–for the most part beyond the means of ordinary working-class readers.

A decline in advertising revenue undoubtedly contributed to the newspaper's financial problems. The number of paid, nonpromotional advertisements per edition had risen from an average of 25 in this sample during the prewar years to about 50 between 1939 and 1948, but the number and variety of these consumer advertisements began to drop in 1949. In the quest to expand readership, the *Guardian* introduced beauty contests, baby competitions, cooking notes and even comics. As Bunting put it, however, "the only thing that worked was politics." Although some advertisers were political "sympathisers," many others were "ordinary business people" who could, during the war years, "write off the cost against income tax." Advertising "fell away" when the government withdrew this concession.[53]

The *Guardian* was redesigned as a five-column tabloid from January 1951 with larger headlines and advertisements featuring up-market goods anchoring each page of the newspaper, but the change in format did not attract more advertising.[54] The number of paid advertisements in this sample declined to an average of 16 in 1951 and 10 in the first five months of 1952, when the newspaper ceased publication under the *Guardian* title. The Guardian League fund-raisers, however, were

Figure 5. Domestic and foreign news in the *Guardian* (in %). Percentages are calculated by dividing the number of story units in each category by the total number of story units. News refers to all story units, including illustrations and informal advertisements classified as news. Formal advertisements are excluded. The *Guardian* had 1, 883 story units.

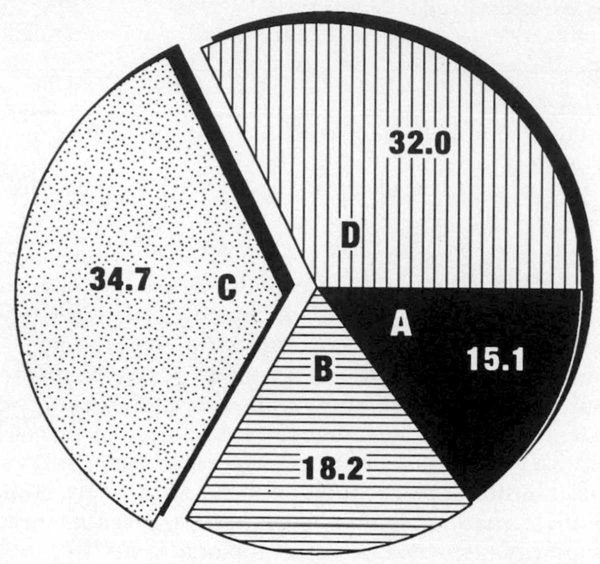

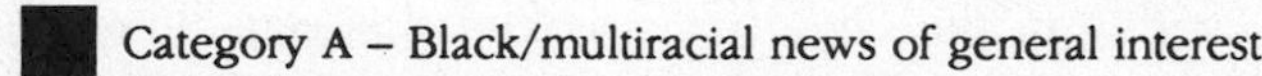

Category A – Black/multiracial news of general interest

Category B – White/multiracial news

Category C – Black/multiracial political and trade union news

Category D – Foreign news

very successful: donations from readers provided more than one-third of the newspaper's "income," for example, in the first 10 years of its existence.[55] Promotional items regularly appealed to readers to support its rummage sales, bazaars, film shows and dances, and most contributions were recognized in a column dubbed "*Guardian* Angels."[56]

News Agenda

The *Guardian*'s news agenda was clearly dominated by Category C, domestic political and trade union news, and Category D, foreign news (Figure 5).

The *Guardian* devoted relatively little space to Category A, general-interest news, in the test sample (Table 23).

Society news (A.2) comprised a calendar of social events (designated in part as

Table 23. *Category A news in the* Guardian (*% of story units*)

Category	%
A. Black/multiracial news of general interest (284 units)	15.1
A.1 Education and religion	1.7
A.2 Society	2.7
A.3 Sports	3.0
A.4, A.5 Living and working conditions in urban and rural areas	2.8
A.6 Independent economic activities	1.7
A.7 Crime and accidents	0.7
A.8 Other: Promotional and miscellaneous[a]	2.5

[a]"Miscellaneous" includes a few public notices, thanks to readers, cooking recipes, homilies and crossword puzzles.

classified advertising in the "What's On" column) together with obituaries, personality profiles, and reviews of films, plays, dances, concerts and art exhibitions. All the commercial movie theaters in Cape Town, moreover, advertised in the newspaper. In contrast to the African protest press, there was little religious or educational news (A.1). Stories in this sample were concerned with conditions in black schools, the grievances of black teachers' organizations, student protests and dissident statements from African church bodies.[57]

Sports (A.3) appeared irregularly on the last page before World War II, but during the 1940s there were virtually no sports stories, except for some on horse racing. A column entitled "World of Sport" began to appear sporadically on the back page in 1949 and 1950,[58] and it became a permanent fixture dominating the page in 1951–52. Horse racing remained a regular feature on the back page throughout the life of the *Guardian*, which reputedly had "the best racing tips in Cape Town."[59]

Very little space was devoted to black economic activities (A.6) or to conditions of life for ordinary black workers and peasants (A.4, A.5). There were stories on unemployment, job reservation and other restrictions placed on black wage earners and entrepreneurs, price hikes in essential commodities, increases in rent and train fares, lack of food in the rural areas, overcrowding and disease in the segregated urban African townships, and the plight of African squatters, but coverage was superficial and erratic before the 1950s.[60]

News targeted at women played a significant role in the *Guardian*'s news agenda. As Bunting later put it: "Editorial policy was always to promote [the] interest of women, and to stress the relationship between the women's struggle for equality and the liberation struggle in general."[61] A "Women in the News" section appeared regularly between September and December 1945, and this was followed by "Women's Platform" between January 1946 and January 1947.[62] Another feature, entitled "The Home Front," in the early 1950s was also aimed primarily at women.[63] Stories intended for women formed a substantial portion of the Society news subcategory (A.2) as well as advice items and cooking recipes coded as "Other" (A.8).

Women, however, were still stereotyped primarily as decorative objects and homemakers. Fashion, cosmetics, health care, household topics and personality profiles saturated the articles and advertisements targeted at women readers in the

Guardian.[64] "Shopping reporter" Margery Willett offered suggestions on the week's best buys, and "Jane," the "*Guardian* Beauty Expert," offered advice on a range of topics from clothes to cosmetics. The admonition "Lipsticks Are Politics! Be Political," for example, explained the use of makeup: "Who is there who does not want to look attractive? Why shouldn't we then make use of the aids which science has provided to even up the bad deal we may have had from nature and from our environment?"[65] "Miss *Guardian*" beauty competitions for "working girls" were held on occasion, and the promotion would last for several weeks before the winners were announced.[66]

White Authoritarian Context

Category B news, concerned with South Africa's dominant white political, economic and social institutions, also comprised a relatively small proportion of the domestic and foreign agenda (Table 24).

The *Guardian*, however, highlighted parliamentary activities more than any other alternative newspaper–in terms of its coverage of legislation affecting blacks, probably more than any other South African newspaper–during the 1940s and 1950s. They were covered before the war in a column entitled "Parliamentary Merry-go-Round," by "Hurdy-Gurdy" (author unknown). As noted earlier, Hyman Basner offered a commentary on parliament in a regular by-lined article during the 1947 session,[67] and Sam Kahn began offering parliamentary reports from January 1949. His regular column entitled "In Parliament–and Out" was a feature of the newspaper from August 1950 to May 1952.[68] One legal advice column entitled "Barrister" (author unknown) examined the impact of apartheid measures as they were enacted. Launched in August 1950, it appeared regularly in the newspaper for more than 10 years.

The *Guardian* was generally critical of the ruling, mainly English-speaking United Party (1939–48) as well as its principal coalition partner, the Labour Party. Members of the reunited National Party under Daniel Malan were regarded throughout the period as fascists. For the *Guardian*, there could be no compromise with the "Malanazis," as the following open letter to "Adolf Hitler" on a page 1 edition in 1945 suggests:

> Dear Adolf Hitler, If you are wondering where to make your new home, may we suggest South Africa—a country where you still have many ardent admirers... We know you will feel at home here in the atmosphere of anti-Semitism and race-hatred which prevails and you will not be hindered in continuing the work you started in Europe... Yours with admiration, D. F. MALAN, H. VAN RENSBURG, O. PIROW.[69]

Labour Party activities were covered fairly regularly and United Party activities much less regularly before and during the war, but white political party news was on the wane by the later 1940s.

Various civil rights groups linked mainly to established mission-church bodies, the South African Institute of Race Relations, student organizations (mainly from English-language universities) and the National Council of Women also received some coverage during the 1940s. Provincial or municipal council news was published when CPSA officials were involved or when black grievances and/or aspirations were under discussion, and the same was true of reports issued by government departments and commissions of inquiry.

Table 24. *Category B news in the* Guardian (*% of story units*)

Category	%
B. White/multiracial news (343 units)	18.2
B.1 Political, legislative and administrative	10.0
B.2 Economic and social	8.2

Most stories in Category B were concerned with official and unofficial acts of discrimination. Like other alternative newspapers, the *Guardian* did not shrink from making its views known, off as well as on the editorial page. For example, it noted in 1941, during a period of crisis in the allied war effort, that the South African government's "civilised labour" and "colour bar" policies had condemned "four-fifths of our population to remain unskilled labourers earning very low wages. Let us admit it–as regards its attitude to eight million [African] citizens of this country, the European section of the population is FASCIST... Truly, the real fight for democracy is on the home front. WHOSE SIDE ARE YOU ON?" As this quotation suggests, when the editor really wanted to emphasize a point, parts of the story were printed in capital letters or italics:

> THE GOVERNMENT SHOULD PROVE THE SINCERITY OF ITS DESIRE FOR A BETTER ORDER IN THE POST-WAR WORLD, BY PAYING ITS NON-EUROPEAN RAILWAY AND HARBOUR WORKERS A LIVING WAGE NOW.[70]

Legislation directed against Africans, especially after the National Party's election triumph in 1948, provided a focal point of dissent. Other targets of the newspaper's wrath included anti-Soviet propaganda in the media, antisemitic speeches and activities wherever they occurred, racism in white trade unions, public and private sector employers who mistreated or underpaid their employees and, of course, police brutality.

Black Politics and Trade Unions

The *Guardian*'s role in chronicling the transition from protest to resistance during this period is revealed primarily in Category C, political and trade union activities (Table 25).

The *Guardian* was not the official mouthpiece of a political body or population group, but a majority of the staff writers and editors were probably CPSA members by the time Bunting was installed as editor, and the newspaper itself was closely identified with party objectives: "It is *The Guardian* which consistently supports the Communist Party of South Africa, in the conviction that the policies it advocates... make it the only political party capable of achieving a successful solution to South Africa's problems."[71] As anticipated, stories about the CPSA and affiliated bodies (Friends of the Soviet Union, Medical Aid for Russia and especially the Left Book Clubs) comprised most political news in Subcategory C.1, Personalities and organizations. The newspaper covered CPSA local and provincial branch meetings and national congresses, promoted CPSA candidates in elections at all levels, carried appeals from CPSA newspapers and even advised readers on how to communicate grievances to CPSA officials.[72]

Table 25. *Category C news in the* Guardian (*% of story units*)

Category	%
C. Black/multiracial political and trade union news (653 units)	34.7
C.1 Personalities and organizations	24.4
C.2 Confrontation and consciousness	10.3

The *Guardian* also covered the activities of militant, white-dominated anti-apartheid groups like the Springbok Legion, which, as we have seen, had its own mouthpiece in *Fighting Talk*, and the Torch Commando (launched in 1951), which was made up largely of English-speaking war veterans. Loosely aligned with other opposition groups, the Torch Commando opposed the loss of the Cape Coloured franchise in 1951 and supported the 1952 Defiance Campaign but became hopelessly divided over the issue of allowing African veterans to join the movement. The Torch Commando virtually dissolved after the National Party won the 1953 general election.[73]

Only 5.3 percent of the news in Subcategory C.1 was concerned with the ANC–about the same percentage of news devoted to the various government consultative bodies for Africans. The report of the ANC's crucial 1949 conference was typical of the *Guardian*'s somewhat tenuous and perfunctory coverage of African nationalist activities during the 1940s. The Programme of Action was summarized in one paragraph, and editorial comment concerned the failure of the ANC and AAC to achieve unity (they held separate conferences at the same time in Bloemfontein).[74] "This reflected the reality," as Bunting later put it. "The day to day agitation, organisation and mobilisation was in the hands of the CPSA more than any other body at that time."[75]

Trade union news, however, comprised about 50 percent of the stories in this subcategory: "The Guardian ... is the only newspaper which fosters the fundamental community of interest between all South Africa's workers, by publication of their news and by giving support to their struggles."[76] Coverage was given mainly to all-white and mixed unions until World War II, when the newspaper became more vocal in its opposition to "colour bars and racial discrimination."[77] Workers' groups cited in the *Guardian* thereafter were associated mainly with the militant nonracial wing of the TLC and its independent African counterpart, the CNETU.

Confrontation and Consciousness

No alternative newspaper before the 1960s except the CPSA mouthpiece *Inkululeko* and perhaps the ICU mouthpiece *Inkundla ya Bantu* matched the *Guardian* in the proportion of news–10.3 percent of the news agenda–devoted to Subcategory C.2, Confrontation and consciousness. Confrontation stories constituted about one-half of this subcategory. They were concerned with strikes (including threatened strikes) by students and various kinds of workers, and boycotts, protest marches and demonstrations initiated mainly by community-action groups in the urban areas. No rural confrontations were cited in this sample.[78]

A majority of the consciousness-raising stories were concerned with the socialist project inside and outside South Africa. The writers and editors of the *Guardian* recognized that all social groups sought to represent reality in their own interests. News coverage was not neutral, and they agreed with their colleagues in the Communist Party press that white commercial newspapers served primarily to represent the interests and concerns of those who ruled. *Guardian*'s task was nothing less than to project an alternative news discourse in the workers' struggle for South Africa.

The Socialist Project outside South Africa

International events dominated the *Guardian*'s news agenda during the war, and page 1 news and editorials continued to focus on foreign affairs after the war. The *Guardian* sought to establish an international context for South African socialists in their perceived struggle against the twin forces of fascism/Nazism and capitalism/colonialism (Table 26).

Foreign news was found on virtually every page, and foreign affairs was a topic in at least six weekly columns and on the editorial page during the lifetime of the newspaper. The *Guardian*'s coverage of fascism abroad (and at home) before World War II was apparently without precedent in the South African press.

Harold Baldry ("Vigilator") wrote the most significant foreign affairs column, which was entitled "Behind the Overseas News." His analyses of events leading to the war were influential, according to Bunting, "because this was the only source of information about what was happening from the Left point of view." Among other things, Baldry urged Africans to support the Allied war effort, which elicited praise from the govemment and "attracted a lot of attention to the paper."[79] The newspaper achieved national acclaim when Radford published a collection of Baldry's columns entitled *The Munich Swindle* (October 1938), which sold more than 25,000 copies.[80]

Baldry continued writing his column during the war, and regular foreign news features appeared under his by-line after the war until about July 1947, when Baldry and his wife Carina Pearson were probably beginning to distance themselves from left-wing causes. Harry Bloom ("Walter Storm") wrote a foreign news feature between July 1947 and about March 1948, but no regular commentary on foreign news appeared in the last four years under the *Guardian* title.[81]

In terms of the *Guardian*'s foreign news biases, the policies of Germany, Italy and Japan were clearly unacceptable between 1937 and 1945, and Republican Spain was clearly acceptable during the final stages of its struggle for survival in the 1936–39 Spanish Civil War.[82] News emanating from Britain, France and the United States was given negative to neutral coverage before the war and neutral to favorable coverage during and immediately after the war, but the wartime Allies were clearly unacceptable with the dawning of the Cold War in the late 1940s. The emerging postcolonial world after the war was given generally favorable news coverage. The Soviet Union and its communist allies, of course, were clearly acceptable throughout the lifetime of the newspaper.

The Soviet Union itself was depicted as a virtual paradise. For example, in a series entitled "Life in the USSR" that ran from 5 September through 12 December 1940 children were singled out as subjects of special concern:

> As children in the USSR have more and better facilities for education than other children, so is their leisure and playtime more richly endowed... Consider the Palaces of Youth... There they can employ their leisure time in ballet dancing, sculpture, painting, music–in electrical engineering, in learning about wireless transmitting, in making model trains, aeroplanes. All without charge![83]

Table 26. *Category D news in the* Guardian (*% of story units*)

Category	%
D. Foreign news (603 units)	32.0
D.1 International socialism at war and peace	21.4
D.2 Other international	10.6

The gospel of socialism offered the best religious environment, because it catered to all beliefs:

> The law on religion in [the] USSR is: "Anyone is free to preach and teach any religion. Anyone is free to preach and teach no religion. The Soviet Government has no interest in anyone's religious beliefs."[84]

The Soviet Union was a role model for the poor in the nonsocialist world, who were forced to depend on a "Workman's Compensation Act" or on "charity services, which are unreliable and dwindling year by year":

> In the USSR this system does not exist. The chief characteristics of the Soviet medical system are that medical service is free and open to all, prevention is in the foreground of medical care, and the medical service is centralized.[85]

In a similar vein, the Soviet version of a nonracial democracy was held out as an example for South Africa. One edition, for example, ran a photograph of an African-American actor, now "a naturalised Soviet citizen," dropping his ballot into a ballot box. The caption read in part: "All citizens of all races have the right to vote in the USSR."[86]

Like the Communist Party press, the *Guardian* was stunned by the signing of the Soviet–German nonaggression pact in August 1939 and urged its readers not to take sides: "The whole world, we're told, was shocked by the news ... The most that a nonaggression pact between Russia and the Reich means is Soviet neutrality. Not 'alliance' or 'co-operation,' but a disinterested attitude for the time being–towards the affairs of Western Europe."[87] The newspaper vacillated until October 1939, when it finally opted against the war. The *Guardian* stood by the Communist Party and tried rather halfheartedly for the next 20 months to convince readers to maintain an antiwar position. This ended abruptly when Germany invaded the Soviet Union in June 1941.

The *Guardian*'s support for the Soviet war effort was unqualified, and tensions among the Allies were invariably described as the fault of the Western democracies, as in the following reply to a demand that the Soviets respond to the bombing of Pearl Harbor in December 1941:

> Some people complain because Soviet bombers haven't yet attacked Tokyo or Osaka. After abusing and ridiculing the USSR for years, they now expect it to win both western and eastern wars for them. The Soviet reply to them is simple. "We know, friends," Russian spokesmen might say, "that our intervention in the East could be decisive. But so could your intervention in the West. Our resources may be enough for a second front against Japan, if yours will provide a second front against Hitler."[88]

The struggle against fascism/Nazism in the *Guardian* was replaced by the struggle against capitalism/colonialism in the early years of the Cold War. The capitalist mode of life fostered imperialism, fought for the continuation of colonial empires and resisted left-wing independence movements throughout the colonial world. The world news prism was now divided into these two camps.[89]

The struggle against fascism/Nazism provided 55 percent of the *Guardian*'s foreign stories between 1937 and 1945 and 10 percent between 1946 and 1952. The struggle against capitalism and colonialism provided 14 percent and 41 percent of the foreign stories during the same periods. World War II, then, ended "a period of truce between the classes. In the Allied countries the differences were obscured during the war years, when there was a common enemy."[90]

The *Guardian* targeted Cold War resistance to socialism and to popular liberation movements in western Europe's colonial possessions as the two main areas of conflict with the capitalist West from the later 1940s.[91] Whereas before the war the United States in particular was depicted as a bulwark against fascism,[92] after the war it was depicted as the direct heir to fascism. The United States government was using biological weapons in the Korean War[93] and contemplating the use of atomic weapons to contain the Chinese communists.[94] The United States continued to support the Franco regime in Spain[95] and was determined to rearm the "West German puppet government" by the early 1950s.[96] Nevertheless, American public opinion was often depicted as being against war, as in the Korean conflict:

> A growing movement in favour of ending the war and withdrawing American forces from Korea is drawing in both the broad masses of trade unionists, churchmen and genuine lovers of peace as well as the extreme right-wing isolationists who are becoming alarmed by the weakening of America's business and strategic position throughout the world.[97]

The *Guardian* called for decolonization around the world:

> We may hope that the new, progressive governments in Britain, France, Holland and other colonial powers will welcome ... the carrying out of a programme to put an end to the colonial system. Yet it is the colonial people themselves, and not their "owners," whom we must expect to provide the main driving force behind their demand for freedom.[98]

Independence movements were deemed to be on the march everywhere after the triumph of India's independence movement in 1947, and the *Guardian* sought to chronicle their activities. The Suez Canal crisis, for example, signaled the end of the British Empire: "Britain has signed in blood her death warrant in the Middle East."[99] Nevertheless, national capital would continue to serve the interests of metropolitan capital in these postcolonial states. As *Guardian* correspondent H. A. Naidoo, a South African delegate to a British Empire conference in London in 1947, noted:

> Perhaps the most important fact revealed at Conference was the gradual elimination of British monopoly capital in the Dominions (Canada, Australia, New Zealand and South Africa) as an influential factor and the growth and concentration of home capital, thus indicating the main line of imperialist tendencies among the Dominions themselves.[100]

The *Guardian* called for a "new order" in the postwar world under the leadership of an international workers' movement:

> Out of the ruins of a war-wrecked world will arise a new order of society, in which mankind will at long last be able to live in peace, free from poverty and insecurity, and able to explore all the possibilities that are open only to those who are secure in the

> essentials of life... The responsibility falls upon the Labour movement. For it is the organised working class, and it alone, that has the vision and the strength required to reshape the world and free humanity of its burden of poverty, ignorance, racial arrogance, and class privileges.[101]

The Socialist Project inside South Africa

The *Guardian* devoted considerable space to the socialist project inside South Africa in the ongoing effort to educate its readers.[102] Socialism, of course, was depicted as a virtual paradise. Wages would improve as the economy improved, and in the socialist utopia food, health-care facilities, schools and jobs would be available for everyone in a nonracial society:

> you will pay nothing for medical attention to yourself or your family... You will have paid holidays. Your Trade Union will have holiday homes at pleasure resorts... The education of your children will cost you nothing... Your factory will run a restaurant where you will be able to get very cheap meals at all times. Your Trade Union will be able to supply you with tickets to the cinema and theatre at nominal prices.[103]

Three major themes appear to have dominated the *Guardian*'s socialist agenda for South Africa before the 1950s. First, all workers–urban and rural, female and male, black and white–were to be educated in collective action and in the principles of socialism. Second, primary support was to be given to the nonracial trade union movement. Third, the socialists and their allies (*contra* the Unity movement and its mouthpiece, the *Torch*) were encouraged to become actively involved in parliamentary politics–to stand as candidates and/or lobby for or against legislation that was of concern to workers.

The educational process began in the very first issue of the newspaper in a commentary by "Ernest Verity":

> The Trades' Union movement in the modern state has become as important as Parliament itself. Through organisation, the working class has indirect democratic representation... [but] achievements which have been won only by long-drawn-out battles could have been more rapidly gained if the leaders of the movement had developed and cultivated the class consciousness of the workers.

Employers resisted worker organization and tried to "play one worker against the other."

> When the worker learns the elementary lesson that by standing shoulder to shoulder with his fellow worker he has nothing to fear he will earn the respect of every right-thinking employer as well as... secure for himself the safety and permanence of his job.

The Afrikaner worker could not be ignored, but the major problem was the African worker: "It is his cheap labour in the industry, and particularly in the basic industries, which depresses the whole wage stratification of the workers of the Union of South Africa. And he of all workers is least of all organised."[104]

The *Guardian* also tried to raise the consciousness of women workers. One of the first series of articles devoted to this issue raised the question, "Can Women Obtain Emancipation in a Capitalist State?"

> Equal pay for equal work is clearly quite impossible under Capitalism... Women are employed mainly because they are cheap. On an equal wage basis with men the man would probably get the jobs and so we again come back to the Capitalist failure to absorb the workers of the world into the industry of the world.

By comparison, women in the Soviet Union "are an example and an inspiration to the women of Capitalist countries... Soviet women enjoy equal rights with men, the right to rest, the right to work and education, and equal pay for equal work."[105]

The *Guardian* was first and foremost a mouthpiece for organized labor, and this theme was crucial to the socialist project inside South Africa. Contributors to the newspaper played an active role in workers' activities, and, as noted earlier, trade union news dominated the news agenda.

The relationship between the *Guardian* and trade union activity was clearly demonstrated during the 1946 African miners' strike, perhaps the best example of confrontation news in the newspaper during the 1940s.[106] Readers were told of the strike plan before it occurred, and a "strike diary" chronicling events was issued, together with detailed descriptions of the violence and mass arrests. The arrest of 52 strike leaders was recorded: "They included representatives of all South Africa's people – black, white and coloured, Afrikaners, English-born, Africans, Indians, Jews... They were all people who had identified themselves, over the years, with the struggle of the oppressed of this country and with the international struggle against Fascism and Capitalism."[107] About half of those accused of sedition and conspiring to initiate an illegal strike were members of the Communist Party.[108]

Among others, the *Guardian* cited the advocate Abram Fischer, then a member of the Johannesburg District Committee and one of the accused, who explained why the party had supported the striking miners:

> Communists were concerned with the welfare of all workers in South Africa. Resolutions taken by national conferences of the Communist Party showed that the party was out to help the workers to obtain better conditions of life. One way of doing this was through support to the trade union movement... Mr. Fischer said the Communist Party not only claimed to represent the workers, it actually did so, and when the workers were in trouble there was nothing a Communist could do but help them.

Fischer was not in Johannesburg when the strike broke out, but he "pleaded guilty because if he had been in town he would naturally have helped in distributing leaflets when called upon."[109]

Police raids following the strike hit the offices of the *Guardian* in both Cape Town and Durban, and pamphlets, correspondence and some newspaper copy were confiscated. The issue of 26 September 1946 was printed with half of one page blank, perhaps the first such act of defiance in the history of the South African press. The page bore the following statement in capital letters:

> WITH ACKNOWLEDGEMENTS TO MR. HARRY LAWRENCE, MINISTER OF JUSTICE, AND THE FREEDOM OF THE PRESS IN DEMOCRATIC SOUTH AFRICA AND APOLOGIES TO OUR READERS. CAPE TOWN, DURBAN AND OTHER NEWS WHICH SHOULD HAVE APPEARED ON THIS PAGE IS IN THE HANDS OF THE POLICE.

And below, on the same page:

> TO ALL WHO VALUE FREEDOM, Communist Statement on Police Raids... The Union-wide police search of the offices of the Communist Party, trades unions, the *Guardian* and the Springbok Legion, as well as the houses of numerous individuals must be a matter of serious concern to all South Africans who value democracy and individual liberty... The only possible reason for this step is that the Government is persecuting the progressive movement in South Africa for the political ends of the United Party.[110]

The *Guardian* sued the minister of justice, and the police were ordered to return the documents they had seized. Two years later, the government finally dropped all charges against those who had been accused of sedition and conspiring to initiate an illegal strike.

Finally, the *Guardian*'s perception of the socialist project found concrete expression in its support of antisegregationist, pro-trade union candidates (especially CPSA members) for political office. The 1948 general election was depicted as a turning point in South African political life: "Fear and hate are the basis of the Nationalist Party's approach...for the time being, Smuts will stay this side of banning the Communist Party in South Africa, while Malan would lump together Communists and all who belong to any progressive organisation and incarcerate the lot."[111]

The Communist Party's election strategy was made clear in the *Guardian* five months before the election was actually held: "Everything possible will be done by the Communist Party in the forthcoming general elections to work for the defeat of the extreme reactionary and pro-Fascist forces represented in the Nationalist Party."[112] In comparing the election manifestos of the United Party and the Nationalists, the newspaper declared:

> While the United Party policy contains the seeds of Fascism, yet it provides opportunity for progressive advances; while the Nationalist Party policy, if adopted, would immediately place South Africa under a Fascist regime in which the right of the working people and the non-Europeans would become non-existent.[113]

The National Party election victory, of course, was a blow to the *Guardian* and other anti-Nationalist newspapers. As Edwin Mofutsanyana, editor of *Inkululeko*, put it: "All sections of the South African people, irrespective of colour, are terribly shaken."[114] The survival of the CPSA as a political organization was now in jeopardy, and in the next 18 months the *Guardian* mounted a spirited defense of the party and its policies.

Resistance to the Suppression of Communism Bill embraced Protestant churches such as the Baptists and Presbyterians as well as Jewish congregations; veterans' groups such as the Springbok Legion; the National Council of Women; scores of trade union and political groups, including the SAIC, the All-African Convention and the ANC. A stay-at-home day organized by the National Day of Protest Coordinating Committee was widely honored when the Suppression of Communism Act was passed in June 1950: "In...Port Elizabeth, Durban and most of the Natal areas a complete stoppage occurred...In Johannesburg and the Reef towns the majority of the Non-European people stayed at home."[115] Sam Kahn told members of the House of Assembly in a prophetic statement that "Communism will outlive the Nationalist Party. Democracy will still be triumphant when members of this Government will be manuring the fields of history."[116]

The Suppression of Communism Act silenced the Communist Party but not the *Guardian*, which continued to fight for the rights of the oppressed in South Africa:

> Within the limits of the Act, we feel it is still open to The *Guardian* to further its main task–to give publicity to the wrongs and injustices which are daily perpetrated in this country, to fight against the tyranny of the colour bar, to give expression to the grievances and aspirations of the oppressed peoples of this country, to press for social reform, and to continue the struggle for the achievement of equal rights for all South Africans, irrespective of race, creed or colour. Above all we intend to carry on with the utmost vigour and determination the struggle against the Nationalist Government

and its apartheid policy. We remain convinced that the longer this Government is in power, the nearer we shall be driven towards the excesses of open fascism... So long as the Nationalists remain in power, there is no prospect of peace and progress in our country."[117]

Conclusion

The banning of the *Guardian* 23 months later had no impact whatsoever on the production of its successor. The first issue of the *Clarion* was published 29 May 1952, exactly one week after the last issue of the *Guardian*, and its tone was more strident than ever:

> BY ITS ACTIONS... THE GOVERNMENT HAS MADE IT PERFECTLY CLEAR IT IS STAKING ALL IN A DESPERATE BID TO ENTRENCH ITSELF IN POWER... THEY WILL PERPETRATE ANY ILLEGALITY IF THEY THINK THEY CAN GET AWAY WITH IT.

Bunting, in a front-page editorial, attacked the banning as neither "just" nor "lawful" and declared "the struggle of the people for full democratic rights... must continue, and the voice of the people must continue to be heard in the land."[118]

News and opinion in the *Guardian* in the 1930s and 1940s had focused on the trade unions, and the vast majority of its readers were whites and Coloureds living in Cape Town and surrounding areas.[119] News and opinion during the 1950s and 1960s, however, shifted dramatically to focus on the ANC and its allies–the trend was already noticeable by 1950–51–and on living and working conditions for blacks in the urban townships. "Non-European affairs," for example, was Number 1 on a list of 19 priorities set by Bunting for the newspaper in January 1951. When the Defiance Campaign was launched in June 1952, the *Clarion* provided more coverage of day-to-day events than any other newspaper in South Africa, and circulation rose again to 40,000. A majority of the readers in the post-*Guardian* era were Africans living in areas outside the mother city, especially Johannesburg and the surrounding Witwatersrand (where *Inkululeko* had recruited a small but solid core of readers), Durban, Port Elizabeth and East London.[120]

The *Guardian*'s successors continued to offer an international "anti-imperialist, anti-capitalist" agenda that was linked directly to issues of national concern, but they now reflected a political agenda that was African nationalist as well as socialist. The banning of the Communist Party actually helped to accelerate this trend. "The feeling that there was a rival [to the ANC] disappeared," as Bunting pointed out. "I think both sides [communists and nationalists] learned to appreciate one another in a way which hadn't been possible before."[121] The newspaper focused coverage on African political activities, and as *New Age* it became the mouthpiece of the Congress Alliance in the mid-1950s. The newspaper was rightly regarded by Albert Lutuli (ANC president general from December 1952 to his death in July 1967) as "the fighting mouthpiece of African aspirations."[122]

The *Guardian* in the 1950s redefined the concept of an opposition press for mainstream opposition newspapers like the *Rand Daily Mail* in the next generation. The *Guardian* also provided a new set of journalistic standards for the resistance press–a role model for those who would continue the struggle in the final decades of the apartheid era. As Bunting expressed it many years later: "We did regard ourselves as a platform for the whole liberation movement."[123]

Notes

1. *Guardian*, 3 September 1937, 3. The South African Typographical Workers' Union called the *Guardian* in 1937 "purely a Trades Union paper, free from all prejudice such as race and colour, and will stand for democracy in the true sense of the word." *Guardian*, 19 February 1937, 10.
2. This position runs counter to the view that forces external to the labor process, namely racism (often perceived as a systemic disease dividing the working classes) and Afrikaner nationalism, were instrumental in shaping the trade union movement in South Africa. Labor scholars also argue that racial discrimination in its various forms was employed by capital to accelerate the development of the industrial economy in South Africa.
3. The founding father of scientific management in the United States at the beginning of the twentieth century, for example, was Frederick W. Taylor, and Taylorism was being applied to the reorganization of industrial labor in South Africa from the 1930s.
4. The section on trade-union activities is based mainly on J. Lewis, *Industrialisation and trade union organisation in South Africa, 1924–55: The rise and fall of the South African Trades and Labour Council* (Cambridge, 1984); and B. Hirson, *Yours for the union: Class and community struggles in South Africa, 1930–1947* (London, 1990). See also S. Greenberg, *Race and state in capitalist development* (Johannesburg, 1980), Chaps. 13–14; E. Webster, *Cast in a racial mould: Labour process and trade unionism in the foundries* (Johannesburg, 1985), esp. Chap. 1; D. E. Kaplan, "The politics of industrial protection in South Africa, 1910–1939," *Journal of Southern African Studies* 3, 1(1976), 70–91; M. Stein, "Max Gordon and African trade unionism on the Witwatersrand, 1935–1940," *South African Labour Bulletin* 3, 9 (1977), 41–57.
5. Lewis, *Industrialisation and trade union organisation in South Africa,* 133, 159.
6. Industrial trade union activities outside the Transvaal were concentrated in the port cities, especially in the Cape, where working conditions were often very different. The western Cape, for example, had its own autonomous coordinating bodies, the main one during this period being the Western Province Federation of Labour Unions (founded in 1941).
7. Lewis, *Industrialisation and trade union organisation in South Africa*, 67, 165.
8. On the confrontation between white labor and the state during the early 1920s, see R. H. Davies, *Capital, state and white labour in South Africa, 1900–1960* (Brighton, 1979), esp. Chap. 4.
9. The Industrial Conciliation Act (No. 28) of 1956 banned the registration of new racially mixed unions and tried to force existing mixed unions to establish independent or segregated parallel bodies for each racial group.
10. Hirson, *Yours for the union*, 38 (Table 4.1). The official statistics do not include certain categories of workers who established unions and participated in strikes during this period. According to Hirson, they ranged from newspaper vendors and golf caddies to electricity workers, tree plantation and plant nursery workers, nurses, shoe repairers and car, van and bus drivers.
11. The Wage Act of 1925 created a Wage Board with the authority to investigate pay rates and working conditions in the industrial sector, but for many years it made few recommendations on behalf of white or black labor and refrained from inquiring into mine labor. The Wage Board gained more freedom to explore black workers' problems after a restrictive clause requiring the board to recommend "civilised" wages in grievance cases was dropped in 1937. African labor leaders and their white liberal allies (such as the Johannesburg Joint Council and the Society of Friends of Africa) had some success in gaining concessions from the Wage Board, and these victories contributed to the growth of the independent African trade union movement.
12. The number of blacks involved in strikes–they were the main strikers during the war years–reached a peak of 12,800 in 1942 (with 58 strikes) and 14,700 in 1945 (with 63 strikes). Hirson, *Yours for the Union*, 87 (Table 7.1).

13. T. Karis and G. M. Carter, *From protest to challenge*, Vol. 2, *Hope and challenge*, by T. Karis (Stanford, 1973), Document 29b ("Africans' Claims in South Africa" manifesto, 16 December 1943), 211; P. Walshe, *The rise of African nationalism in South Africa* (Berkeley and Los Angeles, 1971), 269–70.
14. Trotskyite groups like the Progressive Group of Trade Unions (PTU) attacked the CNETU repeatedly. PTU leaders were expelled from the CNETU in 1945, and a breakaway group in 1947 established the short-lived Council of African Trade Unions.
15. Lewis provides detailed breakdowns for specific occupational categories. As a percentage of the white work force, for example, unskilled white males dropped from 8.42 to 4.03 percent, and semiskilled white operatives remained more or less constant at 14–15 percent between 1936 and 1951. White supervisors in manual labor rose from 3.48 to 7.24 percent between 1936 and 1946. Lewis, *Industrialisation and trade union organisation in South Africa*, 134 (Table IX).
16. Ibid., 170.
17. This section is based on Lodge, *Black politics*, Chap. 11; C. Bundy, "Land and liberation: Popular rural protest and the national liberation movements in South Africa, 1920–1960," in S. Marks and S. Trapido (eds.), *The politics of race, class and nationalism in twentieth-century South Africa* (London, 1987), Chap. 8; Hirson, *Yours for the Union*, esp. Chaps. 10–12.
18. Ray (Alexander) Simons to Switzer, June 1991.
19. Stewart also printed the leading Coloured newspaper at the time, the *Cape Standard* (May 1936–November 1947), and Trom was his works manager. Stewart, however, made his living as a commercial printer, and most of his clients were staunch supporters of the political order. He installed a rotary press in the mid-1940s and raised his prices, forcing the proprietors of the *Guardian* to seek an alternative printer. The Prudential Printing and Publishing Company, an Indian firm probably associated with Stewart, obtained the contract in 1947. Prudential also printed the main Indian passive resistance newspaper at the time, the *Passive Resister* (July 1946–October 1948). The *Guardian* was printed briefly by an Afrikaans printing company (Unie-Volkspers), which produced the United Party opposition newspaper *Die Suiderstem* (October 1936–July 1950). Stewart apparently went into considerable debt with the purchase of the rotary press, and he finally "committed suicide when he could not meet his financial commitments." Len Lee-Warden, an English immigrant who had worked for Stewart as a linotype operator and compositor for about four years during the mid-1940s, started his own company (Pioneer Press) in 1948 and printed the *Guardian* and successor titles from the 1950s. A. J. Friedgut, "The non-European press," in E. Hellmann (ed.), *Handbook on race relations in South Africa* (Cape Town, 1949), 502; Don Pinnock interview with Brian Bunting in London, 1988; Len Lee-Warden to Switzer 25 June 1991.
20. The Fleggs, who came from a wealthy family, held regular Christmas Eve fundraising dances on behalf of the *Guardian*. Norman Flegg, an accountant, was business manager of the Cape Town office for 10 years. He was killed in a plane crash in 1951. James Zug, personal communication.
21. Ray (Alexander) Simons to Switzer, 22 June 1991. The *Guardian* even had a subscription subdepartment in the circulation department. James Zug, personal communication. Radford was also unpaid, but her successor Brian Bunting was paid, as were those in charge of the branch offices. Black clerical and circulation staff were also paid, as were the business and circulation managers. Switzer interview with Naomi (Shapiro) Barnett, 5 June 1991.
22. *Guardian*, 18 February 1938, 1.
23. The banned titles were the *Guardian* (May 1952), *Advance* (October 1954) and *New Age* (November 1962). The apartheid government declared a State of Emergency in South Africa on 30 March 1960, and the police seized the April 7 edition of *New Age* for allegedly violating the emergency regulations in the previous March 31 issue. The newspaper was not published for the remaining months the emergency regulations were in force because most of the staff had been detained. James Zug, personal communication.

24. E. Roux, *Time longer than rope: A history of the black man's struggle for freedom in South Africa* (Madison, 1964), 382.
25. Copies of the *Guardian* during the war years, for example, were sent to readers in Europe and North America, elsewhere in Africa and even Australia. James Zug, personal communication. There is some evidence to suggest that the *Guardian* and the CPSA organ *Inkululeko* were the only newspapers in South Africa to be granted an increase in newsprint allocation during World War II (Zug cites the *Cape Times*, 24 May 1952, for the *Guardian*). Shortages of ink and paper pushed newsprint prices up 700 percent during the war years. Both publications were relatively new and did not have ready access to newsprint as did the commercial press. Ray (Alexander) Simons to Switzer, 22 June 1991.
26. *Guardian*, 16 August 1945, 1; Len Lee-Warden to Switzer, 25 June 1991.
27. The *Guardian* was five columns between February 1937 and August 1945, seven columns between August 1945 and December 1950, and five columns again between January 1951 and May 1952. The introduction of the northern and southern editions apparently coincided with the adoption of the seven-column format, which was introduced when restrictions on newsprint were lifted after World War II. The seven column format considerably increased the size of the newspaper.
28. Don Pinnock interview with Brian Bunting in London, 1988. The company board met twice a year but apparently had little or no influence on *Guardian* editorial policies. James Zug, personal communication.
29. There is evidence in the 1930s that the *Guardian* was decidedly paternalistic on the "Native" question: "we must... act as guardians to people who are emerging from one civilisation to another... it does mean a sense of responsibility on the part of the more advanced European race." *Guardian*, 4 February 1938. See also 16 September 1938: "nobody but a fool is arguing for intermarriage." According to James Zug, coverage of African affairs during the war years was found mainly in letters to the editor. The news quotations and description of Radford's personal idiosyncracies are taken from Zug's unpublished manuscript on the *Guardian* and successor newspapers, which has the working title "The anvil of struggle" (1995).
30. Ray (Alexander) Simons to Switzer, 22 June 1991.
31. *Guardian*, 2 September 1948, 1; 24 March 1949, 4; Zug, "The anvil of struggle." Radford and Pearson now rejected all individuals and activities associated with the Communist Party, and both families left South Africa for England in 1960.
32. Bunting grew up in Johannesburg and received his B.A. (Honours) degree from the University of the Witwatersrand, where he was president of the Students' Representative Council in 1939. He was an airplane mechanic and later an information officer in the South African Army during the war. Brian Bunting to Switzer 24 July 1991.
33. *Clarion* and *People's World* were the only titles not banned or otherwise suppressed by the authorities under Bunting's editorship. The titles were changed because of disputes with other publications claiming the same titles, so the newspaper could not be registered with the government and qualify for reduced postal and rail tariffs. Len Lee-Warden to Switzer 25 June 1991. For a detailed account of these and other events surrounding the *Guardian*'s many title changes, see Zug, "The anvil of struggle."
34. Bunting settled in England and was active in exile politics in subsequent years. He was the editor of the *African Communist*, organ of the South African Communist Party, for 18 years between 1972 and 1990, and he wrote several books on themes relating to South Africa and the resistance movement. Bunting and his wife returned to live in South Africa in 1991. Brian Bunting to Switzer, 24 July 1991, 1 September 1993.
35. Sam Kahn's speeches in parliament were regarded as outrageous by the ruling National Party, and at least one of them, in which he claimed that a cabinet minister had fathered a child with a Coloured woman, was stricken from the parliamentary record. The media (including the English-language press) agreed to participate in this conspiracy of silence. *Sunday*

Times, 5 June 1994, 20 (Joel Mervis's column).

36. See also n. 19. Lee-Warden was a member of the Springbok Legion and national vice-chair of the Congress of Democrats. He was supported by the communists when he stood for election as a Native Representative, and according to Carneson the Africans would not have voted for Lee-Warden without their endorsement. The newspaper never missed an edition under Lee-Warden's supervision, although he was served with banning orders twice, forced to defend himself in court on various charges and detained during the marathon December 1956–March 1961 Treason Trial. Len Lee-Warden to Switzer, 25 June 1991; Don Pinnock interviews with Len Lee-Warden in Cape Town and Fred Carneson in London, 1988.
37. Carneson was the son of a skilled railway worker from Pietermaritzburg, Natal. Largely self-taught–his formal education stopped at Standard 8 (tenth grade)–Carneson joined the CPSA at an early age and was soon fully engaged in party activities. He organized the parliamentary campaigns for party candidates during these years. Don Pinnock interview with Fred Carneson in London, 1988.
38. Other members of the UN delegation were Xuma, the ANC president general; Hyman Basner, a former CPSA member and cofounder of the abortive African Democratic Party in 1946; and Sorabjee Rustomjee, a leader in the Indian passive resistance campaign.
39. Zug, "The anvil of struggle."
40. Numerous other individuals were known to readers only by their pseudonyms. These included trade unionists ("Ernest Verity"), sports writers ("Custodian," "Jack o' Lantern," "VM," "Full Back," "Turf Notes"), teachers ("Don Q," "RKH") and unidentified workers ("Crate-Shifter"). As Bunting put it: "Pseudonyms were invariably used to avoid harassment and intimidation or by people who for one reason or another did not want to be openly associated with the paper, which was always a target of attack and abuse by... right-wing sources." Brian Bunting to Switzer, 24 July 1991; Zug, "The anvil of struggle."
41. Switzer interview with Naomi (Shapiro) Barnett, 5 June 1991; Brian Bunting to Switzer, 24 July 1991; Don Pinnock interviews with Brian Bunting and Fred Carneson in London, 1988; Zug, "The anvil of struggle."
42. Naomi also served as acting editor in the Johannesburg branch office for three months in 1948. She resigned from the *Guardian* toward the end of 1952 when her husband Jack Barnett, an architect, accepted a contract to work in Israel. The family ended up staying two years, and Naomi did not return to the newspaper until the end of 1954. Brian Bunting to Switzer, 24 July 1991; Switzer interview with Naomi (Shapiro) Barnett, 5 June 1991.
43. Don Pinnock interviews with Brian Bunting and Fred Carneson in London, 1988; James Zug, personal communication.
44. *Guardian*, 26 February 1947, 4; H. J. Simons and R. E. Simons, *Class and colour in South Africa, 1850–1950* (Middlesex, 1969), 538; Brian Bunting to Switzer, 24 July 1991; Zug, "The anvil of struggle" (for the figure of 19,000 in 1950).
45. Estimates varied, but up to six adults were believed to be reading each issue. A. K. Brooks, "From class struggle to national liberation: the Communist Party of South Africa, 1940 to 1950," M.A. thesis (University of Sussex, 1967), 42–43 (citing Edwin Munger for the *New Age* figures); Brian Bunting to Switzer, 24 July 1991.
46. Ray (Alexander) Simons to Switzer, 22 June 1991. It was a "weekly duty" for Communist Party members living in Cape Town. Wolfie Kodesh, who was born and raised in Woodstock, was apparently the top *Guardian* hawker in the party during the 1940s. Zug, "The anvil of struggle."
47. Don Pinnock interview with Fred Carneson in London, 1988.
48. T. Schreuders, "The social and intellectual life of the left in Cape Town during the second world war," in H. Bradford and B. Nasson (eds.), *South African research papers 5* (Cape Town, June 1988), 12.
49. Zug, "The anvil of struggle."
50. Don Pinnock interviews with Brian Bunting and Fred Carneson in London, 1988; Brian Bunting to Switzer, 1 September 1993; James Zug, personal communication.

51. Bunting was forced to raise the price of the newspaper to 2 pence in January 1950 and 3 pence in August 1952. *Guardian*, 5 January 1950, 1; Zug, "The anvil of struggle" (citing *Clarion*, 24 July 1952).
52. For a brief but revealing outline of left-wing support groups in Cape Town at the time, see Schreuders, "The social and intellectual life of the left in Cape Town," esp. 13–22.
53. Brian Bunting to Switzer, 24 July 1991, 1 September 1993. According to Zug, the *Guardian* lost many white readers and advertisers in the aftermath of the 1946 African miners' strike. In addition, sales to railway commuters plummeted when the newspaper was banned from railway bookstalls and private shops on railway concourses in March 1949. Zug, "The anvil of struggle."
54. The *Guardian* also achieved a "new look" with a clearer text and more sharply defined photos when the newspaper switched from a rotary to a flat-bed press about August 1951, but printing costs almost doubled. *Guardian*, 23 August 1951, 2.
55. *Guardian*, 27 February 1947, 4–5. There was evidence of widespread support for the newspaper in this tenth anniversary edition. Birthday greetings outside South Africa suggest that the newspaper was distributed virtually everywhere a Communist Party existed around the world. South African greetings came from clergymen and municipal councillors, the Indian Congresses and the Passive Resistance Council, Cape ANC leader Z. K. Matthews and the "Ciskei Africans" (the *Guardian* had launched a feeding scheme to fight hunger in the eastern Cape's Ciskei reserve), and various CPSA-affiliated organizations.
56. Ray (Alexander) Simons to Switzer, 22 June 1991. Readers in 1948, for example, were told that the newspaper would collapse unless they contributed £600 a month. *Guardian*, 5 February 1948, 1. Some individuals donated money that was not acknowledged in the newspaper, but this was by request. Bunting says they were "mostly business people who were afraid of victimisation." He also insists that "to my knowledge we received not a penny from the Soviet Union or any related source, apart from one donation of £3,000 from China which came unsolicited out of the blue sometime in the 1950s." Brian Bunting to Switzer, 24 July 1991.
57. *Guardian*, e.g., 14 March 1946, 3 (headline: "First Indian Bursary"); 4 July 1946, 3 (headline: "African Teachers Militant"); 11 July 1946, 5 (headline: "Teachers Want Race Equality"); 23 July 1946, 4 (headline: "The Church and Michael Scott").
58. *Guardian*, e.g., 13 January 1949, 6; 21 April 1949, 6; 16 March 1950, 6.
59. Schreuders, "The social and intellectual life of the left in Cape Town," 21.
60. Virtually all the stories in these subcategories were concerned with specific events rather than issues, most were published from 1945 onward, and only a few were placed on the front page in this sample: *Guardian*, e.g., 6 January 1944, 1 (on the plight of sugar workers in Natal); 20 September 1945, 1 (food fund for Africans); 4 September 1947, 1 (on the plight of squatters in Moroka near Johannesburg).
61. Brian Bunting to Switzer, 24 July 1991.
62. The feature, along with others highlighting women, reappeared intermittently in later years. *Guardian*, e.g., 6 March 1947, 5 (an International Women's Day feature on women in South Africa); 3 July 1947, 7; 10 July 1947, 7; 17 February 1949, 3 ("Women's Platform").
63. *Guardian*, e.g., 8 February 1951, 10 (headline: "A Nightie to Make in an Hour").
64. "Advertising, as well as the 'domestic' columns... stressed appearance, clothing and femininity." Schreuders, "The social and intellectual life of the left in Cape Town," 22.
65. *Guardian*, 9 June 1939, 8.
66. *Guardian*, e.g., 25 March 1948, 3; 8 April 1948, 3; 15 April 1948,1; 22 April 1948,1; 6 May 1948, 1 ("These pretty girls are all workers who have earned their own living for many years").
67. *Guardian*, e.g., 23 January 1947, 3; 12 June 1947, 5.
68. *Guardian*, e.g., 2 August 1950, 4. Kahn's column continued in the post-*Guardian* era.
69. *Guardian*, 1 February 1945, 1; 20 September 1945, 1.
70. *Guardian*, 10 April 1941, 2 (headline: "What It Means to You"); 25 June 1942, 6 (headline: "Sweated Labour").

71. *Guardian*, 27 February 1947, 4. Alan Brooks argues that "by the end of the war the *Guardian* was an organ of the CPSA in everything but name." Brooks, "From class struggle to national liberation," 42.
72. *Guardian*, e.g., 1 October 1942, 1–2, 6; 15 April 1943, 1–3; 11 November 1943, 6; 6 January 1944, 2; 20 July 1944, 1–2, 5; 2 January 1947, 1, 3. The number of CPSA stories in this sample steadily increased between 1941 and 1950, but they virtually vanished from the pages of the newspaper after the Suppression of Communism Act in 1950.
73. Lee-Warden, the *Guardian*'s printer from the 1950s until the newspaper ceased publication in 1963, was chairman of the organization in the Cape. Len Lee-Warden to Switzer, 25 June 1991. On the Springbok Legion, see the Introduction.
74. *Guardian*, 22 December 1949, 1. On more than one occasion, anticommunist statements by right-wing Africanists triggered *Guardian* coverage of ANC activities during the 1940s: e.g., 15 December 1949, 3 (headline: "Red-Baiting at A.N.C. Conference?").
75. Brian Bunting to Switzer, 24 July 1991. This assessment was shared by every staff member interviewed who worked on the *Guardian* during the 1940s. "The ANC was a shadow," as Rusty Bernstein put it. "It was an idea that might have had a lot of sympathy, but as an organisation it almost didn't exist." Don Pinnock interview with Hilda (Watts) Bernstein and Lionel "Rusty" Bernstein in London, 1988.
76. *Guardian*, 27 February 1947, 4.
77. *Guardian*, 3 May 1940, 2 ("African Craftsmen" editorial). The newspaper had virtually given up on the Labour Party by this time: e.g., 6, 13 January 1939, 4 (two editorials).
78. On strike-related stories in the *Guardian* sample, see 17 May 1940, 1 (garment workers); 24 October 1940, 3 (tobacco workers; 27 November 1941, 10 (rope workers); 1 October 1942, 5 (candy workers); 15 April 1943, 1, 3 (CNETU demonstration in Port Elizabeth, shoe repairers, distributive workers, students); 11 November 1943, 1, 4, 5, 7 (distributive workers, fish workers); 6 January 1944, 2, 5 (fruit pickers, miners); 20 July 1944, 4–6 (trawlermen, tobacco workers); 5 April 1945, 6 (mint workers); 20 September 1945, 5, 8 (brush and broom workers); 2 January 1947, 1 (miners); 4 September 1947, 1, 5–6, 8 (building workers); 21 April 1949, 1 (box factory workers); 14 July 1949, 5 (garment workers).

    On stories concerned with nonunion boycotts, demonstrations, passive resistance and acts of violence in the *Guardian* sample, see 1 October 1942, 7 (Fort Hare students); 14 March 1946, 1 (violence in Orlando Township near Johannesburg), 2 (Kliptown bus boycott); 27 June 1946, 1–5 (Indian passive resisters, Anti-Pass conference); 2 January 1947, 3, 6 (Anti-Pass conference, Indian passive resisters), 4 September 1947, 1, 4 (violence in Moroka Township near Johannesburg); 5 February 1948, 1, 3, 5 (Indian passive resisters, Indian school protests), 21 April 1949, 1 (railway bus boycott), 14 July 1949, 1 (Africans stone Indian buses in Durban), 3 May 1951, 1–2, 6–7, 9–10, 12 (Franchise Action Council, Transvaal Peace Council, Rand War Veterans' Committee, various African, Coloured and Indian political groups in Durban, fast by Manilal Gandhi, son of the Mahatma); 24 April 1952, 7 (Natal Indian Congress protest photograph).
79. Don Pinnock interview with Brian Bunting in London, 1988. A commentary entitled "Survey on the Left" also featured foreign affairs before the war.
80. Zug, "The anvil of struggle."
81. *Guardian*, e.g., 31 July 1947, 6; 25 March 1948, 4. Three other columns ("Topical" by Betty Radford, "Comment" by Brian Bunting and "By the Way" by Michael Harmel as "Alan Doyle") sometimes addressed foreign events and issues. Bunting's column appeared for a few months after Radford's last known "Topical" column was published in March 1949. Harmel's column first appeared in June 1949 and continued until about August 1951. *Guardian*, e.g., 7 April 1949, 4 ("Comment); 9 June 1949, 4; 2 August 1951, 2 ("By the Way").
82. *Guardian*, e.g., 17 September 1937, 3: "the huge majority of the Spanish people are backing the Republican Government in Spain, whereas on the other side the vast majority of the supporters are Moors and foreign Fascist soldiers."

83. *Guardian*, 14 November 1940, 4.
84. *Guardian*, 21 November 1940, 4.
85. *Guardian*, 1 September 1939, 5.
86. *Guardian*, 3 July 1941, 3.
87. *Guardian*, 25 August 1939,1.
88. *Guardian*, 18 December 1941, 3.
89. Capitalism, however, was always represented in the *Guardian* as an alien, rapacious force. The workers in Spain and Czechoslovakia before World War II, for example, were betrayed by the capitalists: "Spain and Czechoslovakia must be numbered among the states where the workers have suffered–not defeat–but betrayal, betrayal at the hands of men of their own nationality and culture, who sold them and their country to an alien Fascist state with the approval and aid of French and British profit-seekers." *Guardian*, 28 April 1939, 4. English metropolitan capitalists were targeted for special disapproval: "War Aim No. 1 is to make England and the Empire safe for the stock-holder." *Guardian*, 21 March 1940, 3.
90. *Guardian*, 1 May 1947, 4.
91. On the French in Vietnam, for example, see the *Guardian*, 16 January 1947, 3: "*To-day, while the Vietnamese scorch their native earth and fight desperately from behind barricades made of rickshaws, kitchen-tables, prams, beds, desks, and rocking-chairs, the French bomb them from the air. It's an all-too-familiar story* [italics in original]."
92. *Guardian*, e.g., 24 February 1939, 2: "It [the United States] has taken the place morally, politically and physically which has been abdicated by Britain in the last few years. Where the British and French Governments align themselves more and more openly with the anti-progressive forces in the world, the Government of the U.S.A. expresses the sentiments of the nation when it dissociates from the dark and backward-flowing trends of Fascism."
93. *Guardian*, e.g., 24 April 1952, 8 (headline: "Control Measures Beating Germ War in Korea").
94. *Guardian*, e.g., 25 January 1951, 7 (headline: "They're Itching for Atomic War").
95. *Guardian*, e.g., 22 March 1951, 6 (headline: "Barcelona Strikers Shake Fascist Dictatorship: U.S. Bombers Supported Franco").
96. *Guardian*, 1 February 1951, 4.
97. *Guardian*, 4 January 1951, 3.
98. *Guardian*, 16 August 1945, 4 (headline: "Freedom for the Colonies").
99. *Guardian*, 31 January 1952, 3.
100. *Guardian*, 10 April 1947, 3. The conference was sponsored by 11 communist parties from Britain's dominions and colonies. Naidoo and Danie Du Plessis were the South African delegates.
101. *Guardian*, 26 April 1945, 4.
102. One 20-article series entitled "Socialism for S.A.," for example, ran from 27 June 1946 through 9 January 1947. It was based on a CPSA publication entitled "Economics and Politics." The articles were entitled "Communist Theory" (27 June 1946, 3), "The Class Struggle" (4 July 1946, 3), "Capitalism" (11 July 1946, 7), "The Source of Profit" (18 July 1946, 7), "Wages under Capitalism" (25 July 1946, 7), "What Keeps Wages Low" (1 August 1946, 7), "Wages and Colour Bars" (8 August 1946, 7), "Unemployment and Crisis" (22 August 1946, 7), "Poverty in the Midst of Plenty" (29 August 1946, 7), "Imperialism" (12 September 1946, 7), "The Cost of Living" (19 September 1946, 7), "Fascist Dictatorships" (3 October 1946, 7), "The Aims of Fascism" (10 October 1946, 7), "Changing over to Socialism" (17 October 1946, 7), "How it Works" (24 October 1946, 7), "Socialist Wages and Wealth" (7 November 1946, 7), "From Socialism to Communism" (21 November 1946, 7), "Work for All" (28 November 1946, 7), "Soviet Russia" (12 December 1946, 7), "Socialist Russia" (9 January 1947, 7).
103. *Guardian*, 11 August 1939, 8.
104. *Guardian*, 19 February 1937, 5 (headline: "The Obvious Benefits of Trade Unionism"). On the Afrikaner worker: "Most of them have left the rural areas only recently. Years of sentimental attachment to the Nationalist Party are not so easily forgotten." *Guardian*, 29 April 1938, 2.
105. *Guardian*, 30 April 1937, 7, 10.
106. See also Chapter 11 (*Inkululeko*) in the present volume.
107. *Guardian*, 29 August 1946,1. See also

Guardian, 8 August 1946, 1 (headline: "Miners Plan Strike, Africans Demand 10s. a Day"); 15 August 1946, 1 (headline: "Greatest Strike in S.A. History, More than 50,000 Out").

108. *Guardian*, 19 September 1946, 1.
109. *Guardian*, 3 October 1946, 2.
110. *Guardian*, 26 September 1946, 5.
111. *Guardian*, 4 March 1948, 1; 18 March 1948, 4.
112. *Guardian*, 8 January 1948, 1.
113. *Guardian*, 29 April 1948, 1, 5; see also 13 May 1948, 1; 20 May 1948, 1. Danie Du Plessis (Troyeville) and Michael Harmel (Hilbrow) in Johannesburg and Fred Carneson (Cape Flats) in Cape Town contested seats in parliament for the Communist Party in the 1948 general election.
114. *Guardian*, 3 June 1948, 1 (citing Edwin Mofutsanyana, editor of *Inkululeko*).
115. *Guardian*, 29 June 1950, 1 (citing a National Day of Protest committee statement).
116. *Guardian*, 22 June 1950, 1.
117. *Guardian*, 29 June 1950, 1 (statement of editorial policy by Brian Bunting).
118. Clarion, 29 May 1952, 1.
119. Don Pinnock interview with Fred Carneson in London, 1988. The newspaper claimed that 85 percent of its readers were "non-European" in 1948, but these were clearly Coloureds living mainly in Cape Town. Zug, "The anvil of struggle" (citing *Guardian* in August 1948).
120. Zug, "The anvil of struggle" (citing *Guardian*, 4 January 1951 and 12 June 1952).
121. Don Pinnock interview with Brian Bunting in London, 1988.
122. R. Ainslie, *The press in Africa* (New York, 1966), 83.
123. Don Pinnock interview with Brian Bunting in London, 1988.

CHAPTER 10

Writing Left

The Journalism of Ruth First and the *Guardian* in the 1950s

Don Pinnock

By whichever way you measure it, financial or political, the *Guardian* was a newspaper that had little hope of survival. From week to week it teetered on the brink of closure, with pennies in the bank and policemen at the door. Titles were banned, and the newspaper was sued, firebombed, spied on and had its presses sealed. It was banned from railway news stands and raided by the police. Two commissions of inquiry investigated its activities. Its editors received personal banning orders, most staff members were arrested and charged at one time or another, its street sellers were harassed and beaten up, and eight staffers went on trial for high treason. And yet, except for the State of Emergency in 1960, the *Guardian* under its many names came out every week for 26 years, the longest run of any left-wing newspaper in South African history.

A journalist who was central to this history was Ruth First. This chapter is an attempt to understand her writing in the context of resistance politics during the 1950s. She belonged to a journalistic tradition that required its practitioners to be activists. Behind this conception was an intuition that the journalist was not a technical entity, like a camera recording the day's events, but a social entity, a listener, a communicator and an actor. At the heart of this form of journalism was the conception of readers as active human beings, able to change their world. For Ruth First and her colleagues, all journalism was in some sense political. It was less useful to ask questions about *what* was reported (or whether it was true) than about *how* it was reported, *how* the reader was positioned by the writer and *what* social values and norms were encoded into the text. These journalists did not mystify the reader with news reports that were deemed to be objective snapshots of a distant reality. They viewed journalism as a social practice that intervened in and represented reality.

Ruth First's parents had migrated to South Africa from a ghetto known as the Pale of Settlement in what was then western Russia, where the vast majority of Russian Jews were forced to live. The ghetto was subjected to repeated pogroms, and hundreds of thousands of Jews left the area for England, the United States and various other parts of the world between the 1880s and World War I. First's father Julius had arrived in South Africa from Latvia at the age of 10 in 1907 and her mother Tilly from Lithuania at the age of 4 in 1901. They met while attending the same Jewish government primary school in Doornfontein, a Johannesburg suburb with a large population of Jewish immigrants. They were married in 1924, and Heliose Ruth First was born on 4 May 1925.

The Firsts were ardent socialists, a political tradition they had probably inherited from their own immigrant parents, and founding members of the Communist Party of South Africa. The issues so central to the CPSA during these formative years were debated daily in the First household (Julius himself was elected party chair in 1925), and First was reared in this revolutionary political tradition. Myrtle Berman, one of First's classmates in primary school, remembers that they were the only persons in their history class who had ever heard of the Soviet Union. First invited Myrtle home to meet her mother, and Myrtle's memory of that meeting captures something of the atmosphere in which First grew up:

> One day after school I went home with Ruth. Got there about three o'clock and emerged at six with my head reeling, having had a three-hour lecture from Tilly on the history of socialism, the Russian Revolution, the origins of religion ... without me saying a word! And I remember wandering home and telling my mother, who nearly had a fit at this seditious stuff. But Tilly educated me. She gave me stuff to read. She was the main person who formed my early views.[1]

First and her mother often had rows, "fighting like two people who are very close," according to Berman. As First sought to develop an identity of her own, relations with her mother became the source of increasing conflict.

Ruth First's father Julius spent much time at the mattress factory that he and his brother owned and little time raising the children. According to one informant, Julius was "sweet and soft ... [but] you wouldn't call him an intellectual giant. Far from it."[2] In one of Ruth First's final works, the beautifully crafted biography of Olive Schreiner that she wrote with a young British academic by the name of Ann Scott, one is tempted to see some of First's own predicament in their description of Schreiner: "She felt herself to be a motherless child: her mother had been superior, distant and severe; her father tender but ineffectual, and a foreigner, ever uncomfortable in Africa."[3]

First was a voracious reader and a keen debater–for example, she became a fixture in the junior version of Johannesburg's Left Book Club after she joined at age 14–but she suffered from an overactive thyroid that left her intermittently hyperactive and lethargic as a youth. These symptoms cleared up when medication was available, but in later years she suffered from a low pulse rate and a persistent weight problem. In dealing with a dominant and at times abrasive mother, an absent and passive father, nonstop politics and a long-term physical ailment, Ruth developed a mixture of toughness and vulnerability, an emotional ambivalence that was also projected in the Schreiner biography: "How could a free woman validate herself? Perhaps by experiencing herself as a man ... We see Olive as someone struggling to come to terms with her identity as a whole ... she cut a lonely, isolated figure, issuing prophetic warnings about the future of the country and retreating into a shy personal life."[4]

First graduated from Jeppe Girls High (Johannesburg) in 1941 with an unexceptional second class matriculation certificate, but she knew what she wanted to do next. The following year she registered to do a degree in social science at the University of the Witwatersrand. In the next three years she would discover the political and social agenda, and the personal comradeship, that would sustain her for the rest of her life.

A Passionate Political Journalist

First was a passionate political journalist who used her skills as a means to target an oppressed social class and mobilize them to challenge the social order. The tools of her trade were the pen, notebook and typewriter. She wrote insightfully, and at times brilliantly, about what she saw and heard, but she was also in a sense *written* by the political and social context. She recorded the voices of the historical protagonists, and at the same time history transformed her into a key protagonist.

First's journalistic frame of reference was South Africa from the late 1940s to the early 1960s. It was drawn from the perspective of the Communist Party and the Congress Alliance, from the position of an educated white woman who was both an observer of the life around her and a social participant in what she observed. But it would be incorrect to say that First was merely a propagandist for the political Left. Hers was a probing, dissident perspective, setting ideas and events against one another, sharpening and clarifying differences and thereby intensifying commitment to certain ideologies and discourses. She was to develop ideas that were in advance of, and at times out of step with, the communist, nationalist and liberal thinkers and activists around her. The Congress Alliance and the Communist Party provided her with a platform, but they were not a cage for her ideas. An integral relation was to develop between her private and her social destiny, and this was to be reflected in her writing. Gavin Williams has identified three underlying ideas that run through her work:

- The proper focus of social explanation should be on capitalism.
- The masses at times are able to seize the political agenda from the hands of their rulers and shape the political agenda.
- First was committed to socialism, despite the difficulties of achieving it.[5]

First's journalism, then, was characterized by certain basic themes. One theme that underlies most of her work is the conflict between nonracialism and apartheid. But it was the *form* in which these two ideological discourses manifested themselves that captured her attention. The Congress Alliance sought to demonstrate the moral superiority of nonracialism over apartheid and to explore to the full the frontiers of the existing social order without crossing its boundaries. The moral positivism of the Congress Alliance incorporated a commitment to nonviolence and a preparedness to rest its case on the intrinsic justice of its cause. This was a justice which, Congress activists felt, no rational being in possession of evidence could deny. The evidence was presented as argument. As Stephen Clingman was to point out: "The Defiance Campaign demonstrated the indignities of *apartheid*...The gathering of the women in Pretoria and the Congress of the People, both events high in symbolic value, were also presented as a kind of social testimony: of the dedication, dignity and vitality of an alternative South Africa."[6]

The apartheid challenge to a nonracial society did not yet suggest social revolution. Increasing state attacks on the Congress Alliance not only entrenched this perspective but demanded that it be spelled out in great detail during the 1956 Treason Trial that kept 156 activists in the dock for four years. After Sharpeville in 1960, it became clear that the state would leave no grounds on which to base a moral stand: reason could not win against apartheid, and races could not be equal when the material conditions of equality did not exist.

Another theme, and perhaps the dominant one in First's writing, was the conflict between labor and capital. First's marxist perspective led her to measure

Photo 34. Ruth First (Slovo) in the 1950s.

progress by a set of indices different from that of the commercial press. Mainstream reporters might see a relationship between the wealth of whites and the poverty of Africans, but First placed these social relations in a contextual framework by showing how apartheid cemented in place the racial and class divisions of an emerging industrial capitalist state.

During the 1950s, National Party government attempted to empower racial capitalism as a natural social practice. Through Acts of Parliament, by-laws, regulations and a massive ideological onslaught, apartheid began to take on the character of an immutable, eternal and God-given order. For people of all colors it became almost common sense that whites should be the rulers and be wealthy and that blacks should be poor and be workers. For apartheid to be effective as an ideology, it had to be framed as a rational bureaucratic discourse, a discourse that represented apartheid as mechanical necessity and as universal common sense.

Immediately after their election victory, the Nationalists began restructuring social relations through legislation, burying apartheid in bureaucratic institutional practices. While the parliamentary opposition and the commercial press attacked the cruder icebergs of this policy, the vast, bureaucratically submerged reordering of society proceeded largely unchallenged, either because it was not seen or because it simply accelerated the practices of racial capitalism already in place in 1948.

The main difference between First's journalism and that of her contemporaries in the white-owned and controlled commercial press was the degree to which this process was accepted as common sense. In its ideological dimension, common sense is itself an effect of power. But power is the outcome of political contest, and if people become aware that a particular aspect of common sense is sustaining power inequalities at their own expense, it ceases to be common sense and may cease to have the capacity to sustain power inequalities. It is not clear whether First understood this by political deduction or intuition, but her attempts to disorganize state legitimacy by focusing on the bureaucratic processes of apartheid labor organization – on the daily indignities of passes, grimy court proceedings, prison conditions, township squalor and farm conditions – was to strike at the heart of apartheid ideology and leave state officials beside themselves with anger. The effect of such reporting, connecting as it did with the daily lives of ordinary people, fed into the calls by Congress Alliance politicians for an end to apartheid and to inequalities of wealth.

Two distinct discourses emerged from the ideological struggles of the 1950s. The dominant discourse was couched in the language of anticommunist racism and was inculcated by the holders of state power; the alternative discourse was a mixture of socialism, nonracialism and moral outrage, communicated by the Congress Alliance and other leftist and liberal groups, which found weekly expression in the *Guardian, Fighting Talk* and various smaller publications. Of course, neither discourse sprang into the arena fully armed. The ideas and language were worked up over the years by activist politicians, bureaucrats, orators, preachers, journalists, pamphleteers and others. Both discourses, however, were to develop their own core themes and forms of expression, and in 1956 these discourses were also in the dock at the Treason Trial.

It was for this reason that the radical press was so central to the political struggles of the era. These newspapers reflected the events of the day, but they also developed a popular antidominant discourse as a conscious alternative to the dominant discourse. It was an attempt to control the contours of the political world, to delegitimize state policy and to shift existing power relations toward the Congress Alliance and the working class. Radical newspapers reported the daily indignities of apartheid, the activities of the Congress Alliance and the world of international socialism, but they also highlighted the issues that would galvanize their readers into action.

This study is an attempt to understand some of these issues by focusing on Ruth First's reporting and, in so doing, throw light on the processes and effects of political journalism in South Africa.

The Plight of Black Farm Workers

In June 1947, First, the newly appointed Johannesburg editor of the *Guardian*, was shown a report in a daily newspaper by the Anglican priest Michael Scott. The "rather cryptic little paragraph," as she put it, indicated that the Boere Arbeid Vereeniging (Farm Labour Union) in Bethal had decided not to supply laborers to farmers who ill-treated their workers.[7] Ruth followed the report back to the Bethal newspaper *De Echo*, which cited a court case against a farm foreman named Johannes Brenkman. He had been tried for setting dogs on farm laborers attempting to flee the farm and for having them beaten with *sjambok*s (whips). After the assaults, according to evidence, the laborers were bound together with donkey chains and taken to the compound, where they were forced to sleep naked and chained together. Ruth and Michael Scott decided to investigate, and they were shocked by what they found.

The trip to Bethal marked the beginning of First's investigative labor journalism and opened a window into the subterranean processes of apartheid. As she recorded the event: "The sort of thing that happens on these farms sounds like a story from the history of some ancient slave empire. Labourers are cursed, beaten, locked in their compounds at night, have their clothes taken from them and savage dogs set over them in case they should try to escape."[8]

Farm workers were found "squatting on heaps of sacks which were also their working clothes." They had no blankets, no boots and worked from 4 A.M. to 6 P.M. under the eye of overseers with whips. They were served "a clod of mealie meal and a pumpkin wrapped in a piece of sacking, each man taking a handful at a time."[9] First reported: "it is not every day that the Johannesburg reporter of the *Guardian* meets an African farm labourer who, when asked to describe conditions on the farm on which he works, silently takes off his shirt to show large weals and scars whipped on his back, shoulders and arms."[10] First and Scott returned to Johannesburg on a Thursday night, too late to make that week's edition of the *Guardian*. Eager to release the story, Scott contacted the *Rand Daily Mail*, which published the exposé on Friday, June 27, under the headline "Near Slavery in Bethal District." It caused an uproar.

Both the *Rand Daily Mail* and the *Guardian* called for a full and independent investigation. Prime Minister Smuts, concerned "that South Africa's efforts at the forthcoming General Assembly meeting of the United Nations may be jeopardized by the behaviour of a few farmers," summoned his minister of justice, H. G. Lawrence, to Pretoria's Union Buildings and insisted that he "remedy the position once and for all with the most drastic means at his disposal."[11] Lawrence conferred with the acting secretary of justice, the attorney general of the Transvaal, the acting commissioner of police and the minister of Native affairs. Officials of the Department of Native Affairs "worked until 2 o'clock [in the morning] preparing a report for the Prime Minister."[12] In a letter to the *Rand Daily Mail*, the general manager of "Native Labour" for the mines vehemently denied any collusion between farmers and the Chamber of Mines in the procurement of labor, but Lawrence announced that the police would "act at once to clean up the unsatisfactory conditions on some farms in the Bethal district."[13]

Michael Scott was invited back to Bethal to "place his case before the farmers." He and First agreed to return to the town, fully expecting trouble from the angry white farmers. The tensions surrounding their return must have been considerable. First was to recall that Bethal "could probably compare well with any small town in the Southern States just before a lynching." About 1,500 farmers and townspeople packed the hall, and Scott was to confess that confronting them was "among the most frightening episodes of [my] life."[14] The farmers demanded that Scott publicly withdraw his "unfounded allegations," and when he refused the crowd became threatening: "Tar and feather him. He is an Uitlander [foreigner], deport him."[15]

First and Scott barely escaped the crowd, but on the way out of town they quietly met a group of workers at a meeting in the Bethal African location, who had collected £17 to "send six representatives to Johannesburg to state their case and views to the press."[16] According to First, they considered "that Michael Scott, far from exaggerating the bad conditions of farm labourers, [had] not told the worst aspects of the story."[17]

Despite the initial flurry, the scandal was downplayed by the government, which attempted to "buy off incensed farmers by promising them convict labour – one shilling a day and guaranteed docile."[18] The commercial press lost interest, and the affair was soon buried in the run-up to the 1948 election, but First refused to let the matter drop and began digging deeper.

Farming in the Bethal area was intensive agriculture with an emphasis on maize and potatoes. This required a large seasonal labor force and did not lend itself to the provision of space for black tenants to farm or raise stock. Workers could not be attracted to the Bethal farms because conditions were so harsh and the work so poorly paid. They were often expected to dig in manure, and to dig out potatoes with their bare hands instead of spades so the potatoes would not be damaged.[19] As far back as 1930, the historian W. M. Macmillan had written that "High Veld maize farmers about Bethal [must] draw supplies of labour from the Cape Reserves, from anywhere except from the neighbouring Low Veld."[20]

First was to discover the full extent of this "anywhere." In July 1947 she unearthed a government notice stating that from March of that year "unregistered foreign Native labour" was to be "rounded up" in the towns and given the alternative of leaving South Africa or working on the farms.[21] The following month she found that 1,853 of these foreigners had been arrested in Johannesburg "by seven special police sections working by motor-car, motor-cycle and on foot to bring foreign Natives to the book."[22] Others were being recruited for the farms as they stepped over the border at Messina in the northern Transvaal:

> About 20,000 Nyasaland Africans come to South Africa on their own every year. Many walk all the way, taking as long as two months to walk through Rhodesia to the Limpopo [River] and over the border into the Union. At Messina, even on the banks of the river, no obstacles are put in their way – as long as they are prepared to work on the farms. This is their alternative to repatriation.[23]

She discovered there were no less than 40,000 foreign contract labourers working in the Bethal area. But she also found it was not only foreigners who were being recruited. In the reserves, recruitment had been taking place for generations, and she was to discover the precise relationship between the collapse of the reserves and capitalist needs:

> Recruitment of labour [in Bethal] depends on poverty. In times of drought and poor crops, recruiting figures soar. In better times, fewer men present themselves at the depot of the recruiter... Labour agencies recruit farm labour [but] recruiting on a really tremendous scale is done on behalf of mining interests in South Africa.[24]

In November 1948 another pool of labor was opened for exploitation. Johannesburg was declared a "closed area" by a law passed to fulfill a National Party election pledge, another amendment to the Urban Areas Act. Police and pass officials were encouraged to interpret this legislation as a way to force people arrested for pass "offenses" into farm labor. Urban policemen became labor catchers for the farming sector, a task they took up with enthusiasm. Police vans prowled the cities checking people's passes for "irregularities," and at the Johannesburg train station hundreds of people were arrested as they came in to work.[25] By 1949 the pass offices in Johannesburg were "comparatively deserted" after hundreds of workers queuing to get their passes stamped were deported to the farms.[26] In June 1949, First made a sensational discovery: court officials were "selling" pass offenders to farmers:

> Early each morning the pick-up vans drive up [to the Native Commissioner's Court in Fordsburg, a working-class area in Johannesburg]. They bring the men – and some

> women – picked up by the police raids the night before… Lining the streets outside this court can be seen cars and lorries with an assortment of Platteland number plates. From the maize and potato belts come the farmers looking for cheap labour. In a shed near the court, as they wait, Africans are pressed to accept farm work. The prisoners, none of whom have yet appeared before the court, let alone been found guilty, are told… if they accept work the charges against them will be withdrawn.[27]

The men were told that the alternative to "voluntary" farm labor was months or even years in a penal colony. They were required to place their thumb prints to contracts that had not been read to them or to sign away their freedom by touching the pencil in the hands of a white official. The truth of the matter was that most offenders, if they appeared in court, would have been fined only a few pounds for failure to produce their pass. When this exposé was published, "police, Bantu Affairs Department officials and farmers denied knowledge and responsibility for it, accused and counter-accused one another, trying to shrug off any part in the operation of its irregularities."[28] The deputy minister of Bantu administration and development(formerly the Department of Native Affars) claimed that "not a single Native is working as a farm labourer in lieu of prosecution for minor offenses."[29] A Native Commissioner said it was "made plain to the men that this is a voluntary scheme," and the police said that "if there was any irregularity in the contract, the Native Commissioner's office is to blame."[30]

But the practice continued unabated, and into First's office at the *Guardian* poured a steady stream of information and groups of brutalized laborers who had escaped from the farms. In 1954 she was to unearth concrete proof of collusion between the police and farmers in procuring labor in the form of a secret circular from the secretary of justice and the commissioner of police sent to all Native Commissioners and magistrates. It was common knowledge, read the circular,

> That large numbers of Natives are daily being arrested and prosecuted for contraventions of a purely technical nature. These arrests cost the State large sums of money and serve no useful purpose. The Department of Justice, the South African Police (and Native Affairs) have therefore… evolved a scheme, the object of which is to induce unemployed Natives now roaming the streets… to accept employment outside such urban areas.[31]

The circular laid down that Africans held for violations of the Urban Areas Act or the Natives Tax Act would be "removed under escort to the district labour bureau and handed over to the employment officer… Priority should be given to farm labour."[32] To be unemployed was a crime but to obtain a job in an urban area a worker needed to have registered accommodation. Given the massive housing shortage in Johannesburg during the 1950s, at least one-third of all Africans were liable to be "canalized" by the state into less desirable jobs in the economy, notably farming. As her investigations progressed, the alliance between mining, agriculture and the state in the maintenance of poverty and cheap labor became increasingly clear. First was to reflect that "no other country with a comparable degree of industrialisation exists on a semi-slave labour force in the rural areas, with the state acting as a recruiting force for bad farmers who cannot attract labour by normal means."[33]

The flurry of state activity around these exposés did nothing to alleviate the problem; if anything, it got worse. But with encouragement from an extraordinary ANC activist, Gert Sibande, the farm workers began to fight back. Sibande, who became known as the Lion of the East, had been a farm laborer in Bethal. Now he was a crusader against South Africa's semifeudal farm labor system. Sibande would sit in the Bethal court, "a silent monitor, his very presence a rock ruffling the stream of legal proceedings, discomforting the dispensers of justice, intervening on behalf of [farm] deserters."[34] It was Sibande who had led Scott and First past watchdogs onto the Bethal farms and into the smoke-filled compounds. He was driven out of Bethal by the authorities, but throughout the 1950s he continued his campaign against farm conditions. With the assistance of Sibande and the brutalized farm workers, First and the newspaper began taking farmers to court, and interdicts were sought to release men detained on farms against their will.

In 1951 a farmer named Max Mann was sentenced to five years' imprisonment with hard labor after being found guilty of 39 assaults on farmworkers. Mann had been charged originally with 87 assaults with whips, pick handles and *sjambok*s, and evidence was presented that some workers had been locked up each night in a room too small for them to lie down in. In another case, a *New Age* informant was charged with perjury after signing an affidavit about the death of a farm laborer; the newspaper helped fight the case and won.[35] In yet another case, following allegations of forced labor by First in *New Age*, the Supreme Court ordered the release of two workers.[36]

Beaten, bruised and dazed men and women continued to flow into the *New Age* offices, and farmers were beginning to feel the effect of negative publicity on their labor supply.[37] Years earlier in 1949, "owing to a shortfall of 60 percent in Native farm labour requirements," the Bethal Farm Labour Bureau had announced plans to build a farm prison to supply convict labor.[38] Although South Africa has always had convict labor, the model then in use dated back to 1932 and was known as the "6 pence a day scheme."[39] It was stopped initially in 1947, following criticism from the Lansdowne Commission, but almost immediately reintroduced after a concerted appeal from various farm interests. More than 40,000 prisoners were working on farms in 1952, and the figure was 100,000 two years later. In 1957 nearly 200,000 prisoners were sent to designated white-owned farms from 165 jails throughout the Union.[40] *New Age* found the previous year that 90 percent of the farmers in the Ladismith (Cape) area, for example, were using convict labor.[41]

Treatment of both convict and farm labor in the eastern Transvaal continued to be brutal, and First investigated and exposed the system wherever she could. For example, *New Age* was asked by a distraught mother in 1959 to help find her 13-year-old son, who had disappeared near Umtata in the Transkei. First traced the boy to a potato farm where he had been abducted by a farmer, and her investigations led to the boy's release. She then started to investigate child labor and found as the reserves became poorer recruits tended to become younger. Some were only 11 years old: "This is where the recruiting bodies cash in, literally, with a price paid for the head of every (youth) 'bought' in this trading in human beings."[42]

New Age also linked the "sale" of children to the issue of passes for women, who were warned that when they were given reference books they could be picked up on police raids and sent to farms.[43] The following month she uncovered "hair-raising details of a new scandal in farm semi-slavery, enough to move South Africans hardened even to Bethal."[44] On a farm owned by a P. J. Potgieter, two men died after assaults and were buried on the farm. Beatings were found to be the order of the day, and workers were cut deliberately on the feet with hoes to prevent them from running away. First assisted in obtaining an urgent court application for the release of one of the workers, a herbalist called Musa Sadika. Following a habeas corpus application by his wife, Musa was freed, and affidavits citing the terrible conditions on the farm were made public. They claimed that about 80 workers had escaped from the farm in previous months, but because Potgieter's son-in-law worked for the local farm labor depot the farm always had a fresh supply of men. Treatment of workers was severe: "Whenever Potgieter arrived and hooted in his car the boss boys immediately started moving among the workers, hitting out at anyone within striking distance of their knobkerries (sticks or clubs). Potgieter would shout: 'Slaan hulle dood!' (Hit them dead!)."[45]

Using *New Age* as its mouthpiece, the ANC called for a public commission of inquiry into farm labor, and the lawyer in the Potgieter case sent a letter to the minister of police demanding action. Sibande, now Transvaal president of the ANC, challenged the government to put him on a commission to investigate farm conditions.[46] In the following edition, First wound the campaign into high gear. She had found a Bantu Affairs Department "youth camp" in the eastern Transvaal that was "selling" 15-year-old boys to Bethal farmers for labor. The camp was supposedly a "place of safety" for youths "picked up off the streets." Some boys were being sent to the camp without their parents knowing where they were. She also found that the previous year the camp's director had been convicted of sodomy.[47]

Three days after this story, the ANC's National Anti-Pass Conference in Johannesburg, responding to the court cases and *New Age* reports, called for a national boycott of potatoes.[48] The police had prohibited ANC president general Albert Lutuli from attending the conference and then prohibited the mass rally planned to welcome him. The Anti-Pass delegates retaliated by calling for a total consumer boycott on 26 June 1959, after which the potato boycott would begin. This move was "the first use of the economic boycott weapon in the struggle," according to Ruth, and it was launched "as a protest against the horrifying conditions of farm labourers on the big potato farms in the Transvaal."[49] The report of the conference planning committee noted that Africans were the greatest economic asset in the country: "What is our economic power? It is the power of our LABOUR [and] our PURCHASING POWER ... by withdrawing our purchasing power we can punch them in the stomach."[50] The conference also recommended a boycott against the products of Nationalist-controlled industries.

In announcing the boycott, *New Age* again demanded a judicial inquiry into farm labor. This call coincided with another appearance in court of the Heidelberg farmer Potgieter, following a court ruling that he release two workers. A number of organizations and individuals (including Ambrose Reeves, the Anglican bishop of Johannesburg) responded to the campaign by setting up a committee to help trace missing farm workers and establish a legal and medical bureau for victims of the system.[51]

New Age reported five more court cases involving farm laborers in the next edition, together with a judgment rendered by Mr. Justice de Wet in the Potgieter case that struck at the roots of the farm labor system. He echoed what First had been saying for years:

> The court would not countenance a procedure where a man was arrested and told he must either go to a farm or to jail. What authority is there for this? Is it not compounding an offense? It was a breach of the policeman's duty for him to arrest and not charge a man. What right has he to hand him over to someone else?[52]

The lead story in the newspaper following the case was headlined "Farm Slave Scheme Cracks":

> First sign that the exposure of the evils of the forced labour system is having effect came this week when an Eastern Transvaal farmer who had been taken to court to produce some of his labourers surrendered his entire labour force and drove them back to Johannesburg. By Tuesday his example had been followed by five other farmers.[53]

Under the slogan "Awadliw ga de jeoe!" ("We don't eat them!", in Tswana) the potato boycott picked up speed. Newspapers reported potatoes piling up in markets and shops in Johannesburg, Durban and Port Elizabeth. As the day for the national boycott drew nearer, mass rallies were planned, fake leaflets calling on people to boycott mealies (maize) appeared and the minister of police warned of mass arrests. The day before the June 1959 boycott, *New Age* ran the headline "Potatoes: Supply Good, Demand Poor." The boycott campaign was remarkably successful and spread from the cities to the smaller centers. For the next two months First was tireless in pursuit of farm exposés. In one edition alone, 23 July 1959, she unearthed no less than four "scandals" about farm conditions.

The Farmers' Union and the Bantu Affairs Department each appointed independent commissions of inquiry into farm labor. Under pressure, the government appointed a parliamentary commission of inquiry, but, as First pointed out, "the conclusions of the Agricultural Union's commission is that abuses on farms were isolated. The [Bantu Affairs Department] commission has also completed its inquiry. The Government commission consists of police, farmers and BAD officials, and it starts its work with these two whitewashing reports already before it."[54]

Two weeks before the potato boycott ended on 31 August 1959, First produced a 24-page booklet entitled *The Farm Labour Scandal,* documenting in her clear, concise style the farm labor scandal from its inception to the boycott. On June 17, the state had suspended the forced labor scheme, pending the findings of its inquiry. A government spokesman admitted there had been a "technical fault" in the allocation of labor.[55] First's newspaper ran the headline, "*New Age* did this! Without *New Age* You Would Never Have Known." Reports about farm labor abuses declined dramatically after the potato boycott, but they did not disappear, and First continued to keep a watchful eye on the countryside. She had proved her point: journalists need not only report about the world, they could also change it.

The Women's Anti-Pass Campaigns

Another aspect of First's journalism can be seen in her attempts to build an identity for African women during the Anti-Pass campaigns of the 1950s. South Africa had given the world two new words–"passes" and Sharpeville–by the time the bullet-riddled bodies of the victims at Vereeniging and Cape Town were buried in 1960. By then passes were the central issue in South African resistance politics. They had always been key documents for most Africans, but the process by which they moved from being irritating paper to being symbols of oppression was an exercise in ideological mobilization by the Congress Alliance, the Federation of South African Women and *New Age* against the state's labor laws and practices.[56]

The Anti-Pass campaigns also played a significant role in the reemergence, after 40 years, of African women into the political arena. The first clash between African women and the government had taken place in the Orange Free State in 1913.[57] It was a struggle that pitted the self-esteem and survival of urban women against the government's determination to banish them initially from the cities as "undesirables" and bring them back later as superexploitable migrants. It was fought out in the streets, on buses, in workers' compounds and in courtrooms, and it was also fought out in laws of parliament, government notices, political speeches, scholarly studies and in the popular press. In a sense, it was a struggle over the soul of African women, who were emerging as a new force in industry and in the cities of postwar South Africa.

African women in the 1950s found themselves struggling against three very different perceptions of themselves–as labor units (by the state), as "harmlessly inferior" (by African men) and as passive adults with the rights of minors in a "traditional" African social order (which prevailed most effectively in the reserves). These contending discourses were to be central to the Anti-Pass campaigns.

The National Party's conception of African women was linked to its urban labor policy. This policy lay at the core of apartheid ideology and was to be the product of intense debates and power struggles within the party hierarchy.[58] One pole of the argument within the ruling group, which Deborah Posel characterizes as that of the "purists," pushed for total geographical and cultural separation of the races. This position was based ultimately on the fear that whites would be "swamped" by Africans migrating to the cities. In its most virulent form it was embodied by Nazi-inspired right-wing movements like the Ossewa Brandwag, but it was also given a biblical twist by Afrikaner preachers who mixed religious pronouncements and secular politics in the pulpit with fluency:

> The black giant of Africa is eating bread for which he has not sweated, he wants to wear clothes which do not fit him, he wants to pay with what he does not have yet, distribute what he does not possess yet, wants to talk about things he does not yet comprehend, wants to be where he still is not...David taught us that a Philistine cannot be merely prayed away–he must also be beaten away. We must unite in the face of common danger. The black masses of Africa do not seek the white man's friendship but his destruction. The snakes of unrest and agitation have crept out of their holes.[59]

Apartheid's solution lay in the control of labor, and to that end it was necessary to conceptualize all Africans as being foreigners in white South Africa, temporary sojourners enjoying the privileges of a capitalist economy but with no rights. Section 10 of the Native Laws Amendment Act of 1952 divided African laborers in the cities into three categories–those who could live in proclaimed "white" urban areas under certain conditions, those who were legal migrants and finally the "undesirables," who would be relocated to the reserves or (if needed) to white commercial farms. The Natives (Abolition of Passes and Co-ordination of Documents) Act of the same year did not abolish passes: it renamed them "reference books" and required that all African males above 16 years of age carry them. Both acts made provision for the extension of these documents to African women. A government notice in October 1952 established labor bureaus throughout the Union and required all work-seekers to register with a labor bureau.[60] The main objective of these laws was to reverse the flow of African workers from rural to urban areas and ensure that additional labor in the cities was supplied only by temporary migrants living in the reserves.

Being unemployed was now a crime. A worker declared "undesirable" under these laws could be "removed from the urban or proclaimed area and detained until removal or sent to a work colony." All definitions of race, place and status were embedded in the pass book. In 1959 Lewis Nkosi captured the mood of millions when he wrote:

> I do not live apart from my own reference book any more. In fact I have decided I AM THE REFERENCE BOOK! It stands for my personality. It delineates my character. It defines the extent of my freedom...It has become my face. What began as a system purporting to smooth my efforts to earn a living and move about with sufficient proof of my claim to the citizenship of this country has now completely subordinated me.[61]

Another – perhaps even harder – political barrier to cross was the way African women were perceived by African men. When the Federation of South African Women (FSAW) was launched in April 1954, *Advance* (another successor to the *Guardian*) failed to report the new organization for more than a week. Cherryl Walker has suggested the newspaper did not regard the founding of the FSAW "as an event of major importance on the calendar," and "perhaps the men of the Congress Alliance were more apprehensive about a conference to promote women's rights than they were prepared to admit."[62] A month later, *Drum* magazine posed the question "Should women have equal rights with men?" to its readers, and 101 out of the 159 who replied said no. The winner of the prize for the best letter wrote: "Let us give them courtesy but no rights. They should continue to carry no passes for they are harmlessly inferior; put on their bonnets everywhere, for it is a shame for a woman to go bareheaded."[63]

As women gradually moved to the front ranks of the resistance movement, the FSAW continued to be frustrated by the reluctance of the ANC to take up the fight against passes. This was manifested as a general ANC passivity toward, rather than active opposition to, the Anti-Pass struggle. Although the coordinating committee of the Congress Alliance insisted on claiming a leadership role in the Anti-Pass campaigns, the FSAW did not succeed in getting Congress activists to mobilize on behalf of women after the Pretoria demonstrations. In 1958, the FSAW was still complaining that the men had not made an "active entry" into the Anti-Pass campaigns and the women "awaited this with impatience."[64] The ANC did not decide to organize an Anti-Pass campaign until late in 1959, but the Pan-Africanist Congress (PAC) jumped in ahead of the ANC in a March 1960 pass-burning campaign that was to end at Sharpeville.

The women's Anti-Pass campaigns did not end sexist attitudes or abolish passes, but they did succeed in building a new gender identity through the mobilization of thousands of African women throughout the 1950s. Central to this process was the interplay between the Anti-Pass campaigns and the radical press.

The FSAW's protest style was to organize mass marches, petitions and public demands addressed to the government. This had emotional high points, particularly the march by 20,000 women to Pretoria's Union Buildings in 1956, which followed a similar demonstration a year earlier. Other key moments were the drafting of the FSAW-sponsored Women's Charter in 1954, the wave of campaigns that followed the issuing of passes to women in the Orange Free State town of Winburg in 1956, the rural Anti-Pass campaign in Zeerust (western Transvaal) in 1957, a massive demonstration in Johannesburg the following year and the women's uprising in Natal in 1959. Anti-Pass protests took place in dozens of cities and towns throughout the Union between 1955 and 1959, giving the impression of a rolling demonstration that tended to coincide with the arrival in each area of the state's mobile pass-issuing unit.

A new image of African women emerged during these campaigns, an image created in part through First's reporting in *New Age*. In responding to the marches and FSAW statements, she provided readers with the impetus and ground rules for further demonstrations and built, as she did so, new myths, heroes and symbols in the struggle. This was done by linking together events and issues into a particular world view and by using language and ideas in individual stories that sharpened the focus on particular associations of events.

The 1955 march on Pretoria, for example, was a bold strategy, an assault on the symbolic seat of government by women. They were told that if they undertook the march they would be arrested. The Pretoria City Council refused permission for the march, canceled transport licenses for the women and tried to get the railways to refuse them train tickets. But still they came. Helen Joseph, one of the organizers, was apprehensive about the demonstration, "but as I drove alongside a railway embankment I saw a train high above me; it was filled with African women leaning out of the windows and singing in triumph. I couldn't hold back my tears of joy and pride. We were on our way to Pretoria."[65]

New Age had begun reporting the Anti-Pass initiative in January 1955, covering demonstrations in Cape Town and Durban as well as the run-up to the Pretoria march in October. Nobody reading the newspaper could have been in any doubt about the issues at stake. Predictably, the government refused to meet a delegation from the assembled women and afterward called the affair a "scandalous incitement." It vowed to prevent any further "desecration" of the seat of government.[66]

First's journalism in the Anti-Pass campaign, in step with FSAW leadership, helped to empower and mobilize African women in the resistance struggle. By seeking out, reporting and supporting every militant action by the women, embedding within each story a tacit approval and a heroic dimension to their actions, she helped to build a new self-image for African women, especially those living in urban areas.

Readers are always positioned according to the presumptions of journalists, but they need not comply with the demands of the reading position constructed for them. Left-wing journalists like First sought to subvert the dominant reading position and use news stories to construct an alternative position, an alternative discourse for apartheid's lowest-ranked victims.[67]

This can be illustrated by contrasting the reports by *New Age* and the *Star*, South Africa's main commercial daily, of the last major demonstration by African women against passes. By mid-1958, government pass-issuing units had begun operations in the larger towns, a sign of increased confidence, and in October they approached Johannesburg. Their strategy was to start with the huge army of domestic workers in the white suburbs, and a circular was sent to employers instructing them to send their "Native female servants" to the Native Commissioner's offices to be issued with reference books.[68] Sophiatown women marched to the commissioner's offices on 21 October 1958 to stop the domestic workers taking out passes. Police intercepted them and arrested 249 women. The demonstrations continued, and by the end of the week nearly 2,000 women had been arrested.[69]

In one of the biggest headlines ever used on its front page, *New Age* told its readers: "Jo'burg Women Say 'No' to Passes." First and her colleague Tennyson Makiwane, who covered the march, gave graphic descriptions of the arrests and the snowballing demonstrations. Jails were "overflowing with the women and their children," and in The Fort (Johannesburg's main prison) there was "no space left for a rat."[70] In rowdy demonstrations "reminiscent of the Defiance Campaign and the bus boycott," African men in admiration "handed over pants to the women," who were beaten and herded into vans singing "a new song with the words: 'The enemy of the African is the pass.'"[71] The newspaper also reported that the pass laws had "claimed their first woman sacrifice," Martha Qoba, who was trampled to death in a pass queue.[72] The *Star* also pictured the women on its front page, but the accompanying headline clearly reflected the preoccupation of most perceived readers: "500 Women Arrested in Reference Book Protest – No Nannies Today."[73] The next day the lead editorial was headlined: "No Servants? Why, it's easy to do without them!"[74]

Following the 1955 march on the Union Buildings, First tracked the Anti-Pass campaign tirelessly. In one week she investigated and wrote about the position of African women in Welkom, Stilfontein, Krugersdorp, Roodepoort, Boksburg, Springs, Germiston, Brakpan and Johannesburg.[75] In November 1955, some 600 people attended an Anti-Pass meeting in Bloemfontein, described by *New Age* as the largest such meeting ever held there. In early 1956 First found out that the government was to begin issuing reference books to African women in Winburg in the Orange Free State, and she began a media campaign to block the move.[76] She also discovered the route of the pass-issuing teams and made it public, forewarning women in other Free State towns.[77] The National Party organ *Die Transvaler* responded to the exposé with irritation and complained of "screaming headlines in which gall is spewed against the issue of reference books to women which are appearing in periodicals and newspapers distributed among Natives."[78]

A week later the national secretary of the ANC Women's League (ANCWL), Mary Ranta, warned that "if Africans in the Free State could oppose the pass system 40 years ago, they can easily do so today!"[79] At first, the pass-issuing teams met with no resistance, and 1,429 reference books had been issued by March 22. Then the newly elected national president of the ANCWL, Lilian Ngoyi, slipped into the district and held a meeting with the Winburg women.[80] Spurred by the presence of their national leader, they decided that the only response to the newly issued passes was to burn them. The next day the women collected a pile of reference books, marched to the magistrate's office and publicly torched the lot.[81]

The burning of passes in Winburg had deep significance for African women and for the women's campaign. A huge wave of protests swept the country. In the first seven months of 1956, the FSAW estimated that about 50,000 women took part in 38 demonstrations against the pass laws in 30 different centers. These protests fed into the second historic march of 20,000 women on the Union Buildings (9 August 1956), and the Anti-Pass campaigns carried on unabated through 1957 and 1958.[82]

During these demonstrations a new self-image was being built by the women: they had seen African men "disappear" in pass raids and families destroyed by imprisonment for failure to have passes in order, and they were not going to have it happen to them. The mood of the time was captured in a Zulu freedom song directed at Prime Minister Johannes Strijdom and first sung on the steps of the Union Buildings: "Strijdom uthitta abafazi, uthinti imbokotho" (Strijdom, you've tampered with the women, you've knocked against a rock). From the moment passes burned in Winburg, their incineration became a symbolic retrieval of self-esteem. Passes represented state control and banishment from the cities. The women responded by invading city centers and instituting "cleansing rituals" around an "open altar where passes are burnt."[83] This perspective was reinforced by the state's response to pass burning – outrage and mass arrests.

The rural Anti-Pass demonstrations at Zeerust in the western Transvaal led to exceptional police brutality, a State of Emergency and the deposition of the local chief, Abraham Moiloa.[84] Police actions were exposed by First in a series of searing articles that led to a complete ban on press access to the region.[85] The mood of the time was reflected in a *Fighting Talk* report about an "unknown man" who appeared beside the road in the wake of the mobile pass column in the Zeerust area and lit a large bonfire. Some women asked him why he had lit the fire, and he replied:

> I do not incite you to burn your Reference Books. I am a man of peace. I do not snatch away your books or threaten you. I sit quietly by my fire and I say only this: If you have rubbish to burn, if you envy the women of the other villages who have freed themselves of the passes – well, the fire is here and it will save you trouble.[86]

By this time, opposition to the pass had become the most powerful symbol of opposition to the apartheid government. A woman from Zeerust told First: "We have been murdered because of passes. Machine guns have been used against the people. I have seen people being shot. Men have been handcuffed hands and feet. I have escaped from hell at Zeerust. But there are still those in this hell who stand firm against passes."[87]

In Natal, two years later, women took action against African livestock dipping tanks, African beer halls and African passes in a series of demonstrations that were to turn violent. Hundreds would be arrested and face court proceedings.[88] During these uprisings, a rural woman in Cato Manor provided an answer to the suggestion in the 1954 letter to *Drum* that women were harmlessly inferior and should put on their bonnets: "They forced us to take off our headdoeks [bonnets, so that they could be photographed for passes]. It was against our custom but we had to do it... The light got to our brains. We woke up and saw the light. And the women have been demonstrating ever since."[89]

In the end, African women were to lose the battle against passes. After the pass-burnings and shootings at Sharpeville and Langa, the pass laws were suspended. But in February 1963, with the state emboldened and the ANC and its allies banned, they were made compulsory again. The Anti-Pass campaigns of the 1950s, however, had a radicalizing impact on women's perceptions of themselves and their place in society.

Poverty In Johannesburg's African Townships

Ruth First's investigations of poverty in the urban African townships of metropolitan Johannesburg began during a freezing July in 1951. That month the Johannesburg City Council voted to virtually double rents in all its African locations and townships. The daily press reported that L. Venables, the council's manager of non-European affairs, had "retired" due to ill health, but First found out he had resigned in protest over the rent increase.[90] She discovered that the increase had emanated from the council's Finance Committee, which had insisted that the Native Revenue Account be reduced drastically. First swung into action on the front page of the *Guardian*.

The Finance Committee's squeeze, she said, placed the burden "on the shoulders of the poorest, instead of the wealthiest ratepayers in Africa's wealthiest city." She ended the article with a warning that proved prophetic and was to be a major focus of her investigative journalism:

> Placing new burdens on the Africans – the city's poorest, hardest hit by the soaring cost of living, at the lowest end of the cost of living allowance scale, the most fleeced by profiteers and black-marketeers in every shortage, carrying the heaviest burden of transport fares, because they are pushed into the furthest locations – can only cause trouble. Has the City Council forgotten the tragic aftermath of the increase in Western Areas tram fares?[91]

Two weeks later, informed by her investigations into the link between farm labor and capitalist accumulation, First began looking at the underpinnings of the South African economy. Under a front page lead entitled "South Africa Drifting towards Economic Crisis," she used a slowdown by railway artisans as a point of departure to show how state inefficiency in the transport networks, together with bad labor relations, was leading to massive shortages of coal, maize, sugar and cement. The result, she said, would be more unemployment and more urban problems.[92] The following month she took a closer look at these problems. "The average African family on the Reef," she wrote, "is struggling to meet an essential budget of £17.4s.4d. with an income of only £12.6s.6d. The basic wages of most African workers have remained unchanged for the last six years, and are wholly inadequate to maintain healthy existence."[93]

She found that between 1944 and 1951 food prices had risen by 48 percent, which was having "a disastrous effect on the expenditure of Africans," who had to spend 87 percent of their meager wages on food alone. These wages did not meet even the minimum requirements for subsistence, "not to speak of emergency requirements such as doctors' fees and medicines, the replenishment of furniture, crockery and other utensils, blankets or other bedding, or the claims of civilised life, such as church dues and children's school books."[94] These conditions, she said, would lead to conflict with ordinary workers about transport services and would accelerate urban crime. First was particularly emphatic about the transportation problem: "All transport between locations and the city should be cheap and adequate. If not it should be subsidised. Africans should not be forced to pay the penalty for the Europeans' insistence that they must live far from European residential areas."[95]

Early in 1952 the economic squeeze on township residents in Johannesburg took an ugly turn. In Newclare a Sotho gang known as the "Russians" went on the rampage, killing 9 residents and injuring at least 100. Contrary to assertions by the police, the *Sunday Times* and *Die Transvaler* that the attack was "communist inspired," First discovered that the Russians had been extorting money from residents:

> Their tactics were to round up peaceful citizens in the dead of night or early morning and compel heads of families to pay £1. [Then] so bold did they become that their womenfolk went from door to door in daytime, demanding 5s. from every woman they met, threatening with violence those who resisted... In a little over a day the Russians collected £200 in this fashion.[96]

When residents resisted, the Russians attacked with heavy sticks, pieces of iron, battle axes and other sharp instruments. The following week, under the headline "Life a 'Hell' in Newclare," First asked: "Why is the government doing so little about the situation? Why are the police not cooperating with the [Newclare] Civic Guard? Why don't they remove the Russian menace and restore law and order to Newclare? Where will all this end?"[97]

The Alexandra Bus Boycotts

Over the next five years, First's reporting focused on the activities of the Congress Alliance. In January 1957, however, her attention was suddenly brought back to grassroots struggles in the townships, when the Public Utility Transport Corporation (PUTCO) decided to raise its bus fares to 5 pence–an increase of 1 pence. "Like a single shot fired," she wrote, people in the affected townships on the Reef refused to board the buses and voted to walk.[98] First reported their action movingly, convinced she was witnessing a new and significant level of grassroots struggle:

> The streets were strangely quiet. First the great lumbering green buses came … empty. [Then] over the rise that obscures Alexandra Township from the main road came the eruption of workers in the dawn hours when mists and brazier fires mingle indistinguishably together. End to end the road was filled with shadowy, hurrying figures. Then the forms thinned out as the younger men with the firmest, sprightly step drew away from the older people, the women, the lame …
>
> Later … the same crowds turned their backs on the city and again took to the roads. Down the hill the footsloggers found it easier … the spindly-legged youngsters trotted now and then to keep up, the progress of the weary women was slower still, here a large Monday washing bundle carried on the head, there a paraffin tin, or a baby tied securely to the back. In pelting rain, running the gauntlet of police patrols, the boycotters walked on.[99]

Alexandra had a history of struggle over bus fares. In 1939 bus companies operating in the township proposed a 1-pence rise in fares. A committee of residents was formed, and Alexandra fought the increase for eight months until it was disallowed by the Road Transportation Board.[100] In 1942, 1943 and again in 1944 the bus owners tried to increase the fares. For six weeks in 1944, for example, the people of Alexandra walked to work, and in the seventh week the bus companies caved in. They were taken over by PUTCO, which moved the fares back to 4 pence.

Although Alexandra had demonstrated that the boycott weapon could produce results, First pointed out that the 1957 boycott would be different:

> The United Party Government in 1944 was still to some extent sensitive to public opinion, to public pressures. The Government of Mr. Strijdom is intransigent, intractable, unyielding. And nine years under this Government has changed African opinion too. It is not only more united, but also more demanding, more angry, increasingly suspicious because of promises never fulfilled, of undertakings that were never realised.[101]

Employers and the Johannesburg City Council were keen to settle the affair. Before the boycott, PUTCO was transporting 45,000 African workers a day. From January 7 this number was practically zero, with streams of tired, often late and hungry workers flowing into the city from the townships of Alexandra, Sophiatown, Lady Selborne, Eastwood and Mooiplaas. Sympathy boycotts soon broke out in the Soweto townships of Moroka, Jabavu and Dube as well as in Randfontein, Brakpan, Port Elizabeth, East London, Bloemfontein and Worcester.[102]

The government, however, took a hard line. The minister of transport, Ben Schoeman, announced that the boycott must be broken. It was "a political movement," he said, "launched by the African National Congress to test its strength and to find out how much support and discipline it could exact from the Bantu through intimidation."[103] He appealed to "all the thousands of law-abiding Natives who are not in favour of the boycott to repudiate their leaders."[104]

The police took this as a signal to victimize boycotters as well as those who assisted them by offering lifts. Drivers were ordered to produce their licenses, passengers had their papers checked, African taxi drivers were harassed for minor traffic oversights, a ban was placed on the operation of taxis outside the municipal area and about 100 Africans were arrested for crossing an intersection on foot against a traffic light at 5.30 A.M. when there were no cars in sight.[105] Police raids were conducted in Alexandra, and nearly 15,000 people were arrested or subpoenaed for minor offenses.[106]

These tactics initially created anger in the white community. In an article reviewing the boycott, First noted that calls were made to increase the PUTCO subsidy or to increase the Native Services Levy through which employers subsidized the bus company. The City Council, under pressure from employers, offered to contribute to a subsidy scheme, the boycott committees announced their willingness to negotiate, and in the first few weeks white public sympathies were clearly with the walkers. But the government stood in the way of a settlement. In February it moved an amendment to the Native Labour Regulations Act that would ban all meetings of Africans who had not obtained the minister's permission, and PUTCO threatened to withdraw its services permanently from Alexandra. As the boycott continued, the mainstream press began to reflect a "break-the-boycott" perspective.[107] A month after the boycott began, the *Rand Daily Mail* placed a banner seven-column headline across its front page asking employers to "warn their workers" against those who had "branded themselves as unworthy leaders of their people." The *Mail* called on African township residents not to be misled by these "agitators."[108]

Behind the *Mail*'s call was the perception that there was a factor in the 1957 Alexandra boycott not present in earlier boycotts: the long walk was not being led by the ANC or any other organized political body. This was not a demonstration coordinated from above but a popular surge of anger from below. In reality, African political leaders, many caught up in the Treason Trial, were bystanders to a new kind of politics. And First, reporting on the issue almost daily, had a close-up view of the new political processes developing in the streets of Alexandra.

The issue of the 1-pence fare increase was first taken up by a group called the Alexandra Standholders and a hastily created Vigilance Committee formed to confront PUTCO. The bus company's intransigence led to the formation of the Alexandra People's Transport Action Committee, which helped to establish similar committees in Sophiatown, Lady Selborne, Eastwood and other affected black townships in the Johannesburg area.[109] Despite the ad hoc nature of these organizations, attempts by the central government, the police, PUTCO and the press to bully and threaten the boycotters simply strengthened their resolve. Beerhalls began to be boycotted, and the bus boycott network continued to spread beyond Alexandra.[110]

The City Council, the Native Affairs Department and the Chamber of Commerce held secret talks with African "moderates" in an attempt to reach a solution, but these discussions were ignored by the walkers. First reported that "the boycott could not be more solid ... One man said: 'If it has to be, this can be a boycott without an end.'"[111] The ANC fared no better. In a leaflet issued by the Alexandra People's Transport Committee, Congress was labeled an organization of "purely loud-mouthed self advertisers":

> The ANC leaders are from time to time the main anti-boycott spokesmen. A struggle properly conducted–a struggle in which the interests of the people are placed

> FIRST–above the individual leader–above self-importance–above organisations–such a struggle will always expose quislings in our midst. We must take note. A man in the police uniform is easy to spot, but a man dressed in strong talk and weak actions–has to be DISCOVERED through his actions. This is the case with the ANC.[112]

First realized that the people had found a method of struggle that could not be stamped out easily by the authorities. "It might come to that," she wrote. "But there is not yet a law on the Union statute book imposing penalties on Africans for walking to work and home again by way of protest against a bus company."[113] In her assessment of the government's role in the boycott, she was also to rethink the strategies hammered out in left-wing Discussion Clubs four years earlier:

> The Government denunciation of the boycott as "political" was one of the sticks it hoped to use to beat the boycott, to ruin all chances of settlement, to frighten employers ... and White South Africa as a whole. The bus boycott did, undoubtedly, develop into a political campaign. [But] the economic facts, the poverty of a people that reckons its income in pennies, sparked off the boycott, and those who argue the economic basis for this protest could not be on firmer ground. But those who would separate the economic background from the political, who would see the African protesting only against a penny rise in fares ... erect distinctions which must be blown over in the first gusts of any African protest or campaign.[114]

African workers, she said, were no longer bewildered, mute, tribal creatures. The boycott had shown that they were industrialized, politically aware, articulate and purposeful. Their organizations were mature and resourceful. The boycott had shown them that "active campaigning for basic human and *economic* demands" held the key to success. First was echoed by the director of the South African Institute of Race Relations:

> The African people have ... shown that amazing ability to communicate and organise without an organisation, which has been apparent on other occasions in the past. The 1944 bus boycott, the mineworkers' strike, the shantytown movement, the Port Elizabeth strike – each of these has shown this quite amazing ability. *It is significant.*[115]

The Alexandra bus boycott alerted many activists to the importance of material issues in the political struggle, and these events clearly shaped First's understanding of popular resistance in the years that followed. The boycott formally ended in April 1957, by which time each Alexandra worker would have walked about 2,000 miles. But the walkers had won, and the fares were restored to 4 pence. Oliver Tambo, general secretary of the ANC, hailed the victory as the beginning of a new phase in the struggle.[116] The newly formed South African Congress of Trade Unions (SACTU) immediately launched a campaign to secure £1 a day for all workers. The campaign did not succeed, but economic demands were elevated to a prominent position in the Congress Alliance's political agenda.

The bus boycott shifted the focus of Ruth First's journalism. She returned to the urban themes she had examined initially in the early 1950s, and she began campaigning for better housing, improved living conditions and a living wage. Between the Alexandra boycott and the State of Emergency in 1960, her journalism increasingly reflected the discourse of ordinary Africans living in the urban townships. Alexandra remained a key focus, and here she traced the growth of gangs, poverty and alcoholism. She also drew links between poverty and official neglect, crime and police inaction:

> Each year the picture gets uglier: new batches of school leavers strike out to find their first jobs, many get them, only to have them snatched from their grasps at the pass offices… So the township turns in on itself. Life must go on. A man must eat, dress, do something in his working hours. Some are caught in the daily manhunt in the township for farm labour. Some take another road. The crime wave in Alexandra Township…is one of the by-products of this throttled community. There are small-time gangs, the pick-pockets, the bag-snatchers, the thieves who waylay people at night and strip them of their clothes. There are youngsters who pounce on the…bus queues, rush a victim from the queue, surround him and empty his pockets.[117]

When the authorities threatened to "clean up" Alexandra, First in her usual style demanded to know exactly what this meant:

> Native Affairs Department "clean-ups" are suspect and the people live in fear of them. In the Western Areas slum clearance meant the abolition of freehold, the death of a long-established township, the forcible removal of an entire community. In Evaton the clean-up meant the vicious imposition of influx control. Will it be the same in Alexandra?[118]

Her solution was more (and more involved) policing. By 1958 she had dubbed Alexandra "Hell's Kitchen," a township with 63,000 people and only 105 policemen. It was, she said, full of "trigger-happy cowboys" firing shots at random. "Let's face facts. Can 105 policemen of whom 86 are Africans rid Alexandra Township of this unruly element…gangsters? Or control crime? Definitely NOT."[119] In Evaton, where the "Russians" ruled, she accused the police of colluding with the gangsters:

> Why have no prosecutions followed the attacks on Evaton homes, the looting and stealing and the assaults? No serious attempt has been made to disarm the "Russians"…Police policy seems to be to let the trouble run on. Their attitude seems to imply that they believe the [bus] boycotters are the "agitators" behind the trouble…Could that be a reason why the police have their hands in their pockets in Evaton where some prompt action by them could bring an end to armed attacks?[120]

First's worst fears about government intentions were realized in 1959, when it was announced that Sophiatown would be completely demolished. First added her voice to demands to halt the demolitions (which had been going on since 1955), set up an emergency housing scheme for stranded families and stop police raids. The demolitions continued, and with anger and disgust she documented the human suffering: "Old people, children, even new-born babies sleep each night in the open, while daily demolitions go on in Sophiatown and even more families are turned out of their homes… What will happen," she asked, "when the rainy season starts next month?"[121]

In March 1960 the State of Emergency was declared, and First was forced to flee to Swaziland. She decided to return to Johannesburg, but she was prevented from attending any political gatherings by a banning order that was extended later to cover all social gatherings. First's days as an investigative journalist in South Africa were coming to an end. In 1963 she was arrested and jailed in the wake of a series of arrests leading to the Rivonia Trial.

After months of solitary confinement, she tried to commit suicide, fearing she would not be able to resist her interrogators. Finally released, she fled into exile, and this time she did not return to South Africa.[122] Ruth First was finally silenced in Mozambique in 1982 when a letter bomb, planted by South African security agents, exploded in her hands and killed her. But she left behind a style of political journalism that was the bedrock from which a left-wing press was to reemerge in the 1980s.

Notes

1. Don Pinnock interview with Myrtle Berman, 1988. Myrtle later joined the CPSA and became the editor of *Viewpoints and Perspectives*, a journal that documented crucial debates within the underground party after it was banned in 1950. She and husband Monty were founder members of the African Resistance Movement in the early 1960s.
2. Don Pinnock interview with Rica Hodgson, 1988.
3. R. First and A. Scott, *Olive Schreiner* (New Brunswick, N.J., 1980), 334.
4. Ibid., 17, 23, 335.
5. G. Williams, "Ruth First: Alle radici dell'apartheid," Seminario sull 'Africa Australe, Rome, October 1984, 4.
6. S. R. Clingman, *The novels of Nadine Gordimer* (Johannesburg, 1986), 62.
7. *Guardian*, 3 July 1947.
8. Ibid.
9. *Rand Daily Mail*, 27 June 1947.
10. *Guardian*, 3 July 1947.
11. *Rand Daily Mail*, 7 July 1947.
12. Ibid.
13. *Rand Daily Mail*, 2, 8 July 1947.
14. F. Troup, *In face of fear: Michael Scott's challenge to South Africa* (London, 1950), 136.
15. *Guardian*, 17 July 1947.
16. Ibid.
17. Ibid.
18. *Guardian*, 24 July 1947.
19. Often this had to be done virtually at a jog, bending double, 12 hours a day.
20. W. M. Macmillan, *Complex South Africa: An economic footnote to history* (London, 1930), 249.
21. *Guardian*, 3 July 1947.
22. *Guardian*, 7 August 1947.
23. Ibid.
24. *Guardian*, 11 December 1947.
25. *Guardian*, 26 May 1949.
26. Ibid.
27. *Guardian*, 2 June 1949.
28. R. First, *The farm labour scandal* (New Age pamphlet, n.d.), 6.
29. Ibid.
30. Ibid., 9 (Circular 23 of 14 June 1954).
31. Ibid.
32. Ibid., 10.
33. Ibid., 22.
34. *New Age*, 6 September 1956 (profile by Alfred Hutchinson).
35. *New Age*, 19 January 1959.
36. *New Age*, 11 July 1959.
37. *New Age*, e.g., 11 October 1956. (See story about the construction of special compounds for women laborers at Bethal. Some of the workers were 15 years old or younger).
38. *Guardian*, 3 March 1949.
39. First, *The farm labour scandal*, 16.
40. Ibid.
41. *New Age*, 4 October 1956.
42. *New Age*, 5 February 1959.
43. *New Age*, 26 March 1959. In the same issue, First reported the death of a laborer named Bethuel Khosi, who was buried in a shallow grave on a farm in Nigel after being assaulted by the farmer.
44. *New Age*, 30 April 1959.
45. *New Age*, 7 May 1959.
46. *New Age*, 21 May 1959.
47. *New Age*, 28 May 1959.
48. B. Bunting, *The rise of the South African reich*, rev. ed. (Harmondsworth, 1969), 170.
49. *New Age*, 4 June 1959.
50. Ibid.
51. Ibid.
52. *New Age*, 11 June 1959.
53. Ibid.
54. *New Age*, 23 July 1959.
55. *Rand Daily Mail*, 17 June 1959.
56. Although the gatherings at Langa and Sharpeville were called by the Pan-Africanist Congress, which had been organizing in these areas, the PAC had done little preparatory work and had not previously challenged the state on the pass issue. They merely jumped in ahead of the ANC's already announced Anti-Pass campaign.
57. See J. Wells, *We have done with pleading: The women's 1913 anti-pass campaign* (Johannesburg, 1991).
58. See D. Posel, "The construction of apartheid, 1948–61," unpublished paper; and J. Lazar, "Verwoerd vs. the 'Visionaries': The South African Bureau of Racial Affairs and apartheid," paper presented at "South Africa in the 1950s" conference, Oxford University, Institute of Commonwealth Studies, 1987.
59. Quoted in B. Sachs, *Mist of memory* (London, 1973), 162.
60. Government Notice No. 2495 of 31 October 1952.

61. *The Black Sash*, June/July 1959, 16.
62. C. Walker, *Women and resistance in South Africa* (London, 1982), 143.
63. Ibid., 149 (citing *Drum*, May 1954).
64. "Report by FSAW on the anti-pass campaign," FSAW document C1 6, 6. FSAW collection, Witwatersrand University.
65. H. Joseph, *Side by side* (London, 1986), 71.
66. *New Age*, 3 November 1955.
67. Of course, no text is merely absorbed passively by a reader. Consequently, every reading involves some reconstitution of the text. G. Kress, *Linguistic process in sociocultural practice* (Oxford, 1989), 42.
68. Walker, *Women and resistance*, 216; *New Age*, 30 October 1958.
69. Walker, *Women and resistance*, 216.
70. *New Age*, 30 October 1958.
71. Ibid.
72. Ibid.
73. *Star*, 21 October 1958.
74. *Star*, 22 October 1958.
75. *New Age*, 10 May 1956.
76. *New Age*, 6, 12 January 1956; 22 March 1956; 5 April 1956.
77. *New Age*, 22 March 1956.
78. *Die Transvaler*, 7 January 1956.
79. *New Age*, 12 January 1956.
80. Walker, *Women and resistance*, 192.
81. These events are summarized in *New Age*, *Drum* and Walker, *Women and resistance*.
82. An FSAW fact sheet listing women's demonstrations during those two years ran to seven closely typed pages. See "Resistance of women to Passes during 1957," FSAW C1 5, and "Resistance of women to passes during 1958," FSAW C1 6. FSAW collection, Witwatersrand University.
83. *New Age*, 8 August 1957.
84. He was replaced by Lucas Mangope, who was to become president of the Bophuthatswana "homeland."
85. *New Age*, 10 June 1957.
86. *Fighting Talk*, November 1960.
87. *New Age*, 29 January 1959.
88. *New Age*, cf. 13 August 1959 and following issues.
89. J. Yawitch, "Natal 1959 – the women's protests," paper presented at the "History of Opposition in South Africa" conference, University of the Witwatersrand, January 1978.
90. She reported that Venables' health was excellent. *Guardian*, 5 July 1951.
91. Ibid.
92. *Guardian*, 19 July 1951.
93. *Guardian*, 30 August 1951.
94. Ibid.
95. Ibid.
96. *Guardian*, 13 March 1952.
97. *Guardian*, 20 March 1952.
98. R. First, "The bus boycott," in *Africa South*, 1, 4 (September 1957), 56.
99. Ibid., 55.
100. Ibid., 59.
101. Ibid., 60.
102. SAIRR, *A Survey of Race Relations in South Africa, 1956–1957* (M. Horrell, comp.), 131.
103. Hansard, 1957 *Debates*, 1 cols. 131–132.
104. Ibid.
105. SAIRR, *Survey of Race Relations*, 1956–1957, 132.
106. Ibid.
107. First and Scott, *Olive Schreiner*, 62.
108. *New Age*, 28 February 1957.
109. SAIRR, *Survey of Race Relations*, 1956–1957, 130.
110. *New Age*, 31 January 1957.
111. *New Age*, 7 February 1957.
112. T. Karis and G. M. Carter, *From protest to challenge*, Vol. 3, *Challenge and violence, 1953–1964* by T. Karis and G. M. Gerhart (Stanford, 1977), Document 22 ("Azikwelwa! leaflet on the bus boycott), 395.
113. First, "The bus boycott," 63.
114. Ibid., 64.
115. SAIRR, *Survey of Race Relations*, 1956–1957, 138.
116. *New Age*, 25 April 1957. Michael Harmel, however, complained of the ANC's failure to give the bus boycott positive leadership. *New Age*, 4 April 1957.
117. *New Age*, 12 June 1957.
118. *New Age*, 27 June 1957.
119. *New Age*, 20 February 1958.
120. *New Age*, 9 August 1957.
121. *New Age*, 24 September 1959.
122. First wrote several books during the next two decades, including *South West Africa* (Harmondsworth, 1963); *The barrel of a gun* (London, 1970); *Libya, the elusive revolution* (New York, 1974); *Olive Schreiner* (cited earlier); *Black gold: The Mozambican miner, proletarian and peasant* (Sussex, 1983); One hundred seventeen days (New York, 1965).

CHAPTER 11

Inkululeko

Organ of the Communist Party of South Africa, 1939–1950

Elizabeth Ceiriog Jones

The roots of the Communist Party of South Africa (CPSA) can be traced back to the South African Labour Party and in particular its radical antiwar wing, the War on War League, during World War I. The League became the International Socialist League (ISL) in September 1915 and began publishing a new weekly journal called the *International*, which is generally regarded as South Africa's first communist newspaper. Five years later the ISL requested membership in the Communist International (Comintern) along with a number of other organizations in South Africa. Since the Comintern would allow only one communist party in each country, these groups joined forces to establish a unified communist party on 30 July 1921.*

The Communist Party and Its Press before World War II

The CPSA, like its predecessor the International Socialist League, was sympathetic to the plight of African workers, but their interests were subordinated in the early years to those of white workers. The party's racial dilemma was revealed during the tumultuous January–March 1922 strike on the Witwatersrand. White miners were striking for the retention of the color bar in their industry, which the communists claimed to oppose. But the white workers were striking against two adversaries of the communists – the government and the Chamber of Mines – who favored the removal of the color bar only in order to open the way for further exploitation of African workers.

The CPSA chose to support the striking white workers, arguing that the interests of Africans were best served by protecting the position of whites and trying to improve conditions for blacks when and where it was possible. Founding members

*This chapter is based on my M. Phil. thesis at the London School of Economics. I would like to thank Les Switzer, who originally suggested the topic and guided me through my research all along the way. Tom Nossiter, my supervisor at the LSE, directed me to several important Communist Party sources, read through the many drafts of my thesis, and arranged for financial assistance. I am grateful to Robert Edgar and Edwin Mofutsanyana, and to those South African communists living in England whom I had the opportunity to interview for this study. A special thanks to my former work colleague Helen Broome, who was an independent coder for the quantitative content analysis of *Inkululeko*. I am grateful to the LSE, which paid for two years of my tuition. LSE also provided a Helen Simpson Lynett scholarship and a subsequent research travel grant to fund trips to South Africa and Lesotho and employ a research assistant.

of the party, including men like David Ivon Jones, who had a reputation as a "negrophile," viewed the barrier as "the best possible condition for cooperation of white with black." To remove the barrier, he argued, would result in direct competition between the two communities and an end to their state of relative harmony. Such muddled thinking meant that the communists found themselves parading under banners such as this: "Workers of the World, Fight and Unite for a White South Africa."[1]

The CPSA turned over its offices and its resources to the militant Council of Action, which believed white workers should embark on a general strike. Two other white workers' groups, the South African Industrial Federation and the Joint Strike Committee, took a more moderate view and worked for reform. But many white workers refused to align themselves with any group and formed irregular commando units. The strikers were divided, but any hope the communists had of uniting them was dashed by March 1922. The Council of Action had ignored the moderates and called on all white workers to participate in the strike, which had degenerated into bloody clashes between white and black workers, armed gangs and government forces. On 18 March 1922, the strike was called off, 76 days after it was launched by the coal miners, and hundreds of people had been killed or injured. White workers were granted their wish, and a legal color bar was established that preserved their privileged position in the South African economy.

The CPSA's attraction to white workers did not improve in the aftermath of the strike, so the communists embarked on a new policy of recruiting Africans to the party. One of the ways in which the CPSA hoped to connect with African workers was through Clements Kadalie's Industrial and Commercial Workers' Union (ICU). As noted in Chapter 5, the ICU was the first national African workers' organization in South African history, claiming a membership of 100,000 at its peak in 1927. A number of Coloured and African communists had worked their way into key positions in the ICU by the mid-1920s, including Jimmy La Guma, Johnny Gomas and Eddie Khaile.

The CPSA, however, had not yet abandoned the notion that the white working class would lead the proletarian revolution. And the ICU never had a clear policy on how to deal with white workers and their trade unions. Nevertheless, the major points of conflict between the ICU and the communists concerned Kadalie's fear that the CPSA was trying to take control of his organization. The communists wanted to dismantle the bureaucratic elite that controlled the ICU and make it a more disciplined and democratic industrial union with greater rank-and-file control over funds and the election of union officials.[2] Kadalie's leadership was also an issue; among other things, the communists had accused him of misusing union funds. Kadalie called an urgent meeting of the ICU's national council in December 1926 and secured a resolution stating that no ICU official could be a member of the Communist Party. When the communists refused to resign from the ICU, Kadalie ordered their expulsion, and the party lost an important lifeline to the African working classes. It would be more than a decade before the CPSA had such close links to an influential African mass organization again.

The communists, however, were involved in organizing a number of autonomous trade unions during the 1920s. CPSA member Fanny Klenerman, for example, organized white waitresses and sweet (candy) workers. Her activities led to the creation of the short-lived South African Women Workers' Union, which focused on areas of the economy – cafés, tea shops and laundries – employing large numbers of white women.[3] Solly Sachs, Willie Kalk, Ben Weinbren and the Trotskyite Max Gordon were active in the garment, furniture and catering industries. A number of newly recruited African communists–Johannes Nkosi, Gana Makabeni and Moses Kotane among them–were working in African trade union bodies like the Native Clothing Workers' Union and the Laundry Workers' Union. The CPSA also initiated two short-lived trade union federations in the late 1920s, the South African Federation of Non-European Trade Unions, and the African Federation of Trade Unions.

There was much debate within the party during these years over the thorny issue of interracial unions.[4] But as Iris Berger notes, most efforts to unite white women and black men in the same union at this time were thwarted by "racial hysteria."[5] By the early 1930s, the communists had worked out their guiding principle of trade union organization, which was to create and register mixed white, Coloured and Indian trade unions, and create parallel, unregistered African trade unions.[6] The communists and other left-wing groups during this decade made considerable headway in organizing urban workers on the Rand and in the western Cape, where a group of dedicated activists (including Ray Alexander, Johnny Gomas and Jimmy La Guma) were based.

In addition to trade unionism, the CPSA found other ways to connect with urban African workers during the 1920s and 1930s. The party began offering night school classes to Africans, for example, in 1925. The first school, located in a Ferreirastown (Johannesburg) slum, was described by Eddie Roux, who was then a party member: "They taught by candlelight, without blackboards or desks. The pupils sat on benches and struggled with complicated political doctrine as they learnt their letters." This school flourished for about five years but was closed during the party purges of the early 1930s. Other schools were established in the mid- to late 1930s.[7]

The party also held impromptu gatherings in black neighborhoods during these years, which attracted many Africans to the party. Edwin Mofutsanyana, the future editor of *Inkululeko*, first made contact with the communists in this way. He was already an active member of the African National Congress (ANC) and had been since 1923, but he "didn't know anything about Marxism" or the CPSA.[8] By chance, he attended a public meeting where a white communist by the name of Jimmy Shields was speaking (with William Thibedi, a party veteran, interpreting). The police came to arrest Shields, but the crowd surrounded his car and threatened violence. Shields was allowed to return to the platform, where he pleaded with the audience to remain peaceful. The crowd let the police take Shields away, but the police returned with their prisoner a short time later, since they lacked evidence to lay charges, and released him. Mofutsanyana was so moved that a white man would allow himself to be arrested for siding with Africans that he started attending CPSA meetings and signed up for the Ferreirastown night school to learn more about the party and its policies.[9]

The African night schools, impromptu public gatherings, party meetings and trade union activities proved effective in recruiting blacks to the party in the mid- to late 1920s. Many future CPSA leaders, including J. B. Marks, Moses Kotane, Albert Nzula, Johnny Gomas, Johannes Nkosi and Jimmy La Guma, were drawn into the party through these channels. Before 1925, the communists had only one black member, William Thibedi. By 1928, of the party's 1,759 members, 1,600 were Africans.[10] Three of them–Thibedi, Gana Makabeni and Eddie Khaile–had been elected to the central committee.[11] The communists appeared to be making great strides in the direction of Africanization, when the party was suddenly thrust into a long and intense period of internal turmoil.

Political Turmoil in the 1930s

CPSA policy until 1928 was to fight for a socialist South Africa by advancing the cause of workers, black and white. Class struggle was all-important. The "national question," meaning the African nationalist movement, was of little importance. This policy changed dramatically in 1928, when the sixth congress of the Communist International (the Comintern) passed a resolution supporting the idea of a "Native Republic" as a prelude to the creation of a socialist state in South Africa.[12] The Native Republic slogan led to bitter divisions within the CPSA and ultimately to the expulsion of the party's most senior members.

At the core of the debate was the Comintern's implied concept of a two-tiered revolution in which African self-determination would be the first stage of a movement toward socialism. Party leader Sydney P. Bunting[13] regarded the slogan as racist. He believed the common interests of all workers, black and white, should be the party's main concern, not African working-class interests alone. This view was shared by many other white members of the CPSA, including Rebecca Bunting and Eddie Roux, and several key black members of the central committee, notably Jimmy La Guma, the prominent Coloured trade unionist who had once been the assistant general secretary of the ICU. On the other side of the debate, Molly and Douglas Wolton,[14] relative newcomers to the party, who spoke for what was then regarded as the radical wing, objected to such "white chauvinism" and argued that working-class solidarity depended on the political empowerment of Africans.[15]

Bunting's position was favored by a majority of the party's central committee at a meeting held in May 1928. But at the party's yearly conference, held in December 1928–January 1929, the Native Republic slogan was debated with a ferocity that on occasion led to physical violence.[16] In the end, the Wolton faction won the debate, and the party adopted a new constitution and program based on the Native Republic slogan. Wolton was elected CPSA general secretary, but soon after the conference ended he and his wife embarked on a trip to England and the Soviet Union, where they studied at the Lenin School in Moscow. Wolton's responsibilities as general secretary and editor of the party newspaper were given to Albert Nzula,[17] the first time an African had held either position.

The Woltons returned to South Africa in late 1930, armed with a Comintern resolution that ordered a purge of all so-called "rightists," meaning those CPSA members who had opposed the Native Republic directive. Douglas Wolton proceeded with the expulsions, beginning with party stalwarts Bunting and Bill Andrews.[18] Amid the sectarianism and ideological confusion, however, most CPSA members simply quit the party of their own accord. Membership had dropped to 300 or less by 1932.

Although the Woltons left South Africa in 1933,[19] the party was still in turmoil. A Latvian-born emigré named Lazar Bach took over as party leader and initiated a new round of expulsions. Eddie Roux, a key member of the party's political bureau who had been a fervent follower of Bunting but had remained loyal when the Native Republic resolution was introduced, was now forced out of the party.[20] Moses Kotane, an ANC activist and future CPSA general secretary (1939–50), and Josiah Ngedlane and Johnny Gomas, leaders in the CPSA-inspired trade union movement, were also among those purged in 1935. Kotane wanted to promote a "united front" of black organizations in which the Communist Party would not necessarily play a leading role. Bach called this "*petit bourgeois* national reformism" and warned that it was ideologically unsound for the party to participate in movements in which the middle class could usurp power.[21]

Soon after Bach purged Kotane and his supporters, however, a directive arrived from the Comintern outlining a new orientation toward the kind of "united front" Kotane had been promoting. The so-called United Front policy against rascism was officially adopted by the Comintern at its seventh congress in 1935. Bach, as it turned out, had contravened Comintern policy. He left South Africa for the Soviet Union soon afterward to present his case but was never heard from again. The CPSA leader and two South African colleagues were arrested and shot for allegedly Trotskyite activities.[22]

The CPSA in fact had made several earlier attempts to forge the kind of alliances that would lead to a United Front. The ICU experience was one example. Another was the attempt by ANC president general Josiah Gumede to bridge the ideological gap between Congress and the CPSA. This effort was thwarted by African nationalists who disapproved of Gumede's close association with the communists. Their fears were heightened after Gumede returned from a visit to the Soviet Union in 1928 proclaiming that he had "seen the new Jerusalem."[23] When he stood for reelection in 1930, he was ousted by Pixley Seme, a leader of the conservative majority within Congress.

The threat of fascism loomed large on the international horizon by the mid-1930s, and within South Africa the white government was busy expanding the boundaries of the segregationist state. With the blessing of Moscow and the return of several members of the purged leadership cadre to the party, the CPSA sought to put the United Front directive into practice by attempting to forge links with other antifascist organizations. One result was the formation of the League against Fascism and War in March 1934, which aimed to awaken South Africans to the threat of fascism. A similar group, the National Liberation League, was formed in December 1935, and its membership included a number of Trotskyites from the Cape.

The most promising political development in the 1930s was the founding in December 1935 of the All-African Convention. An estimated 112 organizations, including the Communist Party and the National Liberation League, were represented at the second meeting in June 1936, when the AAC was established as a permanent federal body. It seemed for a time that the AAC might succeed in bringing together the various groups within the protest movement, but it was not to be. The AAC never developed into a national political movement, although it attracted a number of influential communists (mainly in the Cape) during the 1940s.[24]

The National Liberation League tried to fill the vacuum. Delegates to a League conference in 1939 agreed to form the Non-European United Front (NEUF), an alliance of Africans, Coloureds and Indians that went a step farther than the AAC at the time in voicing support for racial equality and working-class solidarity. But the NEUF was riddled with internal divisions from the beginning–between the CPSA and the Trotskyites, between those who wanted whites barred from the leadership cadre and those who did not, between conservatives who adhered to principles of passive resistance and militants who wanted to confront the state. Like the AAC, the NEUF soon lost its momentum.

The Africanization of the Communist Press

The official party newspaper had undergone several changes during the interwar period, mirroring the CPSA's own transition from an almost exclusively white party to a predominantly African party in terms of membership. In the wake of the 1922 strike disaster, the CPSA recognized the need to attract a black working-class readership. As a first step in that direction, the name of the party organ was changed, on 2 July 1926, from the *International* to the *South African Worker* (or the *Worker*). Articles written in the vernacular began to appear with increasing regularity, comprising 25 and 35 percent of the newspaper in 1928 and 1931.[25]

During the late 1920s and 1930s, the Communist Party and its press were going through a process of "indigenizing" marxism, a process described by Eileen Flanagan as having two key themes: the marxist critique would be applied to South Africa, and the marxist discourse would be translated into the vernacular.[26] Many early non-English articles in the *South African Worker* were written under the pseudonym "Twedie," who Flanagan speculates was really Sydney Bunting, the editor until 1927. As the number of multilingual African communists writing for the newspaper increased–Albert Nzula, Edwin Mofutsanyana, J. W. Nkosi and Moses Kotane among them–the stories by "Twedie" tapered off and disappeared altogether in 1930.

Bunting was replaced as editor by Jimmy Shields, who in turn was replaced by Douglas Wolton. As noted earlier, when Wolton traveled to the Soviet Union in 1929, Albert Nzula was named acting editor, but he resigned before Wolton's return and was replaced by Eddie Roux in 1930. At Roux's request, the newspaper was moved from Johannesburg to Cape Town in 1930 to reduce production costs.[27] Under his editorship, the *Worker* moved farther in the direction of Africanization. Its name was changed to *Umsebenzi*, the Zulu and Xhosa word for "worker." News content changed to reflect African rather than European interests. Less space, for example, was given to international socialism and more to events in South Africa and Lesotho, especially the activities of the CPSA and the ANC. Roux also initiated the use of cartoons to present political ideas in simple terms that would cut across language barriers.

Roux's creative editorship of *Umsebenzi* came to an end in early 1931. The party was reeling from its first purge at the time, and Wolton insisted the newspaper be moved back to Johannesburg so that it could be controlled directly by the political bureau.[28] Roux continued to do "technical work" in connection with the newspaper until he left the party in 1936,[29] but Wolton himself took charge of overall editorial content. Under his direction, the journal became "a theoretical publication filled with abstruse political essays."[30] The use of African languages increased somewhat, but the focus returned to international affairs.[31] Sales slumped: at the end of 1930 they had stood at 5,000 a week, but a year later they were only 5,000 every two weeks. Production, moreover, was irregular during Wolton's tenure.[32]

After Wolton's departure from South Africa in 1933, Moses Kotane took over the editorship. Except for Albert Nzula's brief tour of duty as acting editor, this was the first time an African had been placed in a position of editorial control. With the party's leading theoreticians gone, it became, in Roux's words, "more readable."[33] The newspaper was enlarged and published weekly again rather than fortnightly. Sales increased dramatically with the Italian invasion of Ethiopia in February 1935, a conflict that represented a loss of freedom to Africans across the continent. *Umsebenzi*'s weekly circulation reached 7,000, and its revival as a newspaper in the mid- to late 1930s coincided with the party's efforts to pursue the United Front strategy in South Africa.

The newspaper's title was changed back to *South African Worker* with *Umsebenzi* remaining as the subtitle. This was probably done to encourage progressive whites to read the newspaper and join the United Front. The new slogan displayed across the newspaper's masthead read: "For a United Working Class Front against Imperialism and War." Similarly, the space given to news and comment in the vernacular pages was reduced considerably to avoid looking too much like a journal directed exclusively at the African working class.[34]

South African Worker/Umsebenzi became one of the more widely read African political publications in South Africa, and letters to the editor revealed that its readership stretched into the surrounding protectorates.[35] The use of African languages in developing a marxist perspective aimed at African workers was a crucial innovation, but Africans were not interested in the heady theorizing of communists like Wolton, even when presented to them in their own languages. They were drawn to a newspaper only when it represented their grievances and aspirations. It also seemed clear that stories of working-class struggles would reflect more accurately the perceptions of African workers if they were presented by Africans.

Despite the success of the party newspaper, the party itself continued to languish in the mid- to late 1930s. After years of internal turmoil, it still had a mere 280 members, 150 of whom were in Johannesburg, at the beginning of World War II.[36] And it was in serious financial trouble. In March 1938, the party mouthpiece *South African Worker/Umsebenzi* was forced to close down, after 23 years of continuous publication.

The Communist Party during the 1940s

In December 1938, the headquarters of the Communist Party was moved from Johannesburg to Cape Town to give it some "breathing space" from its troubled past.[37] A new central committee was elected in Cape Town with Moses Kotane as general secretary. The first task facing the CPSA's leadership was to respond to the war in Europe. The declaration of war in September 1939 had sparked a parliamentary crisis in South Africa, which split the ruling Smuts–Hertzog coalition government. Jan Smuts, now the leader of the United Party, who won a slender majority in favor of supporting the allied war effort, took over as prime minister.

The war posed a dilemma for South Africa's communists, especially in view of the Soviet–German nonaggression pact signed in August 1939. On the one hand, the CPSA had been committed antifascists, and there was considerable concern about the growing attachment of certain right-wing South African groups to fascist ideas. Thus the Allied war effort was supported initially by some CPSA members, who left the party and joined the South African armed forces.[38] The majority in the party hierarchy, however, opposed the war on the grounds that it was a struggle between rival imperial powers, Britain and Germany, for world domination.

The CPSA was forced to rethink its position on the war when the Germans invaded the Soviet Union in June 1941. As Michael Harmel later wrote: "The workers of the world could not stand aside when the first workers' state was in peril."[39] The new CPSA policy included renewed attacks on the hypocrisy of a South African government that remained blatantly racist while supporting the war. Blacks, for example, were prohibited from carrying arms and restricted to noncombat duties. Communist headlines that had denounced the war were now replaced with slogans like "Arm the Non-European Soldiers."[40]

The CPSA's new war agenda was in harmony with official ANC policy, but this convergence of views on the war did not constitute an alliance. The ANC was still a reformist organization, whereas the communists wanted to transform the social order. The CPSA was also perceived by the African petty bourgeoisie to be "white-led and white-controlled," as Fatima Meer put it. "Its ideology, too, was seen as white." Although most Africans were peasants and workers, and they experienced class divisions every day of their lives, they continued to be skeptical about a working-class organization that was still believed to be dominated by whites.[41] Nevertheless, the reorganization of the ANC in the 1940s provided an opening for the two groups to work together, especially in recruiting urban African workers.[42] Under the influence of men with high profiles in both organizations – men like Moses Kotane, J. B. Marks, David Bopape and Edwin Mofutsanyana – the CPSA pushed ahead with its United Front policy of "nationalist in form, socialist in content."[43]

The Communist Party also encouraged members to become active in other political organizations that enjoyed grassroots support, including government-sponsored organizations like the Natives' Representative Council (NRC), the Location Advisory Boards, Local/District Councils and the Ciskei and Transkei General Councils in the reserves. The trade unions were an obvious potential ally, and by the early 1940s CPSA organizers were in the forefront of a revived African trade union movement.[44] In addition, Indian communists displaced the conservative merchant leaders of the Transvaal Indian Congress in 1945, and the Springbok Legion, the main servicemen's organization during and after World War II, and its mouthpiece *Fighting Talk*, were dominated by communists.

The war, then, was a catalyst: it was the issue that forced a reconfiguration of protest politics, bringing together organizations with vastly different political goals and traditions. By 1945 the communists had constructed an impressive network of alliances and support groups across the country, and this support was reflected in a fourfold increase in party membership between 1941 and 1943.[45] The CPSA supported three African candidates for the NRC in 1942 (Edwin Mofutsanyana, J. Lekhota and Alpheus Maliba), and it fielded nine candidates in the 1944 whites-only general election. Although none were successful, the party polled a surprising 11 percent of the national vote. Betty Radford and Sam Kahn won seats on the Cape Town City Council in 1943, and Hilda Watts Bernstein was returned to her seat on the Johannesburg City Council by an all-white electorate in 1944. Overall, these were years of unprecedented growth in terms of party membership and influence.

The CPSA also maintained friendly relations with socialist parties in other countries, particularly with the Communist Party in Britain. Perhaps the CPSA's most intriguing association outside South Africa was with Lekhotla la Bafo (Council of Commoners), a conservative nationalist movement founded in 1919 and anchored in rural Basutoland (Lesotho). The organization's association with the CPSA extended back to the 1920s, when the party was attempting to shake off its reputation as a white-dominated organization and looking for links with African-based movements. Lekhotla leaders, seeking publicity in their campaign to confront the British colonial administration, accepted an offer to publish their views in *South African Worker* and successor publications.

The CPSA–Lekhotla alliance was a complex political relationship based on mutual need rather than ideological compatibility.[46] Some members of Lekhotla did become communists, but the CPSA itself was not active in the protectorate. Nevertheless, British administrators in Basutoland were highly suspicious of Lekhotla's links with the party and were continually looking for ways to jail Lekhotla's leadership. The new party newspaper *Inkululeko*, moreover, was actually banned in Basutoland during the war years.[47]

The reemergence of passive resistance as a tool of mass protest during the 1940s had little to do with the CPSA, Congress or other organized protest groups. As Baruch Hirson has argued, they had failed to offer any leadership to the masses at the community level. Various urban township groups–including church groups, youth clubs, organizations of stand holders (individuals with property), craftsmen, herbalists and tenants–formed their own alliances. Resistance in these communities, when it occurred, tended to be spontaneous and from the bottom up.[48]

Such was the case with three Alexandra township bus boycotts between 1942 and 1944, when thousands of Africans walked the 10 miles from Alexandra Township to Johannesburg, where they worked, to protest decisions by the Central Transport Board to increase the bus fare. While residents walked, the CPSA was too deeply embroiled in disagreements over tactics with other opposition groups to offer any real leadership.[49] It was sheer determination on the part of the residents that prevented an increase in bus fares during these years.

Nevertheless, the CPSA never wavered in its support for the weapon of passive resistance during the 1940s. The communists, for example, were in the forefront of the 1943–44 National Anti-Pass Campaign and the 1946–48 Indian passive resistance campaign.[50] Party members were influenced in part by the fact that the South African Indian Congress (SAIC), traditional advocate of nonviolent resistance, had become a crucial component in an emerging coalition of resistance groups. "The Communist Party had never been dogmatic or inflexible concerning methods and techniques of struggle," wrote Michael Harmel. "Passive resistance in South Africa at that time was a method of action going beyond verbal protests, traditional to South Africa and particularly to the Indian community, understood and accepted by the masses."[51]

The CPSA's commitment to passive resistance was never greater than in June 1946, when the Asiatic Land Tenure and Indian Representation Bill became law. The "Ghetto Bill," as the Indian community called it, was "a further step along the road of segregation which spells ruin and Fascism for the country as a whole."[52] This legislation reinforced an anti-Indian measure in 1943 called the "Pegging Act," which was designed to restrict the acquisition of property by Indians by prohibiting land transfers between Indians and non-Indians. The SAIC called for a "Resistance Day" on 13 June 1946, and Indians across the country observed a one-day strike. In Durban, thousands of protesters camped out on land designated for whites only. The Indian passive resistance campaign lasted intermittently for about two years. To the extent that such acts of protest represented a degree of unity between the communists and one or more of its allies, they were successful, but such protests usually revolved around single issues that affected a particular slice of the resistance coalition. The masses as a whole remained unmoved by the calls of protest leaders for action.

The communists were even less successful at tapping into the African protest movement in the rural areas than they had been in the urban townships. Alpheus Maliba, a communist and leader of the Zoutpansberg Cultural Association (ZCA), provided one link between the party and the African reserves. From the mid-1930s through the mid-1940s, the ZCA was embroiled in a struggle against the state's attempts to implement the 1936 Land Act, which, among other things, was being used to reduce the size of allotments given to peasants living on rocky and infertile terrain in the northern Transvaal. Maliba's organization was based in the CPSA offices in Johannesburg, and he tried to chronicle the peasants' struggle in the party press. As starvation spread, resistance to the Land Act increased, and so did the presence of police and army units in the Zoutpansberg (Venda) reserve. The peasants were beaten and otherwise intimidated, arrested and jailed. There were even rumors that some villages had been bombed.[53]

The Zoutpansberg case was only one of many examples of peasant unrest where the communists could have played a role, but they failed to seize the moment. As Baruch Hirson notes, the problems of rural dwellers were not high on the party's political agenda during the war years. The ZCA had virtually ceased to function by 1944, and Maliba himself became something of a "nonperson" as far as the party's hierarchy was concerned.[54]

The CPSA did connect successfully with the struggles of the 1940s concerning the mines. The communists actively participated in and helped to coordinate the African miners' strike of 1946, the most serious act of defiance during the decade. The bitterness of the miners came to the surface after their repeated demand for a minimum wage of 10 s. a day was met with silence from the Chamber of Mines. Thousands of delegates at an African Mine Workers' Union conference in Johannesburg in August 1946 voted in favor of a strike, openly defying War Measure Act No. 1425, which prohibited such action. For 3 days between 12 August and 15 August 1946, an estimated 70,000 to 100,000 miners and their supporters brought mining production on the Witwatersrand to a halt.

The Chamber of Mines and the government met the strikers with brute force, using thousands of armed police. The strike was broken, 9 Africans were killed and 1,248 injured, and the strike leaders were arrested, along with the entire membership of the CPSA's Johannesburg district committee and the party's general secretary, Moses Kotane. In the end, 52 people were accused of sedition and conspiring to bring about an illegal strike. They were convicted of the second charge, but the first was dropped. The government was not content to let the matter rest, and within months all members of the CPSA's executive committee in Cape Town were arrested on charges relating to the strike. The court proceedings dragged on for 2 years until the charges were finally dropped.[55]

The National Party gained control of the government in 1948 and wasted little time in erecting the legislative pillars of the apartheid system. A most ominous piece of legislation for the resistance movement was the Suppression of Communism Bill, which was worded in such a way as to encompass virtually all forces outside parliament opposed to the government. Labeled "the Gestapo Bill" by the communists, it was "[Prime Minister Daniel] Malan's latest and greatest measure to make South Africa a Nazi state." The objective was to outlaw communists first and then every other protest group. "No people's organizations will be safe from attack under this vicious law," the editors wrote, in what proved to be the final issue of the party's newspaper, *Inkululeko*. "The law will place in the hands of the government the right to declare illegal any organization which they think spreads the ideas of communism or which they think tries to bring about any social, political, industrial, or economic change by means of disturbances or illegal acts."[56]

The 17-member central committee was summoned to Cape Town to discuss the future of the party. Only 2 members, Michael Harmel and Bill Andrews, voted in favor of continuing the struggle illegally and underground. The others felt the CPSA membership was not prepared for the dangers involved in clandestine work. Although the executive voted to dissolve the party a few weeks before the Suppression of Communism Act became law, its decision was hotly disputed by rank-and-file members, who felt the party should not have given up without a fight.

Case Study of *Inkululeko*

Inkululeko (Freedom) was the party's flagship newspaper, and arguably the most militant and outspoken protest publication in South Africa during the turbulent 1940s. The closure of *South African Worker/Umsebenzi* in 1938 had left the communists without an official mouthpiece for the first time in their history, and it was more than a year before the party came out with another newspaper.

Soon after the CPSA moved its headquarters from Johannesburg to Cape Town in December 1938, members of the Johannesburg district committee (including Michael Harmel, Michael Diphuko and Edwin Mofutsanyana) began publishing a party newsletter under the title *'Nkululeko* (the date of the first issue is unknown). The issues appeared sporadically in a modest mimeographed format. In December 1940, the party began publishing a printed newspaper under the same title, and *Inkululeko*, as it was now spelled, appeared initially as an irregular monthly.[57]

The CPSA produced a number of other publications in addition to *Inkululeko* during the 1940s. A Cape-based, English-language newspaper also entitled *Freedom* was published irregularly every other month between August 1939 and the summer of 1948, and thereafter it appeared as a fortnightly newsletter. Unlike *Inkululeko*, it was a staid theoretical journal, filled with official statements and speeches and read largely within party circles. It was edited initially by Cape Town surgeon Dr. George Sachs (husband of *Guardian* editor Betty Radford Sacks) and later by CPSA general secretary Moses Kotane. In an effort to reach the Afrikaans-speaking working class, the communists started a publication called *Die Ware Republikein* (the True Republican) in May 1940, but it ceased publication after a few issues. A newsheet called the *Cape Party Organizer*, founded in 1944, also faded quickly, as did a monthly produced for a few months in 1945 entitled *Inkululeko Newsletter*.[58] CPSA members were linked to several nonparty journals during the 1940s, the most famous of which was the *Guardian*, the independent socialist weekly discussed in Chapters 9 and 10 of the present volume.

This case study explores *Inkululeko*'s role in chronicling the national and international political environment of the 1940s, describing its writers and editors, circulation and advertising, and the news agenda. The analysis focuses exclusively on the English-language section of the newspaper. English-language stories made up about one-third of the news agenda, and English-language advertisements comprised about 90 percent of the advertising agenda.

Editors and Writers

From the time *Inkululeko* was founded in 1939 until well into its fourth year as a printed publication, it was produced cooperatively by members of the Johannesburg CPSA district committee.[59] In September 1944, *Inkululeko* announced that Michael Diphuko was to be the newspaper's first editor in chief. A Communist Party member since 1939, Diphuko was trained as a teacher and later became an organizer for the African Building Workers' Union on the Witwatersrand.[60] He had been associated with the newspaper for several years, first as a contributor and then as editor of the Tswana (Sechuana) section. He had also written a party booklet in Tswana called *Mmusho le Ma-Afrika*, which was described as "a theoretical work in Sechuana on socialist principles."[61]

As editor in chief, Diphuko worked closely with an editorial board whose membership comprised Edwin Mofutsanyana, J. B. Marks, Michael Harmel,

Photo 35. Michael Diphuko, editor of *Inkululeko* (1944–45).

Photo 36. Abner A. Kunene, a member of *Inkululeko*'s editorial board, was one of many African correspondents whose by-lines appeared in the newspaper.

Photo 37. Edwin Thabo Mofutsanyana, editor of *Inkululeko* (1945–50).

Photo 38. Michael Harmel, the most influential editorial figure in *Inkululeko*, apart from his close friend Mofutsanyana, in the 1940s. Harmel also wrote a regular column in the *Guardian* between 1949 and 1951.

C. S. Ramohanoe,[62] Armstrong Msitshana, Z. Kgomo, J. Muthibe and Abner A. Kunene. Editorial policy was laid down entirely by this board, and Diphuko made decisions only within the parameters of established policy. The party's central committee had no direct role in deciding the content of its official journal, but many committee members were regular contributors.[63]

Edwin Thabo Mofutsanyana replaced Diphuko as editor in chief in June 1945. The reason for the change is not clear, but Diphuko continued to work for *Inkululeko* as an assistant editor in charge of the Tswana-language section. Mofutsanyana left his full-time position as a party organizer in Johannesburg to take over the editorship, and he soon began to make his mark on the newspaper. He redesigned the masthead, used more boxes to highlight stories – especially on the front page – and introduced more story by-lines. A regular column entitled "Notes and Comments" now appeared under the pseudonym "Umlweli" on page 4 or 5. Advertisements began to appear on page 1, and cinema listings were positioned on the back page. In essence, he redesigned parts of the newspaper to give it a cleaner, more professional facade. More important, he announced his intention to make *Inkululeko* "the organ not only of the CP but also the mouthpiece of the African people and all democratic South Africans."[64]

Mofutsanyana strengthened the editorial board by inviting distinguished foreign observers as well as South Africans to become contributing editors, and some of them were noncommunists. The new members included Moses Kotane, secretary general of the CPSA; Charles Mzingeli, chairman of the African branch of the Southern Rhodesia Labour Party; Hilda Watts Bernstein, the first CPSA member elected to the Johannesburg City Council and editor of a communist magazine called *Soviet Life*; Betty Radford Sacks, editor of the *Guardian* and a member of the Cape Town City Council; Rajani Palme Dutt, vice-chairman of the Communist Party of Great Britain and editor of *Labour Monthly*; Govan A. Mbeki, secretary of a militant opposition group in the Transkei called Transkeian Organised Bodies, a member of the National Anti-Pass Council and the Transkei African Voters' Association; and T. A. Bankole, president of the Trade Union Congress of Nigeria.

The main contributors whose by-lines appeared consistently over the years were Mofutsanyana, Harmel, Diphuko, Kotane, Dadoo, Daniel Tloome,[65] John Kebopetsoe, David W. Bopape[66] and Maphutseng Lefela, the newspaper's Basutoland correspondent. Others included Armstrong Msitshana, L. P. Nqotolo, Abner Kunene, J. B. Marks, Hilda Watts Bernstein,[67] C. S. Ramohanoe, A. Kgomo, Alpheus Maliba, J. Muthibe and Gaur Radebe.[68] On the basis of by-lines alone, it would seem that the vast majority of stories were written by Africans.

Many party workers, black and white, were involved with news production as translators, photographers and editors who scrutinized the copy and designed the layouts. Among those who worked under Mofutsanyana as assistant editors in charge of the different language sections were Michael Diphuko (Tswana), Alpheus Maliba (Venda), (? first name unknown) Mulaudzi (Thonga), Armstrong Msitshana (Xhosa) and Ben Mnisi (Zulu). Mofutsanyana understood these languages but read only some of them, so he had the assistant editors read material to him before accepting it for publication.[69] Most contributors did not receive any kind of renumeration for their work, although many were on the party's payroll for work in other capacities. The only full-time paid staff were the editor in chief (Diphuko and then Mofutsanyana), the business manager (John Nkadimeng), who dealt with packaging and distribution, and a messenger-cum-clerk (John Kebopetsoe), whose salary was apparently paid by the Johannesburg district committee.[70]

From the beginning, the two most influential editorial figures at *Inkululeko* were Mofutsanyana (1899–1995) and his close friend Michael Harmel (1915–1974). They came from completely different backgrounds, and there was nothing in the early life of either to suggest that they would grow up to be lifelong revolutionaries. Mofutsanyana was born in Witzieshoek in the Orange Free State. His mother was a descendant of King Moshoeshoe I of Lesotho, and his father was a farmer who was sympathetic to the Afrikaners to the point of actively assisting them during the South African War. After passing the Standard V (seventh grade) examinations, Mofutsanyana moved to the Cape, working first at Saldanha Bay and then at Stellenbosch in a factory. He returned to school for a time before moving to Johannesburg, where he found work as an attendance clerk in the gold mines and observed firsthand the exploitation of African miners. He joined the Communist Party in 1928.

Friends remember Mofutsanyana as an intense and serious man, clever and deliberate in speech.[71] His commitment to the party was total, and he rose quickly through the ranks. After a period of immersion in the finer points of marxism at the party's school in Johannesburg, he was sent to Potchefstroom in the heart of Afrikanerdom as a regional organizer. It was a particularly tough assignment: his three predecessors had been subjected to relentless intimidation by local Afrikaners and the police and had eventually fled for their lives. Mofutsanyana promised himself he would throw himself wholeheartedly into his work there, even if it cost him his life. It very nearly did. In December 1929 he narrowly survived an assassination attempt as he rose to speak at a mass rally. The bullet intended for him killed his colleague Hermanus Lethebe.

Mofutsanyana was summoned by the Comintern in 1933 to study in the Soviet Union. He traveled first to Berlin and then to Moscow, using Eddie Roux's passport.[72] For two-and-a-half years he studied at the University of the East, a training college for party cadres primarily from Asia and Africa. When he returned to South Africa in 1936, he had added Russian to the other seven languages he spoke. Although Mofutsanyana was continually harassed, detained and jailed by the police, he gained a reputation in the next decade as one of the party's key organizers and leading theoreticians. He became chairman of the CPSA's Johannesburg district committee while continuing as a high-ranking member of the ANC. Mofutsanyana also served on the Advisory Board of Orlando Township and twice contested NRC elections (in 1937 and 1942), but the election process was stacked against left-wing candidates, and he had no chance of winning.

Michael Harmel's parents emigrated to South Africa from Ireland. Born in Johannesburg, he grew up in what was then the largely Jewish suburb of Doornfontein, where his father owned a pharmacy. His mother died when he was an infant, and he was raised by his father, a well-read man with progressive views on racial issues. Harmel became a political activist as a young man studying for a degree in economics at Rhodes University in Grahamstown. He was sent to London after he graduated, where his father hoped he would tone down his political views. Instead, they were hardened. He stood on street corners selling copies of the *Daily Worker*, the British communist newspaper, and supported himself by washing dishes in restaurants. He returned to South Africa in 1937 and immediately joined the CPSA. Like Mofutsanyana, he worked for the Johannesburg district committee and was widely recognized as a key tactician.

Both men contributed more stories to *Inkululeko* than even their by-lines would suggest. Like other left-wing journalists of the day, they often used pseudonyms.

Registered at the G.P.O. as a newspaper — Workers of the World, Unite!

UMSEBENZI
THE SOUTH AFRICAN WORKER

Organ of the Communist Party — Incorporating the "International"

No. 622 — Capetown, Friday, 11 July, 1930 — Price 1d.

TONJENI AT GRAAFF REINET
Agitator Comes to Country Dorp

CONDITIONS IN A TYPICAL LOCATION

"Promoting Hostility"

Dear Comrade Editor,

Kindly publish this report in "Umsebenzi" for general information.

I arrived in Graaff-Reinet a few weeks ago and addressed some meetings in the location, which is inhabited both by Coloured and Native people. The location superintendent, a Euro-

them. If any person in the location, after he or she has faced severe expense in building a house, falls into arrears with the rent, the earthly god can proceed to such house, throw out the belongings and lock it up. It makes no difference even if the husband is away or the wife is sick; the slave family must suffer and sleep outside. That is the kind of civilisa-

citizens of this country to learn that the Native women of Graaff-Reinet are carrying passes. After 9 p.m. Native women are arrested if found walking in the streets without passes. If any woman works in a kitchen up to 9.30 p.m., before she may leave for the location she must get a special pass in the form of a written note from

INKULULEKO

No. 78. — JOHANNESBURG, 9th JUNE, 1945. — 1d.
Registered at the G.P.O. as a Newspaper.

MOFUTSANYANA TAKES OVER "INKULULEKO" EDITORSHIP

Mr. E. T. Mofutsanyana has been released from his work as organiser for the Johannesburg District of the Communist Party in order to take over the post of Editor-in-Chief of "Inkululeko." He will assume his duties immediately.

Mr. Mofutsanyana is known throughout South Africa for his

Mr. Mofutsanyana is one of the most respected figures in the Afri-

IN CAPETOWN

5,000 MARCH AGAINST PASSES

THE Africans of Capetown demonstrated clearly their protest against Prime Minister Hofmeyr's undemocratic refusal to meet the Anti-Pass Deputation representing seven million Africans. They marched in their thousands through the main streets of Capetown, led by the Anti-Pass Deputation, to the Houses of Parliament. They carried banners inscribed "Down with the Pass Laws!" and "Democracy for All!"

The procession followed a mass meeting at the parade addressed by Dr. Y. M. Dadoo, Cr. R. V. Selope Thema, D. W. Bopape, R. G. Baloyi, Moses Kotane and Mrs. J. Palmer. When passing the Houses of Parliament, the demonstration took up the cry "Down with Pass Laws — we want Freedom." The noise from the procession penetrated into both Houses of Parliament and many Members of Parliament went out to watch it.

Chanting the African National anthem, "Nkosi Sikelela i Afrika," the procession turned down through Plein Street back to the parade, where the crowd gathered round the platform and, addressed by members of the deputation, passed resolutions protesting against the unwillingness of the Acting Prime Minister to meet the deputation.

INTERVIEW

Immediately after their arrival in Capetown on Saturday, 2nd June, they contacted the Parliamentarians representing the Africans and asked them to arrange an interview with the Acting Prime Minister. On Monday they were told that the Acting Prime Minister, being very busy, was unable to meet them; but that he could meet them in Pretoria, and that he had suggested that the

he had asked the Minister of Native Affairs to see the deputation. Further representations were made with the same results.

MAJOR VAN DER BYL

Meanwhile, members of the deputation had also been in contact with the Secretary for Native Affairs, who had also explained the Acting Prime Minister's inability for the reasons stated. The Council had asked to see the Ministers of Native Affairs and Justice with Mr. Hofmeyr, but owing to pressure of Parliamentary duties, it was arranged that the two first-mentioned Ministers should meet the deputation separately, and an interview with Major Van der Byl was arranged for 9.45 a.h. on June 7th, notwithstanding the fact that the Minister had prior engagements wh.ch had to be cancelled.

The Minister was available at the appointed time, but the deputation failed to attend and gave no prior explanation to Major Van der Byl or his department. Later a letter was handed in to the effect that in a matter of such grave importance no audience would be satisfactory if not accorded by the Supreme Head. This attitude is totally at variance with a statement made on the day before to the Secretary for Native Affairs that, if the Acting Prime Minister was unable to receive the deputation they would meet his nomi-

them to arrange the interview. On Monday the deputation was informed by them that the Acting Prime Minister, owing to his parliamentary duties, was unable to see the deputation in Cape Town but was willing to meet them in Pretoria.

After discussing the situation the deputation decided to directly contact the Acting Prime Minister by a letter pointing out the importance of the Pass-Law question and the decision of the National Anti-Pass Conference. To this request the Acting Prime Minister replied that he was too busy, but said that the Deputation could meet the Minister for Native Affairs.

On the point made by the Bureau of Information that the Deputation had agreed to meet the Minister of Native Affairs and the

MORE 1425 ARRESTS

Four Africans have been summoned to appear in the Germiston Magistrate's Court on Thursday, June 21st. They are Messrs. Arthur Damane, Daniel Lempe, Lucas Phillips and Mr. Zuma.

It is alleged that they contravened Regulation 1425 of the War Emergency Regulations, by holding a meeting of the Communist Party at Germiston, attended by more than twenty persons, on gold-proclaimed land.

Photo 39. Front pages of *Umsebenzi* in July 1930 and of *Inkululeko* in June 1945, when Mofutsanyana was appointed editor.

This was partly for reasons of personal security, particularly when the issue being addressed was controversial. In *Inkululeko*'s case, pseudonyms also gave the newspaper the appearance of having more contributing writers–and especially African writers–than it actually had. Mofutsanyana wrote under the name "Umlweli." Michael Harmel used the pseudonyms "A. Lerumo" (which means "a teacher," in several African languages) and "The Spectator."

Circulation and Advertising

From the beginning, about two-thirds of *Inkululeko* was published in vernacular African languages in an attempt to lure African readers. A small box on the front page of each issue listed the languages used within. The pages alternated between Zulu, Sotho, Tswana, Venda and to a lesser extent Thonga (Tsonga) and Xhosa. Nevertheless, two key pages were always in English–the front page and the editorial page (page 4)–and the back page of this eight-page newspaper usually appeared in English as well.[73]

Inkululeko relied mainly on street sales to reach a national audience. Only a small percentage of the newspaper was distributed by mail. Party members were given stacks of the newspaper to take back to their townships or villages to sell themselves or to deliver to commission agents, who sold them to locals. Newspapers were sold door to door and hawked at public meetings, beer halls, bus stops and train stations.[74] Although readership figures were almost certainly inflated, there is no doubt that *Inkululeko* was the most widely read of the Communist Party's official journals. At its peak in May 1942, the newspaper claimed a print run of 20,000 copies an issue.[75] In its 9 January 1943 issue–the day *Inkululeko* became a fortnightly, appearing on the first and third Thursday of each month–it reported a print run of 20,000, or 40,000 copies a month. This compared with a print run of 12,000 in August 1941 and 18,000 in December 1941. When *'Nkululeko* was a mimeographed newspaper, only 1,400 copies of any one issue were printed.[76]

After the CPSA's decision to throw its support behind the war effort, the Smuts government set aside its ideological prejudices and began encouraging communists to speak on the radio and at pro-war rallies, in the hope that this would generate support for the war among Africans. For the same reason, the government allotted the CPSA more newsprint during the war to boost *Inkululeko*'s circulation. At a penny a copy, however, *Inkululeko* was not a money-making venture. Advertising was an important source of revenue, but it was accepted only from small-scale local merchants and self-employed entrepreneurs offering a service, for example, tailors, shoemakers and repairmen.[77] *Inkululeko*, by its own account, depended for survival on donations from readers. A fund for voluntary donations called the "*Inkululeko* Fighting Fund" was announced on the front page of the December 1940 issue, and periodic updates kept readers informed of the newspaper's financial status. A sample report in 1941 gives some insight into the various sources of funding, which included what appears to have been a regular subsidy from the party:

> In September, the readers supported us with £46 6s 10d. Let us see what they did during October. As usual we received from the Communist Party £25.00; from MC 1s; social £2 7s 9d; jumble sale £14 3s 0d; A.H. £1; Collection card £29 6s; R.A. 5d; Mrs. S. 2s 6d; B.M. 6d; M.M. 3d; Vereeniging collections 5s; Meyerton collections 4s 9d; Altogether £43 11s 2d.[78]

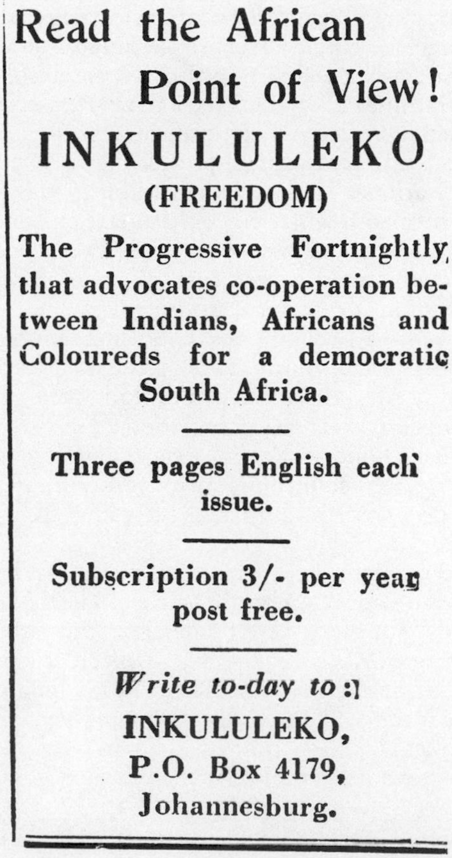

Read the African Point of View!

INKULULEKO

(FREEDOM)

The Progressive Fortnightly that advocates co-operation between Indians, Africans and Coloureds for a democratic South Africa.

Three pages English each issue.

Subscription 3/- per year post free.

Write to-day to:

INKULULEKO,
P.O. Box 4179,
Johannesburg.

Photo 40. A typical subscription notice in *Inkululeko* during the 1940s.

The newspaper's advertising content suggested an intended audience that was poor, urban and African. Essential goods and services, mainly medicine, furniture, clothing and food comprised about 63 percent of the advertisements. Many pharmaceutical advertisements, for example, were for African products: "Kama" was proclaimed "The Great Blood Medicine," "Sana Buchu" kidney pills claimed they relieved chronic back pain, and "Mlamlankunzi Remedies" was a staple health advertisement (although it did not specify what the medicine remedied). The medical advertisements in particular point to a readership concerned with basic health needs.

Some advertisements were more obviously directed at small businessmen and the self-employed. London Sales Agency (actually based in Johannesburg) ran regular advertisements that read: "Important to African Storekeepers – Piece Goods, Men's Vests, Shops, Shirts." City Leather sold its wares with the words "for better leather, machinery and everything for the shoemaker."[79]

A small classified advertising section appeared regularly under the heading "For Sale," the most popular items being coal stoves, bricks, flue pipes and spare parts for stoves, and buckets and wash tubs. On the services side, there were a large number of advertisements for local chemists (pharmacists) and opticians. One for "the African Pharmacy" regularly filled a large slot across the bottom of one of the African-language pages. A major advertiser during these years was "Raphael's," which promoted itself as "the first opticians to cater solely for Africans." The accompanying illustration initially depicted a pair of glasses; later, the drawing was changed to show a bespectacled African reading a book.[80]

Nonessential goods and services comprised about 20 percent of the advertisements. The African National Theatre (Johannesburg) was a major advertiser, and one that targeted Africans. Regular cinema advertisements listed films playing in the African townships along the Witwatersrand. There were also notices for concerts and dances. Manufactured cigarette brands promoted themselves with images of white men. Springbok, for example, sold itself as the "sportsman's cigarette" with images of white men playing cricket, boxing, football and tennis – two of which were not major African sports. There were no advertisements for alcoholic beverages: Africans at the time were prohibited from buying European-brand liquor. Other luxury goods and services included advertisements for jewelers, hairdressers, photographers, nonessential household items like sewing machines, "The People's Bookstore" (which sold communist literature) and an African real estate firm specializing in property "sold in areas restricted for Natives, Coloureds and Indians."[81]

Educational advertisements – correspondence courses, books and African night school programs – were also an important feature. The CPSA, of course, advertised its own night schools, but there were numerous other advertisements for educational services catering to Africans. Lyceum College (a correspondence school in Johannesburg), for example, promoted itself with an illustration of a talking African figure telling readers: "I am earning more money." The advertisement went on to explain that Lyceum College offered Africans a full range of academic courses from Standard V (seventh grade) to matriculation as well as shorthand, typewriting, bookkeeping, motor mechanics, "native" law and administration, agricultural science and "bilingual certificates."[82] The Farming Correspondence College in Stellenbosch (Cape) asked readers: "Can You Cook?" For those who could not, it offered a home economics course.[83]

Promotions for the Communist Party and its flagship newspaper comprised about 17 percent of the advertisements. These included notices of meetings and rallies, updates on Communist Party membership, advertisements for CPSA night school classes, Communist Party pamphlets and membership applications, and *Inkululeko* subscription forms. Updates on the status of the *Inkululeko* Fighting Fund were a regular feature. They often appeared under bold capital headlines, such as "Inkululeko Means Freedom," "Only You Can Save Our Paper," "You Must Be the Doctor" and "What Will YOU Give for Freedom?"[84] Other appeals for financial assistance appeared in the form of letters from the editors[85] and periodic announcements encouraging readers to support *Inkululeko* by becoming sales agents or by submitting stories.

One interesting item was a play called *Africa Comes to Egoli*, which was performed as a fund-raiser for the CPSA.[86] It told the story of an African who goes to Johannesburg in search of work. He is robbed and then thrown into prison for being "idle and unemployed." He is "sorely puzzled about the way the city has treated him," but on his release he is given a copy of *Inkululeko*. "Now he understands things," the reviewer wrote, "and he joins a trade union and supports the workers' leaders in calling out a strike."

Table 27. *Paid advertising in* Inkululeko

Year	Number
December 1940	0
1941	2
1942	19
1943	6
1944	49
1945	124
1946	183
1947	260
1948	139
1949	125
1950 (six months)	34

Most advertisers were based in or around Johannesburg, which suggests that much of the readership was as well. One must assume there was no money or personnel to track down potential advertisers in other parts of the country, and the number of advertising units varied dramatically from year to year.

Paid advertisements – those not concerned with the party or *Inkululeko* – were sparse until after the war (Table 27). It is unclear why advertising began to fall so dramatically in the last two and-a-half years of *Inkululeko's* existence, but one can speculate that advertisers were worried about having any connection with the newspaper after the 1948 general election, when the Nationalists were in a position to act on their threat to suppress the CPSA.[87]

Photographs and Other Illustrations

Another clue to *Inkululeko*'s limited financial resources was the use of photographs and other illustrations. Cartoons, for example, were used much less frequently than in *South African Worker/Umsebenzi*. Roux had made his own cartoons out of linocuts, and apparently no one at *Inkululeko* in the 1940s had this skill. News photographs (photographs taken at the scene of an event) were costly and rarely used. But stock photos of South African communists, mostly Africans associated with the newspaper, were used again and again.

The first printed issue (December 1940) contained four photographs: Venda editor Alpheus Maliba, CPSA general secretary Moses Kotane, prominent Indian communist Yusuf Dadoo and communist trade union organizer Max Joffe. The January 1941 issue contained photographs of Mofutsanyana and Maliba, and Maliba and Dadoo reappeared in the third issue (published in March). Four photographs appeared in the April issue – Zulu editor Ben Mnisi, Xhosa editor Armstrong Msitshana, a leader of the Communist Party in Britain named D. N. Pritt and Indian leader Jawaharal Nehru. A photograph of Dadoo reappeared in May and one of Mofutsanyana in June. In the first six issues of *Inkululeko* as a printed publication, then, 11 of 14 photographs were of persons associated with the newspaper, and only 1 photograph depicted a noncommunist (Nehru).

Inkululeko's first attempt at photojournalism appeared in the August 1941 issue: two cover photographs showed protestors outside the Vereeniging Magistrate's Court, where 56 people were detained after a meeting about lodgers' permits in Vereeniging's African location. The event had taken place the previous month. In September, the newspaper produced its first full-page photo essay with four photographs and full captions describing the Vereeniging event in detail. It was typical of *Inkululeko* to use photographs in this way when it had access to such material, but the photographs usually appeared some months after the event. They were placed mainly on the English-language pages with captions in English.

Between August 1941 and the end of the war, a large part of the newspaper's photographic content involved pro-Soviet propaganda. Most were stock photos supplied by the Soviet Union; there were very few news photos of the war itself. The stock photos depicted soldiers parading in Red Square, Soviet military hardware, and head-and-shoulder pictures of the main military commanders. Non-war photos depicted happy black children, satisfied factory workers and state-owned housing projects. The use of non–South African communist propaganda photos increased dramatically during the war years. The photo credits suggest that more than one-half of the photos appearing in *Inkululeko* in 1943, for example, were supplied to the newspaper by overseas Soviet and Chinese Communist Party sources.

After World War II, there was another dramatic shift in photo priorities. Only 4 of 28 photographs that appeared in 1946 concerned the Soviet Union, and in the next three years only 20 of 179 photos in *Inkululeko* could be classified as stock Soviet propaganda photos. The images of a turbulent South Africa – mass rallies, protests and mug shots of CPSA and ANC activists—now filled the news pages. In fact, more than one-half of the photographs in *Inkululeko* between 1946 and 1950 depicted ANC leaders and activities. The photos of white CPSA leaders rarely appeared, even though the party's central committee was still dominated by whites. The intention was clearly to present the party as having an African face. Few international leaders other than Lenin and Stalin ever appeared in *Inkululeko*. Roosevelt and Churchill each made a single appearance, and Nehru a few more. Photos of the leading figures in white South African politics were virtually excluded. Only one photo of General Smuts ever appeared in *Inkululeko* – immediately after he lost the 1948 election.

Inkululeko tried to make the best use of very limited resources when it came to photographs or anything else. Full-page photographs and double-page photo essays were especially effective. Overall, the product was as bold in design as it was in message. *Inkululeko*'s masthead changed three times in 10 years,[88] but its basic format remained largely the same. A tabloid-sized newspaper, it often carried headlines 120 points (1.75 inches) high. Its layout involved the use of drop letters to introduce paragraphs and boxed-in caption stories. For the first two years, its size fluctuated between 8, 10 and 12 pages, but eventually it settled at 8. Its frequency also fluctuated somewhat because of financial constraints and paper shortages, although government interference was also a factor both during and after the war. *Inkululeko* appeared initially as a monthly, but in January 1943 it was produced more frequently as a fortnightly. The newspaper was a weekly from October 1948 to June 1950.[89] There were 189 issues in all before the newspaper ceased publication.

News Agenda

Inkululeko projected contradictory notions about the concept of news. On the one hand, news was to conform to the credo of the capitalist press. In a revealing

Photos 41, 42, 43. Three key leaders of the resistance movement during the 1940s and 1950s writing regularly for *Inkululeko* and other left-wing newspapers were Daniel Tloome (Council of Non-European Trade Unions, Communist Party and ANC) top left, Yusuf Dadoo (South African Indian Congress, Communist Party and ANC) top right, and Moses Kotane (Communist Party and ANC) above.

two-column, back-page story that appeared in 1944, the editor offered some practical instructions to would-be reporters:

> *Inkululeko* has no paid writers. Those who write for our paper are ordinary people who have no training in journalism. From towns and villages in all parts of South Africa they send news to *Inkululeko* of what is happening in their lives ... What is news? Well, as you can see from the name, it means something new. *Inkululeko* readers want to know what is happening now, not what happened a long time ago ... Suppose that in some location there is no street lighting and a donga [hole] in the road. A man is walking on this road at night and falls and breaks his leg. That's news – and we want to hear about it.

The story went on to outline some basic rules for news, which included:

> 1. Accuracy. If you want to be of assistance to the paper, make sure that everything you send us is true.
> 2. Stick to the facts. *Inkululeko* wants to know what happened. Comment, that is opinions about what is happening, should not be mixed up with a story giving news ... Don't put in your own comment. Don't philosophise about the news.[90]

This advice can be compared with the journalistic philosophy of Moses Kotane, as expressed in the first issue of the newspaper:

> Of what use is a newspaper to a people? A newspaper is a very useful weapon in the hands of a people or a class or to whosoever possesses it. Without a newspaper we would never know what other people want, see, think or do; and what was happening in the world today. Through a newspaper people and parties make known to the public their views and ideas. It organises and informs the opinion of those whose interests it serves ... Africans have no newspaper which truly serves their interest, a newspaper which teaches them the value of organisation, unity and struggle for the betterment of their political, economic and social conditions ... We need a paper which will tell the people the truth of what is happening and what is to be done.[91]

Clearly, there was some confusion in the minds of party leaders over precisely what kind of newspaper *Inkululeko* was supposed to be. On the one hand, news originated in African urban and rural communities and on factory floors: news could be something as seemingly insignificant as a man breaking his leg, but to *Inkululeko* it was news. On the other hand, news was something determined from above, something to be used to educate the masses and prepare them for the struggle ahead.

Both definitions of news in *Inkululeko* emphasized the importance of news as "truth," a social reality that could be recaptured and recorded. But the first definition perceived truth as a factual reality embodied in an accurate rendering of newsworthy issues. Commentary was to be separate from "the news," which was to be written in an objective, informative manner. The editors were anxious to reach African workers by targeting events of concern to them, but stories about everyday life were rare in this newspaper.

The second definition focused on truth in a larger context. *Inkululeko* had a responsibility to educate readers by (1) examining the ways in which most Africans were being exploited as workers and as members of a subordinated racial caste, and (2) mobilizing Africans to take action in concert with other deprived castes and classes in South Africa. In essence, truth was linked to class interest. *Inkululeko*'s pedagogical tone was particularly noticeable during the war years.[92] Headlines sometimes took the form of questions to be answered in the story. In the first

Figure 6. Domestic and foreign news in *Inkululeko* (in %). Percentages are calculated by dividing the number of story units in each category by the total number of story units. News refers to all story units, including illustrations and informal advertisements classified as news. Formal advertisements are excluded. *Inkululeko* had 2,780 story units.

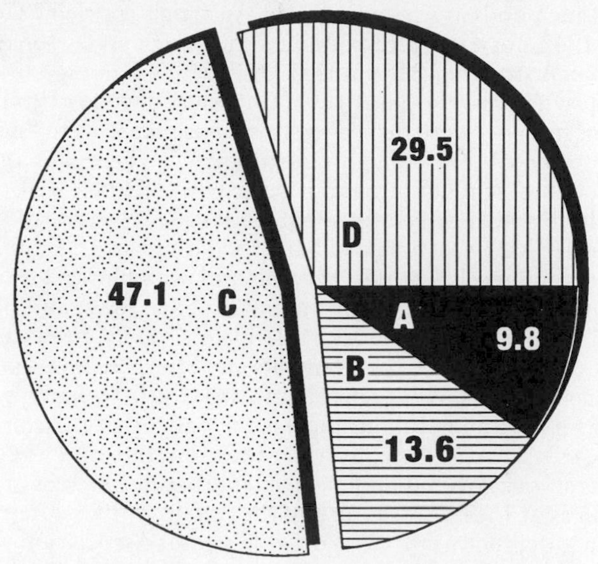

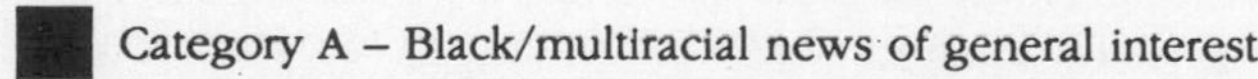

edition, for example, a headline posed the question "What Is Fascism?" and the story responded: "The sort of Government they have in Germany and Italy is called Fascism. Fascism is a cruel and brutal form of oppression of the people by the rich bosses."[93] Headlines were often in the imperative voice: "Don't Pay More for Goods" and "Demand More Pay."[94]

Inkululeko in practice adhered to the second definition of news, and it was an almost exclusively issue-oriented newspaper. Individual events were not ignored, but they were used mainly as reference points for commentaries and broad, ideological statements. Like news photos, news events were often recorded long after they had happened, and it was not uncommon for an event to be mentioned in a big headline but then barely touched upon in the accompanying story.

Black political and trade union activities, as anticipated, dominated *Inkululeko*'s news agenda during the 1940s (Figure 6).

Nonpartisan news of general interest to the African community received very little space in the newspaper (Table 28).

Although Category A is defined as nonpolitical news concerning everyday life in the African community, in *Inkululeko* most stories had political implications. Education news (A. 1) dealt with the quality of African education and conditions for teachers and pupils in African schools. An article entitled "Teachers' Starvation Wages" in 1942, for example, examined the salary scales for African teachers in the Transvaal. A story in 1945 entitled "A People's School" outlined the problems that developed in Orlando (an African township outside of Johannesburg), when thousands of students were turned away because there were "not enough schools, not enough teachers, not enough classrooms."[95] There was only one story that could be identified as religious, and it dealt with a Dutch Reformed Church decision to establish a "Bantu" educational facility.[96]

Society news (A.2) was more ordinary, including birth announcements and obituaries, notices about celebrations, festivals and nonpolitical group meetings. It also included entertainment – music, theater and film reviews, and occasionally poems (featuring a poet named Moses K. Mphahlele).[97] Only a few African success stories, mainly about scholastic achievements and bursaries (grants), were found in the English-language pages. A big surprise, in view of *Inkululeko*'s aspiration to be a mouthpiece for African nationalism, was the paucity of African social news.

Sports news (A.3) was virtually absent from *Inkululeko*'s news agenda as well. A few sports stories covered events, such as African victories at the 1948 summer Olympic games or Joe Louis's return to the ring in 1949.[98] A few others were more political in nature, such as the World Table Tennis Association's rejection of South Africa's color bar, efforts to save an African sports ground under threat as a result of lack of funding, and negotiations between the Bantu Cricket Union and the South Africa Cricket Board.[99]

Living and working conditions in Johannesburg's urban African townships (A.4) comprised by far the leading subject in Category A. Stories included the plight of squatters, high rents, inflationary prices, the selling of goods and services on the black market, food and water shortages in the townships, conditions in workers' hostels and in factories and mines, and inadequate public lavatory facilities and public transportation. In an editorial entitled "Black Man's Burden,"[100] for example, the newspaper addressed the problem of disease in African society as a result of poverty and poor living conditions. Another editorial, entitled "Hospital Overcrowding,"[101] exposed the inadequacy of health care for Africans and overcrowding in Johannesburg's non-European hospital. Letters from readers often relayed individual experiences of racism, discrimination or injustice, such as a letter from a man who had lost both legs in a mining accident and was awarded only £12 in compensation.[102]

There were virtually no stories of conditions in rural areas (A.5),[103] and no stories dealt specifically with African entrepreneurial activities (A.6). There were a few crime stories (A.7), but these were commentaries linking crime with low wages and poor working conditions rather than reports of specific incidents.[104] Accidents were never reported unless they involved someone known to the CPSA community.[105]

Only one example of a straight news report could be found in the English-language pages of *Inkululeko*. This was a front-page story on the 1949 Orlando train crash that killed 68 people and injured 49. Even then, the report was accompanied by a statement from the CPSA's Johannesburg district committee, which, in addition to extending sympathy to the families of the victims, blamed the accident

Table 28. *Category A news in* Inkululeko (*% of story units*)

Category	%
A. Black/multiracial news of general interest (273 units)	9.8
A.1 Education and religion	0.7
A.2 Society	1.7
A.3 Sports	0.3
A.4, A.5 Living and working conditions in urban and rural areas	6.9
A.6 Independent economic activities	0.0
A.7 Crime and accidents	0.2
A.8 Other: Promotional and miscellaneous	0.0

on a system of segregation that "forces workers to live far from work and take transport from crowded, segregated areas."[106]

Inkululeko did not offer recipes, gardening hints, crossword puzzles or other miscellaneous recreational reading. The newspaper did not have a regular letters' section, but letters to the editor frequently appeared, especially on the vernacular pages. Stories promoting the newspaper or the party in this content analysis were classified as advertisements. The only item classified as "Other" (A.8) was a book review. The book dealt with relations between Africans and the police.[107]

White Authoritarian Context

Stories concerning political, economic and social activities involving whites comprised 13.6 percent of the news story units (Table 29).

News about white political activities (B.1) included items in which government officials commented on the African community.[108] There were also several political cartoons. One illustration, for example, showed a bowl with a bone in it. On the bone were the words "Administration of Reserves," and in the distance was a door with an oversized lock and the message "Democratic Rights." A note tacked to the door read "For Europeans Only." The caption was a quotation from Smuts: "We must give the Natives' Representative Council a bone to chew on."[109] *Inkululeko* occasionally reported incidents of infighting in white politics, such as the controversy over the government's plan to establish a South African republic.[110] "Umlweli" once wrote a piece in which he named individuals who were "traitors to the cause." These alleged collaborators included a man of Jewish descent who wanted to join the National Party in the Transvaal (from which he was banned) and a Cape Coloured who wanted to form a Coloured organization to fight communism.[111]

Many stories focused on specific pieces of racist legislation, such as an immigration policy that boosted the inflow of whites, a plan to exclude African workers from the unemployment insurance fund and the influx-control laws.[112] One editorial, entitled "Laws That Make Criminals," presented an overall look at the impact of repressive legislation.[113] Stories attacking government attempts to criminalize the African trade union movement and the Communist Party formed a significant proportion of these news stories. One editorial, entitled "A Bill to Smash Trade Unions," contended that "it is in the interests of employers to destroy the existing African trade union movement and to weaken greatly the trade union movement

Table 29. *Category B news in* Inkululeko (*% of story units*)

Category	%
B. White/multiracial news (379 units)	13.6
B.1 Political, legislative and administrative	12.6
B.2 Economic and social	1.0

as a whole."[114] A story in 1941 entitled "Threat to Gag Communists – Swart Declares War on Free Speech" quoted the minister of justice, who was trying to ban all communist meetings held on Sundays.[115]

Stories that focused on official acts against squatters, including police raids on squatter camps and attempts to arrest squatter leaders and evict or resettle squatter families, also comprised part of this sub-category. A story entitled "Squatters' Leaders in Jail – Authorities' New Plans," for example, described how three members of the Alexandra Shanty Town Committee – one of whom was Abner Kunene, a member of *Inkululeko*'s editorial board – had been arrested by police and charged with assault and extortion. News of the arrests was followed by an editorial comment on the government's new housing plan:

> These arrests take place at the same time as the publication in the *Government Gazette* of the most viciously repressive regulations designed to stamp out the squatter's movement, which itself is merely the reflection of the criminal neglect of the authorities to provide housing for the tens of thousands of African workers whom their policy has forced into the cities. At the same time, the Johannesburg City Council has announced a new plan for the establishment of a single giant Shanty Town under its control, to which 100,000 squatters from existing camps will eventually be moved.[116]

Numerous stories chronicled the development of the apartheid state between 1948 and 1950. Headlines – such as "New Nazi Threats," "Nazi Scheme For S.A.'s Education" and "The Malan Government on the Hitler Road" – invariably linked the National Party with the Nazis.[117] *Inkululeko* stepped up the frequency of its attacks on the government by becoming a weekly in September 1948 (although, to cut down on expenses, the number of pages per issue was cut from the usual eight to four or six). News coverage shifted away from communist activities abroad and protest rallies at home to the activities of the new government and the impact of apartheid on the African population.

At least two conclusions can be drawn from this shift in news priorities. First, the CPSA was increasingly interested in the welfare of Africans once apartheid became a reality. Self-serving propaganda stories, domestic as well as foreign, virtually disappeared from the English-language pages. Second, the CPSA was more solidly African working class in the mid-to late 1940s than it had ever been in the past. *Inkululeko*'s readership and editorial concerns apparently reflected this fact.

Until the National Party election victory in 1948, the communists still exhibited a degree of optimism about what they could achieve by working within the white political system. The communists, however, were absorbed in their own affairs and had little interest in white party politics. They promoted their parliamentary candidates but ignored the fact that Smuts had lost the support of the voting public. An editorial that appeared in February 1948, four months before the election, mirrored the prevailing attitude:

> True, the Communist Party has the right and the opportunity to enter its candidates, so that there may at least be a few true and courageous voices raised amid the clamour of contending herrenvolkists. But the great mass of people are excluded from the franchise. That is why the basic issues affecting us are not decided in this election. That is why the Parliament to be elected this year will be narrow, undemocratic, biased, racialistic and reactionary, as has been the case with every Parliament elected since Union in 1910.[118]

Having said little about the 1948 election in advance, *Inkululeko* responded to the Nationalist victory with the banner headline, "Threat of Fascism to Non-Europeans, Workers." The accompanying story outlined the implications of the Nationalist victory for Africans:

> Shortly before the election the Nationalist Party issued a statement of policy regarding "apartheid" (segregation). This statement favours a policy which would result in Africans becoming slaves in South Africa. The Nationalists aim to drive Africans from settlement in the towns, and into the countryside. They want Africans to be dislodged from skilled or permanent employment, and to condemn Africans permanently to the inferior position of cheap, casual unskilled labourers.[119]

This was the first time *Inkululeko* had explained what National Party policy would mean to its mainly African readership. This was also the first time the newspaper had used the word "apartheid" and defined it as meaning "segregation," although the term had been part of the Nationalist vocabulary since 1943.[120]

The most serious incident of sabotage against *Inkululeko* occurred in February 1943, when four white men forced their way into the offices of the newspaper, doused the rooms with paraffin and set them alight. There was much damage to books, papers and furniture, and most of the stories for the February issue had to be rewritten. The newspaper boldly published a statement on the incident that directly implicated the Nationalists:

> This act of vandalism and sabotage is to our minds a direct response to the Fascist incitements of Zeesen and of pro-Axis propagandists such as Eric Louw in the Union Parliament ... Infuriated by the Allied victories in North Africa and in the Soviet Union, the friends of Hitler in South Africa were frenziedly slandering and attacking the Communist Party. In Parliament, Nationalist Party leaders call for its suppression. They do so because they know that the Communist Party is the foremost standard-bearer in South Africa of national unity for victory in the war, and for a 100 percent South African war effort against the Axis ... Acts of violence, of sabotage, of political murder and terrorism, of treasonable and fifth column propaganda, will continue until the men at the top are interned and checked.[121]

The United Party government under Smuts, however, threatened *Inkululeko* with closure in September and again in December 1943 for "inciting" its readers against government policy.[122] In February 1944 it was discovered that a secret postal ban had been operating against the newspaper for almost a year. Acting on a tip from a sympathetic postal worker, Harmel and Mofutsanyana established that copies of *Inkululeko* destined for subscribers were going as far as the postal officials but no farther. They approached the deputy chief censor in Johannesburg, who confessed that a postal ban had been in effect but said that the authorities had now lifted it.[123] According to *Inkululeko*, the censors had apparently discriminated between "what could be printed in an African paper and what Europeans were allowed to read."[124]

Stories about social activities of whites (B.2) were rare, but they sometimes highlighted the ridiculous situations produced by white racism. "Umlweli" wrote a column entitled "Shakespeare's Crime," for example, about a decision by the Witwatersrand University Council to ban a proposed performance of Othello by the English Department. Shakespeare's crime, it turned out, was to cast a black man in the leading role. "One is tempted to dismiss such ignorant cultural barbarism with contempt," he said. "But it should not be dismissed too lightly, as a sign of the times. One should not forget the obscene scenes in Germany, when the Nazis burnt publicly the greatest works of literature."[125]

A more amusing story by "Umlweli" described how a certain Nationalist MP by the name of Dr. Van Nierop "raised a most serious question in the House of Assembly." Van Nierop apparently had a letter returned to him by the post office with a stamp on it that read: "Address unknown. Inconnue. Vertrek." The writer continued:

> The learned doctor was most upset. "Inconnue" he declared was a word from a Native language. Why should such a "kaffir" word appear on his envelope–particularly above the Afrikaans! It was a disgrace. The government was going communist, etc. Students of African languages scratched their heads. What strange language was this? Sesuto? Then some slightly more cultural genius of the Nationalist Party discovered the clue. "Inconnue" is French. It means [like the Afrikaans vertrek]"unknown."[126]

The handful of economic stories concerning whites (B.2) focused on the actions of government and industry vis-á-vis the economy. These included editorials about government budgets, reports and proposals relating to the economy and the hiring practices of big mining companies.[127]

Black Politics and Trade Unions

Black political and trade union news comprised almost one-half of the news story units and, as anticipated, the vast majority of stories were concerned with the Communist Party (Table 30).

Stories about CPSA personalities and activities and related items featuring its allies and rivals in the resistance movement comprised almost 95 percent of the story units in Subcategory C. 1. As the CPSA's official organ, *Inkululeko* was very concerned with the statements and actions of party members and sympathizers, people like Yusuf Dadoo, H. A. Naidoo, Sam Kahn, Moses Kotane and Michael Diphuko.[128] Open letters from the editor and official party statements were also significant, especially when they were inserted in non-CPSA items. A story headlined "Alex. Fares Stay at 4d," for example, said very little about bus fares in Alexandra Township. It was actually a statement about township transportation by Johannesburg city councillor Hilda Watts Bernstein.[129] Reports about communist activities were often camouflaged in the same way. An item entitled "Alexandra People Want Better Transport," for example, turned out to be an account of a CPSA meeting called to discuss the transportation situation.[130]

The Communist Party's main allies–the ANC, the South African Indian Congress and some key left-wing trade unions (especially the African Mine Workers' Union, Garment Workers' Union and Iron and Steel Workers' Union)–were also important elements in *Inkululeko*'s political agenda. Protest meetings, rallies and campaign strategies–these were the usual topics that featured in the newspaper.[131] But *Inkululeko* did not ignore squabbles between the party and

Table 30. *Category C news in* Inkululeko (*% of story units*)

Category	%
C. Black/multiracial political and trade union news (1,308 units)	47.1
C.1 Personalities and organizations	27.5
C.2 Confrontation and consciousness	19.6

allies like the ANC and the Indian Congress.[132] The newspaper reserved some of its sharpest barbs for the Trotskyites, its main ideological rivals, who were deemed to be "unscrupulous wreckers and enemies of the workers."[133]

Stories about the activities of government organizations for Africans comprised only about 5 percent of the story units in Subcategory C.1. The newspaper rarely covered these groups except at election time or when issues were discussed that affected the CPSA's own political agenda. *Inkululeko* was sympathetic to the Natives' Representative Council (NRC), for example, during the early to mid-1940s,[134] but disillusionment set in after the 1946 miners' strike and the NRC's subsequent adjournment. Negative stories began to appear more regularly, the NRC being characterized as "a fraud." [135]

The communists led a movement to boycott the 1948 NRC election, but the ANC leadership was not willing to participate, and a bitter war of words ensued between the CPSA and the ANC. Stinging editorials suggested that the time had come "for Africans to do some serious thinking about the future of the African National Congress. Clearly there is something seriously wrong with our national organization ... [The ANC is] an instrument for the personal ambitions of a small group of intellectuals."[136] Congress finally agreed to support the boycott, but the CPSA rejected this decision because it was made too close to the election to make a difference. The party then reversed its own boycott decision, and a banner headline appeared in *Inkululeko* announcing "Mofutsanyana for NRC." The communists would rather be in than out of this "dummy" organization.[137]

The CPSA had a similar response to the urban African township Advisory Boards. They were treated sympathetically in *Inkululeko* during the early 1940s but increasingly criticized during the later 1940s. Thus the 1941 Advisory Board in Orlando (an African township outside Johannesburg) had two communist members, who had "succeeded in obtaining many reforms for the people." Advisory Boards by 1947, however, had "no value whatsoever... They are institutions without legal administrative powers. They are merely machinery through which the municipality introduces its bylaws. They serve as rubber stamps. There is no wonder that they have come to be regarded by most Africans as dummies and toy town councils, just as the Natives' Representative Council is a toy parliament.[138]

Confrontation and Consciousness

Among alternative newspapers in South Africa, *Inkululeko* was unique in its emphasis on confrontation and consciousness raising (C.2). No other text analysed before the 1950s was found to devote as much space to calls for direct action and appeals for a united front in opposition to the state. This is a crucial point that is best highlighted by looking at the types of stories and the language used to mobilize the black population.

News headlines were distinguished by calls for strikes, boycotts and other acts of confrontation. Direct-action headlines tended to be straightforward, as in "Cape Broom and Brush Workers to Strike," "Two Thousand Mining Workers Strike," "Biggest Rent Strike in History" and "6 Weeks of Tram Boycott."[139] Other headlines appealed to readers to support these activists, as in "Support African Teachers," "An Appeal to Workers" or "A Call to Action."[140] Sometimes headlines were written in the imperative, as in "Now–Down to Work" (an appeal to readers to be "evangelists" in the Anti-Pass Campaign) or "Answer the Crisis."[141] In other cases, the call for action was contained in the body of the story, as in "The People's Food."[142]

But *Inkululeko* often made much of marginal events and completely misread the significance of mainstream events. Take two examples from the 1940s, the Alexandra bus boycotts and the 1946 miners' strike. In the first case, the CPSA did not play a major role in the boycotts and gave these events little positive coverage. In the second case, the CPSA was very active in the organization of the strike and the coverage was positive, but the event itself elicited few stories of any kind.

News of the 1943 Alexandra bus boycott was first delivered to *Inkululeko*'s readers in a one-column, front-page story in August. The report merely announced that the boycott had been a success and fares would not be increased. Page 1 of this edition was dominated by a three-column story with a photograph headlined "Red Army Drives On." The 1944 bus boycott received considerably more attention in *Inkululeko*, but much of it was a scathing attack on a "group of political adventurers" who were trying to mobilize the Alexandra community.[143] In reality, the boycotts had been a spontaneous protest against a specific grievance, and they were not organized by any mainstream political opposition group. Both the ANC and CPSA shied away from involvement, the CPSA having decided not to take part in illegal forms of protest until the war was over. Party officials chose to sit back and criticize the tactics of the boycotters, and this strategy was reflected in the party newspaper's coverage of these events.

By contrast, communists were actively involved in organizing the 1946 miners' strike. When *Inkululeko* went to press at the end of the second day, 50,000 miners were out on strike, and J. B. Marks, the communist leader of the African Mine Workers' Union, had been arrested. The newspaper called it a "life and death struggle" and published a powerful editorial calling for an end to the "cheap labour" policy:

> African workers are driven from their homes to work for 2d a day, to live in crowded and unsanitary compounds away from their homes and families, to face sudden death from falls ... and slow death from silicosis and tuberculosis. It is to safeguard the profits of the mine magnates, of John Martin and Ernest Oppenheimer, of Hans Pirow and Carleton Jones, of British, American and South African financiers and millionaires, that the African people have been herded into five morgen strips [1 morgen = 2.12 acres] in the reserves, that the young men have been driven to the towns by the poll tax, but the pass laws have been designed to force African men into employment at miserable wages.

The editorial closed with the fighting words: "This is the first organised strike of African miners. It will not be the last."[144]

Inkululeko's editors were clearly aware of the significance of the event. In words that reveal a lingering elitism within the leadership of the party, the newspaper saluted the African miners: "Blanketed and uncultured, now bruised and bitter, from the heart of our countryside they are the standardbearers and the pioneers of a better South Africa. They are the men of the future."[145] Only four stories about this crucial event, however, appeared in the party newspaper. Mofutsanyana later claimed the staff was so involved in helping to organize the strike they had little time to write about it.[146] The failure to cover adequately the most important conflict story of the decade, however, may have been simply a case of poor news judgment.

Although *Inkululeko* devoted considerable space to calls for action in the form of strikes and boycotts, the most common news story in Subcategory C.2 was in the form of an appeal for unity and solidarity. A letter to the editor in 1941 (under the headline "Africans, Wake Up!"), for example, argued that so long as Africans were not united, their freedom "was stolen from them ... It is not enough to sit at home and speak about oppression – we must come out and support those who fight against it. Africans wake up! Unity is strength and through unity we shall overcome all our difficulties."[147]

In the 1940s, *Inkululeko* criticized several groups inside and outside the resistance movement for dividing the black population. "Umlweli," in a column in 1945, for example, blamed such disparate groups as the Labour Party and the Unity Movement for lack of leadership. "The people of South Africa need unity as dry and thirsty soil needs water," he wrote. "Sooner or later they will find their way to it."[148] The newspaper's repeated calls for unity and action, however, were premature. The party did not even succeed in mobilizing its main constituents, Africans who lived in urban townships in the Johannesburg metropolitan area, during this decade.

The Socialist Project outside and inside South Africa

Foreign news constituted 29.5 percent of the news story units (Table 31), and the struggle against fascism /Nazism during, and to a limited extent after, World War II was the major international story.

The early issues of the mimeographed newspaper *'Nkululeko* reflected the rift within the party over how to respond to the war. A page 1 editorial in September 1939, for example, suggested that Germany and its pro-fascist supporters in South Africa had to be opposed, but this was not an imperialist war:

> Of the war of 1914–1918 it was correct to say that on both sides the war was fought by imperialists, solely for imperialist interests. Today this is not the case. There is a sharp division between fascist countries which have brought about the war by their policy of aggression, and democratic countries in which the people can hope for progress only if they resist aggression and fascism, both inside their countries and outside them.[149]

Two months later, another page 1 editorial urged Africans to stop giving money to support the war effort. Instead, they should concentrate on advancing their position in South Africa:

> Clearly there can be no talk of fighting oppression inside South Africa. But also outside South Africa, in the war against Germany, we have no war against oppression. In fact it is a war to retain oppression. Great Britain wants to continue oppressing and exploiting the colonial peoples under her, and is fighting to defend her rights of exploitation and oppression from Germany, which wishes to seize some of her colonies. The British working class is demanding peace, and is demanding that a government of the people should be formed in England in place of the present government

Table 31. *Category D news in* Inkululeko (*% of story units*)

Category	%
D. Foreign news (820 units)	29.5
D.1 International socialism at war and peace	18.7
D.2 Other international	10.8

of the rich. We in South Africa support the British working people in these demands. We declare that this is an unjust war in which we have no interest except our desire to end it.[150]

'Nkululeko's editors followed the party line in maintaining the imperialism thesis for almost two years. The Soviet Union was depicted as a moral country, to which the workers of the world were looking with pride and hope. "The Soviet Union will not bring its 180 million people into the war on either side of imperialists," one editorial writer declared in July 1940. "They will keep up their policy of neutrality and struggle to bring peace to the world."[151]

The first mention of the invasion of the Soviet Union in *Inkululeko* appeared in August 1941. There was no attempt to rationalize the previous party line, no suggestion of soul searching over the possible misreading of previous events. Instead, in its first article after the invasion, the newspaper launched straight into a scathing attack on Nazi Germany in a classic page 1 story headlined "How to Beat Hitler." It began, in the usual imperative voice, with the words "*Inkululeko* says," and continued:

The free people of Soviet Russia are showing the world how to stop and defeat the hateful Fascist slavery of Hitler Germany. Decent and freedom-loving people all over the world stand side by side with the Soviet Union for the defeat of Nazism ... Hitlerism, the brutal dictatorship of the rich, is a threat to the very hope of the advancement and freedom for all workers and oppressed peoples. Therefore the African people wish in every way to help this great fight to rid the world forever of the Fascist menace to humanity ... BUT PEOPLE WHOSE HANDS ARE IN CHAINS CANNOT PROPERLY FIGHT FASCIM. ONLY A FREE PEOPLE CAN FIGHT FOR FREEDOM.

As was typical in *Inkululeko*'s war stories, the article went on to link the freedom to fight fascism with the need to free black South Africans. It demanded an end to pass laws, provision of land for the starving people in the countryside, proper wages and reasonable rents, an end to police raids and terrorism, and "democratic rights" for the "great mass of the people of South Africa." It ended with the usual plea for unity:

Give the people democratic rights, give them a country and a decent life, give them arms and there is nothing which they will not do to defend their freedom and their rights from all enemies within and outside South Africa ... There is no time to waste! The people must unite their forces now![152]

Throughout the war, there was strong support for a two-track, activist approach that involved the workers' front and the battlefront. As one reader put it: "Comrades, we can produce music on the white keys of a piano, and we can produce music on the black keys. But to produce good harmony we must play on both keys at the same time."[153]

The war, then, had distinct international and domestic implications. During its first five years, *Inkululeko* considered itself more of a mouthpiece for international communism than an organ of South African communism. For example, there were 49 stories specifically about the Soviet Union's war campaign between 1941 and 1945, 41 of which appeared on page 1, but there was only one editorial on the subject. Stories about other aspects of the war – the campaign for a second front, the activities of the Allied and Axis powers, the postwar agreements – were treated in a similar way, with a large number of front-page stories but few editorials. In terms of content, moreover, these stories reflected the war from a Soviet perspective. When the war was linked to issues of freedom and democracy inside South Africa, there was room for editorial comment from a South African perspective. For example, between 1941 and 1945 there were 47 stories involving the war as a catalyst for internal change in South Africa; 11 appeared on page 1 and 13 on the editorial page.

The CPSA never claimed in the pages of *Inkululeko* that it was a Stalinist organization, and many prominent members from this era insist in retrospect that the party did not follow Moscow's line at all.[154] In the content analysis, there was more nonconflict Western news items than domestic USSR news items, even during the war years. Nonconflict Western news after the war was virtually all from the United States, Britain and Western Europe, a leading topic being news reports about communist candidates in various elections (Britain, France, West Germany, Portugal and Italy).[155] As with other protest newspapers, *Inkululeko* covered the British royal family, even though their activities were perceived as frivolous. Nevertheless, coverage of the Soviet war effort and the glowing images of Soviet life clearly suggest that the party continued to support Stalin's policies during the 1940s. These uncritical portraits were less obvious after the war, because news priorities shifted to the domestic front.

The switch in emphasis from foreign to domestic news after the war may have reflected in part a disillusionment with Cold War politics among key party members. Edwin Mofutsanyana's appointment as editor in chief of *Inkululeko* in 1945 hinted at a possible distancing of the CPSA from Moscow. Mofutsanyana himself insisted, in later life, that he was never a Stalinist. His primary interest, he said, was to promote the marriage of socialism and African nationalism.[156] Mofutsanyana's claim is supported to some extent by the evidence. There were 20 Soviet propaganda stories and 104 Soviet-supplied photographs before Mofutsanyana's editorship (December 1940–June 1945), whereas there were only 12 propaganda stories and 25 such photographs during his editorship (June 1945–June 1950).

As with the *Guardian*, the struggles against capitalism and colonialism were linked together in *Inkululeko* during the early years of the Cold War. This topic were often found in editorials that appeared under such headlines as "The Last Days of Capitalism," "The End of an Empire" and "Empire Plot against Workers."[157] Most nonconflict, non–Western news stories dealt with events in southern Africa (including Angola and Nyasaland). But the only country in the region to receive any significant attention was Basutoland. This was a reflection of the CPSA's close ties to Lekhotla la Bafo and of Mofutsanyana's close friendship with Josiel Lefela. *Inkululeko* published 81 stories on southern African countries outside South Africa in this sample, and 43 of these were about Basutoland. The reports were concerned mainly with three issues – the political development of Basutoland (especially the destruction of the precolonial power structure by the

British colonial administration), the banning of *Inkululeko* from the protectorate, and the harassment and imprisonment of members of Lekhotla la Bafo.[158]

Conclusion

The 1940s were critical years in the history of black politics in South Africa. Rapid industrial expansion during and after the war brought hundreds of thousands of Africans to the major cities in search of work and generated a highly politicized African working class. Like the ANC, the Communist Party recognized the potential power of this new urban constituency and sought to capitalize on it. Unlike the ANC, the Communist Party had to overcome doubts about its foreign ideology, its subservience to the international communist movement and its history of white elitism.

Inkululeko represented the party's best chance to project an African image to a mass audience. The newspaper never had a white editor, and only one of the 10 editorial board members and 2 of the 9 contributing editors were white. Most of the newspaper's regular contributors were African, and the most important white contributor, Michael Harmel, published much of his work under an African pseudonym. The work of white communists (people like Rusty Bernstein), who devoted much time behind the scenes to produce the newspaper, was never acknowledged in print. Photographs and stories about African communists like Mofutsanyana, Maliba, Diphuko, Marks and Kotane helped to elevate these men to the status of political celebrities. They were, in a sense, the party's showpieces.

Africans who rose to the top of the CPSA were enormously capable, but they were part of an elite, a small band of dedicated and hard-working comrades who made up the core of the CPSA. The Communist Party was a vanguard party, which helps to explain the pedantic tone of *Inkululeko*. The newspaper could not hope to represent "the masses"; it could only hope to offer an expression of what the Communist Party leadership, black and white, perceived as the concerns of the African working class and to express those concerns in terms that might advance the struggle as a whole.

Inkululeko certainly regarded the plight of African workers as central to the struggle for power, but the party and its newspaper were trying to represent the needs of a much larger, more disparate population during the 1940s. Ideological purity was of little importance to the CPSA at a time when the party had resolved to join forces with other groups actively confronting the segregationist state. The party was prepared to sacrifice ideology for the sake of its allies, and this strategy was reflected in the party newspaper's coverage of the resistance movement.

Inkululeko's whole raison d'etre was to organize, unify and especially to mobilize the political groups that were trivialized or denounced (when they could not be ignored) in the mainstream white commercial press. The newspaper was least successful at mobilization, because the party itself was not organized at the community level.[159]

The newspaper was more successful at promoting unity when it addressed issues – like equality for non-European soldiers and the abolition of the pass laws – that affected Africans, Indians and Coloureds alike. On the other hand, the kinds of parochial problems that affected the burgeoning black townships – housing and food shortages, transportation problems and low wages – were downplayed in *Inkululeko*. They were treated as symptoms of a sick society rather than substantial issues in and of themselves. The prescription was always more of the same–organization and unity. The newspaper did not attempt to examine the ambiguities of South African history or to present a blueprint for the proletarian revolution. Outside the brief period before the German invasion of the Soviet Union, moreover, there was no evidence in *Inkululeko* of ideological conflicts within the party during the 1940s.

For a newspaper that claimed to be a mouthpiece of the ANC,[160] there were virtually no stories about black consciousness, black leisure-time activities or black culture–art, music, theater or sports. Like the ANC, however, the Communist Party was determined to be successful in electoral politics, and the achievements of black and white communists were highlighted in *Inkululeko*. Participation in government-sponsored bodies like the NRC and the Location Advisory Boards for black communists and their sympathizers, and the municipal/provincial councils and parliament for their white counterparts, was encouraged even when the organizations themselves were attacked. White party politics, however, was dismissed as irrelevant, and most general elections during the 1940s were ignored.

The newspaper never issued statements that advocated the overthrow of the government, although it made vague suggestions about the potential of the African masses to respond to violence with violence. A story headlined "Africans and the Police," for example, advised the police not to arm themselves with machine guns or use sjamboks (whips) against Africans: "That would be a very good way to provoke and goad the Africans, most long-suffering and peaceful peoples, beyond endurance. That would be a good way to fan the flames of Moroka [an African township near Johannesburg] into a mighty blaze that might destroy South Africa."[161] The party's ultimate objectives, as mirrored in *Inkululeko*, remained ambiguous during the 1940s: the newspaper oscillated between demands for a democratic South Africa with a universal franchise, a "Native Republic" and a worker-controlled state. It was an uneasy blend of liberal reformist and revolutionary rhetoric.

Nevertheless, the triumph of the Afrikaner Nationalists in 1948 galvanized *Inkululeko*, as it did other protest journals. Reform was no longer possible, and in the last two years of its existence the newspaper confronted the rhetoric of apartheid in a way that would transform the rhetoric of resistance in the next generation: "Only cowards and panic-mongers will think of surrendering to this threat [of apartheid]. To every true South African patriot and lover of freedom, of whatever race, there can only be one course of action: Build the unity of the people ... [for] our freedom and our country!"[162]

Notes

1. H. J. Simons and R. E. Simons, *Class and colour in South Africa, 1850–1950* (Harmondsworth, 1969), 285.
2. K. Luckhardt and B. Wall, *Organize or starve! The history of the South African Congress of Trade Unions* (London, 1980), 43.
3. I. Berger, *Threads of solidarity: Women in South African industry, 1900–1980* (London, 1992), 93.
4. Ray Harmel recalls this debate within the party in the early 1930s. She also had numerous discussions with Garment Workers' Union (GWU) leader Solly Sachs about the need to merge black and white unions. Ray and her husband Michael were leading party activists and trade unionists during the 1930s and 1940s. Ray had worked as a seamstress and was a GWU steward for many years. Elizabeth Jones interview with Ray Harmel, August 1992.
5. Berger, *Threads of solidarity*, 91.
6. Luckhardt and Wall, *Organize or starve!*, 50–51.

7. E. Roux, *Time longer than rope: A history of the black man's struggle for freedom in South Africa*, 2nd ed. (Madison, 1964), 354. Continued police harassment also helped to undermine the night schools during these years. (One in Durban was forced to shut down.) Nevertheless, a party school in District Six (Cape Town) was opened in 1936 in premises loaned to the party by the Anglican Church. It lasted three years, but the outbreak of World War II forced its closing owing to a lack of teachers. A group of liberal-minded whites also founded a school, called the "African College," in Johannesburg in 1939, and Roux says nearly 100 students (many of whom had to sit on the floor) attended classes each night during the early 1940s.
8. According to Mofutsanyana, these meetings were first held during the later years of World War I, predating the formation of the CPSA in 1921. White communists in the International Socialist League initiated contacts with Africans in the back of shops on Fox Street in a black section of Johannesburg. As more Africans were recruited into the party, the meetings were led by African communists, including Mofutsanyana himself. Elizabeth Jones interview with Edwin Mofutsanyana, October 1990.
9. Interview conducted by Robert Edgar (Department of African Studies, Howard University, Washington, D.C.) with Edwin Mofutsanyana, 1981 (hereafter "Edgar interview").
10. B. Bunting, *South African communists speak: Documents from the history of the South African Communist Party, 1915–1980* (London, 1981), 80.
11. Simons and Simons, *Class and colour*, 388.
12. The exact wording of the new slogan called for the creation of "an independent native South African republic as a stage towards a workers' and peasants' republic with full equal rights for all races, black, coloured and white." B. Hirson, "Bukharin, Bunting and the 'Native Republic' slogan," in *Searchlight South Africa*, 1, 3 (July 1989), 60.
13. Bunting was born in Britain in 1873 and arrived in South Africa with the British military forces during the South African War. He first became politically active in South Africa as a member of the South African Labour Party. He then joined the International Socialist League and was one of those who broke away from the ISL to form the Communist Party. He was elected party secretary in 1922 and party chairman two years later.
14. Molly and Douglas Wolton emigrated to South Africa – Molly from Lithuania in 1919 and Douglas from Yorkshire, England, in 1921. They met shortly after joining the CPSA in 1925, and they were married later that year.
15 Nyawuza [Brian Bunting], "Left, right on the road to the black republic," *African Communist*, 123 (1990), 54–55.
16. Mofutsanyana told the author that a fight broke out at the conference over the Native Republic issue. The police were called, but when they found out the communists were fighting among themselves they refused to intervene. Elizabeth Jones interview with Edwin Mofutsanyana, October 1990.
17. Nzula's rise in the CPSA was meteoric. Although he only joined the party in August 1928, within six months he had taken over from Wolton. Nzula was born in Rouxville, Orange Free State, in 1906 and went to mission schools in the eastern Cape. He was trained to be a teacher and also worked as a court interpreter. He was secretary of the Aliwal North (Cape Province) branch of the ICU before joining the Communist Party. Nzula played a key role in Wolton's efforts to Africanize the CPSA hierarchy. He was also a member of the ANC, and he supported left-wing leader Josiah Gumede in his abortive attempts to broaden the base of Congress during his presidency between 1927 and 1930. Nzula joined Eddie Roux in 1929 in launching the League of African Rights, a CPSA-inspired organization that tried but failed to counter the conservative ANC in appealing for an African nationalist workers' movement. Nzula was chosen to lead the Federation of Non-European Trade Unions in 1930, but he left for the Soviet Union within a few months to study at the Lenin School in Moscow and remained to work on the Comintern newspaper, the *Negro Worker*. Mofutsanyana described him as "brilliant," but he was also a "serious drinker." One night in

Moscow he fell asleep in a snowbank, came down with pneumonia and died at the age of 27 in 1933. T. Karis and G. M. Carter (eds.), *From protest to challenge: A documentary history of African politics in South Africa* (Stanford, 1972–1977), Vol. 4: *Political profiles,* by G. M. Gerhart and T. Karis, 123–124; Elizabeth Jones interview with Edwin Mofutsanyana, October 1990.

18. "Comrade Bill" Andrews was a pioneer of the South African trade union movement and the first general secretary of the CPSA. Born in Britain in 1870, he was the first chairman of the South African Labour Party (and an SALP member of parliament), and a charter member of the International Socialist League and the CPSA. In the 1920s, Andrews was not in favor of the CPSA devoting its energies to organizing African workers, and during the mid-1920s he partially withdrew from party activities. Although he was one of the first members to be expelled during the purge of the early 1930s, Andrews was readmitted to the party in 1938 and served as chair of the party's central committee during the turbulent 1940s. He died in December 1950. Gerhart and Karis, *Political profiles*, 3.
19. Molly Wolton suffered from a heart condition, which was the reason the Woltons finally left South Africa. The weather was too hot, and Molly required treatment that was more advanced in Britain. The couple moved first to Sheffield, where Douglas tried but failed to start his own newspaper. They then moved to north London, where Douglas took up a job as an industrial paints salesman. Molly Wolton died of a heart attack in February 1945. Douglas Wolton remarried and remained in Britain until his death in 1988 at the age of 89. Elizabeth Jones interview with sons Greg and Jim Wolton, September 1992.
20. Roux was born in South Africa in 1903 and joined the CPSA in 1923. After completing his doctorate in botany at Cambridge University in England, he returned to South Africa in 1930 and became a full-time party activist. Roux was removed from the political bureau in 1935 but not officially expelled from the party. Nevertheless, he was treated as a pariah by remaining party members, and he felt ashamed that he had accepted the expulsion of his mentor Sydney Bunting. Roux quit the party in 1936 and never returned. He dropped out of politics for 20 years, went back to his botanical studies and after World War II took up a faculty position in the botany department at the University of the Witwatersrand. He joined the Liberal Party in 1957 but was forced to resign in 1963 under a government edict forbidding members or former members of illegal or banned organizations to be members of legally recognized political organizations. Roux died in 1966. Gerhart and Karis, *Political profiles*, 133–134.
21. Nyawuza, "Left, right on the road to the black republic," 60; H. Pike, *A history of communism in South Africa*, 2nd ed. (Germiston, South Africa, 1988), 183, 189.
22. These executions were eventually acknowledged publicly by the South African Communist Party. Elizabeth Jones interview with Ray Harmel, August 1992.
23. Simons and Simons, *Class and colour*, 402.
24 Several party members in the mid- to late 1930s, including Eddie Roux, had urged the party to work with the All-African Convention as "the permanent organization of Africans, Coloureds and Indians." Ibid., 478.
25. E. Flanagan, "Indigenizing marxism: The *South African Worker* and *Umsebenzi*, 1926–1930," paper presented at the Southern Africa Research Program, Yale University (New Haven, 1988), 12. Articles in Afrikaans, aimed at Coloured workers in Cape Town, were introduced in 1930.
26. Ibid., 1.
27. Ibid., 24.
28. E. Roux and W. Roux, *Rebel pity: The life of Eddie Roux* (London, 1970), 94.
29. Pike, *A history of communism in South Africa*, 182.
30. L. Switzer and D. Switzer, *The black press in South Africa and Lesotho, 1836–1976* (Boston, 1979), 78.
31. Flanagan, "Indigenizing marxism," 31.
32. B. Bunting, *Moses Kotane: South African revolutionary* (London, 1975), 62.
33. Roux, *Time longer than rope*, 283.
34. Simons and Simons, *Class and colour*, 479.

35. Flanagan, "Indigenizing marxism," 34–35.
36. A. K. Brooks, "From class struggle to national liberation: The Communist Party of South Africa, 1940 to 1950," M.A. thesis (University of Sussex, 1967), 25.
37. A. Lerumo (M. Harmel), *Fifty fighting years: The Communist Party of South Africa, 1921–1971* (London, 1971), 77.
38. Elizabeth Jones interview with Rusty Bernstein, October 1991.
39. Michael Harmel, "The Communist Party of South Africa," in A. La Guma (ed.), *Apartheid: A collection of writings on South African racism by South Africans* (London, 1972), 214.
40. *Inkululeko*, August 1941, 1.
41. F. Meer, "African nationalism – inhibiting factors," in H. Adam (ed.), *South Africa: sociological perspectives* (London, 1971), 133.
42. On ANC reforms in the 1940s, see the Introduction to the present volume.
43. L. Callinicos, "The Communist Party during the war years: Beginnings of grassroots politics," *South African Labour Bulletin* 15, 3 (September 1990), 102.
44. On communist leadership of the trade unions in the 1940s, see the Introduction.
45. *Inkululeko*, 23 January 1943, 1. The CPSA went on a recruiting drive between 1941 and 1943 and added more than 1,300 members during these years.
46. According to Mofutsanyana, the Lekhotla–CPSA connection was maintained in part because of his close personal friendship with the organization's leaders, Josiel and Maphutseng Lefela. The Lefela brothers were members of a commoner family from Mapoteng in Basutoland. Josiel, the better known of the two, was born about 1885 and educated to about Standard III (fifth grade). He worked in the mines in South Africa and was employed as a policeman in Bechuanaland (Botswana) before returning to Basutoland, where he owned a butchers shop and practiced medicine as a herbalist. Josiel Lefela founded Lekhotla la Bafo in 1919. His brother Maphutseng (born about 1895) was relatively well educated (having studied at Lovedale) and worked as a teacher in various Roman Catholic schools. Maphutseng Lefela was a propagandist for Lekhotla, which included writing stories on Basutoland issues for *Inkululeko*. R. Edgar, *Prophets with honour: A documentary history of Lekhotla la Bafo* (Johannesburg, 1988), 6–7; Elizabeth Jones interview with Edwin Mofutsanyana, October 1990.
47. *Inkululeko* makes reference in 1942 to the newspaper being banned in Basutoland the previous year, and it was still banned in 1944. *Inkululeko* does not indicate when the ban was lifted, but we can assume it was in effect during the war years. E.g., January 1942, 1.
48. B. Hirson, *Yours for the union: Class and community struggle in South Africa, 1930–1947* (London 1990), Chaps. 1–2.
49. Ibid., 144–145.
50. On these protest activities, see the Introduction to the present volume.
51. Lerumo, *Fifty fighting years*, 84.
52. *Inkululeko*, 4 April 1946, 6.
53. Hirson, *Yours for the union*, 131.
54. Ibid., 133.
55. On the 1946 strike, see Simons and Simons, *Class and colour*, Chap. 24.
56. *Inkululeko*, June 1950, 1.
57. For example, the newspaper did not appear three times – in February 1941, July 1941 and April 1942 – during the first 18 months. The change in orthography from '*Nkululeko* to *Inkululeko* was presumably made for linguistic reasons. This is the same word for freedom.
58. Switzer and Switzer, *The Black press*, 75, 79.
59. Elizabeth Jones interview with Rusty and Hilda Watts Bernstein, October 1991.
60. "The people of Vereeniging remember him well for his efforts there to spread political education and enlightenment." *Inkululeko*, 9 September 1944, 1.
61. Ibid. The newspaper also referred to Diphuko as a "proprietor," but this reference appeared for administrative reasons and did not mean he had a financial interest in the publication. Elizabeth Jones interview with Rusty and Hilda Watts Bernstein, October 1991.
62. Ramohanoe, provincial president of the Transvaal ANC from 1944 to 1950, was a leading organizer of the National Anti-Pass Campaign in the mid-1940s.
63. Elizabeth Jones interview with Rusty and Hilda Watts Bernstein, October 1991.
64. *Inkululeko*, 9 June 1945, 1.
65. Tloome joined the CPSA in the 1930s and became active in trade unions and also the

ANC. He was narrowly defeated by Walter Sisulu for the post of ANC secretary general in 1949, but he was elected to the ANC's national executive. Tloome would play a prominent role in the 1952 Defiance Campaign. Gerhart and Karis, *Political profiles*, 158.

66. Bopape, who was trained as a teacher, was a militant ANC activist who joined the CPSA in the 1940s. He was elected Transvaal provincial secretary of the ANC in 1944 and retained this post until he was banned and forced to resign in 1952. Bopape was secretary of the National Anti-Pass Council and played a role in other protest actions during the 1940s and early 1950s. Ibid., 10–11.
67. Hilda Watts Bernstein emigrated from Britain in 1915. She joined the CPSA, along with husband-to-be Rusty Bernstein, in the late 1930s. She was the first communist elected to the Johannesburg City Council, representing Hillbrow in 1943, and she held the seat for three years. Hilda was active in the 1946 miners' strike and various other protest actions during the 1940s and 1950s. The Bernsteins left South Africa following the Rivonia Trial in 1964. Ibid., 6.
68. Radebe was a militant activist in numerous dissident organizations between the 1930s and the 1960s. He helped establish the African Mine Workers' Union in 1941 while holding the portfolio of secretary for mines in the Transvaal ANC. He was temporarily expelled from the CPSA in 1942 for what *Inkululeko* described as suspicious business dealings. He helped launch the abortive African Democratic Party in 1943 and was a leader in the 1943–44 Alexandra bus boycotts. He was elected to the ANC's national executive committee in 1949, but he gradually moved away from Congress during the 1950s and eventually ended up with the Pan-Africanist Congress. Ibid., 130.
69. Rusty Bernstein made this point when interviewed by the author, October 1991.
70. *Ibid.* Abner Kunene apparently also helped out the business manager: his name in fact appeared in many issues of *Inkululeko* as the business manager and sometimes in promotional stories concerned with fundraising. Bernstein did not recall that Kunene had ever worked full time for *Inkululeko*, but like many other party members (including Bernstein) he worked without pay in a variety of newspaper jobs.
71. Elizabeth Jones interview with Ray Harmel, Summer 1991.
72. Elizabeth Jones interview with Edwin Mofutsanyana, October 1990.
73. The modern spellings are given for these languages. In *Inkululeko*, Tswana was "Sechuana", Thonga (or Tsonga) was "Shangaan", and Sotho was Sesotho or "Sesuto".
74. Elizabeth Jones interview with Edwin Mofutsanyana, October 1990; Elizabeth Jones interview with Rusty Bernstein, October 1991.
75. *Inkululeko*, May 1942, 1.
76. *Inkululeko*, 9 January 1943, 1; Elizabeth Jones interview with Rusty Bernstein, October 1991. According to Bernstein, circulation was limited to 1,400 because after that many were run off the stencils began to disintegrate. The last issue of *'Nkululeko* was produced in October 1940.
77. Mofutsanyana and business manager John Nkadimeng were also responsible for soliciting advertising, since the newspaper did not have an advertising manager. Elizabeth Jones interview with Edwin Mofutsanyana, October 1990.
78. *Inkululeko*, November 1941, 1.
79. *Inkululeko*, e.g., 4 April 1946, 8 ("The City Leather," a regular back-page advertisement).
80. *Inkululeko*, e.g., January 1942, 7; June 1946, 8.
81. *Inkululeko*, e.g., June 1948, 5; 29 October 1945, 8.
82. *Inkululeko*, e.g., February 1947, 6.
83. *Inkululeko*, e.g., 28 January 1946, 8.
84. *Inkululeko*, e.g., December 1940, 2; 30 July 1949, 1; 13 August 1949, 1; 16 October 1948, 1.
85. *Inkululeko*, e.g., September 1948, 1 (Mofutsanyana).
86. *Inkululeko*, 23 October 1948, 4.
87. *Inkululeko* felt the impact of the Suppression of Communism Bill weeks before it became law. There was virtually no advertising, and in a note on the front page of the final issue the editors apologized for a six-week delay in getting the newspaper to its readers. *Inkululeko* had been printed

by Prompt Printing and Publishing Co. (Johannesburg) throughout the 1940s, but the contract was cancelled suddenly, and it took several weeks before a new printer was found – Hygrade Printers, of Johannesburg – to produce the last issue.

88. The first masthead, beginning with the December 1940 issues, had the name *Inkululeko* in boldface with the translation "Freedom" in smaller type underneath. Next to "Freedom" was a drawing of a man with his fists in the air. The drawing was removed from the masthead for several months in 1943, a period of paper shortages, when the size of the tabloid-sized newspaper was reduced even further, and the print run was also reduced to 12,750 from the normal 20,000 copies an issue. The second masthead appeared when Mofutsanyana's editorship began. The title was still in bold type, but the English translation was removed. Superimposed over the title was a drawing of the map of Africa. The third masthead was introduced when *Inkululeko* began appearing as a weekly on 9 October 1948. The word *Inkululeko* was written on a flag planted in the drawing of Africa. Underneath the drawing was the word "weekly."
89. The day of publication is missing from most monthly issues, many fortnightly issues and even some weekly issues.
90. *Inkululeko*, 8 July 1944, 8 ("How To Write News For *Inkululeko*").
91. *Inkululeko*, December 1940, 1.
92. *Inkululeko*, e.g., 20 November 1943, 2 ("The Story of the Communist Party").
93. *Inkululeko*, December 1940, 2.
94. *Inkululeko*, 11 April 1943, 5; 24 April 1943, 4.
95. *Inkululeko*, e.g., January 1942, 8; 9 June 1945, 8. Other educational news items dealt with African teachers' conferences, new teaching appointments and relations between parents and teachers.
96. *Inkululeko*, December 1947, 4.
97. *Inkululeko*, e.g., 29 May 1944, 4.
98. *Inkululeko*, 12 March 1949.
99. *Inkululeko*, e.g., April 1941, 8; 25 June 1949, 1; July 1947, 4.
100. *Inkululeko*, 28 August 1943, 1.
101. *Inkululeko*, 20 November 1943, 5.
102. *Inkululeko*, 10 June 1944, 4.
103. The urban profile of *Inkululeko*'s readership is reflected in the fact that in 10 years there were only seven farming stories in the English-language section. One was concerned with farming conditions in the Transkei and another with African farmers clashing with white farmers who had plowed over their land. Several stories focused on working and living conditions of farm laborers in Bethal (Orange Free State) and included the photograph of a farm laborer. *Inkululeko*, e.g., September 1947, 8.
104. *Inkululeko*, e.g., 20 June 1943, 4 ("War on Crime"); July 1947, 4 ("How to Stop Crime").
105. *Inkululeko*, e.g., June 1942, 1: the editors extended their sympathy to two leaders of the Transvaal ANC, S. S. Maloka and S. Mokoape, who were seriously injured in a car accident.
106. *Inkululeko*, 7 May 1949, 1.
107. *Inkululeko*, September 1941, 5.
108. *Inkululeko*, e.g., 23 January 1943, 4 (headline: "Smuts on the Africans"). This was a report describing the prime minister's response to the Christian Council Emergency Committee, a church-sponsored pressure group investigating African economic and political conditions.
109. *Inkululeko*, May 1947, 1.
110. *Inkululeko*, 30 October 1948, 1.
111. *Inkululeko*, 23 October 1948, 1.
112. *Inkululeko*, 4 March 1944, 4 ("Immigration"); September 1948, 4 ("The Facts About Unemployment Pay"); 19 November 1949, 1 ("Africans Must Keep Out").
113. *Inkululeko*, August 1941, 6.
114. *Inkululeko*, June 1947, 1.
115. *Inkululeko*, 28 May 1949, 1.
116. *Inkululeko*, April 1947, 1.
117. *Inkululeko*, 29 January 1949, 1; 16 April 1949, 4; September 1948, 1.
118. *Inkululeko*, February 1948, 4. The newspaper did cover right-wing opposition groups, including the Nuwe Order (New Order) and the Ossewa Brandwag (Oxwagon Guard), during the early 1940s. Because the CPSA was a primary target, incidents of harassment were usually reported. *Inkululeko*, e.g., 6 February 1943, 1 ("Nazi Terrorism on the Rand"); 10 July 1943, 5 ("Communist Meeting Broken Up").

119. *Inkululeko*, June 1948, 1.
120. Brian Bunting, "The origins of apartheid," in La Guma, *Apartheid*, 23.
121. *Inkululeko*, 20 February 1943, 1. In a smaller story on the same page, the newspaper reported a decision by Colin Steyn, minister of justice, not to take action against the Communist Party on the basis of the "vague allegations" presented to the House of Assembly by Eric Louw. Louw had been pressing the government to break off consular relations with the Soviet Union and suppress the communists in South Africa.
122. *Inkululeko*, 18 December 1943, 1: the editors were called before the chief magistrate in Johannesburg and warned that unless the newspaper stopped publishing "its present type of article" it would be banned. The story made the point that "openly anti-war, pro-Nazi papers like the *Transvaler*, organ of the Nationalist Party, and the *Workers' Voice*, organ of the Trotskyists, have been appearing regularly without any interference from the Government. *Inkululeko*, by contrast, is known for its support of the war." The story concluded that the banning threats could only be "because the paper has ceaselessly fought for an end to the colour bar, for democratic rights and higher wages for all sections of the people."
123. Elizabeth Jones interview with Edwin Mofutsanyana, October 1990.
124. *Inkululeko*, 4 March 1944, 1.
125. *Inkululeko*, June 1947, 4.
126. *Inkululeko*, 28 April 1945, 5.
127. *Inkululeko*, e.g., 18 December 1948, 1 ("Nazi Plan for Trust Farms"); March 1947, 4 ("Rich Man's Budget"); 8 November 1945, 4 ("Cheap Labour on the Mines").
128. *Inkululeko*, 16 October 1948, 1 ("Dadoo Interviewed in Paris"); 30 October 1948, 1 ("We Will Win Again Says Dadoo"); 6 November 1948, 1 ("Dadoo Answers Louw"); July 1947, 1 ("H. A. Naidoo Arrested"); 6 November 1945, 1 ("Kahn for Parliament"); 16 October 1948, 1 ("Sam Kahn Gaining Widespread Support"); 29 January 1949, 1 ("Sam Kahn Takes His Seat"); November 1942, 5 ("Moses Kotane Arrested"); 27 November 1948, 4 ("Diphuko in Court").
129. *Inkululeko*, 13 February 1945, 1.
130. *Inkululeko*, 8 September 1945, 5.
131. *Inkululeko*, e.g., March 1941, 5 ("International Women's Day"), which was billed as an opportunity for women to come out and air their grievances; May 1942, 4 ("Non-European Leaders Call People's Conference"); October 1942, 4 ("African Workers... Mass Rally"); 20 May 1944, 4 ("Union Defends Miners"). On plans to resist the pass laws and the anti-Indian legislation, see *Inkululeko*, e.g., 14 August 1944, 5 ("Anti-Pass Marches On"); August 1946, 4–5 ("Indian Struggle Grows" and "Thousands Take Anti-Pass Pledge").
132. *Inkululeko*, e.g., 3 December 1945, 4 ("Towards a Real Unity"), a story attacking "a most stupid and dangerous proposal" to be considered at the ANC's national conference that would exclude members of other organizations from being Congress officials. *Bantu World* editor Selope Thema was attacked for trying to turn the ANC into "just another sect." Sometimes internal ANC politics was included in the news agenda. *Inkululeko*, e.g., 5 March 1949, 1 (ANC official R. G. Baloyi supports a National Party candidate for the Senate in the 1948 general election). "Umlweli" wrote in 1946 that Anton Lembede was associating himself with "aggressive" nationalists, a "questionable crowd" who called themselves the African Improvement Society and were hostile to the communists. *Inkululeko*, 21 June 1946, 5. Indian passive resisters were criticized for their pacifist tactics: "The pages of history bear proof that 'turning the other cheek' brings defeat and disillusionment, not victory and progress." *Inkululeko*, July 1946, 4 ("Salute to the Indians").
133. *Inkululeko*, e.g., 28 January 1946, 4 ("Timber Workers' Tragedy"). The newspaper blamed the Trotskyites for encouraging timber workers to strike and then abandoning them. The Non-European Unity Movement, heavily influenced by "Trotskyites," was an "unrepresentative" organization. *Inkululeko*, 3 December 1945, 4.
134. *Inkululeko*, cf. June 1942, 4 ("The election does offer the Africans a chance to show that we are a united people determined to win and maintain freedom");

30 August 1944, 4 (The NRC "served a valuable purpose").

135. *Inkululeko*, 26 November 1946, 1.
136. *Inkululeko*, December 1947, 14.
137. *Inkululeko*, February 1948, 1.
138. *Inkululeko*, January 1941, 8; April 1947, 5.
139. *Inkululeko*, 8 August 1945, 5; 23 August 1944, 1; July 1947, 1; 8 October 1949, 1.
140. *Inkululeko*, March 1942, 4; 23 October 1948, 4; 28 May 1949, 1.
141. *Inkululeko*, 29 May 1944, 4; 16 April 1949, 4.
142. *Inkululeko*, May 1946, 4. It reads in part: "STAMP OUT THE BLACK MARKET by taking drastic action."
143. Rival anticommunist groups involved in the boycott action (namely the Workers' Transport Action Committee and its ally the African Democratic Party), according to "Umlweli," were dividing the protesters. *Inkululeko*, 25 November 1944, 1, 4.
144. *Inkululeko*, August 1946, 4.
145. *Inkululeko*, September 1946, 1.
146. Elizabeth Jones interview with Edwin Mofutsanyana, October 1990.
147. *Inkululeko*, December 1941, 4.
148. *Inkululeko*, 29 January 1945, 4.
149. *'Nkululeko*, September 1939, 1.
150. *'Nkululeko*, 15 November 1939, 1.
151. *'Nkululeko*, July 1940, 3.
152. *Inkululeko*, August 1941, 1.
153. *Inkululeko*, December 1941, 6.
154. Ray Harmel, for example, says the CPSA did not support Stalin. Members of the party were aware of Stalin's "treacherous" policies and did not agree with him. Rusty and Hilda Bernstein also insisted, in an interview, that the CPSA did not follow Moscow's instructions. Elizabeth Jones interviews with Ray Harmel, August 1992; Rusty and Hilda Bernstein, October 1991.
155. *Inkululeko*, e.g., February 1947, 4. See also 14 July 1945, 8 (George Bernard Shaw supports a British communist candidate in an election); 4 March 1950, 4 (headline: "Traitors to Socialism," an editorial about the British Labour Party); 30 April 1949, 4 (speech by African American Paul Robeson at a conference in Paris on the "Negro people"); 14 April 1945, 1 (death of U.S. President Franklin Roosevelt); 9 June 1945, 1 (headline: "British Communist Candidates").
156. Edwin Mofutsanyana told the author that friends accused him of being a Stalinist because he kept a photograph of Stalin in his home, but he says he kept it not out of admiration but "to throw darts at it!" Elizabeth Jones interview with Edwin Mofutsanyana, October 1990.
157. *Inkululeko*, 30 July 1949, 4; 7 May 1949, 4; 19 March 1949, 1.
158. Mofutsanyana fled South Africa to Basutoland in 1959, and Josiel Lefela provided him with a hiding place in the mountains. He worked with Lefela in subsequent years, drafting letters and petitions to the United Nations and various Western governments on behalf of the Lekhotla opposition movement. Robert Edgar to Elizabeth Jones, 25 September 1992.
159. For the party's overall impact on African workers during the 1940s, see D. Fortescue, "The Communist Party of South Africa and the African working class in the 1940s," *International Journal of African Historical Studies*, 24, 3 (1991), 481–512.
160. *Inkululeko*, e.g., June 1945, 1.
161. *Inkululeko*, September 1947, 4. Suggestions of looming violence became increasingly graphic, as in a story headlined "Apartheid's Savages," about attempts by right-wing whites to torch schools in Johannesburg's African townships: "The burning of the schools is the start of operations by the savages of *apartheid*. Let the people be warned. This is South Africa's Reichstag fire, which ushers in the rule of the sjambok and the cut throat." *Inkululeko*, September 1948, 4.
162. *Inkululeko*, June 1948, 1.

Appendix

A Content Analysis of Six Alternative Newspapers in a Time Series (1919–1952)

Six newspapers were targeted for quantitative analysis, using a classification system developed by Les Switzer after years of examining various kinds of black and white commercial and non-commercial publications in South Africa. There were three stages in refining a method for analyzing the content of the alternative press.

In Stage 1, conducted in South Africa, conventional news categories devised by U.S. scholars in the 1950s and 1960s were used. The content analyses were conducted by postgraduate honors students working under Switzer's supervision between 1979 and 1984, when he was a member of the Department of Journalism and Media Studies at Rhodes University (Grahamstown, South Africa). Nofikile Nxumalo, Jo-Anne Richards, Brian McCulloch, Lizeka Mda, David O'Sullivan and David Bristow deserve a special word of thanks for these efforts. The categories employed at this stage were eventually abandoned – they did not really interrogate the texts of alternative publications – but except for two newspapers (the *Guardian* and *Inkululeko*) the test samples were retained, and the knowledge gained from these experiments proved to be most beneficial in later stages of the analysis.

Switzer examined samples from these newspapers again in Stage 2 of the project, conducted in Houston in 1987–88. New news categories and subcategories were constructed, and they were refined further in Stage 3, conducted in Houston in 1991–92. Stories rather than column inches were used as units of measurement. No significant differences in the ranking of categories were recorded in two test samples where both measurements were used.

The four categories used in the final analysis are as follows:

Category A—Black [multiracial, where applicable] news of general interest in South Africa. Stories assigned to this category were defined as general-interest stories involving blacks, in which the headline and "news peg" or central theme did not feature a political organization or trade union. Multiracial stories were placed in this category when the controlling agent or agency was perceived to be black or to represent primarily blacks.

Category B—White [multiracial, where applicable] news in South Africa. Stories assigned to this category were political, economic and social stories involving whites, the acts of individuals and institutions embracing the hegemonic culture. Multiracial stories were placed in this category when the controlling agent or agency was perceived to be white or to represent primarily whites.

Category C—Black [multiracial, where applicable] political and/or trade union news in South Africa. Stories assigned to this category were political and trade union stories involving blacks. Multiracial stories were placed in this category when the controlling agent or agency was perceived to be black or to represent primarily blacks.

Category D—Foreign news. Stories assigned to Category D were stories generated outside South Africa, even when South Africans featured in these stories.

These categories generated 14 subcategories – 8 in black general-interest news (Category A), 2 in white political, economic and social news (Category B), 2 in black political and trade union news (Category C), and 2 in foreign news found in the socialist press (Category D).

Category A stories were subdivided into 5 conventional subject areas retained from earlier data analyses – Education and religion (A.1), Society (A.2), Sports (A.3), Crime and accidents (A.7) and Other: Promotional and miscellaneous (A.8) – and 3 new subject areas – Living conditions in urban areas (A.4), Living conditions in rural areas (A.5), and Independent economic activities (A.6). Stories concerned with health, poverty and welfare or with any other grievance expressed by ordinary blacks about situations that disrupted their everyday lives (often in letters to the editor), and all reports of activities by black entrepreneurs, were placed in the new subcategories.

Category B stories were subdivided into Political, legislative and administrative (B.1), and Economic and social (B.2) – and Category C stories into Personalities and organizations (C.1), and Confrontation and consciousness (C.2). Confrontation stories deal with passive and active resistance, including strikes and other types of work stoppages, boycotts, protest marches and rallies, civil disobedience and armed struggle. Consciousness-raising stories include appeals for workers' unity, class consciousness, racial solidarity and self-reliance, appeals to opposition groups to unite against the segregationist state, appeals for an end to capitalism or the promotion of socialism or any other statement that confronted the dominant ideological discourse.

Category D is very significant for the socialist press between the 1930s and 1950s, so 2 subcategories were established for the *Guardian* and *Inkululeko* in the final stage of the analysis. International socialism in war and peace (D.1) is concerned essentially with the international workers' movement and the socialist project before, during and after World War II. Conflict news in this subcategory highlights the struggle against fascism/Nazism and the struggle against capitalism and ..colonialism/imperialism. Nonconflict news in this subcategory highlights political, economic and cultural developments in the Soviet Union. Other international (D.2) is concerned essentially with nonconflict Western and nonconflict non-Western news.

The percentage of formal advertising was also determined for each of the six newspapers. Informal advertising – advertisements disguised as news stories – was classified as news, and most of these stories were promotional (A.8). Formal advertising content was evaluated in three newspapers – each owned by a different interest group with a different political agenda: *Bantu World*, a white-owned commercial newspaper; *Inkundla ya Bantu*, an independent African nationalist newspaper; and the *Guardian*, an independent socialist newspaper.

All formal advertisements in the three newspaper samples were itemized, and each advertisement regardless of size or placement was counted as a unit in the analysis. Binary categories were used in coding the advertising units. First, we distinguished between advertising units featuring "white" and "black" goods and services. Second, we distinguished between goods and services advertised by white-owned businesses that were deemed to be essential and nonessential. The four advertising categories are White businesses: Essential goods and services; White businesses: Nonessential goods and services; Black goods and services (essential and nonessential); Promotional. In each newspaper sample, the same businesses usually appeared as advertisers and offered the same goods and services from year to year.

1. *Imvo Zabantsundu* (English/Xhosa), the *Workers' Herald* (English/Xhosa/Zulu/Sotho).

The content analysis of *Imvo Zabansundu* (for which back issues were available only on microfilm) focused on the 1920s, a crucial decade in the history of the African nationalist movement. A random probability sampling method was used to select 22 issues of the newspaper for a period of 11 years between January 1919 and December 1929. As a weekly, *Imvo* comprised 52 issues a year. Each issue was given a number from 1 to 52, and 2 issues each year were selected for analysis using a random numbers table.

The Xhosa-language section usually comprised seven pages of the eight-page newspaper during the 1920s. Switzer supplemented this data with an analysis of selected stories drawn from English-language editorial pages between 1918 (to examine coverage of black political/trade union activities and strikes/boycotts by black workers in South Africa in the final year of World War I) and 1930 (to examine coverage of the onset of the Great Depression).

The content analysis of the *Workers' Herald* was based on the English-language pages of all known issues of the newspaper. The dates and numbers printed in the text suggest that no more than 53 issues of the newspaper, an irregular monthly, were produced between May 1923 and December 1928. A total of 37 issues (69.8 percent) of the known universe had been found by 1991, and 68.5 percent of these stories were in English. Two surviving issues (February, April 1925) stemmed from the period when the newspaper was edited by James Thaele, and the rest were produced under Henry Tyamzashe's editorship in Cape Town and Johannesburg. As a broadsheet, one or two pages were normally in African languages before September 1926, and three pages between October 1926 and May 1928. As a tabloid, up to four pages were in the vernacular between August and December 1928. The newspaper was normally eight pages between April 1925 and December 1928. Stories about ICU activities in colonial South-West Africa, Rhodesia and Nyasaland were considered domestic rather than foreign news items.

In both newspapers, all stories – news items, columns, editorials, poems, songs, essays, homilies, obituaries, jokes, letters to the editor and advertisements disguised as news stories – were evaluated as units and included in the test samples. Stories that jumped to other columns on the same page or to other pages were assigned extra units.

Catherine Nawa-Gwamanda, a South African living in Houston who is fluent in Xhosa, reexamined, reclassified and recoded all story units in the original *Imvo* sample, and Switzer repeated this procedure, using her English translations of the story unit headlines and central themes. News items previously thrown together in general-interest columns (Category A) such as "Izinto Ngezinto" (This and That) were itemized separately, and about 15 stories in Xhosa that could not be deciphered due to the poor quality of the microfilm were not included. Intercoder discrepancies between Nawa-Gwamanda and Switzer in the *Imvo* sample were within 8.3 percent of the 535 story units examined. Intercoder discrepancies between Switzer and Ime Ukpanah (the second coder) in the *Workers' Herald* sample were within 5.2 percent of the 1,222 story units examined.

2. *Bantu World* (English/Afrikaans/Xhosa/Zulu/Sotho/Tswana/Venda/Thonga or Tsonga).

The content analysis of *Bantu World* focused on the 1930s between the founding of the newspaper in April 1932 and December 1939 following South Africa's entry into World War II. A random probability sampling method was employed to select issues of the newspaper (for which back issues were available only on microfilm). As a weekly, *Bantu World* comprised 52 issues a year. Each issue was given a number from 1 to 52, and 2 issues a year for a total of 16 issues were selected for analysis using a random numbers table.

All news stories except those in Sotho/Tswana – 16.3 percent of the total – and a few items in Venda and Thonga were examined in the test sample. English-language stories comprised about 7 pages of a typical 20-page newspaper, or about 35 percent of the news items. Each story, regardless of size or placement, was counted as a unit in the analysis. Stories that jumped to other columns on the same page or to other pages were assigned extra units. News items included columns, editorials, essays, poems, short stories, homilies, obituaries, jokes and advertisements disguised as news stories. There was no advertising on page 1 until December 1936, but in the last three years of this sample a two-column cigarette advertisement featured regularly on the front page. Only the English-language editorial page was without advertising during the 1930s. Switzer reexamined, reclassified and recoded the story and advertising units in the original sample (the headlines and central themes of all story and advertising items in African languages had been translated into English). Intercoder discrepancies between Switzer and Ime Ukpanah (the second coder) were within 7.5 percent of the 1,554 story units and 3.5 percent of the 608 advertising units examined.

3. *Inkundla ya Bantu* (English/Zulu/Sotho).

The content analysis of *Inkundla ya Bantu* was accomplished over a period of 3 months, between March and May 1992. A random probability sampling method was used to select the editions of the newspaper (for which back issues were available only on microfilm), and the analysis was based on the entire data base of the newspaper.

Inkundla appeared as a monthly (1938–43), bimonthly (1944–46), weekly (1947–49) and an irregular bimonthly (1950–51). The number of sample issues was linked to the frequency of publication: Switzer decided on 2 issues a year for the monthly, 3 issues a year for the fortnightly, and 4 issues a year for the weekly. Each issue was given a number corresponding to the frequency of publication in that year, and 40 issues were selected (1 extra issue was included in 1946) using a random numbers table – 14 before and 26 after *Inkundla* began to perceive itself as the unofficial organ of the Congress Youth League (from June 1944). Stories that jumped to other columns on the same page or to other pages were assigned extra units. All stories in English, Zulu and Sotho – news items, columns, editorials, essays, homilies, obituaries, letters to the editor, promotional stories and advertisements disguised as news stories – and all advertising units were included in the test sample.

Three coders analyzed the news content of *Inkundla*. Catherine Nawa-Gwamanda (Coder 1) translated all African-language news headlines, summarized the stories and conducted the initial coding of the *Inkundla* test sample. She is fluent in Zulu in addition to Xhosa, and Sotho is her home language. Ukpanah (Coder 2) and Switzer (Coder 3) independently coded the news stories, based on their reading of the English-language stories and Nawa-Gwamanda's English translations of headlines and stories in the two African languages. Intercoder discrepancies in the placement of 1,620 story units in the four news categories was 4.3 percent between Coder 1 and Coder 2 and 7.6 percent between Coder 1 and Coder 3. Gwamanda and Ukpanah analyzed the advertising content of *Inkundla*, and intercoder discrepancies were within 2.1 percent of the 654 ad units examined.

4. The *Guardian* (English).

The content analysis of the *Guardian* (for which back issues were available only on microfilm) was based on a random probability sample of the entire data base under this title. As a weekly, the newspaper normally appeared 52 times a year. Each issue was given a number from 1 to 52. Two issues each year from February 1937 to May 1952 were selected for analysis using a random numbers table. All stories in the 32 issues examined – news items, columns, editorials, book and movie reviews, sports, obituaries, letters to the editor, illustrations (photographs and drawings), occasional poems and advertisements disguised as news – were evaluated as single units in the test sample. Stories that jumped to other columns on the same page or to other pages were assigned extra units.

Switzer and Jonathan Hook, a graduate student in history at the University of Houston who was the second coder, examined, classified and coded the story and advertising units. Intercoder discrepancies were within 5.7 percent of the 1,883 story units examined. There were virtually no intercoder discrepancies (less than 0.5 percent) in the 1,230 advertising units examined.

5. *Inkululeko* (English/Afrikaans/Xhosa/Zulu/Sotho/Tswana/Venda).

The content analysis of *Inkululeko* (for which back issues were available only on microfilm) was undertaken by Elizabeth Jones, who had written to Switzer at the University of Houston in 1989 in search of a possible thesis topic. He suggested *Inkululeko* as one South African newspaper that remained largely unresearched. Using conventional categories similar to ones devised by Switzer and his students at Rhodes University, Jones undertook a preliminary study of *Inkululeko* in 1990 as part of her graduate research at the London School of Economics.

English-language stories comprised about one-third of the news items, and all English-language news items were classified – news reports, letters to the editor, editorials, columns, short stories and poems, film, theater and book reviews, birth and death notices. Stories that jumped to other columns on the same page or to other pages were assigned extra units. All advertisements in English or partly in English where the product or service could be identified (which was virtually all of them) on the English and African-language pages were also classified. In addition, all illustrations (photographs and drawings) were classified, regardless of the language used for the caption, except in a few cases where the quality of the illustration was too poor to identify and/or the caption was not informative.

The content analysis was based on 159 of 189 issues of the newspaper, which appeared as an irregular monthly, fortnightly and weekly during the 1940s. Jones did not have access to 30 cyclostyled (mimeographed) issues under the '*Nkululeko* title, which were published before December 1940. Jones and Helen Broome, a full-time researcher for a major American news organization who was well versed in South African affairs, examined, classified and coded the story and advertising units. Intercoder discrepancies in the first stage of the project were within 18 percent (218 units) of the 1,226 story and advertising units examined.

Jones consulted with Switzer again, who examined the results and suggested that she reexamine the newspaper using the new categories and subcategories he had developed. After discussions with Switzer on the categories he was using, Jones reexamined, reclassified and recalculated all stories in the English-language section of *Inkululeko* (and in the African-language sections in terms of advertising and news illustrations). This analysis generated 2,780 story units and 1,136 advertising units. Using a random numbers table, Broome (the second coder) selected 20 issues of the known universe – two issues for each year between 1941 and 1949, the December 1940 issue and one issue in 1950 – and examined all story items in the English-language section and all advertisements and illustrations in the English and vernacular-language sections. Intercoder discrepancies dropped to 3.3 percent (20 units) of the 612 story and advertising units examined. Jones was not able to make a further distinction between white and black consumer advertising before this book went to press, so the editor did not use the data she compiled on *Inkululeko*'s advertising agenda.

6. The terms "black" and "multiracial" as defined in this study.

The term "black" refers to Africans, Coloureds and Indians as these population groups are identified in South Africa. The term "multiracial" did not really apply to Category A, because there were virtually no nonpolitical, multiracial news items of general interest to blacks in these test samples. A few only were recorded in *Imvo* during the 1920s, *Bantu World* during the 1930s and the socialist press during the 1940s.

The term "multiracial" when applied to Category B embraces virtually all extraparliamentary groups *dominated by whites*. These groups are mentioned particularly in the texts of newspapers before World War II, and they include the Joint Councils and other welfare organizations, the South African Institute of Race Relations, student groups such as the Student Christian Association and the National Union of South African Students, and various mission and church bodies.

The term "multiracial" when applied to Category C includes all extraparliamentary groups *dominated by blacks*. In addition, whites who represented Africans in parliament were included in this category, along with African members of various government-sponsored African agencies (the Native Conferences, Native Advisory Boards, Natives' Representative Council, Ciskei and Transkei local and district councils and the two General Councils), and the Communist Party of South Africa.

The CPSA – fully committed to organizing black workers by 1924 – was the only multiracial political organization of any significance represented in Category C test samples drawn during the 1920s and 1930s. Beside the Communist Party and numerous affiliated organizations, multiracial items in Category C during the 1940s and 1950s included a few white-dominated, extraparliamentary opposition groups like the Springbok Legion, and unions associated with the nonracial South African Trades and Labour Council. Virtually no stories on multiracial trade unions, other than the Industrial and Commercial Workers' Union, appeared during the interwar era. Stories on multiracial trade unions where the membership was mainly white – all of them in socialist newspapers in the late 1930s and early 1940s – were placed in Category C.

Index